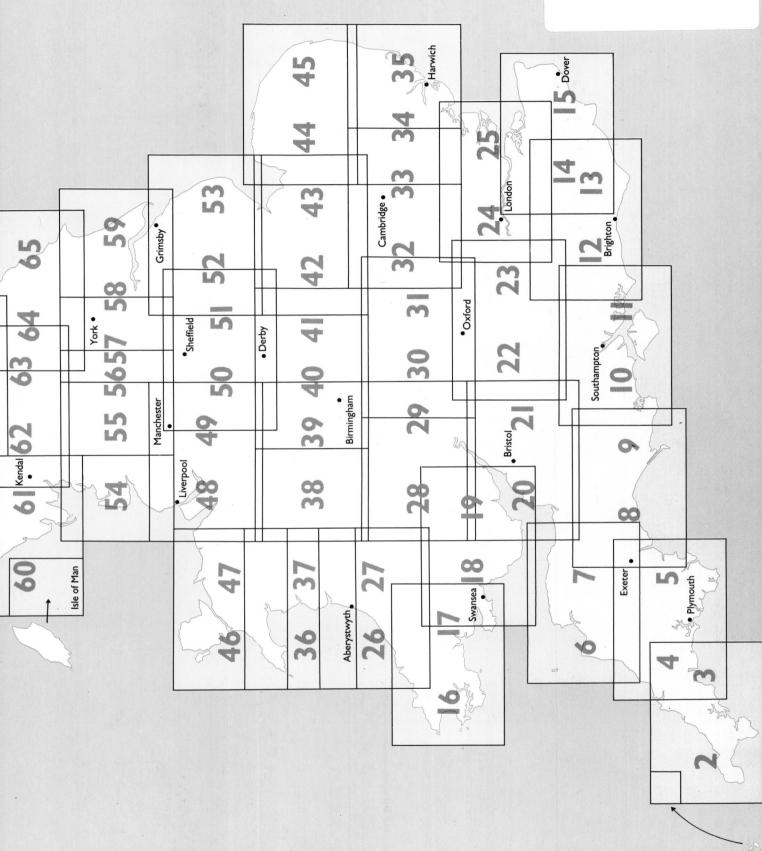

THE
MOTORIST'S
ATLAS OF BRITAIN

THE MOTORIST'S ATLAS OF BRITAIN

JOHN BARTHOLOMEW & SON LTD

First published MCMLXXXVI as
Barts Motorist's Atlas of Britain
This edition published MCMLXXXVII by
John Bartholomew & Son Ltd
Duncan Street
Edinburgh EH9 ITA

ISBN 0 7028 0806 7
Maroon presentation edition 0 7028 0807 5
Blue presentation edition 0 7028 0808 3
Black leather presentation 0 7028 0809 1

Index typesetting by C.R.Barber & Partners

Photography by Andy Williams
Title page: Tal-y-llyn, Snowdonia, Wales
Opposite page from top:
Corfe Castle, Dorset
Kyle of Lochalsh to Kyleakin ferry, Isle of Skye
Grange, Borrowdale, Cumbria

Printed in Scotland by John Bartholomew & Son Ltd

Details included in this atlas are subject to change without
notice. Whilst every effort is made to keep information
up to date John Bartholomew & Son Ltd will not be
responsible for any loss, damage or inconvenience caused
by inaccuracies in this atlas. The publishers are always
pleased to acknowledge any corrections brought to their
notice, and record their appreciation of the valuable
services rendered in the past by map users in assisting to
maintain the accuracy of their publications.

CONTENTS

Motoring Information VI-VII

Distance Charts VIII

Key 1

Main Map Section 2-115

Distance Finder Diagrams 116-119

Channel Ferries 120

London Guide 121

London Through Routes 122-123

London Central Plan 124-131

London Central Plan Index 132-136

Town Plan Guide 137

Town Plans 138-168

Main Map Section Index 169-216

INDEPENDENT LOCAL RADIO

		Med. Wave metres/KHz	VHF MHz
1	Aberdeen (North Sound)	290/1035	96.9
2	Ayr (West Sound)	290/1035	96.2
3	Dundee (Radio Tay)	258/1161	95.8
4	Edinburgh (Radio Forth)	194/1548	96.8
2	Girvan (West Sound)	290/1035	97.1
5	Glasgow (Radio Clyde)	261/1152	95.1
6	Inverness (Moray Firth Radio)	271/1107	95.9
3	Perth (Radio Tay)	189/1584	96.4
7	Bradford (Pennine Radio)	135/1278	96.0
8	Humberside (Viking Radio)	258/1161	102.7
9	Isle of Man (Manx Radio)	219/1367	96.9
10	Leeds (Radio Aire)	362/828	94.6
11	Liverpool (Radio City)	194/1548	96.7
12	Manchester (Piccadilly Radio)	261/1152	97.0
13	Preston and Blackpool (Red Rose Radio)	301/999	97.3
14	Rotherham (Radio Hallam)	194/1548	95.9
14	Sheffield (Radio Hallam)	194/1548	95.2
15	Teesside (Radio Tees)	257/1170	95.0
16	Tyne & Wear (Metro Radio)	261/1152	97.0
17	Wrexham and Deeside (Marcher Sound/Sain-Y-Gororau)	238/1260	95.4
18	Birmingham (BRMB Radio)	261/1152	94.8
19	Cardiff (Red Dragon Radio)	221/1359	96.0
20	Coventry (Mercia Sound)	220/1359	95.9
21	Gloucester & Cheltenham (Severn Sound)	388/774	95.0
22	Hereford (Radio Wyvern)	314/954	95.8
23	Leicester (Leicester Sound)	238/1260	97.1
19	Newport (Red Dragon Radio)	230/1305	104.0
24	Northampton (Hereward Radio)	192/1557	102.8
25	Nottingham (Radio Trent)	301/999	96.2
24	Peterborough (Hereward Radio)	225/1332	95.7
26	Stoke-on-Trent (Signal Radio)	257/1170	104.3
27	Swansea (Swansea Sound)	257/1170	95.1
28	Wolverhampton and Black Country (Beacon Radio)	303/990	97.2
22	Worcester (Radio Wyvern)	196/1530	96.2
29	Bedford (Chiltern Radio)	378/792	95.5
30	Bristol (Radio West)	238/1260	96.3
31	Bury St. Edmunds (Saxon Radio)	240/1251	96.4
32	Chelmsford (Essex Radio)	220/1359	96.4
33	Ipswich (Radio Orwell)	257/1170	97.1
34	London (Capital Radio)	194/1548	95.8
35	London Broadcasting Company	261/1152	97.3
29	Luton (Chiltern Radio)	362/828	97.6
36	Norwich (Radio Broadland)	260/1152	97.6
37	Reading (Radio 210)	210/1431	97.0
32	Southend (Essex Radio)	210/1431	95.3
38	Swindon (Wiltshire Radio)	258/1161	96.4
38	West Wiltshire (Wiltshire Radio)	321/936	97.4
39	Ashford (Invicta Radio)	497/603	96.3
40	Bournemouth (2 CR)	362/828	97.2
41	Brighton (Southern Sound)	227/1323	103.4
39	Canterbury (Invicta Radio)	497/603	95.1
39	Dover (Invicta Radio)	497/603	97.0
42	Exeter (Devon Air Radio)	450/666	95.8
43	Guildford (County Sound)	203/1476	96.6
44	Plymouth (Plymouth Sound)	261/1152	96.0
45	Portsmouth (Radio Victory)	257/1170	95.0
39	Thanet (Invicta Radio)	497/603	95.9
42	Torbay (Devon Air Radio)	314/954	95.1
46	Reigate and Crawley (Radio Mercury)	197/1521	103.6
39	West Kent (Invicta Radio)	242/1242	103.8

NATIONAL TRAVEL SUMMARIES

Road	01-246 8031
Rail	01-246 8030
Sea	01-246 8032
Air	01-246 8033

AIRPORTS

Aberdeen	0224 722331
Edinburgh	031-333 1000
Glasgow (Abbotsinch)	041-887 1111
Newcastle upon Tyne	0632 860966
Tees-side	Darlington (0325) 332811
Leeds & Bradford	0532 509696
Manchester	061-489 3000
Liverpool	051-494 0066
East Midlands	Derby (0332) 810621
Birmingham	021-743 4272
London (Heathrow)	01-759 4321
London (Gatwick)	Crawley (0293) 28822

BBC NATIONAL RADIO

		Med. Wave metres/KHz	VHF MHz
Radio 1		285/1053	88-91
		275/1089	88-91
		202/1485	88-91
Radio 2		433/693	88-91
		330/909	88-91
Radio 3		251/1197	90-93
		247/1215	90-93
Radio 4		(1500/200 LW)	92-95
	Aberdeen	207/1449	92-95
	Carlisle	202/1485	92-95
	London	417/720	92-95
	Newcastle	497/603	92-95
	Plymouth	388/774	92-95
	Redruth	397/756	92-95
Radio Scotland		370/810	92-100
Radio Wales		340/882	-
Radio Cymru		- -	92-95
		- -	96.8

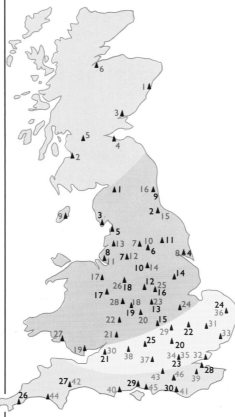

It is anticipated that some independent and BBC local radio stations will change their VHF frequencies during 1986.

TRAVELINE

Scotland	031-246 8021
Northern England	Newcastle upon Tyne (0632) 8021
South & West Yorkshire	Leeds (0532) 8021
North West England	061-246 8021
Midlands	021-246 8021
South Wales	Cardiff (0222) 8021
London	01-246 8021
South West England	Bristol (0272) 8021

WEATHER CENTRES

Glasgow	041-248 3451
Newcastle upon Tyne	0632 26453
Manchester	061-832 6701
Nottingham	0602 384092
London	01-836 4311
Southampton	0703 28844

BBC LOCAL RADIO

			Med. Wave metres/KHz	VHF MHz
1	Radio Cumbria	(Carlisle)	397/756	95.6
		(Whitehaven)	206/1458	96.1
2	Radio Cleveland	(Cleveland)	194/1548	96.6
		(Whitby)	194/1548	95.8
3	Radio Furness		358/837	96.1
4	Radio Humberside		202/1485	96.9
5	Radio Lancashire	(Lancashire)	351/855	96.4
		(Lancaster)	193/1557	103.3
6	Radio Leeds	(Leeds)	388/774	92.4
		(Wharfedale area)	388/774	95.3
7	Radio Manchester		206/1458	95.1
8	Radio Merseyside		202/1485	95.8
9	Radio Newcastle	(Newcastle)	206/1458	95.4
		(N.E.Northumberland)	206/1458	96.3
10	Radio Sheffield		290/1035	97.4
			290/1035	88.6
11	Radio York	(York)	450/666	90.2
		(Scarborough)	450/666	97.2
12	Radio Derby		269/1116	96.5
			269/1116	94.2
13	Radio Leicester		358/837	95.1
14	Radio Lincolnshire		219/1368	94.9
15	Radio Northampton	(North)	271/1107	103.3
		(South)	271/1107	96.6
16	Radio Nottingham	(North)	189/1584	95.4
		(South)	197/1521	95.4
17	Radio Shropshire	(North)	397/756	96.0
		(South)	189/1584	95.0
18	Radio Stoke-on-Trent		200/1503	94.6
19	Radio WM (West Midlands)			
		(Birmingham)	206/1458	95.6
		(Wolverhampton)	362/828	95.6
20	Radio Bedfordshire	(Bedford)	258/1161	96.9
		(Luton)	476/630	103.7
21	Radio Bristol	(Bristol)	194/1548	95.5
		(Taunton)	227/1323	95.5
22	Radio Cambridgeshire	(North)	207/1449	96.0
		(South)	292/1026	96.0
23	Radio London		206/1458	94.9
24	Radio Norfolk	(Norfolk)	351/855	95.1
		(King's Lynn)	344/873	96.7
25	Radio Oxford		202/1485	95.2
26	Radio Cornwall	(N.& E.)	457/657	95.2
		(Mid & W.)	476/630	96.4
		(Isles of Scilly)	-	97.3
27	Radio Devon	(Plymouth)	351/855	97.5
		(Exeter)	303/990	97.0
		(Torbay)	206/1458	97.5
		(Okehampton)	303/990	96.2
		(N.Devon)	375/801	103.9
28	Radio Kent	(W.Kent)	290/1035	96.7
		(E.Kent)	388/774	104.2
		(Tunbridge Wells)	187/1602	96.7
29	Radio Solent	(IOW, Hants, W.Sussex.)	300/999	96.1
		(Bournemouth & Poole)	221/1359	96.1
30	Radio Sussex	(S.Sussex)	202/1485	95.3
		(E.Sussex)	258/1161	104.5
		(N. & Central Sussex)	219/1368	104.0

WEATHERLINE

Dundee, Tayside, Fife and Central	Dundee (0382) 8091
Edinburgh and Lothian	031-246 8091
Glasgow Area	041-246 8091
Grampian and Aberdeen	Aberdeen (0224) 8091
Anglesey and North Wales Coast	Chester (0244) 8091
Humberside	Lincoln (0522) 8091
Lake District and Cumbria	Carlisle (0228) 8091
N. E. England inc. N.Yorks	Newcastle (0632) 8091
North West England	061-246 8091
South Yorkshire and Peak District	Sheffield (0742) 8091
West Yorkshire	Leeds (0532) 8091
East Midlands	Nottingham (0602) 8091
Glamorgan and Gwent	Cardiff (0222) 8091
Lincolnshire	Lincoln (0522) 8091
South West Midlands	Hereford (0432) 8091
Staffordshire and Salop	Stoke-on-Trent (0782) 8091
West Midlands and Warwickshire	021-246 8091
East Anglia	Ipswich (0473) 8091
Essex Coast	01-246 8096
Herts., Beds. and Inland Essex	01-246 8099
London Area	01-246 8091
Oxon., Berks. and Bucks.	01-246 8090
Somerset and Avon	Bristol (0272) 8091
Devon and Cornwall	Exeter (0392) 8091
Dorset and Hants Coast	Southampton (0703) 8091
North Kent Coast	01-246 8096
North Downs and the Weald	01-246 8092
Sussex Coast & South Kent Coast	01-246 8097

MOTORING INFORMATION

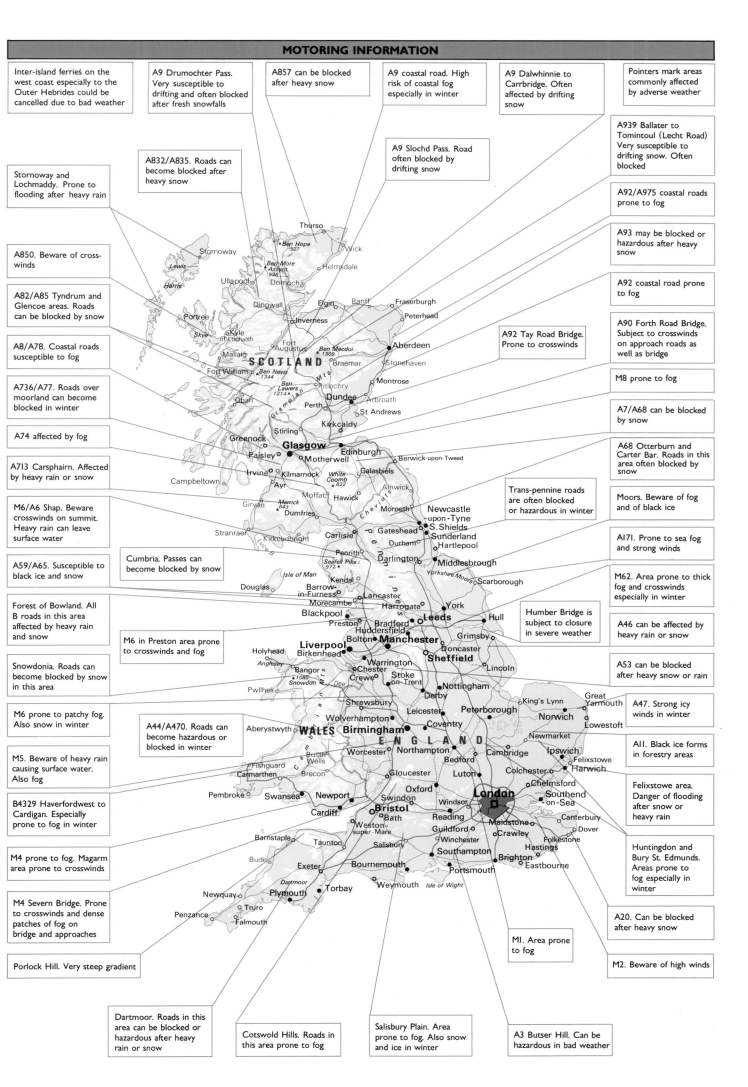

Inter-island ferries on the west coast especially to the Outer Hebrides could be cancelled due to bad weather

A9 Drumochter Pass. Very susceptible to drifting and often blocked after fresh snowfalls

A857 can be blocked after heavy snow

A9 coastal road. High risk of coastal fog especially in winter

A9 Dalwhinnie to Carrbridge. Often affected by drifting snow

Pointers mark areas commonly affected by adverse weather

A9 Slochd Pass. Road often blocked by drifting snow

A939 Ballater to Tomintoul (Lecht Road) Very susceptible to drifting snow. Often blocked

A832/A835. Roads can become blocked after heavy snow

Stornoway and Lochmaddy. Prone to flooding after heavy rain

A92/A975 coastal roads prone to fog

A93 may be blocked or hazardous after heavy snow

A850. Beware of cross-winds

A92 coastal road prone to fog

A82/A85 Tyndrum and Glencoe areas. Roads can be blocked by snow

A90 Forth Road Bridge. Subject to crosswinds on approach roads as well as bridge

A8/A78. Coastal roads susceptible to fog

A92 Tay Road Bridge. Prone to crosswinds

M8 prone to fog

A736/A77. Roads over moorland can become blocked in winter

A7/A68 can be blocked by snow

A74 affected by fog

A68 Otterburn and Carter Bar. Roads in this area often blocked by snow

A713 Carsphairn. Affected by heavy rain or snow

Trans-pennine roads are often blocked or hazardous in winter

Moors. Beware of fog and of black ice

M6/A6 Shap. Beware crosswinds on summit. Heavy rain can leave surface water

A171. Prone to sea fog and strong winds

Cumbria. Passes can become blocked by snow

M62. Area prone to thick fog and crosswinds especially in winter

A59/A65. Susceptible to black ice and snow

Humber Bridge is subject to closure in severe weather

A46 can be affected by heavy rain or snow

Forest of Bowland. All B roads in this area affected by heavy rain and snow

M6 in Preston area prone to crosswinds and fog

A53 can be blocked after heavy snow or rain

Snowdonia. Roads can become blocked by snow in this area

A47. Strong icy winds in winter

M6 prone to patchy fog. Also snow in winter

A44/A470. Roads can become hazardous or blocked in winter

A11. Black ice forms in forestry areas

M5. Beware of heavy rain causing surface water. Also fog

Felixstowe area. Danger of flooding after snow or heavy rain

B4329 Haverfordwest to Cardigan. Especially prone to fog in winter

M4 prone to fog. Magarm area prone to crosswinds

Huntingdon and Bury St. Edmunds. Areas prone to fog especially in winter

M4 Severn Bridge. Prone to crosswinds and dense patches of fog on bridge and approaches

A20. Can be blocked after heavy snow

Porlock Hill. Very steep gradient

M1. Area prone to fog

M2. Beware of high winds

Dartmoor. Roads in this area can be blocked or hazardous after heavy rain or snow

Cotswold Hills. Roads in this area prone to fog

Salisbury Plain. Area prone to fog. Also snow and ice in winter

A3 Butser Hill. Can be hazardous in bad weather

DISTANCE IN KILOMETRES

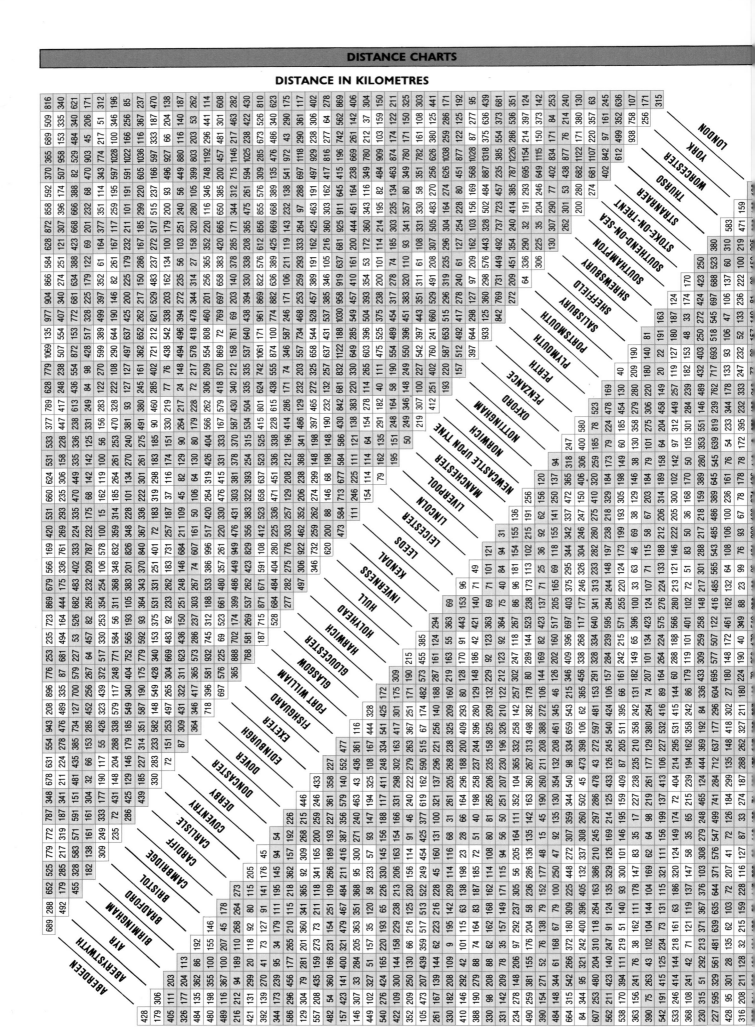

DISTANCE IN MILES

KEY

motorway autoroute Autobahn M5 — Service Area — Under const.	**county/regional boundary** limite de comté/région Bezirksgrenze
junction number numéro d'accès Anschluß-nummer 12 Junction — 13 Restricted Access	**national park** parc nationale Naturschutzpark
dual carriageway chaussées séparées getrennte Fahrbahnen A35 — Under const.	**forest park** réserve geschützt Forst
primary route itinéraire principal 'Primary Route' A39 — Under const.	**height in metres** altitude en mètres Höhe in Meter 456
'A' road route 'A' Hauptstraße 'A' A370 — Under const.	**abbey, cathedral, priory** abbaye, cathedrale Abtai, Dom
'B' road route 'B' Straße 'B' B 3188 — Under const.	**historic house** château ou maison historique historisches Haus
other road autre route übrige Straße	**historic house and garden** maison historique et jardin historisches Haus und Garten
narrow road with passing place route à voie unique Straße, einbahnig	**castle** château Schloß
distance in miles distance en miles Entfernung in 'miles' 15 9 6	**garden** jardin Garten
gradient rampe Steigung	**country park** parc naturel Naturpark
toll péage Zoll Toll	**information centre** syndicat d'initiative Informationszentrum
railway chemin de fer Eisenbahn Sta.	**motor racing circuit** circuit de course Motodrom
car ferry bac pour autos Autofähre	**race course** champ de courses Pferderennbahn
canal canal Kanal	**golf course** terrain de golf Golfplatz
airport aéroport Flughafen	**ancient monument** site antique antikes Denkmal
national boundary limite nationale Landesgrenze	**battle site** site de bataille Schlachtfeld 1685

4 MILES TO INCH / 1 : 253 440

0 1 2 3 4 5   10   15 kilometres
0 1 2 3 4 5   10 miles

at the same scale

Seven Stones

—50°

I

White Island
St Helen's
St Martin's
Bryher
Tean
Higher Town
Tresco
Eastern Isles
Crow Sound
Samson
The Road
A3110
A3111
Hugh Town
St Mary's
The Garrison
Scilly Isles
A3112
To Penzance
Crim Rocks
Broad Sound
Annet
Gugh
St Mary's Sound
St Agnes
ISLES OF SCILLY
Bishop Rock
Western Rocks
Smith Sound

6°20'

A   **B**

Seven Stones

Nev
Pentir
Kelsey Head
West Pentire
Crant
Holywell Bay
Holy
Penhale Point
Cube
Ligger Point
Ligger or Perran Bay
Penhale Sands
Bawden Rocks or Man and his man
Perranporth
St Agnes Head
Trevellas
Perra
Penh
St Agnes
Mithian
Goonbell
Callestick
A30
Porthtowan
Mount Hawke
Tregavethan
Kenw
Mawla
Blackwater
Chacewater
Portreath
Illogan
Pool
Scorrier
Cross Lanes
Crane Islands
Coombe
Carn Brea
St Day
Twelvehea
Navax Point
Red
Kehelland
Redruth
Bissoe
Godrevy Island
Gwithian
Roseworthy
Tuckingmill
Camborne
Carharrack
Pennance
Gwennap
Perranwell Sta
The Island
St Ives
St Ives Bay
Connor Downs
Barripper
Four Lanes
Lanner
Carn Naun Point
The Carracks
Phillack
Angarrack
Troon
Penhalvean
Perranarworthal
Gurnard's Head
Zennor
Halsetown
Carbis Bay
Gwinear
Carnhell Green
Praze-an-Beeble
Ponsanooth
Porthmeor
Trendrine Hill
Towednack
Lelant
Hayle
Rosewarne
Stithians
Pe
Trencrom Hill
Amalebra
Cripplesease
St Erth Praze
Crowan
Crowan Beacon
Rame
Long Downs
Mabe Burnthouse
Pendeen Watch
Morvah
Canonstown
St Erth
Leedstown
Edgcumbe
Lower Boscaswell
Bojewyan
Newmill
Townshend
Porkellis
Treverva
Falm
Trewellard
Pendeen
Ludgvan
Nancegollan
Brill
Botallack
Carnyorth
Madron
Gulval
Crowlas
Godolphin Cross
Wendron
Sewergan
Penjerrick
Cape Cornwall
St Just
Newbridge
Heamoor
Penzance
Longrock
Marazion
Crowntown
Constantine
Mawnan Smith
The Brisons
Bosavern
Tremethick Cross
Buryas Bridge
Chyandour
St Michael's Mount
Goldsithney
Trescowe
Helston
Porth Navas
Kelynack
Sancreed
Tredavoe
Newlyn
Relubbus
St Hilary
Germoe
Tregonning Hill
Gweek
Helford
Brane
Drift
Catchall
Paul
Perranuthnoe
Ashton
Sithney
Breage
Gwek
Crows-an-wra
Kerris
Mousehole
St Clement's Isle
Praa Sands
Rinsey
Porthleven
Garras
Mawgan
St Martin's Green
Manacc
Whitesand Bay
Sennen Cove
Sennen
Trevescan
St Buryan
Boleigh
Cudden Point
Trewavas Head
Loe Pool
Gunwalloe
Berepper
Newtown
Tregidden
St Kever
Longships
Land's End
Porthcurno
Treen
Cury
Traboe
St Levan
Cribba Head
Logan Rock
Lamorna Cove
Mount's Bay
Poldhu Cove
Poldhu Point
Goonhilly Downs
Gwennap Head
Runnel Stone
To Isles of Scilly
Mullion
Porth Mellin
Mullion Cove
Gwenter
Coverack
Mullion Island
Predannack Wollas
Ruan Major
Vellan Head
Ruan Minor
Cadgwith
Grade
Kynance Cove
Landewednack
Hot Point
Lizard
Lizard Point

0 1 2 3 4 5 10 15 kilometres
0 1 2 3 4 5 10 miles

A B C D E

Moor
Halwill Forest
ill Junctio
Halwill 18
Beaw

Titson
Coppathorne
Week?chard
Yeomadon
Herdicott
Clawton
Upcott
Dizzard Point
Poundstock
Tregole
Trewint
Whitstone
Tinney
Coffcott Green
Quoditch
Broadbury
St Gennys
A39
North Tamerton
Tetcott
Lana
Ashwater
Crackington Haven
Cambeak
Wainhouse Corner
Jacobstow
Trebarrow
Henford
Germansweek
Eworthy
Crackington
19
South Wheatley
Maxworthy
West Curry
Luffincott
Northcott
A388
Boas
Tresparrett Posts
Collamoor Head
Langdon
Canworthy Water
Caudworthy
Clubworthy
Bennacott
Boyton
East Panson
Fire Beacon Point
Matshgate
Troswell
St Giles-on-the-Heath
Carey
Brat Clov
Boscastle
B3263
Lesnewth
Otterham
Penwenham
Warbstow
North Petherwin
Brazacott
Bridgetown
Polapit Tamar
Broadwoodwidger
Trevalga
Davidstow
Tremaine
Treneglos
Tresmeer
Cross Green
Tintagel Head
Trewarmett
Tintagel
Bossiney
B3263
Trewassa
Tremail
Hallworthy
Egloskerry
Langore
Werrington
Thrushelton
Stowford
Lewdown
Start Point
Trebarwith
Rockhead
A39
St Clether
Laneast
Trewen
Downhead
Red Down
Piperspool
Tregadillett
St Stephen's
Newport
Launceston
Liftondown
Lifton
Tinhay
Portgate
A30
18
Lewtre
Delabole
Camelford
Newpark
Lower Moor
Butterm Hill
Bray Down
Altarnun
Fivelanes
Lewannick
South Petherwin
Lezant
A30
Allerford
Coryt
Port Isaac Bay
Lanteglos
Tresinney
400
346
346
369
Polyphant
Trebullett
Coad's Green
Treburley
Rezare
Dunterton
Marystow
Chillaton
Kelly
Port Isaac
Port Gaverne
Trewalder
Helstone
Rough Tor
Brown Willy 420
Codda
Trebartha
North Hill
Bathpool
Linkinhorne
Rilla Mill
Luckett
Downgate
Bradstone
Felldownhead
Milton Abbot
South Brer
Longcross
Portquin
Trelights
LONG CROSS VICTORIAN GARDENS
Pendoggett
Michaelstow
Garrow Tor
Bolventor
Bodmin Moor
Henwood
Golberdon
Kelly Bray
Kit Hill
Chilsworthy
Hingston Down
Gunnislake
Highe Walred
St Minver
St Endellion
Trelill
St Kew
St Breward
Row
Smallacombe Downs
Kilmar Tor 390
Upton Cross
South Hill
Harrowbarrow
St Ann's Chapel
Albaston
A390
Chapel Amble
St Kew Highway
St Tudy
Temple
Dozmary Pool
Minions
Caradon Hill
Darite
Pensilva
Haye
Trevigro
Callington
Ashton
COTEHELE (NT) THE GARDEN HO
Harewood
Calstock
Bodieve
Kelly
St Mabyn
Blisland
Colliford Reservoir
Browngelly Downs
Common Moor
Middlehill
Newbridge
St Dominick
Bere Alston
evanson
Wadebridge
Egloshayle
Helland
Maidenwell
Siblyback
Warleggan
St Neot
St Cleer
Tremar
St Ive
Merrymeet
Pengover Green
Quethiock
St Mellion
BUCKLAND
Milton Com
Burlawn
Cardinham Moor
Cardinham
Mount
Ley
Doublebois
Dobwalls
Liskeard
Menheniot
Blunts
Pillaton
Bere Fe
k Downs
Washaway
Lane-end
PENCARROW
Ruthernbridge
Nanstallon
St Lawrence
Dunmere
Bodmin
Lanivet
Trebyan
Bodmin Parkway Sta.
LANHYDROCK (NT)
West Taphouse
East Taphouse
St Pinnock
CORNWALL
Hatt
Botusfleming
Landrake
Cargreen
Landulph
Tamerto Foliot
Withiel
Victoria
Roche Sta.
Lockengate
Redmoor
Boconnoc
St Keyne
Horningtops
Tideford
A38
Trematon
Markwell
Saltash
St Bude
A30
Roche
Bilberry
Bugle
Bridgend
Couchsmill
Bocaddon
Herodsfoot
Trewidland
Bylane End
Widegates
Hessenford
Trerule Foot
St Germans
St Stephens
Polbathic
Sheviock
ANTONY (NT)
Torpoint
Devonport
Dennis
Hensborough Downs
Stenalees
Penwithick
Trethurgy
Lanlivery
Luxulyan
Penpillick
Lanreath
Lerryn
Muchlarnick
Sandplace
Morval
St Martin
Crafthole
Portwrinkle
Antony
Cremyll
Stor
Turn Dra Islan
Nanpean Carthew
A391
Ruddl
Foxhole
St Blazey
Tywardreath Highway
Tywardreath
Golant
St Veep
Penpoll
Pelynt
Trenewan
East Looe
Downderry
Seaton
St John
Freathy
Millbrook
Mount Edgcumbe
Plymou Breakw
ST AUSTELL
Boscoppa
Holmbush
Par
Lescrow
Bodinnick
Lanteglos
Lansallos
West Looe
Porthallow
St George's or Looe Island
Kingsand
Cawsand Bay
Cawsand
Rame
High Street
Trewoon
St Mewan
A390
Charlestown
Menabilly
Fowey
Polruan
Polperro
Whitsand Bay
Rame Head
Penlee Point
He
Sticker
Polgooth
Porthpean
St Austell Bay
Carlyon Bay
Pencarrow Head
Lantivet Bay
Hewas Water
Trenarren
Black Head
Gribbin Head
St Ewe
Polkerris
assick
Pentewan
Penare Point
Mevagissey Bay
St Michael Caerhays
Trevarrick
Mevagissey
Chapel Point
Gorran Churchtown
Gorran Haven
Maenease Point
Boswinger
Penare
Veryan Bay
Dodman Point

To Roscoff & Santander
Eddystone Rocks

Jacobstowe · Exbourne · North Tawton · Bow · Clannaborough Barton · Coleford · Knowle · Creedy Park · Thorverton · Efford

Inwardleigh · Shilstone · Sampford Cot · Broadnymet · Nymet Tracey · Colebrooke · Yeoford · Crediton · Shobrooke · Brampford Speke · Nether Exe · KILLERTON (NT) · ewe · Budlake · Clyst St Lawrenc

hlew · Oak · Itton · Colebrooke · Uton · Hookway · Newton St Cyres · Upton Pyne · Stoke Canon · Westw

bury · Folly Gate · Taw Green · Spreyton · Court Barton · Oldridge · Cowley · Poltimore · Pinhoe · Broadclyst · Dog Village · Whir

Southcott · Yelland · **Okehampton** · South Tawton · Whiddon Down · Crockernwell · Cheriton Bishop · Tedburn St Mary · Whitestone · Exwick · **EXETER** · Whipton · Clyst Honiton · A30 · Rock

Meldon · Belstone · Sticklepath · South Zeal · Cawsand Hill · Throwleigh · Drewsteignton · Cheriton Cross · Longdown · Pocombe Bridge · Ide · Alphington · Countess Wear · Sowton · Clyst St Mary · Farringdon

Sourton · Okehampton Camp · Yes Tor,619 · High Willhays · Wonson · Gidleigh · CASTLE DROGO · Easton · Dunsford · Dunchideock · Shillingford St George · Topsham · Exminster · Clyst St George · Woodbur · Salterton

Downton · Bridestowe and Sourton Common · Hangingstone Hill · Great Kneeset · Whitehorse Hill · Murchington · Chagford · Doccombe · Bridford · Christow · Higher Ashton · Lower Ashton · DEVON AND EXETER · Kennford · Kenn · Powderham · Exton · Woodbu

Beardon · Shortacombe · Amicombe Hill · Cranmere Pool · Frenchbeer · Moretonhampstead · Trusham · Whiteway House · Bickham House · Oxton House · Starcross · Lympstone · A LA RONDE · Withycom · Raleigh

Willsworthy · DARTMOOR · Teign Head · North Bovey · Sanduck · Easdon Tor · Lustleigh · Hennock · Mamhead · Cockwood · EXMO

Cut Hill · Warren House · Hameldown Tor · Manaton · Bovey Tracey · Chudleigh Knighton · Ideford · Langdon House · Dawlish Warren Sta.

Lynch Tor · Rough Tor · Higher White Tor · Sittaford Tor · White Ridge · Widecombe in the Moor · Haytor Vale · Ilsington · Heathfield · Chudleigh · Ugbrooke House · Luton · Little · **Dawlish**

Cudliptown · Cocks Hill · Postbridge · Bellever · Cator Court · Dunstone · Liverton · Coldeast · Preston · Sandygate · Bishopsteignton · Holcombe

Peter Tavy · Great Mis Tor · Babeny · Corndon Tor · Ponsworthy · Sigford · Teigngrace · Kingsteignton · **Teignmouth** · Shaldon

Merrivale · Two Bridges · Whiteworks · Dartmeet · Hexworthy · Buckland in the Moor · Bickington · Highweek · **Newton Abbot** · Netherton · Milber · Combeinteignhead · Stokeinteignhead

Princetown · Sampford Spiney · Walkhampton Common · Royal Hill · Poundsgate · Rew · Caton · Combe Cross · Wolborough · East Ogwell · Haccombe · Babbacombe Bay

Yelverton · Sheepstor · Holne Ridge · Cater's Beam · Ryder's Hill · Holne · **Ashburton** · RIVER DART · Forder Green · Woodland · Denbury · Abbotskerswell · Coffinswell · Daccombe · Maidencombe

Meavy · Burrator Resr · Abbot's Way · Dean Moor · **Buckfastleigh** · Buckfast · Landscove · Torbryan · Ipplepen · Kingskerswell · Barton · St Marychurch

Clearbrook · Shaugh Bridge · Shaugh Prior · Shell Top · Stall Moor · Shipley Bridge · Dean · Woolston Green · Staverton · Broadhempston · North Whilborough · Compton · Cockington · Edginswell · Shiphay · Babbacombe

Bickleigh · Lee Moor · Penn Moor · Harbourneford · Didworthy · Dean Prior · Rattery · Shinner's Bridge · Dartington · Dart Valley Rly · Red Post · Marldon · Torre Sta. · **Torquay** · Hope's Nose

Cornwood · Harford · Ugborough Beacon · South Brent · Tigley · Berry Pomeroy · Blagdon · KIRKHAM · **TORBAY**

Plympton · Drakeland Corner · Lutton · Bittaford · Belsford · Harberton · **Totnes** · Collaton St Mary · **Paignton** · Tor Bay

Plym Bridge · Sparkwell · Colebrook · Ivybridge · Lee Mill Bridge · Ugborough · Avonwick · Diptford · Lincombe · Sharpham House · Stoke Gabriel · Goodrington

OUTH · Westlake · Ermington · Brownston · North Huish · Rolster · Harbertonford · Crabadon · Ashprington · Tuckenhay · Cornworthy · Churston Ferrers · **Brixham** · Berry Head

Elburton · Bickham Bridge · Gara Bridge · East Cornworthy · Dittisham · Higher Brixham · Sharkham Point

ymstock · Brixton · Yealmpton · Dunstone · Flete · Modbury · Halwell · Washbourne · Allaleigh · Capton · Downton · Raddicombe · Woodhuish

Goosewell · Kitley · Torr · Ford · Holbeton · Moreleigh · Hemborough Post · Boohay · Scabbacombe Head

Thomas ighton · Newton Ferrers · Battisborough Cross · Ashford · Aveton Gifford · Blackawton · Millcombe · **Dartmouth** · Kingswear · COLETON FISHACRE (NT)

Wembury · Noss Mayo · Netton · St Ann's Chapel · Houghton · Loddiswell · Woodleigh · East Allington · Coombe · Bowden · Mew Stone

Worswell · Kingston · Ringmore · Bigbury · Venn · Churchstow · Goveton · Merrifield · Cole's Cross · Strete · Stoke Fleming

Stoke Point · Beacon Point · Bigbury-on-Sea · Burgh Island · West Alvington · Upton · Buckland-tout-Saints · Slapton

Bantham · Buckland · South Milton · **Kingsbridge** · Sherford · Slapton Ley · Start

Thurlestone · South Huish · Charleton · Frogmore · Chillington · Torcross · Start Bay

Galmpton · Hope · Malborough · South Pool · Beeson · Beesands

Bolt Tail · **Salcombe** · Kellaton · Hallsands

Bolberry · OVERBECKS · Soar · East Portlemouth · Chivelstone · Start Point

Bolt Head · East Prawle · Lannacombe Bay · Prawle Point

0 1 2 3 4 5   10   15 kilometres

0 1 2 3 4 5   10 miles

A   B   C   D   E

1

2

3

4

5

6

7

North West Point

Lundy

Rat Island

Shutter Point

Widmouth Head

Combe Martin Bay

Ilfracombe

Hele

Bull Point   Lee Bay   Lee   Slade   Berrynarbor   Sterridge

Rockham Bay   Morte Point   Mortehoe

West Down

Woolacombe   Morte Bay   Trimstone   Bittadon   East

Pickwell   North Buckland   Milltown   Mudd

Baggy Point   Georgeham   Halsinger   Youls

Croyde Bay   Croyde   Knowle   Marwood   Kingshear

Saunton   Pippacott   MARWOOD HILL

Braunton   Heanton Punchardon   Prixford

Saunton Sands   Wrafton   Ashford   Pilton

BARNSTAPLE   Braunton Burrows

OR   Taw

BIDEFORD BAY   The Neck   Bickington   Goo

A39   Fremington   Ba

Appledore   Bickleton   New

Westward Ho!   Instow   Lan

Tapeley   St John's Chapel   Bish

Northam   Westleigh   Tawstock   Taw

Bideford   Eastleigh   Horwood   Newton Tracey   Ensis

Abbotsham   East-the-Water   Loveacott   Fishle

Hartland Point   Gammaton Moor   Hiscott   Barto

Titchberry   Windbury Point   Fairy Cross   Ford   Yeo Vale   Woodtown   Alverdiscott   Yarnscombe

Gallantry Bower   Clovelly   Landcross   Atheri

Hartland Quay   Clovelly Bay   Buck's Mills   Horns Cross   Weare Giffard   Langridge

Stoke   Hartland   Dyke   Clovelly Cross   Goldworthy   Huntshaw Cross   Lar

Milford   Philham   Buck's Cross   Littleham   High Bullen   Sherwo

Elmscott   Edistone   Tosberry   Cranford   Parkham Ash   Parkham   Monkleigh   Great Torrington   Green

Woolfardisworthy   Buckland Brewer   St Giles in the Wood

South Hole   Almiston Cross   Frithelstock   Taddiport   Kingscott

Welcome   Melbury   Frithelstock Stone   ROSEMOOR   Rot

Ashmansworthy   Powler's Piece   Little Torrington   Villavi

Meddon   Northmoor   Kismeldon Bridge   Langtree   Beaford

Gooseham   Youlstone   Dinworthy   East Putford   Stibb Cross   Winswell

Morwenstow   Eastcott   West Putford   Peters Marland   Merton   Heanton Satchville

Higher Sharpnose Point   Shop   Bradworthy   Bulkworthy   Woollaton   Do

Lower Sharpnose Point   Woodford   Brendon   Abbots Bickington   Newton St Petrock   Huish   Dow

Taylors Cross   Upper Tamar Lake   Sutcombe   Milton Damerel   North Town   Ido

Coombe   A39   Alfardisworthy   Shebbear   Petrockstowe

Kilkhampton   Lower Tamar Lake   Soldon Cross   Waldon   Buckland Filleigh   Ash   Meeth

Stibb   Youldonmoor Cross   Thornbury   Sheepwash

Rhude Cross   Youldon   Holsworthy Beacon   Bradford   Torridge   Hele Bridge

Poughill   STAMFORD HILL   Chilsworthy   Black Torrington

Bude   Flexbury   X 1643   Grimscott   Cookbury   Monkokehampto

Bude Haven   Stratton   Launcells Cross   Brandis Corner   Highampton

Bude   A3072   Pancrasweek   Anvil Corner   Lydacott   Hatherleigh

Bay   Launcells   Holsworthy   Dunsland Cross   Basset's C

Helebridge   Red Post   Rydon   Hollacombe   13   Graddon Moor   Jacobsto

Marhamchurch   Ryworthy   Chasty   A3072

Widemouth Bay   Bridgerule   Halwill Forest   Lew

Titson   Yeomadon   Deer   Halwill Junction   Inwardleigh

Coppathorne   Week Orchard   Herdicott   Clawton   Halwill   18   Beaworthy   Northlew   A386

Dizzard Point   Tinney   Coffcott Green   Upcott   Ashbury   Oak   Folly Gate

Poundstock   Whitstone   North Tamerton   Quoditch   Broadbury

Tregole   Week St Mary   Trebarrow   Tetcott   B 3248

St Gennys   Trewint   Lana   Ashwater   Southcott

Crackington Haven   Jacobstow   Luffincott   Henford   Germansweek   Eworthy   Yelland

Cambeak   Wainhouse Corner   A39

Crackington   South Wheatley   West Curry   Northcott   Boasley Cross

Fire Beacon Point   Tresparrett Posts   Collamoor Head   Maxworthy   Clubworthy   Boyton   Virginstow   Hewton

Langdon   Caudworthy   Bennacott   East Panson   Bratton Clovelly

Boscastle   Marshgate   Canworthy Water   Troswell   Brazacott   St Giles-on-the-Heath   Meldon

Trevalga   Otterham   Warbstow   Wolf   Bridestowe   Sou

B 3263   enwenham   Petherwin   Bridgetown   Broadwoodwidger   A30   A386   Yes T

Bossiney   Tremaine   Polapit Tamar   Cross Green   W. Okement   Bridestowe and Sou

Treneglos   Ladycross

A377   A361   A386   A388   A3079   B 3254   B 3343   B 3230   B 3231   B 3232   B 3237   B 3248   B 3266

62

EXMOOR FOREST — EXMOOR NATIONAL PARK

Brendon Hills

A B C D E

Towns and places (selected):

Lynton · Lynmouth · Countisbury · Foreland Point · Countisbury Cove · Lynmouth Bay · Valley of Rocks · Heddon's Mouth · Woody Bay · Trentishoe · Martinhoe · Heale · Parracombe · Kentisbury · Blackmoor Gate · Kentisbury Ford · Arlington · Knightacott · Loxhore · Bratton Fleming · Benton · Challacombe · Leworthy · Stoke Rivers · Gunn · Charles · Brayford · High Bray · North Radworthy · North Heasley · South Radworthy · Heasley Mill · East Buckland · West Buckland · Swimbridge · Castle Hill · Filleigh · Chittlehampton · Clapworthy · Satterleigh · Warkleigh · Chittlehamholt · Hudscott · South Molton · Bishop's Nympton · George Nympton · Alswear · Mariansleigh · Rose Ash · Ash Mill · Knowstone · Romansleigh · King's Nympton · Rowley · Meshaw · Creacombe · Rackenford · Chulmleigh · Copy Lake · Ashreigney · Ashley · Eggesford Barton · Wembworthy · Chawleigh · Cheldon · West Worlington · East Worlington · Witheridge · Nomansland · Thelbridge Barton · Hele Lane · Puddington · Pennymoor · Cruwys Morchard · Templeton · Withleigh · Tiverton · Calverleigh · Washfield · Loxbeare · Bolham · Chevithorne · Chettiscombe · Knightshayes Court · East Mere · Bickleigh · Cadeleigh · Upham · Well Town · Black Dog · Woolfardisworthy · Poughill · Stockleigh English · Cheriton Fitzpaine · Kennerleigh · East Village · Morchard Bishop · Oldborough · Lapford · Eastington · Forches Cross · Coldridge · Nymet Rowland · Brushford Barton · Taw Bridge · Bondleigh · East Leigh · Zeal Monachorum · Down St Mary · Ash Bullayne · Clannaborough Barton · Coleford · Knowle · Copplestone · Sandford · Upton Hellions · Stockleigh Pomeroy · Crediton · Shobrooke · Creedy Park · Cadbury · Bickleigh · Ravenshayes · Bradninch · Silverton · Up Exe · Thorverton · Efford · Nether Exe · Rewe · Killerton · Brampford Speke · Upton Pyne · Stoke Canon · Poltimore · Broadclyst · Dog Village · Whimple · Cowley · Newton St Cyres · Hookway · Court Barton · Uton · Oldridge · Whitestone · Exwick · Exeter · Pinhoe · Whipton · Clyst Honiton · Marsh Green · Rockbeare · West Hill · Ottery St Mary · Fairmile · Wiggaton · Tipton St John · Harpford · Venn Ottery · Newton Poppleford · Aylesbeare · Woodbury Salterton · Clyst St George · Clyst St Mary · Sowton · Countess Wear · Ide · Alphington · Shillingford St George · Dunsford · Cheriton Bishop · Tedburn St Mary · Crockernwell · Drewsteignton · Castle Drogo · Spreyton · South Tawton · North Tawton · Bow · Broadnymet · Nymet Tracey · Sampford Courtenay · Honeychurch · North Tawton · Taw Green · Whiddon Down · South Zeal · Throwleigh · Gidleigh · Easton · Murchington

Exmoor area: Brendon · Leeford · Malmsmead · Oare · Culbone · Porlock Weir · W.Porlock · Porlock · Allerford · Selworthy · Bossington · Minehead · Alcombe · Marsh Street · Dunster · Blue Anchor · Watchet · St Decumans · St Audries · West Quantox · East Quantox · Bicknoller · Williton · Old Cleeve · Washford · Sampford Brett · Orchard Wyndham · Monksilver · Nettlecombe · Stogumber · Combe Sydenham Hall · Lower Vexford · Elworthy · Raleighs Cross · Brompton Ralph · Treborough · Willett · Tolland · Combe · Clatworthy · Pitsford Hill · Tarr · Langley Marsh · Wiveliscombe · Huish Champflower · Maundown · Ford · Milverton · Chipstable · Waterrow · Nunnington Park · Bathealton · Langford Budville · Runnington · Appley · Thorne St Margaret · Holywell Lake · Greenham · Hockworthy · Holcombe Rogus · Westleigh · Burlescombe · Nicholashayne · Sampford Arundel · Culmstock · Hackpen Hill · Uffculme · Craddock · Ashill · Sheldon · Kentisbeare · Blackborough · Dunkeswell · Broadhembury · Luton · Upton · Awliscombe · Cheriton · Buckerell · Feniton · Fenny Bridges · Gittisham · Alfington

Hills and features: Dunkery Hill · Dunkery Beacon 519 · Codsend Moors · Lype Hill 423 · Haddon Hill · Haddon Hill · Selworthy Beacon · North Hill 252 · Hurtstone Pt. · Hoaroak Hill · Dure Down · Span Head 439 · Worth Hill · Molland Common · Withypool Hill · Winsford Hill · Dry Hill 444 · Shoulsbarrow Common · Pinkworthy Pond 480 · Challacombe Common · Brendon Common · South Common · Lucott Cross · Holnicote Estate · Cawsand Hill 550 · Butter Hill 413 · Croydon Hill · Rodhuish · Bilbrook · Withycombe · Wimbleball Reservoir · Clatworthy Reservoir · Heydon Hill · Battleton · Dulverton · Bury · Skilgate · Morebath · Petton · Shillingford · Clayhanger · Stawley

Roads: A39 · A361 · A377 · A373 · A396 · A30 · M5 · B3223 · B3224 · B3221 · B3222 · B3227 · B3358

EXETER

0 1 2 3 4 5 10 15 kilometres
0 1 2 3 4 5 10 miles

Hawkridge • Brompton Ralph
Clatworthy Reservoir
Upton ·317
Clatworthy • Pitsford Hill • Tarr • Langley Marsh
Combe Florey • Toulton • Cushuish
Eastcombe • Bishop's Lydeard • Fulford
Thurloxton • North Newton
Burrow Brick
Hedging • Lyng • Athelney

Dulverton • Battleton • Bury • Skilgate
Haddon Hill • Huish Champflower • Maundown • Ford
Wiveliscombe • Fitzhead • Halse • Ash Priors
Kingston St Mary • West Monkton • Bathpool
Creech St Michael • Durston • Meare Green • Oath • Stoke St Gregory
Curload

East Anstey • Nightcott • Brushford
Exebridge • Morebath • Petton
Chipstable • Waterrow • Nunnington Park • Milverton
Heathfield • Staplegrove • Monkton Heathfield
TAUNTON • SOMERSET
Ruishton • Ham • Knapp • North Curry • Thorn Falcon

Oldways E • Exebridge • Shillingford
Bathealton • Stawley • Langford Budville • Nynehead
Chipley Park • Oake • Hillfarrance • Bishop's Hull • Wilton
Henlade • Stoke St Mary • Wrantage • Curry Mallet • West Hatch • Beer Crocombe • Fivehead • Isle Abbotts • Isle Brewers

Nether Newton • Oakford
Huntsham • Ashbrittle • Appley • Runnington • Thorne St Margaret
Bradford-on-Tone • Trull
West Buckland • Hatch Beauchamp
Bickenhall • Ashill • Puckington • Stoch

Stoodleigh • Stoodleigh Beacon • Cove
Hockworthy • Greenham • Holcombe Rogus • Westleigh • Burlescombe
Wellington • Rockwell Green • Sampford Arundel • Wrangway • Ford Street
Angersleigh • Blackmoor • Pitminster • Corfe • Blagdon Hill
Staple Fitzpaine • Curland • Windmill Hill • Broadway • Whitelackington

Loxbeare • Washfield
Knightshayes Court (NT) • East Mere • Chevithorne • Chettiscombe • Bolham
Pit • Whitnage • Uplowman • Ayshford
Nicholashayne • Rosemary Lane • Clayhidon • Widcombe
Blackdown Hills
Churchstanton • Stapley • Otterford • Fyfett • Buckland St Mary
Horton • Broadway • Ilminster • Donyatt

Templeton Bridge • Silverleigh
Templeton • Withleigh • TIVERTON • Bolham • Lowman
Sampford Peverell • Halberton • Waterloo Cross • Appledore
Uffculme • Culmstock • Hemyock • Bolham Water
Churchinford • Northay • Whitestaunton • Combe St Nicholas • Wadeford • Cudworth • Chaffcombe
Crock Street • Cricket Malherbie • Knowle St Giles

Cruwys Morchard • Withleigh
Ash Thomas • Tiverton Junc. • Smithincott • Craddock • Ashill • Hackpen Hill
Madford • Smeatharpe • Howley • Marsh • Whitestaunton
Newcott • Yarcombe • Wambrook • Chard • Forton
Chard Junction • Thorncombe • Holditch

Well Town • Upham • Cadeleigh • Cheriton Fitzpaine
Halberton • Willand • Bradfield • Blackborough • Sheldon
Kentisbeare • Dunkeswell • Luppitt • Upottery
Rawridge • Stockland • Furley • Chardstock • Tatworth • South Chard • Tytherleigh • Membury

Butterleigh • Cadbury • Ravenshayes • Bradninch
CULLOMPTON • Colebrook • Westcott • Dulford • Kerswell • Broadhembury
Beacon • Monkton • Dalwood • Smallridge • Hawkchurch • Birdsmoor • Marshals

Stockleigh Pomeroy • Up Exe • Silverton • Hele • Langford
Mutterton • Norman's Green • Plymtree • Luton • Upton
Combe Raleigh • Awliscombe • Cotleigh • Wilmington • Axminster • Wootton Fitzpaine

Thorverton • Efford • Nether Exe • Rewe • Clyst Hydon
Higher Tale • Payhembury • Cheriton • Buckerell • Feniton
HONITON • Hamlet • Offwell • Widworthy • Shute • Kilmington • Seaton Junction • Whitford

Brampford Speke • Upton Pyne • Stoke Canon • Budlake
Clyst St Lawrence • Aunk • Colestocks • Talaton
Fenny Bridges • Gittisham • Alfington • Church Green • Northleigh • Farway
Colyton • Musbury • Uplyme • Charm

Newton Cyres • Cowley • Poltimore • Westwood • Broadclyst
Dog Village • Whimple • Fairmile
OTTERY ST MARY • Wiggaton • Broad Down • FARWAY
Southleigh • Colyford • Combpyne • Rousdon • Morcombelake • Pinhay • LYME REGIS

A377 • EXETER • Exwick • Whipton • Pinhoe
Rockbeare • Marsh Green • West Hill • Tipton St John • Sidbury • Harcombe
Weston • Branscombe • Seaton • Axmouth • Dowlands • Pinhay

Pocombe Bridge • Ide • Alphington • Countess Wear
Clyst Honiton • Sowton • Farringdon • Aylesbeare • Venn Ottery • Harpford
Sidford • Salcombe Regis • Beer Vicarage • Beer Head • Seaton Bay

Shillingford St George • Exminster • Topsham • Ebford • Exton
Woodbury Salterton • Hawkerland • Newton Poppleford • Houghton • Bowd
Sidmouth • Weston

Haldon House • Higher Ashton • Ashton • Kennford • Kenn
Woodbury • Colaton Raleigh • Bicton • Pinn • Otterton • East Budleigh

Bickham House • Devon and Exeter • Kenton • Oxton House • Starcross
Powderham • Lympstone • Withycombe Raleigh • Knowle • Littleham
BUDLEIGH SALTERTON

Chudleigh • Ugbrooke House • Ideford • Luton
Mamhead • Ashcombe • Cockwood • EXMOUTH • Littleham

Sandygate • Langdon House • Dawlish Warren Sta. • Holcombe
DAWLISH

Kingsteignton • Bishopsteignton • Combeinteignhead • Shaldon
TEIGNMOUTH

Netherton • Milber • Haccombe • Coffinswell • Stokeinteignhead
Babbacombe Bay

Daccombe • Maidencombe • St Marychurch • Babbacombe
Edginswell • Torre Abbey • TORQUAY • Hope's Nose
Cockington • Marldon • TORBAY • PAIGNTON • Goodrington

Tor Bay • To Guernsey, Alderney & Jersey

LYME

Exe Valley • Vale of Taunton Deane • Culm Valley • Blackdown Hills

High Ham · Littleton · Kingweston · Copley Wood · Lydford · Lovington · Cary · Shepton Montague · Barrow · Penselwood · Barrow Street · Fonthill Gifford

A · Bramwell · Bradley Hill · Charlton Mackrell · Babcary · North Barrow · Bratton Seymour · Charlton Musgrove · Bourton Common · Huntingford · **E** · East Knoyle · **I**

Wearne · Pitney · Somerton · Charlton Adam · Yarlington · Wincanton · Stoke Trister · Milton on Stour · Sedgehill · Newtown · Hatch · Tisbury

Huish Episcopi · Pibsbury · Kingsdon Hill · Kingsdon · North Cadbury · Holton · Lattiford · Gillingham · Coppleridge · A350 · Semley

Muchelney · Long Sutton · Sparkford · Compton Pauncefoot · South Cadbury · Blackford · N. Cheriton S. · Buckhorn Weston · Cucklington · Peacemarsh · Motcombe · Donhead St Andrew

Thorney · Long Load · Podimore · West Camel · Queen Camel · Sutton Montis · Charlton Horethorne · Horsington · Kington Magna · West Stour · Knap Corner · East Stour · **Shaftesbury** · Donhead St Mary · Ludwell

E · Northover · Yeovilton · Marston Magna · Corton Denham · Stowell · Abbas Combe · Temple Combe · Fifehead Magdalen · Stour Row · Guy's Marsh · Cann · Charlton

Stapleton · Witcombe · Ilchester · Chilton Cantelo · Rimpton · Milborne Wick · Yenston · Henstridge Marsh · Todber · Twyford · Cann Common · Melbury Abbas · Win Green · **12**

Ash · Limington · Ashington · Mudford · Sandford Orcas · Poyntington · **Milborne Port** · Henstridge · Marnhull · Margaret Marsh · Bedchester · Compton Abbas · Ashmore

Martock · Tintinhull · Chilthorne Domer · Yeovil Marsh · Adber · Trent · Oborne · Purse Caundle · Stalbridge · Hinton St Mary · Orchard · Manston · Fontmell Magna · Sutton Waldron

East Lambrook · Bower Hinton · Stoke sub Hamdon · Montacute · **YEOVIL** · Over Compton · **Sherborne** · Nether Compton · Goathill · Stalbridge Weston · Stourton Caundle · **Sturminster Newton** · Hammoon · Child Okeford · Iwerne Minster

South Petherton · Norton sub Hamdon · Odcombe · Preston Plucknett · BRYMPTON D'EVERCY · Haydon · North Wootton · Bishop's Caundle · Lydlinch · Sturminster Common · Iwerne Courtney or Shroton · Tarrant Gunville

Over Stratton · West Chinnock · East Chinnock · Chiselborough · West Coker · Barwick · Bradford Abbas · Thornford · Folke · Allweston · Longburton · Holwell · Fifehead Neville · King's Stag · Okeford Fitzpaine · Shillingstone · Pimperne Down · Tarrant Hinton

Lopen · Merriott · Haselbury Plucknett · Hardington Mandeville · Pendomer · Yeovil Junc. · Stoford · Yetminster · Leigh · Sandhills · Holwell · Crouch Hill · Kingston · Stourpaine · Durweston · Pimperne · Tarrant Launceston

Misterton · Clapton Court · North Perrott · Hardington Marsh · Ryme Intrinseca · Beer Hackett · Lillington · Holnest · Pulham · Hazelbury Bryan · Ibberton · Turnworth · Blandford Camp · Tarrant Monkton

Seaborough · South Perrott · Mosterton · Corscombe · Closworth · Melbury Osmond · Chetnole · Hermitage · Glanvilles Wootton · Woolland · **Blandford Forum** · Blandford St Mary · Tarrant Rawston

Drimpton · Chedington · Benville Lane · West Chelborough · Melbury Bubb · Melbury Sampford · Hilfield · Middlemarsh · Duntish · Mappowder · Bulbarrow Hill · Bryanston · Langton Long Blandford · Tarrant Keyneston

Broadwindsor · Toller Down Gate · Toller Whelme · Evershot · Holywell · Batcombe · Lyon's Gate · Minterne Magna · Buckland Newton · Higher Ansty · Melcombe Bingham · Hilton · Winterborne Stickland · Charlton Marshall · Tarrant Crawford

Beaminster · Mapperton · Hooke · Higher Kingcombe · Uphall · Rampisham · Up Cerne · Alton Pancras · THE GIANT (NT) · Folly · Plush · Winterborne Houghton · Winterborne Clenston · Thornicombe · Spetisbury

Stoke Abbott · Netherbury · Melplash · Lower Kingcombe · Frome St Quintin · Chalmington · Up Sydling · Cerne Abbas · Piddletrenthide · White Lackington · Bingham's Melcombe · Milton Abbas · Whatcombe · Charlton Down · Sturminster Marsh

South Bowood · Waytown · North Poorton · Toller Porcorum · Chilfrome · Cattistock · Sydling St Nicholas · Cheselbourne · Winterborne Whitechurch · Almer

Salwayash · Toller Fratrum · Maiden Newton · Nether Cerne · Dewlish · Winterborne Kingston · Anderson · Winterborne Zelston

Dottery · Bradpole · Loders · Uploders · Powerstock · Wynford Eagle · West Compton · Godmanstone · Piddlehinton · Milborne St Andrew · A31 · Bloxworth · Morden · Lytchett

Nettlecombe · Eggardon Hill · Forston · Puddletown · Tolpuddle · Bere Regis · Turners Puddle · Slepe

Bridport · Walditch · Bothenhampton · Askerswell · Grimstone · Stratton · Charminster · Affpuddle · Briantspuddle · Lane End · Wareham Forest · Holton Heath

Eype · Shipton Gorge · Chilcombe · Kingston Russell · Compton Valence · Bradford Peverell · WOLFETON HOUSE · Burton · Stinsford · Burleston · Tincleton · A35 · Trigon Hill · Sandford

West Bay · Seatown · North Hill · Litton Cheney · Long Bredy · Winterborne Abbas · **Dorchester** · Lower Brockhampton · Woodsford · Moreton Sta. · Bovington Camp

Burton Bradstock · Punknowle · Littlebredy · Winterborne Steepleton · Winterborne Came · West Stafford · Moreton · East Burton · Stokeford · **Ware**

West Bexington · Swyre · Martinstown · Winterborne Monkton · Whitcombe · West Knighton · Winfrith Heath · Wool · East Stoke · Stoborough · Stok

White Hill · Black Down · Bronkham Hill · Portesham · Broadmayne · Warmwell · Owermoigne · East Knighton · West Holme · Rid

Abbotsbury · Rodden · Upwey · Bincombe · Sutton Poyntz · Poxwell · Winfrith Newburgh · Coombe Keynes · East Lulworth · Grange Heath · East Creech

Langton Herring · Broadway · Upwey Sta. · Preston · Osmington · Toll · Holworth · Chaldon Herring or East Chaldon · Lulworth Camp · Steeple

Chickerell · Radipole · Melcombe Regis · Osmington Mills · Chaldon Down · West Lulworth · Purbeck Hills

East Fleet · Charlestown · **WEYMOUTH** · Weymouth Bay · Ringstead Bay · Worbarrow Bay · Broad Bench · Tyneham · Kimmeridge

Westham · Wyke Regis · Ferry Bridge · Portland Harbour · Lulworth Cove

West Bay · **Fortuneswell** · Easton · Grove · Isle of Weston · Southwell · Portland

Bill of Portland

To Jersey, Guernsey (summer only) · To Cherbourg (summer only)

0 1 2 3 4 5   10   15 kilometres

0 1 2 3 4 5   10 miles

DOWN PLANS: **BRIGHTON & HOVE** P141   **MAIDSTONE** P155
EASTBOURNE P149   **ROYAL TUNBRIDGE WELLS** P161
GUILDFORD P150   **WORTHING** P168
HASTINGS & ST LEONARDS P151

22	23	24	25		
10	11	12	13	14	15

13

KENT

EAST SUSSEX

THE WEALD

ASHDOWN FOREST

MAIDSTONE

ROYAL TUNBRIDGE WELLS

TONBRIDGE

Southborough

Sevenoaks

East Grinstead

Crowborough

Haywards Heath

Burgess Hill

Lewes

BRIGHTON

Newhaven

Seaford

EASTBOURNE

BEXHILL

HASTINGS

Heathfield

Hailsham

Battle

Beachy Head

Pevensey Bay

DWN PLANS: **CANTEBURY** P142 **HASTINGS & ST LEONARDS** P151
CHATHAM & ROCHESTER P143 **MAIDSTONE** P155
DOVER P147 **ROYAL TUNBRIDGE WELLS** P161
FOLKESTONE P149

24 25
12 13 14 15

15

A   B   C   D   E

To Vlissingen

Warden Point
Leysdown-on-Sea

South Channel
Long Nose Spit   Foreness Point
MARGATE
Westgate on Sea   Cliffonville   White Ness
Reculver   Birchington   North Foreland
Birchington Bay   QUEX PARK   St Peter's
HERNE BAY   ISLE OF THANET   **BROADSTAIRS**
Harty   Shell Ness   Hillborough   St Nicholas   Acol
WHITSTABLE   Swalecliffe   at Wade   Manston
Whitstable Bay   West   Broomfield   Gore   Monkton   Minster   **RAMSGATE**
Seasalter   End   Herne   Highstead   Street   Cliffsend   St Augustine's
Chestfield   Boyden   Sarre   Pegwell Bay
Graveney   Clapham Hill   Maypole   Gate   Chislet   West   Sandwich
Yorkletts   Pean Hill   Hoath   Upstreet   Stourmouth   East   Bay
Goodnestone   Dargate   Honey   Calcott   Hersden   Grove   Stourmouth   Westmarsh
Preston   Hernhill   Hill   Broadoak   Westbere   Stodmarsh   Preston   Ware   Stonar   Cut
Boughton Street   Blean   Tyler   Sturry   Elmstone   Hoaden   Cop Street   Great Stonar
Dunkirk   Hill   Hales   Fordwich   Wickhambreaux   Ash   Sandwich
Overland   Harbledown   Place   Ickham   Hoaden   **SANDWICH**
Selling   Chartham   **CANTERBURY**   Littlebourne   Wingham   Marshborough   Woodnesborough   Toll
Old Wives   Hatch   Thanington   Bramling   Staple   Worth
Lees   Chartham   Bekesbourne   Goodnestone   Eastry   Hacklinge   The Small Downs
Shottenden   Street End   Patrixbourne   Ham   Finglesham
Chilham   Nackington   Bridge   Adisham   Chillenden   Knowlton   Northbourne   **DEAL**
Molash   Lower   Aylesham   Betteshanger   Great   Sholden
Godmersham   Hardres   Bishopsbourne   Nonington   Easole   Tilmanstone   Mongeham   Ripple
Lees   Bilting   Petham   Kingston   Barham   Womenswold   Street   Elvington   East Studdal   Sutton   Walmer
Crundale   Sole Street   Upper Hardres   Barfreston   Eythorne   West   Ringwould   Kingsdown
Olantigh   Waltham   Court   Derringstone   Woollage   Shepherdswell   Langdon
Hassell   Bossingham   Green   or   East   Martinmill Sta.
Wye   Street   Stelling   Breach   Denton   Sibertswold   Langdon   St Margaret's
Bodsham   Minnis   Bladbean   Coldred   Guston   at Cliffe
Hastingleigh   Green   Wingmore   Lydden   West   The Downs
Kennington   Brook   Lymbridge   Rhodes   Elham   Selstead   Whitfield   Cliffe   St Margaret's Bay
Hinxhill   Green   Minnis   Wootton   Temple Ewell   Buckland   South Foreland
Stowting   Ottinge   Acrise   Ewell Minnis   St Radigunds   To Zeebrugge
Brabourne   Place   Swingfield   To Oostende
Willesborough   Lyminge   Minnis   Alkham   **DOVER**   To Calais
Sevington   Brabourne Lees   Densole   Drellingore   West   Maxton
Mersham   Smeeth   Newbarn   Paddlesworth   Hawkinge   Hougham   Farthingloe   East Wear Bay
Cheeseman's   Sellindge   Postling   Etchinghill   Capel
Green   Stanford   Beachborough   le Ferne
Aldington   Court-   Westenhanger Sta.   Newington
Bonnington   at-Street   Lympne   Saltwood
Ruckinge   Lympne   PORT LYMPNE   W. Hythe   **FOLKESTONE**
Street   Burmarsh   Sandgate
ROMNEY   Newchurch   **Hythe**
MARSH   Romney, Hythe   & Dymchurch Rly   **Dymchurch**
St Mary in   the Marsh   St Mary's Bay
Ivychurch
New Romney   East
Old Romney   Littlestone-   Romney   Road
on-Sea   Sands
Lydd   Greatstone-on-Sea
Denge Marsh
Lydd-on-Sea   Varne
Denge Beach   Dungeness

STRAIT OF DOVER

To Boulogne

A   B   C   D   E

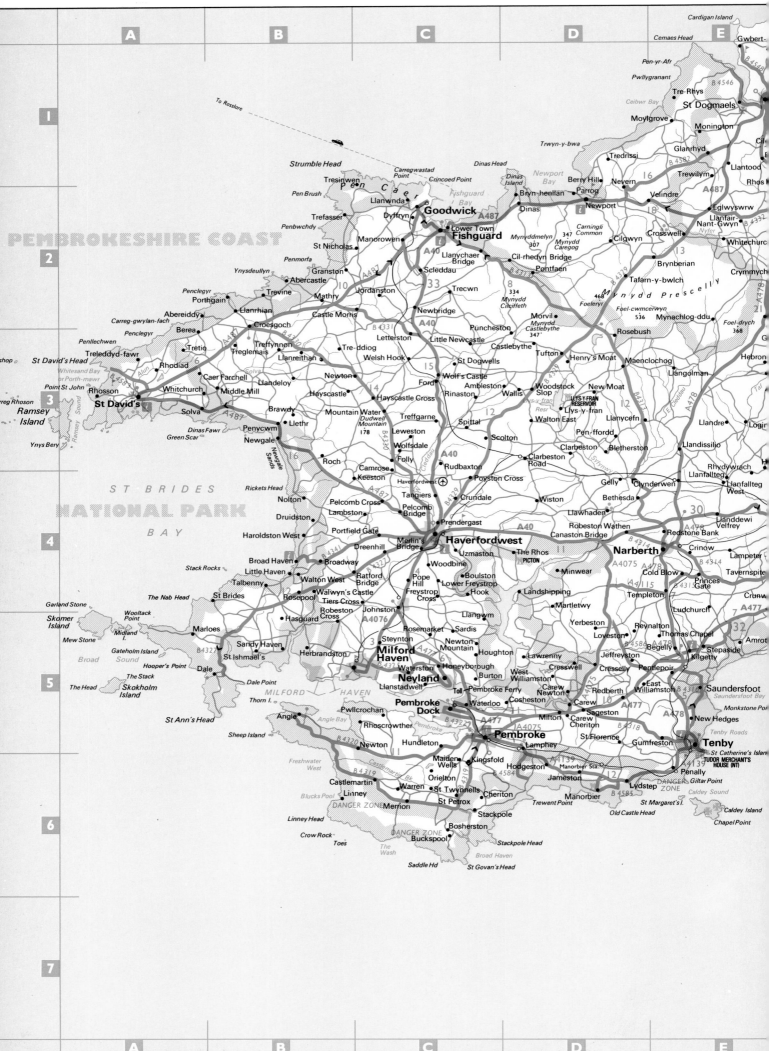

Parcllyn Penpnbach Penbryn Pentregat Talgarreg Gors-goch Capel St Silin Cribyn Bettws Bledrws Silian Bryn Brawd Llanfair Clydogau
Aberporth Sarnau Bryn nant Wstrws Capel Cynon Aber Cwrt-newydd Lampeter Cellan Carn Nant-yr-ast
Tresaith Tan-y-groes Glynarthen Castell Howell Cwmsychpant Llanwenog Llanwnnen Pont-faen Crug Siarls Garthynty
Tremain Blaenporth Bettws Evan Rhydlewis Ffostrasol Moel-y-mor Pontshaen Rhydowen Drefach Alltyblaca Ram Llanycrwys Farmers
Noyadd Trefawr Beulah Hawen Penrhiwpal Tre-groes Pren-gwyn Highmead Pencarreg Llanybther Pen Tas-eithin
Pantgwyn Ponthirwaun Brongest Troedyraur Maesllyn Horeb Capel Dewi Abergiar Maesycrugiau Pumsaint Llandre Rhyd Galed
Capel Tygwydd Pont Ceri Llandyfriog Aberbanc Penrhiwllan Llandyssul Llanfihangel ar-Arth Mynydd Llanllwni Rhydcymerau DOLAUCOTHI Caeo
Abercych Cenarth Newcastle Emlyn Bangor Teifi Pontwelly Llanllwni Rhydcymerau Llidiadnenog Llansawel Aber Bowlan Cilyc
Clyn-fiew Penrherber Aberarad Pentre-cagal Drefach Velindre Pentre-cwrt Banc-y-ffordd Pencader New Inn Gwernogle Abergorlech Edwinsford Porthyrhyd
Glaspant Capel Iwan Cwmpengraig Penboyr Bwlch-clawdd Rhos Dol-gran Gwyddgrug Talley Waunclynda Llanwrda
Clydey Cilrhedyn Cwm Morgan Gorllwyn Alltwalis Brechfa Pen-y-garn Mynydd Cynros Cwmdu Halfway
Star Tegryn Hermon Cwmduad Llanllawddog Llanfynydd Capel Isaac Salem Manordeilo Felindre Dyffryn Ceidrych
Dinas Trelech Esgair Llanpumsaint Pontarsais Plas Rhydargaeau Court Henry Broadoak Penybanc Rhosmaen Bethlehem Llangadog
Llanwinio Trelech a'r Betws Blaen-y-coed Bwlchnewydd Felingwm Uchaf Llanfihangel-uwch-Gwili Pentrefelin Llandeilo Capel Gwynfe
Cwmfelin Mynach Cwmbach Talog Newchurch Capel Gwyn Nantgaredig Llanegwad Felindre Llangathen Ffairfach Maerdy
Gellywen Abernant Ffynnon-ddrain Abergwili Llanarthney Dryslwyn Golden Grove GELLI AUR Trapp
Castell Gorfod Meidrim Merthyr Tre-vaughan Carmarthen Tanerdy Capel Dewi Penrhiwgoch Derwydd Llandyfan
Llangynin Bron-y-Gaer Sarnau Llanllwch Johnstown Llangunnor Pensarn Cwmffrwd Porthyrhyd Maesybont Carmel Pentre-Gwenlais Tair Carn Isaf
Boeth Picton Ferry Bancyfelin Llangain Cwmisfael Heol-ddu Mynydd Cerrig Cefneithin Gorslas Llandybie Glanaman
St Clears Pwll Trap Llangynog Croesyceiliog Llanddarog Cwmisfael Fach Drefach Cross Hands Penygroes Saron Tir-y-dail Garnant Gwaun-leision
Llanddowror Llandeilo Abercywyn Pontantwn Crwbin Pontyberem Tumble Ammanford Capel Hendre Pantamba Gwaun-Cae-Gurwen Cwmgors
Llandawke Cwmllyfri Llanybri Is-coed Llandefaelog Meinciau Ponthenry Llannon Tycroes Betws Pantyffynnon Cwmgors
Llansadurnen Brook Laugharne Broadway Ferryside Four Roads Pen-rhos Pontyates Sylen Capel Hendre Pentrebach Garnswllt
Broadway Cliff Broadlay Llansaint Mynydd-y-Garreg Pont-henri Felinfoel Llangennech Hendy Pontardulais Felindre Pontardawe Trebanos
Kidwelly (Cydweli) Carway Cynheidre Llannon Fforest Bolgoed Craigcefnparc Vardre
East Marsh Laugharne Burrows Ginst Point Five Roads Horeb Mynydd Sylen Pembrey Forest Pentrebach Cefn Drum
Laugharne Sands Pendine Sands Llandyry Trimsaran Waun-y-clyn Felinfoel Burry Port Pwll Llangennech Dafen Bryn Grovesend Pontlliw Clydach Ynystawe
Pembrey Cefn Padrig LLANELLI Bynea Llwynhendy Gorseinon Penllergaer Llangyfelach Birchgrove Glais
Whiteford Point Whiteford Burrows Llanrhidian Sands Salthouse Pt Pen-clawdd Loughor Cadle Tir-deunaw Morriston Llansamlet Skewen
Llanmadoc Cheriton Landimore Crofty Gowerton Fforest-fach Pen-filia Landore Pentre-dwr Port Talbot
Llangennith Fairyhill Oldwalls Llanmorlais Pound-ffald Waunarlwydd Cockett Sketty Cwm Bon-y-maen Pentre-chwyth
Reynoldston Cefn Bryn Three Crosses Dunvant Killay Kilvey Hill Llanddewi Knelston Parkmill Ilston Upper Killay CLYNE VALLEY Black Pill West Cross SWANSEA
Rhossili Penrice Nicholaston Penmaen Bishopston Pennard Newton The Mumbles Mumbles Head
Middleton Oxwich Oxwichgreen Oxwich Bay Langland Bay Pwlldu Head SWANSEA BAY
Port Eynon Overton Horton Port Eynon Point

CARMARTHEN BAY

To Cork

TOWN PLANS: **CARDIFF** P143
NEWPORT P157
SWANSEA P165

26	27		
16	17	28	29
18	19	20	21

19

0 1 2 3 4 5   10   15 kilometres
0 1 2 3 4 5   10 miles

A   **B**   **C**   **D**   **E**

Troedyrhiw
Bedlinog
Deri
Hollybush
Markham
St Illtyd
Cwm Frrwd-oer
Pontnewynydd
Little Mill
Gwernesney
Trelleck Grange
Tintern Parva
Brackweir
Hewe
Aberfan
Cefn
Merthyr Vale
Merthyr
Aberbeeg
Glandwr
Trevethin
PONTYPOOL
Glascoed
sk
A 447
Wolve Newton
New Inn
Chapel Hill
Tidenham Chase
Wool
Wibdr
Bargoed
Gilfach
Gelli-gaer
Oakdale
Rock
Trinant
Griffithstown
New Inn
Llanbadoc
Llangwm
Kilgwrrwg Common
Devauden
Chepstow Park Wood
Brook
Treharris
Trelewis
Gilfach
Bedwellty
Argoed
Crumlin
Penmaen
Sebastopol
Coed-y-paen
Llanllowel
Newchurch
Itton Common
St Arvans
Woodcroft
Tutshill
Boughspring
Tidenham
Blackwood
Newbridge
Upper Cwmbran
Pont-rhydyrum
Llangybi
Llantrisant
Gaer llwyd
Pen-y-cae-mawr
Mynydd-bach
Mounton
Chepstow
Gelligaer
Penybryn
Cefn Hengoed
Pontllanfraith
Abercarn
Pontnewydd
Croesyceiliog
Llandegveth
Newbridge-on-Usk
Caerwent
Highmoor Hill
Crick
Pwllmeyric
Beachley
Severn Road Bridge
Hengoed
Maesycwmmer
CWMBRAN
Llanfrechfa
Tredunnock
Kemeys Inferior
Llanvaches
Llanvair-Discoed
Runston
Mathern
22
Oldbury Sands
Ystradmynach
Ynysddu
Cwmcarn
Henllys
Llantarnam
Pont-hir
Llanhennock
Christchurch
Llanbeder
Penhow
Caerwent
Caldicot Castle
Portskewett
Sudbrook
Aust Ingst
Llanbradach
Abertridwr
Wattsville
Risca
Pontymister
NEWPORT
Malpas
Llanmartin
St Brides Netherwent
Llanvihangel
Rogiet
Caldicot
Rogiet
Magor
DANGER ZONE
Severn Tunnel
Almor
Bedwas
Machen
Rhiwderin
Bassaleg
Milton
Underwood
Llanwern
Bishton
Wilcrick
Undy
Summerleaze
Redwick
Severn Beach
CAERPHILLY
Rudry
Draethen
Lower Machen
Rogerstone
Pentre-poeth
Pye Corner
Broadstreet Common
Whitson
Goldcliff
Welsh Grounds
Redwick
Northwick
Pilning
Upper Boat
Treforest Industrial Estate
Nantgarw
Thornhill
Cefn Mably
Michaelston-y-Fedw
Castleton
Coedkernew
Nash
Caldicot Level
Easter Compton
Glanyllyn
Lisvane
Llanedeyrn
Pentwyn
Blacktown
Marshfield
St Bride's Wentlooge
Whitson
Hallen
Taff's Well
Tongwynlais
CASTELL COCH
Llanishen
Whitchurch
Llanrumney
St Mellons
Peterstone Wentlooge
Avonmouth
Henbury
Radyr
Llandaff North
Roath
Rumney
Battery Point
West Hill
Shirehampton
Horf
Llandaff
Canton
Ely
Fairwater
CARDIFF (CAERDYDD)
Sheepway
Portishead
Redcliff Bay
Pill
Easton-in-Gordano
Ham Green
Clifton
St Brides-super-Ely
St Fagans
Grangetown
Weston-in-Gordano
Portbury
Clapton-in-Gordano
Lt Failand
Leigh Woods
Abbots Leigh
Failand
BRISTOL
Redla
St Peterston-super-Ely
St George's
Leckwith
Michaelston-le-Pit
Llandough
Walton-in-Gordano
M5
Wraxall
Long Ashton
St Nicholas
Caerau
Cogan
CLEVEDON COURT
Tickenham
Nailsea
East End
Flax Bourton
Barrow Gurney
Dundry
St Andrews Major
Dinas Powys
Lower Penarth
PENARTH
Clevedon
West End
St Mary's Grove
Chelvey
Backwell
West Town
Colcot
Palmerstown
Sully
Cosmeston
Lavernock
Kenn
North End
Claverham
Brockley
Downside
Upper Town
Felton
Winford
North Wick
Cadoxton
Merthyr Dyfan
BARRY
Lavernock Point
Sully Island
Kingston Seymour
Chelvey
Cleeve
Lulsgate Bottom
Chew Magna
Barry Island
Flat Holm
Woodspring Priory
Sand Point
Wick St Lawrence
Bourton
Hewish
Puxton
Yatton
Congresbury
Redhill
Butcombe
Ridgehill
Chew Stoke
Porthkerry
Rhoose
Porthcer
Sand Bay
Kewstoke
Steep Holm
Milton
Worle
West Wick
East Rolstone
Wrington
Lower Langford
Rickford
Blagdon
Ubley
MOUTH OF THE SEVERN
WESTON-SUPER-MARE
Weston Bay
Toll
Locking
Churchill
Sandford
Burrington
Rowberrow
Nempnett Thrubwell
Brean Down
Uphill
Hutton
Banwell
Star
Shipham
Compton Martin
Brean
Bleadon
Christon
Winscombe
Sidcot
Cross
KING JOHN'S HUNTING LODGE
Axbridge
Cheddar
Charterhouse
East Harptree
Lympsham
Eastertown
Lower Weare
Weare
Cheddar Gorge
Mendip Forest
Berrow
Brent Knoll
Tarnock
Badgworth
Clewer
Nyland Hill
Draycott
Priddy
Rodney Stoke
Rooks Bridge
East Brent
Stone Allerton
Westbury-sub-Mendip
Burnham-on-Sea
Edithmead
Chapel Allerton
West Stoughton
Cocklake
Wookey Hole
Wells
Stert Island
Mark Causeway
Mark
Blackford
Wedmore
Heath House
Mudgley
Theale
Wookey
Dulcote
Highbridge
Watchfield
Bason Bridge
Westham
Panborough
Henton
Stolford
Steart
Huntspill
Cote
East Huntspill
River Bridge
Tadham Moor
Westhay Moor
Upper Godney
Polsham
Coxley
Worminster
Lilstock
Knighton
Stockland Bristol
Stretcholt
Puriton
Woolavington
Cossington
Chilton Polden
Edington
Catcott
Shapwick
Westhay
Lower Godney
Watchet
East Quantoxhead
Kilton
Burton
Shurton
Kilve
Stringston
Stogursey
Otterhampton
Pawlett
Down End
Knowle Hall
Bawdrip
Chilton Trinity
Stawell
Ashcott
Glastonbury
Glastonbury Tor
West Pennard
Edgarley
East Pennard
St Decumans
St Audries
West Quantoxhead
Holford
Dodington
Fiddington
Nether Stowey
Cannington
Street
Walton
Overleigh
Butleigh Wootton
Baltonsborough
Ham Stree
Bicknoller
Stogumber
Over Stowey
Rodway
Combwich
Dunball
Chilton Trinity
Chedzoy
Sutton Mallet
Greinton
Moorlinch
Pedwell
Nythe
Butleigh
Parbrook
Yellow
Crowcombe
Quantock Forest
Spaxton
Four Forks
BRIDGWATER
Wembdon
SEDGEMOOR 1685
Westonzoyland
Dundon
Compton Dundon
Barton
Kingweston
Lydford
COMBE SYDENHAM HALL
Flaxpool
Lower Aisholt
Merridge
Enmore
Durleigh
Goathurst
Huntworth
Woolmersdon
North Petherton
Northmoor Green or Moorland
Middlezoy
Henley
Henley Corner
High Ham
Dundon
Willett
West Bagborough
Broomfield
Courtway
Thurloxton
North Newton
Burrow Bric
Othery
Pathe
Kingweston
Elworthy
Cothelstone
Toulton
Cushuish
Huntworth
Lyng
Low Ham
Littleton
Copley Wood
Charlton Mackrell
Bab

Pitsford Hill
Langley Marsh
Combe Florey
Tart
Bishop's Lydeard
Kingston St Mary
West Monkton
Hedging
West Lyng
Stathe
Bradley Hill
Somerton
Charlton Adam
Maundown
Lydeard St Lawrence
Ash Priors
Fulford
Fitzhead
North Curry
Wrantage
Pitney
Keinton Mandeville

OWN PLANS: **BATH** P138
BRISTOL P141
CARDIFF P143
NEWPORT P157

	28	29	30	31
18	19			
	20	21	22	23
6	7			
	8	9	10	11

21

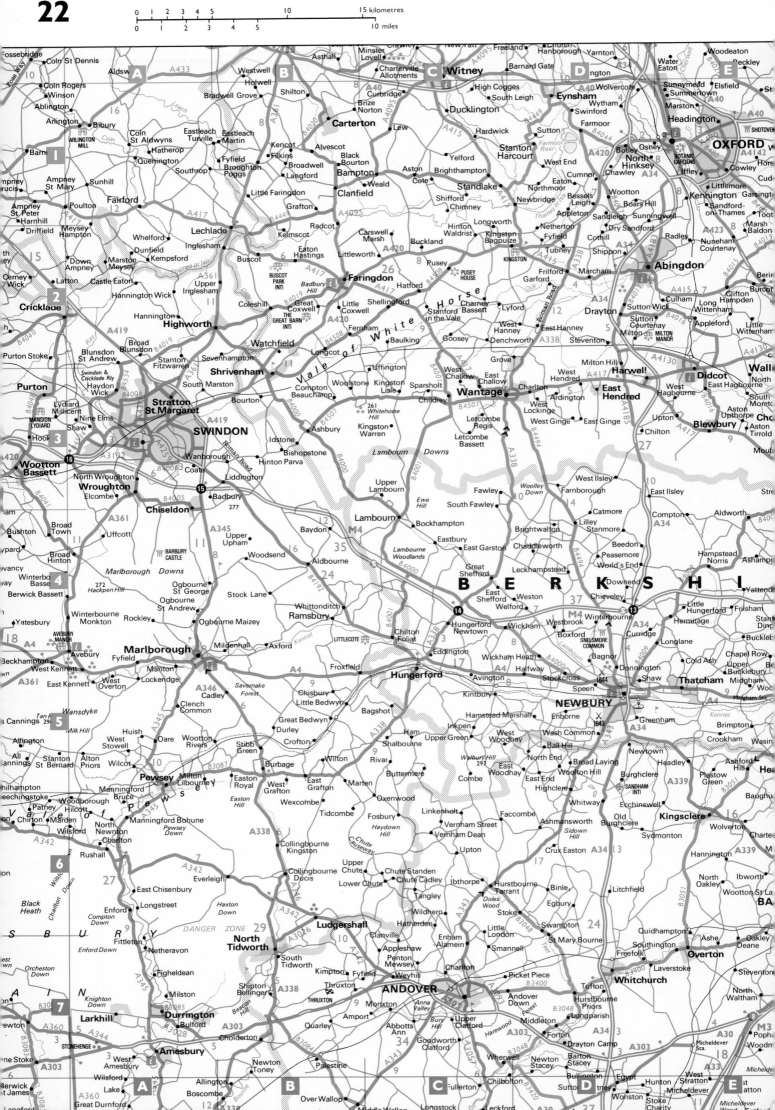

OWN PLANS: **BASINGSTOKE** P138   **SWINDON** P165
GUILDFORD P150   **WINDSOR** P167
OXFORD P158
READING P161

28	29	30	31	32	33
20	21	22	23	24	25
8	9	10	11	12	13

23

WN PLANS: **CHATHAM & ROCHESTER** P143 **LUTON** P150
CHELMSFORD P144 **MAIDSTONE** P155
CROYDON P146 **SOUTHEND-ON-SEA** P163
GUILDFORD P150

30	31	32	33	34	35
22	23	24	25		
		12	13	14	15

25

ESSEX

CHELMSFORD

Witham

Maldon

BLACKWATER

West Mersea

Mersea Island

Burnham-on-Crouch

Southminster

BRENTWOOD

Billericay

BASILDON

RAYLEIGH

Rochford

SOUTH BENFLEET

Foulness Island

Maplin Sands

SOUTHEND-ON-SEA

Westcliff-on-Sea

Leigh-on-Sea

Shoeburyness

CANVEY ISLAND

THAMES

GRAYS

Tilbury

NORTHFLEET

GRAVESEND

Swanscombe

Isle of Grain

Sheerness

Minster

SHEPPEY

Leysdown-on-Sea

WHITSTABLE

ROCHESTER

CHATHAM

GILLINGHAM

Queenborough

Eastchurch

SITTINGBOURNE

Faversham

MAIDSTONE

DOWNS

KENT

0 1 2 3 4 5   10   15 kilometres
0 1 2 3 4 5   10 miles

A   B   C   D   E

C A R D I G A N

B A Y

1

2

Aberystwyth
The Bar
Penpar
Rhydyf
Llanfar
Blaenplwyf
3
Rhôd
A487
Llandde
Carreg Ti-pw
Llanrhystud
Mabws
Rhyd
Llansantffraid
Llanon
Nebo
4
Aberarth
Cross Inn
Penant
Aberaeron
Monachty
Foss-y-ffin
Llanayron
New Quay Head   New Quay
New Quay Bay
Llwyn-onn 38
Llwyncelyn
Cilcennin
Bwlchllan
Gilfachrheda
Cwmtudu
Ciliau-Aeron
Cross Inn
Neuadd Oakford
Brynog
Trefilan
Nanternis
Llanarth
Talsarn
Ynys-Lochtyn
Llwyndafydd
Dihewyd
Ystrad Aeron
Aber
Llangranog
Mydroilyn
Temple Bar
5
Synod Inn
Caledrhydiau
13
Wervil Brook
Plwmp
A487
Penbryn
Bettws
Sarnau
Pentregat
Talgarreg
Capel St Silin
Sil
Pencribach
Aberporth
Brynhoffnant
Gors-gôch
Cribyn
Parcllyn
Tresaith
324
Aber
A487
Wstrws
Moel-y-mor
311
Cardigan Island
Gwbert-on-Sea
Verwig
Blaenannerch
Tan-y-groes
15
Glynarthen
Capel Cynon
8
Castell Howell
Cwrt-newydd
Lampeter
Cemaes Head
Penparc
Tremain
Blaenport
Bettws Evan
Rhydlewis
Ffostrasol
Cwmsychpant
Llanwnen
A475
Pen-yr-Afr
Pwllygranant
Noyadd Trefawr
Beulah
Hawen
Pontshaen
12
Llanwenog
Drefach
Alltyblaca
Ceibwr Bay
Tre-Rhys
St Dogmaels
Cardigan
Llangoedmor
Pantgwyn
Brongest
Troedyraur
Penrhiwpal
Tre-groes
Rhydowen
Highmead
Pencarreg
Llanybyther
grove
Monington
Ponthirwaun
Maesllyn
29
Pren-gwyn
Capel Dewi
9
Glanrhyd
Cilgerran
Llechryd
Capel Tygwydd
Llandygwydd
Horeb
Llanllwni
Abergiar
Tredrissi
Bridell
Manordeifi
Cwmcou
Pont Ceri
Aber-
banc
Penrhiwllan
Llandysul
Maesycrugiau
16
Trewilym
Llantood
Abercych
Cenarth
Llandyfriog
Llanfair-Orllwyn
Llandyssul
Llanfihangel ar-Arth
Nevern
Rhos Hill
Newcastle
Emlyn
Henllan
Pontwelli
5
arrog
Velindre
Newchapel
Clyn-fiew
Abetarad
Pentre-cagal
Saron
Teifi
A486
Newport
Eglwyswrw
Penrherber
Drefach
Llangeler
Pentre-cwrt
New Inn
8
Llanfair-
Nant-Gwyn
Boncath
Velindre
Glynteg
Banc-y-ffordd
Pencader
Gwyddgrug
Rhydcymera
Cilgwyn
Crosswell
Whitechurch
Blaenffos
Capel Iwan
Cwmpengraig
Penboyr
Bwlch-clawdd
Gwernogle
7
Brynberian
Bwlch-y-groes
Glaspant
335
Penboyr
Bwlch-clawdd
257
Dol-gran
23
Abergo
Tafarn-y-bwlch
Clydey
Cwm Morgan
Rhôs
355
Crymmych
Cilrhedyn
326
29
Alltwalis
Mynydd Prescelly
Tegryn
Gorllwyn
6
Cwmduad
Pen-y-ga
Foel-cwmcerwyn
Hermon
Llanfyrnach
Hermon
Brechfa
Rosebush
Mynachlog-ddu
Pentre-galar
262
368
Llanllawddog
ry's Moat
Glandwr
Dinas
Trelech
Llanpumsaint
Maenclochog
Hebron
Esgair
Pontarsais
Llanfyr

A   B   C   D   E

OWN PLANS: CHELTENHAM *P144*
GLOUCESTER *P149*
HEREFORD *P152*
WORCESTER *P168*

38	39	40	41
26	27		
28	29	30	31
18	19		
20	21	22	23

29

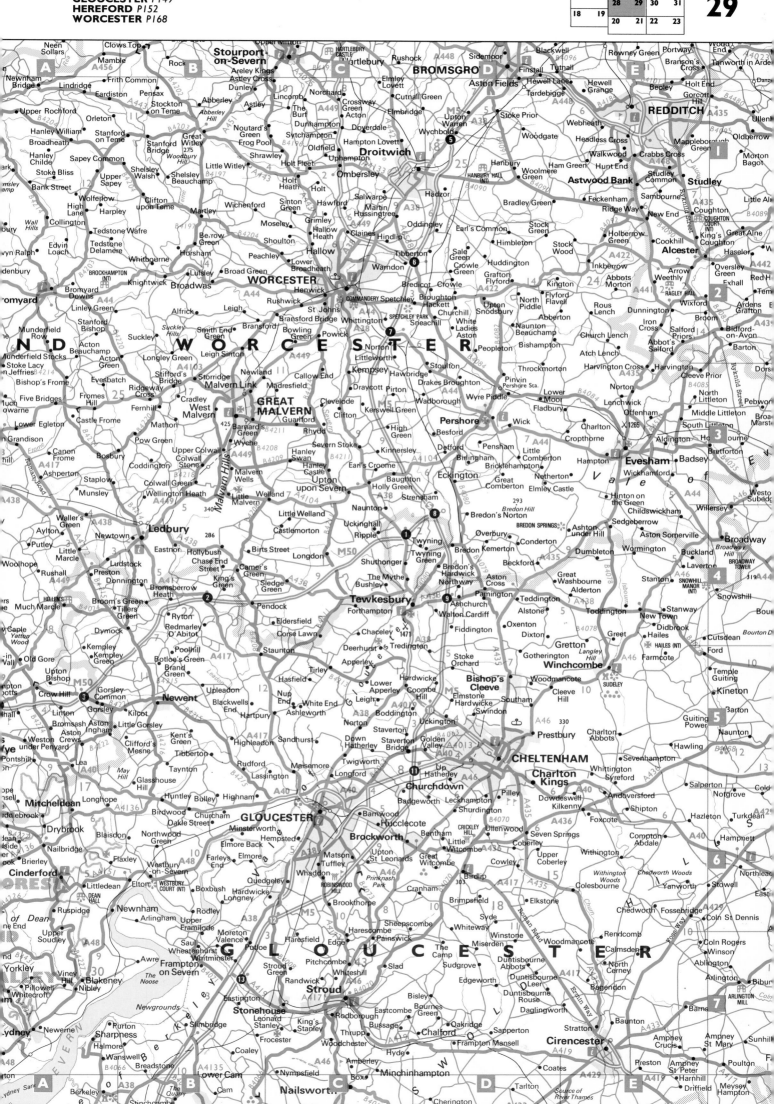

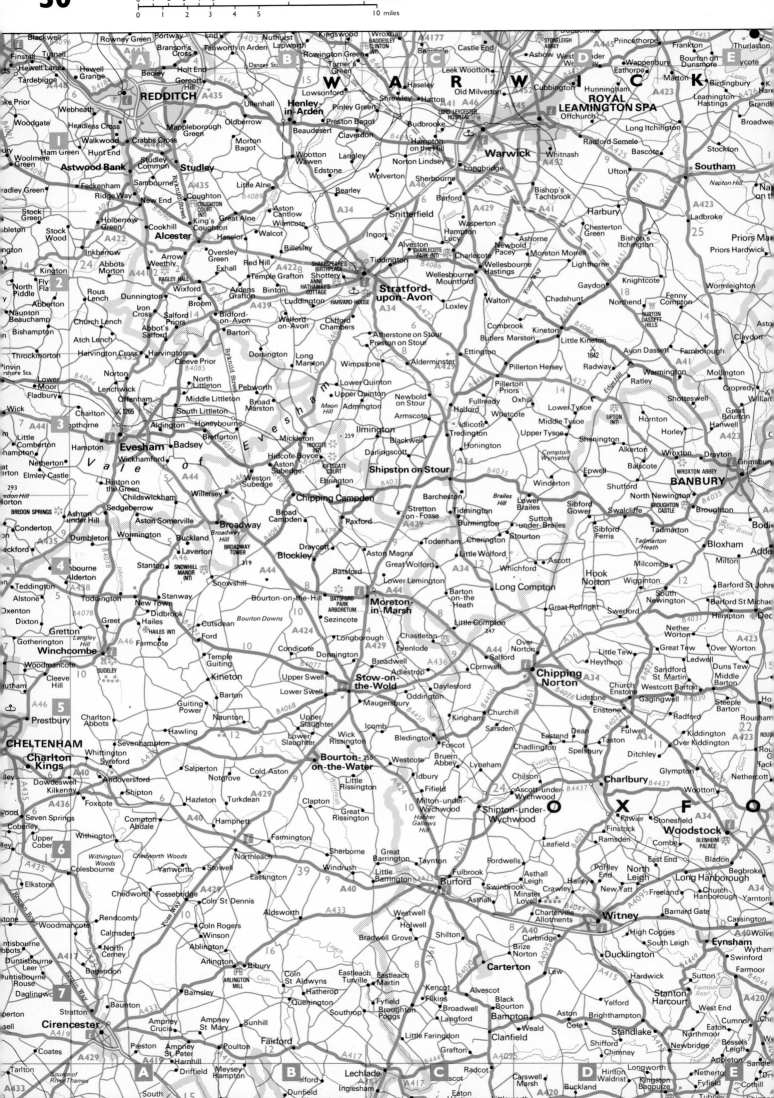

OWN PLANS: **CHELTENHAM** P144 **STRATFORD-UPON-AVON** P164
NORTHAMPTON P157 **WARWICK** P167
OXFORD P158
ROYAL LEAMINGTON SPA P161

38	39	40	41	42	43
28	29	30	31	32	33
20	21	22	23	24	25

31

Major labels on map:

NORTHAMPTON

WELLINGTONBOROUGH

BUCKINGHAM

MILTON KEYNES

OXFORD

Daventry, Brackley, Bicester, Buckingham, Winslow, Bletchley, Wolverton, Newport Pagnell, Aspley Guise, Woburn, Leighton Buzzard, Linslade, Dunstable, Aylesbury, Tring, Berkhamsted, Chesham, Thame, Princes Risborough, Wendover, Towcester, Weedon Bec, Rushden, Higham Ferrers, Kempston, Olney, Irchester, Wollaston, Earls Barton, Flitwick, Toddington

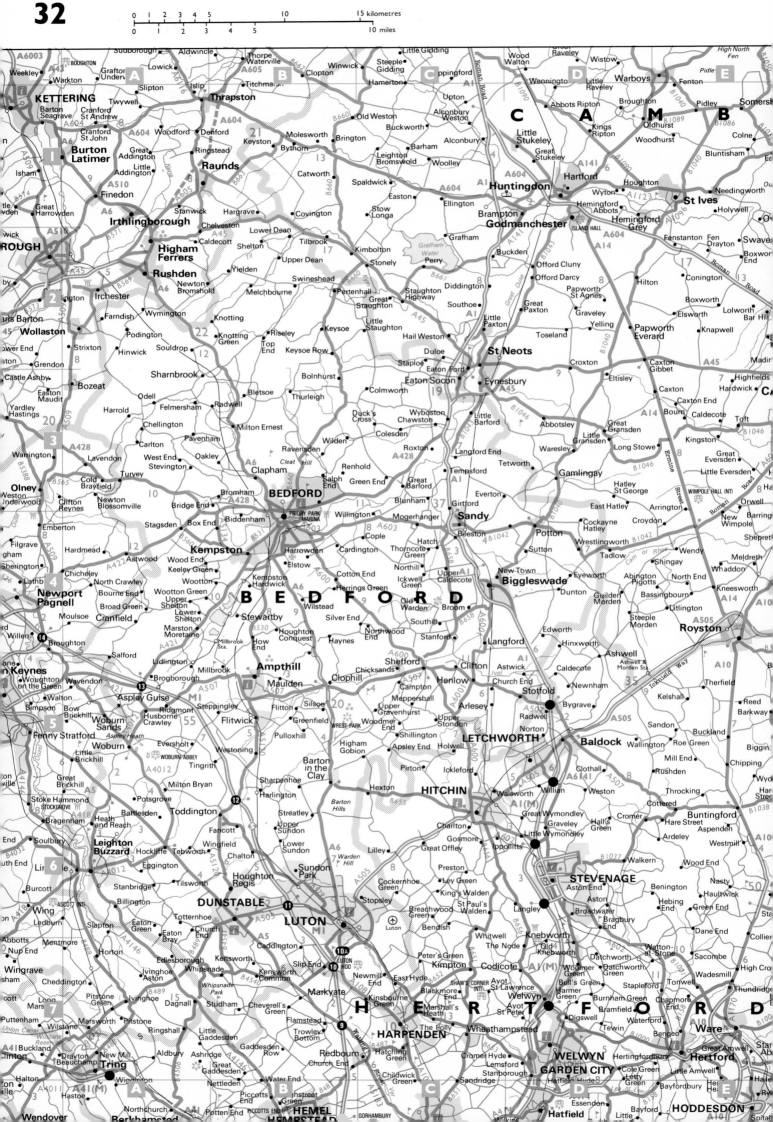

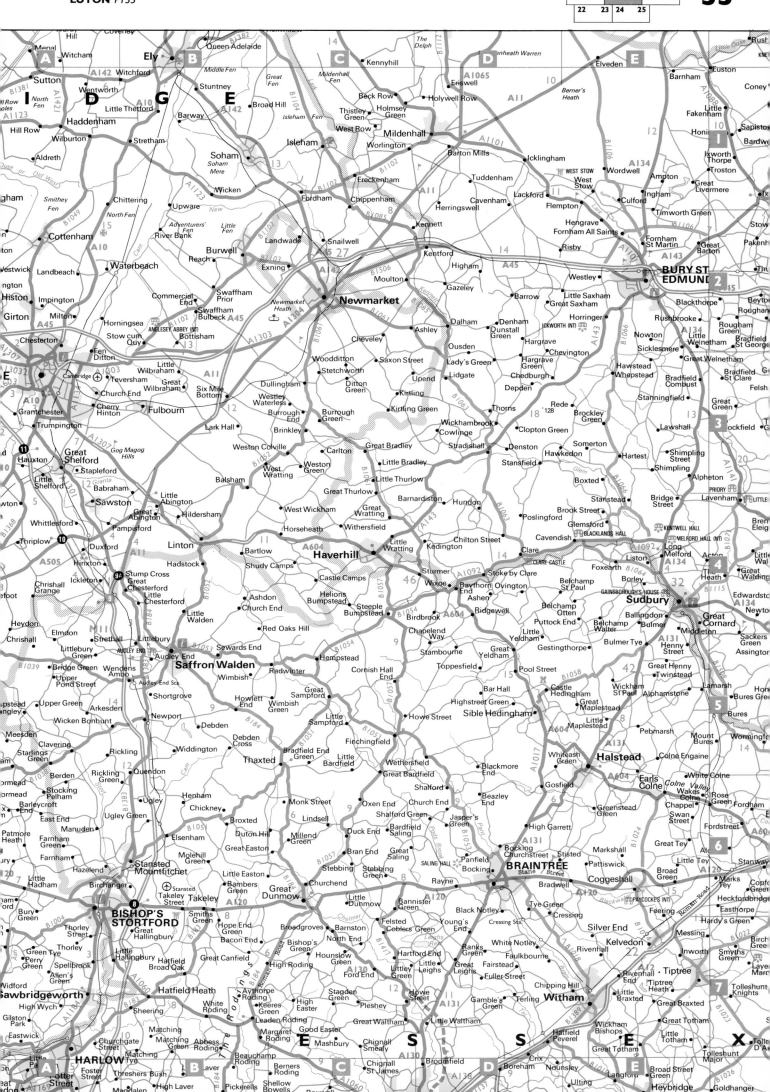

OWN PLANS: **CLACTON-ON-SEA** P145
COLCHESTER P145
HARWICH P151
IPSWICH P152

42	43	44	45
32	33	34	35
	24	25	

35

Diss · Scole · Billingford · Oakley · Hoxne · Brockdish · Dickleburgh · Needham · Withersdale Street · bread · St James South El · Rumburgh · Brampton · Stoven · Covehithe · South Cove

Thelveton · Thorpe Abbotts · Metfield · B1123 · Spexhall · Westhall · Cox Common · Common · Wangford · Mount Pleasant

Eye · Stuston · Brome · Brome Street · Cross Street · Wingfield · Chickering · Fressingfield · Little Whittingham Green · Linstead Parva · Chediston · Broadway · Wissett · Holton · Blyford · Reydon · Blackwater · Southwold

Braiseworth · Occold · Redlingfield · Athelington · Wilby · Brundish Street · Silverley's Green · Cratfield · Halesworth · Cookley · Walpole · Wenhaston · Blythburgh · Thorington · Walberswick

Stoke Ash · Thorndon · Rishangles · Bedingfield · Southolt · Fingal Street · Brundish · Badingham · Heveningham · Laxfield · Ubbeston Green · Poys Street · Sibton · Darsham Sta. · Darsham · Dunwich · Westleton

Wetheringsett · Kenton · Aspall · Bedfield · Worlingworth · Peasenhall · Yoxford · Middleton

Wetherup Street · Debenham · Tannington · Dennington · Bruisyard · Bruisyard Street · Cransford · Rendham · Kelsale · Theberton · East Bridge

Mickfield · Winston · Ashfield · Monk Soham · Saxtead · Saxtead Green · Brabling Green · Swefling · Carlton · LONELY FARM LEISURE PARK · Leiston · Sizewell

Stonham Aspal · Pettaugh · Framlingham · Brandeston · Parham · Stratford St Andrew · Saxmundham · Knodishall · Coldfair Green · Aldringham · Thorpe Ness · Thorpeness · The Mere

Crowfield · Helmingham · Framsden · Cretingham · Hoo Green · Kettleburgh · Easton · Hacheston · Farnham · Sternfield · Friston · Snape

Gosbeck · Ashbocking · Charsfield · Monewden · Letheringham · EASTON FARM PARK · Marlesford · Little Glenham · Blaxhall · Snape Street · Iken · Aldeburgh

Coddenham · Hemingstone · Swilland · Otley · Debach · Dallinghoo · Wickham Market · Pettistree · Campsea Ashe · Tunstall · High Street · Slaughden · Aldeburgh Bay

Barham · Witnesham · Grundisburgh · Bredfield · Ufford · Bromeswell · Rendlesham · Chillesford · Sudbourne

Claydon · Henley · Burgh · Hasketon · Eyke · Tunstall Forest · Butley

Akenham · Culpho · Great Bealings · Melton · Woodbridge · Rendlesham Forest · Orford · Gedrave · Orford Ness

Whitton · Castle Hill · CHRISTCHURCH MANSION · Westerfield · Tuddenham · Playford · Little Bealings · Martlesham · Sutton · Boyton · Orford Beach

IPSWICH · Kesgrave · Waldringfield · Shottisham · Hollesley · Hollesley Bay · Shipwash

Chantry · Ipswich · Newbourn · Brightwell · Hemley · Ramsholt · Shingle Street · Alderton · To Kristiansand (summer only) · To Oslo via Hirtshols (Denmark) · To Göteborg

Belstead · Wherstead · Nacton · Bucklesham · Bawdsey · To Esbjerg

Freston · Woolverstone · Levington · Kirton · Falkenham · To Hamburg

Holbrook · Chelmondiston · Shotley · Trimley St Martin · Trimley St Mary · Trimley Marshes · Walton · Felixstoweferry · Old Felixstowe

Lower Holbrook · Harkstead · Shotley Street · Erwarton · **FELIXSTOWE** · To Hoek van Holland

Stutton · Upper Street · Shop Corner · Shotley Gate · Orwell Haven · Harwich Harbour

Wrabness · Parkeston · **Harwich** · Mill Bay

Bradfield · Ramsey · Little Oakley · Stone Point · Sunk

Bradfield Heath · Great Oakley · Stones Green · Beaumont · Horsey Island · The Naze · To Zeebrugge

Horsleycross Street · Wix · Wix Green · Tendring · Thorpe-le-Soken · Kirby le Soken

Horsley Cross · Weeley · Weeley Heath · Kirby Cross · **Walton on the Naze**

Rough Heath · Little Clacton · Great Holland · **Frinton-on-Sea**

Great Clacton · Sandy Point · **Holland-on-Sea**

Osyth · Jaywick · **CLACTON-ON-SEA**

NORFOLK · SUFFOLK

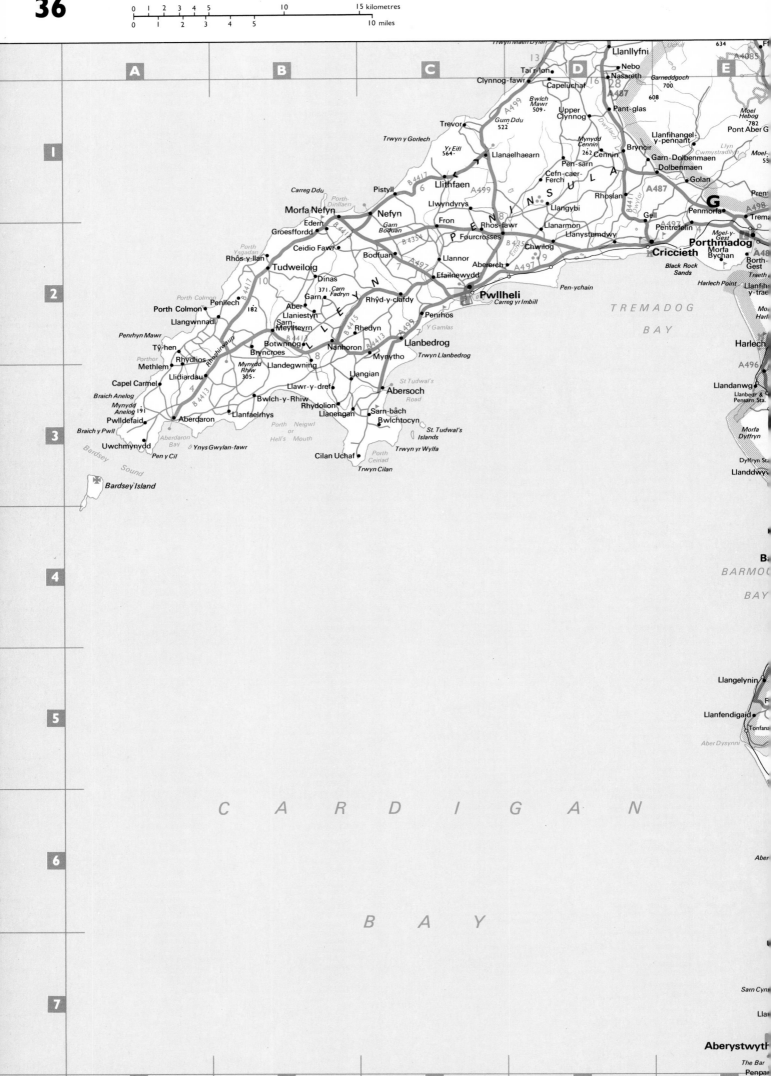

OWN PLANS: **BIRMINGHAM** P139
SHREWSBURY P162
STAFFORD P163
WOLVERHAMPTON P168

46	47	48	49	50	51
36	37	38	39	40	41
26	27	28	29	30	31

39

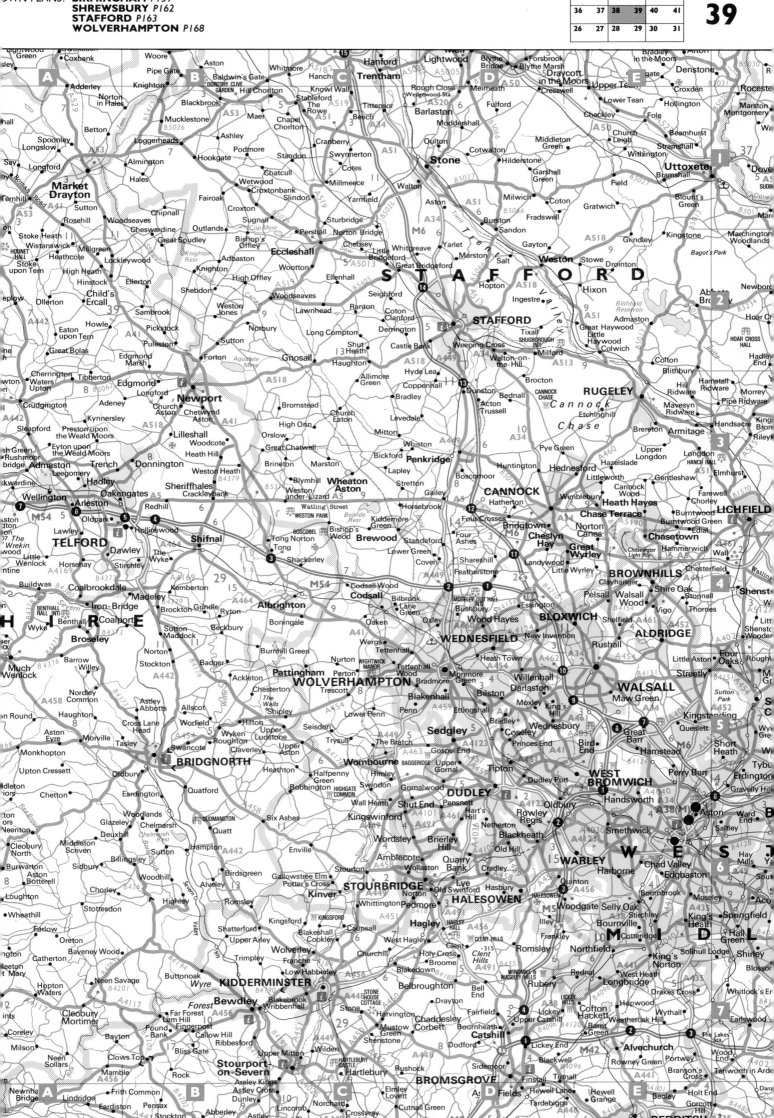

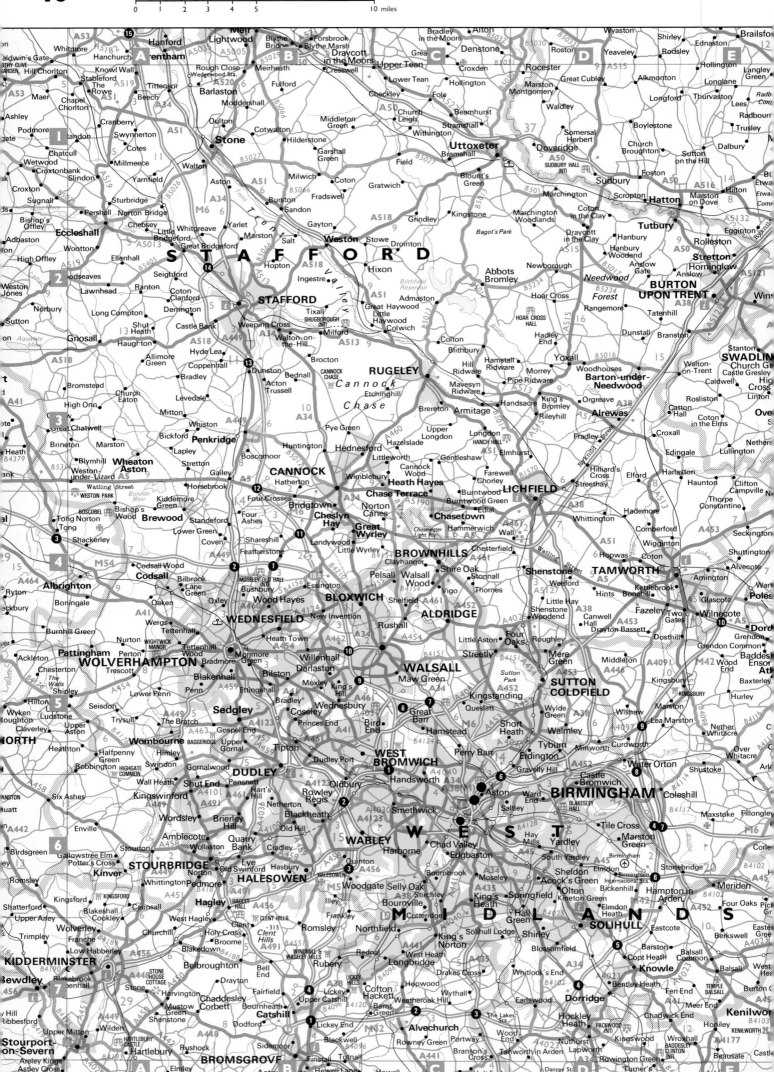

WN PLANS: **BIRMINGHAM** P139 **LEICESTER** P154
BURTON UPON TRENT P142 **NOTTINGHAM** P158
COVENTRY P146 **STAFFORD** P163
DERBY P147 **WOLVERHAMPTON** P168

48	49	50	51	52	53
38	39	40	41	42	43
28	29	30	31	32	33

41

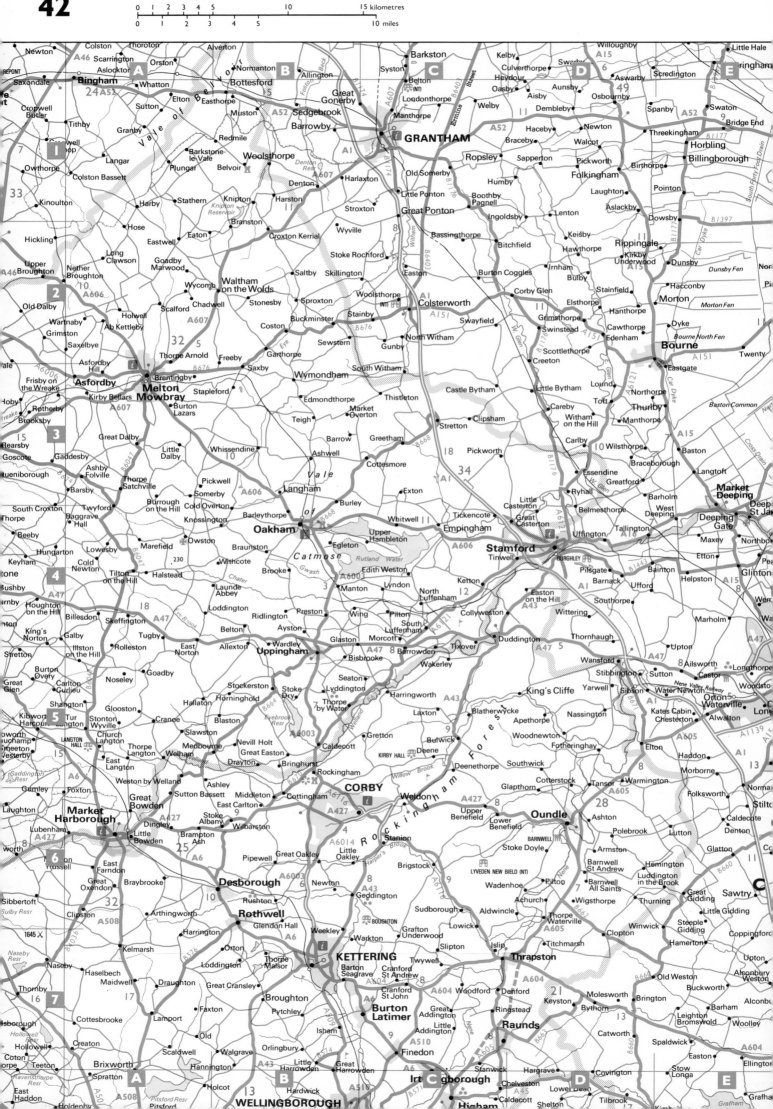

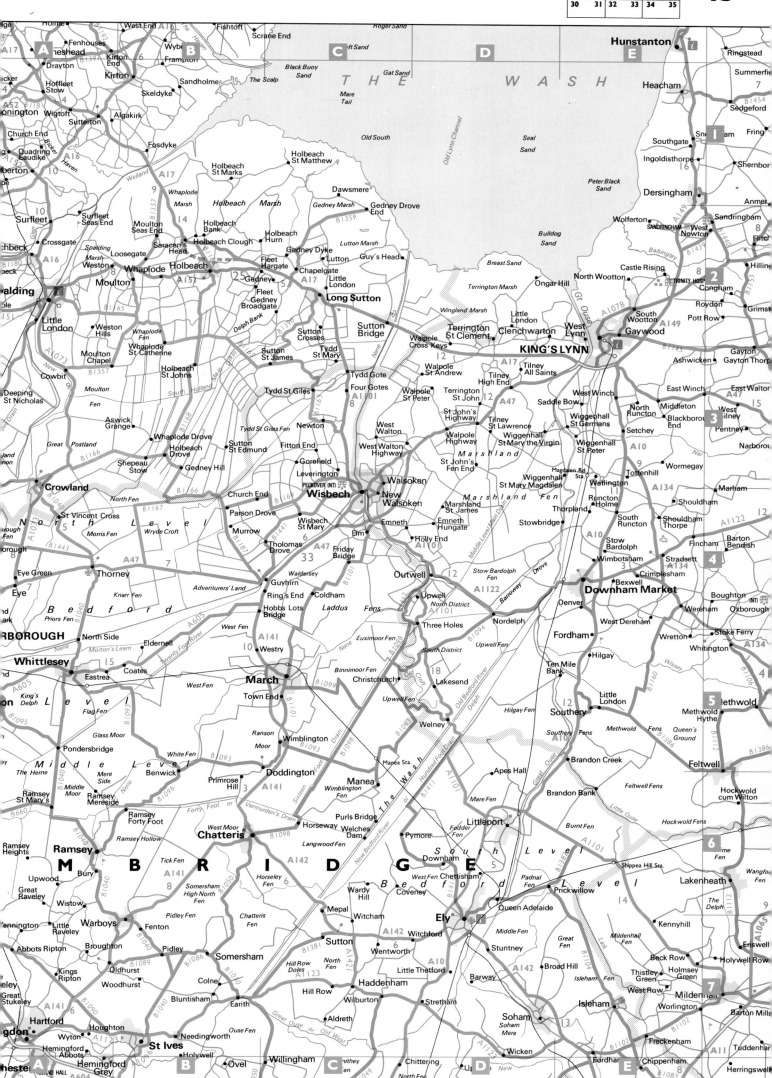

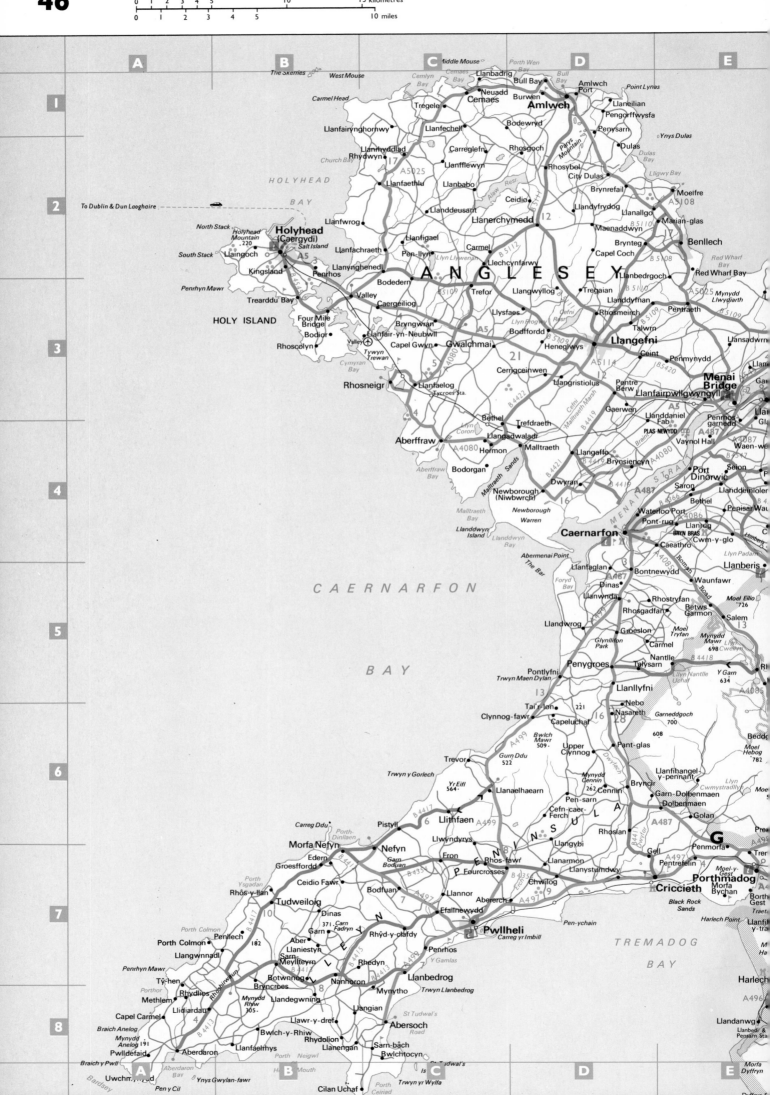

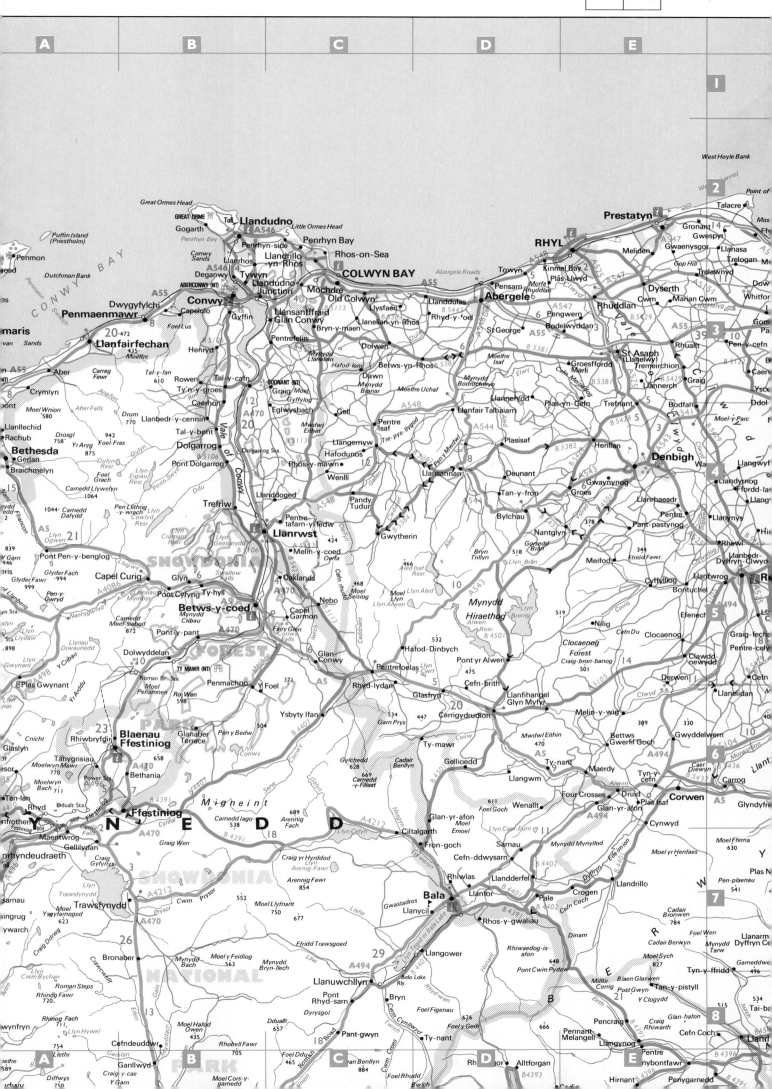

OWN PLANS: BOLTON P140   NEWCASTLE-UNDER-LYME P156
CHESTER P144   STOKE-ON-TRENT P164
CREWE P146   WARRINGTON P166
LIVERPOOL & BIRKENHEAD P154   WIGAN P167
MANCHESTER P155

54	55	56	57
46	47	48	49	50	51
36	37	38	39	40	41

49

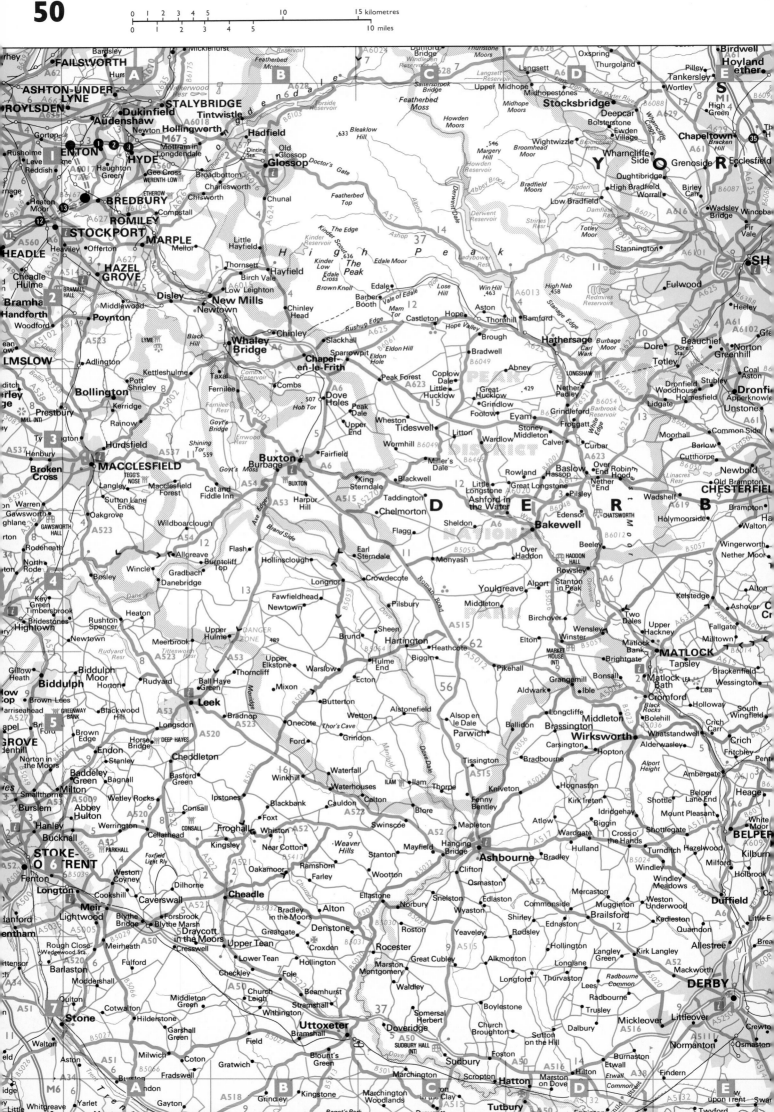

TOWN PLANS: CHESTERFIELD P145 NOTTINGHAM P158
DERBY P147 SHEFFIELD P162
DONCASTER P147 STOKE-ON-TRENT P164
MANSFIELD P156

54	55	56	57	58	59
48	49	50	51	52	53
38	39	40	41	42	43

51

Major towns and places shown on the map include: DONCASTER, ROTHERHAM, Maltby, Tickhill, Bawtry, Bircotes, Harworth, Gainsborough, Morton, Blyton, WORKSOP, RETFORD (East Retford), Saxilby, Langold, Blyth, Whitwell, Clowne, Creswell, Bolsover, Shirebrook, Warsop, Edwinstowe, Ollerton, Boughton, Tuxford, Collingham, MANSFIELD WOODHOUSE, MANSFIELD, SUTTON IN ASHFIELD, KIRKBY IN ASHFIELD, NEWARK-ON-TRENT, Balderton, Southwell, HUCKNALL, Calverton, ARNOLD, Burton Joyce, Bingham, NOTTINGHAM, CARLTON, WEST BRIDGFORD, BEESTON, ILKESTON, LONG EATON, Ruddington, Keyworth, Bottesford, GRANTHAM.

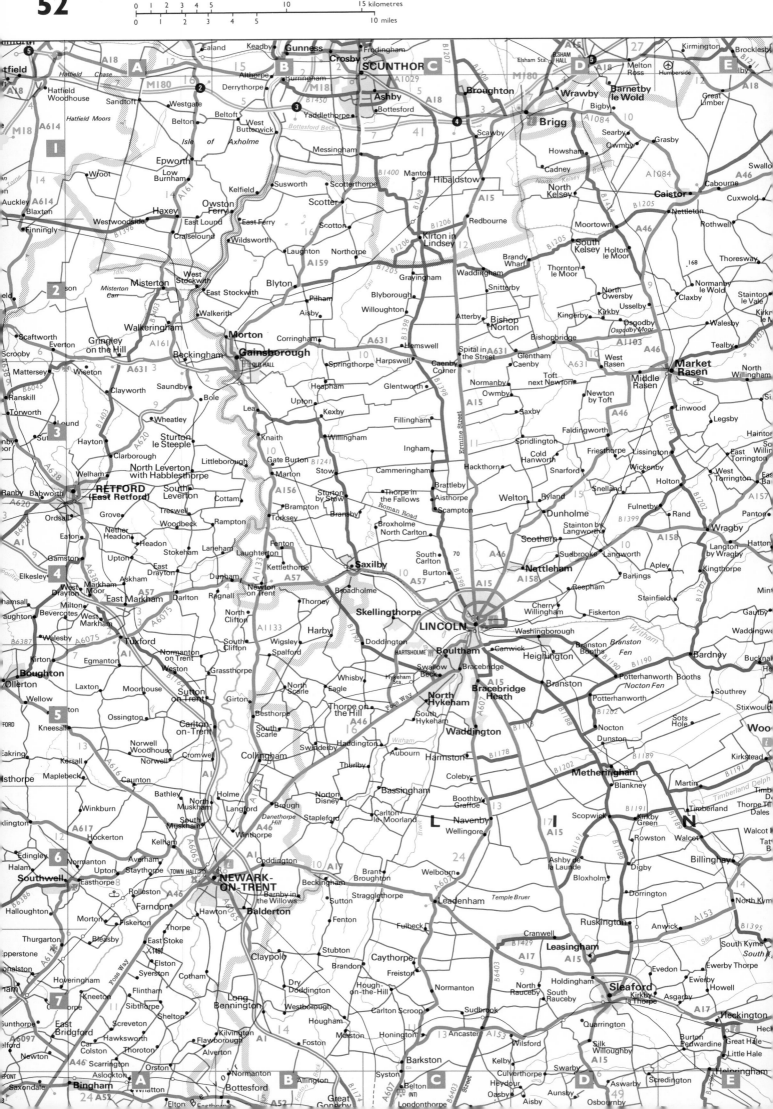

0 1 2 3 4 5   10   15 kilometres
0 1 2 3 4 5   10 miles

I

BARROW-IN-FURNESS
th Scale
Vickerstown
Tummer Hill Scar
Biggar
WALNEY ISLAND
South End
To Douglas
Sheep Island
Piel Island
Foulney Island
Roa Island
Rampside
Roosecote
Newbiggin
Leece
Newbarns
Dendron
Newton
Scales
Gleaston
Aldingham

Cartmel
Wharf
MORECAMBE
BAY
Mort Bank
Yeoman Wharf
Lancaster Sound

Carnforth
Capernwray
Over Kell
Nether Kellet
Bolton-le-Sands
Hest Bank
Slyne
Halton
Aughton Moorgate
Brookhouse
Caton
MORECAMBE
West End
Sandylands
Torrisholme
LANCASTER
Quernmore
HEYSHAM
Oxcliffe Hill
Heaton
Scotforth
Middleton
Overton
Stodday
Clougha Pike
Lee Fell

2

Glasson
Sunderland Point
Sunderland Bank
Lune
Conder Green
Lower Thurnham
Upper Thurnham
Galgate
THURNHAM HALL
Greenbank
Lee
Cockerham
Dolphinholme
Braides
Forton
Street
Wyre
Bernard Wharf
Pilling Lane
Pilling
Fisher's Row
Winmarleigh
Scorton
North Wharf
Knott End-on-Sea
Stake Pool
Rossall Point
FLEETWOOD
Preesall
Stalmine
Garstang
Oakenclough

3

Burn Naze
Staynall
Eagland Hill
Nateby
Calder Vale
Cleveleys
Trunnah
Hambleton Mosside
Churchtown
Bowgreave
Catterall
Claughton
Little Bispham
Norbreck
Hambleton
Ratten Row
St. Michael's on Wyre
White Chapel
Inglewhite
Bispham
Whin Lane End
Out Rawcliffe
Toll
LANCS
Poulton-le-Fylde
Singleton
Great Eccleston
Elswick
Bilsborrow
Thornton
Crossmoor
Inskip
Cuddy Hill
Barton
Goosnargh
Normoss
Thistleton
Roseacre
Newsham
BLACKPOOL
North Shore
Staining
Esprick
Greenhalgh
Wharles
Catforth
Broughton
Haighton Green

4

Great Marton
Weeton
Wesham
Treales
Cottam
Sharoe Green
Common Edge
Great Plumpton
Kirkham
Salwick Sta.
Fulwood Ribbleton
South Shore
Squires Gate
Westby
Clifton
Lea Town
Fishwick
A584
Higher Ballam
Moss Side
Wrea Green
PRESTON
Blackpool St. Anne's
Freckleton
Higher Penwortham
Walton-le-Dale
LYTHAM ST ANNE'S
Ansdell
Lytham
Saltcotes
Warton
Hutton
New Longton
Bamber Bridge
Salter's Bank
RIBBLE
Longton
Farington
Tardy Gate

5

Banks Sands
Walmer Bridge
Midge Hall
Hesketh Bank
Becconsall
Much Hoole
Leyland
Clayton-le-Woods
Whittle-le-Woods
Banks
Hundred End
Tarleton
Bretherton
Horse Bank
Crossens
Marshside
Churchtown
Mere Brow
Sollom
Croston
Euxton
Angry Brow
Eccleston
ASTLEY HALL

6

SOUTHPORT
Holmeswood
Rufford
RUFFORD OLD HALL (NT)
Mawdesley
Heskin Green
Charnock Richard
Birkdale
Brown Edge
Bescar Lane Sta.
Tarlscough
Burscough Bridge
Coppull Moor
Shirdley Hill
Snape Green
Bescar
New Lane
Hoscar Sta.
Newburgh
Parbold
Appley Bridge
Shevington Moor
Ainsdale
Scarisbrick
Pinfold
Burscough
Standish

7

Mad Wharf
Halsall
A570
Dalton
Beacon Park
Shevington
Formby Hills
Freshfield
Barton
Haskayne
Downholland Cross
Aughton Park
Westhead
Roby Mill
Gathurst
Formby Point
Formby
Great Altcar
ORMSKIRK
Scarth Hill
SKELMERSDALE
Up Holland
WIGAN
Hightown
Ince Blundell
Aughton
Town Green
Bickerstaffe
M58
Maghull
Lunt
Thornton
Sefton
Barrow Nook
Crawford
Rainford
Billinge
Little Crosby
Hall Rd Sta.
Netherton
Melling
Melling Mount
Moss Bank
CROSBY
Blundellsands
Waterloo
Great Crosby
LITHERLAND
Aintree
KIRKBY
Kirk Ind Estate

A   **B**   **C**   **D**   **E**

OWN PLANS: **BLACKBURN** P139   **HALIFAX** P151   **WIGAN** P167
BLACKPOOL P139   **HUDDERSFIELD** P152
BOLTON P140   **MORECAMBE** P156
BRADFORD P140   **PRESTON** P160

60	61	62	63
54	55	56	57
48	49	50	51

55

Greta Lonsdale Slatenber Moughton Fell Ribblesdale Darnbrook Fell Arncliffe Hawkswick Conistone Moor Mowbes Stean Moor Ramsgill Bou

High Bentham Clapham Wharfe Studfold Arncliffe Co Grassington Moor Heathfield Moor Pateley

Mill Houses Keasden Clapham Sta. Austwick Helwith Bridge Fells Kilnsey Conistone Grassington Appletreewick Grimwith Resr Moor Greenhow Hill

Lowgill Moor Cock Lawkland Stackhouse Stainforth Kirkby Fell Malham Tarn Bordley Threshfield Grassington Hebden Linton Thorpe Burnsall Pock Stones Moor Simon's Seat

Thrushgill Tatham Fells Moor Eldroth Giggleswick Settle Malham 553 Threapland Cracoe Drebley Howgill Brown Bank Head

Botton Head Catlow Fell Cleatop Mearbeck Kirkby Malham Hanlith Airton Calton Hetton Rylstone Earl Seat

White Hill 544 Brayshaw Long Gill Rathmell Long Preston Otterburn Winterburn Embsay Moor

Salter Fell Wolfhole Crag Croasdale Fell Tosside Wigglesworth Hellifield Bell Busk Flasby Gargrave Embsay Eastby Halton East Bolton Abbey Hill End

Forest Stephen Moor Halton West Coniston Cold Nappa Bank Newton Thorlby Skipton Beamsley Beacon

Slaidburn Paythorne Moor Paythorne Newsholme West Marton East Marton Broughton Carleton Low Bradley Addingham Middle

Hareden Dunsop Bridge Easington Fell 396 Holden Gisburn Bracewell Thornton-in-Craven Elslack Ravenshaw ILKLEY

Bowland Whitewell Marl Hill Moor Sawley Rimington Newby Barnoldswick Earby Cononley Lothersdale Silsden Kildwick Ilkley Moor

Chipping Bashall Eaves West Bradford Chatburn Downham Greystone Salterforth Kelbrook New Road Side Cowling Sutton-in-Craven Glusburn Steeton Utley East Morton

Walker Fold Bashall Town Low Moor Waddington Pendle Hill 557 Weets Hill Whitemoor Resr Foulridge Laneshaw Resr KEIGHLEY Riddlesden Eldwick

Chipping Low Moor Clitheroe Worston Barley Roughlee Blacko Colne Laneshaw Bridge Oakworth Ingrow Worth Valley Railway Harden BINGL

Billington Whalley Wiswell Sabden Newchurch Barrowford Winewall Wycoller Keighley Moor Haworth Cullingworth Wilsden

Ribchester Copster Green Great Mitton Read Simonstone Higham Wheatley Fence Lane NELSON Trawden The Forest of Trawden Stanbury Bronte Parsonage Oxenhope Leeming Denholme Thornton BRAD

Salesbury Wilpshire Langho Padiham Altham Brierfield Haggate Harle Syke Catlow Boulsworth Hill 518 Oldfield Penistone Hill Denholme Clough Clayton

BLACKBURN Clayton-le-Moors Rishton Church Hapton BURNLEY Worsthorne Hurstwood Widdop Walshaw Dean Resrs Wadsworth Moor Ogden Queensbury

ACCRINGTON Oswaldtwistle Huncoat Hameldon Hill Townley Hall Mere Clough Walk Mill High Gate Gorple Resrs Heptonstall Moor Pecket Well Wainstalls Illingworth Buttershaw Shelf

DARWEN Baxenden Crawshawbooth Acre Water Weir Heald Moor Holme Chapel Cornholme Lydgate Heptonstall Mytholm Hebden Bridge Mytholmroyd Luddenden Ovenden Northov

Haslingden Rawtenstall Newchurch Bacup Britannia Walsden Todmorden Lumbutts Cragg Sowerby Bridge Sowerby Halifax Hipperho

Ramsbottom Edgworth Waterfoot Stacksteads Shawforth Warland Calderbrook Summit Ripponden Stainland Greetland Elland

Whitworth Wardle Clough Littleborough Rishworth Booth Wood Slaithwaite Linthwaite

Edenfield Shuttleworth Cheesden Broadley Healey Smallbridge Syke Milnrow Rochdale Marsden Meltham

Tottington BURY HEYWOOD ROCHDALE Slattocks Shaw Diggle Uppermill

BOLTON RADCLIFFE Whitefield MIDDLETON CHADDERTON OLDHAM Mossley

FARNWORTH PRESTWICH Higher Blackley FAILSWORTH

Tyldesley Swinton Pendlebury Cheetham Hill Harpurhey Micklehurst

LEIGH ECCLES SALFORD DROYLSDEN ASHTON-UNDER-LYNE STALYBRIDGE

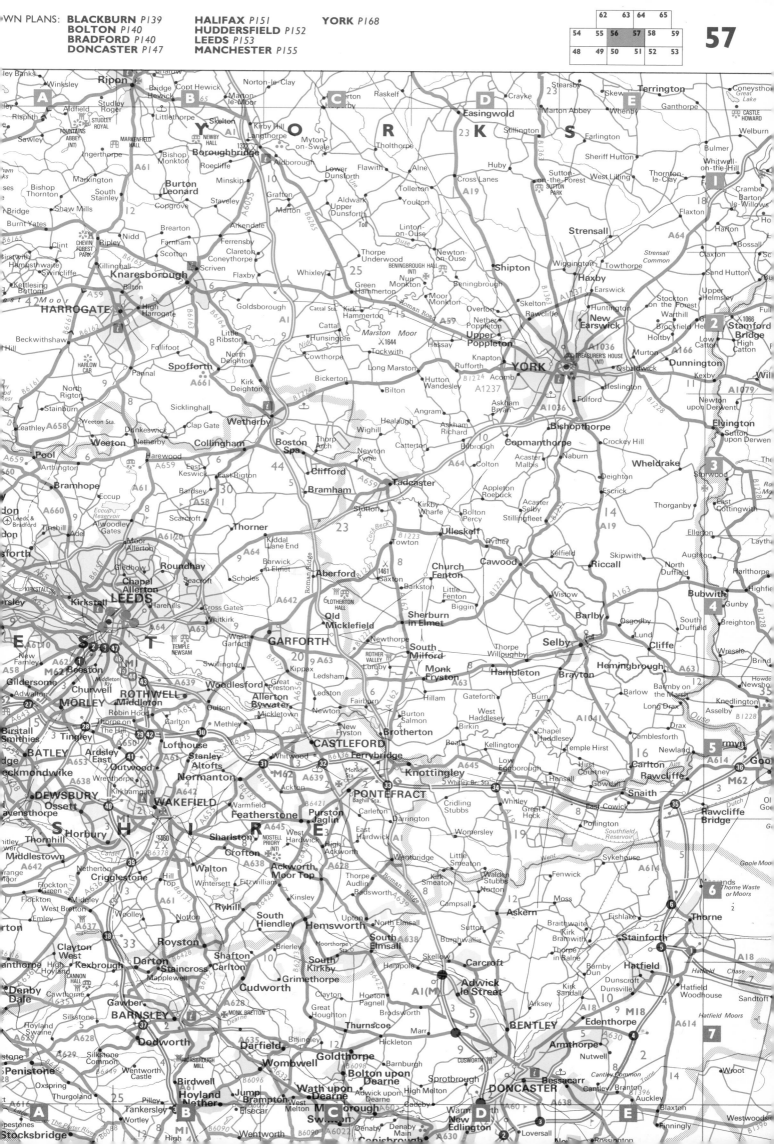

OWN PLANS: **DONCASTER** *P147*
KINGSTON UPON HULL *P153*
YORK *P168*

62	63	64	65
56	57	58	59
50	51	52	53

59

Fleming
Grindale
Bempton
Dane Dyke
Flamborough
Flamborough
Head

A
Thwing
B
A165
C
D
E

Octon
Swaythorpe
Boynton
Sewerby
1

B1253
Rudston
BRIDLINGTON
B R I D L I N G T O N

ngtoft
Kilham
Carnaby
Hilderthorpe
West
Haisthorpe
Bessingby
End
Burton
Thornholme
Carnaby Moor
B A Y

A166
Agnes
Fraisthorpe
Ruston
Harpham
Parva
12
Barmston
Lowthorpe
Gransmoor
Nafferton
Great
Lissett
Kelk
45

Great
Gembling
Ulrome
Driffield
Foston on
the Wolds
Skipsea
2

elywthorpe
Wansford
B1249
Skerne
Brigham
Beeford
nderlandwick
Church
North
End
Frodingham
Dunnington
ton
Rotsea
NUNKEELING
swick
Hempholme
Atwick
Watton Carrs
Burshill
Bewholme
ick

Brandesburton
Hornsea
3

Little
Burton
Seaton
Aike
Catwick
Hornsea
Mere
corborough
B1244
Arram
Leven
Little
Sigglesthorne
Catwick
Rolston
confield
Goxhill
Mappleton
7
Routh
Great
Rise
Hatfield
Tickton
31
BEVERLEY
Great Cowden
Long
Riston
Withernwick
Meaux
New
Marton
Woodmansey
Ellerby
West **Aldbrough**
South
Newton
Wawne
Skirlaugh
13
Thearne
Old
Burton
Dunswell
Ellerby
Constable
Flinton
S
I
D
E
Swine
Garton
4
A165
Coniston
Cottingham
Sproatley
Humbleton
Stoneferry
Ganstead
Lelley
Owstwick
Sutton-
B1238
on-Hull
Bilton
Elstronwick
Tunstall
B1240
Willerby
MAINSTER
Marfleet
B1239
Preston
Burton
Roos
Waxholme
HOUSE
Pidsea
Wadworth
Rimswell
st Ella
A1033
Hill
Withernsea
nlaby
WILBERFORCE
Hedon
HOUSE
Burstwick
20
Hessle
KINGSTON
Thorngumbald
Halsham
Hollym
UPON HULL
Paull
17
Keyingham
4
Winestead
5
Barton-upon-
New
Holmpton
Humber
Holland
Ottringham
A1033
B1218
Barrow
East Halton
Patrington
Out
Haven
Newton
Skitter
Paull Holme
B1445
Goxhill
Sands
7
Welwick
Weeton
Barrow
South
Cherry Cobb
Salthaugh
6
upon Humber
End
Sands
Grange
Skeffling
East
B1206
Halton
Easington
Thornton
Sunk
THORNTON
Island
Burnham
Thornton
Old
Curtis
North
Hall
Kilnsea
Killingholme
Wootton
South
Skeffling
A1077
Killingholme
Clays
Ulceby
A160
Immingham
Kilnsea
Dock
Clays
Brocklesby
Sunk Island Sands
Habrough
Immingham
6
A1173
Elsham
H U M B E R
Brocklesby
A180
Sta.
To Rotterdam,
Croxton
Stallingborough
Zeebrugge
27
Kirmington
Brocklesby
GRIMSBY
Spurn Head
ELSHAM
Melton
Keelby
West
HALL
Ross
Healing
Marsh
5
Great
A18
Coates
Wrawby
Barnetby
Great
A46
le Wold
Limber
Riby
Aylesby
CLEETHORPES
Bigby
Bradley
Scartho
Humberston
gg
A1084
Searby
Grasby
Laceby
7
Owmby
Irby upon
New
Humber
Waltham
owsham
Swallow
Barnoldby
Waltham
Holton
adney
Cabourne
A46
Beelsby
le Beck
Brigsley
le Clay
18
Kelsey
Cuxwold
Caistor
Hatcliffe
Fenby
Tetney
North
Lock
Kelsey
B1205
Nettleton
North Cotes
DANGER
A46
Rothwell
East
West End
Marsh Chapel
Donna Nook
Ravendale
North
Eskham
ZONE
South
Thoresby
Grainsby
Kelsey
Ashby
Wragholme

0 1 2 3 4 5   10   15 kilometres
0 1 2 3 4 5   10 miles

A   **B**   **C**   **D**   **E**

A594 Cameron Little Broughton Bro
Seaton Clifton Bridgefoot Gre
A66 Little Clifton Eag
WORKINGTON Ulloc
Westfield Branthwaite Deans
High Harrington
A596
Distington Gillgarran
Moresby Pica
Parton Asby
Arlecdon
WHITEHAVEN Rowah Me
A5086
Frizington Kirkland
Hensingham
Saltom Bay **Cleator Moor**
Sandwith Wath
B5295 Brow
St Bees Head Cleator
A595
Rottington **St Bees**
How Man **Egremont**
Middletown Snellings
Nethertown Haile
Nethertown Sta. Th
Netherton Sta. Beckermet
Braystones Sta.
Calder Ponsonby
Bridge
Sellafield Gosforth
Sta.
Kokoarrah Raveng
Seascale DANGER
A595 ZON
B5344
Holmrook
Drig
Stub Place
Selker Bay
Annas

I   **2**   **3**   **4**   **5**   **6**   **7**

a   **b**   **c**   **d**   **E**

Roads in Isle of Man are locally classified

Point of Ayre
Rue Point The Ayres
The Lhen Smeale Cranstal
Glentruan Bride
A10 Dhowin
A19 Shellag Point
Sartfield Jurby East **Andreas** A17
Jurby Head Regaby A9
Jurby West Ramsey Bay
Ballasalla Sandygate St Judes Dhoor
Crawyn A10 Churchtown **Ramsey**
The Cronk Sulby A3 Port e Vullen
The Curraghs A18 A15
54° Orrisdale Ballaugh Maughold
20' Orrisdale Head Ravensdale Dreemskerry Head
A14 Maughold
Kirk Michael Slieau Curn Sulby Ballajora Port Mooar
Slieau 565 Corrany
Slieau Dhoo North
Freoaghane Barrule Clagh Port Comaa
Ballacarnane ·488 Snaefell Ouyr
Beg Barregarrow 621 Slieau
ISLE OF MAN Sartfell Lhean Dhoon
Shaughlaige- Bulgham Bay
Gob y Deigan e-Quiggin B10 Snaefell
Knocksharry Little A3 Mountain **Laxey**
Ballagyr Cronk- London Rly I. of Man
Peel y-Voddy Injebreck Railway Laxey Head
St Patrick's Isle Lambfell Moar 422 8 Ballacannell
487· Laxey Bay
Contrary Head Ballig Colden Baldrine To Belfast
Knockaloe Moar Patrick ·478 (summer only)
Neb Slieau Ruy Baldwin To Stranraer
St. John's Greeba A27 Mtn Garwick Bay (summer only)
333· 7 Clay Head
Glenmaye Crosby Hillberry A2
Dalby Point Strang
Dalby A4 Garth Glen **Onchan**
Niarbyl Foxdale Eairy Vine Union Port Groudle
A36 Braid Mills Douglas Bay To Heysham
Niarbyl Bay South Stuggadho **DOUGLAS**
Barrule Close A26 A24 Onchan Head To Liverpool
Stroin Vuigh ·483 Clark St A6 Douglas Head
13 Mark's To Dublin
Lingague Ronague Newtown Quine's Hill (summer only)
Fleshwick Bay A27 Grenaby Ballaveare Little Ness
Ballafesson Ballakilpheric Santon Head
Bradda Head Colby Ballasalla Port Grenaugh
Port Erin Bradda Ballabeg
The Howe A5 Croit A7 A28 Ronaldsway
Cregneish e Caley Balladoole St. Michael's Island
Calf of **Port** Derbyhaven
Man **St Mary** A4 Langness
Chicken Rock Spanish Head **Castletown** Dreswick Point
Bay ny Carrickey Castletown Bay
at the same scale
4° 20'

OWN PLANS: **DARLINGTON** P147
MIDDLESBROUGH P156
SCARBOROUGH P162

70	71		
62	63	64	65
56	57	58	59

65

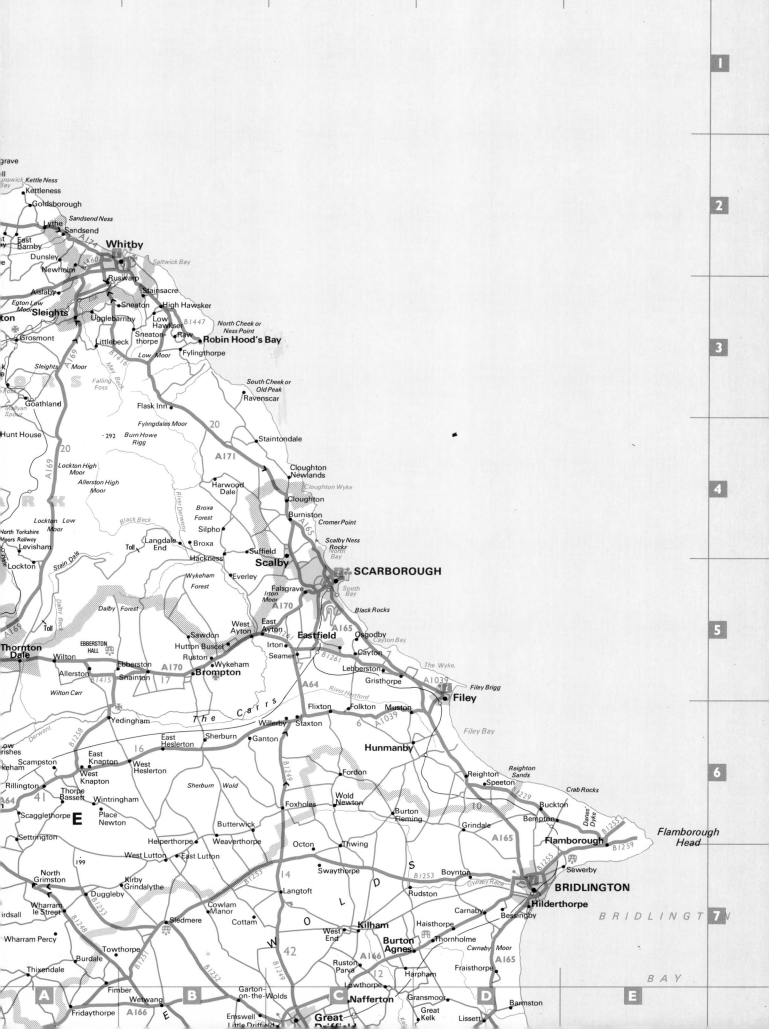

0 1 2 3 4 5   10   15 kilometres

0 1 2 3 4 5   10 miles

A   **B**   **C**   **D**   **E**

Downhill

Deil's

Cra

Ailsa Craig

Chapeldonan

Trochrague

Barg

Dailly

Hadyard Hill

Garleffin Fell

Linfern Loch

Girvan

Old Dailly

B734

Penkill

Glendoune

Saugh Hill

Glengennet

North Balloch

Glendrissaig

Black Neuk

A77

Barr

South Balloch

Ardwell

A714

Pinminnoch

Grey Hill 297

8

Kennedy's Pass

C *Stinchar*

B734

A

Changue Forest

13

R

Pinmore

R

Lendalfoot

Polmaddie Hill 565

Water of Lendal

Aldons

Loch Scalloch

479

GA

Carleton Fishery

Daljarrock

Muck Water

Bennane Head

Poundland

9

Pinwherry

Shalloch Well

Colmonell

Dalreoch

Glenduisk

Black Clauchrie

Loch Moan

A765

Craigneil

Ballochmorrie

Ballantrae Bay

Kirriereoc

Loch

Knockdolian

Mains of Tig

Garwall Hill

B7044

Water of Tig

Loch Goosey

F

Ballantrae

Auchairne

Balkissock

Shiel Hill

Barhill

Feoch Burn

Eldrick

Low Kilphin

A714

30

Downan Point

Glenapp Castle

High Kilphin

Cross Water

Lochton

Corwar House

22

30

Kilantringan Loch

Craigie Fell

Beneraird 439

Drumlamford Loch

Glencaird

A77

Milljoan Hill

Chirmorie

Drumlamford

Carlock Hill

Altimeg Hill

Bargrennan

Loch Dornal

Benbrake Hill

Loch Maberry

Clauchaneasy

Finnarts Point

Markdow

Larg

Milleur Point

Miltonise

Loch Ochiltree

Corsewall Point

Glenwhilly

Polbae

Knowe

Knockville

To Larne

Barnhills

Dalnigap

Urrall Fell

Penninghame

North Cairn

Corsewall

B738

Cairn Point

Loch Ree

Black Burn

Glenrazie

South Cairn

Kirkcolm

Cairnryan

G

Carseriggan

Borela

Dounan Bay

Airies

Ervie

17

Main Water of Luce

Artfield Fell

A

Challoch

Loch Connell

Braid Fell

L

Portobello

B738

St Mary's Croft

Beoch Burn

Balminnoch

Newton S

B718

Knocknain

Leswalt

Soleburn Bridge

Tarf Bridge

Culvennan Fell

Slouchnawen Bay

B7043

New Luce

T H E

M O O R S

Shennanton

4

Lochnaw Castle

A718

Innermessan

Auchmantle

Craig Fell

Galdenoch

Loch Ronald

15

Ber

L O C H

Lochinch Castle

Black Loch

Carscreugh

Barlae

Craighlaw

Baraes

Broadsea Bay

Stranraer

CASTLE KENNEDY

White Loch

Kirkcowan

Portslogan

R

A718

White Loch

Carsreugh

25

Y

N

A75

Castle Kennedy

Dunragit Moor

Whitecairn

Tarf Water

Spittal

A75

Whiteleys

I

Loch Magillie

10

Dunragit

Dernaglar Loch

Clugston Loch

5

N

Lochans

Soulseat Loch

Genoch

Whitecrook

Glenluce

Knock Moss

B733

Black Head

Dinvin

S

Kildrochet

Genoch Square

A715

Knock Fell

Bladn

Cairn Pat

8

Whitefield Loch

Fell Loch

Portpatrick

O

A716

Colfin

8

10

DANGER ZONE

Castle Loch

Corsemalzie

Awhirk

A77

Sands of Luce

Auchenmalg

Mochrum Loch

Stoneykirk

A715

Crows Nest

8

Port of Spittal Bay

F

B7042

W of Malzie

35

Barnba

Balgreggan

G

Culshabben

Cairngarroch Bay

Sandhead

A

A747

Alticry

6

Money Head

L U C E *B A Y*

Elrig Loch

Loch Head

Awhirk

L

Barr Point

Elrig

Ardwell Bay

Ardwell

Longcastle

L

To Douglas (summer only)

Chapel Rossan

Airyhassan

A

Portacree

Port William

Mochrum

O

Drumbreddan Bay

Logan

9

New England Bay

Barwinno

White Loch

M

Mull of Logan

W

Port Logan

Terally

Barsalloch Point

B716

Kilstay

Y

Monreith Bay

Monrei

Clanyard Bay

Drummore

Scares

B7041

Laggantalluch Head

Kirkmaiden

Caillness Point

St

Damnaglaur

7

Crammag Head

Dunman

Maryport

Portankil

Cairnd

Nick of Kindram

East Tarbert

West Tarbert

Mull C *alloway*

A   **B**   **C**   **D**   **E**

DUMFRIES & GALLOWAY

Maratz Hill, Craigengillan, Loch Muck, Windy Standard 698, Countam, Cairnkinna Hill, Drumcruilton

Waterhead, A713, Drumjohn, Lamloch, Brochloch, Cairnsmore of Corsphairn 797, Dodd Hill, Colt Hill, Countam, Auchenbrack, Torbraehead, Auchenhessnane, Holm, Carronbridge, Dabton, Gatelawbridge, Rashy

Craiglee, Coran of Portmark, Garryhorn, Knockgray, Craig of Knockgray, Black Shoulder, Bail Hill, Benbuie, Bennan, Eccles, Thornhill, Burnhead, Penpont, Clonrae, Keir Mill, Closeburn, Croalchapel

Starr, Loch Head, Carsphairn, Bardennoch, Marscalloch Hill, Cornharrow Hill, Carroch, B729, Moniaive, Craigdarroch, Crawfordton, Kirkland, MAXWELTON, Tynron, Keir Hills, Dalsw Comr

Carlin's Cairn, Corserine 813, Loch Harrow, Millfire 716, Castlemaddy, Dalshangan, Forrest Lodge, Burnhead, Knocknalling, Carsfad Loch, A713, B7000, Glencrosh, Crossford, Barndennoch, Glenhead, Blackwood

Merrick 843, Loch Enoch, Dry Loch, Loch Dungeon, Garroch Burn, Earlstoun Loch, Corriedoo, Castlefairn, Holmhead, Lochurr 432, Sundaywell, Milton, Crawston Hill, Dunscore, Friars

Craignaw, Loch Neldricken, Cooran Lane, Garroch, Glenlee, Bogue, St John's Town of Dalry, Blackcraig Hill, Blackcraig, Waterhead, Craigenputtock, Stroquhan, Speddoch, Newtonairds, Gribton, Holy

Buchan Hill, Loch Valley, Trool, 1304, Lamachan Hill 716, Craigencallie, Clatteringshaws Loch, Darnaw, Cairnsmore of Dee, Clatteringshaws, Holme, Balmaclellan, Scroggie Hall, Drumwhirn, Knocklearn, Slongaber, Skeoch Hill, Magreig, Scaur, Terregles

New Galloway, Gibbshill, Garcrogo Forest, Corsock, Glen 398, Shawhead, Henderland, A75

Millfore, Round Fell, Fell of Fleet 471, Shaw Hill, Auchencloy Hill, Bennan, Drumrash, Parton, Shieldhill, Walton Park, Barwhillanty, Merkland, Glenlair, Square Point, Crofts, Brae, Lochfoot, Crocketford or Ninemile Bar, Goldielea, Dalskairth

Castle, Cumloden, Dallash, Cairnsmore of Fleet 711, White Top of Culreoch, Darngarroch, Slogarie, Little Duchrae, Craig, Loch Ken, Lochenbreck Loch, Auchendolly, Old Bridge of Urr, Kirkpatrick Durham, Springholm, Milton, Beeswing, Kinharvie

Bargaly, Cairnsmore, Door of Cairnsmore, Loch Grannoch, Loch Skerrow, Airie Hill, Crossmichael, Mollance, Haugh of Urr, Kirkgunzeon, Stonehouse, Cuil Hill

Blackcraig, Palnure, Craig, Spittal, Barholm, Glenquicken Moor, Rusko, Castramont, Barlay, Glengap, Laurieston, Glenlochar, Townhead of Greenlaw, Clarebrand, Hillowton, Castle Douglas, Dalbeattie

Creetown, Cassencarie, Cairnharrow 456, Glen, Lauchentyre, Anwoth, Ardwall, Gatehouse of Fleet, Barwhinnock, Ringford, Barcaple, Valleyfield, Netherthird, Airieland, Screel Hill 391, Bengairn, Barnbarroch, Palnackie, Dalbeattie Forest, Fairgirth

Wigtown, Wigtown Sands, Carsluith, Kirkdale, Cardoness, Girthon, Barharrow, Twynholm, Cumstoun, Tongland, Barcloy, Kippford or Scaur, Rockcliffe, Colvend, Douglas Hall, Preston

Bladnoch, Baldoon Sands, Kirkinner, Murray's Isles, Islands of Fleet, Ardwall Island, Barlocco I., Sandgreen, Lennox Plunton, Knockbrex, High Borgue, Langlands, Kirkcudbright, Auchnabony, Bankhead, Auchencairn, Hazelfield, Rascarrel, Balcary Point, Port o' Warren

Stewarton, Eggerness, Borgue, Kirkandrews, Senwick, St Mary's Isle, Townhead, Barclay, Dundrennan, Orroland, Barlocco Bay, Almorness Point, Hestan Island, Castlehill Point

Sorbie, Garlieston, Cruggleton Bay, Ringdoo Point, Borness, Ross, DANGER ZONE, Balmae, Port Mary, Little Ross, Abbey Head, Barnhou

Cults, Whithorn, Portyerrock, A746, A750, A747, Isle of Whithorn, Cutcloy, The Devil's Bridge, Burrow Head

A B C D E

Knock Forest
Hart Fell
The Shin
B709
Calkin Rig 450
Glentenmont Height
Paddockhole
Grange Fell
Debate
Callisterhall
Dunnabie
Collin Hags
Bigholms
Craigcleuch
Langholm
Hallcrofts
Raes Knowes
Earshaw Hill
Auchenrivock
B7068
B709
Crumpton Hill
Kirkstile
Bentpath
Arkleton Hill
Watch Hill
Hog Fell
Black Edge
Tinnis Hill
Newcastleton
Newcastleton Forest
Black Knowe
B357
Castleton
Dinlabyre
Fell
Pike
Caplestone Fell
Black Knowe
514
Glendhu Hill
Rough Pike
Jock's Pike
Gill Pike
The Rigg
Reeker Pike
Bolt's Law
KIELDER PARK
Highfield
Hawkhope
White F
Kielder Res
Falstone
Stannersbu
I

Waterbeck
B725
Springkell
Eaglesfield
Chapelknowe
Kirkpatrick-Fleming
Creca
Hollee
B6357
Nutberry Moss
Gretna Green
Springfield
1543
Gretna
Rigg
Eastriggs
A75
Sarkfoot Point
Torduff Point
Bowness-on-Solway
Glasson
Drumburgh
Burgh by Sands
Longburgh
Finglandrigg
Studholme
Kirkbampton
Oughterby
Great Orton
Little Orton
Newby West
CARLISLE
Cummersdale
Baldwinholme
Micklethwaite
Thursby
Dalston
Buckabank
Durdar
Brisco
Wreay
Wigton
West Curthwaite
Red Dial
Warblebank
Rosley
Welton
Raughton Head
Stockdalewath
Gaitsgill
Sebergham
Ivegill
Curmersdale

Solwaybank
Wallacehall
Evertown
Canonbie
A7
Milltown
Riddings
Moat
Easton
Netherby
Chapeltown
Crofthead
Longtown
Kirklinton
Hethersgill
Smithfield
Scalebyhill
Scaleby
Laversdale
Westlinton
Todhills
Rockcliffe
Blackford
Harker
Low Crosby
Houghton
Kingstown
Stanwix
Linstock
Warwick
Scotby
Wetheral
Carleton
Cumwhinton
Cotehill
Low Hesket
Aiketgate
Southwaite
High Hesket

Cauldside
Nook
Arthur Seat
Rowanburn
Catlowdy
Wakey Hill
Baileyhead
Blackpool Gate
Oakshaw Ford
Roughsike
Bewcastle
Lyneholmeford
Stapleton
Spadeadam
Haggbeck
Boltonfellend
Kirkcambeck
West Hall
Walton
Hadrian's Wall
Banks
Newtown
Low Row
Brampton
Milton
Hayton
Talkin Tarn
Farlam
Talkin
Warwick Bridge
Heads Nook
How
Faugh
Castle Carrock
Great Corby
Cumwhitton
Hall's Tenement
Hornsby
Cumrew
Newbiggin
Croglin
Armathwaite
Ruckcroft
Ainstable
Croglin
Renwick
Scale Houses
Haresceugh

Kershopefoot
Kershope Forest
The Flatt
White Preston
Barron's Pike
Green Rigg
Spadeadam Forest
Deer Hill
Sighty Crag 518
Christianbury Crag
Paddaburn Moor
Wiley Sike
Thirlwall Common
Gilsland Spa
Gilsland
CAMBOGLANNA
LANERCOST
Hadrian's Wall Vallum
Greenhead
Haltwhi
Featherstone Castle
Rowfoot
Plenmeller
Denton Fell
Tindale
Midgeholme
Halton Lea Gate
Lambley
Stonehouse
Tindale Fells
Forest Head
Cold Fell 621
King's Forest of Geltsdale
Geltsdale Middle
Gelt
Burnstones
Knarsdale
Slaggyford
Kirkhaugh
Ayle
A689
Alston
Bayles
Le
Gilderdale Forest
Renwick Fell
Black Fell 661
Whitfield Law
A686
Fiend's Fell
Hartside Height
Grey Nag 656
Melmerby Fell
710
Gamblesby
Glassonby
Melmerby
Green Fell
Ousby Fell
Round

Churnside Lodge
Clintburn
Chirdon Burn
Spy Rigg
Round Top
Black Fell
F o r e s t
Whiteside
Hadrian's Wall Vallum
A69
Plenmeller Co
Melkridge
Untha
A691
Asholme Common
18
Glendue Fell
South Tyne
Will Common
A689
South Tynedale Railway
B6277
Mi
A l s t o n
Rotherhope F

Oulton
Lessonhall
Waverbridge
Bolton Low Houses
Brocklebank
Boltongate
B5299
Ireby
Uldale
Whelpo
Parkend
Branthwaite
Caldbeck
Hesket Newmarket
Millhouse
B5305
Sowerby Row
Lamonby
Skelton
Ellonby
HUTTON-IN-THE-FOREST
Hutton Roof
Mosedale
Carrock Fell
Uldale Fells 710 Knott
Great Calva 690
DISTRICT
Skiddaw Forest 931 Skiddaw
Bassenthwaite
Millbeck
Applethwaite
Threlkeld
Keswick
Portinscale
LINGHOLM
A591
Little Tow
Fells

C U M B R I A
High Pike 658
Caldbeck Fells
Blencathra or Saddleback 265
Mungrisdale
Greystoke Forest
Greystoke
Motherby
Penruddock
Hutton
DALEMAIN
Dacre
Great Mell Fell
Little Mell Fell
Matterdale End
Dowthwaitehead
Great Dod
Wreay
Watermillock
Ulcat Row
Dockray
Aira Force
A592
ULLSWATER
Barton Fell
Loadpot Hill 671
Sandwick
Martindale Common
Place Fell

Low Braithwaite
Calthwaite
Hutton End
New Rent
Unthank
Plumpton Hall
Plumpton Head
Laithes
Johnby
Blencow
Newton Reigny
Newbiggin
Eamont Bridge
Penrith
A6
Catterlen
A66
Lazonby
Salkeld Dykes
Great Salkeld
Little Salkeld
Hunsonby
Winskill
Ousby
Kirkoswald
Staffield
Langwathby
Edenhall
Skirwith
Kirkland
Blencarn
847 Knock Fell
Culgaith
Newbiggin
Milburn
Milburn Forest
Temple Sowerby
ACORNBANK
Roman Road
Whinfell Forest
Brougham
Clifton
Lowther Castle
Askham
Lowther
Helton
Pooley Bridge
Melkinthorpe
Cliburn
Tirril
Stainton
Eamont Bridge
Whale
Great Strickland
Kings Meaburn
Morland
Newby
Little Strickland
Sleagill
Reagill
Hoff
Kirkby Thore
Long Marton
Bramp
Dufton
A66
Backstone Edge
Keisley
Appleby-in-Westmorland
Colby
Burrells
Coupland
Great
Crackenthorpe

A B C D E

A B C D E

Bedlington
Nedderton
Cowpen
Bebside
BLYTH
Newsham
East Hartford
Shankhouse
A192
Nelson Village
Cramlington
New Hartley
Seaton
Hartley
St Mary's or Bait Island
Seaton Delaval
To Bergen (summer only)
To Stavanger (summer only)
To Göteborg (summer only)

1

Seaton Burn
Dudley
Seghill
WHITLEY BAY
To Esbjerg (summer only)
Camperdown
Killingworth
Backworth
Monkseaton
Cullercoats
Forest Hall
New York
Marden
Benton Square
Preston
TYNEMOUTH
LONGBENTON
North Shields
SOUTH SHIELDS

2

Kenton
Blakelaw
WALLSEND
Willington
Toll
Jesmond
HEBBURN
JARROW
Harton
Marsden Bay
Heaton
Walker
Monkton
Cleadon
Marsden
FELLING
East Boldon
Whitburn
GATESHEAD
West Boldon
BOLDON
Team Valley
Southwick
Fulwell
Roker
Lamesley
Springwell
Castletown
Whitburn Bay
Birtley
Wrekenton
South Hylton
Monkwearmouth

3

Kibblesworth
Washington
Fatfield
SUNDERLAND
Ouston
Penshaw
Hendon
Pelton
Shiney Row
Herrington
New Silksworth
North of England Open Air Museum
Newfield
Grange Villa
Bournmoor
Silksworth
Ryhope
Chester-le-Street
Waldridge
HOUGHTON-LE-SPRING
SEAHAM
Edmondsley
Great Lumley
Colliery Row
Seaton
Kimblesworth
Plawsworth
Hetton-le-Hole
Dalton-le-Dale
Nose's Point
acriston
FINCHALE
East Rainton
Murton
Cold Hesledon

4

Pity Me
West Rainton
South Hetton
Hawthorn
Hawthorn Hive
Witton Gilbert
Framwellgate Moor
Easington Lane
Beacon Point
Shippersea Bay
Carrville
Pittington
Littletown
Easington
Easington Colliery
DURHAM
Haswell
Little Thorpe
Horden Point
Sherburn
Shadforth
Shotton Colliery
Langley Moor
Shincliffe
Ludworth
Horden
Brandon
Thornley
Shotton
PeterLee
Gore Dene Mouth
Blackhalls Rocks

5

Wheatley Hill
Blackhall Colliery
Cassop
Bowburn
Quarrington Hill
Hesleden
Sunderland Bridge
Kelloe
Castle Eden
Croxdale
Hett
Coxhoe
Wingate
Crimdon Park
Tudhoe
Trimdon Grange
Trimdon Station Town
Hart
Spennymoor
South Wingate
Hutton Henry
Comforth
Sheraton
Byers Green
TRIMDON
High Throston
Middlestone Moor
Ferryhill
Fishburn
Hurworth Burn Resr
Elwick
HARTLEPOOL
Dean Bank
Bishop Middleham
Hartlepool Bay
Kirk Merrington
Coundon
Chilton
Dalton Piercy
Seaton Carew
BISHOP AUCKLAND
Rushyford
Brierton
Tees

6

Coundon Grange
Bradbury
Sedgefield
Greatham
Woodham
Mordon
Newton Bewley
Seal Sands
Middridge
Thorpe Larches
Wolviston
Coatham
Redcar
Newton Aycliffe
Foxton
Stillington
Cowpen Bewley
Dormanstown
Redworth
Thorpe Thewles
Billingham
Haverton Hill
Kirkleatham
Marske-by-the-Sea
Heighington
Aycliffe
Great Stainton
Whitton
Port Clarence
Grangetown
New Marske
Saltburn-by-the-Sea

7

Houghton-le-Side
Brafferton
Bishopton
Carlton
Norton
North Ormesby
South Bank
Wilton
Skelton
Bratton
Coatham Mundeville
Little Stainton
Redmarshall
MIDDLESBROUGH
Cargo Fleet
Lazenby
Dunsdale
Skelton Green
North Skelton
Skinning
Archdeacon Newton
Great Burdon
Sadberge
Hartburn
Acklam
Eston
Ormesby
Normanby
Boosbeck
Loftu
High Coniscliffe
DARLINGTON
Elton
Thornaby-on-Tees
CLEVELAND
Guisborough
Lingdale
Stanghow
Low Coniscliffe
Eastbourne
Eaglescliffe
Allens W.
Stainton
Marton
Upleatham
Liverton
Cleasby
Blackwell
Egglescliffe
Tees-side Airport Sta.
Middleton One Row
High Leven
Hemlington
Nunthorpe
Pinchinthorpe
Moorsholm
Newton under Roseberry
Freebrough Moor
A171
Croft-on-Tees
Hurworth-on-Tees
Neasham
Low Dinsdale
Yarm
Hilton
Newby
Great Ayton
Gisborough Moor
Danby Low Moor
Barton
Girsby
Sockburn
Picton
Crathorne
Tanton
GREAT AYTON
Commondale
Danby
Stokesley
Little Ayton
Kildale
Castleton

0 1 2 3 4 5 10 15 kilometres
0 1 2 3 4 5 10 miles

An Dunan
Rubh an Leim
Sowlandman's Bay
Sron Garbh
Rubh an Leanachais
Eilean Bhride

Point of Knap
Baile Boidheach
Cnoc a Bharaille
Druimdrishaig
Larach na Gaibhre
Dubh Chreag 480
Loch Chaorunn
Meall Reamhar
B8024
Ashens
St eld
Barmore Island
SCOTT
Barfad
Auchalick B800
Tighnabruaich
Rhubodach
Kyles
South Hall
Glaic
Craignafeich
Kames
Shalunt
Stronc Point
Stuck
Cretshengan
Coulaghailtro
Meall Reamhar
Loch a Chaoruinn
Loch Racadal
East Loch Tarbert
Dubhchladach
Tarbert
West Tarbert
Mealldarroch Point
Port Leatham
Derybruich
Portavadie
Low Stillaig
Blair's Ferry
Millhouse
Glenmore
Glecknabae
Kames Hill
Ardmaleish
8
Na Cuiltean
Stotfield Bay
Miller's Bay
Port Ban
Kilberry Head
Keppoch Point
Kilberry
Cruach Airde
Dunmore
B8024
Carse
Ardpatrick
Achadh-chaorrunn
Escart
Corranbuie
Cruach ant Sorchain
5
Achadacaie
Cruach Doire Leithe 421
Cnoc a Bhaile-shios
Redhouse
Whitehouse
Coire nan Capull
Altagalvash
Culindrach
Rubha Lagganroaig
Kilbride Bay
Ardlamont
Kilbride
Carry
Upper Ardroscadale
Meikle Kilmory
St Ninian's Point
Loch Quien
Inchmarnock
Midpark
Ardscalpsie
Pip

Rubha Cruitiridh
Loch Stornoway
Gartnagrenach
A83
Gartavaich
A8001
Glenrisdell
Skipness
Ardlamont Bay
Ardlamont Point
Camas na Ceardaich

Ardpatrick Point
Portachoillan
Quinhill
Clachan
Cruach nam Fiadh 269
Claonaig
Rockfield
B8001
Skipness Point
Skipness
Auchameanach
Scalpsie Bay
Stravanan
Dunagoil B
Garro
Garro
SOUND OF BUTE
Stravanan Bay

To Port Askaig
Port Mor
Ronachan Point
Talatoll 52
Corriechrevie
Loch Ciaran
Ballochroy
Auchinafaud
Cruach Mhic-Gougain
Escairt
Port Fada
(summer only)
Loch Ranza
North
Newton
South
Lochranza
A841
Cock of Arran
To Port Ellen
West Tarbert Bay
East Tarbert Bay
Tarbert
Ardaily
Druimyeon Bay
Rhunahaorine Point
Ardminish Bay
North
South
Crossaig
Cour
Cour Bay
Catacol Bay
Rubha Airigh Bheirg
Glen Catacol
Glen Chalmadale
North Glen Sannox
14

Gigha Island
Ardminish
Craro Island
Grob Bagh
SOUND OF GIGHA
Rhunahaorine
Narachan Hill 285
Cnoc an t-Samhlaidh
Cnoc Reamhar
Sunadale
Grogport
21
Whitefarland Point
Craw
Lenimore
Mid Thundergay
South Thundergay
Pirnmill
Beinn Bhreac 573
Beinn Tarsuinn
711
Beinn Bhreac
Caisteal Abhail
Cir Mhor 798
Cioch-na-h-Oighe
Sannox Bay
Mid Sannox
Corrie

Cara Island
Mull of Cara
Cleit Dhubh
A Chleit
Tayinloan
Killean
Beacharr
Clachaig Water
Deucheran Hill
Cruach nan Gabhar 354
Achaglass
Muasdale 33
Arinanuan
Diollaid Mhor
Rhonadale
Carradale
Dippen
Dougarie Point
Imachar
Balliekine
Glen Iorsa
17
Iorsa Water
Beinn Bharrain 721
Beinn Tarsuinn 825
Beinn Nuis
Goat Fell 874
Glen Rosa
Merkland Point
Loch Tanna
ARRAN

Glenacardoch Point
Belloch
Glenbarr
Barr Water
Beinn Bhreac 426
Beinn an Tuirc 436
Torrisdale
Carradale Bay
Dougarie
A841
Machrie
Glaister
An Tunna
Machrie Water
A'Chruach 512
Tarrnacraig
Brodick Bay
Glencloy
Strathwhillan
Brodick
Corrygills
Clauchlan
5
A841

Bellochantuy Bay
Bellochantuy
Corrylach
Killocraw
Lussa Loch
Meall Buidhe 374
Saddell
Whitestone
Saddell Bay
Bunlarie
Ugadale Point
Machrie Bay
Tormore
Ard Bheinn 511
Benlister Glen
Ballymichael
Beinn Bhreac 503
Glenkiln
Margnaheglis
Lamlash
Holy

Port Crom
Tangy Loch
Tangy
Ballivain
Westport
Skeroblingarry
Drumgarve
Glen Lussa
Callyburn
Peninver
Ballochgair
Ardnacross Bay
Sgreadan Hill 397
13
Torbeg
Shiskine
Blackwaterfoot
Drumadoon Bay
Kilpatrick
Brown Head
Kingscross
Kingscross
Knockenkelly
Kiscadale
458
Whiting Bay
Largymore
Largybeg
Dippin
Whiting B
Glen Scorrodale
Kilmory Water

Machrihanish Bay
Machrihanish
Kilchenzie
A83
East Drumlemble
Kilmichael
Campbeltown
Drumore
Witchburn
Campbeltown Loch
Davaar I.
Corriecravie
Sliddery
Lagg
A841
20
Shannochie
Bennan Head
Kildonan
Sound of Pladda
Pladda

Drumlemble
B843
Dalivaddy
Chiscan
Kilkerran
Davaar
New Orleans
Earadale Point
Killypole
Oatfield
Knocknaha
Kilchrist
Beinn Ghuilean 352
Chiscan Water
Killellan
385
The Slate
Killellan
Arinarach Hill
6
Cnoc Moy 446
Rubha Duin Bhain
Largybaan
Cnoc Reamhar
10
Conie Water
Cnoc Odhar 276
Brecklate
Glen Breackerie
Keprigan
Glen Kerran
Drum Kilavie
Feochaig
Ru Stafnish
Sheanachie
Macharioch
Polliwilline Bay
South Point
Beinn na Lice 428
Strone Glen
Carrine
Garveld
Feorlan
Keil
Southend
Carskey Bay
Sanda Sound
Mull of Kintyre
Borgadelmore Point
Sheep Island
Sanda Island

Ailsa Craig

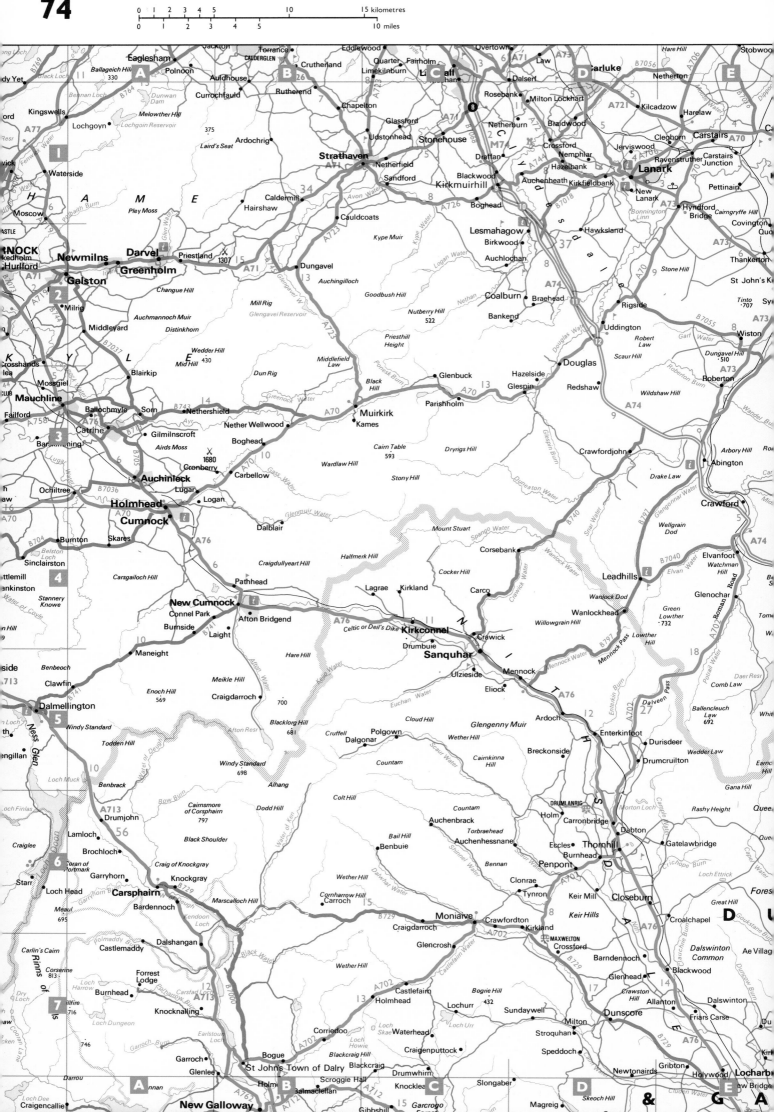

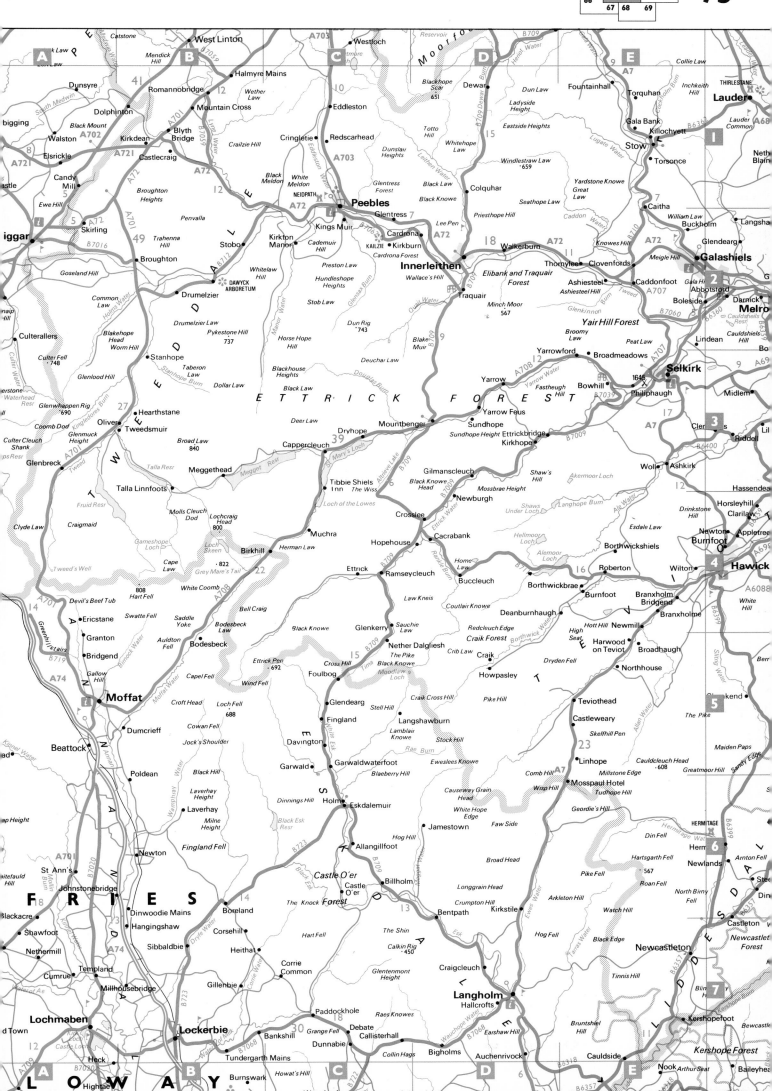

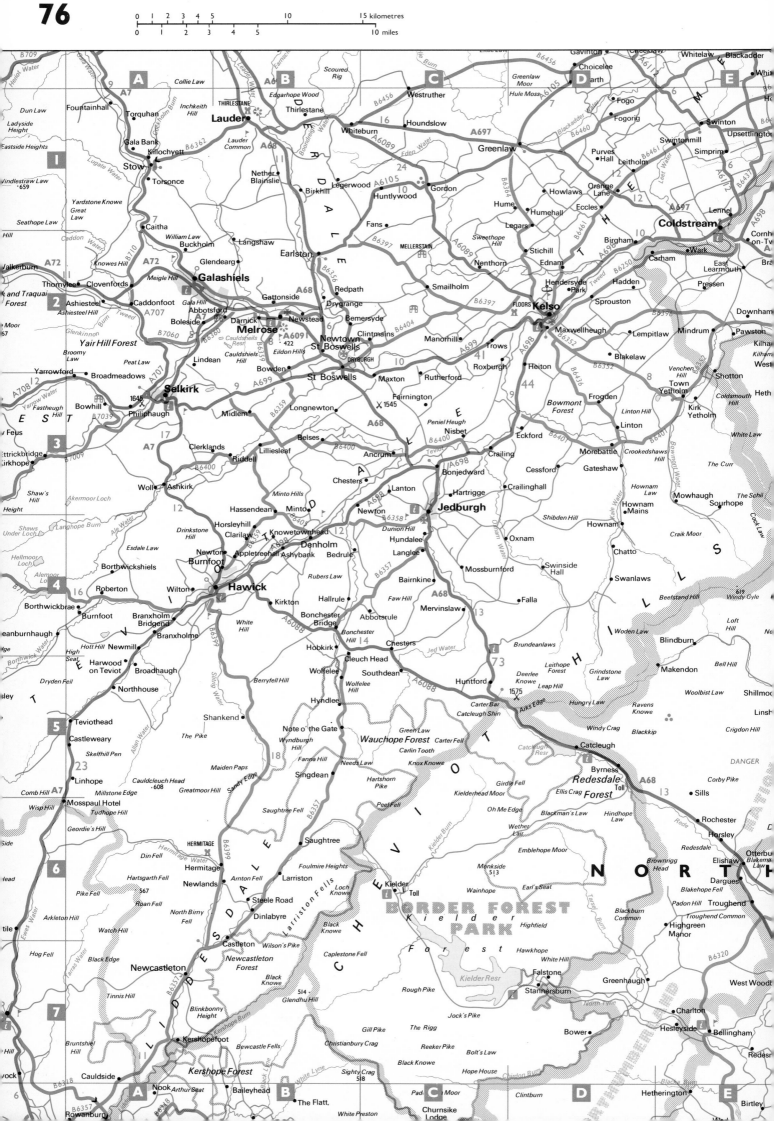

A B C D E

Tweedmouth
East Ord
Longridge Towers
Spittal
Horncliffe
Murton
Redshin Cov
Thornton
Shoresdean
Scremerston
Cheswick
Black Rocks
West Allerdean
Goswick
Duddo
Ancroft
Berrington
Beal
Keel Head
Emmanuel Head
Lindisfarne or
Holy Island
LINDISFARNE (NT)
Kimmerston
Holburn
Holy Island Sands
Castle Point
Etal
Barmoor Lane End
Kyloe
Fenwick
Buckton
Guile Point
Fenham Flats
Ford
Detchant
Elwick
Ross
Budle Point
Longstone
Farne Islands
Staple Sound
Kimmerston
Fenton Town
Nesbit
Doddington
Horton
Middleton
Easington
Budle
Glororum
Bamburgh
Farne Island
Inner Sound
Monks House Rocks
Belford
Spindlestone
Burton
Seahouses
Bradford
Elford
North Sunderland
Newtown
Coupland
Wooler
Bellshill
Warenton
Lucker
Newham Hall
Beadnell
Benthall
Humbleton
Chatton
Greendykes
Adderstone
Twizell House
Newham
Swinhoe
Fleetham
Beadnell Bay
Earle
Haugh Head
Newtown
Chillingham
Rosebrough
Warenford
Newstead
Chathill
Freddenhill
Middleton Hall
Hepburn
Ellingham
Preston
Tughall
Snook Point
High Newton-by-the-Sea
Ilderton
Old Bewick
Bewick Moor
Brockdam
Middle Moor
Christon Bank
Brunton
Low Newton by-the-Sea
Newton Haven or St Mary's
Roddam
New Bewick
West Ditchburn
North Charlton
Embleton
Embleton Bay
Wooperton
Eglingham
South Charlton
Rock
Dunstan
Craster
Beanley
Shipley
Rennington
Stamford
Cullernose Point
Brandon
Powburn
East Bolton
Littlehoughton
Howick
Branton
Glanton
Bolton
Hulne Park
Denwick
Longhoughton
Longhoughton Steel
Prendwick
Great Ryle
Whittingham
Broome Wood
Alnwick
Hawkhill
Boulmer
Boulmer Haven
Alnham
Yetlington
Callaly
Thrunton Wood
Edlingham
Lesbury
Alnmouth Sta.
Alnmouth
Bilton
Alnmouth Bay
Scrainwood
Elilaw
Lorbottle Hall
Alnwick Moor
Shilbottle
High Buston
Netherton
Lorbottle
Long Crag
Bigges Pillar
High Trewhitt
Cartington
Newton-on-the-Moor
Eastfield Hall
Birling
Warkworth
Burradon
Snitter
Guyzance
Gloster Hill
Amble
Coquet Island
Sharperton
Warton
Rothbury
CRAGSIDE
Shirlaw Pike
Longframlington
Swarland Estate
Morwick Hall
Hauxley
Hauxley Haven
Caistron
Newtown
Thropton
Whitton
Swarland
Felton
Acklington
Togston
Radcliffe
Hadston Carrs
Hepple
Great Tosson
Pauperhaugh
East Thirston
South Broomhill
Broomhill
Chevington Drift
Tosson Hill
Simonside
Low Hesleyhurst
BRINKBURN
Eshott
West Chevington
Red Row
Druridge Bay
Billsmoor Park
Dough Crag
Forestburn Gate
Wingates
Widdrington
Elsdon
Harwood Forest
Coldrife
Longhorsley
Causey Park
Widdrington Sta.
Cresswell
Snab Point
Ottercops Moss
Earsdon Moor
Tritlington
Ulgham
Ellington
Raechester
Netherwitton
Stanton
Espley Hall
Fenrother
Lynemouth
Blue Holes
Beacon Point
Ray Fell
High Hartington
Longwitton
Todd Hill
Hebron
Longhirst
Woodhorn
ASHINGTON
Newbiggin-by-the-Sea
Knowesgate
Rothley
Pigdon
Pegswood
Hirst
North Seaton
Kirkwhelpington
Scots Gap
Hartburn
Throphill
Morpeth
Bothal
WANSBECK
Cambois
Cambo
WALLINGTON (NT)
Middleton
Mitford
NEWMINSTER
Shadfen
Guide Post
Stakeford
East Sleekburn
Kirkharle
Middleton Bank Top
Meldon
Tranwell
West Edington
Clifton
Hepscott
Scotland Gate
Bedlington
BLYTH
Capheaton
BOLAM LAKE
Whalton
Nedderton
Cowpen
Bebside
Newsham
Thockrington
Belsay
Saltwick
Stannington
Hartford
Shankhouse
Ogle
Nelson Village

CUMBERLAND

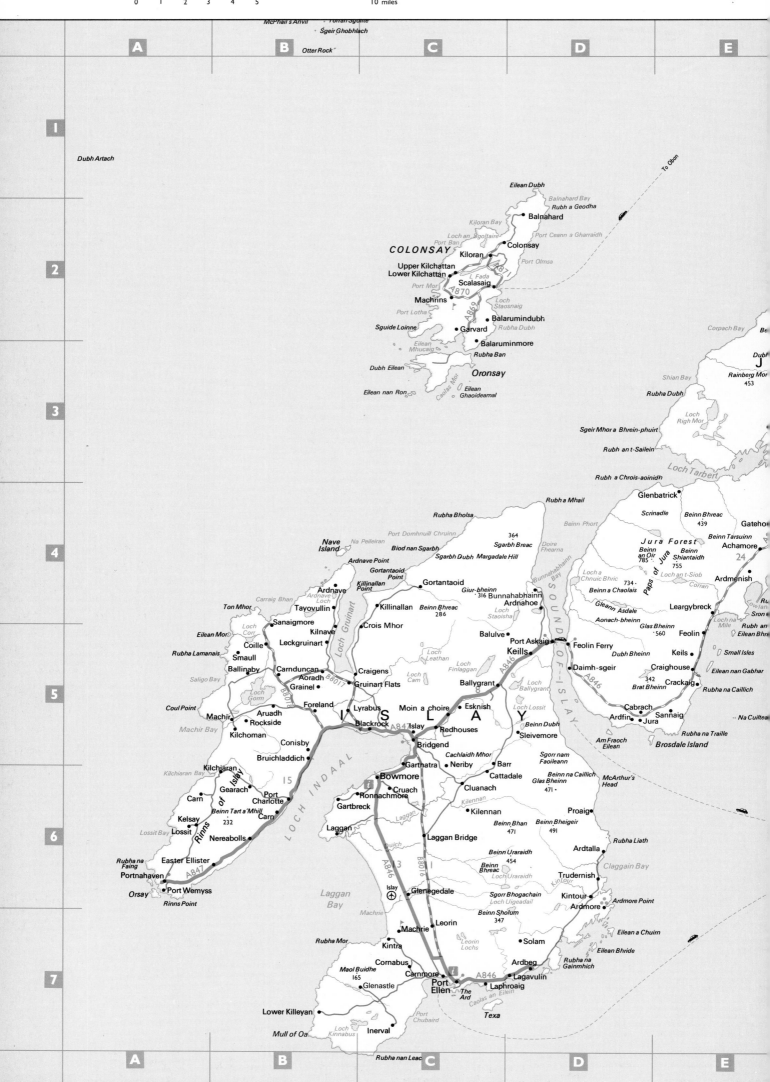

Scale bars:
0 1 2 3 4 5   10   15 kilometres
0 1 2 3 4 5   10 miles

McPhail's Anvil
Torran Sgoilte
Sgeir Ghobhlach
Otter Rock

Dubh Artach

Eilean Dubh
To Oban
Balnahard Bay
Rubh a Geodha
Kiloran Bay
Port Ban
Loch an Sgoltaire
Colonsay
COLONSAY   Kiloran
Port Ceann a Gharraidh
Port Olmsa
Upper Kilchattan
Lower Kilchattan
L Fada
Scalasaig
Machrins   A870
Loch Staosnaig
Port Mor
Port Lotha
Balarumindubh
Sguide Loinne   Garvard
Rubha Dubh
Balaruminmore
Corpach Bay
Be
Eilean Mhucaig
Rubha Ban
Dubh Eilean
Oronsay
Dubl
Rainberg Mor
453
J
Eilean nan Ron
Eilean Ghaoideamal
Shian Bay
Rubha Dubh
Loch Righ Mor
Sgeir Mhor a Bhrein-phuirt
Loch Tarbert
Rubh an t-Sailein
Rubh a Chrois-aoinidh
Glenbatrick
Rubh a Mhail
Scrinadle
Beinn Bhreac 439
Rubha Bholsa
Beinn Phort
Beinn Tarsuinn
Gateho
Port Domhnuill Chruinn
364
Sgarbh Breac
Doire Fhearna
JURA FOREST
Beinn an Oir 785
Beinn Shiantaidh 755
Achamore
Nave Island
Na Peilleiran
Biod nan Sgarbh
Sgarbh Dubh
Margadale Hill
Bunnahabhainn Bay
24
Ardnave Point
Gortantaoid Point
Gortantaoid
Giur-bheinn
Loch a Chnuic Bhric
Beinn a Chaolais 734
Paps of Jura
Ardmenish
Killinallan Point
316 Bunnahabhainn
Loch an t-Siob
Corran
Ardnave
Tayovullin
Killinallan
Beinn Bhreac 286
Ardnahoe
Loch Staoisha
Glenn Asdale
Leargybreck
Ardnave Loch
Carraig Bhan
Balulve
Aonach-bheinn
Feolin
Sanaigmore
Kilnave
Crois Mhor
Glas Bheinn 560
Loch Corr
Coille
Leckgruinart
Port Askaig
Feolin Ferry
Eilean Bhri
Eilean Mor
Keills
Dubh Bheinn
Keils
Rubha Lamanais
Smaull
Daimh-sgeir
Small Isles
Loch Gruinart
Loch Leathan
Ballinaby
Carnduncan
Craigens
Loch Finlaggan
342
Craighouse
Eilean nan Gabhar
Saligo Bay
Aoradh
Gruinart Flats
Brat Bheinn
Crackaig
Grainel
Loch Cam
Ballygrant
Rubha na Caillich
Loch Gorm
Ballygrant
Foreland
Moin a choire
Esknish
Cabrach
Sannaig
Coul Point
Lyrabus
ISLAY
Ardfin
Jura
Machir
Aruadh
Blackrock
Islay
Redhouses
Am Fraoch Eilean
Rubha na Traille
Rockside
Beinn Dubh
Machir Bay
Bridgend
Sleivemore
Brosdale Island
Kilchoman
Conisby
Cachlaidh Mhor
Sgorr nam Faoileann
McArthur's Head
Bruichladdich
Gartnatra
Neriby
Barr
Beinn na Caillich Glas Bheinn 471
Kilchiaran
Bowmore
Cattadale
Gearach
Cruach
Cluanach
Carn
Port Charlotte
Ronnachmore
Kilennan
Proaig
Kelsay
Beinn Tart a'Mhill 232
Carn
Gartbreck
Kilennan
Beinn Bhan 471
Beinn Bheigeir 491
Rinns of Islay
Nereabolls
Laggan
Laggan
Ardtalla
Lossit Bay
Lossit
Laggan Bridge
Beinn Uraraidh 454
Rubha Liath
Easter Ellister
Rubha na Faing
Duich
Beinn Bhreac
Loch Uraraidh
Kintour
Claggain Bay
Portnahaven
A847
Trudernish
Orsay
Port Wemyss
Islay
Glenegedale
Sgorr Bhogachain
Kintour
Ardmore Point
Rinns Point
Laggan Bay
Loch Uigeadail
Ardmore
Machrie
Leorin
Beinn Sholum 347
Eilean a Chuirn
Machrie
Leorin Lochs
Solam
Rubha Mor
Kintra
Eilean Bhride
Cornabus
Carnmore
Rubha na Gainmhich
Maol Buidhe 165
Ardbeg
Glenastle
Port Ellen
Lagavulin
Lower Killeyan
Laphroaig
Mull of Oa
Loch Kinnabus
Inerval
The Ard
Caolas an Eilein
Texa
Port Chubaird
Rubha nan Leac

Scale bar: 0 1 2 3 4 5 10 15 kilometres / 0 1 2 3 4 5 10 miles

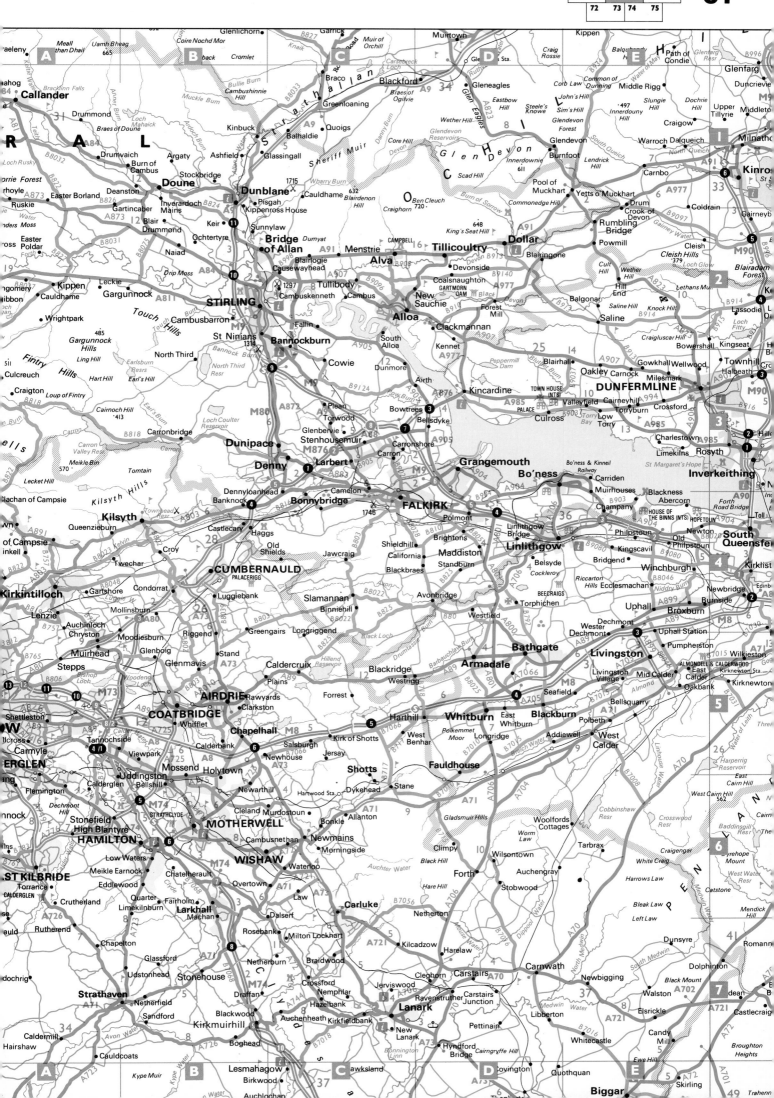

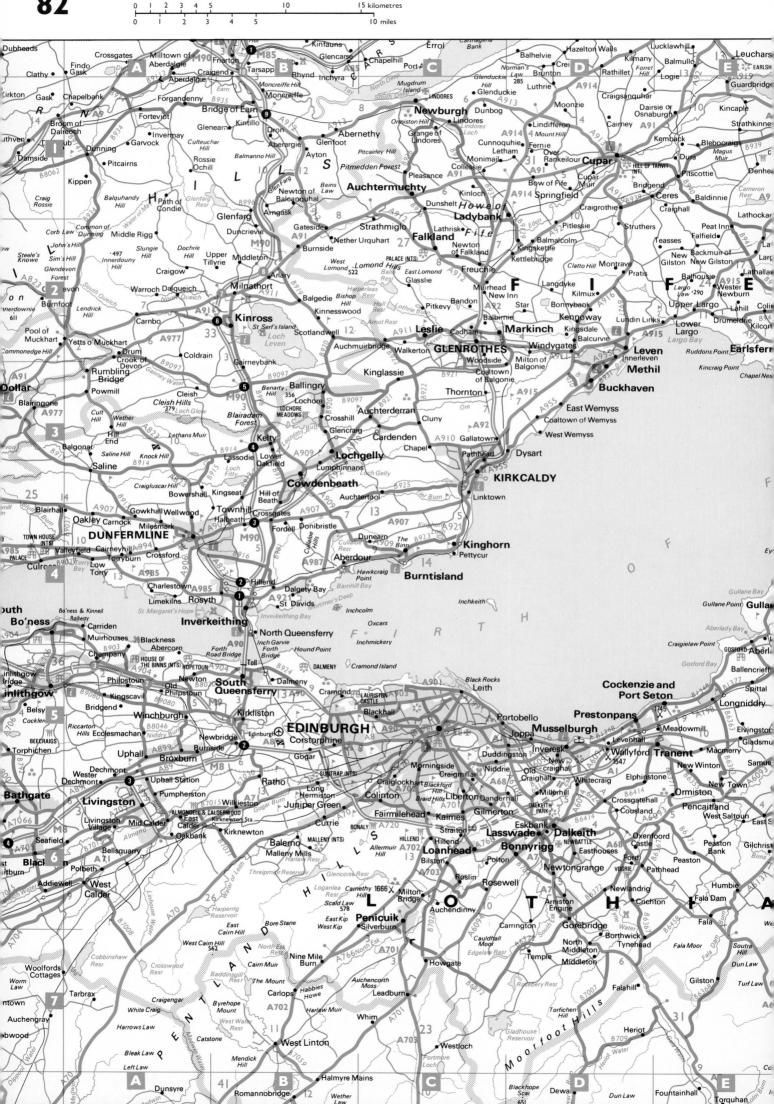

0 1 2 3 4 5   10   15 kilometres
0 1 2 3 4 5   10 miles

A   B   C   D   E

1

2

3

4

5

6

7

Eilean nan Ea
Rubh'an Inb
Rubh'an Inb
Ardnam

To Lochboisdale

To Castlebay

Eag na Maoile   Eilean Mor
Rubha Mor
Rubh' a'Bhinnein   Bousd   Rubha Sgor innis
Loch Fada   Sorisdale
Torastan
Bagh na Coille
Clad Bay
Grishipoll Bay   Arnabost
Grishipoll   •73
Clabhach   Loch Cliad
Hogh Bay   Ballyhaugh   104   2
Totamore   C O L L   Bagh Feisdlum
Port Mine   Arinagour
Totronald   Eilean nam Muc
Feall Bay   Arileod   Acha   5
Uig   B8071   Loch Eatharna
Calgary Point   Crossapol   Gorton   Eilean Ornsay
Crossapol Bay   Port na h-eitheir
Gunna   Friesland Bay
Port a'Mhurain   Rubha Fasachd
Soa
Urvaig   Soa
Miodar
Ruaig   Rubha Dubh
Balephetrish Bay   B8069   Caoles
The Green   Balephetrish Hill   Brock   Port Ban
4   Rubha Liath
T I R E E   Gott Bay
Kilkenneth   B8068   5   Scarinish
Saundaig   B8065   Heylipoll   5   Baugh
Barrapoll   Hynish   Heanish
B8067   Balemartine   Bay
Balephuil   Hynish

Caliach Point
Port
Sunipol   La
Mornis
Cruach Sleibh
Rubha nan Oirean   166•
Calgary Bay
Treshnish Point   Ensay
Treshnish
Beinn Duill
191   Rubh a Chaoil
Reudle
Rubh an t-Suibhein
Cairn na Burgh More   Cairn na Burgh Beg
Fladda   Rubha na Sroi
Sgeir à Chaisteil   Eilean Dioghlum
Lunga   Rubha Maol na Mine   Gometra
Treshnish Isles   Gometra
Maisgeir
Bac Mor or Dutchman's Cap   Little Colonsay
Bac Beag
Staffa   Eilean Dubh
Fingal's Cave   The Causeway
Erisger
Rubha
Aira
Eilean Annraidh
Reidh Eilean   Carraig
Eilean Chalbha
Dun
Port an Duine Mhairbh   Kintra
Iona   Rubha nan Cearc
Fionnphort   Beinn Chladan   Eorab
Ruanaich   Aridhglas   A849
Stac an Aoineidh   Loch na Lathaich
Fidden
Rubha na Carraig-geire   R O S S
Knockvologan   Ardalanish
Soa Island   Erraid   Torr Fada   Ardchia
Eilean Dubh   Aird Mor   Port
Eilean a Chalmain   Eilean Mor   Rubh' Arda
Ruadh Sgeir
Torran Rocks   Dearg Sgeir
West Reef   Na Torrain
McPhail's Anvil   Torran Sgoilte
Sgeir Ghobhlach
Otter Rock

A   B   C   D   E

OF EIGG

Muck

SOUND OF ARISAIG

A B C D E

Rubha Chaolais
Eilean nan Gobhar
Loch Doir a'Ghearrain
Ardnish
Lochailort
Inverailort
Loch Eilt
Ranochan
Glenfinnan Sta.
A830
45
Sgurr na Paite
Beinn Odhar Mhor 870
Meall a' Bhainne 559
Drum

Samalaman Island
Smearisary
Roshven
A861
An Stac
869
Druim Fiaclach 882
Odhar Mhor
Beinn Odhar Bheag 882
Sgor Craobh a'Chaoruinn 775
Meall nan Damh 718
Meall nan Creag Leac

Eilean Shona
Aonach
Bailetonach
Shona Beag 265
Kylesbeg
Cruach Bhrochdadail 357
712
Assary
664 Sgurr Dhomhuill Mor 754
Sgor an Tarmachain 786
Stob Mhic Bheathain 719
Cona Glen

Rubha Aird Druimnich
Ardtoe
Newton of Ardtoe
Shielfoot
Kentra
Carn Mor
Beinn Bhreac 239
Ardmolich
Cliff Dalnabreck
Glen Moidart
Beinn Gaire
Gaskan
Gorstanvorran
Sgurr na Greine 497
Beinn Mheadhoin 889
Sgorr a'Chaorainn
Tighnacomaire
Glen

Faskadale
Plocaig
Achateny
Kilmory
Ockle
Swordle
Branault
Ockle Point
357
Beinn Bhreac
Gortenfern
Arevegaig
Acharacle
Claish Moss
Ardshealach
Dalelia
Achnanellan
Polloch
Glenhurich
Glen Hurich
Druim Garbh
Sgurr Dhomhuill
ARD
Glen Go

Sanna
Achnaha
Achnha
Achosnich
Meall nan Con 437
Ormsaigmore
Kilchoan
Camphouse
Ben Hiant 528
Beinn nan Losgann 313
Ardslignish
Maclean's Nose
ARDNAMURCHAN
Leac Shoilleir 437
Lochan nam Fiann
Salen
Tarbert
Beinn Resipol 845
Resipole
Scotstown
SUNART
Ardery
Anaheilt
Drumnatorran
Garbh Bheinn 885
Sgurr nan Cnam 700
Tigh Ghlinnegal

Beinn na Seilg 342
Kilchoan Bay
Sron Bheag
Meall an Tarmachain 404
Beinn Bhuidhe
Glenbeg
278
Glenborrodale
Laga
B8007
512 Ben Laga
303
Gearr Chreag 339
Meall a Bhroin
Glencripesdale
Woodend
Ardnastang
LOCH SUNART
12
Ranachan
Strontian
25
Achnalea
A861
Glen Tarbert
Gearr Inversan

Oronsay
Risga
Carna
452
Doirlinn
571
Beinn Iadain
Meall a Chaise 522
Achagavel
Liddesdale
Achleek
A884
7
Meall a' Choirein Luachraich
853
Creach Bheinn 620
Glas Bheinn 765
Maol Odhar
Meall nan Each
Kilmalieu

Meall an Inbhire
Tobermory
Mishnish
S Airde Beinn
Calve Island
Torraneidhinn
Rahoy
Barr
Ardtornish
Taobh Dubh
352
Fuar Bheinn 591
Beinn Na Cille
Glengalmadale
13
Am Broilein
A82

Dervaig
Achnadrish
Torr-a-chlachan
AROS
Mishnish Lochs
Caol Lochan
Mains of Drimnin
Ardantiobairt
Kinloch
464
Beinn na h-Uamha
Gleann Dubh
Durinemast
Beinn Chlaonleud
Meall a Chaorainn Loch Uisge
Gleann Geal
MORVEN
Beach
Meall a Chaorainn 481
Sgurr Shalachain
Ceanna Mor
Rubha na h-Airde Uinnsinn
Camasnacroise
Shuna Island

Drimnin
Achleanan
Beinn Bhuidhe 451
550
Sidhean na Raplaich
Loch Arienas
Claggan
Braigh na Glaice Moire
Clounlaid
739
Alltachonaich
568
Caol Bheinn 425
Sgurr a Bhuic
Glensanda
Port a Chaistell
Eilean Ramsay
Eilean Loch Oscair
Ardtur
Port Appin
Portnacro
Ki

Rhemore
Speinne Mor 444
Ardnacross
Lettermore
Ledmore
Meall na Caorach
Killundine
267 Creag Bhan Ard
Beinn an t-Sruthain
336
Beinn Bhan
Larachbeg
Meall Damh
12
Ardtornish
Glais Bheinn
An Sleaghach
462
Loch Tearnait
Port Ramsay
Clachan
Appin Rocks
North Shian
Eigniag
Etiska
South Shian
Loch Co

Achnacraig
315
Cnoc an da Chinn
Fanmore
Ballygown
Kilbrenan
Drium an Fhraoich Mhin 318
Beinn Bhuidhe 383
Meall an Fhiar Mhaim 309
Tenga
Glen Aros
Eilean an Glasa
Fishnish Point
Achnaha
Tighachnoic
Lochaline
Innbeg
478
Mam a'Chullaich 514
Sailean
Achnacroish
Seabank
Eilean Dubh
LORN
Balygrundle
Kiel Crofts
Culcharan

Salen
Pennygown
Killbeg
Maol Buidhe
Bailemeonach
Garmony
Scallastle Bay
Rubha an Ridire
Inninmore Bay
MORVEN
LYNN OF
Bernera
Balure
Ledaig
A828

Knock
Gaodhail
Na Binneinean
Cruach Torran Lochain
Gruline
Beinn nan Lus
Beinn Chreagach Mhor 580
636
Beinn Mheadhon
Scallastle
Craignure Bay
Craignure
Duart Bay
Eilean Musdile
Pladda Island
Rubha Garbh aird
South Ledaig
North Connel
A85

Clachandhu
Dishig
An Gearna
Beinn a Ghraig 591
Creag Dhubh
Beinn Fhada
762
Beinn Talaidh
Dun da Ghaoithe
Maol nan Uan
Duart Point
Lady's Rock
Ganavan Bay
Dunbeg
Connel
Pennyfuir
Cuil-uaine
Stro

MULL
Balmeanach
Coirc Bheinn 560
Ben More 966
Gortenbuie
Beinn Chaisgidle
Sgurr Dearg 740
Lochdonhead
TOROSAY
Ardchoirk
Gorten
Maiden Island
Rubh a Bhearnaig
Ardantrive
Oban Bay
Oban
Ardconnel
Auchnac

Balmeanach
Maol Mheadhonach
Cruachan Dearg 704
Guibean Uluvailt
Cruach Choireadail
Ishriff
Oakbank
Ardachoil
Ardnadrochet
Grass Point
Port Donain
Ruba na Lice
Bailliemore
Soroba
Glencruitten
Strontoiller
A816
Glenamach

Balevulin
Gib Bheinn 519
Dererach
Uluvalt
Ardura
Cruach Ardura
Auchnacraig
Carn Ban
Gortenanrue
Ardmore
Lerags
Gylen
Gallanach
Kilbride
Cleigh
Kilmo
Baligoun
Clachadow

Aird of Kinloch
Derrynaculen
Craig
A849
Glen More
15
Ben Buie 717
Creach Beinn 698
Fellonmore
Rubha na Faoilinn
Bach Island
Rubha Seanach
Dunach
Glenfeochan
Midr

Killinaig
Pennyghael
Beinn na Croise 503
Maol nan Uan
Loch Fuaran
Cruach nan Con
Kinlochspelve
Croggan
Dalnaha
Portfield
Dubh Sgeir
Knipoch
Barrnacarry
Barnacarry Bay
Minard Point

Goirtein Driseach
Brolass
Glenbyre
L. Uisg
Creag nam Fitheach
405
Druim Fada
Maol Ban
Port na Muice Duibhe
Eilean Duin
Kilninver
An Creachan
A Chruach
368
Scamadale
Braglenbeg
Beinn Dea

375
Cruachan Min
Beinn Chreagach 376
Carsaig
Beinn a Bhainne
Rubha Garbh Airde
Ardencaple
Barrachrail
Rarey
Duachy
Kilmore
Glen Euchar
Shellachan
515

Creachan Mor
Nun's Pass
Aoineadh Mor
Carsaig Bay
Rubha Dubh
Inish Island
Ardfad
Seil
Clachan-Seil
Ardshellach
Corriclorne
28
Loch Tralaig

Rubha nam Braithrean
Malcolm's Point
Frank Lockwood's Island
Dun Mor
Ardcaple
Easdale
Balvicar
Caddleton
Henderson's Rock
Loch a Phearsain
Drissa

SCOOR
Rubha nam Braithrean
Garvellachs or Isles of the Sea
To Colonsay
Cullipool
Cuan Sound
Torsay Island
Kilchoan
Ardanstur
Maolachy

FIRTH OF LORN
Eilean an Naoimh
Lunga
Black Mill Bay
Shuna
A'Chuli
Belnahua
Garbh Eileach
Glas Eilean
Degnish
Degnish Point
Ardinamar
Luing
Eilean Dubh Mor
Eilean Gamhna
Tullich
Kilmelford
Lagalochy
43

Guirasdeal
Kames
Arduaine
Tom Soilleir
Cam Loch
491
Lergiechoniemore
A816
Inverliever Forest
Kilmaha
Arinechtan

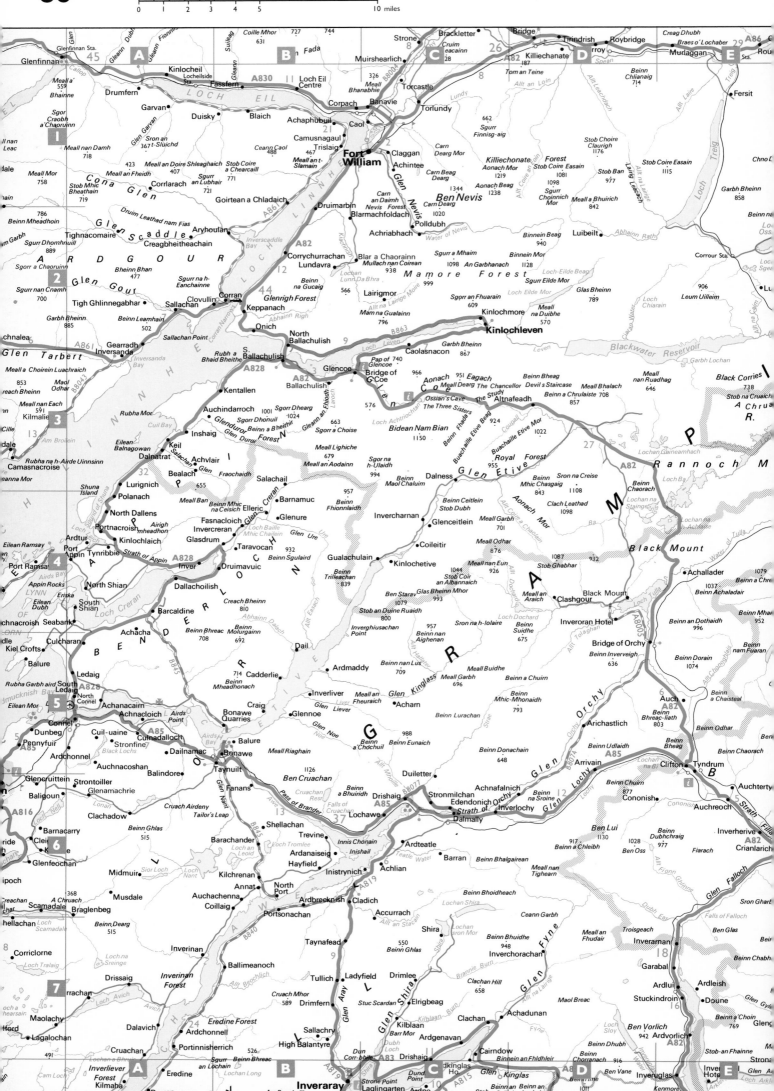

0 1 2 3 4 5   10   15 kilometres

0 1 2 3 4 5   10 miles

A   **B**   **C**   **D**   **E**

Beinn Bhreac

Loch Mhairc

Braigh Sron Ghorm

Tarf Water

Falls of Tarf

An Sligearnach 785

Carn an Righ

Gleann Mor

Glas Tulaichean 1051

An Socach 937

Iutharn Mhor 1044

Beinn Iutharn Bheag 953

Sgor Mor

Carn Aosda 915

Carn an Tuirc 1018

Fafernie 1000

Broad Cairn 996

Cairn of Claise 1062

Tolmount 958

Black Hill of Mark 771

Glen

Glen Tilt

Forest Lodge

Beinn a'Ghlo 1068

1120

Loch Loch

Carn Liath

Meall Breac

Ben Vuirich

Glen Lochsie

The Cairnwell 932

Devil's Elbow

Glas Maol 1068

Creag Leacach

Monega Hill

Caenlochan Forest

Finalty Hill

Craig Mellon

Glen Doll

Glendoll Lodge

Braedownie 865

Loch Brandy

Green Hill

Loch Wharral

Mayar 927

Driesh 947

Hill of Strone 847

564

Tulach Hill

BLAIR

Bridge of Tilt

Blair Atholl

Aldclune

Killiecrankie

Pass of Killiecrankie

Craigower

Ben Vrackie 841

Tarvie

Dalnacarn

Glen Brerachan

Kindrogan Field Centre

Balvarran

Enochdu

Kirkmichael

Spital of Glenshee

Dalmunzie Hotel

Ben Gulabin

Lair

Cray

Dalnaglar Castle

Forter

Folda

Bridge of Brewlands

Glenisla Forest

Hare Cairn

Glenhead Farm

Longdrum

Cat Law 671

Runtaleave

Balnaboth

Glenprosen

Corwharn

Hill of Couternach

Glenmark

Easter Lednathie

Pearsie

Balloch

Queen's View

Pitlochry

Moulin

Port na Craig

Milton of Dalcapon

Ballinluig

Balmyle

Ballintuim

Persey

Ashmore

Netherton

Tullymurdoch

Bamff

Hill of Alyth

Alyth

Ruthven

Shanzie

Craigton

Mile Hill

Ascreavie

Kirkton of Kingoldrum

Bridgend of Lintrathen

Kirkton of Airlie

Baldovie

Westmuir

Lindertis

Kirriemuir

Aberfeldy

Gatehouse

Grandtully

Little Ballinluig

Pitnacree

Ballechin

Logierait

Tulliemet

Balnaguard

Balmacneil

Kincraigie

Kindallachan

Guay

Dowally

Riemore Lodge

Benachally

Riechip

Arlick

Butterstone

Achalader

Lornty

Middleton

Parkhill

Kinloch

Rattray

Blairgowrie

Rosemount

Muirton of Ardblair

Leitfie

Balhary

New Alyth

Jordanstone

Balendoch

Meigle

Kirkinch

Castleton

Eassie and Nevay

Balkeerie

Ark Hill

Nether Handwick

Scotston

Ballinlick

Drumour

Aldville

Trochry

Milton

Dalguise

Dalmarnock

Little Dunkeld

Dunkeld

Birnam

Loch of Lowes

Newtyle Hill

Thornton

Spittalfield

Caputh

Delvine

Kirkton of Lethendy

Clunie

Concraigie

Craigie

Coupar Angus

Keithick

Kettins

Markethill

Ardler

Newtyle

Auchtertyre

Keillor

Bonnyton

Kirkton of Auchterho

Thriepley

Lundie

Auchterhouse

Leoch

Dronley

Muirhead

Birkhill

Amulree

Corrymuckloch

Glenshee

Tullybelton

Bankfoot

West Tofts

Stanley

Waterloo

Upper Obney

Obney Hills

Airntully

Gellyburn

Murthly

Kinclaven

Meikleour

Woodside

Burrelton

Campmuir

Pitcur

Saucher

Collace

Kinrossie

Kirkton of Collace

Abernyte

Rossie Priory

Inchture

Longforgan

Invergowrie

Kingoodie

Harrietfield

Chapelhill

Moneydie

Luncarty

Newmiln

Colenden

St Martins

Balbeggie

Kinnaird

Craigdallie

Ballindean

Knapp

Benvie

Denhead

Buchanty

Tulchan

Pickston

Pitcairngreen

Almondbank

Old Scone

New Scone

Scone Palace

Balthayock

Glendoick

Kinfauns

Rait

Kilspindie

Pitroddie

Grange

Errol

Port Allen

Balmerino

Grundcruie

Busby

Methven

Braegrum

Huntingtower

PERTH

Bridgend

Branklyn

Kinnoull Hill

Crieff

Newmiln

Tibbermore

Dupplin Lake

Milltown of Aberdalgie

Friarton

Tarsappie

Elcho

Rhynd

Inchyra

Glencarse

Chapelhill

Mugdrum Island

Lindores

Newburgh

Dunbog

Luthrie

Brunton

Creich

Balhelvie

Coultra

Monzie

Cultoquhey

Keillour Forest

Madderty

Dubheads

Crossgates

Findo Gask

Aberdalgie

Craigend

Moncreiffe

Bridge of Earn

Kintillo

Dron

Abernethy

Glenfoot

Ormiston Hill

Grange of Lindores

Letham

Cunnoquhie

Fernie

Collessie

Monimail

Over Rankeilour

Cupar

Crieff

Muthill

Millearn

Kinkell Bridge

Machany

Aberuthven

Duncrub

Broom of Dalreoch

Fortviot

Forgandenny

Invermay

Aberargie

Ayton

Dunning

Garvock

Pitcairns

Kippen

Glenfarg

Arngask

Duncrievie

Gateside

Strathmiglo

Falkland

Auchtermuchty

Pleasance

Kinloch

Springfield

Ladybank

Auchterarder

Muirtown

Gleneagles Sta.

Path of Condie

Common of Dunning

Glenfarg Resr.

Newton of Balcanquhal

Auchtermuchty

Howe of Fife

Blackford

Blairgowrie

M90

Dunshelt

Kingskettle

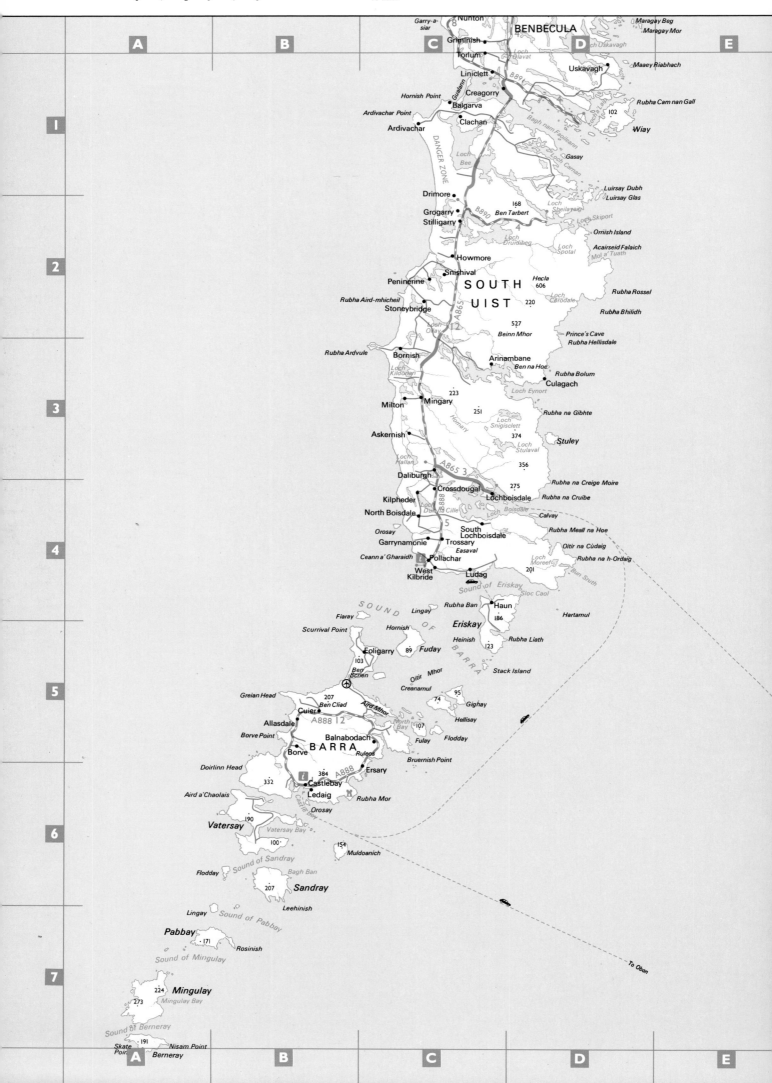

0 1 2 3 4 5   10   15 kilometres

0 1 2 3 4 5   10 miles

BENBECULA

Maragay Beg
Maragay Mor

Garry-a-siar
Nunton
Griminish
Torlum
Loch Olavat
Maaey Riabhach
Uskavagh

Liniclett
Loch Uskavagh
Uskavagh

Creagorry
Hornish Point
Balgarva
Rubha Cam nan Gall
Clachan
Ardivachar Point
Ardivachar
Bagh nam Faoileann
Wiay

DANGER ZONE
102
Loch Bee
Gasay

Loch Carnan
Luirsay Dubh
Luirsay Glas

Drimore
Grogarry
168
Ben Tarbert
Loch Sheilavaig
Loch Skiport
Stilligarry
Ornish Island
Loch Druidibeg
Acairseid Falaich
Mol a' Tuath

Howmore
Snishival
SOUTH
Hecla
606
Peninerine
UIST
Loch Corodale
Rubha Rossel

Rubha Aird-mhicheil
220
Stoneybridge
527
Rubha Bhilidh
Loch Olay
Beinn Mhor
Prince's Cave
Rubha Hellisdale

Rubha Ardvule
Bornish
Arinambane
Loch Kildonan
Ben na Hoe
Rubha Bolum
223
Mingary
Culagach
Milton
Loch Eynort
251
Rubha na Gibhte

Loch Snigisclett
Loch Hallan
374
Askernish
Loch Stulaval
Stuley
356
A865 3
Daliburgh
275
Rubha na Creige Moire
Crossdougal
Lochboisdale
Rubha na Cruibe
Kilpheder
Loch Dun na Cille
Calvay
North Boisdale
Loch Boisdale
Orosay
South
Rubha Meall na Hoe
Garrynamonie
Lochboisdale
Oitir na Cùdaig
Trossary
Ceann a' Gharaidh
Easaval
Rubha na h-Ordaig
Pollachar
201
West
Ludag
Loch Moreef
Bun Sruth
Kilbride

Sound of Eriskay
Sloc Caol

Lingay
Rubha Ban
Haun
Hartamul
Fiaray
186
Scurrival Point
Hornish
Eriskay
Eoligarry
Fuday
Heinish
Rubha Liath
103
89
123
Ben Scrien

Oitir Mhor
Greian Head
207
Creanamul
Stack Island
Ben Cliad
Aird Mhor
74
95
Cuier
A888 12
Gighay
Allasdale
North Bay
107
Hellisay
Borve Point
Balnabodach
Floday
Borve
BARRA
Fulay
Ruleos
Doirlinn Head
384
Bruernish Point
332
Ersary
A888
Aird a'Chaolais
Castlebay
Ledaig
Rubha Mor
Orosay
190
Vatersay
Castle Bay
Vatersay Bay
100
154
Muldoanich
Sound of Sandray
Flodday
Bagh Ban
207
Sandray
Leehinish

Lingay
Sound of Pabbay
Pabbay
171
Rosinish
Sound of Mingulay

To Oban

224 **Mingulay**
Mingulay Bay
273

Sound of Berneray
Skate
Point
191
Nisam Point
Berneray

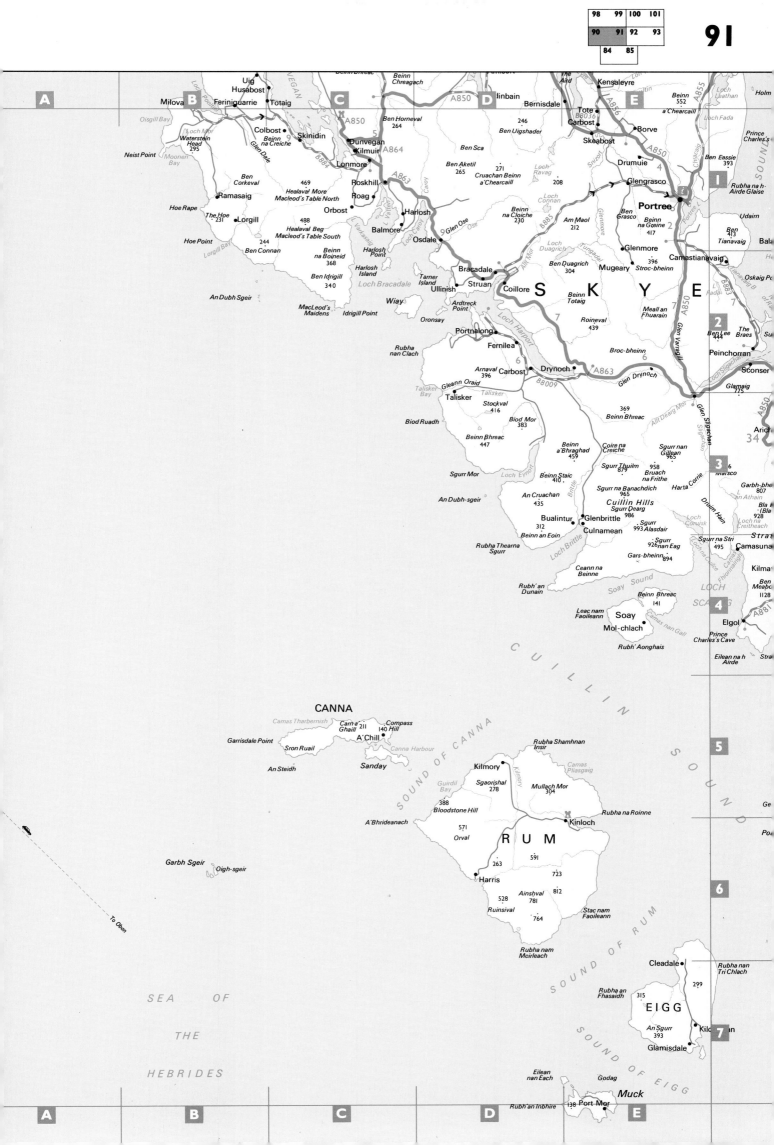

A
B
C
D
E

SKYE

Uig
Husabost
Milova
Feriniquarrie
Totaig
Oisgill Bay
Loch Pooltiel
Colbost
Beinn na Creiche
Skinidin
Waterstein Head 295
Glen Dale
Neist Point
Moonen Bay
Ben Corkeval
Ramasaig
Healaval More
Macleod's Table North
469
Lonmore
Dunvegan
Kilmuir
Roskhill
Roag
A864
A863
Orbost
Healaval Beg
Macleod's Table South 488
Balmore
Harlosh
Osdale
Hoe Rape
The Hoe 231
Lorgill
Hoe Point
Ben Connan 244
Beinn na Boineid 368
Harlosh Point
Harlosh Island
Ben Idrigill 340
An Dubh Sgeir
MacLeod's Maidens
Idrigill Point
Wiay
Oronsay
Tarner Island
Ullinish
Struan
Bracadale
Coillore
Ardtreck Point
Portnalong
Fernilea
Rubha nan Clach
Arnaval 396
Carbost
Drynoch
Talisker Bay
Gleann Oraid
Talisker
Stockval 416
Biod Ruadh
Biod Mor 383
Beinn Bhreac 447
Sgurr Mor
An Dubh-sgeir
Beinn a'Bhraghad 459
Beinn Staic 410
An Cruachan 435
Cuillin Hills
Bualintur
Glenbrittle
Sgurr Dearg 986
Culnamean 312
Beinn an Eoin
Rubha Thearna Sgurr
Loch Brittle
Sgurr nan Eag 926
Gars-bheinn 894
Ceann na Beinne
Rubh'an Dunain
Leac nam Faoileann
Soay
Mol-chlach
Rubh'Aonghais
Soay Sound
Beinn Bhreac 141

Beinn Bhreac
Beinn Chreagach
A850
Dlinbain
Bernisdale
246
Ben Horneval 264
Ben Uigshader
Ben Sca
Ben Aketil 265
271
Cruachan Beinn a'Chearcaill
208
Loch Ravag
Loch Connan
Beinn na Cloiche 230
Am Maol 212
Glen Ose
Osdale
Loch Duagrich
Ben Duagrich 304
Mugeary
Stroc-bheinn
396
Beinn Totaig
Roineval 439
Broc-bheinn
Meall an Fhuarain
Glen Drynoch
Beinn Bhreac
369
Coire na Creiche
Sgurr Thuilm 879
Sgurr nan Gillean 965
Bruach na Frithe 958
Sgurr na Banachdich 965
Harta Corrie
Druim Hain
Sgurr 993 Alasdair
Loch Coruisk
Loch na Creitheach

Kensaleyre
The Aird
Beinn 552 a'Chearcaill
Loch Fada
Holm
Loch Leathan
Tote
Carbost
Borve
Skeabost
Drumuie
Ben Eassie 393
Rubha na h-Airde Glaise
Glengrasco
Ben Grasco
Beinn na Greine 417
Portree
Udairn
Ben 413
Tianavaig
Bala
Glenmore
Camastianavaig
Oskaig Po
of Ra
Ben Lee 444
The Braes
Su
Peinchorran
Sconser
Glamaig 775
Arich
Marsco 736
Garbh-bhe 807
Bla (Bla 928
Sgurr na Stri 495
Camasuna
Kilma
Ben Meabo 1128
LOCH SCA G
Elgol
A881
Prince Charles's Cave
Eilean na h Airde
Stra

CUILLIN SOUND

CANNA
Camas Tharbernish
Carn a' Ghaill 211
Compass Hill 140
A'Chill
Garrisdale Point
Sron Ruail
Canna Harbour
An Steidh
Sanday
SOUND OF CANNA

Rubha Shamhnan Insir
Kilmory
Guirdil Bay
Sgaorishal 278
Camas Pliasgaig
Mullach Mor 304
Rubha na Roinne
388
Bloodstone Hill
A'Bhrideanach
Kinloch
571
Orval
RUM
Garbh Sgeir
Oigh-sgeir
263
591
Harris
723
528
Ainshval 781
812
Ruinsival
764
Stac nam Faoileann
To Oban
Rubha nam Moirleach
SOUND OF RUM

Cleadale
Rubha nan Tri Chlach
Rubha an Fhasaidh
315
299
EIGG
An Sgurr 393
Kilc an
Glamisdale

SEA OF THE HEBRIDES

Eilean nan Each
Godag
138 Port Mor
Muck
Rubh'an Inbhire
SOUND OF EIGG

A
B
C
D
E

1
2
3
4
5
6
7

98	99	100	101	102	103
90	91	92	93	94	95
	84	85	86	87	

93

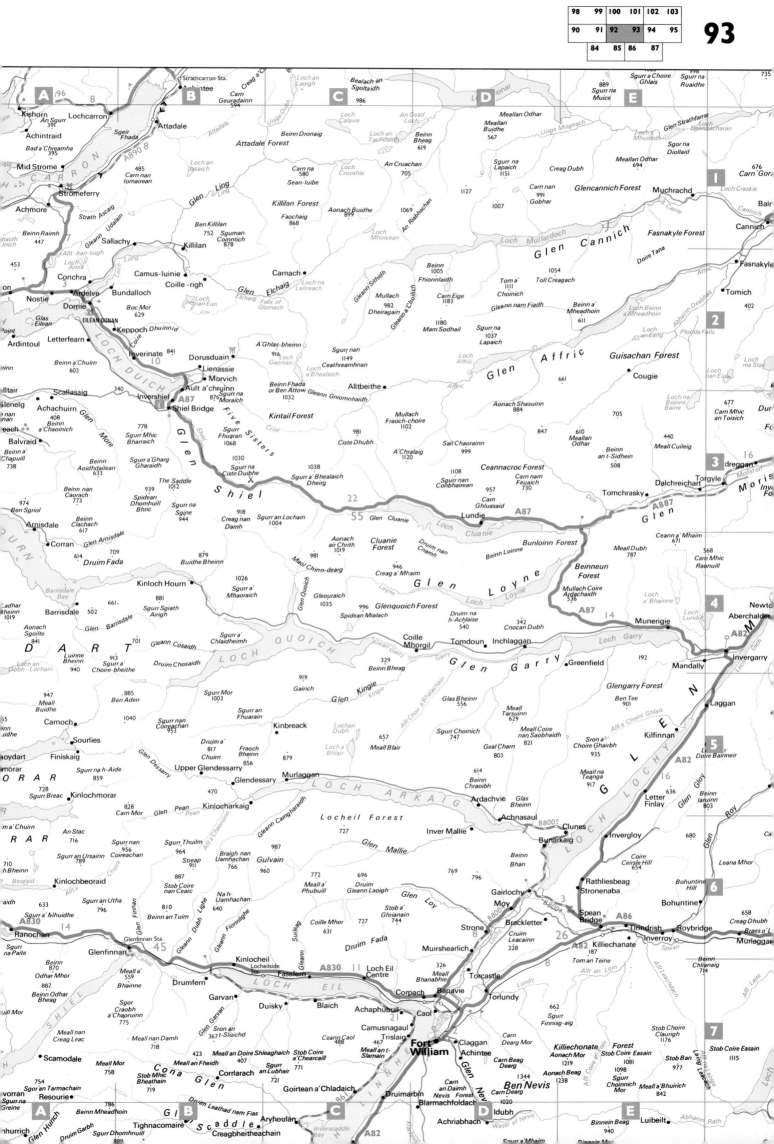

0 1 2 3 4 5   10   15 kilometres
0 1 2 3 4 5   10 miles

Scardroy
Meall na Faochaig 680
Carno
Inverchoran
Glenmeanie
Meall nan Damh 670
Meall Giubhais
Carn na Coinnich 662
Glen Orrin
Orrin Reservoir
Sron nan Saobhaidh 408
Orrin Falls
Faebait A832
Muir of Ord
Kilcoy
Newton
Drumder Ian
A9 B9162 B9161

STRATHCONON FOREST
Bac an Eich 849
laidheimh
787 Sgurr Coire nan Eun
Carn Eiteige 881
An Gorm Loch
Loch na Caoidhe
Sgurr na Cairbe
Meallan Buidhe 764
Sgurr a'Phollan 845
Beinn a' Bha'ach Ard
Carn nan Gobhar 992
1083 Sgurr a'Choire Ghlais
998 Sgurr na Ruaidhe
Carn Ban 735
Gleann Goibhre
Allt Goibhre
Beinn nam Fitheach 431
Cnoc Eille Mor
Erchless Forest
Lochan Fada
Ardnagrask
Windhill A862
Rheindown
Ruilick
Urchany and Farley Forest
Breakachy
Druim Pass Crask of Aigas
Kilmorack
A832 Milton Redcastle
Charlestown
North Kesso
South Kessock
Craigto Lon
BEAULY FIRTH
INVE
Beauly 21 A831 Kirkhill
Achnagairn
B9164 Drumchardine
Easter Moniack
Bunchrew Leachkin A82
onar Forest

889 Sgurr na Muice
Sgurr na Muice
Meallan Odhar
Carn nan 991 Gobhar
Glencannich Forest
Muchrachd
Meallan Odhar 694
Loch Craskie
Sgor na Diollaid
Glen Strathfarrar
Loch a' Mhuillidh
Locha Bhennacharan
Farrar
Struy
Eskadale
Mauld
Crelevan
Carnoch
Oldtown of Aigas
Craigdhu
Strathglass
Culligran
Culligran Falls
Culburnie
Kiltarlity
Druimkinnerras
Boblainy Forest
Camault Muir
Foxhole
Tomnacross
Belladrum
An Leacainn
Lagnalean
Dochgarroch
Kirkton
Scaniport
Essich
Carn a' Bhodaich 500
The Aird
Cnoc na Moine 316
Strath Dores
Caledonian Canal
A862

HIGHLAND
urr na paich
Carn nam 991 Gobhar
Glencannich Forest
Carn Gorm 676
Glassburn
Balmore
Cannich
Grange
Corrimony
Millness
Bearnock
Balnain
457 Carn nam Bad
Carn Mor
Lochan an Tairt
Meall nan Caorach
Meall Gorm 413
Cudrish
Balchraggan
A831 Balbeg
Gartally
Achmony
Glen Urquhart
Milton Drumnadrochit
465
Meall na h-Eilrig
Abriachan
Loch Laide
243
Brachla
Ashie Moor
Tor Point Dores
Loch Ashie
Balnafoi
Tordarro
Creag a Chlachain
Loch Duntelchaig
Stac na Cathaig
Achnabat
Loch a' Choire
Tullich
Brinm
Strathnairn

Fasnakyle Forest
Doire Tana
Fasnakyle
Tomich
402
Balmacaan Forest
Meall a' Chrathaich
Loch a' Chrathaich
525
Carn Macsna
Glen Coiltie
Lewiston
Strone
Urquhart Bay
Urquhart
Lenie
Torness
Abersky
Aberarder
Loch Ceo Glais
East Croachy
Carn na
Tom Bailgeann
Whitefield
1054 Toll Creagach
Beinn a' Mheadhoin 611
Loch Beinn a' Mheadhoin
Loch an Eang
Ploda Falls
Suidhe Ghuirmain 578
Coiltie
Divach Burn
Balbeg
Bunloit
Grotaig
Inverfarigaig
Aultnagoire
Dhuhallow
Errogie
Farraline
Loch Conagleann
Beinn Bhuidhe 710
Carn Ghriogair
Beinn B

Affric
661
Guisachan Forest
Cougie
705
Loch nan Eun
Invermoriston Forest
Loch na Beinne Baine
677 Carn Mhic an Toisich
Dundreggan Forest
Levishie
A82
Alltsigh
Loch nam Breac Dearga
696
Meall Fuarvounie
Easter Boleskine
Foyers
Lyne of Gorthleck
Lochgarthside
Beinn Dubhcharaidh
Carn Odhar 798

nach Shasuinn 884
847
610 Meallan Odhar
440 Meall Cuileig
Carn Mhic an Toisich
Dundreggan
Loch na Stairne
Torgyle
Glen Moriston
Inverwick Forest
605
Portclair Forest
Invermoriston
Allt Saigh
Loch Ness
Glen Albyn or Glen Mor
Loch Kemp
Whitebridge
Easter Drummond
Strath Errick
Knockie
Faichlin
656
Carn Fliuch-bhaid
Doire Meurach 787
Carn na Laraiche Maoile
Carn na Saobhaidhe 810
U
Beinn an t-Sidhein 508
acroc Forest
Carn nam Feuaich 730
Tomchrasky
Dalchreichart
A887
Doe
A87
Bunloinn Forest
Loinne
Meall Dubh 787
Ceann a' Mhaim 671
568 Carn Mhic Raonuill
Inchnacardoch
Fort Augustus
Glendoebeg
710
Loch Tarff
Loch nan Eun
Glen Brein
Allt Breisleig
778 Carn Easgann Bana
Carn a' Choire Ghlaise 779
Glen Matkie
Burrach Mor
855
Coignafearn Forest
Dalbeg Forest
Calpa Mor
Sgaraman nam Fiadh

Beinneun Forest
Mullach Coire Ardtachaidh
yne
Loyne
A87 14
Munerigie
Loch Lundie
Newtown
Aberchalder
Loch a' Bhainne
Glen Doe
Glendoe Forest
Carn a' Chuilinn 816
Coire Oghar
941 Carn Ban
Cairn Ewen
Loch na Lairige
Carn Dearg
Loch Dubh
941
A'C

342 Cnocan Dubh
laggan
Garry
Greenfield
Loch Garry
192
Mandally
Invergarry
Glen Tarff
Culachy Forest 891
Corrieyairack Hill
Corrieyairack Pass
Gairbeinn 893
Meall na h-Aisre 962
Geal Charn 925
Carn an Leth-choin
817
Dalballoch Gle
A8

Glengarry Forest
Ben Tee 901
Laggan
Carn Dearg 816
Corrieyairack Forest
Melgarve
Creag Mhor
Carn Leac 881
Spey
Feith Talagag
Beinn a' Chrasgain
Marg na Craige
A8

Meall arsuinn 629
Meall Coire nan Saobhaidh 821
Sron a' Choire Ghairbh 935
Kilfinnan
637 Leacann Doire Bainneir
Leckroy
Loch Spey
Garvamore
Loch Crunachdan
Crathie
Sherramore
Black Craig 563
Blargie
Laggan
Balgowan
8

Meall na Teanga 917
Letter Finlay
636
Glen Gloy
Beinn Iaruinn 803
Turret Bridge
Glen Roy
834 Carn Dearg
Loch Roy
Lochan a' Choire
1005 Carn Liath
Cromra
1128 Creag Meagaidh
Aberarder
Ardverikie
Loch Laggan
Kinloch Laggan
Loch Caoldair
A889
Loch Ericht
Falls of Truim
Cruban Beag
Glen Truim
Dalwhinnie
A9

Glas Bheinn
Clunes
Bunarkaig
Invergloy
680
Glen Roy
Carn Dearg
Leana Mhor
Bohuntine Hill
913
991 An Cearcallach
Moy Forest
Binnein Shuas
Coille Coire Chrannaig
A86
Linn of Pattack
Beinn Eilde
Beinn Bhan
Rathliesbeg
Stronenaba
Coire Ceirsle Hill 654
Bohuntine
834
Leana Mhor
Moy
1128
Creag Meagaidh
Loch na h-Earba
1049
Ardverikie Forest
Geal Charn 896
Creagan Mor
A9

Spean Bridge A86
Tirindrish
Roybridge
Murlaggan
Tulloch Sta.
Roughburn
Bohuntine
658 Creag Dhubh
Braes o' Lochaber
Craigbeg
Binnein Shuas
Beinn a' Chlachair
Geal-charn
916 An Torc or Boar of Badenoch
936

Killiechanate
Inverroy
187
Tom an Teine
Allt an Loin
Beinn Chlianaig 714
Fersit
Meall Luidh Mor
1088
An Lairig
Meall Cruaidh
A'Bhuidheanach Bheag

Grantown-on-Spey

Kingussie

Newtonmore

Aviemore

Carrbridge

Boat of Garten

Braemar

Tomintoul

CAIRNGORM MOUNTAINS

GLENMORE FOREST PARK

Cairn Nature Reserve

Glenfeshie Forest

Gaick Forest

Glen Ey Forest

Abernethy Forest

The Queen's Forest

Rothiemurchus

Braes of Abernethy

Forest of Glenavon

Mar Forest

Invercauld Forest

Darnaway Forest

Culloden Forest

Scootmore Forest

Ben Macdui 1309
Braeriach 1296
Cairn Toul 1293
Cairn Gorm 1245
Sgor an Lochain Uaine
Beinn a'Bhuird 1173
Ben Avon 1171
Monadh Mor 1113
Beinn Bhrotain 1157
Beinn Mheadhoin 1184
Bynack More 1089
Derry Cairngorm 1155
Sgoran Dubh Mor 1111
Sgor Gaoith 1115
Mullach Clach a'Bhlair 1019
Beinn a'Chaorainn 1083
North Top 1196
South Top 930
Stob an t-Sluichd 1083

Loch Morlich
Loch Garten
Loch Vaa
Loch Insh
Loch Alvie
Loch Einich
Loch Avon
Loch Etchachan
Loch Builg
Loch an Eilein

A9, A95, A939, A938, A940, A96

Inverness
Moy
Tomatin
Daviot
Culloden
Slochd
Carrbridge
Dulnain Bridge
Duthil
Nethy Bridge
Dulsie
Ferness
Dava
Cromdale
Speybridge
Congash
Advie
Knockando
Cardow
Marypark
Bridge of Avon
Tomnavoulin
Knockandhu
Glenlivet
Tomintoul
Delnabo
Inchrory
Braemar
Inverey
Muir
Kincraig
Feshiebridge
Alvie
Kinrara
Inverdruie
Coylumbridge
Glenmore Lodge

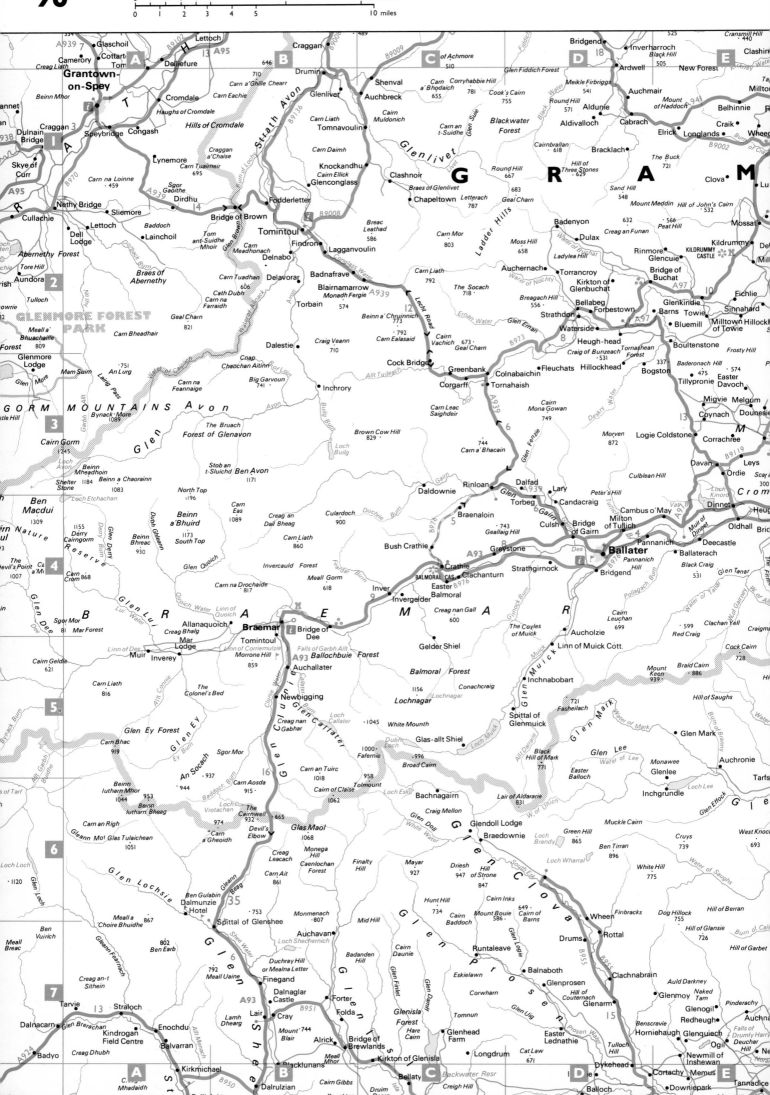

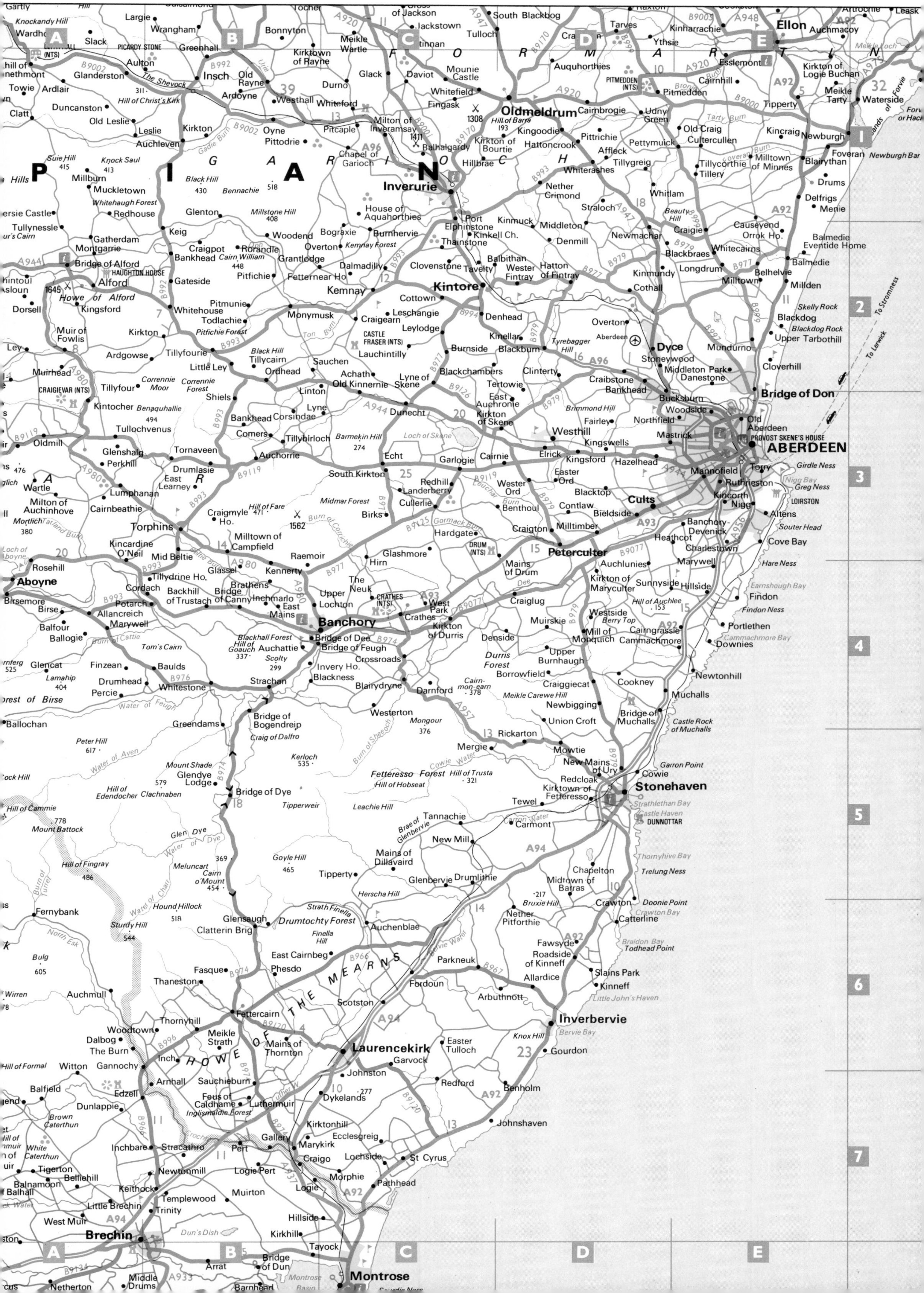

Major towns and places (map labels):

ABERDEEN, Ellon, Oldmeldrum, Inverurie, Kintore, Dyce, Bridge of Don, Old Aberdeen, Peterculter, Cults, Banchory, Torphins, Aboyne, Stonehaven, Inverbervie, Laurencekirk, Montrose, Brechin

Region names: *P I C A R D Y P L A I N*, *F O R M A R T I N E*, *G A R I O C H*, *THE MEARNS*, *HOWE OF THE MEARNS*

Selected place names:
Knockandy Hill, Wardhouse, Largie, Wrangham, Greenhall, Bonnyton, Kirktown of Rayne, Meikle Wartle, Jackstown, South Blackbog, Tarves, Kinharrachie, Auchmacoy, Slack, PICARDY STONE (NTS), Insch, Old Rayne, Glack, Daviot, Mounie Castle, Auquhorthies, Ythsie, Esslemont, Kirkton of Logie Buchan, Durno, Whitefield, Fingask, Cairnbrogie, Udny Green, Pitmedden (NTS), Cairnhill, Tipperty, Whiteford, Oldmeldrum, Kingoodie, Pittrichie, Affleck, Old Craig, Cutercullen, Kincraig, Newburgh, Foveran, Milton of Inveramsay, Balhalgardy, Kirkton of Bourtie, Hattoncrook, Pettymuick, Tillycorthie, Milltown of Minnes, Blairython, Drums, Delfrigs, Menie, Causeyend, Orrok Ho., Balmedie, Whitecairns, Blackbraes, Longdrum, Belhelvie, Milltown, Millden, Blackdog, Upper Tarbothill, Cloverhill, Bucksburn, Woodside, Mastrick, Northfield, Kingswells, Hazelhead, Mannofield, Ruthrieston, Kincorth, Nigg, Torry, Girdle Ness, Greg Ness, Altens, Cove Bay, Souter Head, Hare Ness, Portlethen, Findon, Newtonhill, Muchalls, Cowie, Garron Point, Dunnottar, Catterline, Crawton, Johnshaven, Gourdon, St Cyrus

Hills and features: Hill of Barra 193, Bennachie 518, Brimmond Hill, Tyrebagger Hill, Tap o' Noth, Mount Battock 778, Clachnaben 589, Kerloch 535, Cairn-mon-earn 378, Mongour 376

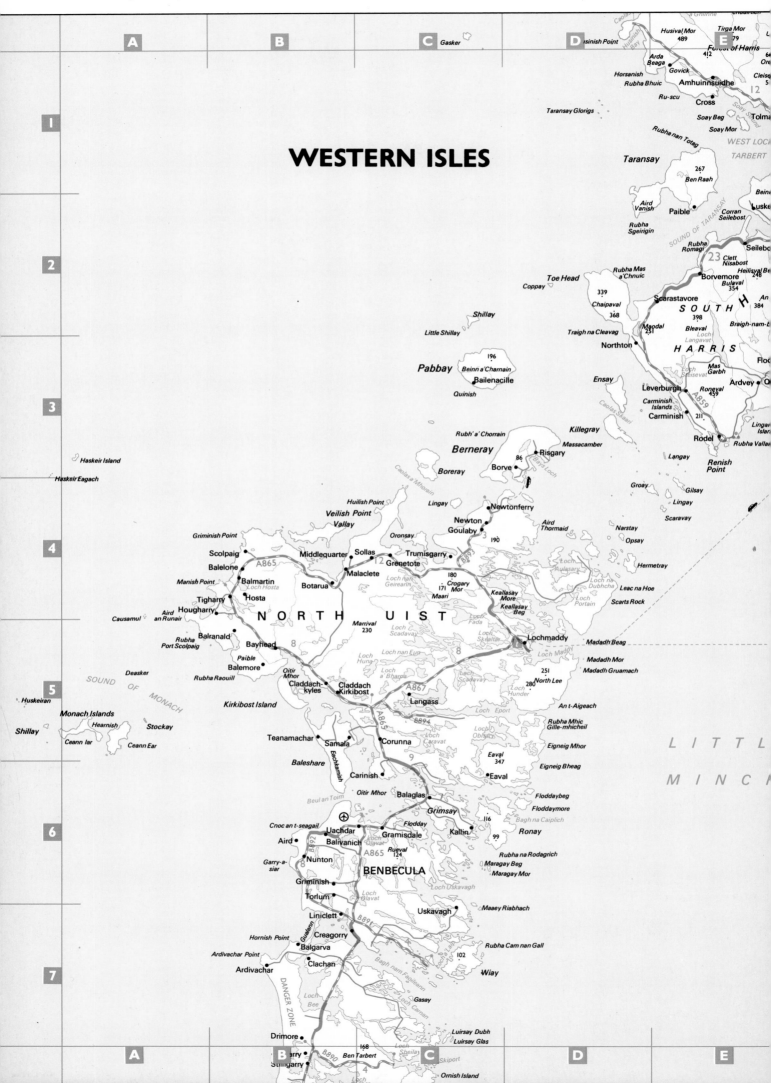

WESTERN ISLES

Scale: 0 1 2 3 4 5 10 15 kilometres
0 1 2 3 4 5 10 miles

Harris / Taransay area

Forest of Harris
Husival Mor 489
Tirga Mor 679
Arda Beaga 412
Ore
Cleise 5
Horsanish
Rubha Bhuic
Govick
Amhuinnsuidhe
Ru-scu
Cross
Soay Beg
Soay Mor
Tolma
Rubha nan Totag
Taransay Glorigs
WEST LOCH TARBERT
Taransay
Ben Raah 267
Aird Vanish
Paible
Corran Seilebost
Luske
Rubha Sgeirigin
Clett Nisabost
Seilebo
Toe Head
Rubha Mas a'Chnuic
Heilisval Be 248
Coppay
339
Borvemore
Bulaval 354
Chaipaval 368
Scarastavore
SOUTH
An 384
Traigh na Cleavag
Maodal 231
Bleaval
Braigh-nam-b
Northton
Loch Langavat
HARRIS
398
Mas Garbh

Pabbay / Berneray area

Shillay
Little Shillay
Pabbay
Beinn a'Charnain 196
Bailenacille
Quinish
Ensay
Leverburgh
Roneval 459
Ardvey
Carminish Islands
Carminish 211
Lingar Islar
Rubh' a' Chorrain
Killegray
Massacamber
Rodel
Rubha Vallar
Berneray
Langay
Renish Point
Boreray
Risgary
Borve 86
Groay
Gilsay
Lingay
Scaravay
Lingay

North Uist

Haskeir Island
Haskeir Eagach
Huilish Point
Veilish Point
Vallay
Oronsay
Newtonferry
Newton
Goulaby
Aird Thormaid
Narstay
Opsay
Hermetray
Griminish Point
Scolpaig
Middlequarter
Sollas
Trumisgarry
190
Loch Aulasary
Leac na Hoe
Balelone
A865
Malaclete
Grenetote
180
Crogary Mor 171
Keallasay More
Loch na Dubhcha
Scarts Rock
Manish Point
Balmartin
Botarua
Loch Hosta
Loch nan Geireann
Maari
Keallasay Beg
Loch Portain
Tigharry
Hosta
Hougharry
NORTH UIST
Loch Scadavay
Loch Fada
Lochmaddy
Madadh Beag
Causamul
Aird an Runair
Marrival 230
Loch Skealtar
Madadh Mor
Balranald
Bayhead
8
Loch nan Eun
8
Madadh Gruamach
Rubha Port Scolpaig
Loch Huna
Loch a'Bharpa
Loch Scadavay
251
Paible
Loch Maddy
North Lee 280
Deasker
Balemore
Oitir Mhor
Claddach-kyles
Claddach Kirkibost
Langass
An t-Aigeach
Rubha Raouill
A867
Loch Eport
Huskeiran
Shillay
SOUND OF MONACH
Kirkibost Island
Loch Hunder
Rubha Mhic Gille-mhicheil
Monach Islands
Hearnish
Stockay
Teanamachar
Samala
Corunna
Loch Obisary
Eigneig Mhor
Ceann Iar
Ceann Ear
Baleshare
Eachkamish
Carinish
Eaval 347
Eigneig Bheag
LITTLE MINCH
Beul an Toim
Oitir Mhor
Balaglas
Eaval
Floddaybeg
Floddaymore

Benbecula / Grimsay

Grimsay
Bagh na Caiplich
Cnoc an t-seagail
Uachdar
Flodday
Kallin
Ronay
Aird
Balivanich
Gramisdale
116
99
Garry-a-siar
Nunton
A865
Rueval 124
Rubha na Rodagrich
BENBECULA
Maragay Beg
Griminish
Loch Olavat
Maragay Mor
Torlum
Uskavagh
Maaey Riabhach
Liniclett
Loch Uskavagh
Creagorry
Hornish Point
Balgarva
Rubha Cam nan Gall
Ardivachar Point
Clachan
102
Ardivachar
Wiay
DANGER ZONE
Gasay
Loch Bee
Luirsay Dubh
Luirsay Glas
Drimore
arry
Ben Tarbert 168
Loch Sheilay
Skiport
Stilligarry
Ornish Island
Loch Corran

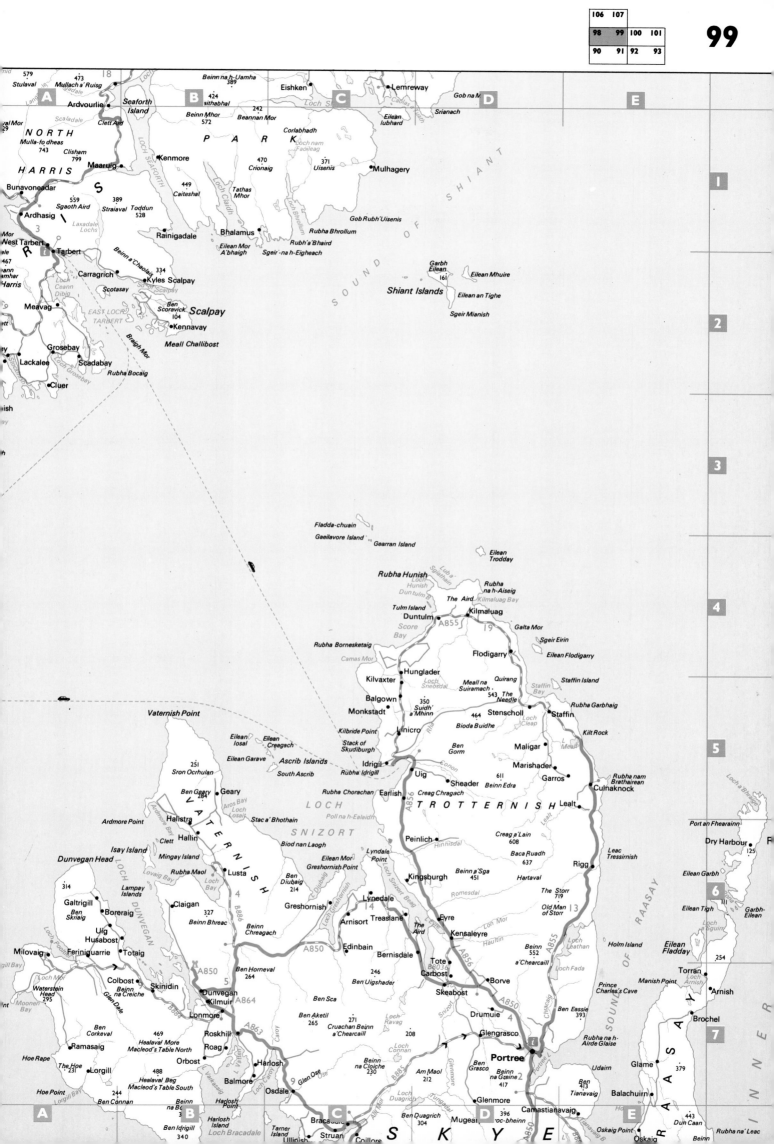

0 1 2 3 4 5   10   15 kilometres

0 1 2 3 4 5   10 miles

A   **B**   **C**   **D**   **E**

h-Uamha 389
Eishken
Lemreway
Gob na Milaid

242
Beannan Mor
Corlabhadh
Loch nam Faoileag
Srianach
Eilean Iubhard

1

Loch Shell

THE   MINCH

470 Crionag
371 Uisenis
Mulhagery

Tathas Mhor

Gob Rubh'Uisenis

halamus

ilean Mor M'bhaigh

Rubha Bhrollum
Rubh'a'Bhaird
Sgeir-na h-Eigheach

SOUND OF SHIANT

Garbh Eilean 161
Eilean Mhuire

2

Shiant Islands
Eilean an Tighe
Sgeir Mianish

Rubha Reidh
Camas Mor
Loch an Draing
Sron Eilean an Air

296 An Cuaidh

Melvaig
Aultgrishan

3

293 Cnoc B
Peterburn

Fladda-chuain
Gaeilavore Island
Gearran Island
Eilean Trodday

North Erradale

B8021

Big Sand
Longa Island

GAIR LO

To Lochbisdale

Rubha Hunish
Loch Hunish
Lub a' Sgiathain
Dun tulm
The Aird
Rubha na h-Aiseig
Kilmaluag Bay

4

Tulm Island
Duntulm A855
Kilmaluag
Galta Mor
Sgeir Eirin
Eilean Flodigarry

Score Bay
19

Port Henderson
Opinan
Loch Clair

South Erradale

Rubha Bornesketaig
Camas Mor

Flodigarry

Kilvaxter
Hunglader
Meall na Suiramach
Quirang
543 The Needle
Staffin Island
Staffin Bay

Redpoint
Maol Ruadh

Red Point

Balgown
350 Suidh' a'Mhinn
464
Stenscholl
Rubha Garbhaig

5

Eilean Iosal
Eilean Garave
South Ascrib
Ascrib Islands

Monkstadt
Linicro
Bioda Buidhe
Staffin
Loch Cleap
Kilt Rock

Kilbride Point
Stack of Skudiburgh
Rubha Idrigill
Idrigil

Ben Gorm
Maligar
L Meall

Sgeir na Trian
Meall Uamh 287
Crai

Geary
Aros Bay
Loch Losait
Stac a'Bhothain

Uig
Sheader
611 Beinn Edra
Marishader
Garros
Rubha nam Brathairean
Culnaknock

Rubha na Fearn
Rubha na Fearn
Fearnmore
Fearnbeg
LOCH TORRIDON

Conon
Ria

Rubha Chorachan
Earlish

Creag Chragach
TROTTERNISH
Lealt

Lealt

Ob na h-Uamha
Ob Chuaig
Arinacrinachd
Cuaig
Kenmore

LOCH
SNIZORT
Poll na h-Ealaidh

Peinlich
Creag a'Lain 608
Baca Ruadh 637
Rigg

Port an Fhearainn
RONA
Dry Harbour 125

Ardheslaig
Inverbai
Loch a Chreaich

Biod nan Laogh
Hinnisdal

6

Eilean Mor
Greshornish Point
Lyndale Point
Kingsburgh
Beinn a'Sga 451
Hartaval
The Storr 719

An Garbh-mheall 492
Loch Gaineamhach
Croic-bheinn 493

Ben Diubaig 214
Loch Diubaig

Romesdal

Old Man of Storr
13

Eilean Garbh
Kyle Rona
Eilean Tigh 111
Garbh-Eilean

Lonbain
An Dubh loch
Meall na Fhuaid 518

Greshornish
14
Lyndale
Treaslane
Eyre
Kensaleyre
Lon Mor
Haultin

626

Arnisort
The Aird

Holm Island
Eilean Fladday
254

Loch han Eun
Applecross

Edinbain
A850
Bernisdale
Tote B8036
Carbost
Borve
Beinn 552 a'Chearcaill
Loch Leathan
Loch Fada
Torran
Manish Point
Loch Arnish
Arnish

Hartfield
Carn De 646
Applecross

Ben Horneval 264
Ben Sca
Skeabost
A850
Prince Charles's Cave
Glame 379
Brochel

Milton
Camusteel

invegan
A864
ilmuir
A850
Ben Aketil 265
Cruachan Beinn a'Chearcaill 271
Loch Ravag
Drumuie
Ben Eassie 393
Rubha na h-Airde Glaise
Udairn

Camasterach
Loch Braigh an Achaidh

7

oskhill
bag
Ben Uigshader
208
Loch Connan
Skeabost
Glengrasco
Glen Ose

SKYE

Beinn na Cloiche 230
Am Maol 212
B885
Ben Grasco
Benn na Greine 417
Portree 2
Glame

Ben Tianavaig
Balachuirn

Sron-na h-Airde Baine
Culduie

Harlosh
Balmore
Glen Ose
Beinn na Gneine
Loch Duagrich
Ben Duagrich 304
Mugeary
Stroc-bheinn
396
Camastianavaig
443 Dun Caan
Rubha na' Leac
Toscaig
Toscaig

Harlosh Point
Osdale
Bracadale
Tarner
Oskaig Point
Eilean na Ba

SOUND OF RAASAY

INNER SOUND

A   B   C   D   E

Eilean Mullagrach
Isle Ristol
Polbain
Aird of Coigach
Inverpolly Forest
849 Cul Mor 612
Stac Polly
Drumrunie Forest
Elphin
Knockan
1

Summer Isles
Glas-leac Mor
Achiltibuie
Achvraie
489
.601
Cul Beag
769
Loch Doire Dhubh
Coigach
17
Cromalt Hills
516
307 Cnoc na Glas Choille

Tanera Beg
Tanera Mor
Glas-leac Beag
Horse Island
743
Culnacraig
Geodha Mor
Camas Mor
Strathcanaird
Strath Canaird
408 Na Dromannan
Meall an Fhuarain 578
578 Meall an Fhuarain

Priest Island
Bottle Island
Eilean Dubh
Carn nan Sgeir
Leac Dhonn
Isle Martin
Cul a'Bhogha
Ardmair
Rhidorroch Forest
Meall Liath 548
Rhidorroch
Choire
Knockdamph

Greenstone Point
Opinan
Rubha Mor
Leac Mhor
Rubha Beag
Cailleach Head
Stattic Point
Achmore
Scoraig
Rhireavach
Rhue
Morefield
Ullapool
Braes of Ullapool
Rhidorroch
516

Mellon Udrigle
Achgarve
Gruinard Island
DANGER ZONE
GRUINARD BAY
Badluachrach
Beinn Ghobhlach 635
Allt na h'Airbhe
578 Beinn Eilideach
Loggie
Loch Achall
Glen Achall
2

Mellon Charles
Ormiscaig
Bualnaluib
Aultbea
Laide
Coast
Durnamuck
Mungasdale
A832
Badcaul
Cnoc a'Bhaid-rallaich 543
Badrallach
Blarnalevoch
Rhiroy
Ardcharnich
Leckmelm
Meall Dubh 642
Meall nam Bradhan 677

Isle of Ewe
INVEREWE (NTS)
Loch a'Bhaid luachraich
Ardessie
Camusnagaul
Dundonnell
Sail Mhor
Carn na Beiste 300
Ardindrean
Letters
Eilean Darach
30
Carn nam Buailtean 391
Creag-mheall Beag 347
Gruinard Forest
Carn Mor 647
Inverlael Forest
Eididh nan Clach Geala 926
Freewater Forest

Loch Thurnaig
Boor
Poolewe
Londubh
Loch Kernsary
Little Gruinard
Bidein a'Ghlas Thuill 1061
An Teallach
1059 Sgurr Fiona 989
Dundonnell Forest
Inverlael
Lael
Inverbroom
Auchlunachan
Meall nan 976
3
Glenbeg
Meall a'Chuaille

347
Fisherfield Forest
Beinn a'Chaisgein Mor 854
Beinn Dearg Mhor 906
Strath na Sealga
Beinn a'Chlaidheimh
Glackour
Beinn Enaiglair 889
Ceapraichean
Carn Breac Beag
Braemore
Fasagrianach
Beinn Dearg 1081

Charlestown
Kerrysdale
Meall Aundrary 326
791 Beinn Airigh Charr
Dubh Loch
Fuar Loch Mor
Sgurr Ban 989
Fain
A835
Dirrie More
Meall Leacachain 618
522
Lochdrum
Strathvaich Forest
Ban Mor 742

Eilean Ruairidh Mor
Letterewe
Eilean Subhainn
859
Beinn Lair
Beinn Mhialairidh 960
Mullach Coire Mhic Fhearchair
Meall an t-Sithe
Creag Rainich
807
601
Creag Dubh
Meall a'Chrasgaidh 933
Sgurr Mor 1109
Loch a'Mhadaidh
Beinn Liath Bheag 662

18
Furnace
Slattadale
980 Slioch
Loch Garbhaig
Beinn Tarsuinn 930
Beinn Bheag
Groban 739
A'Chailleach
Sgurr Breac
Sgurr nan Clach Geala 999
4
20
Au Inn

Beinn an Eoin 705
Baosbheinn 874
855 Ruadh-stac Mor
Meall a'Ghiubhais
Gleann Bianasdail
Beinn a'Mhuinidh 680
Kinlochewe Forest
Heights of Kinlochewe
Meallan Chuaich
Meallan Chuaich
948 Meall Gorm
923 An Coileachan
Beinn Dearg
Fannich Forest
680 Meall Mhic Iomhair 605

WESTER ROSS
619
Beinn Bhreac
Beinn Dearg 913
Beinn Alligin 921
Sail Mhor 981
Beinn Eighe Nature Reserve
Kinlochewe
Rhu Noa
Taagan
Leckie
Strath Chrombuill
Beinn nan Ramh 711
Loch Fannich
Lochrosque Forest
512
Carn Daraich 558
5
Lochluichart Sta.

708
Torridon Forest 1053
Liathach 1024
A'Ghairbhe
46
Glen Docherty
Fionn Bheinn 933
Knockban
A832
Strath Bran
312
461

UPPER LOCH TORRIDON
Fasag
Torridon 436
Seana Mheallan
Sgurr Dubh 782
Carn Loisgte
Loch Coulin
Lubmore
Badavanich
Achnasheen
Ledgowan Forest
Sgurr a'Ghlas Leathaid 847
Meallan nan Uan 867
Milltown
6
Porin

Annat
Balgy
Ben-damph Forest
Beinn na h-Eaglaise 735
Beinn Liath Mhor 925 868
Coulin Forest
Carn Breac 678
550
Glen Carron
Cnoc an t-Sidheim 371
Carn Liath 857
538 Carn Mhartuin
Scardroy
Carn an 561 Leanaidh
Meall na Faochaig
Gleann Meinich
680
Carnoch
Inverchoran
Meall Giubhais 662

Ben Shieldaig 516
Beinn Damh 901
Maol Chean-dearg 933
Sgorr Ruadh
Craig
55
Moruisg 928
Glencarron Forest
874 Carn Gorm
STRATHCONON
849 Bac an Eich

513
An Staonach
Meall na Saobhaidhe 368
Fuar-Tholl 905
An Ruadh-stac 890
Balnacra
Coulags
Achnashellach Forest
Gleann Fiodhaig
Maoile Lunndaidh 1007
FOREST
787 Sgurr Coire nan Eun
Carn Eiteige 881
Carn nan Gobhar 992
7

Kishorn
Lochcarron
Achintraid
Strathcarron Sta.
Achintee
Attadale
Carn Geuradainn 594
Creag a'Chaorainn Eaglain
Sgurr na Feartaig
863
Sgurr na Ceannaichean
Beinn Tharsuinn 863
West Monar Forest
Sgurr a'Chaorachain 1053
East Monar Forest
Bealach an Sgoltaidh 986
Beinn Dronaig 567
Meall Odhar
Meallan Buidhe
Sgurr na Muice 889
1083 Sgurr a'Choire Ghlais
998 Sgurr na Ruaidhe

A   B   C   D   E

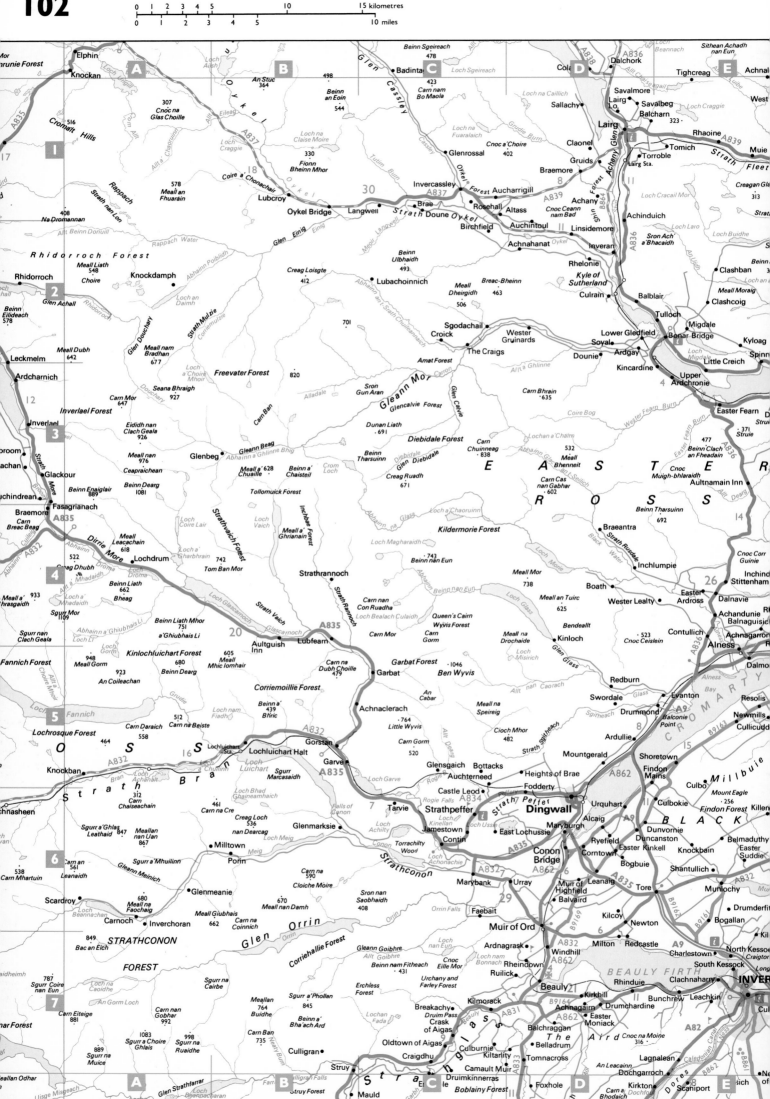

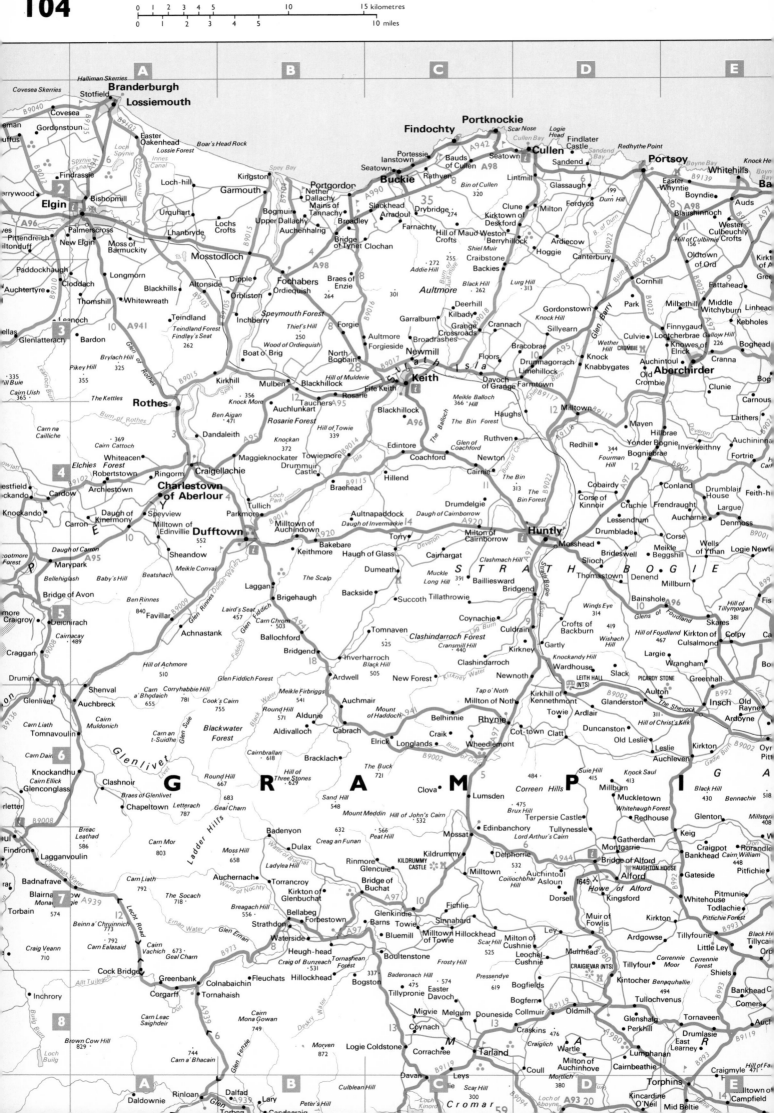

WN PLANS: **ABERDEEN** P138

102 103
94 95
104 105
96 97

105

0 1 2 3 4 5   10   15 kilometres
0 1   2   3   4   5   10 miles

A   B   C   D   E

1

2

3

Aird Mh
Mas Sgeir   Ga
Old Hill   Creagearr
Bearasay   Borrowston
  Loch Carlowa
WEST   Floday
  Harsgeir   Little   Creag Mhor
LOCH ROAG   Bernera

Gallan Head   Tobson   Breaclet
  Pabay   Camas
Aird Uig   Mor   Sandig
Geodha Nasavig   Forsnaval   Vacsay   Great
  204   Valtos   Bernera
Fiavag Bagh   Nissa   Vuia
  Miavaig   Mhor   Mor   Hacklete   Barrag

4

Timsgarry   Uigean   B8011
Ard More   Camas   Crowlista   Floday   Vuia Beg   Crulivig
Mangersta   Uig   Caryshader   Ben
Loch   Ardroil   Drovinish
Caslavat   Suainaval   256
Mangersta   428   Teahaval   Loch
Aird Fenish   Tungava
  Loch   Enaclete
  Suainaval
Islivig   Mealisval   Loch   Scaliscro
Aird Brenish   574   Raonasgail   Loch   B8011
  Gisla   Grunavat
Brenish   515   L   16   E   Beinn M
  Tahaval   Gisla   207

5

Greineim   514   265   226
  Cracaval   Skeun   Caltrashal
  Tamanaisval   Loch   241   Beg
  467   Dibadale   Coduinn
  Beinn   228
Mealista   Mealista   397   Caltrashal
Island   Mheadhonach   Mhor
Griomaval   Maghannan   Loch Morsgail   Loch
  Coirigerod
Liongam   Loch na   Loch Benisval
Duisker   Craobheig   Scalaval
  Aird   Loch   Sandig
  Bheag   Bodavat

6

Kearstay   Gob na-h   Aird   Morsgail Forest
  Airde Moire   Mhor   Loch Resort   Beinn a'Bhoth
Sgeir Moil Duinn   307
  308   Ulladale   Ke
Scarp   Sron Romul   329   386   295   Rapaire   492
  Mas Garbh   Mas a' Chnoic   Mullach na   453   Liutha
Manish   Loch   chuairtich   Reidheachd   579   473
  a'Ghlinne   Loch   Stulaval   Mullach a'Ru
  Husiva Mor   Tirga Mor   Voshimid   gadale
Gasker   489   679   Ullaval   Ardvou
Husinish Point   Forest of Harris   656   Scaladale

7

Husinish   Arda   412   660   Uisgnaval Mor   NORTH
Bay   Beaga   Oreval   729
Horsanish   Govick   Cleisqval   Mulla-fo dheas
Rubha Bhuic   Amhuinnsuidhe   511   743   Clisham
Ru-scu   12   799
Taransay Glorigs   Cross   B887   HARRIS
  Soay Beg   Tolmachan
Rubha nan Totag   Soay Mor   Soay Sound
  WEST LOCH   Bunavoneadar
  TARBERT   Teilesnish Bay   559
  Isay   Sgaoth Aird

WESTERN ISLES

Taransay   Ardhasig   Laxadar
  267   Geo Mor   Loch
  Ben Raah   506   West Tarbert   R
Aird   Beinn Dhubh   Beesdale   R   Tarbert
Vanish   Paible   Corran   467   287   Ceann   Car
  ebost   Luskentyre   Reamhar   Loch
Rubha   South   R   Harris   Ceann
Sgeirigin   Forest   Dibig
Rubha   SOUND OF TARANSAY   Seilebost   Meavag
Romagi

A   B   C   D   E

Butt of Lewis

A B C D E

Port Sto

Cunndal
Eoropie
Bad an Fhitich
Five Penny Ness

Eorodale
Port of Ness
Cross Sands
Swainbost
Lionel
Skigersta
Port Skigersta
North Dell
Habost
Aird Dell
Cross
Seilastotar
South Dell
Meall Geal

Dell
Glen Cross
Port Alasdair

Toa Galson
North Galson
South Galson
Airigh na Glaice
Maoim
Cellar Head

Melbost Borve
Roinn a Bhuic
Ben Dell
Airighean Beinn nan Caorach

Five Penny Borve
Breihascro
Loch Langavat

Upper Shader
Lower Shader
Airighean Loch Breihavat
Sguinean nan Creagan Briste

Rubha Leathann
Aird Barvas
Ballantrushal
Diaval
Dun Othail

Rubh'a'Bhiogair
Goile Chroic
Loch Mor Barvas
Glen Shader
Loch Mor Sandaval

DANGER ZONE

Aird Mhor Bragair
Rinn Druim Tallig
Port Arnol
Brue
Torray
Geiraha
Port Geiraha

Labost
Fivig
Arnol
Barvas
Loch Gress

Shawbost
Bragar
Loch Urrahag
Loch Casgro
Airigh na Glaice
New Tolsta
North Tolsta

Beinn Choinnich 210
Gleann Bhruthadail
Gearraidh Euscleit
L. Kearstavat
248 Muirneag
Loch na Cloich
Tolsta Head
Port nam Bothag

261 · 248 *Beinn Rahacleit*
Roishal Mor 174
Loch na Scaravat
Loch Mor Sandaval
L. Sgeireach Mor
Glen Tolsta
Port Bun a'Ghlinne

Loch Sandaval
Loch an Tobair
Loch an Tuim
Gress

291 Ben Barvas
Glen More Barvas
Creag Fhraoich

Stacashal 216
Loch nam Breac
Loch nan Stearnag
Back
Coll
Breivig
Sgeir Leathann

Loch Garvaig
Vatisker Point
Tiumpan Head

Beinn nan Surrag 199
Newmarket
Laxdale
Coll Sands
Gob Cha-leig
Portnaguiran
Rubha Deas

Garynahine
Eitshal 223
Achmore
Laxdale
Stornoway
Melbost Sands
BROAD BAY
OR
LOCH A TUATH
Aird Tunga
Sron Ruadn
Gob Hunisgeir
East Roisnish
Shulishader
Sheshader
Rubha na Greine

Beinn a'Bhuna
Beinn a'Bhota Bridein
Sandwick
Melbost
Aignish
Knock
Eye Peninsula
Garrabost
Rubha na Bairneach

Arnish Moor
Stornoway Harbour
Arnish Point
Branahuie Banks
Swordale
Upper Bayble
Lower Bayble
Bayble Bay
Rubha Dubh

Rubh a'Bhaigh Uaine
Chicken Head

Leurbost
Grimshader
Grimshader

Crossbost
Raerinish Point
Barkin Isles
Tavay Mor

Laxay
Keose
Eilean Chaluim Chille
Orinsay
Cromore
Rosay
Balallan
Kershader
Caversta
Torray
Habost
Marvig

Arivruaich
Seaforth Head
Malasgair 172
Calbost
Rubha Iosal

Aird an Troim
Mor Mhonadh 401
Feirihisval 327
Gravir
Tom an Fhuadain
Kebock Head

Sidhean an Airgid 381
Glen Ouirn
Loch Shanndabhal

Beinn na h-Uamha 389
Eishken
Lemreway
Gob na Milaid

424 *Muaithabhal*
Loch Shell
Srianach
Eilean Iubhard

242 *Beannan Mor*
Beinn Mhor 572
Corlabhadh
THE MINCH

P A R K

Kenmore
470 *Crionaig*
371 *Uisenis*
Mulhagery

449 *Caiteshal*
Tathas Mhor
Rainigadale
Bhalamus
Gob Rubh'Uisenis
Rubha Bhrollum
SOUND OF SHIANT

334
yles Scal
Eilean Mor A'bhaigh
Rubh'a'Bhaird
Sgeir-na h-Eigheach

Garbh Eilean
Eilean Mhuire
Shiant Islands
Eilean an Tighe

Sgeir Mianish

To Ullapool

1 2 3 4 5 6 7

0 1 2 3 4 5 10 15 kilometres

0 1 2 3 4 5 10 miles

A B C D E

1

Cape Wrath

Du

A'Chailleach
Am Bodach

Kear

Geodha Ruadh
na Fola

Bay of Keisgaig

297
Cnoc a'
Ghiubhais

Loch
Keisg

2

Am Balg

Rubh' an
Fhir Leithe

Sandwood
Bay

Sandwood
Loch

Beinn

Strath Shinar

Abhainn an t-Sra

48
Creag Ria
465
An Grianan

Loch na
Gainimh

Sheigra
Balchrick
Blairmore
Polin

257

355

Eilean an
Roin Mor

Loch Clash

Kinlochbervie

Rubha na Leacaig

Achriesgi

B80

3

Bagh Loch
an Roin

Loch Ti

Achlyness

B80

Rhiconich

Ardmore Point
Rubha Ruadh

Loch Dughaill

LOCH LAXFORD

Fanagmore
Tarbet

Foindle

Laxford Bridge

Handa Island

Sound of Handa

7
Badnabay
Gorm
Loch

La ford

4

Scourie More
Scourie

Scourie Bay

Rubh' Aird an
t-Sionnaich

Badcall

Badcall Bay

52

10

Ben Auskaird
386

Loch
Crocach

721
Ben
Stack
Strath

R Ste

Ad

F

A894

Eilean a'
Bhreitheimh

Meall Mor

Rubh' a'
Mhucard

Calbha
Beag

Ben Strome
419

L. an
Leathaid
Bhuain

Crei

5

Point of Stoer

Cirean Geardail

Sgeir nan Gall
Rubha nan Cosan

Oldany
Island

EDDRACHILLIS
BAY

Calbha
Mor

Kylestrome

Glendhu F

162
Eilean
Chrona

Loch Nedd

Ardvar

LOCH CAIRNBAWN

Loch Glendhu

B

Culkein

Cluas Deas

Achnacarnin

Drumbeg

B869

B869

24

Nedd

Loch
Poll

Gleann Leireag

778

Unapool

Loch Glencoul

B869

53

Balchladich

Clashnessie

Clashnessie
Bay

Stoer

Rubh' a' Mhill Dheirg

Bay of
Stoer

Clachtoll

Loch an
Leothaid

Loch
Crocach

Loch
Beannach

809
Quinag

764
Spidean
Coinich

G

7

6

Rubha Leumair

Achmelvich Bay

B869

Achmelvich

Rubha Rodha

Soyea Island

Kirkaig Point

A'Chleit

Ardroe

Baddidarach

LOCH INVER
Lochinver

Badnaban
Strathan

Loch
Culag

Inverkirkaig

Loch Kirkaig

Rubha na Breige

Rubha Coigeach

Eilean Mor

ENARD BAY

Camas
Eilean Ghlais

Camas Coille

Rubha Mor

Reiff

Rubh' a'
Choin

Eilean Mullagrach

Isle Ristol

Loch
Osgaig

Aird of Coigach

Loch Inver

Alt an
Traghaich

Inver

Loch
Assynt

10

A837

Loch Feith
an Leothaid

Beinn Gharbh
539

775
Glas Bheinn

Skiag Bridge

Bei

Inchnadamph

Inch
Gleann
Traili

9

Stronechrubie

Glencanisp
Forest

Fionn
Loch

731
Suilven

Loch nan
Gainimh

847
Canisp

Cam
Loch

A837

Loch
Veyatie

Loch
Awe

Loch
Sionascaig

Loch
Borralan

7

-leac Mor

Summer Isle

Polbain

Achiltibuie

Inverpolly
Forest

612
Stac Polly

849
Cul Mor
Drumrunie Forest

769
Cul Beag

Ledmore

Elphin

Knockan

A835

Loch Un

Loch
Borralan

307
Cnoc r
Glas Che

A B C D E

Tanera Beg

489

Loch an
Doire Dhuibh

Loch Lurgann

110

0 1 2 3 4 5   10   15 kilometres
0 1 2 3 4 5   10 miles

A   B   C   D   E

1

Strathy Point

Whiten Head
Geodh' a' Bhrideoin
Eilean Cluimhrig
Cnoc Ard an t-Siuil 184
Rubha Thormaid
Port Vasgo
Port Allt a'Mhuilinn
Totegan
Sandside Head
Red Point
Fresgoe
Sandside Bay
Do

2
Ben Hutig 408
Midfield
Rabbit Islands
Eilean nan Ron
Neave or Coomb Island
Caol Raineach
Farr Point
Kirtomy Point
Kirtomy Bay
Ardmore Point
Aultiphurst
Brawl
Armadale Bay
Baligill
Strathy
Melvich
Bighouse
Red Point
Sandside House
Reay
Isa
ll
Inverhope
A'Mhoine Moine Ho
Talmine
Midtown
Skerray
Modsarie
Achtoty
Swordly
Farr
Kirtomy
Armadale
Lednagullin
Strathy
169
Beinn Chuldail
Strathy Forest
Kirkton
Golval
Beinn Ratha 242
Drum Hollistan
Achidigill Loch
Loch Akran

230
en boll
22
A838
Loch Maovally
Lochside
Achuvoldrach
Tongue Bay
Skullomie
Torrisdale
Bettyhill 28
Achina
Invernaver
Naver Rock
Leckfurin
Loch Meadie
Beinn nam Bo 229
Loch Buidhe Mor
Loch na Seilge
Bowside Lodge
Achiemore
Upper Bighouse
Craigtown

3
Loch Hope
262
Druim nan Cliar
Tongue Ho
A836
Coldbackie
Borgie
Borgie Forest
Loch Buidhe
Loch Slaim
Loch Craggie
Lochan nan Carn
Skelpick Burn
Loch Mor na Caorach
254
Beinn Ruadh
Cnoc Bad Mhairtein
Dalhalvaig
Croick
Cnoc an Fhuarain Bhain 243
Loch Tuim Ghlais
Ribigill
Cnoc Craggie 318
Cunside
Loch na Moine
Lochan nan Ealachan
Meall an Spothaidh 527
Dunviden Lochs
Loch nan Clach
Cnoc Badaireach na Gaoithe
Trantlemore
Trantlebeg
Dyke
Forsinain

Creag Riabhach Bheag 464
Loch na Seilg
Ben Hope 927
Loch a' Ghobha-Dhuibh
Meallan Liath
Ben Hiel
765
Ben Loyal
Beinn Stumanadh 527
Meall an Spothaidh
Rhifail
Loch Rifa-gil
Beinn Rifa-gil
Loch Strathy
Loch nam Breac
Loch Saobhaidhe
280 Sletill Hill
Loch Sletill
Loch Leir

4
Lettermore
Cnoc nan Cuilean 557
Loch Haluim
Inchkinloch
A836
Loch Syre
Syre
Skail
Strathnaver
Creagan Dubha 338
Reidhe Bhig
345
Cnoc nan Tri-chlach
Loch Crocach
Ben Griam Beg 580
Loch Druim a' Chliabhain
Meall a' Bhealaich
275 Cnoc nan Gall
Loch Rumsdale
Cnoc Crom-uillt 365
Forsinard

Allnabad
Loch Meadie
Cnoc an Daimh Mor 356
245
Cnoc an Daimh Beag
Cnoc a' Mhoid
Loch Staing
Loch Eileanach
Pole Hill 294
Loch Rosail
Rhifail Loch
Allt Lon a' Chuil
Rimsdale Burn
403
Rimsdale Hill
Loch Coire nam Mang
Ben Griam Mor 590
Allt Airigh-dhamh
Loch an Ruathair
Achentoul Forest
Knockfin Heights 438

346 nam Bad
oire na Duibhe
Meall na Tear 365
Mudale
Meall a' Bhrollaich 226
Loch Naver
270 Beadaig
Maillart
Garbh
Badanloch Forest
Loch Rimsdale
Loch nan Clar
284 Cnoc Ach 'na h-Uai'
Loch Arichlinie
Lochside
Achentoul
Bannock Burn

5
Altnaharra
Klibreck
Strath Vagastie
Klibreck Burn
Ben Klibreck 721
Loch Choire Forest
Loch Truderscaig
Loch an Alltan Fhearna
Loch Badanloch
Badanloch
Loch Achnamoine
Kinbrace
Kinbrace Burn
Gobernuisgach

Meall an Fhuarain 472
Cnoc an Alaskie
962
Meall nan Con
Loch nan Uan
Loch Choire Lodge
694
Gearnsary
Loch na Gainimh
Allt nan Achadhean
Burnfoot
437 Cnoc Coire na Fearna
Cnoc an Eireannaich 518

6
ask Inn
265
Strath a' Chraisg
Cnoc a' Ghiubhais
Loch Gaineamhach
Meall a'Bhata 581
Cnoc an Liath-bhaid Mhoir
Borrobol Forest
Altanduin
364 Cnoc na Breun-choille
Creag nam Fiadh 388
Abhainn na Frithe
Loch Ascaig
Strath of Kildonan
Cnoc Salislade 482
554 Creag Scalabsdale

Loch an Ulbhaidh
Sithean Freiceadain 487
Creag Riabhach na Greighe
Ben Armine Forest
Creag Mhor 713
Gorm-loch Beag
Gorm-loch Mor
Strath na Seilge
382 Cnoc na Feannaig
Strath Skinsdale
Skinsdale Burn
337 Cnoc na h'Innse Moire
Tuarie Burn
Kildonan
416 Duible
A897
Torrisl

7
Arscaig
The Airde
Shinness
Rhian
Dalmichy
Dalnessie
Meallan Liath Mor 462
Meall a' Phiobaire
Strath na Seilge
Dalbreck
Pollie
Cnoc Meadhonach 345
Ben Uarie
482 The Craggan
Meallan Liath Beag
624 Beinn Dhorain
Beinn Mhealaich 591
Glen Sletdale
Craggie
Craggie Water
Col-bheinn 539
Creag a' Chrionaich 394
Glen Loth
Culgower

A   B   C   D   E

Colaboll
Dalchork
A838
Tighcreag
Achnaluachrach
Grumby Rock
West Langwell
Scibercross
Kilbraur
Kilbraur Hill
324 Carrol Rock
onbush
A9
Kintradwell
beg Point
Lothmo

Savalmore
Lairg Lo.
Savalbeg
Sallachy
Loch na Caillich
Loch Craggie
Strath Brora
Tannachy

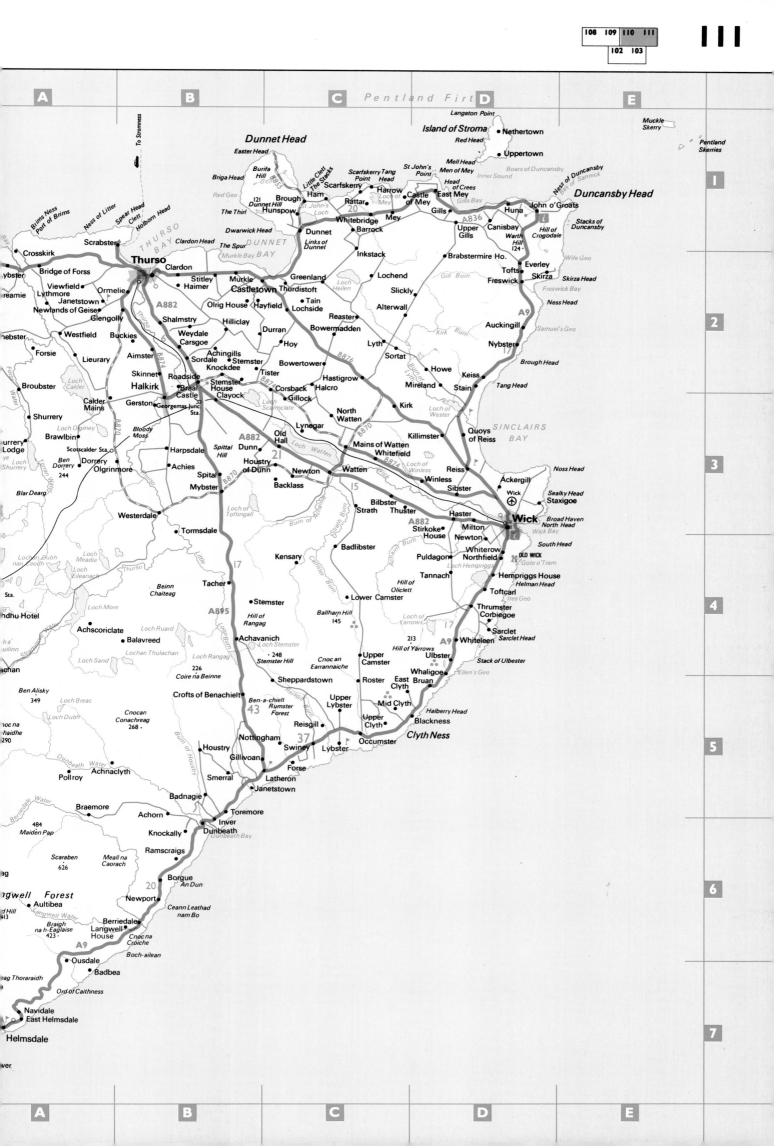

0 1 2 3 4 5 10 15 kilometres
0 1 2 3 4 5 10 miles

ORKNEY

NORTH RONALDSAY
Dennis Head
North Ronaldsay
Linklet Bay
Hollandstoun
Strom Ness

North Ronaldsay Firth

SANDAY
Tafts Ness
Scuthvie Bay
Start Point
Northwaa
Bay of Lopness
Newark
Bay of Newark
Tres Ness
Sanday Roadside
Overbister
Burness
Otters Wick
Scar
Els Ness
Kettletoft
Sty Wick
Broughtown
Holms of Ire
Backaskaill
Backaskaill Bay
Braeswick
Stove
Spur Ness
B9069
B9068
B9070

SANDAY SOUND

STRONSAY
Papa Stronsay
Odness
Whitehall
Everbay
Odin Bay
Burgh Head
Aith
Kirbister
Lamb Head
Dishes
Holland
Odie
Sronsay
Grobister
Bay of Holland
Tor Ness
Rothiesholm
Rothiesholm Head
Links Ness
Linga Holm
St Catherine's Bay
Mill Bay
Huip Ness
Holm of Huip
B9060
B9061
B9062

Auskerry
Auskerry Sound

STRONSAY FIRTH

EDAY
Calf of Eday
Red Head
Calfsound
Guith
Millbounds
Eday
Backaland
War Ness
Fers Ness
Kili Holm
Muckle Green Holm
Faray
Sound of Faray
B9063

THE NORTH SOUND

PAPA WESTRAY
Mull Head
Holland
Papa Westray
Backaskaill
Head of Moclett
Spa Ness
Papa Sound

WESTRAY
Noup Head
Bow Head
Aikerness
Rackwick
Westray
Pierowall
Broughton
Braehead
Midbea
Langskaill
Berst Ness
Inga Ness
Skelwick
Rapness
Stanger Head
Bay of Tuquoy
Skea Skerries
Point of Huro
Rapness Sound
B9066
B9067

WESTRAY FIRTH

EDAY SOUND

ROUSAY
Sacquoy Head
Costa Head
Saviskaill Bay
Wasbister
Westness
Blotchnie Fiold 250
Brinyan
Muckle Water
Faraclett Head
Rousay Sound
B9064

Egilsay
Wyre
Gairsay
Gairsay Sound

SHAPINSAY
Ness of Ork
The Galt
Veantrow Bay
Edmonstone
Sandgarth
Haco's Ness
Balfour
Car Ness
Head of Holland
Renwick Head
B9058
B9059

SHAPINSAY SOUND

WIDE FIRTH

Eynhallow
Eynhallow Sound
Aiker Ness
Redland
Gorseness
Broad Taing
Isbister
Bay of Firth
A965
A966
Costa
Georth
Milldoe 726
Hackland
Netherbrough
Bimbister
Firstown
Heddle
Kirbuster
Beaquoy
Dounby
Mirbister
Brough
Loch of Harray
A986
B9057
Twatt
Isbister
Quoyloo
Skeabrae
Aith
Voy
Tenston
Loch of Stenness
A967
A966
B9055
B9056
Birsay
Birsay Bay
Marwick
Marwick Head
Northdyke
Bay of Skaill
Row Head
Skaill
Yesnaby
Neban Point
Loch of Swannay
Loch of Hundland
Loch of Boardhouse
Brough Head

FIRTH

AUSKERRY SOUND

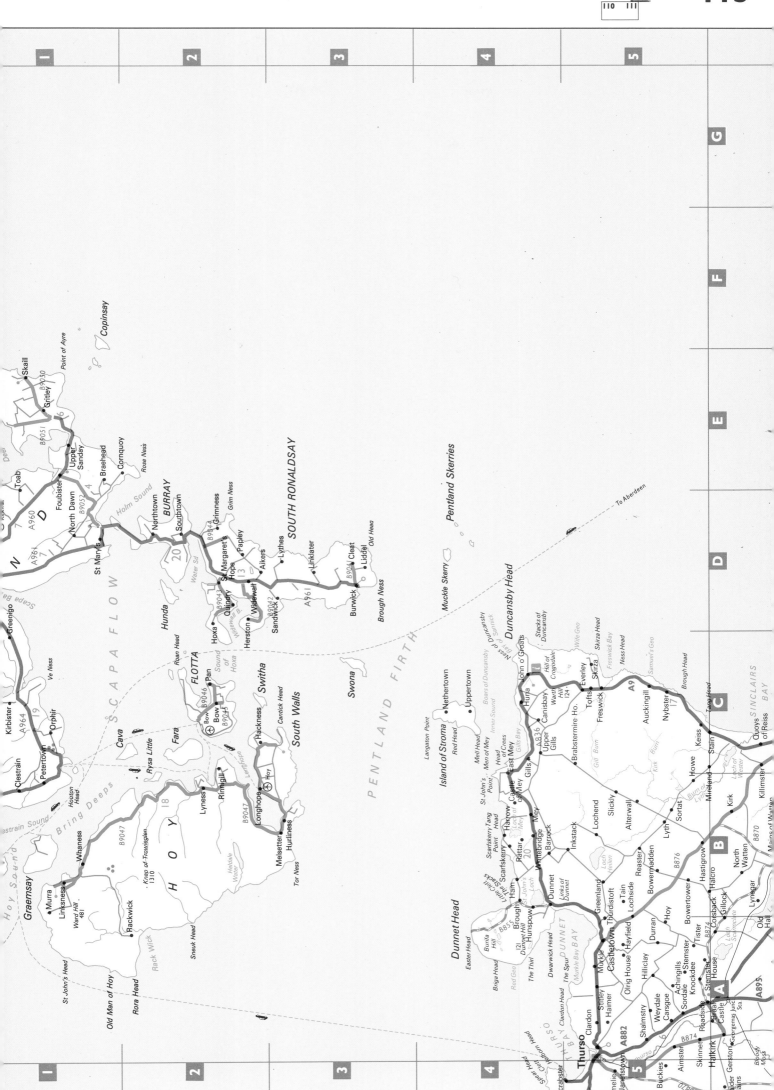

0 1 2 3 4 5   10   15 kilometres

0   1   2   3   4   5   10 miles

SHETLAND

UNST

Lamba Ness
Skaw
Saxa Vord
Norwick
285
Valsgarth
The Nev
Haroldswick
Balta
Burra Firth
B9086
Quoys
Hagdarth
Buness
Harold's Wick
Burrafirth
A968
Baltasound
Caldback
Sand Wick
Mu Ness
Baliasta
Herma Ness
Loch of Cliff
Valla Field
Westing
Unst
Uyeasound
Clivocast
Muckle Flugga
Newgord
Lund
A968
Uyea
Belmont
Sound
Bluemull Sound

FETLAR
Strandburgh Ness
Wick of Gruting
Funzie
Aith B9088
The Snap
Houbie
Fetlar
Tresta
Wick of Tresta
Rams Ness
Oddsta
Brough Lodge
Lamb Hoga
Hascosay
Colgrave Sound

Breakon
B9083
Gloup
North Neaps
Cullivoe
Stonganess
South Garth
B9082
Gutcher
Sellafirth
Colvister
Cunnister
North Sandwick
Basta Voe
Burra Ness
Basta
Camb
A968

YELL
Aywick
Gossabrough
Otters Wick
East Yell
B9081
Otterswick
Mid Yell
Hamnavoe
Burravoe
Brough
Heoga Ness
Hamna Voe
Ulsta
Copister
West Yell
West Sandwick
A968
Clothan
Bigga
Grimister
Whale
Nev of Stuis
Samphrey
Mossbank
Brother Isle
Uynarey
Mio Ness
Linga
Lunna Holm
Ness

YELL SOUND
Ramna Stacks
Point of Fethaland
Lamba
Little Roe
Brough
Toft
Oil Terminal
Graven
Scatsta A9076

Isbister
Burra Voe
North Roe
North Roe
Housetter
Collafirth
Colla Firth
A970
Voe
Ollaberry
B9079
Gluss
Uyea
Roer Water
Ronas Hill
450
Eela Water
Sullom
A970
Ronas Voe
Urafirth
Ura Firth
Scalsta
Heylor
Burnside
Hillswick
The Faither
Hamnavoe
Scarff
B9078
Braehoullagh
Ure
Tangwick
Stenness
Esha Ness
Baa Taing
Brae Wick
Hamna Voe
Sullom Voe

Bruray
Muckle Skerry
Out

FAIR ISLE
Skroo
Bu Ness
Sheep Rock
Stonybreck
Malcolm's Head

27 miles south west of Sumburgh Head

FOULA
at the same scale
Strem Ness
Ham
The Kame
The Sneug 418
South Ness

27 miles west of Scalloway

Inset (C6): at the same scale

Ve Skerries

PAPA STOUR

WHALSAY

BRESSAY

Isle of Noss

Noup of Noss

Bard Head

To Tórshavn (Faroes) &
Seyðisfjörður (Iceland)
(summer only)

To Bergen (Norway) &
Hanstholm (Denmark)
(summer only)

To Aberdeen
To Stromness

Lerwick

Scalloway

West Burra
East Burra

Mousa

Sumburgh Head

Sumburgh Roost

Fitful Head

Skaw Taing
Skaw
Whalsay
Isbister
Huxter
Brough
Marrister
Symbister
Clett Head

Lunning
West Linga
Lunning Sd
Swining
Vidlin
Lunnasting
Hillside
Laxo
Voe
Dury Voe
Stava Ness
The Keen
South Nesting Bay
Moul of Eswick
Neap
Laxfirth
North Nesting
Bretabister
Skellister
Freester
Gletness
Hawks Ness
Kebister Ness
Score Head
Gunnista
Heogan
Manfield
Setter
Brough
Grindiscol
Ward of Bressay 226
Kirkabister
Bressay Sound
Holmsgarth
Gulberwick
Helli Ness
Okraquoy
Cunningsburgh
Fladdabister
Mail
Mousa Sd
No Ness
Sandwick
Northpunds
Levenwick
Leebotten
Hoswick
Channerwick
Ireland
Bigton
St Ninian's Isle
Fora Ness
Maywick
Kettla Ness
South Havra
Royl Field 293
Cliff Hills
Cliff Sound
Bridge End
Hamnavoe
Oxna
Hildasay
Trondra
Burwick
Cutts
Uradale
Quarff
Veensgarth
Whiteness
Loch of Strom
Girlsta
Loch of Girlsta
Gott
Laxfirth
Catfirth
Lax Firth
Cat Firth
The Kames
Voe
Hillside
Swining
Wethersta
Burravoe
Busta
Roesound
Muckle Roe
Vementry
Papa Little
West Burrafirth
Unifirth
Brindister
Noonsbrough
Clousta
Aith
Aithsting
Twatt
Bixter
Stanydale
Browland
Gruting
Bridge of Walls
Walls
Vaila
Dale
Skarpigarth
Melby
Garth
Sandness
Sandness Hill 249
Biggings
Mu Ness
Wats Ness
Skelda Ness
Culswick
Wester Skeld
Westerwick
Silwick
Reawick
Easter Skeld
Sand
Garderhouse
Semblister
Westerfield
Sound
Tresta
Heglibister
Setter
Weisdale
Hellister
Huxfer
Scalla Field 281
East Burrafirth
Gonfirth
Olna Firth
Linga
Busta Voe
Aith Voe
Sullom Voe
Papa Stour
Sound of Papa
Effirth
Sandsound
Weisdale Voe
South View
White Ness
Whiteness Voe
Loch of Tingwall
The Deeps
Gruting Voe
Browland

Sumburgh inset (G/C6):
Fora Ness
Scousburgh
Skelberry
Hillwell
Quendale
Loch of Spiggie
Bay of Quendale
Boddam
Exnaboe
Toab
Sumburgh
Grutness
283
A970
Sumburgh Roost

A970
A971
B9071
B9074
B9073
B9075
B9122
B9011

Scousburgh
Skelberry

Fifteen Route Centres - key points in the nation's network of motorways and main roads - have been selected to represent different areas throughout Britain. They are as follows:

London
Aberdeen
Birmingham
Bristol
Cardiff
Edinburgh
Exeter
Glasgow
Inverness
Leeds
Liverpool
Manchester
Newcastle
Norwich
Southampton

For each Route Centre a set of useful destinations has been selected e.g. major cities, holiday resorts, cross-channel ferry ports - and the shortest road distances to these destinations using motorways and A roads are indicated. The distances are shown in miles, with the kilometric equivalent in italics.

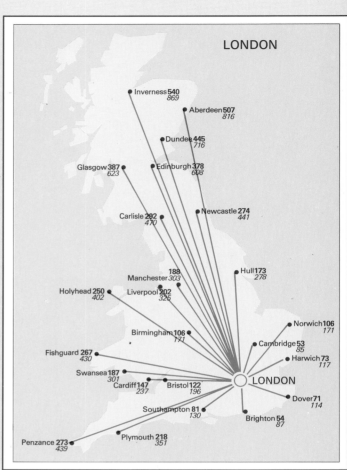

LONDON

Inverness 540 / 869
Aberdeen 507 / 816
Dundee 445 / 716
Glasgow 387 / 623
Edinburgh 378 / 608
Carlisle 292 / 470
Newcastle 274 / 441
Manchester 188 / 303
Hull 173 / 278
Holyhead 250 / 402
Liverpool 202 / 326
Norwich 106 / 171
Birmingham 106 / 171
Cambridge 53 / 85
Fishguard 267 / 430
Harwich 73 / 117
Swansea 187 / 301
Cardiff 147 / 237
Bristol 122 / 196
LONDON
Dover 71 / 114
Southampton 81 / 130
Brighton 54 / 87
Penzance 273 / 439
Plymouth 218 / 351

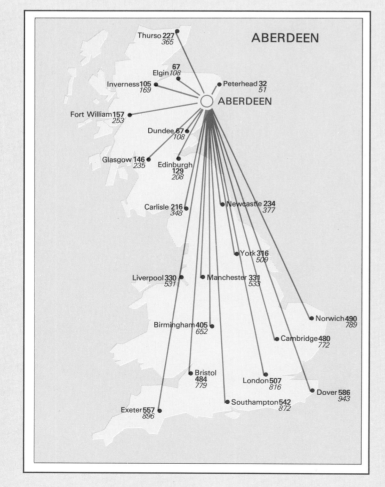

ABERDEEN

Thurso 227 / 365
Elgin 67 / 108
Inverness 105 / 169
Peterhead 32 / 51
ABERDEEN
Fort William 157 / 253
Dundee 67 / 108
Glasgow 146 / 235
Edinburgh 129 / 208
Carlisle 216 / 348
Newcastle 234 / 377
York 316 / 509
Liverpool 330 / 531
Manchester 331 / 533
Norwich 490 / 789
Birmingham 405 / 652
Cambridge 480 / 772
Bristol 484 / 779
London 507 / 816
Dover 586 / 943
Exeter 557 / 896
Southampton 542 / 872

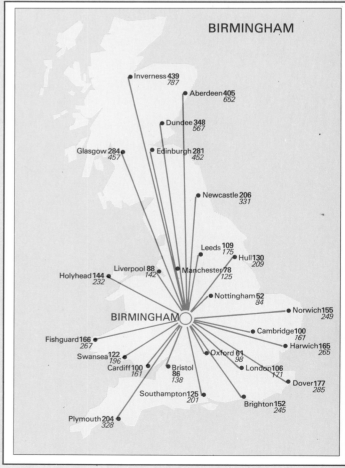

BIRMINGHAM

Inverness 439 / 787
Aberdeen 405 / 652
Dundee 348 / 567
Glasgow 284 / 457
Edinburgh 281 / 452
Newcastle 206 / 331
Leeds 109 / 175
Hull 130 / 209
Holyhead 144 / 232
Liverpool 88 / 142
Manchester 78 / 125
Nottingham 52 / 84
BIRMINGHAM
Norwich 155 / 249
Cambridge 100 / 161
Fishguard 166 / 267
Harwich 165 / 265
Swansea 122 / 196
Oxford 61 / 98
Cardiff 100 / 161
Bristol 86 / 138
London 106 / 171
Dover 177 / 285
Southampton 125 / 201
Brighton 152 / 245
Plymouth 204 / 328

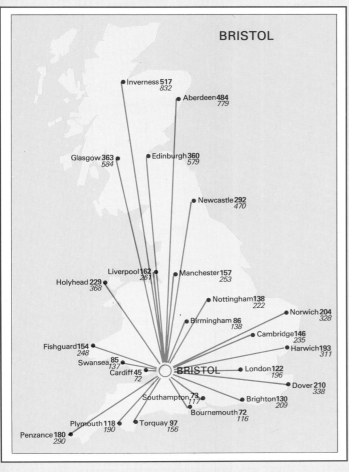

BRISTOL

Inverness 517 *832*
Aberdeen 484 *779*
Glasgow 363 *584*
Edinburgh 360 *579*
Newcastle 292 *470*
Liverpool 162 *261*
Manchester 157 *253*
Holyhead 229 *368*
Nottingham 138 *222*
Birmingham 86 *138*
Norwich 204 *328*
Cambridge 146 *235*
Fishguard 154 *248*
Harwich 193 *311*
Swansea 85 *137*
Cardiff 45 *72*
BRISTOL
London 122 *196*
Dover 210 *338*
Southampton 73 *117*
Brighton 130 *209*
Bournemouth 72 *116*
Plymouth 118 *190*
Torquay 97 *156*
Penzance 180 *290*

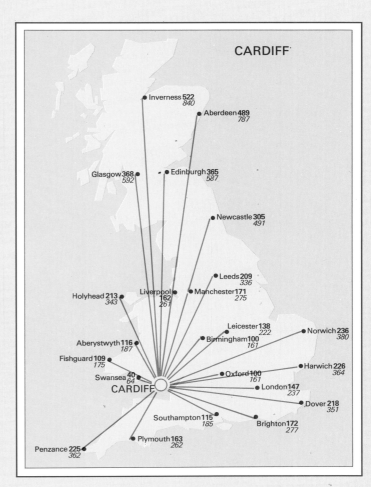

CARDIFF

Inverness 522 *840*
Aberdeen 489 *787*
Glasgow 368 *592*
Edinburgh 365 *587*
Newcastle 305 *491*
Leeds 209 *336*
Holyhead 213 *343*
Liverpool 162 *261*
Manchester 171 *275*
Leicester 138 *222*
Aberystwyth 116 *187*
Birmingham 100 *161*
Norwich 236 *380*
Fishguard 109 *175*
Oxford 100 *161*
Harwich 226 *364*
Swansea 40 *64*
CARDIFF
London 147 *237*
Dover 218 *351*
Southampton 115 *185*
Brighton 172 *277*
Plymouth 163 *262*
Penzance 225 *362*

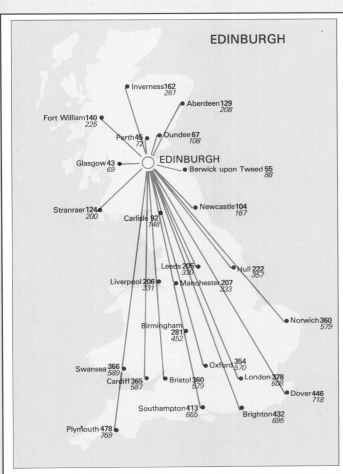

EDINBURGH

Inverness 162 *261*
Aberdeen 129 *208*
Fort William 140 *225*
Perth 45 *72*
Dundee 67 *108*
Glasgow 43 *69*
EDINBURGH
Berwick upon Tweed 55 *88*
Stranraer 124 *200*
Newcastle 104 *167*
Carlisle 92 *148*
Leeds 205 *330*
Hull 222 *357*
Liverpool 206 *331*
Manchester 207 *333*
Norwich 360 *579*
Birmingham 281 *452*
Oxford 354 *570*
Swansea 366 *589*
London 378 *608*
Cardiff 365 *587*
Bristol 360 *579*
Dover 446 *718*
Southampton 413 *665*
Brighton 432 *695*
Plymouth 478 *769*

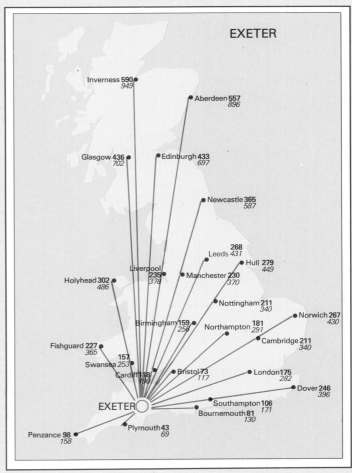

EXETER

Inverness 590 *949*
Aberdeen 557 *896*
Glasgow 436 *702*
Edinburgh 433 *697*
Newcastle 365 *587*
Leeds 268 *431*
Hull 279 *449*
Liverpool 235 *378*
Manchester 230 *370*
Holyhead 302 *486*
Nottingham 211 *340*
Northampton 181 *291*
Birmingham 159 *256*
Norwich 267 *430*
Fishguard 227 *365*
Cambridge 211 *340*
Swansea 253 *157*
Cardiff 113 *190*
Bristol 73 *117*
London 175 *282*
Dover 246 *396*
Southampton 106 *171*
EXETER
Bournemouth 81 *130*
Penzance 98 *158*
Plymouth 43 *69*

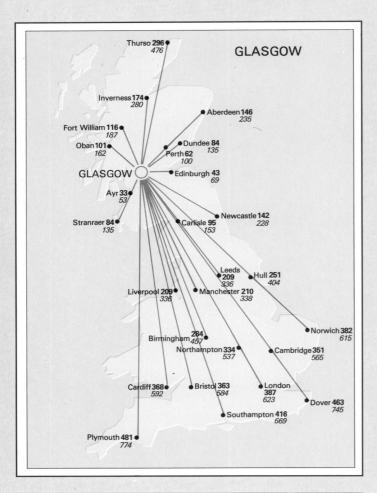

GLASGOW

Thurso 296 / 476
Inverness 174 / 280
Fort William 116 / 187
Oban 101 / 162
Aberdeen 146 / 235
Dundee 84 / 135
Perth 62 / 100
GLASGOW
Edinburgh 43 / 69
Ayr 33 / 53
Stranraer 84 / 135
Carlisle 95 / 153
Newcastle 142 / 228
Leeds 209 / 336
Hull 251 / 404
Liverpool 209 / 336
Manchester 210 / 338
Birmingham 284 / 457
Northampton 334 / 537
Norwich 382 / 615
Cambridge 351 / 565
Cardiff 368 / 592
Bristol 363 / 584
London 387 / 623
Dover 463 / 745
Southampton 416 / 669
Plymouth 481 / 774

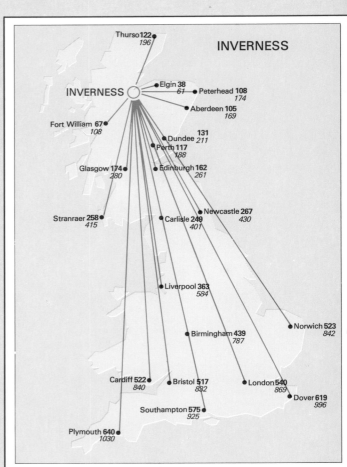

INVERNESS

Thurso 122 / 196
Elgin 38 / 61
Peterhead 108 / 174
INVERNESS
Aberdeen 105 / 169
Fort William 67 / 108
Dundee 131 / 211
Perth 117 / 188
Glasgow 174 / 280
Edinburgh 162 / 261
Stranraer 258 / 415
Carlisle 249 / 401
Newcastle 267 / 430
Liverpool 363 / 584
Birmingham 439 / 787
Norwich 523 / 842
Cardiff 522 / 840
Bristol 517 / 832
London 540 / 869
Dover 619 / 996
Southampton 575 / 925
Plymouth 640 / 1030

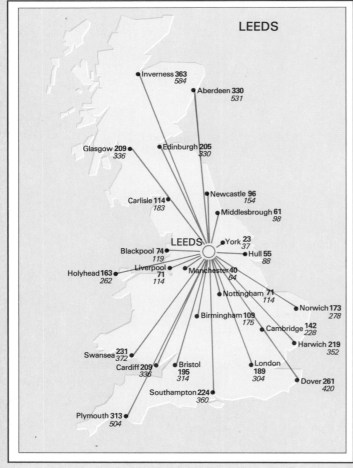

LEEDS

Inverness 363 / 584
Aberdeen 330 / 531
Glasgow 209 / 336
Edinburgh 205 / 330
Carlisle 114 / 183
Newcastle 96 / 154
Middlesbrough 61 / 98
LEEDS
York 23 / 37
Blackpool 74 / 119
Hull 55 / 88
Holyhead 163 / 262
Liverpool 71 / 114
Manchester 40 / 64
Nottingham 71 / 114
Norwich 173 / 278
Birmingham 109 / 175
Cambridge 142 / 228
Harwich 219 / 352
Swansea 231 / 372
Cardiff 209 / 336
Bristol 195 / 314
London 189 / 304
Dover 261 / 420
Southampton 224 / 360
Plymouth 313 / 504

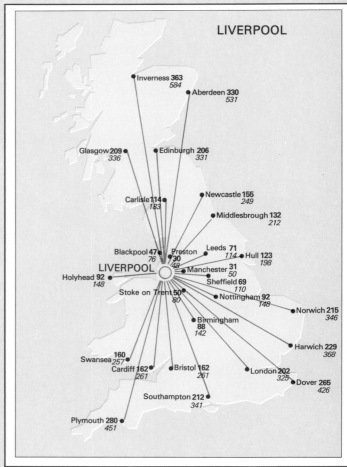

LIVERPOOL

Inverness 363 / 584
Aberdeen 330 / 531
Glasgow 209 / 336
Edinburgh 206 / 331
Carlisle 114 / 183
Newcastle 155 / 249
Middlesbrough 132 / 212
Blackpool 47 / 76
Preston 30 / 48
Leeds 71 / 114
Hull 123 / 198
LIVERPOOL
Manchester 31 / 50
Holyhead 92 / 148
Sheffield 69 / 110
Stoke on Trent 50 / 80
Nottingham 92 / 148
Norwich 215 / 346
Birmingham 88 / 142
Harwich 229 / 368
Swansea 160 / 257
Cardiff 162 / 261
Bristol 162 / 261
London 202 / 325
Dover 265 / 426
Southampton 212 / 341
Plymouth 280 / 451

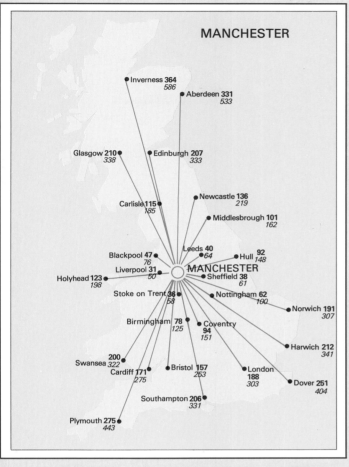

MANCHESTER

Inverness **364** *586*
Aberdeen **331** *533*
Glasgow **210** *338*
Edinburgh **207** *333*
Carlisle **115** *185*
Newcastle **136** *219*
Middlesbrough **101** *162*
Leeds **40** *64*
Hull **92** *148*
Blackpool **47** *76*
Liverpool **31** *50*
MANCHESTER
Holyhead **123** *198*
Sheffield **38** *61*
Stoke on Trent **36** *58*
Nottingham **62** *100*
Norwich **191** *307*
Birmingham **78** *125*
Coventry **94** *151*
Harwich **212** *341*
Swansea **200** *322*
Cardiff **171** *275*
Bristol **157** *263*
London **188** *303*
Dover **251** *404*
Southampton **206** *331*
Plymouth **275** *443*

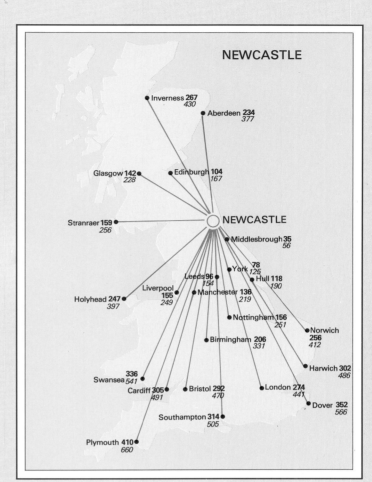

NEWCASTLE

Inverness **267** *430*
Aberdeen **234** *377*
Glasgow **142** *228*
Edinburgh **104** *167*
Stranraer **159** *256*
NEWCASTLE
Middlesbrough **35** *56*
York **78** *125*
Leeds **96** *154*
Hull **118** *190*
Liverpool **155** *249*
Manchester **136** *219*
Holyhead **247** *397*
Nottingham **156** *251*
Norwich **256** *412*
Birmingham **206** *331*
Harwich **302** *486*
Swansea **336** *541*
Cardiff **305** *491*
Bristol **292** *470*
London **274** *441*
Dover **352** *566*
Southampton **314** *505*
Plymouth **410** *660*

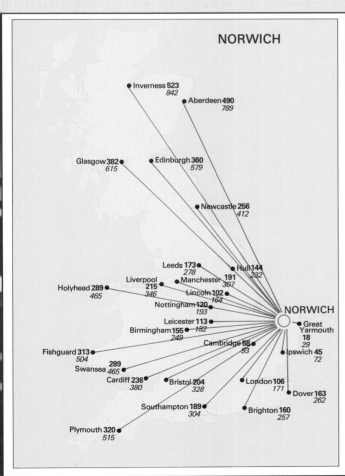

NORWICH

Inverness **523** *842*
Aberdeen **490** *789*
Glasgow **382** *615*
Edinburgh **360** *579*
Newcastle **256** *412*
Leeds **173** *278*
Hull **144** *232*
Liverpool **215** *346*
Manchester **191** *307*
Holyhead **289** *465*
Lincoln **102** *164*
Nottingham **120** *193*
Leicester **113** *182*
NORWICH
Birmingham **155** *249*
Great Yarmouth **18** *29*
Cambridge **58** *93*
Ipswich **45** *72*
Fishguard **313** *504*
Swansea **289** *465*
Cardiff **236** *380*
Bristol **204** *328*
London **106** *171*
Dover **163** *262*
Southampton **189** *304*
Brighton **160** *257*
Plymouth **320** *515*

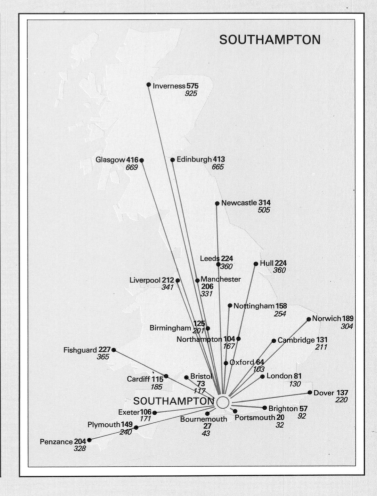

SOUTHAMPTON

Inverness **575** *925*
Glasgow **416** *669*
Edinburgh **413** *665*
Newcastle **314** *505*
Leeds **224** *360*
Hull **224** *360*
Liverpool **212** *341*
Manchester **206** *331*
Nottingham **158** *254*
Norwich **189** *304*
Birmingham **125** *201*
Northampton **104** *167*
Cambridge **131** *211*
Fishguard **227** *365*
Oxford **64** *103*
London **81** *130*
Cardiff **115** *185*
Bristol **73** *117*
Dover **137** *220*
SOUTHAMPTON
Exeter **106** *171*
Brighton **57** *92*
Plymouth **149** *240*
Bournemouth **27** *43*
Portsmouth **20** *32*
Penzance **204** *328*

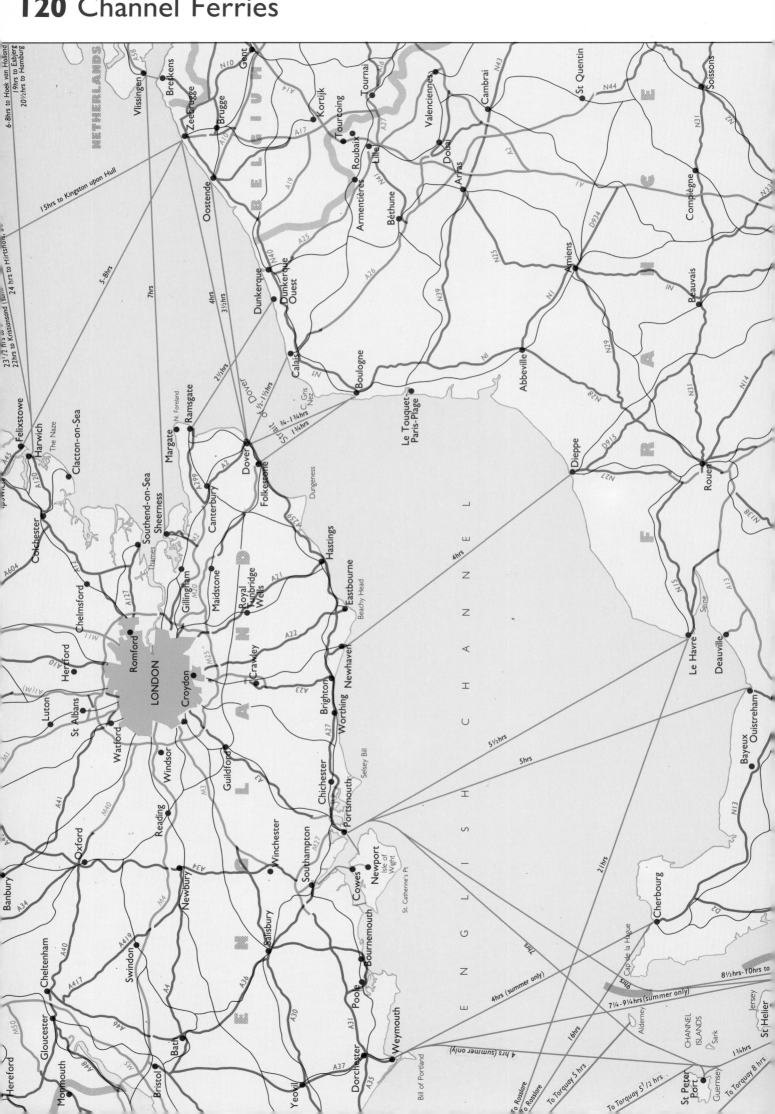

LONDON GUIDE CONTENTS

London Through Routes **122-123**

London Central Plan **124-131**

London Index **132-136**

KEY TO MAP PAGES

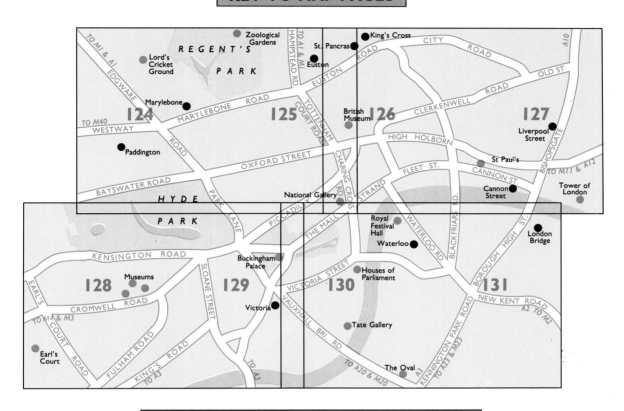

KEY TO LONDON CENTRAL PLAN

motorway
autoroute
Autobahn

dual carriageway
chaussées séparées
Straße mehrbahnig

main link road
axe secondaire
Verbindungsstraße

other roads
autres rues
sonstige Straßen

lane, drive
petite rue, allée
Gaße, Einfahrt

walkway
passage
Fußgängerweg

restricted zone
zone d'accès limité
Zugangsbeschränkung

tourist information centre
syndicat d'initiative
Informationsbüro

car park
parking
Parkplatz

toilets
toilettes
Toiletten

post office
bureau de poste
Postamt

principal hotel
hôtel important
führendes Hotel

public building
bâtiment public
offentliches Gebäude

tower block
immeuble élevé
Hochhaus

hospital
hôpital
Krankenhaus

museum or gallery
musée ou galerie d'art
Museen

library
biblotheque
Bibliothek

church
église
Kirche

synagogue
synagogue
Synagoge

railways
lignes ferroviaires
Eisenbahnlinien

passenger station
gare
Bahnhof

main station
gare principale
Hauptbahnhof

underground station
métro
U-Bahnhof

airport coach terminal
aérogare
Abfahrt zum Flughafen

embassy
ambassade
Botschaft

police station
poste de police
Polizeiwache

one-way street
sens unique
Einbahnstraße

built-up area
terrain bâti
bebaute Fläche

public park
jardin public
Park

private garden
jardin privé
Privatpark

cemetery
cimetière
Friedhof

sports ground
terrain de sports
Sportplatz

bowling green
boules
Bowlingplatz

tennis court
tennis
Tennisplatz

swimming pool
piscine
Schwimmbad

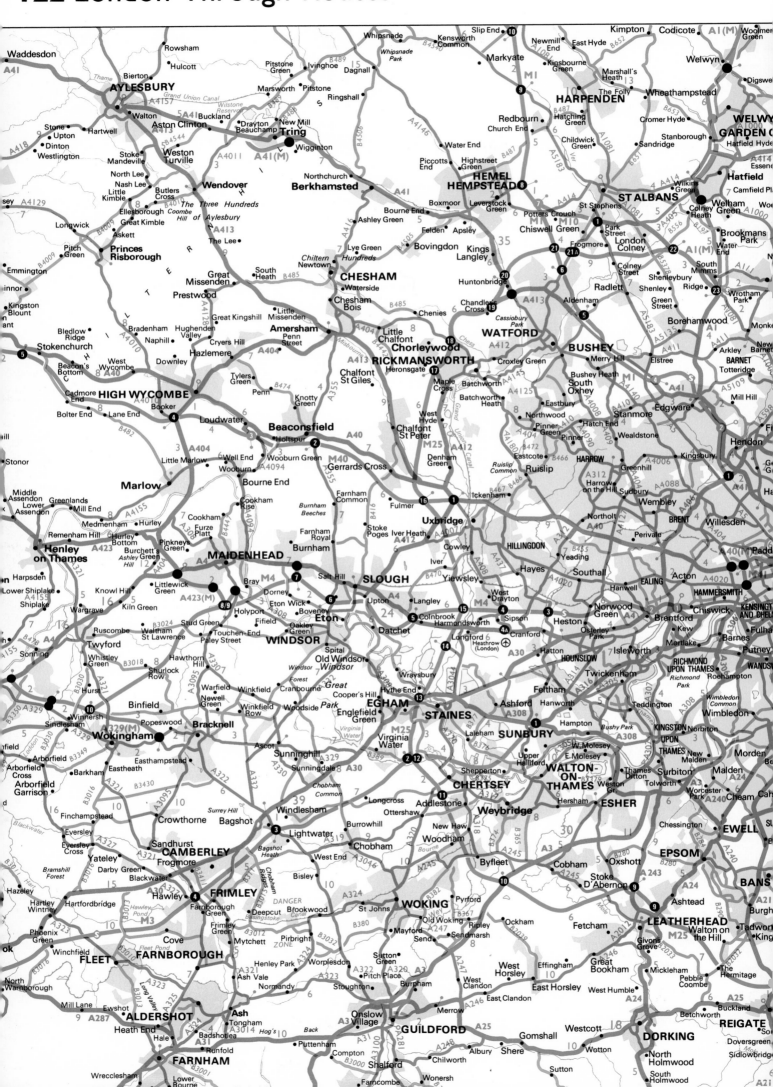

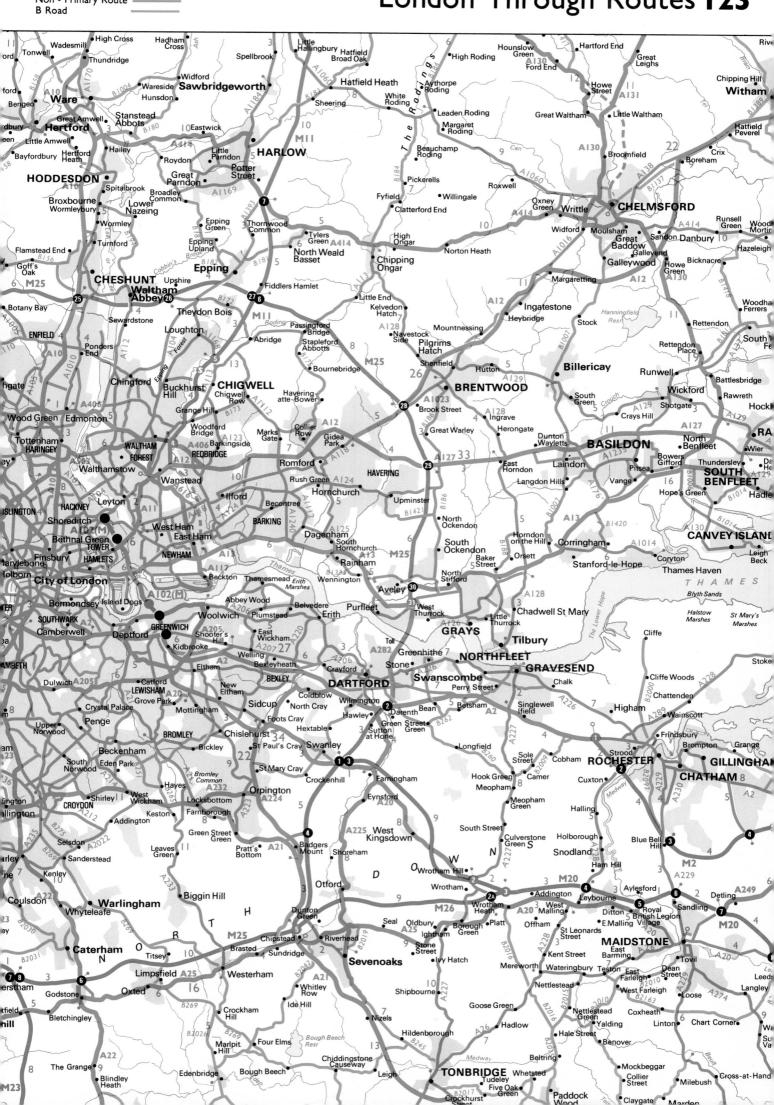

0   0.25   0.5 kilometre

0   0.25   0.

A

I

asgow
Ho.

Falkirk
Ho.

Edinburgh
Ho.

Elgin
Ms

The Lane

Marlborough Pl.

Aubrey

Violet Hill

Abbey Gdns.

Hamilton Terrace

Nugent Terr.

Hall

Abbey Rd

Garden
Rd.

Arna

Mans

Abbey Gdns

Grove End

B

Hosp. of St. John
& St. Elizabeth

Wellington
Road

Circus

Cochrane Street

St. John's Wood High Street

Barrow Hill
Est.

Allitsen Rd.

Chalbert St.

C

Grand Union Canal

PRINCE ALBERT RD.

Winfield
Ho.

R E G

Nuffield
Foundation

St. John's Wood

Public
Gardens

Mosque
Regent's
Lodge

**Regent's Park
Lake**

A

2

SUTHERLAND

Randolph

Crescent

Castellain

Warrington

Bristol
Gdns

Clifton
Villas

Blomfield

Delamere
Ter.

MAIDA VALE

HALL

Lanark Road

Vale
Clo.

Lanark

ABERCORN PLACE

ABBEY ROAD

Lord's
Cricket
Ground
(M.C.C.)

WOOD ROAD

LISSON GROVE

Lisson Green
Estate

PARK ROAD

GLOUCESTER

Royal Coll. of
Obstetr. & Gynaec.

Sussex Place

MARYLEBONE

MARYLEBONE

A

3

BISHOP'S

WESTBOURNE

Hallfield
Estate

Little Venice

Warwick Cr.

WARWICK
AVENUE

CLIFTON GDNS

Maida

Warwick
Avenue

AVENUE ROAD

John Aird
Court

EDGWARE ROAD

Braithwaite Tower
Hall Tower

Tech.
Coll.

Paddington
Green Hosp.

Paddington
Green

WESTWAY

PADDINGTON

Paddington Basin

North Wharf Road

St. Mary's
Hospital

PADDINGTON

PADDINGTON

SUSSEX GARDENS

PRAED STREET

Broadley

EDGWARE ROAD
(Bakerloo)

EDGWARE ROAD
(Met. &
Circle)

Old Marylebone Rd.

Samaritan
Hosp.

MARYLEBONE RD.

SEYMOUR

**MARBLE
ARCH**

**MARBLE
ARCH**

A

4

Inverness

Queensborough Terrace

Porchester Terrace

Leinster Gdns

CRAVEN HILL

Queen's Gardens

Craven Hill Gdns

Lancaster

BAYSWATER

Lancaster
Gate

**LANCASTER
GATE**

Westbourne
Gate

Victoria Gate

BAYSWATER ROAD

The Ring

Albion Gate

Stanhope
Gate

Speaker's
Corner

**HYDE
PARK**

The Fountains

Speke's Monument

Peter Pan
Statue

Nursery

Bird Sanctuary

New Lodge

A   **B**   **C**

0   0.25   0.5 kilometre
0   0.25   0

0   0.25   0.5 kilometre
0   0.25   0

A   **B**   **C**

NOTTING HILL GATE
NOTTING HILL GATE

Black Lion Gate
Orme Sq. Gate
The Broad Walk
Speke's Monument
Budge's Walk
Peter Pan Statue
The Long Water
Buck Hill Walk
The Ring

Clock Tower

KENSINGTON

The Orangery
Temple Lodge
Magazine

The Round Pond

Kensington Palace

GARDENS

Bandstand
Serpentine Gallery
Serpentine Bridge
Restaurant
The Lido

Queen Elizabeth College

Kensington Palace Gardens

Kensington Palace Barracks

Lancaster Walk
The Flower Walk
Albert Memorial

South Carriage Drive

KENSINGTON ROAD

Palace Gate
Queen's Gate
Alexandra Gate

KENSINGTON

Kensington Gore
Royal Geographical Society
Royal College of Art
Royal Albert Hall

KNIGHTS

Kensington & Chelsea Town Hall

HIGH STREET KENSINGTON

Maria Assumpta College
AER LINGUS
Royal College of Music
Prince Consort Road
Imperial College
Royal College of Science

2

St. Mary Abbots Hospital

Science Museum
Natural History Museum
Geological Museum
Victoria and Albert Museum
The Oratory

Cornwall Gardens

CROMWELL ROAD

WEST LONDON

CROMWELL ROAD

GLOUCESTER ROAD

Fr. Univ. College

SOUTH KENSINGTON

SOUTH KENSINGTON

Melton Ct.

Brompton Hospital
Royal Marsden Hosp.

3

EARL'S COURT

EARL'S COURT

FULHAM

Coleherne Court

The Boltons

St. Luke's Hosp.
Chelsea Hosp. (for Women)

Earl's Court Exhibition Building

Princess Beatrice Hosp.

WEST BROMPTON

Chelsea College
School of Art

West Brompton

4

Brompton Cemetery

St. Stephen's Hospital

KING'S

Western Hospital

A   **B**   **C**

0   0.25   0.5 kilometre
0   0.25   0.5

A   **B**   **C**

PICCADILLY
REGENT STREET
PALL MALL EAST
New Zealand Ho.
Trafalgar
Duncannon St.
Villiers St.
Cleopatra's Needle
King's Reach
IBM Bldg.

ST. JAMES'S
St. James's Square
Cockspur Sq.
CHARING CROSS
Nelson's Column
Northumberland Av.
CHARING CROSS
EMBANKMENT
Victoria Embankment Gardens
Charing Cross Pier
Hungerford Bridge (Footbridge)
National Theatre
Queen Elizabeth Hall
Hayward Gallery

THE MALL
Admiralty Arch
Whitehall
Ministry of Defence
Hispaniola
P.S. Tattersall Castle
Royal Festival Hall
Shell Centre Downstream Bldg.
Corn Ho.

RAC
Marlborough Ho.
Horse Guards Parade
Ministry of Defence
Dept. of Trade
South Bank
WATERLOO
Shell Centre Tower

St. James's Palace
Clarence Ho.
Cake House
Duck Island
Horse Guards'
The Treasury
Ministry of Defence
Downing St.
Richmond Ter.
WATERLOO

Lancaster House
ST. JAMES'S PARK
St. James's Park Lake
Foreign & Commonwealth and Home Offices
King Charles St.
Cenotaph
Parliament
Westminster Pier
The County Hall
General Lying-in Hospital

Queen Victoria Memorial
BIRDCAGE WALK
Government Offices
WESTMINSTER
Gassiott Ho.

2

Guards Chapel
Anne's Gate
Old Queen St.
Storey's Gate
Gt. George St.
Guildhall
Westminster Hall
Bridge St. Westminster Bridge

Wellington Barracks
Central Hall
Westminster Abbey
Houses of Parliament
St. Thomas's Hospital

Buckingham
Petty France
ST. JAMES'S PARK
Tothill St.
Broad Sanctuary
St. Margaret's
Old Palace Yd.
Victoria Tower Gardens
St. Thomas's Medical School
Lambeth Palace Gardens
LAMBETH

Passport Office
Caxton Hall
New Scotland Yard
Westminster School
Burghers of Calais

Westminster City Hall
Tel. Exchange
Dean's Yd.

VICTORIA
Howick Place
Greycoat Pl.
Greycoat Hosp.
College
Dept. of Environment
Smith Square
Lambeth Pier
Lambeth Palace
China Walk Estate

Westminster Cathedral (R.C.)
Tech College
Medway St.
Romney St.
Lambeth Bridge
FERRY ROAD
LAMBETH ROAD

Westminster Hosp.
Westminster School Playing Field
WESTMINSTER
Thames Ho.
Fire Brigade H.Q.

3

Children's Hosp.
Gordon Hosp.
Grosvenor Hosp.
Page Street
Millbank Tower
Queen Alexandra's Hospital
Coverley Pt.
Hayman Pt.
Ethelred Estate

BELGRAVE ROAD
Lillington Gdns. Estate
Tate Gallery
Millbank Barracks
Vauxhall

WARWICK WAY
Bessborough St.
PIMLICO
BESSBOROUGH ST.
Glasshouse Walk

GROSVENOR ROAD
Tachbrook Estate
R.H.M. Centre
VAUXHALL BRIDGE
Bridgefoot
KENNINGTON LANE

Churchill Gardens Estate
Pimlico Gardens
VAUXHALL
HARLEYFORD RD.
The Oval (Surrey County Cricket Ground)

4

Dinorvic Wharf Boating Centre
NINE ELMS LANE
New Covent Garden Market
Vauxhall Park
KENNINGTON OVAL

Jetty   Jetty

A   **B**   **C**

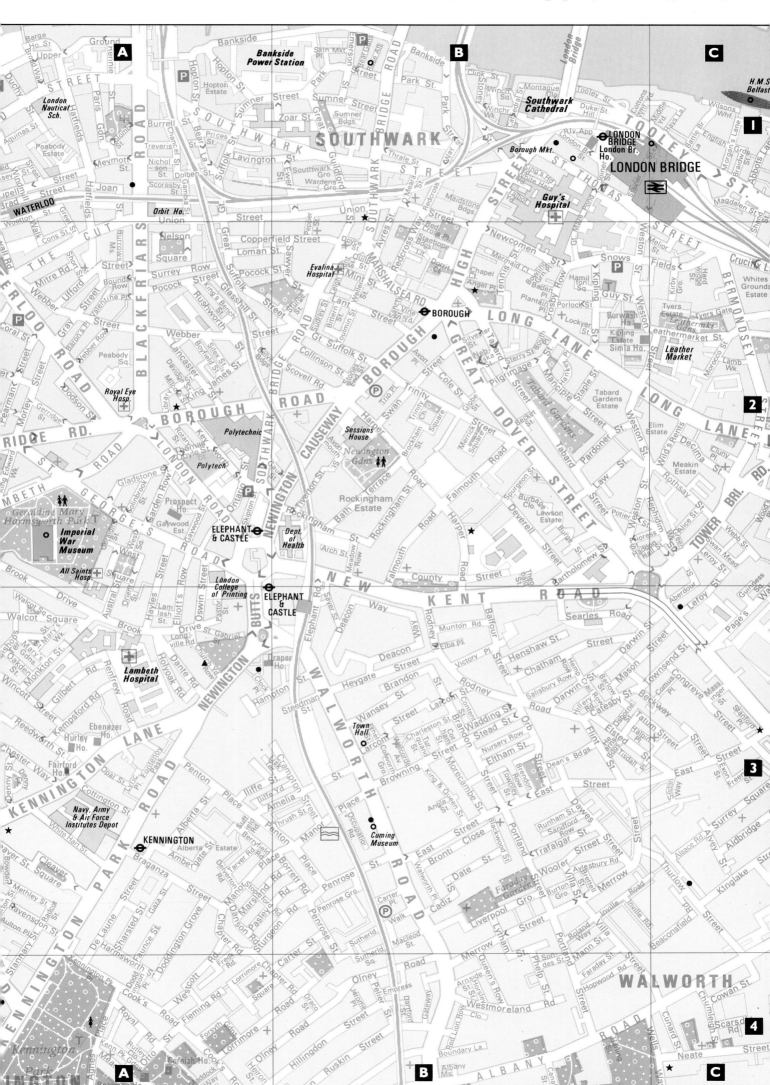

A
Abbey Gdns. 124B1
Abbey Lo. 124C2
Abbey Orchard St. 130A2
Abbey Rd. 124B1
Abbey Rd. Mans. 124B1
Abbots La. 131C1
Abchurch La. 127B4
Abercorn Clo. 124B1
Abercorn Pl. 124B2
Aberdeen Pl. 124B2
Aberdour St. 131C3
Abingdon Rd. 128A2
Abingdon St. 130B2
Abingdon Villas 128A2
Achilles Statue 129B1
Acton St. 126B2
Adam St. 126B4
Adam & Eve Mews 128A2
Adam's Row 125A4
Addington St. 130B2
Adelaide St. 126B4
Adeline Pl. 125B3
Admiralty Arch 130A1
Adpar St. 124B3
Aeolian Hall 125A4
Aer Lingus, air terminal 128A2
Agar St. 126B4
Agdon St. 126C2
Air St. 125B4
Albany, The 125B4
Albany Mews 131B4
Albany Rd. 131B4
Albany St. 125A2
Albany Ter. 125A2
Albemarle St. 125B4
Albert Embank. 130B3
Albert Gate 129A2
Albert Mem. 128B2
Albert Mews 128B2
Albert Pl. 128A2
Alberta Estate 131A3
Alberta St. 131A3
Albion Clo. 124C4
Albion Gate, Hyde Park 124C4
Albion Mews 124C4
Albion Pl. 126C3
Albion St. 124C3
Aldbridge St. 131C2
Aldenham St. 125B1
Aldermanbury 127B3
Alderney St. 129B3
Aldersgate St. 127B3
Aldford St. 125A4
Aldgate 127C3
Aldgate East Sta. 127C3
Aldgate High St. 127C3
Aldgate St. 127C3
Aldwych 126B4
Aldwych Sta. 126B4
Alexander Pl. 128C3
Alexander Sq. 128C3
Alexandra Gate 128B2
Alford St. 127B1
Alfred Mews 125B3
Alfred Pl. 125B3
Alice St. 131C2
Aliens Office 126B3
All Saints Hosp. 131A2
Allen St. 128A2
Allington St. 129B2
Allitsen Rd. 124C1
Allsop Pl. 124C2
Alma Sq. 124B1
Alma Ter. 128A2
Alpha Cl. 124C2
Alpha Pl. 129A4
Alsace Rd. 131C3
Alvey St. 131C3
Ambergate St. 131A3
Ambrosden Av. 130A2
Amelia St. 131B3
Amen Ct. 127A3
America Sq. 127C4
American Embassy 125A4
Ampton Pl. 126B2
Ampton St. 126B2
Amwell St. 126C2
Anderson St. 129A3
Andrew Borde St. 125B3
Angel Ct. 127B3
Angel Pas. 127B4
Angel Pl. 131B2
Angel Sta. 126C1
Angel St. 127B3
Angle St. 131B3
Anning St. 127C2
Ansdell St. 128A2
Ansdell Ter. 128A2
Apple Tree Td. 125B4
Appold St. 127C3
Apsley Ho. (Wellington Mus.) 129B2
Aquinas St. 131A1
Arch St. 131B2
Archbishop's Park 130B2
Archer St. 125B4
Archery Clo. 124C3
Archibald Mews 125A4
Arden Estate 127C1
Argyle Sq. 126B2
Argyle St. 126B2
Argyll Rd. 128A2
Argyll St. 125B3
Arlington St. 129C1
Arlington Way 126C2
Arne St. 126B3

Arnold Cir. 127C2
Arnside St. 131B4
Arthur St. 127B4
Artillery La. 127C3
Artillery Row 130A2
Arts Council 125B4
Arundel St. 126B4
Ashbridge St. 124C2
Ashburn Gdns. 128B3
Ashburn Mews 128B3
Ashburn Pl. 128B3
Ashby St. 127A2
Ashford St. 127C2
Ashland St. 125A3
Ashley Pl. 129C2
Ashmill St. 124C3
Ashworth Rd. 124A2
Astell St. 129A3
Astwood Mews 128C3
Atterbury St. 130B3
Attneave St. 126C2
Aubrey Pl. 124B1
Auckland St. 130B3
Augustus St. 125A1
Aulton Pl. 131A3
Austin Friars 127B3
Austin Friars Sq. 127B3
Austin St. 127C2
Austral St. 131A3
Australia Ho. 126B3
Ave Maria La. 127A3
Aveline St. 130C3
Avery Row 125A4
Avon Pl. 131B2
Avonmouth St. 131B2
Aybrook St. 125A3
Aylesbury Rd. 131B3
Aylesbury St. 126C2
Aylesford St. 130A3
Ayres St. 131B2
B
Babmaes St. 125B4
Baches St. 127B2
Baden Pl. 131B2
Bainbridge St. 125B3
Baird St. 127B2
Baker St. 124C3
Baker Street Sta. 124C2
Baker's Mews 125A3
Baker's Row 126C2
Balcombe St. 124C2
Balderton St. 125A3
Baldwin St. 127B2
Baldwin's Gdns. 126C3
Balfe St. 126B1
Balfour Pl. 125A4
Balfour St. 131B3
Baltic St. 127B2
Banner St. 127B2
Bank of England 127B3
Bank St. 127B3
Bankside 131A1
Bankside Power Sta. 131A1
Banner St. 127B2
Barbican Arts Centre 127B3
Barbican, The 127B3
Barge House St. 131A1
Barkston Gdns. 128A3
Barlow Pl. 125A4
Barlow St. 131B3
Barnby St. 125B1
Baron St. 126C1
Baroness Rd. 127C2
Barons Pl. 131A2
Barrett St. 125A3
Barrow Hill Estate 124C1
Barrow Hill Rd. 124C1
Barter St. 126B3
Bartholomew Clo. 127B3
Bartholomew La. 127B3
Bartholomew Sq. 127B2
Bartholomew St. 131B2
Barton St. 130B2
Basil St. 129A2
Basinghall Av. 127B3
Basinghall St. 127B3
Bastwick St. 127B2
Bateman Ho. 131A4
Bateman St. 125B3
Bateman's Row 127C2
Bath Pl. 127C2
Bath St. 127B2
Bath Ter. 131B2
Bathurst Mews 124B4
Bathurst St. 124B4
Battersea Wh. 129B4
Battle Bridge La. 131C1
Bayley St. 125B3
Baylis Rd. 131A2
Bayswater Rd. 124A4
Beaconsfield Rd. 131C3
Beak St. 125B4
Bear Gdns. 131B1
Bear La. 131A1
Beauchamp Pl. 129A2
Beauchamp St. 126C3
Beaufort Gdns. 129A2
Beaufort St. 128B4
Beaumont Mews 125A3
Beaumont St. 125A3
Becket St. 131B2
Beckway St. 131B3
Bedford Av. 125B3
Bedford Coll. 124C2
Bedford Ct. 126B4
Bedford Gdns. 128A1
Bedford Pl. 126B3
Bedford Row 126B3

Bedford Sq. 125B3
Bedford St. 126B4
Bedford Way 125B2
Bedfordbury 126B4
Beech St. 127B3
Beeston Pl. 129B2
Belfast, H.M.S. 131C1
Belgrave Mews,N. 129B2
Belgrave Mews,S. 129B2
Belgrave Mews, W. 129B2
Belgrave Pl. 129B2
Belgrave Rd. 129B3
Belgrave Sq. 129B2
Belgrave St. 126B2
Belgravia 129B3
Bell La. 127C3
Bell St. 124C3
Bell Wharf La. 127B4
Bell Yd. 126C3
Belvedere Bdgs. 131A2
Belvedere Rd. 130B2
Bendall Mews 124C3
Benjamin St. 126C3
Bennet's Hill 131A1
Bennett St. 129C1
Bentinck Mews 125A3
Bentinck St. 125A3
Berkeley Mews 124C3
Berkeley Sq. 125A4
Berkeley St. 125A4
Bermondsey St. 131C2
Bernard St. 126B2
Berners Mews 125B3
Berners Pl. 125B3
Berners St. 125B3
Berry Pl. 127A2
Berry St. 127A2
Berryfield Rd. 131A3
Berwick St. 125B3
Bessborough Gdns. 130A3
Bessborough Pl. 130A3
Bessborough St. 130A3
Bethnal Green Rd. 127C2
Betterton St. 126B3
Bevenden St. 127B2
Bevin Ct. 126B2
Bevin Way 126C2
Bevis Marks 127C3
Bickenhall St. 124C3
Bidborough St. 126B2
Billiter St. 127C3
Bina Gdns. 128B3
Bingham Pl. 125A3
Binney St. 125A3
Birchin La. 127B3
Bird St. 125A3
Birdcage Walk 130A2
Birkenhead St. 126B2
Bishop's Bridge Rd. 124A3
Bishop's Ter. 131A3
Bishopsgate 127C3
Bittern St. 131B2
Black Hill 126C2
Black Lion Gate 124A4
Black Prince Rd. 130B3
Blackburne's Mews 125A4
Blackfriars Bri. 126C4
Blackfriars La. 126C3
Blackfriars Rd. 131A2
Blackfriars St. 126C4
Blackfriars Tube Sta. 126C4
Blackhall St. 127C2
Blacklands Ter. 129A3
Blackwood St. 131B3
Blandford Mews 125A3
Blandford St. 124C3
Bletchley Ct. 127B1
Bletchley St. 127B1
Blithfield St. 128A2
Blomfield Rd. 124A3
Blomfield St. 127B3
Blomfield Villas 124B3
Bloomfield Ter. 129B3
Bloomsbury 126B3
Bloomsbury Pl. 126B3
Bloomsbury Sq. 126B3
Bloomsbury St. 125B3
Bloomsbury Way 126B3
Blossom St. 127C2
Bolsover St. 125A2
Bolton Gdns. 128A3
Bolton Gdns. Mews 128B3
Bolton St. 129B1
Boltons, The 128B3
Bond Ct. 127B4
Bond St. 125A4
Bond St. Sta. 125A3
Bondway 130B4
Bonhill St. 127B2
Bonnington Sq. 130B4
Boot St. 127C2
Borough High St. 131B2
Borough Mkt. 131B1
Borough Rd. 131A2
Borough Sta. 131B2
Borrett Rd. 131B3
Boscobel Pl. 129B3
Boscobel St. 124B2
Boston Pl. 124C2
Boswell St. 126B3
Botolph La. 127C4
Boundary La. 131B4
Boundary Row 131A2
Boundary St. 127C2
Bourchier St. 125B4
Bourdon St. 125A4
Bourlet Clo. 125B3
Bourne St. 129B3

Bourne Ter. 124A3
Bouverie Pl. 124B3
Bouverie St. 126C3
Bow Ch. 127B3
Bow La. 127B3
Bow St. 126B3
Bow St. Court 126B3
Bowden St. 131A3
Bowling Green La. 126C2
Bowling Green Pl. 131B2
Bowling Green St. 130C4
Bowling Green Wk. 127C2
Boyfield St. 131A2
Boyle St. 125B4
Brad St. 131A1
Braganza St. 131A3
Braidwood St. 131C1
Braithwaite Tower 124B3
Bramerton St. 128C4
Bramham Gdns. 128A3
Brandon St. 131B3
Bray Pl. 129A3
Bread St. 127B3
Bream's Bdgs. 126C3
Brechin Pl. 128B3
Bremner Rd. 128B2
Brendon Row 131B3
Brendon St. 124C3
Bressenden Pl. 129B2
Brettell St. 131B3
Brewer St. 125B4
Briant Estate 130C2
Brick La. 127C2
Brick St. 129B1
Bride La. 126C3
Bridewell Pl. 126C3
Bridford Mews 125A3
Bridge St. 130B2
Bridgefoot 130B3
Bridgeman St. 124C1
Bridgewater Sq. 127B3
Bridgeway St. 125B1
Bridle La. 125B4
Briset St. 126C2
Bristol Gdns. 124A2
Britannia St. 126B2
Britannia Wk. 127B2
Britannic Tower 127B3
British Airways Air Terminal 129B3
British Med. Assoc. 125B2
British Museum 126B3
British Steel Corp. 129B2
Britten St. 128C3
Britton St. 126C2
Broad Sanctuary 130A2
Broad Street Sta. 127C3
Broad Wk., The 124A4
Broad Wall 131A1
Broadbent St. 125A4
Broadcasting Ho. (B.B.C.) 125A3
Broadley St. 124C3
Broadley Ter. 124C2
Broadway 130A2
Broadwick St. 125B3
Brockham St. 131B2
Brompton 129A2
BromptonCem. 128A4
BromptonHosp. 128B3
Brompton Pl. 129A2
Brompton Rd. 128C3
Brompton Sq. 128C2
Bronti Clo. 131B3
Brook Dr. 131A2
Brook MewsN. 124B4
Brook St. 124B4
Brook St. 125A4
Brooke St. 126C3
Brooke's Ct. 126C3
Brooks Mews 125A4
Brown Hart Gdns. 125A4
Brown St. 124C3
Browning Clo. 124B2
Browning St. 131B3
Brownlow Mews 126B2
Brownlow St. 126B3
Brune St. 127C3
Brunswick Gdns. 128A1
Brunswick Mews 124C3
Brunswick Pl. 127B2
Brunswick Sq. 126B2
Brushfield St. 127C3
Bruton La. 125A4
Bruton Pl. 125A4
Bruton St. 125A4
Bryanston Mews E. 124C3
Bryanston Mews W. 124C3
Bryanston Pl. 124C3
Bryanston Sq. 124C3
Bryanston St. 124C3
Buck Hill Wk. 124B4
Buckingham Gate 130A2
Buckingham Palace 129B2
Buckingham Palace Gdns. 129B2
Buckingham Palace Rd. 129B3
Buckingham Pl. 129C2
Buckingham St. 126B4
Buckland St. 127B1
Bucklebury 125B2
Bucklersbury 127B3
Bucknall St. 125B3
Budges Wk. 128B1
Bulinga St. 130B3
Bulls Gdns. 129A3
Bulstrode St. 125A3

Bunhill Fields 127B2
Bunhill Row 127B2
Burbage Clo. 131B2
Burdett St. 131A2
Burge St. 131B2
Burghers of Calais 130B2
Burleigh St. 126B4
Burlington Arcade 125B4
Burlington Gdns. 125B4
Burlington Ho. (Royal Academy) 125B4
Burnsall St. 129A3
Burrell St. 131A1
Burrows Mews 131A2
Burton Gro. 131B3
Burton St. 125B2
Burton's Ct. 129A3
Burwash Ho. 131B2
Burwood Pl. 124C3
Bury Ct. 127C3
Bury Pl. 126B3
Bury St. 130A1
Bury St. 127C3
Bury Wk. 128C3
Bush Ho. 126B3
Bush La. 127B4
Bute St. 128B3
Buttesland St. 127B2
Byng Pl. 125B2
Byward St. 127C4
Bywater St. 129A3
C
Cabbell St. 124C3
Cadiz St. 131B3
Cadogan Gate 129A3
Cadogan Gdns. 129A3
Cadogan La. 129B2
Cadogan Pl. 129A2
Cadogan Sq. 129A3
Cadogan St. 129A3
Caesar St. 127C2
Cake Ho. 130A2
Cale St. 128C3
Caledonia St. 126B1
Caledonian Rd. 126B1
Callow St. 128B4
Calshot St. 126B1
Calthorpe St. 126B2
Calvert Av. 127C2
Calvin St. 127C2
Cambridge Cir. 125B3
Cambridge Gate 125A2
Cambridge Gate Mews 125A2
Cambridge Pl. 128A2
Cambridge Sq. 124C3
Cambridge St. 129B3
Cambridge Ter. 125A2
Cambridge Terrace Mews 125A2
Camden Town Hall 125B2
Camera Pl. 128B4
Camlet St. 127C2
Camomile St. 127C3
Campbell St. 124B2
Campden Gro. 128A2
Campden Hill Rd. 128A2
Campden House Clo. 128A2
Campden St. 128A1
Canal St. 131B4
Canning Pas. 128B2
Canning Pl. 128B2
Cannon Row 130B2
Cannon St. 127B3
Cannon St. Sta. 127B4
Capland St. 124B2
Capper St. 125B2
Carburton St. 125A3
Cardigan St. 130C3
Cardington St. 125B2
Carey St. 126B3
Carlisle La. 130B2
Carlisle Pl. 129C2
Carlisle St. 125B3
Carlos Pl. 125A4
Carlton Gdns. 125B4
Carlton House Ter. 130A1
Carlyle St. 128B3
Carlyle's Ho. 128C4
Carmelite St. 126C4
Carnaby St. 125B3
Caroline Ter. 129B3
Carpenter St. 125A4
Carriage Rd., The 129A2
Carter La. 127A3
Carter Pl. 131B3
Carter St. 131B4
Carteret St. 130A2
Carthusian St. 127B3
Carting La. 126B4
Cartwright Gdns. 126B2
Castellain Rd. 124A2
Castle Baynard St. 127A4
Castle La. 130A2
Castlereagh St. 124C3
Catesby St. 131B3
Cathcart Rd. 128A4
Cathedral St. 131B1
Catherine Pl. 129C2
Catherine St. 126B4
Cato St. 124C3
Catton St. 126B3
Causton St. 130A3
Cavaye Pl. 128B4
Cavendish Av. 124B1
Cavendish Clo. 124B2
Cavendish Pl. 125A3
Cavendish Sq. 125A3

Cavendish St. 127B1
Caversham St. 129A4
Caxton Hall 130A2
Caxton St. 130A2
Cayton St. 127B2
Cenotaph, Whitehall 130B2
Centaur St. 130B2
Central Criminal Ct. 127A3
Central Hall 130A2
Central London Air Terminal 129B3
Central St. 127B2
Centre Point 125B3
Chadwell St. 126C2
Chadwick St. 130A2
Chagford St. 124C2
Chalbert St. 124C1
Chalton St. 125B1
Chambord St. 127C2
Chance St. 127C2
Chancel St. 131A1
Chancery La. 126C3
Chandos Pl. 126B4
Chandos St. 125A3
Chapel Ct. 131B2
Chapel Pl. 125A3
Chapel St. 124C3
Chapel St. 129B2
Chapter Rd. 131A3
Chapter St. 130A3
Charing Cross Sta. 130B1
Charing Cross Pier 130B1
Charing Cross Rd. 125B3
Charing Cross Tube Sta. 130B1
Charles II St. 130A1
Charles Sq. 127B2
Charles St. 129B1
Charleston St. 131B3
Charlotte Rd. 127C2
Charlotte St. 125B3
Charlwood Pl. 130A3
Charlwood St. 129C3
Chart St. 127B2
Charterhouse Bdgs. 127A2
Charterhouse Sq. 127A3
Charterhouse St. 126C3
Chatham St. 131B3
Cheapside 127B3
Chelsea 129A3
Chelsea Barracks 129B3
Chelsea Bri. 129B4
Chelsea Bridge Rd. 129B3
Chelsea Coll. 128C3
Chelsea Embank. 129A4
Chelsea Gate 129A3
Chelsea Hosp. (for Women) 128B3
Chelsea Manor Gdns. 129A3
Chelsea Manor St. 129A3
Chelsea Park Gdns. 128B4
Chelsea Physic Gdn. 129A4
Chelsea Sq. 128B3
Cheltenham Ter. 129A3
Cheney Rd. 126B1
Chenies Mews 125B2
Chenies St. 125B3
Cheniston Gdns. 128A2
Chequer St. 127B2
Cherbury Ct. 127B1
Cherbury St. 127B1
Chesham Mews 129B2
Chesham Pl. 129B2
Chesham St. 129B2
Cheshire St. 127C2
Chester Clo. 129B2
Chester Clo. N. 125A2
Chester Clo. S. 125A2
Chester Gate 125A2
Chester Mews 129B2
Chester Pl. 125A2
Chester Rd. 125A2
Chester Row 129B3
Chester Sq. 129B3
Chester St. 129B2
Chester Ter. 125A2
Chester Way 131A3
Chesterfield Gdns. 129B1
Chesterfield Hill 129B1
Chesterfield St. 129B1
Cheval Pl. 129A2
Cheyne Ct. 129A4
Cheyne Gdns. 129A4
Cheyne Mews 129A4
Cheyne Row 128C4
Cheyne Walk 129A4
Chicheley St. 130B2
Chichester Rd. 124A3
Chichester St. 130A3
Child's Pl. 128A3
Child's St. 128A3
Chiltern St. 125A3
Chilworth Mews 124B3
Chilworth St. 124B3
China Walk Estate 130B2
Chiswell St. 127B3
Chitty St. 125B3
Christchurch St. 129A4
Christina St. 127C2
Christopher St. 127C2
Chrysanthemum, H.M.S. 126C4
Chumleigh St. 131C4
Church St. 124B3
Church St. Estate 124B2
Church Way 125B2
Church Yard Row 131A3

Churchill Gardens Estate 129C3
Churchill Gardens Rd. 129B3
Churton St. 130A3
Circus Rd. 124B2
City Business Lib. 127B3
City Garden Row 127A1
City of London 127B3
City of London Coll. 127B3
City Rd. 126C1
City Univ. 126C2
Clabon Mews 129A2
Clare Mkt. 126B3
Claremont Clo. 126C1
Claremont Sq. 126C1
Clarence Gdns. 125A2
Clarence Gate 124C2
Clarence Ho. 130A2
Clarence Ter. 124C2
Clarendon Clo. 124C4
Clarendon Gdns 124B2
Clarendon Gate 124C4
Clarendon Mews 124C4
Clarendon St. 129B3
Clarendon Ter. 124B2
Clareville Gro. 128B3
Clareville St. 128B3
Clarges Mews 129B1
Clarges St. 129B1
Claverton St. 130A3
Clay St. 124C3
Clayton St. 130C4
Cleaver Sq. 131A3
Cleaver St. 131A3
Clement's Inn 126B3
Clement's La. 127B4
Clenston Mews 124C3
Cleopatra's Needle 126B4
Clere Pl. 127B2
Clere St. 127B2
Clerkenwell 126B2
Clerkenwell Clo. 126C2
Clerkenwell Gr. 126C2
Clerkenwell Rd. 126C2
Cleveland Gdns. 124B3
Cleveland Mews 125B3
Cleveland Pl. 130A1
Cleveland Row 130A1
Cleveland Sq. 124B3
Cleveland St. 125B3
Cleveland Ter. 124B3
Clifford St. 125B4
Clifton Gdns. 124B2
Clifton Pl. 124C3
Clifton Rd. 124B2
Clifton St. 127C3
Clifton Villas 124B3
Clink St. 131B1
Clipstone Mews 125B3
Clipstone St. 125B3
Clive St. 124B2
Cliveden Pl. 129B3
Cloak La. 127B4
Clock Pl. 131A3
Cloth Fair 127A3
Clover Mews 129A4
Cub Row 127C2
Cluny Pl. 131C2
Cobb St. 127C3
Cobourg St. 125B2
Cochrane St. 124B1
Cock La. 126C3
Cockpit Yd. 126B3
Cockspur St. 130A1
Coin St. 131A1
Colbeck Mews 128A3
Cole St. 131B2
Colebrook St. 131A2
Colebrooke Row 126C1
Coleherne Ct. 128A3
Coleherne Mews 128A3
Coleherne Rd. 128A3
Coleman St. 127B3
Coley St. 126B2
Colinbrook St. 131A2
College Ct. 129A3
College Hill 127B4
College St. 130B2
College St. 127B4
Collier St. 126B1
Collingham Gdns. 128A3
Collingham Pl. 128A3
Collingham Rd. 128A3
Collinson St. 131B2
Colombo St. 131A1
Columbia Sq. 127C2
Colville Pl. 125B3
Colworth Gro. 131B3
Combe, The 125A2
Commercial St. 127C2
Commercial Union Assurance Bdg. 127C3
Compton Pl. 126B2
Compton St. 127A2
Comus Pl. 131C3
Concert Hall App. 130B1
Conduit Mews 124B3
Conduit Pl. 124B3
Conduit St. 125A4
Congreve St. 131B3
Connaught Clo. 124C3
Connaught Mews 124C3
Connaught Pl. 124C4
Connaught Sq. 124C3
Connaught St. 124C3
Cons St. 131A2
Constitution Hill 129B2
Content St. 131B3
Conway St. 125B2
Cook's Rd. 131A4

Coombs St. 127A1
Cooper's Row 127C4
Cope Pl. 128A2
Copperfield St. 131A2
Copthall Av. 127B3
Copthall Ct. 127B3
Coptic St. 126B3
Coral St. 131A2
Coram St. 126B2
Coram's Flds. 126B2
Cork St. 125B4
Corn Exchange 127C4
Cornhill 127B3
Cornish Ho. 131A4
Cornwall Gdns. 128A2
Cornwall Ho. 130C1
Cornwall Mews S. 128B2
Cornwall Mews Wk. 128A2
Cornwall Rd. 130C1
Coronet St. 127C2
Corporation Row 126C2
Corsham St. 127B2
Cosser St. 130C2
Cotham St. 131B3
Cottage Pl. 128C2
Cottesmore Gdns. 128A2
Cottington St. 131A3
Cotton's Gdns. 127C2
Cottons Wharf Yd. 127B4
Coulson St. 129A3
County Hall, The 130B2
County St. 131B2
Courtauld Institute Gallery 125B2
Courtauld Inst. of Art 125A3
Courtenay St. 130C3
Courtfield Gdns. 128A3
Courtfield Rd. 128B3
Cousin La. 127B4
Covent Garden 126B4
Covent Garden Sta. 126B4
Coventry St. 125B4
Coverley Point 130B3
Cowan St. 131C4
Cowcross St. 126C3
Cowley St. 130B2
Cowper St. 127B2
Cox St. 127B3
Craig's Ct. 130B1
Crail Row 131B3
Cramer St. 125A3
Crampton St. 131A3
Cranbourn St. 125B4
Cranleigh St. 125B1
Cranley Gdns. 128B3
Cranley Mews 128B3
Cranley Pl. 128B3
Cranmer Ct. 129A3
Cranwood St. 127B2
Craven Hill 124B4
Craven Hill Gdns. 124B4
Craven Hill Mews 124B4
Craven Rd. 124B4
Craven St. 130B1
Craven Ter. 124B4
Crawford Pl. 124C3
Crawford St. 124C3
Creechurch La. 127C3
Creed La. 127A3
Cremer St. 127C4
Crescent, The 127C4
Crescent Pl. 128C3
Crescent Row 127B2
Cresswell Gdns. 128B3
Cresswell Pl. 128B3
Crestfield St. 126B2
Crispin St. 127C3
Cromer St. 126B2
Crompton St. 124B2
Cromwell Gdns. 128C2
Cromwell Mews 128B3
Cromwell Pl. 128B3
Cromwell Rd. 128A3
Cromwell Tower 127B3
Crondall St. 127B1
Cropley St. 127B1
Crosby Row 131B2
Crosby Sq. 127C3
Cross Keys Clo. 125A3
Crosswall 127C4
Crown Office Row 126C4
Crucifix La. 131C2
Cruickshank St. 126C2
Crutched Friars 127C4
Cubitt St. 126B2
Culford Gdns. 129A3
Cullum St. 127C4
Culross St. 125A4
Culworth St. 124C1
Cumberland Gdns. 126C2
Cumberland Gate 124C4
Cumberland Mkt. 125A2
Cumberland St. 129B3
Cumberland Ter. 125A1
Cumberland Terrace Mews 125A1
Cuming Mus. 131B3
Cumming St. 126B1
Cunard St. 131C4
Cundy St. 129B3
Cunningham Pl. 124B2
Cureton St. 130A3
Cursitor St. 126C3
Curtain Rd. 127C2
Curzon Pl. 129B1
Curzon St. 129B1

Custom Ho. 127C4
Cut, The 131A2
Cuthbert St. 124B3
Cutler St. 127C3
Cygnet St. 127C2
Cynthia St. 126B1
Cypress Pl. 125B2
Cyrus St. 127A2
D
Dacre St. 130A2
Dalehead 125B1
Dallington St. 127A2
Dan-Air Air Terminal 129B3
Dane St. 126B3
Dansey Pl. 125B4
Danson Rd. 131A3
Dante Rd. 131A3
Danube St. 129A3
D'Arblay St. 125B3
Dartford St. 131B4
Dartmouth St. 130A2
Darwin St. 131B3
Date St. 131B3
Daventry St. 124C3
Davidge St. 131A2
Davies Mews 125A4
Davies St. 125A3
Dawes St. 131B3
Dawson St. 127C1
De Laune St. 131A3
De Vere Gdns. 128B2
De Walden St. 125A3
Deacon Way 131B3
Dean Bradley St. 130B2
Dean Farrar St. 130A2
Dean Stanley St. 130B2
Dean St. 125B3
Dean Trench St. 130B2
Deane Mews 125A3
Deanery St. 129B1
Dean's Bdgs. 131B3
Dean's Pl. 130A3
Dean's Yd. 130A2
Decima St. 131C2
Delamere Ter. 124A3
Delverton Rd. 131A3
Denbigh Pl. 130A3
Denbigh St. 130A3
Denman St. 125B4
Denmark St. 125B3
Denning Clo. 124B2
Denning Point 127C3
Denny Cres. 131A3
Denny St. 131A3
Denyer St. 129A3
Dept. of Trade 130B1
Derby St. 129B1
Dereham Pl. 127C2
Dering St. 125A3
Derry St. 128A2
Deverell St. 131B2
Devonshire Clo. 125A3
Devonshire Mews S. 125A3
Devonshire Mews W. 125A2
Devonshire Pl. 125A2
Devonshire Place Mews 125A2
Devonshire Row 127C3
Devonshire Sq. 127C3
Devonshire St. 125A3
Devonshire Ter. 124B3
Dial Walk, The 128A2
Diana Pl. 125A2
Dilke St. 129A4
Dingley Pl. 127B2
Dingley Rd. 127B2
Dinorvic Wharf Boating Centre 130A4
Diss St. 127C2
Distaff La. 127B4
Distin St. 130C3
Doctor Johnson's Ho. 126C3
Doddington Gro. 131A4
Doddington Pl. 131A4
Dodson St. 131A2
Dolben St. 131A1
Dolland St. 130B3
Dolphin Sq. 130A3
Dombey St. 126B3
Dominion St. 127B3
Donegal St. 126B1
Donne Pl. 129A3
Doon St. 130C1
Doric Way 125B2
Dorrington St. 126C3
Dorset Clo. 124C3
Dorset Estate 127C1
Dorset Mews 129B2
Dorset Pl. 130A3
Dorset Rise 126C3
Dorset Sq. 124C2
Dorset St. 124C3
Doughty Mews 126B2
Doughty St. 126B2
Douglas St. 130A3
Douro Pl. 128A2
Dove Mews 128B3
Dovehouse St. 128C3
Dover St. 125A4
Dowgate Hill 127B4
Down St. 129B1
Downing St. 130B2
Doyce St. 131B2
Draco St. 131B4
Draper Ho. 131A3

Draycott Av. 129A3
Draycott Pl. 129A3
Draycott Ter. 129A3
Drayson Mews 128A2
Drayton Gdns. 128B3
Drummond Cres. 125B2
Drummond St. 125B2
Drury La. 126B3
Dryden St. 126B3
Drysdale St. 127C2
Duchess St. 125A3
Duchy St. 131A1
Duck Island 130A2
Dudmaston Mews 128B3
Dufferin St. 127B2
Dufour's Pl. 125B3
Duke of Wellington Pl. 129B2
Duke of York St. 130A1
Duke of York's H.Q. 129A3
Duke St. 125A3
Duke St. 130A1
Duke St. Hill 131B1
Duke's La. 128A2
Duke's Mews 125A3
Duke's Pl. 127C3
Duke's Rd. 125B2
Duncan Ter. 126C1
Duncannon St. 126B4
Dunmore Point 127C2
Dunraven St. 124C4
Dunstable Mews 125A3
Dunster Ct. 127C4
Durham St. 130B3
Dyott St. 125B3
Dysart St. 127C3
E
Eagle St. 126B3
Eardley Cres. 128A3
Earl St. 127C3
Earlham St. 125B3
Earl's Ct. 128A3
Earl's Court Gdns. 128A3
Earl's Court Rd. 128A2
Earl's Court Sq. 128A3
Earl's Court Sta. 128A3
Earls Walk 128A2
Earnshaw St. 125B3
Easleys Mews 125A3
East Harding St. 126C3
East Rd. 127B2
East St. 131B3
Eastbourne Mews 124B3
Eastbourne Ter. 124B3
Eastcastle St. 125B3
Eastcheap 127C4
Easton St. 126C2
Eaton Clo. 129B3
Eaton Gate 129B3
Eaton La. 129B2
Eaton Mews N. 129B2
Eaton Mews S. 129B2
Eaton Mews W. 129B3
Eaton Pl. 129B2
Eaton Row 129B2
Eaton Sq. 129B2
Eaton Ter. 129B3
Eaton Terrace Mews 129B3
Ebenezer Ho. 131A3
Ebenezer St. 127B2
Ebor St. 127C2
Ebury Bri. 129B3
Ebury Bridge Rd. 129B3
Ebury Mews 129B3
Ebury Sq. 129B3
Ebury St. 129B3
Eccleston Bri. 129B3
Eccleston Mews 129B2
Eccleston Pl. 129B3
Eccleston Sq. 129B3
Eccleston Sq. Mews 129B3
Eccleston St. 129B2
Edge St. 128A1
Edgware Rd. 124C3
Edgware Rd. Sta. 124C3
Edinburgh Gate 129A2
Edinburgh Ho. 124A2
Edward Mews 125A3
Egerton Cres. 129A3
Egerton Gdns. 128C2
Egerton Gdns. Mews 129A2
Egerton Pl. 129A2
Egerton Ter. 129A2
Elba Pl. 131B3
Elder St. 127C2
Eldon Rd. 128A2
Eldon St. 127B3
Elephant & Castle 131A2
Elephant & Castle Sta 131A3
Elephant Rd. 131B3
Elgin Av. 124A2
Elgin Mews N. 124A2
Elgin Mews S. 124A2
Elia Mews 126C1
Elia St. 126C1
Elim Estate 131C2
Elizabeth Bri. 129B3
Elizabeth Clo. 124B2
Elizabeth Garrett Anderson Hosp. 125B2
Elizabeth St. 129B3
Elliott's Row 131A3

Ellis St. 129A3
Elm Park Gdns. 128B3
Elm Park Ho. 128B3
Elm Park La. 128B3
Elm Park Mans. 128B4
Elm Park Rd. 128B4
Elm Pl. 128B3
Elm St. 126B2
Elm Tree Clo. 124B2
Elm Tree Rd. 124B2
Elms Mews 124B4
Elsted St. 131B3
Eltham St. 131B3
Elvaston Mews 128B2
Elvaston Pl. 128B2
Elverton St. 130A3
Ely Pl. 126C3
Elystan Pl. 129A3
Elystan St. 128C3
Embankment Sta. 130B3
Emerald St. 126B3
Emerson St. 131B1
Emery Hill St. 130A2
Emperor's Gate 128A2
Empress Pl. 128A3
Empress St. 131B4
Endell St. 126B3
Endsleigh Gdns. 125B2
Endsleigh Pl. 125B2
Endsleigh St. 125B2
Enford St. 124C3
English Grds. 131C4
Ennismore Gdns. 128C2
Ennismore Gdns. Mews 128C2
Ennismore Mews 128C2
Ensor Mews 128B3
Environment, Dept. of 130A2
Epworth St. 127B2
Erasmus St. 130A3
Eros 125B4
Errol St. 127B2
Essex St. 126C4
Essex Villas 128A2
Esterbrooke St. 130A3
Ethel St. 131B3
Ethelred Estate 130B3
Europa Pl. 127B2
Euston Air Terminal 125B2
Euston Centre 125B2
Euston Rd. 125B2
Euston Sq. 125B2
Euston Sq. Sta. 125B2
Euston Sta. 125B2
Euston St. 125B2
Euston Tower 125B2
Euston Tube Sta. 125B2
Evalina Hosp. 131B2
Evelyn Ct. 127B1
Evelyn Gdns. 128B3
Evelyn Wk. 127B1
Eversholt St. 125B1
Ewer St. 131B1
Exeter St. 126B4
Exhibition Rd. 128B2
Exmouth Mkt. 126C2
Exon St. 131C3
Exton St. 130C1
Eye Hosp. 126B3
Eyre Street Hill 126C2
F
Fairford Ho. 131A3
Falconberg Mews 125B3
Falkirk Ho. 124A2
Falkirk St. 127C1
Falmouth Rd. 131B2
Fann St. 127B2
Fanshaw St. 127C2
Faraday Gdn. 131B3
Faraday St. 131B4
Farm St. 125A4
Farmer St. 128A1
Farnell Mews 128A3
Farnham Royal 130B3
Farringdon Rd. 126C2
Farringdon Sta. 126C3
Farringdon St. 127C3
Fashion St. 127C3
Faunce St. 131A3
Fawcett St. 128B4
Featherstone St. 127B2
Fellows St. 127C1
Fenchurch Av. 127C3
Fenchurch St. 127C4
Fenchurch Street Sta. 127C4
Fernsbury St. 126C2
Fetter La. 126C3
Field Ct. 126B3
Field Pl. 126C1
Finborough Rd. 128A3
Finch La. 127B3
Finsbury 126C2
Finsbury Av. 127B3
Finsbury Cir. 127B3
Finsbury Hall 127B2
Finsbury Mkt. 127C2
Finsbury Pavement 127B3
Finsbury Sq. 127B2
Finsbury St. 127B2
Fire Brigade H.Q. 130B3
First St. 129A3
Fish Street Hill 127B4
Fisher St. 126B3
Fisherton St. 124B2
Fisherton Street Estate 124B2
Fishmongers' Hall 127B4

Fitzalan St. 130C3
Fitzhardinge St. 125A3
Fitzmaurice Pl. 125A4
Fitzroy Mews 125B2
Fitzroy Sq. 125B2
Fitzroy St. 125B2
Flaxman Ter. 125B2
Fleet La. 126C3
Fleet St. 126C3
Fleming Rd. 131A4
Flint St. 131B3
Flood St. 129A3
Flood Wk. 129A4
Floral St. 126B4
Flower & Dean St. 127C3
Flower Wk., The 128B2
Foley St. 125B3
Folgate St. 127C3
Foot Hosp. 125B2
Fontenoy Pas. 131A3
Fore St. 127B3
Foreign & Commonwealth and Home Offices 130A2
Formosa St. 124A2
Forset St. 124C3
Forsyth Gdns. 131A4
Fortune St. 127B2
Foster La. 127B3
Foubert's Pl. 125B3
Foulis Ter. 128B3
Fountain St. 127C2
Fournier St. 127C3
Frampton St. 124B2
Francis St. 130A3
Franklin's Row 129A3
Frazier St. 130C2
Frederick Clo. 124C4
Frederick Rd. 131A4
Frederick St. 126B2
Freemasons' Hall 126B3
French Bdgs. 127C3
French University Coll. 128B3
Friday St. 127B4
Friend St. 126C2
Frith St. 125B3
Fulham Rd. 128B3
Fullwood's Mews 127B2
Fulton Mews 124B4
Fulwood Pl. 126B3
Furnival St. 126C3
Fynes St. 130A3
G
Galen Pl. 126B3
Galway Ho. 127B2
Gambia St. 131A1
Ganton St. 125B4
Garbutt Pl. 125A3
Garden Rd. 124B2
Garden Row 131A2
Garden Ter. 130A3
Garden Wk. 127C2
Garnault Pl. 126C2
Garnett St. 127B2
Garrett St. 127B2
Garrick Hill 127B4
Garrick St. 126B4
Gascoigne Pl. 127C2
Gasholder Pl. 130B3
Gaspar Mews 128A3
Gassiott Ho. 130B2
Gate Mews 129A2
Gate St. 126B3
Gateforth St. 124C2
Gateway 131B4
Gateways, The 129A3
Gatliff Rd. 129B3
Gaunt St. 131B2
Gayfere St. 130B2
Gaywood Estate 131A2
Gaywood St. 131A2
Gaza St. 131A3
Gee St. 127B2
Geffrye Mus. 127C1
Geffrye St. 127C1
General Lying-in Hosp. 130B2
General Post Office 127A3
Geological Museum 128B2
George St. 124C3
George Yd. 125A4
Georgina Gdns. 127C2
Gerald Rd. 129B3
Geraldine Mary Harmsworth Pk. 131A2
Geraldine St. 131A2
Gerrard St. 125B4
Gerridge St. 131A2
Gertrude St. 128B4
Gibson Rd. 130B3
Gilbert Pl. 126B3
Gilbert Rd. 131A3
Gilbert St. 125A3
Gillfoot 125B1
Gillingham Mews 129C3
Gillingham St. 129C3
Giltspur St. 127A3
Gladstone St. 131A2
Glasgow Ho. 124A1
Glasgow Ter. 129C3
Glasshill St. 131A2
Glasshouse St. 125B4
Glasshouse Wk. 130B3
Glasshouse Yd. 127B2
Glebe Pl. 128C4
Gledhow Gdns. 128B3
Glendower Pl. 128B3
Glentworth St. 124C2
Globe St. 131B2

Globe Yd. 125A3
Gloucester Gdns. 124B3
Gloucester Mews 124B3
Gloucester Mews W. 124B3
Gloucester Pl. 124C3
Gloucester Pl. Mews 124C3
Gloucester Rd. 128B2
Gloucester Rd. Sta. 128B3
Gloucester Sq. 124B3
Gloucester St. 129C3
Gloucester Ter. 124A3
Gloucester Wk. 128A2
Gloucester Way 126C2
Glynde Mews 129A2
Goding St. 130B3
Godfrey St. 129A3
Godliman St. 127B3
Golden La. 127B2
Golden La. Estate 127B2
Golden Sq. 125B4
Goldsmiths' Hall 127B3
Goodge Pl. 125B3
Goodge St. 125B3
Goodge St. Sta. 125B3
Goodman's Yd. 127C4
Goose Yd. 126C1
Gordon Hosp. 130A3
Gordon Pl. 128A2
Gordon Sq. 125B2
Gordon St. 125B2
Gore St. 128B2
Gorsuch St. 127C2
Gosfield St. 125B3
Goswell Rd. 127A2
Gough St. 126B2
Goulston St. 127C3
Gower Mews 125B3
Gower Pl. 125B2
Gower St. 125B2
Gracechurch St. 127B4
Grafton Mews 125B2
Grafton Pl. 125B2
Grafton St. 125A4
Grafton Way 125B2
Graham St. 127A1
Graham Ter. 129B3
Granby Ter. 125B1
Grand Av. 127C3
Grantham Pl. 129B1
Granville Pl. 125A3
Granville Sq. 126B2
Granville St. 126B2
Grape St. 126B3
Gravel La. 127C3
Gray St. 131A2
Gray's Inn Pl. 126B3
Gray's Inn Rd. 126B2
Gray's Inn Sq. 126C3
Grayson Ho. 127B2
Great Castle St. 125A3
Great Central St. 124C3
Great Chapel St. 125B3
Great College St. 130B2
Great Cumberland Mews 124C3
Great Cumberland Pl. 124C3
Great Dover St. 131B2
Great Eastern St. 127C2
Great George St. 130A2
Great Guildford St. 131B1
Great James St. 126B3
Great Marlborough St. 125B3
Great Maze Pond 131B2
Great Newport St. 126B4
Great Ormond St. 126B3
Great Percy St. 126B2
Great Peter St. 130A2
Great Portland St. 125A2
Great Portland St. Sta. 125A2
Great Pulteney St. 125B4
Great Queen St. 126B3
Great Russell St. 125B3
Great Scotland Yd. 130B1
Great Smith St. 130A2
Great Suffolk St. 131A1
Great Sutton St. 127A2
Great Swan Alley 127B3
Great Titchfield St. 125B3
Great Tower St. 127C4
Great Windmill St. 125B4
Greek St. 125B3
Green Hill Rents 126C3
Green Pk. 129B2
Green Park Sta. 129C1
Green St. 125A4
Green Wk. 131C2
Greenberry St. 124C1
Greencoat Pl. 130A3
Greenwell St. 125A2
Greet St. 131A1
Gregory Pl. 128A2
Grenville Pl. 128B2
Gresham St. 127B3
Gresse St. 125B3
Greville Pl. 126B2
Greville St. 126B3
Grey Eagle St. 127C2
Greycoat Hosp. 130A2
Greycoat Pl. 130A2
Greycoat St. 130A2
Grocer's Hall Ct. 127B3
Groom Pl. 129B2
Grosvenor Cotts. 129B3
Grosvenor Cres. 129B2

Grosvenor Crescent Mews 129B2
Grosvenor Gdns. 129B2
Grosvenor Gdns. Mews N. 129B2
Grosvenor Hosp. 130A3
Grosvenor Mews 125A4
Grosvenor Pl. 129B2
Grosvenor Rd. 129B4
Grosvenor Sq. 125A4
Grosvenor St. 125A4
Grotto Pl. 125A3
Grove End Rd. 124B2
Grove Gdns. 124C2
Grove Hall Ct. 124B2
Guards Chapel 130A2
Guildhall 130A2
Guildhall 127B3
Guildhall Sch. of Music 127B3
Guildhall Yd. 127B3
Guildhouse St. 129C3
Guilford St. 126B2
Guinness Sq. 131C3
Gundulf St. 130C3
Guthrie St. 128C3
Gutter La. 127B3
Guy St. 131B2
Guy's Hosp. 131B1
H
Haberdasher St. 127B2
Hackney Rd. 127C2
Haddon Hall St. 131B2
Half Moon St. 129B1
Halford Rd. 128A4
Halkin Pl. 129B2
Halkin St. 129B2
Hall Gate 124B2
Hall Pl. 124B2
Hall Rd. 124B2
Hall St. 127A2
Hall Tower 124B3
Hallam Mews 125A3
Hallam St. 125A3
Hallfield Estate 124A3
Halpin Pl. 131B3
Hamilton Clo. 124B2
Hamilton Gdns. 124B2
Hamilton Pl. 129B1
Hamilton Sq. 131B2
Hamilton Ter. 124B2
Hampstead Rd. 125B1
Hampton St. 131A3
Hanbury St. 127C3
Handel St. 126B2
Hankey Pl. 131B2
Hanover Gate 124C2
Hanover Sq. 125A3
Hanover St. 125A3
Hanover Ter. 124C2
Hanover Terrace Mews 124C2
Hans Cres. 129A2
Hans Pl. 129A2
Hans Rd. 129A2
Hans St. 129A2
Hanson St. 125B3
Hanway Pl. 125B3
Hanway St. 125B3
Harbert Rd. 124B3
Harcourt St. 124C3
Harcourt Ter. 128A3
Hardwick St. 126C2
Hardwidge St. 131C2
Hare Wk. 127C1
Harewood Av. 124C2
Harewood Row 124C3
Harley Gdns. 128B3
Harley Pl. 125A3
Harley St. 125A3
Harleyford Rd. 130B4
Harling St. 131B4
Harmsworth St. 131A3
Harold Pl. 130C3
Harp La. 127C4
Harper Rd. 131B2
Harpur St. 126B3
Harriet Walk 129A2
Harrington Gdns. 128A3
Harrington Rd. 128B3
Harrington St. 125B2
Harrison St. 126B2
Harrow Pl. 127C3
Harrow Rd. 124B3
Harrowby St. 124C3
Hart St. 127C4
Hasker St. 129A3
Hasley St. 129A3
Hastings St. 126B2
Hatfields 131A1
Hatton Gdn. 126C3
Hatton Pl. 126C3
Hatton St. 124B2
Hatton Wall 126C3
Haverstock St. 127A1
Hay Hill 125A4
Haydon St. 127C3
Haydon St. 127C4
Hayes Pl. 124C2
Hayles St. 131A3
Hayman Point 130B3
Haymarket 125B4
Hayne St. 127A3
Hays La. 131C1
Hay's Mews 129B1
Hayward Gallery 130B1
Hayward's Pl. 126C2
Headfort Pl. 129B2
Health, Dept. of 131B2

Hearn St. 127C2
Hearn's Bdgs. 131B3
Heathcote St. 126B2
Heddon St. 125B3
Heiron St. 131A4
Helmet Row 127B2
Hemp Row 131B3
Hemus Pl. 129A3
Henniker Mews 128B4
Henrietta Pl. 125A3
Henrietta St. 126B4
Henshaw St. 131B3
H.M. Stationery Office 126B3
Herbal Hill 126C2
Herbert Cres. 129A2
Herbrand St. 126B2
Hercules Rd. 130B2
Hereford Sq. 128B3
Hermes St. 126C1
Hermit St. 126C2
Herrick St. 130A3
Hertford St. 129B1
Hesper Mews 128A2
Hewett St. 127C2
Heygate St. 131B3
Hide Pl. 130A3
High Holborn 126B3
High St. Kensington Sta. 128A2
Hill Rd. 124B1
Hill St. 125A4
Hillery Rd. 131B3
Hillgate Pl. 124A3
Hillgate St. 128A1
Hillingdon St. 131B4
Hills Pl. 125B3
Hinde St. 125A3
Hispaniola 130B1
Hobart Pl. 129B2
Hocker St. 127C2
Hogarth Rd. 128A3
Holbein Mews 129B3
Holbein Pl. 129B3
Holborn 126C3
Holborn Cir. 126C3
Holborn Hall 126C3
Holborn Sta. 126B3
Holborn Viaduct 126C3
Holburn Viaduct Sta. 126C3
Holford Pl. 126B2
Holford St. 126C2
Holford St. 126C2
Holland St. 128A2
Hollen St. 125B3
Holles St. 125A3
Hollywood Rd. 128B4
Holme, The 124C2
Holyoak Rd. 131A3
Holywell La. 127C2
Holywell Row 127C2
Homeopathic Hosp. 126B3
Homer St. 124C3
Honourable Artillery Co. H.Q. 127B2
Hopkins St. 125B3
Hopton Estate 131A1
Hopton St. 131A1
Hopwood Rd. 131B4
Hornton Pl. 128A2
Hornton St. 128A2
Horse Guards' Av. 130B1
Horse Guards' Parade 125B4
Horse Guards' Rd. 130A1
Horseferry Rd. 130A2
Horsley St. 131B4
Hosier La. 126C3
Hotspur St. 130C3
Houghton St. 126B3
Houndsditch 127C3
Houses of Parliament 130B2
Howell St. 124B3
Howick Pl. 130A2
Howland St. 125B3
Howley Pl. 124B3
Hoxton Sq. 127C2
Hudson's Pl. 129B3
Hugh Mews 129B3
Hugh St. 129B3
Hull St. 127B2
Hungerford Bri. 130B1
Hunter St. 126B2
Huntley St. 125B2
Huntsworth Mews 124C2
Hurley Ho. 131A3
Hyde Pk. 124C4
Hyde Park Barracks 129A2
Hyde Park Corner 129B2
Hyde Park Cres. 124C3
Hyde Park Gdns. 124B4
Hyde Park Gardens Mews 124B4
Hyde Park Gate 128B2
Hyde Park Sq. 124C3
Hyde Park St. 124C3

I
IBM Building 130C1
Idol La. 127C4
Ifield Rd. 128A4
Iliffe St. 131A3
Iliffe Yd. 131A3
Imperial Coll. 128B2
Imperial Institute Rd. 128B2
Imperial War Mus. 131A2
India Ho. 126B4

India St. 127C3
Information Centre 124B3
Information Centre 125B3
Information Centre 126B4
Information Centre British Tourist Authority 125B4
Ingestre Pl. 125B3
Inglebert St. 126C2
Inner Circle 125A2
Inner Temple Gdns. 126C4
Insurance St. 126C2
International Press Centre 126C3
Inverness Gdns. 128A1
Inverness Mews 124A4
Inverness Pl. 124A4
Inverness Ter. 124A3
Inverness Ter. Gate 124A4
Inville Rd. 131B3
Ironmonger La. 127B3
Ironmonger Row 127B2
Irving St. 125B4
Italian Hosp. 126B3
Iverna Ct. 128A2
Iverna Gdns. 128A2
Ives St. 129B2
Ivor Pl. 124C2
Ixworth Pl. 128C3

J
James St. 125A3
James St. 126B4
Jameson St. 128A1
Jay Mews 128B2
Jermyn St. 125B4
Jerome Pl. 131B4
Jerome St. 127C2
Jewry St. 127C3
Joan St. 131A1
Jockey's Flds. 126B3
John Adam St. 126B4
John Aird Ct. 124B2
John Carpenter St. 126C4
John Islip St. 130A3
John Prince's St. 125A3
John St. 126B2
John's Mews 126B2
Johnson's Pl. 130A3
Joiner St. 131B1
Jonathan St. 130B3
Jubilee Gdns. 130B1
Jubilee Pl. 129A3
Judd St. 126B2
Junction Mews 124C3
Juxon St. 130B3

K
Kean St. 126B3
Keeley St. 126B3
Kelso Pl. 128A2
Kemble St. 126B3
Kempsford Gdns. 128A3
Kempsford Rd. 131A3
Kendall Pl. 125A3
Kendall St. 124C3
Kennings Way 131A3
Kennington 131A4
Kennington Gro. 130B4
Kennington La. 130B3
Kennington Oval 130B4
Kennington Pk. 131A4
Kennington Park Estate 131A4
Kennington Park Gdns. 131A4
Kennington Park Pl. 131A4
Kennington Park Rd. 131A4
Kennington Rd. 131A3
Kennington Sta. 131A3
Kenrick Pl. 125A3
Kensington & Chelsea Town Hall 128A2
Kensington Church St. 128A1
Kensington Church Walk 128A2
Kensington Ct. 128A2
Kensington Court Mews 128A2
Kensington Court Pl. 128A2
Kensington Gdns. 128B1
Kensington Gate 128B2
Kensington Gore 128B2
Kensington High St. 128A2
Kensington Mall 128A1
Kensington Pal. 128A1
Kensington Palace Barracks 128A2
Kensington Palace Gdns. 128A1
Kensington Palace Gr. 128A1
Kensington Pl. 128A1
Kensington Rd. 128B2
Kensington Sq. 128A2
Kenway Rd. 128A3
Kestrel Ho. 127B2
Keyworth St. 131A2
Kiffen St. 127B2
Killick St. 126B1
King & Queen St. 131B3
King Charles St. 130A2
King Edward Wk. 131A2
King Gdns. 128A2
King James St. 131A2
King John's Ct. 127C2
King Sq. Estate 127A2

King St. 130A1
King St. 126B4
King St. 127B3
King William St. 127B3
Kinglake St. 131C3
Kingly St. 125B3
King's Arms Yd. 127B3
King's Bean Ho. 127C4
King's Bench St. 131A2
King's Coll. 126B4
King's Cross Rd. 126B2
King's Cross Sta. 126B1
King's Cross Midland Sta. 126B2
King's Cross Tube Sta. 126B2
King's Head Yd. 131B1
King's Mews 126B2
King's Rd. 128B3
King's Scholar's Pas. 129C2
Kingsland Rd. 127C1
Kingsley Mews 128A2
Kingsway 126B3
Kinnerton St. 129B2
Kipling Estate 131B2
Kipling St. 131B2
Kirby Gro. 131C2
Kirby St. 126C3
Knaresborough Pl. 128A3
Knightsbridge 129A2
Knightsbridge Grn. 129A2
Knox St. 124C3
Kramer Mews 128A3
Kynance Mews 128A2
Kynance Pl. 128B2

L
Lackington St. 127B3
Lamb St. 127C3
Lamb Wk. 131C2
Lambeth 130B2
Lambeth Bri. 130B3
Lambeth High St. 130B3
Lambeth Hill 127B4
Lambeth Hosp. 131A3
Lambeth N. Sta. 130C2
Lambeth Palace 130B2
Lambeth Palace Gdns. 130B2
Lambeth Palace Rd. 130B2
Lambeth Pier 130B2
Lambeth Rd. 131A2
Lambeth Wk. 130B3
Lamb's Conduit St. 126B2
Lamb's Pas. 127B3
Lamlash St. 131A3
Lanark Pl. 124B2
Lanark Rd. 124A1
Lancaster Gate 124B4
Lancaster Gate Sta. 124B4
Lancaster Mews 124B4
Lancaster Pl. 126B4
Lancaster St. 131A2
Lancaster Ter. 124B4
Lancaster Wk. 124B4
Lancelot Pl. 129A2
Lancing St. 125B2
Land Registry 126B3
Landon Pl. 129A2
Lane, The 124B1
Lanfranc St. 131A2
Langham, The 125A3
Langham Pl. 125A3
Langham St. 125A3
Langley La. 130B4
Langley St. 126B3
Langton Clo. 126B2
Lansdowne Ter. 126B2
Lant St. 131B2
Larcom St. 131B3
Laud St. 130B3
Lauderdale Rd. 124A2
Lauderdale Tower 127B3
Launceston Pl. 128B2
Laurence Pountney La. 127B4
Laverton Pl. 128A3
Lavington St. 131A1
Law St. 131B2
Lawn La. 130B4
Lawrence La. 127B3
Lawson Estate 131B2
Laxton Pl. 125A2
Laystall St. 126C2
Leadenhall Pl. 127C3
Leadenhall St. 127C3
Leake St. 130B2
Leather La. 126C3
Leather Mkt. 131C2
Leathermarket Gdns. 131C2
Leathermarket St. 131C2
Lecky St. 128B3
Lee Ho. 127B3
Leeke St. 126B1
Lees Pl. 125A4
Leicester Pl. 125B4
Leicester Sq. 125B4
Leicester Sq. Sta 125B4
Leicester St. 125B4
Leigh Hunt St. 131B2
Leigh St. 126B2
Leinster Gdns. 124B3
Leinster Mews 124B4
Leinster Pl. 124B3
Leinster Ter. 124B4
Lennox Gdns. 129A3
Lennox Gdns. Mews 129A3

Leonard St. 127B2
Leopold Walk 130B3
Lever St. 127B2
Lewisham St. 130A2
Lexham Gdns. 128A3
Lexham Gardens Mews 128A2
Lexham Mews 128A3
Lexington St. 125B4
Leyden St. 127C3
Library St. 131A2
Lidlington Pl. 125B1
Light Horse St. 129B3
Ligonier St. 127C2
Lillie Yd. 128A4
Lillington Gardens Estate 130A3
Lillington St. 130A3
Lime St. 127C4
Limerston St. 128B4
Lincoln St. 129A3
Lincoln's Inn 126B3
Lincoln's Inn Flds. 126B3
Lindsey St. 127B3
Linhope St. 124C2
Lisk Ter. 131A3
Lisle St. 125B4
Lisson Green Estate 124C2
Lisson Gro. 124B2
Lisson St. 124C3
Litchfield St. 125B4
Little Albany St. 125A2
Little Argyll St. 125B3
Little Boltons, The 128A3
Little Britain 127A3
Little Chester St. 129B2
Little Dorrit Ct. 131B2
Little George St. 130B2
Little Newport St. 125B4
Little Portland St. 125B3
Little Russell St. 126B3
Little St. James's St. 130A1
Little Smith St. 130A2
Little Somerset St. 127C3
Little Titchfield St. 125B3
Little Trinity La. 127B4
Liverpool Gro. 131B3
Liverpool Rd. 127C3
Liverpool Street Sta. 127C3
Liverpool Street U'ground Sta. 127C3
Livonia St. 125B3
Lizard St. 127B2
Lloyd Baker St. 126C2
Lloyd Sq. 126C2
Lloyd St. 126C2
Lloyd's 127C3
Lloyd's Av. 127C3
Lloyd's Row 126C2
Lockyer St. 131B2
Lodge Rd. 124B2
Logan Mews 128A3
Logan Pl. 128A3
Lolesworth St. 127C3
Lollard Pl. 130C3
Lollard St. 130B3
Loman St. 131A2
Lombard La. 126C3
Lombard St. 127B3
London Bri. 131B1
London Bridge Ho. 131B1
London Bridge Sta. 131B1
London Bridge St. 131B1
London Bridge Tube Sta. 131B1
London College of Printing 131A2
London Gate 129B3
London Mews 124B3
London Nautical Sch. 131A1
London Rd. 131A2
London School of Economics 126B3
London St. 124B3
London Tourist Board 129B2
London Transport Museum 126B4
London Wall 127B3
London Weekend T V 130C1
Long Acre 126B4
Long La. 127A3
Long La. 131B2
Long St. 127C2
Long Yd. 126B2
Longford St. 125A2
Longmoore St. 129C3
Longridge Rd. 128A3
Longville Rd. 131A3
Lord Nelson St. 130B2
Lord's Cricket Gd. (M.C.C.) 124B2
Lorenzo St. 126B2
Lorne Cr. 124C2
Lorrimore Rd. 131A4
Lorrimore Sq. 131A4
Lost Property Off. 124C2
Lothbury 127B3
Love La. 127B3
Lower Belgrave St. 129B2
Lower Grosvenor Pl. 129B2
Lower Marsh 130C2
Lower Sloane St. 129B3

Lower Thames St. 127B4
Lowndes Clo. 129B2
Lowndes Pl. 129B2
Lowndes Sq. 129A2
Lowndes St. 129B2
Lucan Pl. 128C3
Ludgate Cir. 126C3
Ludgate Hill 126C3
Luke St. 127C2
Lumley St. 125A3
Lupus St. 129C3
Luton St. 124B2
Luxborough St. 125A3
Lyall Mews 129B2
Lyall St. 129B2
Lyons Pl. 124B2
Lyric Pl. 131A3
Lytham St. 131B3

M
Macclesfield Rd. 127B2
Macklin St. 126B3
Mackworth St. 125B2
Macleod St. 131B3
McLeod's Mews 128A2
Madame Tussauds 125A2
Maddock Way 131A4
Maddox St. 125A4
Magdalen St. 131C1
Magee St. 131A4
Maida Av. 124B3
Maida Vale 124B2
Maida Vale Hosp. 124B2
Maida Vale Sta. 124A2
Maiden La. 126B4
Maidstone Bdgs. 131B1
Makins St. 129A3
Malet Pl. 125B2
Malet St. 125B2
Mall, The 130A2
Mallord St. 128B4
Mallow St. 127B2
Malta St. 126C2
Manchester Sq. 125A3
Manchester St. 125A3
Manciple St. 131B2
Mandeville Pl. 125A3
Manette St. 125B4
Mann St. 131B3
Manor Pl. 131A3
Manresa Rd. 128C3
Mansell St. 127C3
Mansfield St. 125A3
Mansion Ho. 127B3
Mansion Ho. Sta. 127B4
Manson Mews 128B3
Manson Pl. 128B3
Maple Pl. 125B2
Maple St. 125B3
Marble Arch 124C4
Marble Arch Sta. 124C3
Marchmont St. 126B2
Margaret St. 125A3
Margaretta Ter. 128C4
Margery St. 126C2
Maria Assumpta Coll. 128A2
Mark La. 127C4
Mark St. 127C2
Market Mews 129B1
Market Pl. 125B3
Market Towers 130B4
Markham Sq. 129A3
Markham St. 129A3
Marlborough Gate 124B4
Marlborough Ho. 130A1
Marlborough Pl. 124B1
Marlborough Rd. 130A1
Marlborough St. 128C3
Marloes Rd. 128A2
Marshall St. 125B3
Marshalsea Rd. 131B1
Marsham St. 130A2
Marsland Rd. 131A3
Mart St. 126B4
Martin La. 127B4
Marylebone 125A3
Marylebone High St. 125A3
Marylebone La. 125A3
Marylebone Mews 125A3
Marylebone Rd. 124C3
Marylebone Stas. 124C2
Marylee Way 130B3
Mason St. 131B3
Mason's Arms Mews 125A3
Masons's Yd. 130A1
Massinger St. 131C3
Matthew Parker St. 130A2
Maunsel St. 130A3
Mayfair 125A4
Mayfair Pl. 129B1
May's Ct. 126B4
Mead Row 131A2
Meadow Row 131B2
Meakin Estate 131C2
Meard St. 125B3
Mecklenburgh Pl. 126B2
Mecklenburgh Sq. 126B2
Mecklenburgh St. 126B2
Medcalf Pl. 126C1
Medway St. 130A2
Melbourne Pl. 126B4
Melcombe Pl. 124C3
Melcombe St. 124C2
Melior St. 131C2
Melina Pl. 124B2

Lower Thames St. 127B4
Melton Ct. 128B3
Melton St. 125B2
Mepham St. 126B4
Mercer St. 126B3
Meredith St. 126C2
Merlin St. 126C2
Mermaid Ct. 131B2
Merrick Sq. 131B2
Merrington Rd. 128A4
Merrow St. 131B4
Methley St. 131A3
Meymott St. 131A1
Micawber St. 127B2
Michael Cliffe Ho. 126C2
Middle St. 127B3
Middle Temple La. 126C3
Middle Yd. 131C1
Middlesex Hosp. 125B3
Middlesex St. 127C3
Midford Pl. 125B2
Midhope St. 126B2
Midland Rd. 126B1
Milborne Gro. 128B3
Milcote St. 131A2
Mildmay Mission Hosp. 127C2
Miles St. 130B4
Milford La. 126C4
Milk St. 127B3
Mill Hill Pl. 125A3
Mill St. 125B4
Millbank 130B2
Millbank Barracks 130B3
Millbank Tower 130B3
Millman St. 126B2
Millner St. 129A3
Mill's Ct. 127C2
Milton St. 127B3
Milverton St. 131A3
Mincing La. 127C4
Minera Mews 129B3
Ministry of Defence 130B1
Minories 127C3
Mint St. 131B1
Mitchell St. 127B2
Mitre Rd. 131A2
Mitre St. 127C3
Molyneux St. 124C3
Monck St. 130A2
Monkton St. 131A3
Monmouth St. 126B3
Montagu Mans. 124C3
Montagu Mews 124C3
Montagu Mews S. 124C3
Montagu Mews W. 124C3
Montagu Pl. 124C3
Montagu Row 124C3
Montagu Sq. 124C3
Montagu St. 124C3
Montague Clo. 131B1
Montague Pl. 125B3
Montague St. 126B3
Montclare St. 127C2
Montford Pl. 130C3
Montpelier Mews 129A2
Montpelier Pl. 129A2
Montpelier Sq. 129A2
Montpelier St. 129A2
Montpelier Wk. 129A2
Montreal Pl. 126B4
Montrose Ct. 128B2
Montrose Pl. 129B2
Monument, The 127B4
Monument Sta. 127B4
Monument St. 127B4
Moor Ho. 127B3
Moor La. 127B3
Moore St. 129A3
Moorfields 127B3
Moorfields Eye Hosp. 127B2
Moorgate 127B3
Mora St. 127B2
Morecambe St. 131B3
Moreland St. 127A2
Moreton Pl. 130A3
Moreton St. 130A3
Moreton Ter. 130A3
Morgan's La. 131C1
Morley St. 131A2
Morocco St. 131C2
Morpeth Ter. 130A2
Mortimer Mkt. 125B2
Mortimer St. 125B3
Morton Mews 128A3
Morton Pl. 130C2
Morwell St. 125B3
Mossop St. 129A3
Motcomb St. 129B2
Mount Pleasant 126B2
Mount Pleasant Sorting Office, G.P.O. 126B2
Mount Row 125A4
Mount St. 124A4
Moxon St. 125A3
Mulberry Wk. 128B4
Mundy St. 127C2
Munster Sq. 125A2
Munton Rd. 131B3
Murphy St. 130C2
Murray Gro. 127B1
Muscovy St. 127C4
Museum of London 127B3
Museum St. 126B3
Myddelton Pas. 126C2
Myddelton Sq. 126C2
Myddelton St. 126C2
Myrtle Wk. 127C1

N
Nassau St. 125B3
National Army Mus. 129A4
National Coal Board 129B1
National Film Thea. 126B4
National Gallery 125B4
National Hosp. 126B2
National Portrait Gallery 125B4
National Temperance Hosp. 125B2
National Westminster Ba... 127B3
National Westminster Tower 127C3
Natural History Mus. 128B2
Navarre St. 127C2
Navy, Army & Air Force Institutes Depot 131A3
Neal St 126B3
Neate St. 131C4
Nebraska St. 131B2
Nelson Pl. 127A1
Nelson Sq. 131A2
Nelson Ter. 127A1
Nelson's Column 125B4
Netherton Gro. 128B4
Netley St. 125B2
Nevern Pl. 128A3
Nevern Rd. 128A3
Nevern Sq. 128A3
Neville St. 128B3
Neville Ter. 128B3
New Bond St. 125A3
New Bridge St. 126C3
New Broad St. 127B3
New Burlington Pl. 125B...
New Burlington St. 125B...
New Cavendish St. 125A...
New Change 127B3
New Compton St. 125B3
New Covent Garden Market 130A4
New Fetter La. 126C3
New Goulston St. 127C3
New Inn St. 127C2
New Inn Yd. 127C2
New Kent Rd. 131B3
New Lo.(Regents Park) 125A2
New Lo. (Hyde Park) 124C4
New North Pl. 127C2
New North Rd. 127B1
New North St. 126B3
New Oxford St. 125B3
New Quebec St. 124C3
New Row 126B4
New Scotland Yd. 130A...
New Sq. 126C3
New St. 127C3
New Street Sq. 126C3
New Union St. 127B3
New Zealand Ho. 130A1
Newburgh St. 125B3
Newburn St. 130B3
Newcastle Pl. 124B3
Newcombe St. 128A1
Newcomen St. 131B2
Newcourt St. 124C1
Newgate St. 127A3
Newington 131B3
Newington Butts 131A3
Newington Causeway 131B2
Newington Gdns. 131B2
Newman Pas. 125B3
Newman St. 125B3
Newnham Ter. 130C2
Newport St. 130B3
Newport St. 125B4
Newport St. 130B3
Newton St. 126B3
Nicholson St. 131A1
Nile St. 127B2
Nine Elms La. 130A4
Noble St. 127B3
Noel St. 125B3
Norfolk Cres. 124C3
Norfolk Pl. 124B3
Norfolk Row 130B3
Norfolk Sq. 124B3
Norman St. 127B2
North Audley St. 125A4
North Bank 124C2
North Cres. 125B3
North Flower Wk. 124B...
North Gower St. 125B2
North Mews 126B2
North Ride 124C4
North Row 124C4
North Ter. 128C2
North Walk 124B4
North Wharf Rd. 124B3
Northampton Rd. 126C2
Northampton Sq. 126C2
Northburgh St. 127A2
Northdown St. 126B1
Northington St. 126B2
Northumberland Av. 130B1
Northumberland Av. 127C3
Northumberland St. 130...
Northwick Clo. 124B2
Northwick Ter. 124B2
Norton Folgate 127C3
Norwich St. 126C3
Notting Hill Gate 128A1

Notting Hill Gate Sta. 128A1
Nottingham Pl. 125A3
Nottingham St. 125A3
Nuffield Foundation 124C2
Nugent Ter. 124B1
Nursery Row 131B3
Nutford Pl. 124C3
O
Oak Tree Rd. 124C2
Oakden St. 131A3
Oakley Gdns. 129A4
Oakley St. 128C4
Oat La. 127B3
Observatory Gdns. 128A2
Occupation Rd. 131B3
Ogle St. 125B3
Old Bailey 126C3
Old Billingsgate Mkt. 127C4
Old Bond St. 125B4
Old Broad St. 127B3
Old Brompton Rd. 128A3
Old Burlington St. 125B4
Old Castle St. 127C3
Old Cavendish St. 125B4
Old Church St. 128B3
Old Compton St. 125B4
Old Court Pl. 128A2
Old Gloucester St. 126B3
Old Jewry 127B3
Old King Edward St. 127B3
Old Manor Rd. 128A3
Old Marylebone Rd. 124C3
Old Nichol St. 127C2
Old Palace Yd. 130B2
Old Paradise St. 130B3
Old Park La. 129B1
Old Pye St. 130A2
Old Quebec St. 124C3
Old Queen St. 130A2
Old Sq. 126C3
Old St. 127B2
Old Street Sta. 127B2
Old Town Hall 126B3
Old Town Hall, The 126B3
Oldbury Pl. 125A3
Olney Rd. 131A4
Olympia Yd. 124A4
O'Meara St. 131B1
Omega Pl. 126B1
Ongar St. 128A4
Onslow Gdns. 128B3
Onslow Mews W. 128B3
Onslow Sq. 128B3
Ontario St. 131A2
Opal St. 131A3
Orange St. 125B4
Oratory, The 128C2
Oratory La. 128B3
Orb St. 131B3
Orbit Ho. 131A1
Orchard St. 125A3
Orchardson St. 124B2
Orde Hall St. 126B2
Orient St. 131A3
Orme Square Gate 128A1
Ormond Clo. 126B3
Ormond Mews 126B2
Ormond Yd. 130A1
Ormonde Gate 129A3
Orsett Mews 124A3
Orsett St. 130B3
Orsett Ter. 124A3
Osborne St. 131B3
Osnaburgh St. 125A2
Osnaburgh Ter. 125A2
Ossulston Estate 125B2
Ossulston St. 125B1
Osten Mews 128A2
Oswin St. 131A3
Otto St. 131A4
Outer Circle 124C2
Oval, The (Surrey C.C. Ground) 130B4
Oval Way 130B3
Ovington Gdns. 129A2
Ovington Sq. 129A2
Ovington St. 129A3
Owen's Row 126C2
Oxendon St. 125B4
Oxenholme 125B1
Oxford Cir. 125B3
Oxford Circus Sta. 125B3
Oxford Sq. 124C4
Oxford St. 124C4
Oxford St. 125B3
P
Paddington 124B3
Paddington Gr. 124B3
Paddington Green Hosp. 124B3
Paddington Stas. 124B3
Paddington St. 125A3
Page St. 130A3
Page's Wk. 131C3
Pakenham St. 126B2
Palace Av. 128A2
Palace Gdns. Mews 128A1
Palace Gdns. Ter. 128A1
Palace Gate 128B2
Palace Gr. 128A2
Palace St. 129C2
Palissy St. 127C2
Pall Mall 130A1
Pall Mall E. 130A1
Pall Mall Pl. 130A1

Palmer St. 130A2
Pan-Am Air Terminal 129B3
Pancras La. 127B3
Pancras Rd. 125B1
Panton St. 125B4
Paradise Wk. 129A4
Pardoner St. 131B2
Paris Gdns. 131A1
Park Cres. 125A2
Park Cres. Mews E. 125A2
Park Cres. Mews W. 125A2
Park La. 124C4
Park Pl. 129C1
Park Palace Villas 124B3
Park Rd. 124C2
Park Sq. 125A2
Park Square E. 125A2
Park Square Mews 125A2
Park Square W. 125A2
Park St. 125A4
Park St. 131B1
Park Village E. 125A1
Park Wk. 128B4
Park West 124C3
Park West Pl. 124C3
Parker St. 126B3
Parliament Sq. 130B2
Parliament St. 130B2
Parry St. 130B4
Pasley Rd. 131A3
Passmore St. 129B3
Passport Off. 130A2
Pastor St. 131A3
Patent Off. 126C3
Pater St. 128A2
Paternoster Row 127B3
Paternoster Sq. 127A3
Paton St. 127B2
Paul St. 127C2
Paultons Sq. 128B4
Paultons St. 128B4
Paveley St. 124C2
Pavilion Rd. 129A2
Paxton Ter. 129B4
Peabody Av. 129B3
Peabody Estate 131A1
Peabody Estate 127B2
Peabody Sq. 131A2
Pear Tree Ct. 126B3
Pear Tree St. 127B2
Pearman St. 131A2
Peel Pas. 128A1
Peel St. 128A1
Peerless St. 127B2
Pegasus Pl. 130C4
Pelham Cres. 128C3
Pelham Pl. 128C3
Pelham St. 128B3
Pelier St. 131B4
Pelter St. 127C2
Pembroke Clo. 129B2
Pembroke Rd. 128A3
Pembroke Sq. 128A2
Pembroke Villas 128A2
Penfold Pl. 124C3
Penfold St. 124B2
Peninsular & Orient Bdg. 127C3
Pennant Mews 128A3
Penrose Gro. 131B3
Penrose St. 131B3
Penton Gro. 126C1
Penton Pl. 131A3
Penton Rise 126B2
Penton St. 126C1
Pentonville Rd. 126B1
Penywern Rd. 128A3
Pepper St. 131B2
Pepys St. 127C4
Percival St. 126C2
Percy Cir. 126B2
Percy Mews 125B3
Percy St. 125B3
Peregrine Ho. 127A2
Perkin Rents 130A2
Peter Pan Statue 128B1
Peter St. 125B4
Petersham La. 128B2
Petersham Mews 128B2
Petersham Pl. 128B2
Peto Pl. 125A2
Petticoat La. 127C3
Petticoat Tower 127C3
Petty France 130A2
Petyward St. 129A3
Phelp St. 131B4
Phene St. 129A4
Phillimore Gdns. 128A2
Phillimore Pl. 128A2
Phillimore Wk. 128A2
Philpot La. 127C4
Phipp St. 127C2
Phipps Mews 129B2
Phoenix Pl. 126B2
Phoenix Rd. 125B2
Phoenix St. 125B3
Piccadilly 129B1
Piccadilly Cir. 125B4
Piccadilly Cir. Sta. 125B4
Pickard St. 127A2
Picton Pl. 125A3
Pilgrim St. 126C3
Pilgrimage St. 131B2
Pimlico 129B3
Pimlico Gdns. 130A4
Pimlico Rd. 129B3
Pimlico Sta. 130A3

Pindar St. 127C3
Pindock Mews 124A2
Pine St. 126C2
Pitfield St. 127C1
Pitt St. 128A2
Pitts Head Mews 129B1
Planetarium 125A2
Plantain Pl. 131B2
Playhouse Yd. 126C3
Plough Yd. 127C2
Plumtree Ct. 126C3
Plympton St. 124C2
Pocock St. 131A2
Poland St. 125B3
Pollen St. 125B3
Polygon Rd. 125B2
Polytechnic 125A3
Polytechnic 131A2
Polytechnic College of Architecture 125A3
Polytechnic of Central London 126B3
Pond Pl. 128C3
Ponsonby Pl. 130A3
Ponsonby Ter. 130A3
Pont St. 129A2
Pont Street Mews 129A2
Pooles Bdgs. 126C2
Porchester Gdns. 124A4
Porchester Gardens Mews 124A3
Porchester Pl. 124C3
Porchester Sq. 124C3
Porchester Ter. 124B4
Porchester Ter. N. 124A3
Porlock St. 131B2
Porter St. 124C3
Porteus Rd. 124B3
Portland Ho. 129C2
Portland Pl. 125A3
Portland St. 131B3
Portman Bdgs. 124C2
Portman Clo. 125A3
Portman Mews 125A3
Portman Sq. 125A3
Portman St. 125A3
Portpool La. 126C3
Portsea Pl. 124C3
Portsoken St. 127C4
Portugal St. 126B3
Post Office Tower 125B3
Postal Sorting Off. 125B3
Postal Sorting Off. 126B3
Potier St. 131B2
Poultry 127B3
Powis St. 126B2
Praed Mews 124B3
Praed St. 124B2
Pratt Wk. 130B3
President, H.M.S. 126C4
Price's St. 131A1
Prideaux Pl. 126B2
Primrose St. 127B2
Prince Albert Rd. 124C2
Prince Consort Rd. 128B2
Prince of Wales Gate 128C2
Prince of Wales Ter. 128A2
Princelet St. 127C3
Prince's Gdns. 128B2
Prince's Gate 128B2
Prince's Gate Mews 128B2
Princes St. 125A3
Princes St. 127B3
Princess Beatrice Hosp. 128A3
Princeton St. 126B3
Prioress St. 131B2
Priory Wk. 128B3
Procter St. 126B3
Prospect Ho. 131A2
Provence St. 127B1
Providence Ct. 125A4
Provost Estate 127B1
Provost St. 127B2
Public Records Office 126C3
Pudding La. 127B4
Purchese St. 125B1
Q
Quaker St. 127C2
Quebec Mews 125A3
Queen Alexandra's Hosp. 130B3
Queen Anne Mews 125A3
Queen Anne St. 125A3
Queen Anne's Gate 130A2
Queen Elizabeth Coll. 128A2
Queen Elizabeth Hall 130B1
Queen Mary's Gdns. 125A2
Queen Sq. 126B2
Queen St. 126B3
Queen Street Mayfair 129B1
Queen Street Pl. 127B4
Queen Victoria Mem. 129C2
Queen Victoria St. 127A4
Queenhithe Dock 127B4
Queen's Elm Sq. 128B3
Queen's Gallery 129B2
Queen's Gdns. 124B4
Queen's Gate 128B2
Queen's Gate Gdns. 128B2
Queen's Gate Mews 128B2

Queen's Gate Pl. 128B2
Queen's Gate Place Mews 128B2
Queen's Gate Ter. 128B2
Queen's Row 131B4
Queen's Wk., The 129C1
Queensberry Mews W. 128B3
Queensberry Pl. 128B3
Queensberry Way 128B3
Queensborough Pas. 124B4
Queensborough Ter. 124B4
Queensway 124A4
Quick St. 126C1
Quilp St. 131B2
R
Rabbit Row 128A1
Radcot St. 131A3
Radley Mews 128A2
Radnor Mews 124B3
Radnor Pl. 124C3
Radnor St. 127B2
Radnor Wk. 129A3
Railway App. 131B1
Railway St. 126B1
Rainsford St. 124C3
Ralston St. 129A3
Ramillies Pl. 125B3
Ramillies St. 125B3
Rampayne St. 130A3
Randall Rd. 130B3
Randall Row 130B3
Randolph Av. 124A2
Randolph Cres. 124B2
Randolph Mews 124B2
Randolph Rd. 124B2
Ranelagh Gdns. 129B3
Ranelagh Gro. 129B3
Ranelagh Rd. 130A3
R.H.M. Centre 130A3
Ranston St. 124C3
Raphael St. 129A2
Rathbone Pl. 125B3
Rathbone St. 125B3
Ravensdon St. 131A3
Ravent Rd. 130B3
Rawlings St. 129A3
Rawstorne St. 126C2
Ray St. 126C2
Raymond Bdgs. 126B3
Red Cross Pl. 131B1
Red Lion Clo. 131B4
Red Lion Row 131B4
Red Lion Sq. 126B3
Red Lion St. 126B3
Red Pl. 125A4
Redanchor Clo. 128B4
Redburn St. 129A4
Redchurch St. 127C2
Redcliffe Clo. 128A3
Redcliffe Gdns. 128A3
Redcliffe Mews 128A3
Redcliffe Pl. 128B4
Redcliffe Rd. 128B3
Redcliffe Sq. 128A3
Redcliffe St. 128A3
Redcross Way 131B2
Redesdale St. 129A4
Redfield La. 128A3
Redhill St. 125A1
Reece Mews 128B3
Reedworth St. 131A3
Reeves Mews 125A4
Regan Way 127C1
Regency St. 130A3
Regent Sq. 126B2
Regent St. 125A3
Regent's Lo. 124C2
Regent's Park 125A2
Regent's Park Barracks 125A1
Regent's Park Sta. 125A2
Relton Mews 129A2
Remington St. 127A1
Remnant St. 126B3
Renfrew Rd. 131A3
Rennie St. 131A1
Rephidim St. 131C2
Reston Pl. 128B2
Rex Pl. 125A4
Richards Pl. 129A3
Richmond Ter. 130B2
Rickett St. 128A4
Ridgmount Gdns. 125B3
Ridgmount St. 125B3
Riding House St. 125B3
Ring, The 124C4
River St. 126C2
Rivington St. 127C2
Robert Adam St. 125A3
Robert Clo. 124B2
Robert St. 125A2
Robert St. 126B2
Roberts Pl. 126C2
Rochelle St. 127C2
Rochester Row 130A3
Rochester St. 130A2
Rockingham Estate 131B2
Rockingham St. 131B2
Rodmarton St. 124C3
Rodney Ct. 124B2
Rodney Pl. 131B3
Rodney Rd. 131B3
Rodney St. 126B1
Roger St. 126B2

Roland Gdns. 128B3
Roland Way 128B3
Roland Way 131B3
Rolls Bdgs. 126C3
Romilly St. 125B4
Romney St. 130B2
Rood La. 127C4
Roosevelt Mem. 125A4
Ropemaker St. 127B3
Rosary Gdns. 128B3
Roscoe St. 127B2
Roscoe St. Estate 127B2
Rose Alley 131B1
Rosebery Av. 126C2
Rosemoor St. 129A3
Rosoman St. 126C2
Rossmore Rd. 124C2
Rotary St. 131A2
Rothsay St. 131C2
Rotten Row 129A2
Roupell St. 131A1
Rowton Ho. 131A3
Roxby Pl. 128A4
Royal Academy 125B4
Royal Academy of Dramatic Art 125B2
Royal Academy of Music 125A2
Royal Air Force Mem. 126B4
Royal Albert Hall 128B2
Royal Army Med. Coll. 130B3
R.A.M.C. Barracks 130A3
Royal Automobile Club 125B4
Royal Av. 129A3
Royal Coll. of Arms 127B4
Royal Coll. of Art 125B2
Royal Coll. of Music 128B2
Royal Coll. of Nursing 125A3
Royal Coll. of Obstetr. & Gynaec. 124C2
Royal Coll. of Organists 128B2
Royal Coll. of Physicians 125A2
Royal Coll. of Science 128B2
Royal Coll. of Surgeons 126B3
Royal Courts of Justice 126B3
Royal Ear Hosp. 125B3
Royal Exchange 127B3
Royal Eye Hosp. 131A2
Royal Festival Hall 130B1
Royal Free Hosp. 126B2
Royal Geographical Soc. 128B2
Royal Hosp. (Chelsea) 129B3
Royal Hosp. Rd. 129A4
Royal Inst. 125A4
Royal Marsden Hosp. 128B3
Royal Mews, The 129B2
Royal Oak Ct. 127C2
Royal Opera Ho. 126B3
Royal Rd. 131A4
Royal St. 130B2
Royal Waterloo Hosp. 126B4
Royal West Hosp. 131A1
Royex Ho. 127B3
Rufus St. 127C2
Rugby St. 126B2
Runham St. 131B3
Rupert St. 125B4
Rushworth St. 131A2
Russell St. 126B2
Russell Sq. 126B2
Russell Sq. Sta. 126B2
Russell St. 126B4
Russia Row 127B3
Rutherford St. 130A3
Rutland Gdns. 129A2
Rutland Gate 128C2
Rutland Mews S. 128C2
Rutland St. 129A2
Rutley Clo. 131A4
Ryder St. 130A1
Rysbrack St. 129A2
S
Sackville St. 125B4
Sadler's Wells Theatre 126C2
Saffron Hill 126C3
Sail St. 130B3
St. Agnes Pl. 131A4
St. Alban's Gro. 128B2
St. Alban's St. 125B4
St. Alphage Ho. 127B3
St. Andrew St. 126C3
St. Andrew's Gdns. 126B2
St. Andrew's Hill 127A4
St. Andrew's Pl. 125A2
St. Anne's Ct. 125B3
St. Ann's St. 130A2
St. Barnabas St. 129B3
St. Bartholomew the Great Ch. 127A3
St. Bartholomew's Hosp 127A3
St. Bartholomew's Med. Sch. 127A2
St. Botolph St. 127C3
St. Bride St. 126C3
St. Chads Pl. 126B2
St. Chads St. 126B2

St. Clare St. 127C3
St. Clement Danes Ch. 126B3
St. Clement's La. 126B3
St. Cross St. 126C3
St. Gabriel St. 131A3
St. George St. 125A4
St. George's Dr. 129B3
St. George's Gdns. 126B2
St. George's Rd. 131A2
St. George's Sq. 130A3
St. George Sq. Mews 130A3
St. Giles High St. 125B3
St. Helen's Pl. 127C3
St. Helen's St. 131A2
St. James' Ct. 130A2
St. James's 130A1
St. James's Pal. 130A1
St. James's Pk. 130A2
St. James's Park Sta. 130A2
St. James's Pl. 130A1
St. James's Row 126B2
St. James's Sq. 130A1
St. James's St. 130A1
St. James's Wk. 126C2
St. John & St. Elizabeth Hosp. 124B1
St. John St. 126C1
St. John's Estate 127B1
St. John's Hall 125A2
St. John's La. 126C2
St. John's Sq. 126C2
St. John's Wood 124B1
St. John's Wood High St. 124C1
St. John's Wood Rd. 124B2
St. Leonard's Ter. 129A3
St. Loo Av. 129A4
St. Luke's 127B2
St. Luke's Estate 127B2
St. Luke's Hosp. 128C3
St. Luke's St. 129A3
St. Margaret St. 130B2
St. Margaret's Ch. 130B2
St. Mark's Hosp. 127A2
St. Martin-in-the-Fields 126B4
St. Martin's La. 126B4
St. Martin's-le-Grand 127B3
St. Martin's St. 125B4
St. Mary's Abbot's Hosp. 128A2
St. Mary-at-Hill 127C4
St. Mary Axe 127B3
St. Mary's Gdns. 131A3
St. Mary's Hosp. 124B3
St. Mary's Mans. 124B3
St. Mary's Sq. 124B3
St. Mary's Ter. 124B3
St. Mary's Wk. 131A3
St. Matthew's Hosp. 127B2
St. Michael's St. 124B3
St. Oswald's Pl. 130B3
St. Pancras 126B2
St. Pancras Sta. 126B1
St. Pancras Tube Sta. 126B2
St. Paul's Cath. 127B3
St. Paul's Churchyard 127A3
St. Paul's Sta. 127B3
St. Stephen's Hosp. 128B4
St. Swithin's La. 127B4
St. Thomas St. 131B1
St. Thomas's Hosp. 130B2
St. Thomas's Medical Sch. 130B2
St. Vincent St. 125A3
Salamanca Pl. 130B3
Salamanca St. 130B3
Sale Pl. 124C3
Salisbury Ct. 126C3
Salisbury Pl. 124C3
Salisbury Row 131B3
Salisbury St. 124C2
Samaritan Hosp. 124C3
Samford St. 124C2
Sancroft St. 130B3
Sanctuary St. 131B2
Sandell St. 131A2
Sandford Row 131B3
Sandland St. 126B3
Sandwich St. 126B2
Sandy's Row 127C3
Sans Walk 126C2
Sarah St. 127C2
Sardinia St. 126B3
Saunders St. 130C3
Savage Gdns. 127C4
Savile Row 125B4
Savoy Hill 126B4
Savoy Pl. 126B4
Savoy St. 126B4
Sawyer St. 131B2
Sayer St. 131B3
Scala St. 125B3
Scarsdale Rd. 131C4
Scarsdale Villas 128A2
School of Pharmacy 126B2
Science Museum 128B2
Sclater St. 127C2
Scoresby St. 131A1
Scott Ellis Gdns. 124B2

Scott's Discovery 131C1
Scovell Rd. 131B2
Scrutton St. 127C2
Seacoal La. 126C3
Seaford St. 126B2
Seagrave Rd. 128A4
Searles Rd. 131B3
Sebastian St. 127A2
Sedan Way 131C3
Seething La. 127C4
Sekforde St. 126C2
Selwood Pl. 128B3
Semley Pl. 129B3
Serle St. 126B3
Serpentine Bri. 128B1
Serpentine Gallery 128B2
Serpentine Rd. 129A1
Sessions Ho. 131B2
Seville St. 129A2
Seward St. 127A2
Seymour Mews 125A3
Seymour Pl. 124C3
Seymour St. 124C3
Seymour Wk. 128B4
Shaftesbury Av. 125B4
Shaftesbury Mews 128A2
Shaftesbury St. 127B1
Shafto Mews 129A2
Shakespeare Tower 127B3
Shand St. 131C2
Sharsted St. 131A3
Shawfield St. 129A3
Sheffield Ter. 128A1
Shell Centre Tower 130B2
Shell Centre 130B1
Shell Mex Ho. 126B4
Shelton St. 125B3
Shenfield St. 127C1
Shepherd Mkt. 129B1
Shepherdess Wk. 127B1
Sherwood St. 125B4
Shillibeer Pl. 124C3
Shoe La. 126C3
Shoreditch 127C2
Shoreditch High St. 127C2
Short St. 131A2
Shorter St. 127C4
Short's Gdns. 126B3
Shouldham St. 124C3
Shroton St. 124C3
Sick Children, Hosp. for 126B2
Siddon's La. 124C2
Sidford Pl. 130B2
Sidmouth St. 126B2
Sidney Gro. 126C1
Silex St. 131A2
Silk St. 127B3
Silvester St. 131B2
Simla Ho. 131B2
Singer St. 127B2
Skin Market Pl. 131B1
Skinner St. 126C2
Skipton St. 131A2
Sloane Av. 129A3
Sloane Ct. E. 129B3
Sloane Ct. W. 129B3
Sloane Gdns. 129B3
Sloane Square Sta. 129B3
Sloane St. 129A2
Sloane Ter. 129B3
Smallbrook Mews 124B3
Smith Sq. 130B2
Smith St. 129A3
Smith Ter. 129A3
Smithfield Central Mkts. 126C3
Smithfield St. 126C3
Smith's Ct. 125B4
Snow Hill 126C3
Snowdon St. 127C2
Snows Fields 131B2
Soho 125B3
Soho Sq. 125B3
Soho St. 125B3
Soley Mews 126C2
Somers Cres. 124C3
Somerset Ho. 126B4
Somerstown 125B2
Sondes St. 131B4
South Africa Ho. 126B4
South Audley St. 125A4
South Bank 130B1
South Bolton Gdns. 128A3
South Carriage Drive 129A2
South Cres. 125B3
South Eaton Pl. 129B3
South End 128A2
South End Row 128A2
South Kensington 128B3
South Kensington Stas. 128B3
South Lambeth Pl. 130B4
South Molton La. 125A3
South Molton St. 125A3
South Parade 128B3
South Pl. 127B3
South Sq. 126C3
South St. 125A4
South Ter. 128C3
South Wharf Rd. 124B3
Southampton Bdgs. 126C3
Southampton Pl. 126B3
Southampton Row 126B3
Southampton St. 126B4
Southwark 131B1
Southwark Bridge 127B4

Southwark Bridge Rd. 131B1
Southwark Cath. 131B1
Southwark Gro. 131B1
Southwark St. 131A1
Southwell Gdns. 128B2
Southwick Mews 124B3
Southwick Pl. 124C3
Southwick St. 124C3
Spa Fields 126C2
Spa Green Estate 126C2
Spanish Pl. 125A3
Speakers Corner 124C4
Spear Mews 128A3
Speke's Mon. 124B4
Spencer St. 126C2
Spenser St. 130A2
Spital Sq. 127C3
Spitalfields 127C3
Spitalfields Mkt. 127C3
Sprimont Pl. 129A3
Spring Gdns. 130A1
Spring St. 124B3
Spur Rd. 130A2
Spurgeon St. 131B2
Stable Yard Rd. 130A2
Stables Way 130C3
Staff St. 127B2
Stafford Cripps Estate 127B2
Stafford Pl. 129C2
Stafford St. 125B4
Stafford Ter. 128A2
Stag Pl. 129C2
Stainer St. 127B4
Staining La. 127B3
Staircross St. 125B2
Stamford St. 130C1
Stamp Pl. 127C1
Stanford Pl. 131C3
Stanford Rd. 128A2
Stanhope Bdgs. 131B2
Stanhope Gdns. 128B3
Stanhope Gate 124C4
Stanhope Gate 129B1
Stanhope Mews E. 128B3
Stanhope Mews S. 128B3
Stanhope Mews W. 128B3
Stanhope Pl. 124C3
Stanhope St. 125B2
Stanhope Ter. 124B4
Stannary St. 131A4
Stanway St. 127C1
Staple Inn Bdgs. 126C3
Staple St. 131B2
Star St. 124B3
Star Yd. 126C3
Stead St. 131B3
Steedman St. 131B3
Stephen St. 125B3
Stephenson Way 125B2
Sterling St. 129A2
Sterry St. 131B2
Steward St. 127C3
Stewart's Gro. 128C3
Stillington St. 130A3
Stock Exchange 127B3
Stone Bdgs. 126B3
Stonecutter St. 126C3
Stones End St. 131B2
Stoney La. 127C3
Stoney St. 131B1
Stopford Rd. 131A3
Store St. 125B3
Storey's Gate 130A2
Stourcliffe St. 124C3
Strand 126B4
Stratford Av. 128A2
Stratford Pl. 125A3
Stratford Rd. 128A2
Strathearn Pl. 124C4
Strathmore Gdns. 128A1
Stratton St. 129B1
Streatham St. 126B3
Strutton Ground 130A2
Strype St. 127C3
Stukeley St. 126B3

Sturge St. 131B2
Sturgeon Rd. 131A3
Sturt St. 127B1
Sudeley St. 127A1
Sudrey St. 131B2
Suffield Rd. 131A3
Suffolk La. 127B4
Suffolk St. 125B4
Summer's St. 126C2
Sumner Bdgs. 131B1
Sumner Pl. 128B3
Sumner St. 131A1
Sun St. 127C3
Surrey Row 131A2
Surrey Sq. 131C3
Surrey St. 126B4
Sussex Gdns. 124B3
Sussex Pl. 124B3
Sussex Pl. 124C2
Sussex Sq. 124B4
Sussex St. 129B3
Sutherland Av. 124A2
Sutherland Row 129B3
Sutherland Sq. 131B4
Sutherland St. 129B3
Sutherland Wk. 131B3
Sutton Dwellings 129A3
Sutton Row 125B3
Swallow St. 125B4
Swan Ct. 129A3
Swan La. 127B4
Swan Mead 131C2
Swan St. 131B2
Swan Wk. 129A4
Swanfield St. 127C2
Swinton St. 126B2
Sydney Ct. 128B3
Sydney Mews 128B3
Sydney Pl. 128B3
Sydney St. 128C3
Sylvia Ct. 127B1
Symon's St. 129A3

T
Tabard Gdns. 131B2
Tabard Garden Est. 131B2
Tabard St. 131B2
Tabernacle St. 127B2
Tachbrook Estate 130A3
Tachbrook Mews 130A3
Tachbrook St. 130A3
Talbot Ct. 127B4
Talbot Sq. 124B3
Talbot Yd. 131B1
Tallis St. 126C4
Tamworth St. 128A4
Tankerton St. 126B2
Taplow St. 127B1
Tarver Rd. 131A3
Tate Gallery 130B3
Tattersall, P.S. 130B1
Tatum St. 131B3
Taunton Mews 124C2
Taunton Pl. 124C2
Tavistock Pl. 126B2
Tavistock Sq. 125B2
Tavistock St. 126B4
Taviton St. 125B2
Tedworth Sq. 129A3
Telephone Exchange 130A2
Telford Ter. 129C4
Temple, The 126C4
Temple Av. 126C4
Temple Ch. 126C3
Temple La. 126C3
Temple Lodge 128B1
Temple Pl. 126B4
Temple Sta. 126B4
Templeton Pl. 128A3
Tennis St. 131B2
Tenterden St. 125A4
Terminus Pl. 129B2
Thackeray St. 128A2
Thames Ho. 130B3
Thanet St. 126B2
Thavies Inn 126C3
Thayer St. 125A3

Theed St. 131A1
Theobald St. 131B2
Theobald's Rd. 126B3
Thirleby Rd. 130A2
Thistle Gro. 128B3
Thomas Doyle St. 131A2
Thoresby St. 127B2
Thorndike St. 130A3
Thorney St. 130B3
Thornhaugh St. 125B2
Thornton Pl. 124C3
Thrale St. 131B1
Thrawl St. 127C3
Threadneedle St. 127B3
Three King's Yd. 125A4
Thrush St. 131B3
Thurloe Pl. 128B3
Thurloe Sq. 128C3
Thurloe St. 128B3
Thurlow St. 131C3
Tilney St. 129B1
Tinworth St. 130B3
Tisdall Pl. 131B3
Titchborne Row 124C3
Tite St. 129A4
Tiverton St. 131B2
Tokenhouse St. 127B3
Tolmer's Sq. 125B2
Tonbridge St. 126B2
Took's Ct. 126C3
Tooley St. 131B1
Topaz St. 130B3
Topham St. 126C2
Tor Gdns. 128A2
Torrens St. 126C1
Torrington Pl. 125B2
Tothill St. 130A2
Tottenham Court Rd. 125B2
Tottenham Court Rd. Sta. 125B3
Tottenham St. 125B3
Toulmin St. 131B2
Tower Bri. App. 131C1
Tower Bridge Rd. 131C2
Tower Hill 127C4
Tower Hill Sta. 127C4
Tower of London 127C4
Tower Pier 127C4
Tower St. 126B3
Town Hall 131B3
Townley St. 131B3
Townsend St. 131C3
Toynbee Hall 127C3
Toynbee St. 127C3
Tracey St. 130C3
Trade Centre, U.S. 125A3
Trafalgar Sq. 125B4
Trafalgar St. 131B3
Traitor's Gate 131C1
Transept St. 124C3
Treasury, The 130B2
Trebeck St. 129B1
Trebovir Rd. 128A3
Tregunter Rd. 128B4
Treveris St. 131A1
Trevor Pl. 129A2
Trevor Sq. 129A2
Trevor St. 129A2
Triangle, The 127A2
Trinity Church Sq. 131B2
Trinity Coll. of Music 125A3
Trinity Ho. 127C4
Trinity Sq. 127C4
Trinity St. 131B2
Trio Pl. 131B2
Triton Sq. 125B2
Tryon St. 129A3
Tudor Pl. 125B3
Tudor St. 126C4
Tufton St. 130B2
Turk's Row 129A3
Turnmill St. 126C2

Turnpike Ho. 127A2
Turquand St. 131B3
Tybald's Estate 126B3
Tyers Estate 131C2
Tyers Gate 131C2
Tyers St. 130B3
Tyers Ter. 130B3
Tysoe St. 126C2
U
Ufford St. 131A2
Underwood St. 127B2
Union St. 131A1
Union Wk. 127C2
University Coll. 125B2
University Coll. Hosp. 125B2
University of London 125B3
University St. 125B2
Upbrook Mews 124B3
Upper Belgrave St. 129B2
Upper Berkeley St. 124C3
Upper Brook St. 125A4
Upper Cheyne Row 128C4
Upper Grosvenor St. 125A4
Upper Ground 130C1
Upper Harley St. 125A2
Upper Marsh 130B2
Upper Montagu St. 124C3
Upper Phillimore Gdns. 128A2
Upper St. Martin's La. 126B4
Upper Thames St. 127B4
Upper Wimpole St. 125A3
Upper Woburn Pl. 125B2
Uxbridge St. 128A1
V
Vale, The 128B4
Vale Clo. 128B4
Valentine Pl. 131A2
Vandon St. 130A2
Varndell St. 125B2
Vauxhall 130B3
Vauxhall Bri. 130B3
Vauxhall Bridge Rd. 130A3
Vauxhall Cross 130B3
Vauxhall Gardens Estate 130B3
Vauxhall Gro. 130B4
Vauxhall Pk. 130B4
Vauxhall Sta. 130B3
Vauxhall St. 130B3
Vauxhall Wk. 130B3
Venables St. 124B3
Vere St. 125A3
Vernon Pl. 126B3
Vernon Rise 126B2
Vernon Sq. 126B2
Verulam St. 126C3
Vestry St. 127B2
Vicarage Gate 128A2
Vicarage Gdns. 128A1
Victoria & Albert Mus. 128B2
Victoria Coach Sta. 129B3
Victoria Embank 126B4
Victoria Embank. Gdns. 126B4
Victoria Gate 124B4
Victoria Gro. 128B2
Victoria Rd. 128B2
Victoria Sq. 129B2
Victoria Sta. 129B3
Victoria St. 130A2
Victoria Tower Gdns. 130B2
Victoria Tube Sta. 129B2
Victory Pl. 131B3
Vigo St. 125B4
Villa St. 131B3
Villiers St. 126B4
Vince St. 127B2
Vincent Sq. 130A3

Vincent St. 130A3
Vincent Ter. 126C1
Vine Hill 126C2
Vine St. 127C3
Vine Yd. 131B2
Vinery Villas 124C2
Violet Hill 124B1
Virgil St. 130B2
Virginia Rd. 127C2
Viscount St. 127B2
W
Wadding St. 131B3
Wakefield St. 126B2
Wakley St. 126C2
Walbrook 127B4
Walcorde Av. 131B3
Walcot Sq. 131A4
Wallace Collection 125A3
Wallgrave Rd. 128A3
Walnut Tree Wk. 130C3
Walpole St. 129A3
Walton Pl. 129A2
Walton St. 129A3
Walworth 131B4
Walworth Pl. 131B3
Walworth Rd. 131B3
Wansey St. 131B3
Wardens Gro. 131B1
Wardour St. 125B3
Warner St. 126C2
Warren St. 125B2
Warren Street Sta. 125B2
Warrington Cres. 124B2
Warrington Gdns. 124B2
Warwick Av. 124A2
Warwick Ct. 126B3
Warwick Cres. 124B3
Warwick La. 127A3
Warwick Pl. 124B3
Warwick Rd. 128A3
Warwick Row 129B2
Warwick Sq. 129C3
Warwick Sq. 127A3
Warwick St. 125B4
Warwick Way 129B3
Water Gdns. 124C3
Watergate 126C4
Waterloo Bri. 126B4
Waterloo Bridge Ho. 130C1
Waterloo Pl. 130A1
Waterloo Rd. 131A2
Waterloo Sta. 130C2
Waterloo Underground Sta. 130B2
Waterson St. 127C2
Watling St. 127B3
Waverton St. 129B1
Webb St. 131C2
Webber Row 131A2
Webber St. 131A2
Weighhouse. St. 125A3
Weirs Pas. 125B2
Welbeck St. 125A3
Welbeck Way 125A3
Well Ct. 127B3
Wellcome Mus. 125B2
Weller St. 131B2
Wellers Ct. 126B1
Wellesley Ct. 124B2
Wellesley Ter. 127B2
Wellington, H.Q.S. 126C4
Wellington Arch 129B2
Wellington Barracks 130A2
Wellington Pl. 124B2
Wellington Rd. 124B1
Wellington Sq. 129A3
Wellington St. 126B4
Wells Mews 125B3
Wells St. 125B3
Wells Way 131C4
Wenlock Rd. 127B1
Wenlock St. 127B1
Wentworth St. 127C3
Werrington St. 125B1
Wesley's Cha. 127B2

West Brompton 128A4
West Brompton Sta. 128A3
West Central St. 126B3
West Eaton Pl. 129B3
West End Hosp. 125B3
West Halkin St. 129B2
West Harding St. 126C3
West London Air Terminal 128A3
West Mall 128A1
West Smithfield 127A3
West Sq. 131A2
West St. 125B3
West Tenter St. 127C3
Westbourne Cres. 124B4
Westbourne Gate 124B4
Westbourne St. 124B4
Westbourne Ter. 124B3
Westbourne Terrace Mews 124B3
Westbourne Terrace Rd. 124B3
Westcott Rd. 131A4
Western Hosp. 128A4
Westgate Ter. 128A3
Westland Pl. 127B2
Westmoreland Pl. 129B3
Westmoreland Rd. 131B4
Westmoreland St. 125A3
Westmorland Ter. 129B3
Weston Rise 126B2
Weston St. 131B2
Wetherby Gdns. 128B3
Wetherby Mews 128A3
Wetherby Pl. 128B3
Weymouth Mews 125A3
Weymouth St. 125A3
Weymouth Ter. 127C1
Wharf Rd. 127B1
Wharfedale St. 128A3
Wharncliffe Gdns. 124B2
Wharton St. 126B2
Wheatley St. 125A3
Wheler St. 127C2
Whetstone Pk. 126B3
Whidborne St. 126B2
Whiskin St. 126C2
Whitby St. 127C2
Whitcomb St. 125B4
White Hart St. 131A3
White Hart Yd. 131B1
White Horse St. 129B1
White Lion Hill 127A4
White Lion St. 126C1
Whitechapel High St. 127C3
Whitecross Pl. 127B3
Whitecross St. 127B2
Whitefriars St. 126C3
Whitehall 130B1
Whitehall Ct. 130B1
Whitehall Pl. 130B1
Whiteheads Gro. 129A3
White's Grounds Estate 131C2
White's Row 127C3
Whitfield Pl. 125B2
Whitfield St. 125B2
Whitgift St. 130B3

Whittaker St. 129B3
Whittington Av. 127C3
Whittlesey St. 131A1
Wickham St. 130B3
Wicklow St. 126B2
Wigmore Hall 125A3
Wigmore Pl. 125A3
Wigmore St. 125A3
Wilbraham Pl. 129A3
Wild Ct. 126B3
Wild St. 126B3
Wilds Rents 131C2
Wilfred St. 130A2
Wilkes St. 127C3
William IV St. 126B4
William Mews 129A2
William Rd. 125B2
William St. 129A2
Willow Pl. 130A3
Willow St. 127C2
Wilmington Sq. 126C2
Wilson St. 127B3
Wilsons Wharf 131C1
Wilton Cres. 129B2
Wilton Mews 129B2
Wilton Pl. 129B2
Wilton Rd. 130A3
Wilton Row 129B2
Wilton St. 129B2
Wilton Ter. 129B2
Wimpole Mews 125A3
Wimpole St. 125A3
Winchester Sq. 131B1
Winchester St. 129B3
Winchester St. 127B3
Winchester Wk. 131B1
Wincott St. 131A3
Windmill St. 125B3
Windmill Wk. 131A1
Windsor Pl. 130A3
Windsor Ter. 127B2
Wine Office Ct. 126C3
Winfield Ho. 124C2
Wingate Centre 127C4
Winsland Mews 124B3
Winsland St. 124B3
Winsley St. 125B3
Winterton Pl. 128B4
Woburn Pl. 126B2
Woburn Sq. 125B2
Wood St. 127B3
Woodbridge St. 126C2
Woodfall St. 129A3
Wood's Mews 124A4
Woodstock St. 125A3
Wooler St. 131B3
Wootton St. 131A1
Worgan St. 130B3
Wormwood St. 127C3
Worship St. 127C2
Wren St. 126B2
Wright's La. 128A2
Wyclif St. 126C2
Wyndham Mews 124C3
Wyndham Pl. 124C3
Wyndham St. 124C3
Wyndham Yd. 124C3
Wynnstay Gdns. 128A2
Wynyatt St. 126C2
Wythburn Pl. 124C3
Y
Yardley St. 126C2
Yeoman's Row 129A2
York Bridge 125A2
York Gate 125A2
York House Pl. 128A2
York Rd. 130B2
York St. 124C3
York Ter. 125A2
York Way 126B1
Y.M.C.A. 127B3
Young St. 128A2
Z
Zoar St. 131B1
Zoological Gdns. 125A1

138 Aberdeen
   Basingstoke
   Bath
   Bedford
139 Birmingham
   Blackburn
   Blackpool
140 Bournemouth
   Bolton
   Bradford
141 Brighton & Hove
   Bristol
142 Burton upon Trent
   Cambridge
   Canterbury
   Carlisle
143 Cardiff
   Chatham & Rochester
144 Cheltenham
   Chelmsford
   Chester
145 Chesterfield
   Clacton-on-Sea
   Colchester
146 Coventry
   Crewe
   Croydon
147 Darlington
   Derby
   Doncaster
   Dover
148 Dundee
   Durham
   Edinburgh
149 Eastbourne
   Exeter
   Folkestone
   Gloucester
150 Glasgow
   Great Yarmouth
   Guildford
151 Hastings & St Leonards
   Halifax
   Harwich
152 Hereford
   Huddersfield
   Ipswich
153 Inverness
   Kingston upon Hull
   Leeds
154 Leicester
   Lincoln
   Liverpool & Birkenhead
155 Luton
   Maidstone
   Manchester
156 Mansfield
   Middlesbrough
   Morecambe
   Newcastle-under-Lyme
157 Newcastle upon Tyne
   Newport
   Northampton
158 Nottingham
   Norwich
   Oxford
159 Perth
   Peterborough
   Plymouth
160 Portsmouth
   Preston
161 Reading
   Royal Leamington Spa
   Royal Tunbridge Wells
162 Salisbury
   Scarborough
   Sheffield
   Shrewsbury
163 Southend-on-Sea
   Southampton
   Stafford
164 Stirling
   Stoke-on-Trent
   Stratford-upon-Avon
   Stranraer
165 Swansea
   Swindon
166 Torquay
   Sunderland
   Warrington
167 Warwick
   Wigan
   Winchester
   Windsor
168 Wolverhampton
   Worcester
   Worthing
   York

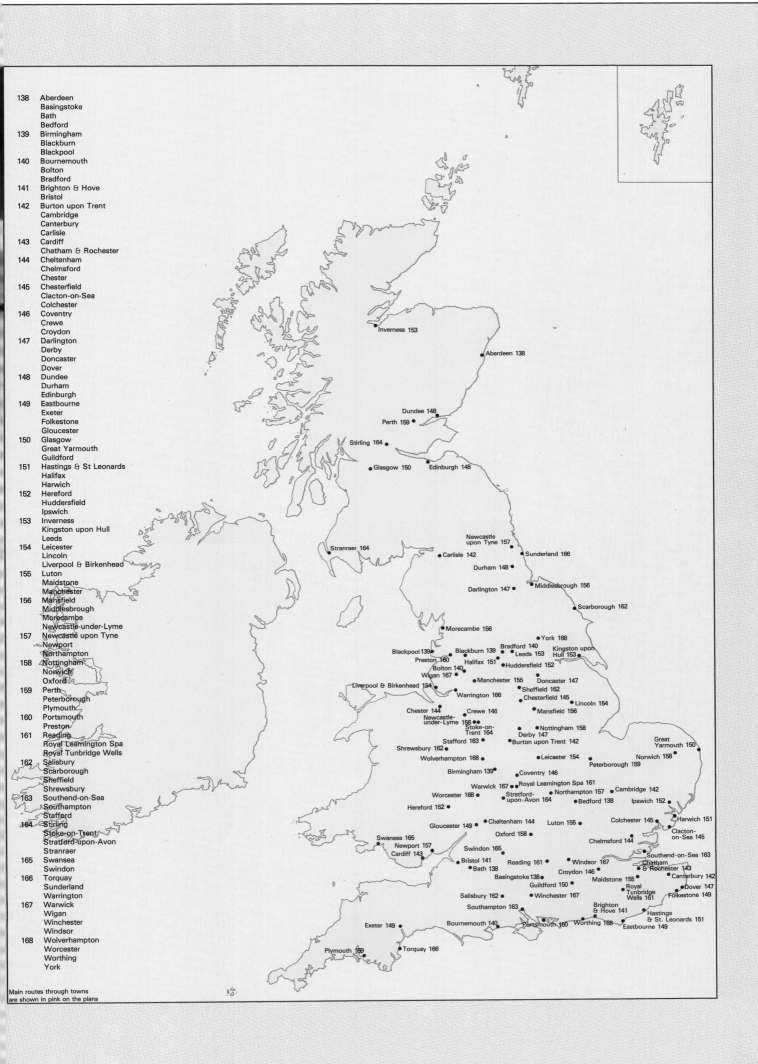

Inverness 153

Aberdeen 138

Dundee 148
Perth 159

Stirling 164

Glasgow 150   Edinburgh 148

Stranraer 164

Newcastle upon Tyne 157
Carlisle 142   Sunderland 166
Durham 148
Darlington 147   Middlesbrough 156
Scarborough 162

Morecambe 156
York 168
Blackpool 139   Blackburn 139   Bradford 140   Kingston upon Hull 153
Preston 160   Halifax 151   Leeds 153
Bolton 140   Huddersfield 152
Wigan 167
Liverpool & Birkenhead 154   Manchester 155   Doncaster 147
Warrington 166   Sheffield 162   Lincoln 154
Chester 144   Crewe 146   Chesterfield 145
Newcastle-under-Lyme 156   Mansfield 156
Stoke-on-Trent 164   Nottingham 158
Stafford 163   Derby 147
Shrewsbury 162   Burton upon Trent 142   Great Yarmouth 150
Wolverhampton 168   Leicester 154   Norwich 158
Birmingham 139   Coventry 146   Peterborough 159
Warwick 167   Royal Leamington Spa 161
Worcester 168   Stratford-upon-Avon 164   Northampton 157   Cambridge 142   Ipswich 152
Hereford 152   Bedford 138
Gloucester 149   Cheltenham 144   Luton 155   Colchester 145   Harwich 151
Oxford 158   Chelmsford 144   Clacton-on-Sea 145
Swansea 165   Southend-on-Sea 163
Newport 157   Swindon 165   Chatham & Rochester 143
Cardiff 143   Bristol 141   Reading 161   Windsor 167   Canterbury 142
Bath 138   Croydon 146   Maidstone 155   Dover 147
Basingstoke 138   Guildford 150   Royal Tunbridge Wells 161   Folkestone 149
Salisbury 162   Winchester 167   Brighton & Hove 141   Hastings & St. Leonards 151
Southampton 163   Portsmouth 160   Worthing 168   Eastbourne 149
Exeter 149   Bournemouth 140
Plymouth 159   Torquay 166

Main routes through towns
are shown in pink on the plans

MAP REFERENCES: ABERDEEN 97E3
BASINGSTOKE
BATH 21B4
BEDFORD 32B4

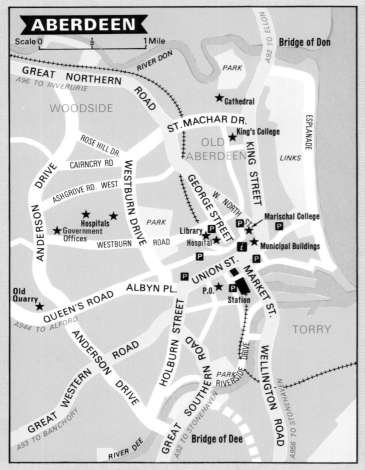

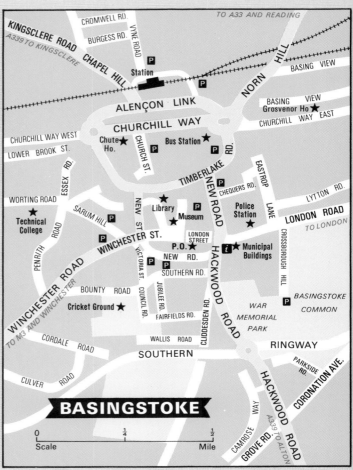

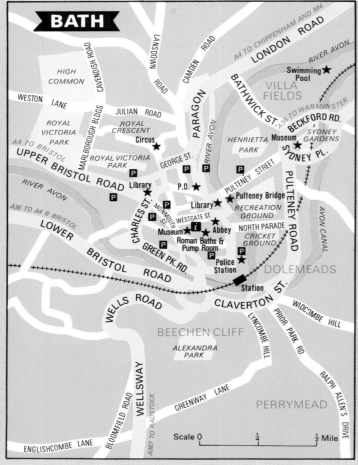

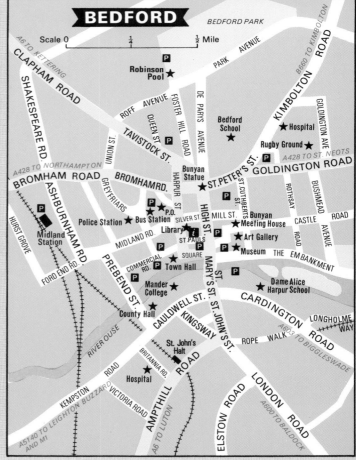

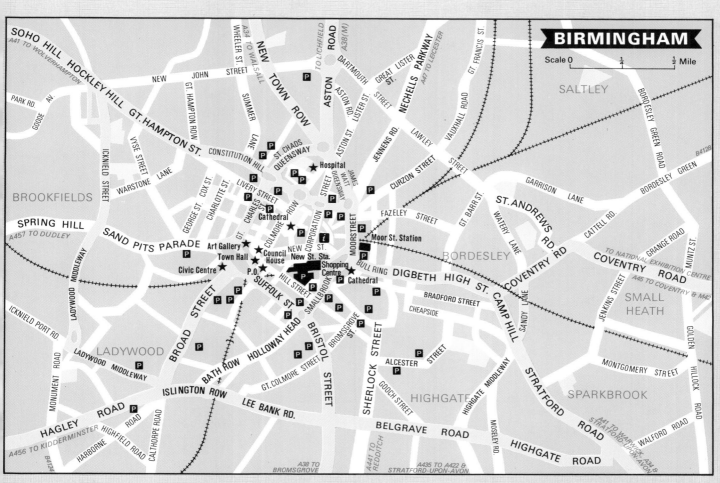

BIRMINGHAM

Scale 0   ¼   ½ Mile

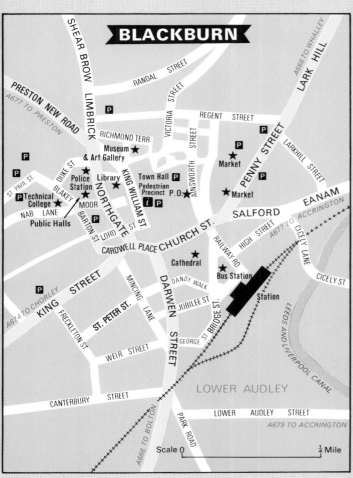

BLACKBURN

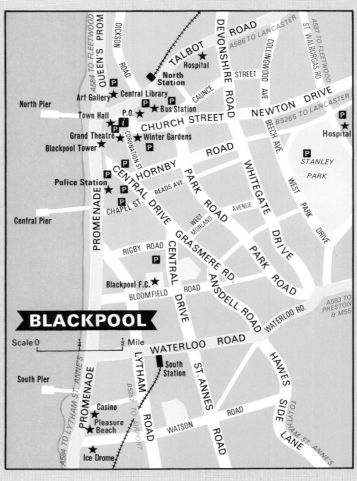

BLACKPOOL

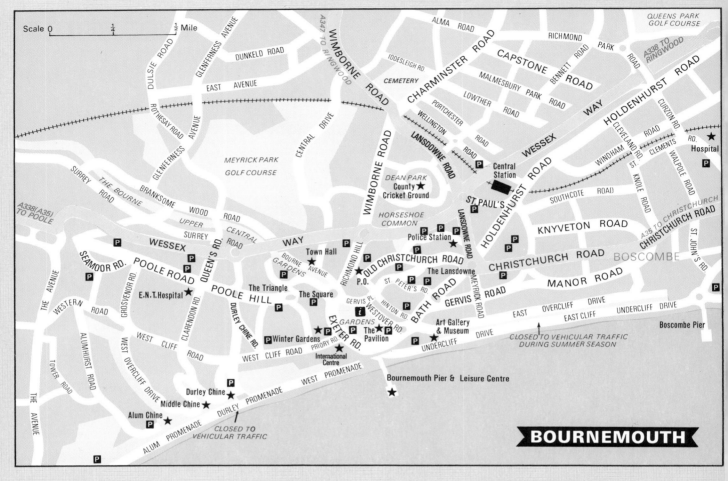

BOURNEMOUTH

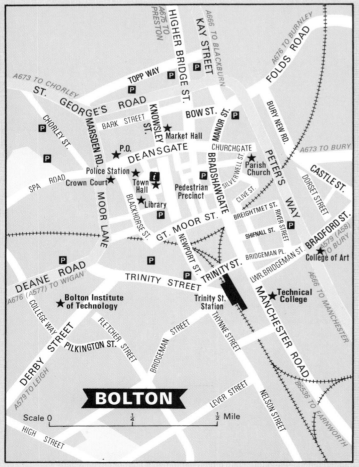

BOLTON

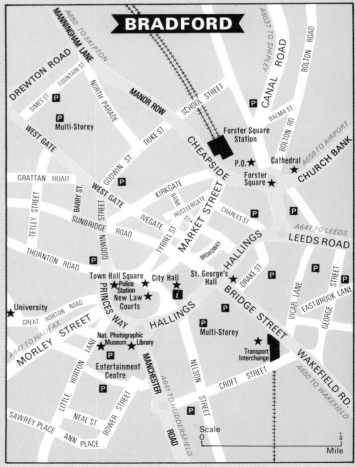

BRADFORD

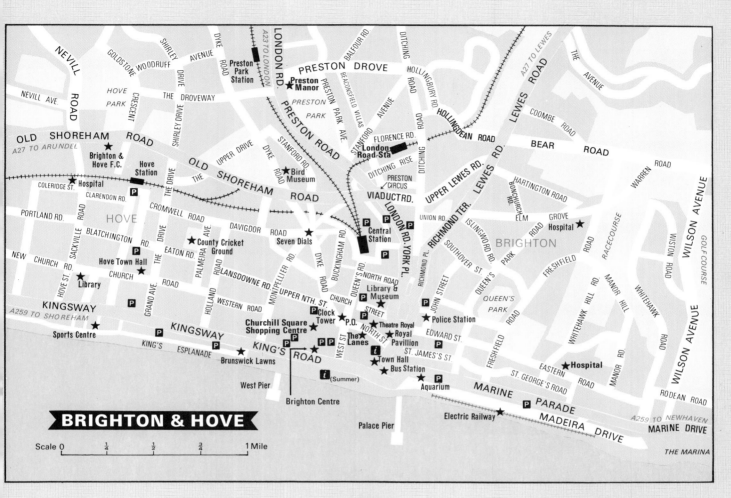

BRIGHTON & HOVE

Scale 0   ¼   ½   ¾   1 Mile

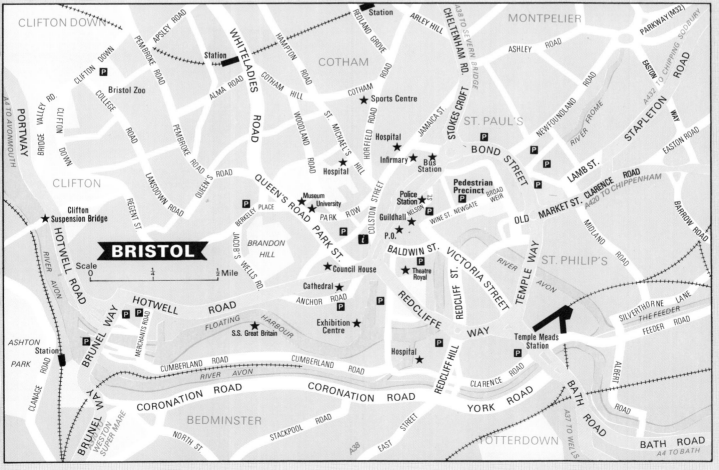

BRISTOL

Scale 0   ¼   ½ Mile

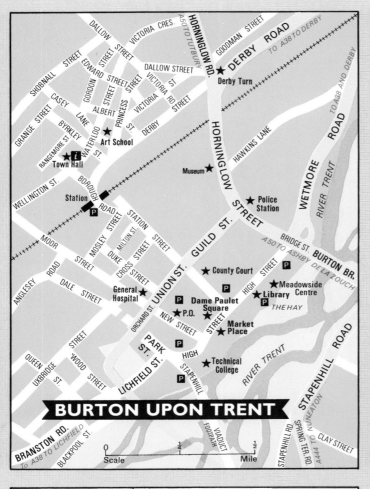

BURTON UPON TRENT

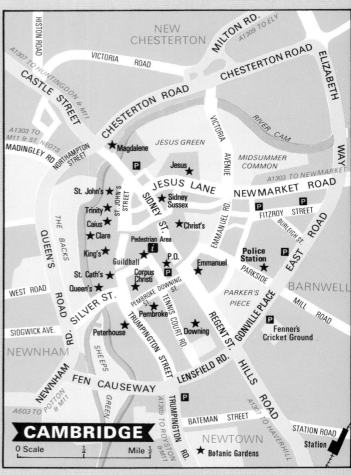

CAMBRIDGE

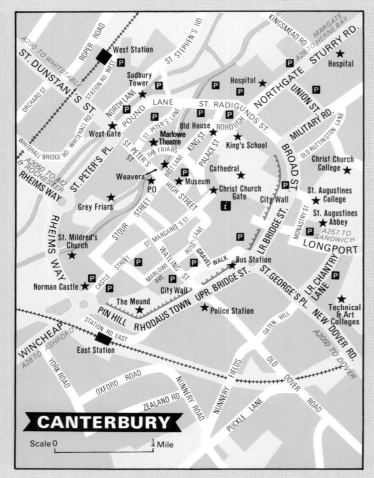

CANTERBURY

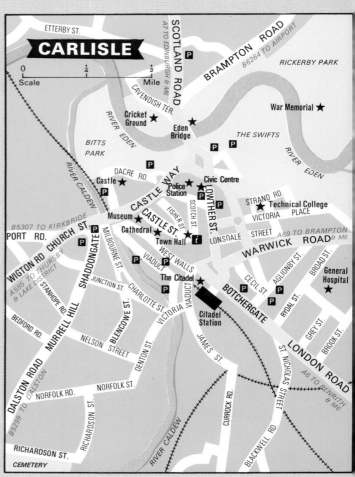

CARLISLE

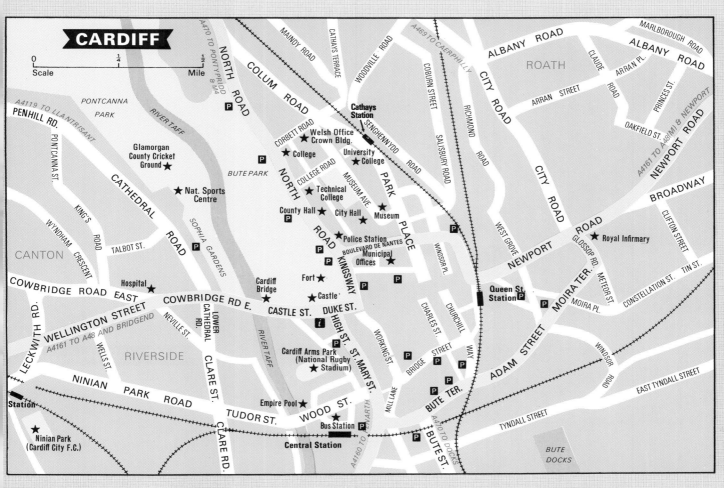

CARDIFF

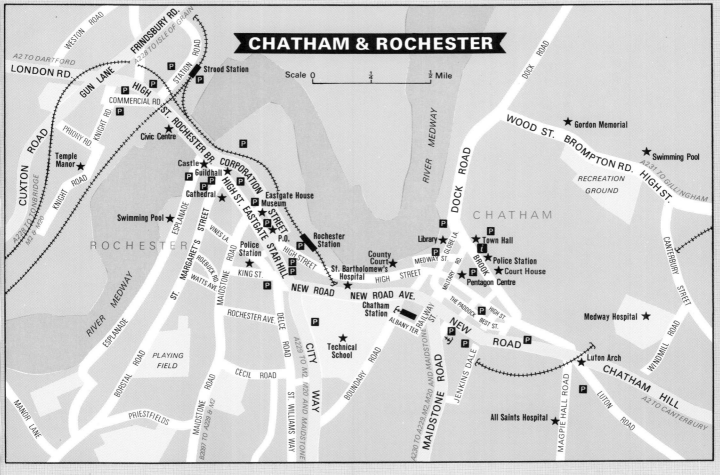

CHATHAM & ROCHESTER

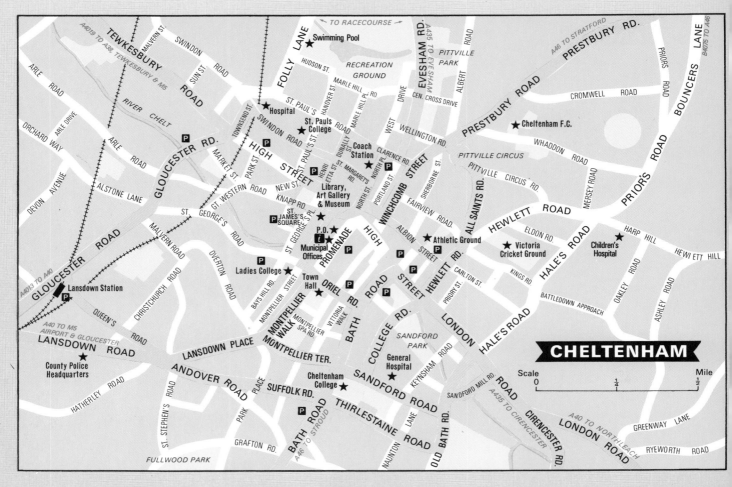

CHELTENHAM

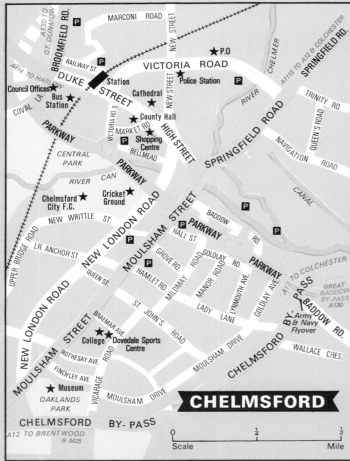

CHELMSFORD

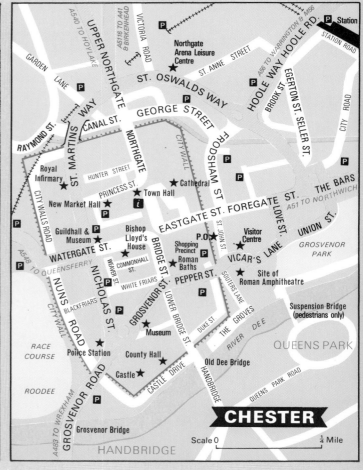

CHESTER

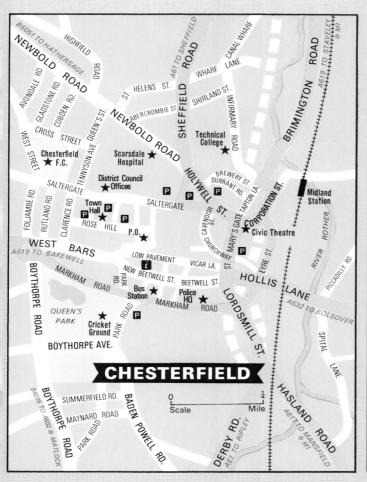

CHESTERFIELD

B6051 TO HATHERSAGE
HIGHFIELD ROAD
NEWBOLD ROAD
AVONDALE RD.
GLADSTONE RD.
COBDEN RD.
CROSS STREET
WEST STREET
Chesterfield F.C. ★
SALTERGATE
FOLJAMBE RD.
RUTLAND RD.
CLARENCE RD.
TENNYSON AVE.
QUEEN'S ST.
ST. HELENS ST.
ABERCROMBIE ST.
SHIRLAND ST.
SHEFFIELD ROAD
A61 TO SHEFFIELD
WHARF LANE
CANAL WHARF
Technical College ★
INFIRMARY ROAD
BRIMINGTON ROAD
A619 TO STAVELEY & M1
Scarsdale Hospital ★
District Council Offices ★
Town Hall P
P
Rose Hill
P.O. ★
WEST BARS
A619 TO BAKEWELL
HOLYWELL ST.
SALTERGATE
BREWERY ST.
DURRANT RD.
TAPTON LA.
ST. MARY'S GATE
CAVENDISH ST.
CHURCHWAY
VICAR LA.
CORPORATION ST.
Midland Station
Civic Theatre ★
i
LOW PAVEMENT
NEW BEETWELL ST.
BEETWELL ST.
HOLLIS LANE
EYRE ST.
RIVER ROTHER
PICCADILLY RD.
A632 TO BOLSOVER
BOYTHORPE ROAD
MARKHAM ROAD
PARK RD.
Bus Station ★
Police HQ ★
MARKHAM ROAD
LORDSMILL ST.
SPITAL LANE
HASLAND ROAD
A617 TO MANSFIELD & M1
QUEEN'S PARK
Cricket Ground ★
PARK ROAD
BOYTHORPE AVE.
SUMMERFIELD RD.
B6015 TO A632 & MATLOCK
MAYNARD ROAD
BADEN POWELL RD.
PARK ROAD
DERBY RD.
A61 TO RIPLEY

Scale 0 — ¼ Mile

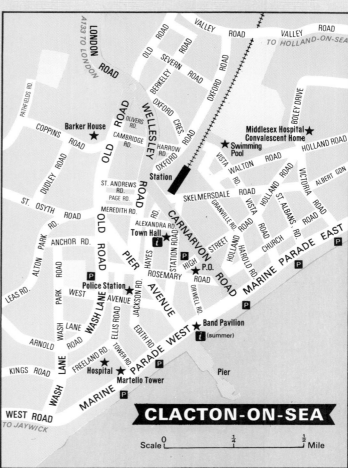

CLACTON-ON-SEA

VALLEY ROAD
VALLEY ROAD TO HOLLAND-ON-SEA
A133 TO LONDON
LONDON ROAD
OLD ROAD
SEVERN ROAD
BERKELEY ROAD
OXFORD ROAD
OXFORD ROAD
BOLEY DRIVE
PATHFIELDS RD.
COPPINS ROAD
Barker House ★
OLIVERS RD.
CAMBRIDGE RD.
WELLESLEY ROAD
HARROW RD.
OXFORD CRES.
Station
Middlesex Hospital Convalescent Home ★
Swimming Pool ★
HOLLAND ROAD
VISTA RD.
WALTON ROAD
ALBERT GDN.
DUDLEY ROAD
ST. ANDREWS RD.
PAGE RD.
SKELMERSDALE ROAD
GRANVILLE RD.
HOLLAND ROAD
VISTA ROAD
ST. ALBANS RD.
VICTORIA ROAD
ST. OSYTH ROAD
MEREDITH RD.
ALEXANDRA RD.
CARNARVON ROAD
STATION ROAD
HIGH STREET
HOLLAND RD.
HAROLD RD.
CHURCH ROAD
ALTON ROAD
ANCHOR RD.
Town Hall ★
i
HAYES RD.
ROSEMARY ROAD
P.O. ★
MARINE PARADE EAST
LEAS RD.
PARK WEST
JACKSON RD.
WASH LANE
AVENUE
PIER AVENUE
ELLIS ROAD
EDITH RD.
ORWELL RD.
P
Police Station ★
ARNOLD ROAD
WASH LANE ROAD
FREELAND RD.
TOWER RD.
Band Pavilion ★
i (summer)
KINGS ROAD
Hospital ★
Martello Tower ★
MARINE PARADE WEST
Pier
WASH LANE
MARINE PARADE WEST
WEST ROAD
TO JAYWICK

Scale 0 — ¼ — ½ Mile

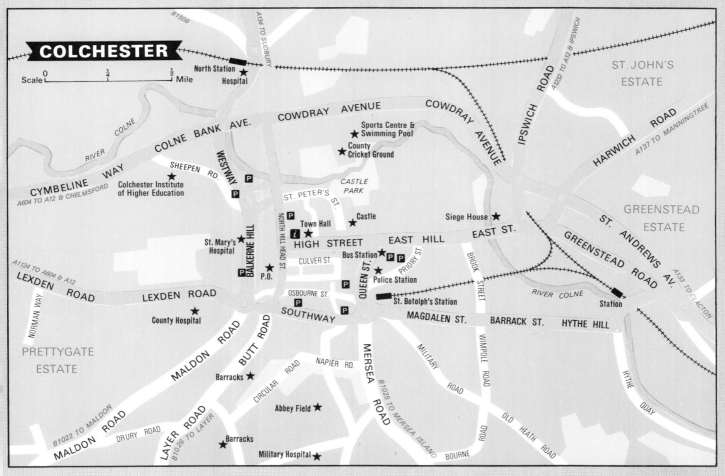

COLCHESTER

Scale 0 — ¼ — ½ Mile
B1508
A134 TO SUDBURY
A1232 TO A12 & IPSWICH
North Station ★
Hospital ★
ST. JOHN'S ESTATE
RIVER COLNE
COWDRAY AVENUE
COWDRAY AVENUE
COLNE BANK AVE.
WESTWAY
SHEEPEN RD.
P
IPSWICH ROAD
HARWICH ROAD
A137 TO MANNINGTREE
CYMBELINE WAY
A604 TO A12 & CHELMSFORD
Colchester Institute of Higher Education
P
Sports Centre & Swimming Pool ★
County Cricket Ground ★
CASTLE PARK
GREENSTEAD ESTATE
St. Mary's Hospital ★
BALKERNE HILL
ST. PETER'S ST.
Town Hall
i
Castle ★
Siege House ★
HIGH STREET
EAST HILL
EAST ST.
ST. ANDREWS AV.
A1124 TO A604 & A12
NORTH HILL
HEAD ST.
CULVER ST.
Bus Station ★
P P
GREENSTEAD ROAD
A133 TO CLACTON
LEXDEN ROAD
P.O.
QUEEN ST.
PRIORY ST.
Police Station ★
BROOK STREET
RIVER COLNE
Station
NORMAN WAY
LEXDEN ROAD
OSBOURNE ST.
SOUTHWAY
St. Botolph's Station
MAGDALEN ST.
BARRACK ST.
HYTHE HILL
PRETTYGATE ESTATE
County Hospital ★
MALDON ROAD
BUTT ROAD
NAPIER RD.
CIRCULAR ROAD
MERSEA ROAD
MILITARY ROAD
WIMPOLE ROAD
HYTHE QUAY
B1022 TO MALDON
DRURY ROAD
Barracks ★
B1025 TO MERSEA ISLAND
MALDON ROAD
LAYER ROAD
B1026 TO LAYER
Abbey Field ★
BOURNE ROAD
OLD HEATH ROAD
Barracks ★
Military Hospital ★

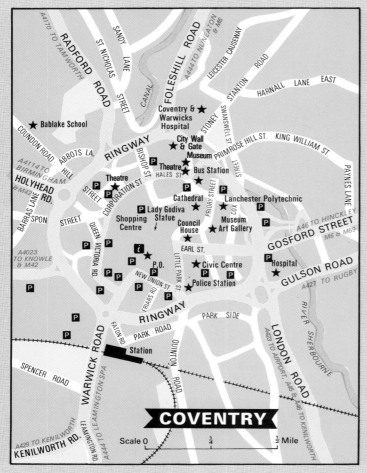

COVENTRY

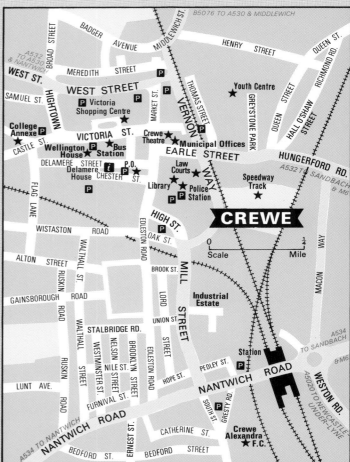

CREWE

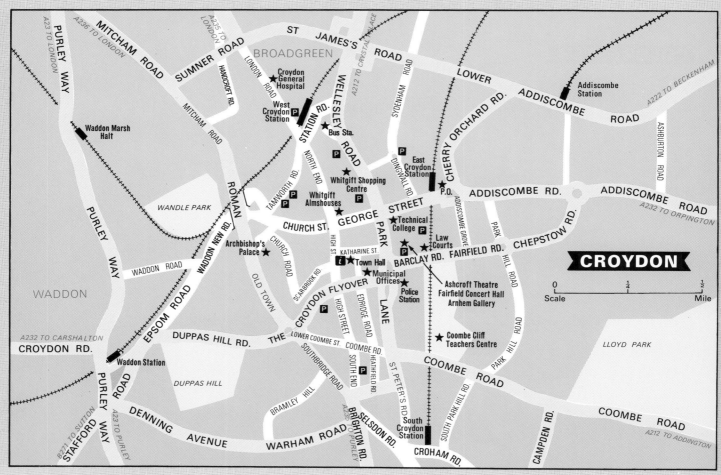

CROYDON

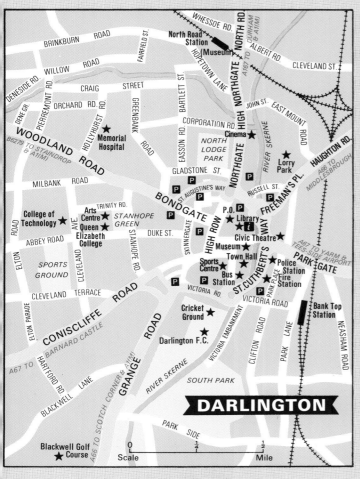

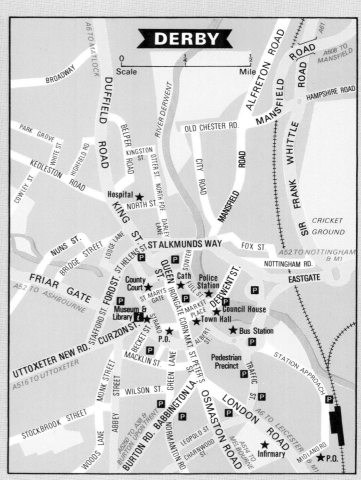

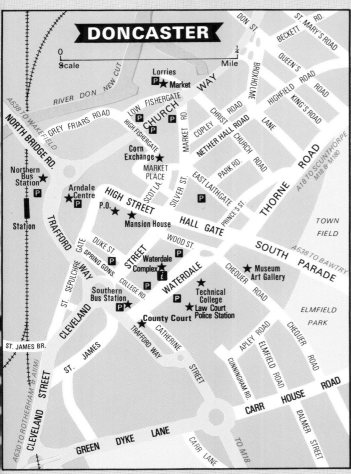

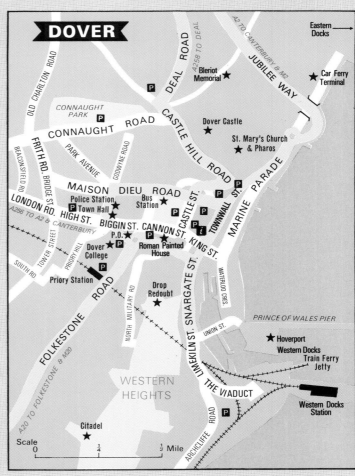

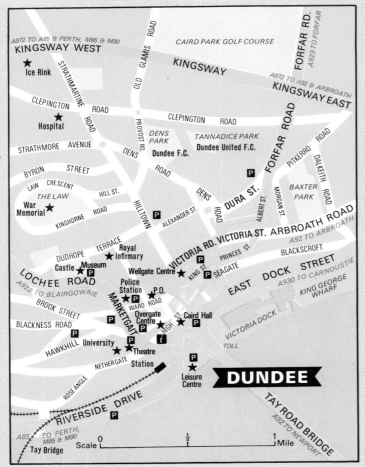

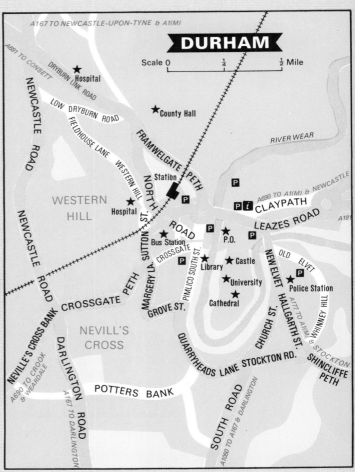

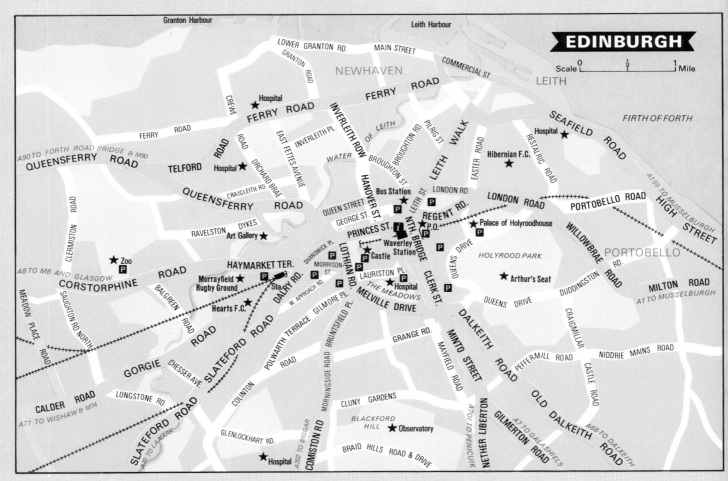

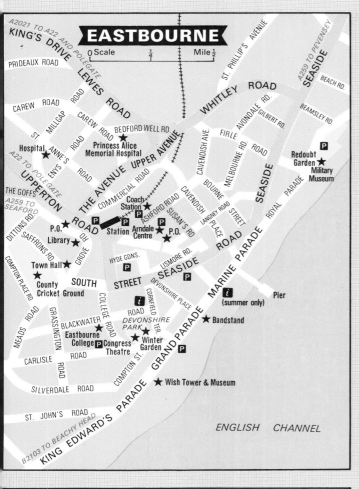

EASTBOURNE

Scale — Mile ½

King's Drive · A2021 to A22 and Polegate
Prideaux Road
Carew Road
St. Millgap Road
Carew Road
Hospital
St. Anne's Road
Enys Road
Upperton Road · A22 to Polegate
The Goffs
A259 to Seaford
Dittons Rd.
Saffrons Rd.
P.O.
Library
Town Hall
Compton Place Rd.
County Cricket Ground
South Street
Meads Road
Grassington Road
Blackwater Road
College Road
Carlisle Road
Eastbourne College
Congress Theatre
Winter Garden
Silverdale Road
St. John's Road
King Edward's Parade · B2103 to Beachy Head
Lewes Road
The Avenue
Upper Avenue
Commercial Road
Princess Alice Memorial Hospital
Bedford Well Rd.
Cavendish Ave.
Ashford Road
Cavendish Road
Coach Station
Station
Arndale Centre
Bourne Street
Susan's Rd.
Hyde Gdns.
Lismore Rd.
Seaside Road
Cornfield Road
Devonshire Place
Devonshire Park
Compton St.
Grand Parade
Whitley Road
St. Phillip's Avenue
Firle Road
Avondale Rd.
Gilbert Rd.
Melbourne Road
Langney Road
Seaside
Marine Parade
Royal Parade
Beamsley Rd.
A259 to Pevensey
Redoubt Garden
Military Museum
P.O.
i (summer only)
Pier
Bandstand
Winter Garden
Wish Tower & Museum

ENGLISH CHANNEL

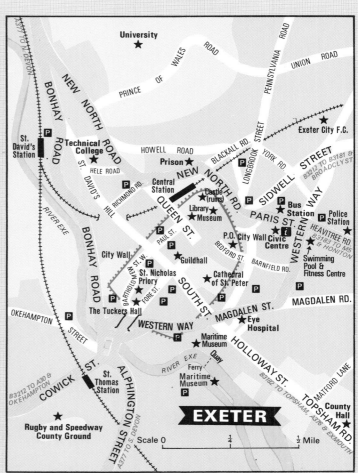

EXETER

Scale 0 — ¼ — ½ Mile

University
A377 to Devon
Bonhay Road
New North Road
Prince of Wales Road
Pennsylvania Road
Union Road
St. David's Station
Technical College
Hele Road
St. David's Hill
Howell Road
Blackall Rd.
Longbrook Street
York Rd.
Exeter City F.C.
Sidwell Street
B3183 & Broadclyst
Prison
Central Station
New North Rd.
Richmond Rd.
Castle (ruins)
Library
Museum
Paris St.
Bus Station
Western Way
Police Station
Heavitree Rd. · B3183 to M5 & Honiton
River Exe
City Wall
Queen St.
Paul St.
St. W.
P.O.
City Wall
Civic Centre
Bonhay Road
St. Nicholas Priory
Bartholomew St. W.
Fore St.
Guildhall
Bedford St.
Barnfield Rd.
Cathedral of St. Peter
Swimming Pool & Fitness Centre
Okehampton Street
South St.
Magdalen St.
Magdalen Rd.
The Tuckers Hall
Western Way
Eye Hospital
B3212 to A30 & Okehampton
Cowick St.
St. Thomas Station
St. Alphington Street
A377 to S. Devon
Maritime Museum
River Exe
Quay
Ferry
Maritime Museum
Holloway St.
B3182 to Topsham
Matford Lane
A376 to Exmouth
County Hall
A38 to Topsham
Rugby and Speedway County Ground

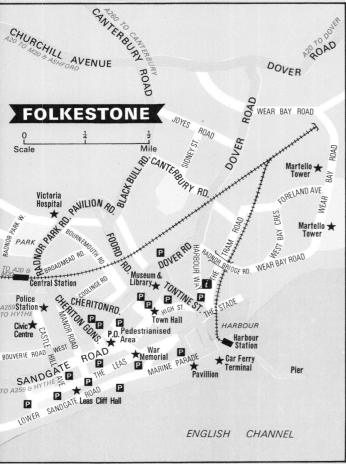

FOLKESTONE

Scale 0 — ¼ — Mile

A260 to Canterbury
Churchill Avenue
Canterbury Road
A20 to M20 & Ashford
A20 to Dover
Dover Road
Wear Bay Road
Joyes Road
Sidney St.
Martello Tower
Foreland Ave.
Wear Bay Road
Martello Tower
Victoria Hospital
Radnor Park W.
Pavilion Rd.
Black Bull Rd.
Canterbury Rd.
Dover Road
West Bay Cres.
Radnor Park
Bournemouth Road
Broadmead Rd.
Foord Rd.
The Tram Road
Radnor Bridge Rd.
Wear Bay Road
To A20 & A259
Central Station
Police Station
To Hythe
Cheriton Rd.
Coolinge Rd.
Cheriton Gdns.
Manor Road
Dover Rd.
Harbour Way
The Stade
Museum & Library
i
Tontine St.
High St.
Town Hall
P.O.
Pedestrianised Area
Harbour
Civic Centre
Castle Hill Ave.
West Road
Bouverie Road
Sandgate Road
The Leas
War Memorial
Marine Parade
Harbour Station
Car Ferry Terminal
Pier
A259 & Hythe
Lower Sandgate Road
Leas Cliff Hall
Pavillion

ENGLISH CHANNEL

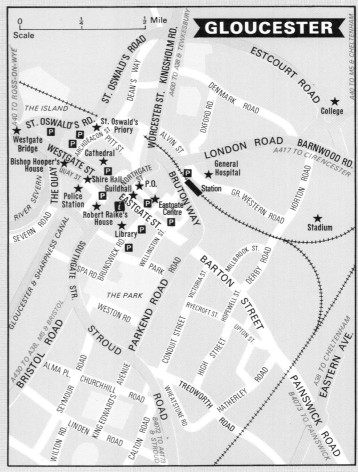

GLOUCESTER

Scale 0 — ¼ — ½ Mile

A40 to Ross-on-Wye
St. Oswald's Road
Dean's Way
Worcester St.
Kingsholm Rd.
A430 to A38 & Tewkesbury
Denmark Road
Estcourt Road
A40 to M5 & Cheltenham
The Island
St. Oswald's Rd.
St. Oswald's Priory
Archdeacon St.
Pitt St.
Alvin St.
Oxford Rd.
London Road
A417 to Cirencester
Barnwood Rd.
College
Westgate Bridge
Westgate St.
Cathedral
Bishop Hooper's House
Quay St.
Shire Hall
Northgate St.
P.O.
General Hospital
Bruton Way
Station
Gr. Western Road
Horton Road
The Quay
River Severn
Guildhall
Police Station
i
Robert Raike's House
Library
Eastgate St.
Eastgate Centre
Wellington St.
Stadium
Gloucester & Sharpness Canal
Severn Road
Southgate Str.
Brunswick Rd.
Spa Road
The Park
Weston Rd.
Victoria St.
Millbrook St.
Derby Road
Barton Street
Bristol Road
A430 to A38, M5 & Bristol
Alma Pl.
Churchill Avenue
Kingsholm Rd.
Stroud Road
Parkend Road
Conduit Street
Ryecroft St.
Hopewell St.
Upton St.
Tredworth
Hatherley Road
Wheatstone Road
Painswick Road
B4073 to Painswick
Eastern Ave.
A38 to Cheltenham
Seymour Road
Linden Road
Wilton Road
King Edward's Avenue
Calton Road
B4072 to A4173 & Stroud

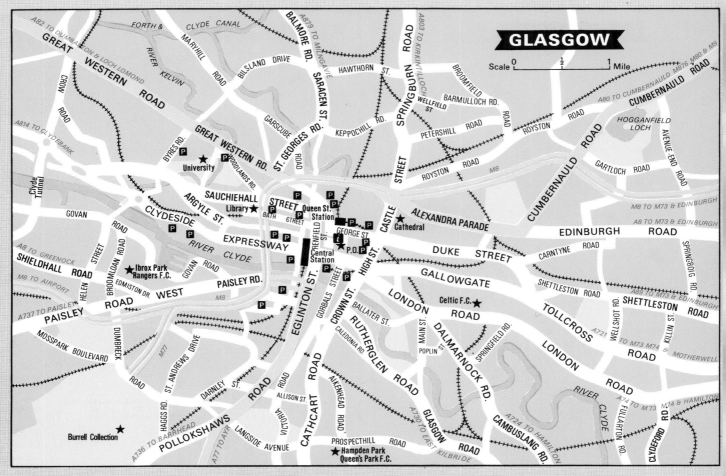

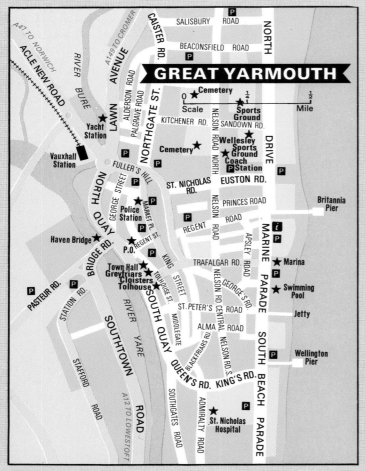

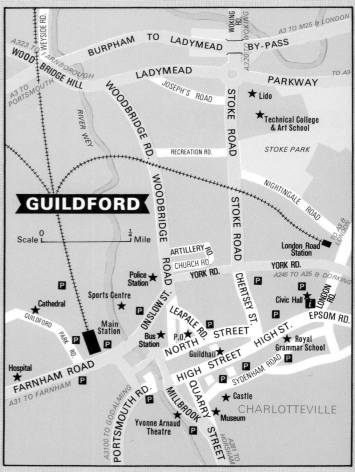

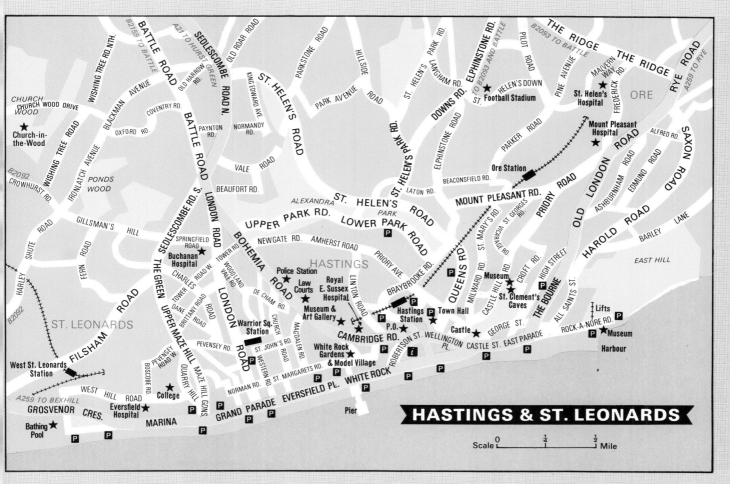

HASTINGS & ST. LEONARDS

Scale 0 — ¼ — ½ Mile

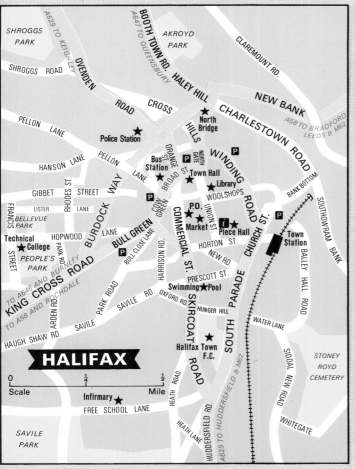

HALIFAX

0 — ¼ — Mile
Scale

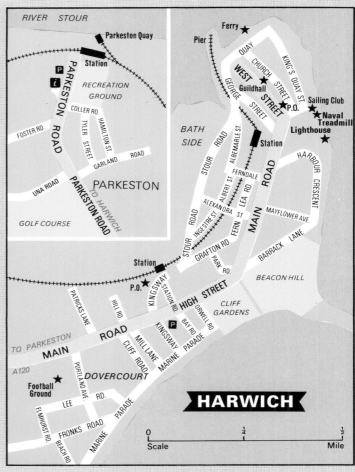

HARWICH

0 — ¼ — ½
Scale — Mile

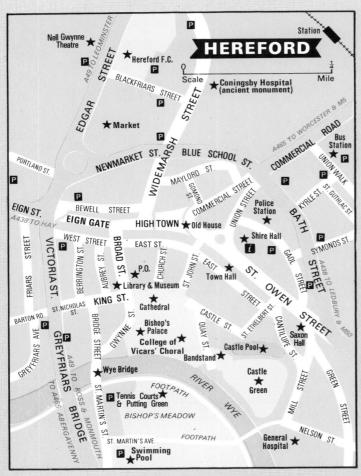

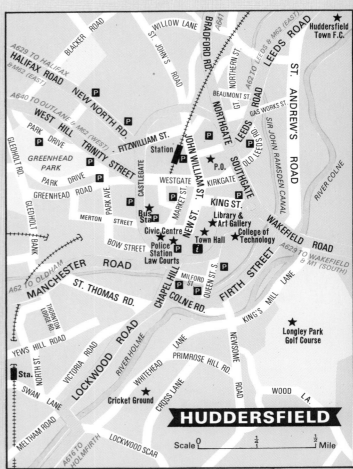

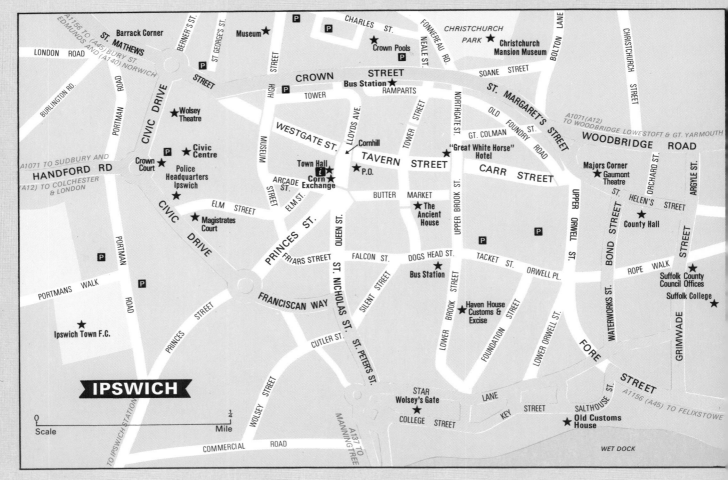

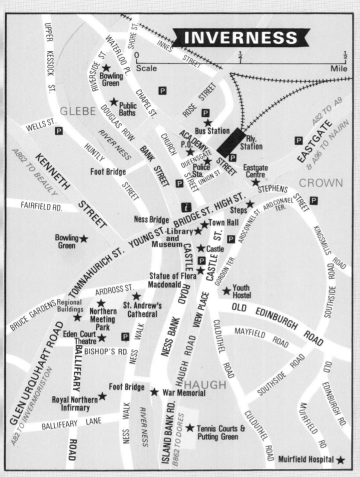

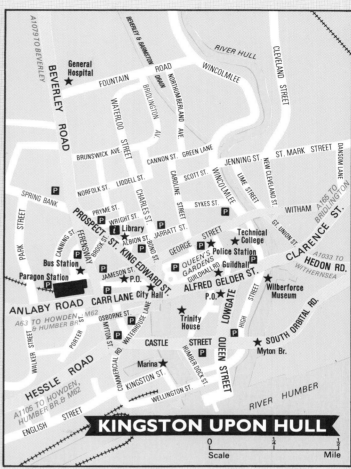

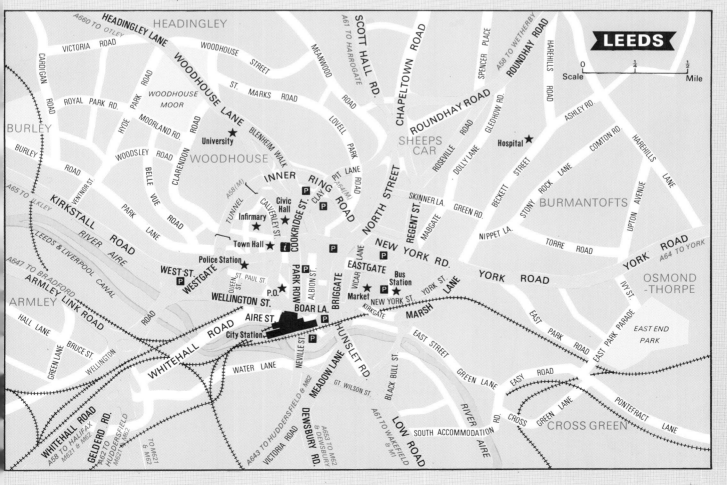

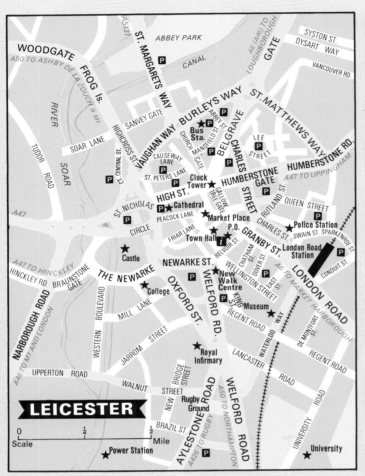

LEICESTER

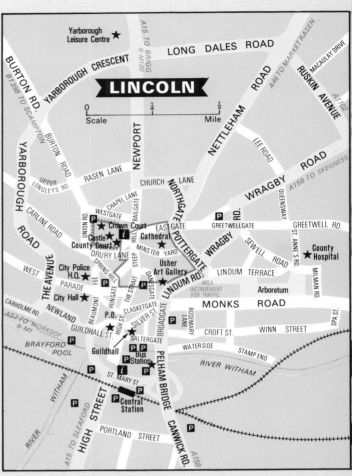

LINCOLN

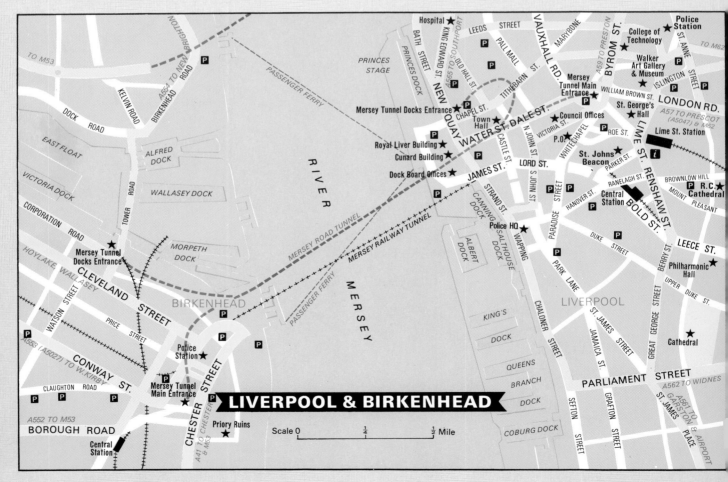

LIVERPOOL & BIRKENHEAD

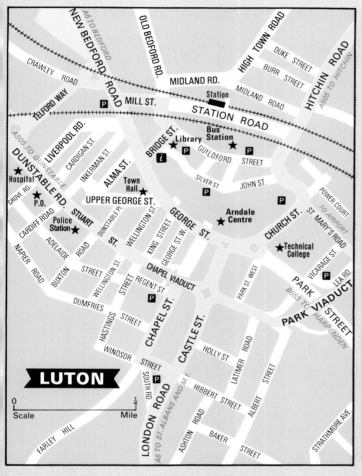

LUTON

0 Scale ½ Mile

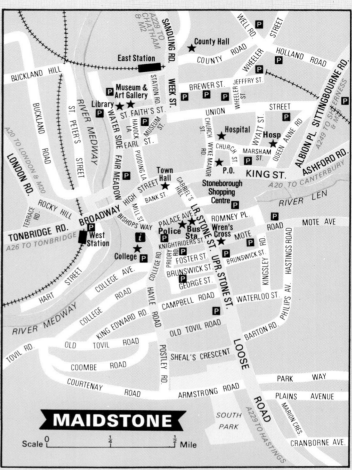

MAIDSTONE

0 ¼ ½ Mile Scale

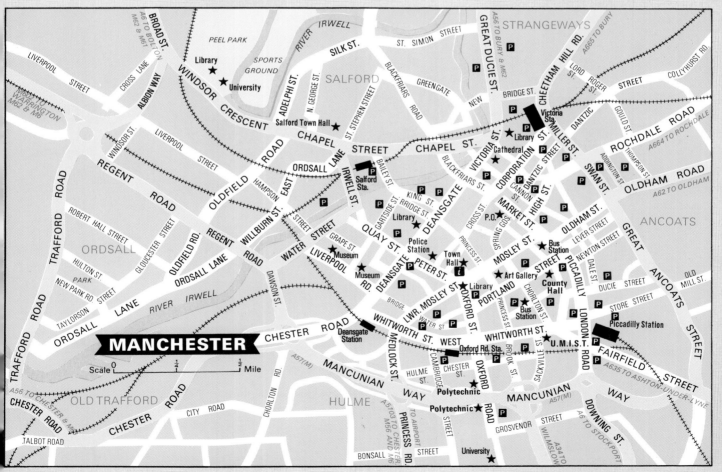

MANCHESTER

0 ¼ ½ Mile Scale

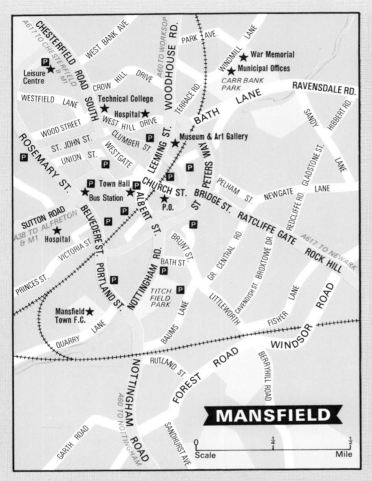

MANSFIELD

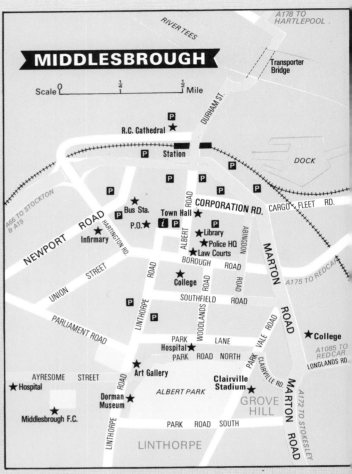

MIDDLESBROUGH

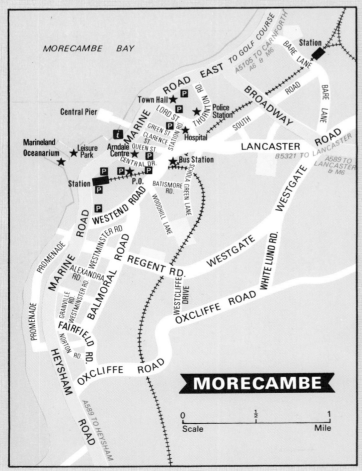

MORECAMBE

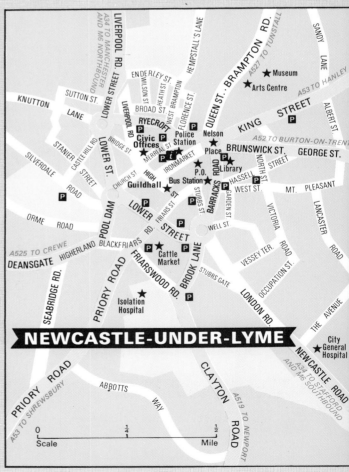

NEWCASTLE-UNDER-LYME

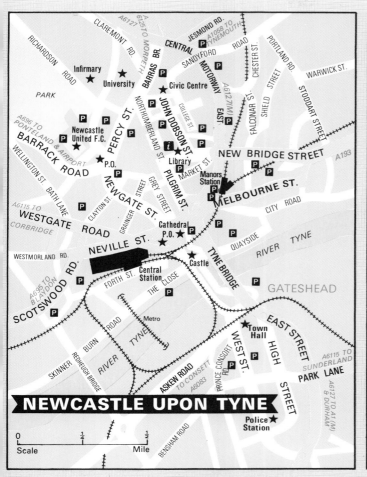

NEWCASTLE UPON TYNE

Scale 0 — ¼ — ½ Mile

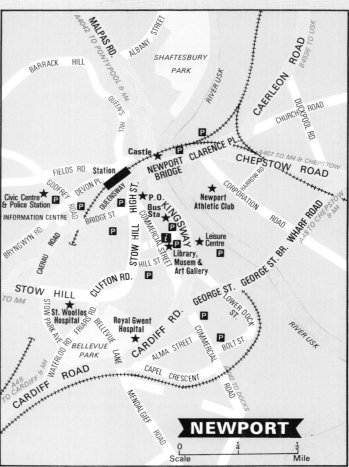

NEWPORT

Scale 0 — ¼ — ½ Mile

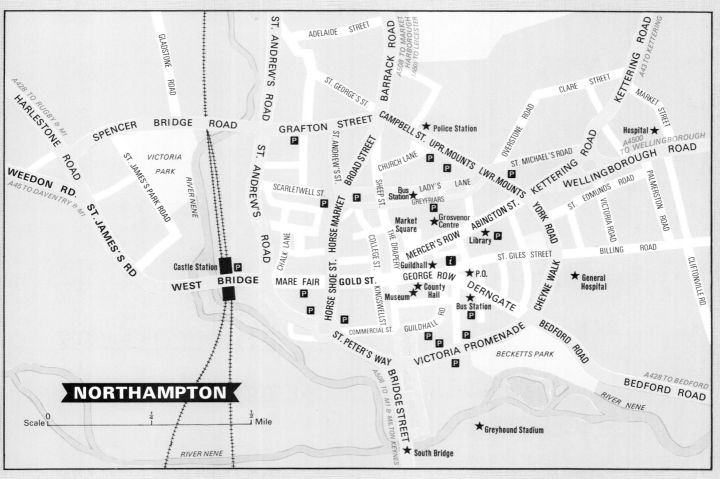

NORTHAMPTON

Scale 0 — ¼ — ½ Mile

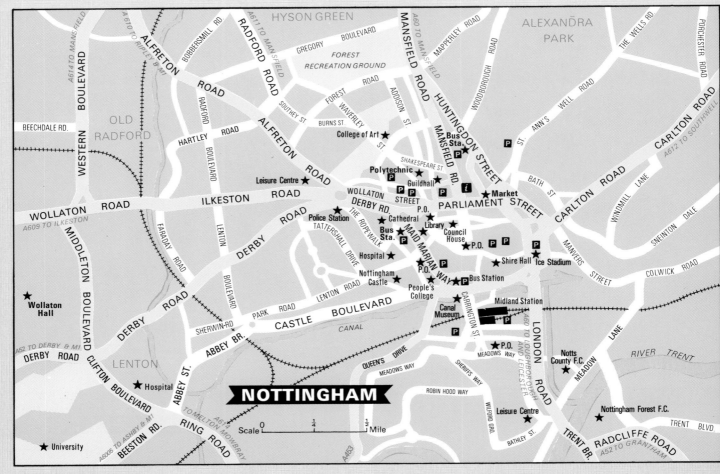

NOTTINGHAM

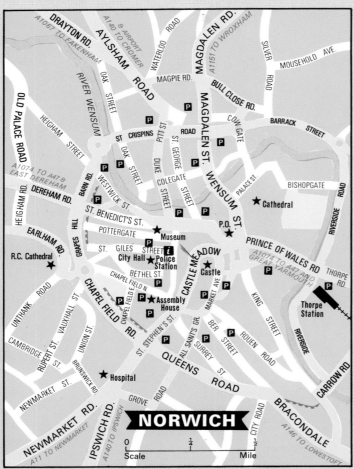

NORWICH

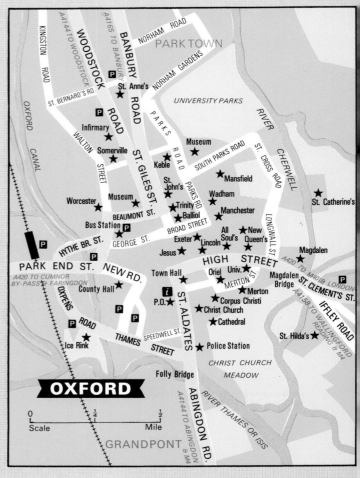

OXFORD

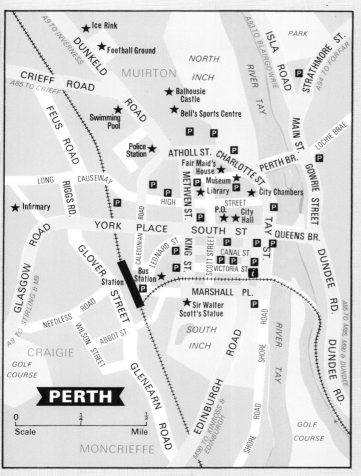

PERTH

- ★ Ice Rink
- ★ Football Ground
- MUIRTON
- NORTH INCH
- A9 TO INVERNESS
- DUNKELD ROAD
- CRIEFF ROAD
- A85 TO CRIEFF
- FEUS ROAD
- ★ Swimming Pool
- ★ Balhousie Castle
- ★ Bell's Sports Centre
- ISLA ROAD
- A93 TO BLAIRGOWRIE
- RIVER TAY
- PARK
- STRATHMORE ST.
- A94 TO FORFAR
- MAIN ST.
- LOCHIE BRAE
- GOWRIE STREET
- PERTH BR.
- CHARLOTTE ST.
- Police Station ★
- ATHOLL ST.
- Fair Maid's House ★
- ★ Museum
- ★ Library
- METHVEN ST.
- HIGH STREET
- ★ City Chambers
- P.O.
- ★★ City Hall
- SOUTH ST.
- QUEENS BR.
- TAY ST.
- LONG CAUSEWAY
- RIGGS RD.
- ★ Infirmary
- YORK PLACE
- KING ST.
- LEONARD ST.
- SCOTT STREET
- CANAL ST.
- VICTORIA ST.
- GLASGOW ROAD
- A9 TO STIRLING & M9
- GLOVER STREET
- Station
- Bus Station
- NEEDLESS ROAD
- WILSON STREET
- ABBOT ST.
- MARSHALL PL.
- ★ Sir Walter Scott's Statue
- CRAIGIE
- GOLF COURSE
- SOUTH INCH
- CALEDONIAN ROAD
- DUNDEE RD.
- A85 TO M85, M90 & DUNDEE
- SHORE ROAD
- RIVER TAY
- GLENEARN ROAD
- EDINBURGH ROAD
- M90 TO KINROSS & EDINBURGH
- MONCRIEFFE
- DUNDEE RD.
- GOLF COURSE

0 ¼ ½
Scale Mile

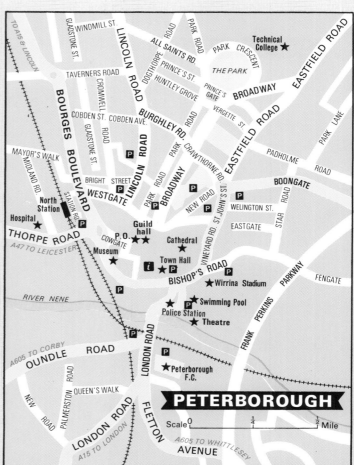

PETERBOROUGH

- A15 & LINCOLN
- WINDMILL ST.
- GLADSTONE ST.
- LINCOLN ROAD
- ALL SAINTS RD.
- PARK ROAD
- PARK CRESCENT
- Technical College ★
- EASTFIELD ROAD
- TAVERNERS ROAD
- CROMWELL ROAD
- DOGTHORPE ST.
- PRINCE'S ST.
- HUNTLEY GROVE
- THE PARK
- PRINCE'S GATE
- VERGETTE ST.
- BROADWAY
- BOURGES BOULEVARD
- COBDEN ST.
- COBDEN AVE.
- GLADSTONE ST.
- BURGHLEY RD.
- PARK ROAD
- CRAWTHORNE RD.
- PADHOLME ROAD
- PARK LANE
- MAYOR'S WALK
- MIDLAND RD.
- BRIGHT STREET
- WESTGATE
- LINCOLN ROAD
- BROADWAY
- NEW ROAD
- ST. JOHN'S ST.
- BOONGATE
- North Station
- STATION RD.
- ★ Hospital
- THORPE ROAD
- A47 TO LEICESTER
- COWGATE
- Guild Hall
- P.O.
- ★★★ Museum
- WELINGTON ST.
- EASTGATE
- STAR ROAD
- ★ Cathedral
- i Town Hall
- BISHOP'S ROAD
- VINEYARD RD.
- FRANK PERKINS PARKWAY
- FENGATE
- ★ Wirrina Stadium
- RIVER NENE
- ★ Swimming Pool
- ★ Police Station
- ★ Theatre
- A605 TO CORBY
- OUNDLE ROAD
- LONDON ROAD
- NEW ROAD
- PALMERSTON ROAD
- QUEEN'S WALK
- ★ Peterborough F.C.
- FLETTON AVENUE
- A15 TO LONDON
- A605 TO WHITTLESEY

Scale 0 ¼ ½ Mile

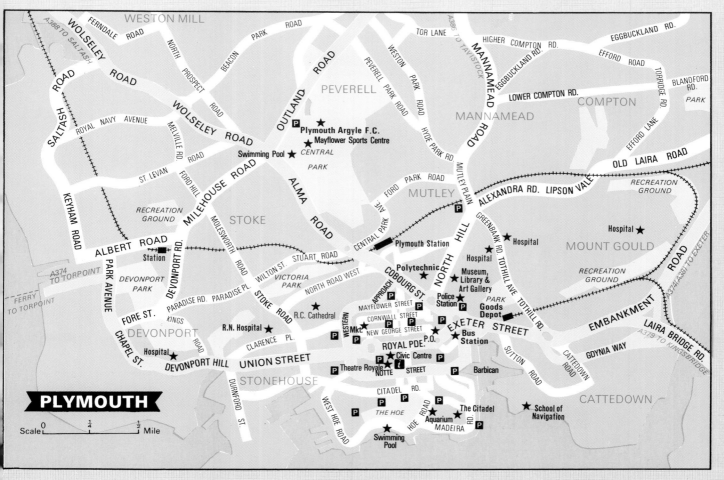

PLYMOUTH

- WESTON MILL
- FERNDALE ROAD
- WOLSELEY ROAD
- A388 TO SALTASH
- NORTH PROSPECT ROAD
- BEACON PARK ROAD
- PARK ROAD
- TOR LANE
- A386 TO TAVISTOCK
- HIGHER COMPTON RD.
- EGGBUCKLAND RD.
- SALTASH ROAD
- WOLSELEY ROAD
- PEVERELL
- WESTON PARK ROAD
- PEVERELL PARK ROAD
- MANNAMEAD ROAD
- EGGBUCKLAND RD.
- EFFORD ROAD
- ROYAL NAVY AVENUE
- MELVILLE RD.
- ★ Plymouth Argyle F.C.
- ★ Mayflower Sports Centre
- LOWER COMPTON RD.
- COMPTON
- TORRIDGE RD.
- BLANDFORD RD.
- ST. LEVAN ROAD
- FORD HILL
- MILEHOUSE ROAD
- OUTLAND ROAD
- ★ Swimming Pool
- CENTRAL PARK
- HYDE PARK RD.
- MANNAMEAD
- EFFORD LANE
- PARK
- KEYHAM ROAD
- RECREATION GROUND
- STOKE
- MOLESWORTH ROAD
- ALMA ROAD
- FORD PARK ROAD
- MUTLEY
- MUTLEY PLAIN
- OLD LAIRA ROAD
- RECREATION GROUND
- ALBERT ROAD
- Station
- DEVONPORT RD.
- WILTON ST.
- STUART ROAD
- CENTRAL PARK
- Plymouth Station
- NORTH HILL
- ALEXANDRA RD.
- LIPSON VALE
- A374 TO TORPOINT
- DEVONPORT PARK
- PARADISE RD.
- PARADISE PL.
- VICTORIA PARK
- NORTH ROAD WEST
- Polytechnic ★
- GREENBANK RD.
- ★ Hospital
- ★ Hospital
- MOUNT GOULD
- FERRY TO TORPOINT
- FORE ST.
- KINGS ROAD
- STOKE ROAD
- ★ R.C. Cathedral
- MAYFLOWER STREET
- CORNWALL STREET
- Museum, Library & Art Gallery ★
- ★ Police Station
- Goods Depot
- RECREATION GROUND
- A374/A381 TO EXETER
- ★ R.N. Hospital
- CLARENCE PL.
- WESTERN Mkt
- NEW GEORGE STREET
- EXETER STREET
- TOTHILL AVE.
- TOTHILL RD.
- EMBANKMENT ROAD
- LAIRA BRIDGE RD.
- A379 TO KINGSBRIDGE
- CHAPEL ST.
- ★ Hospital
- DEVONPORT HILL
- UNION STREET
- ROYAL PDE.
- P.O.
- Bus Station
- SUTTON ROAD
- GDYNIA WAY
- DEVONPORT
- ★ Civic Centre
- i
- NOTTE STREET
- ★ Theatre Royale
- ★ Barbican
- CATTEDOWN ROAD
- STONEHOUSE
- DURNFORD ST.
- CITADEL RD.
- WEST HOE ROAD
- THE HOE
- HOE ROAD
- MADEIRA RD.
- ★ The Citadel
- ★ School of Navigation
- CATTEDOWN
- Aquarium ★
- ★ Swimming Pool

0 ¼ ½
Scale Mile

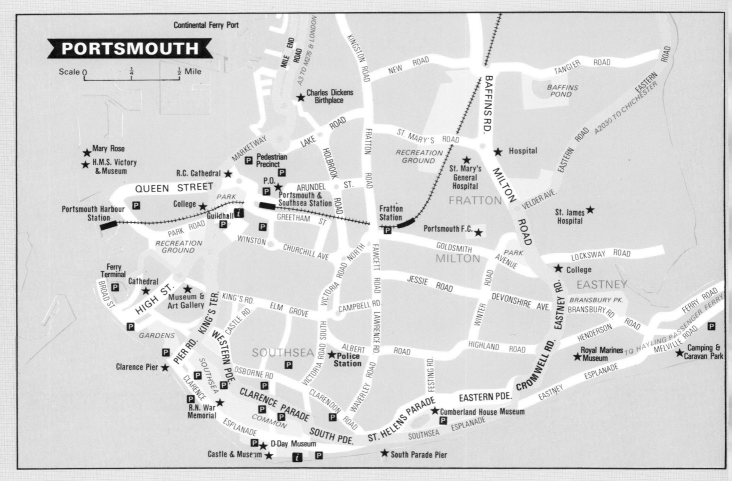

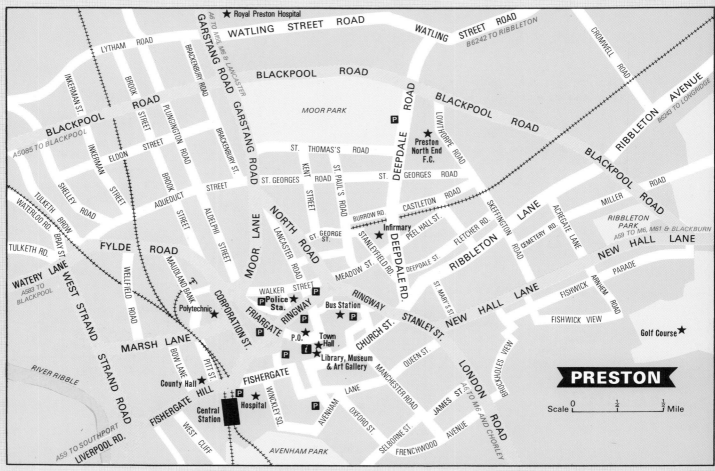

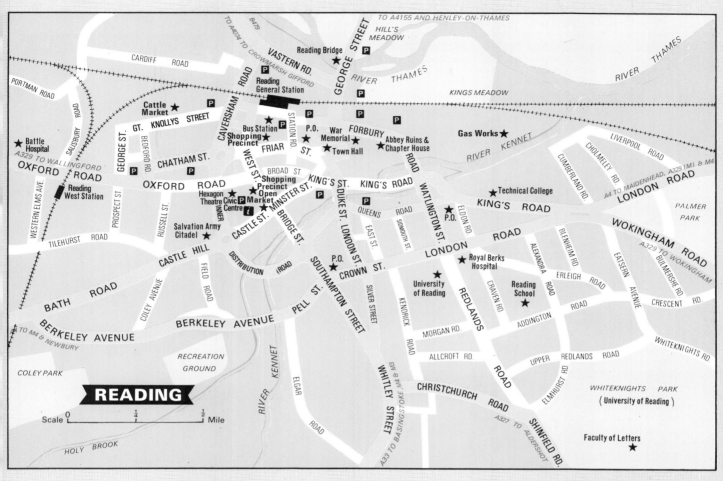

READING

Scale 0 — ¼ — ½ Mile

ROYAL LEAMINGTON SPA

Scale 0 — ¼ Mile

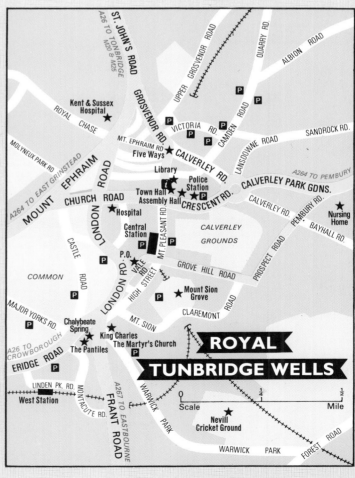

ROYAL TUNBRIDGE WELLS

Scale 0 — ¼ — ½ Mile

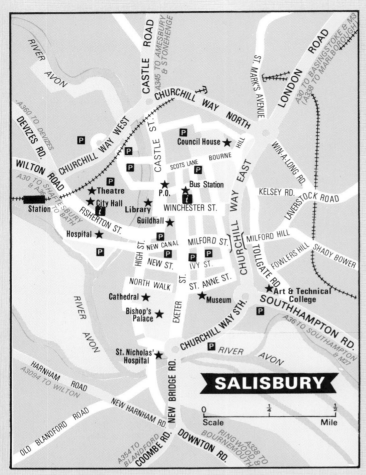

SALISBURY

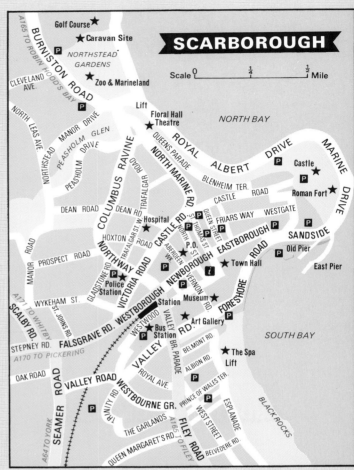

SCARBOROUGH

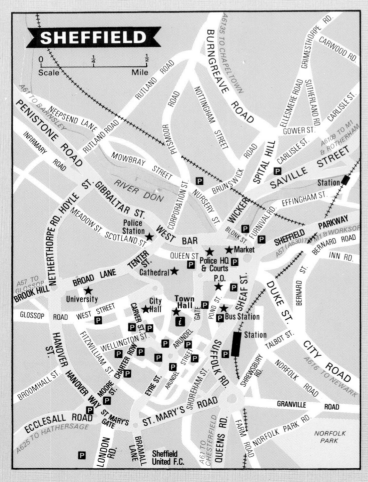

SHEFFIELD

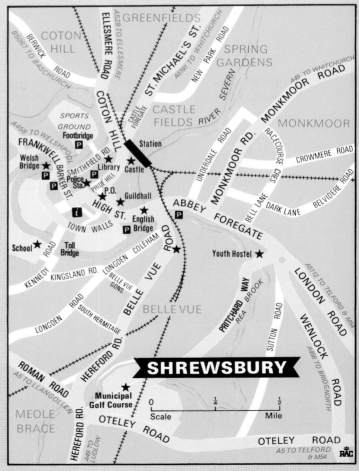

SHREWSBURY

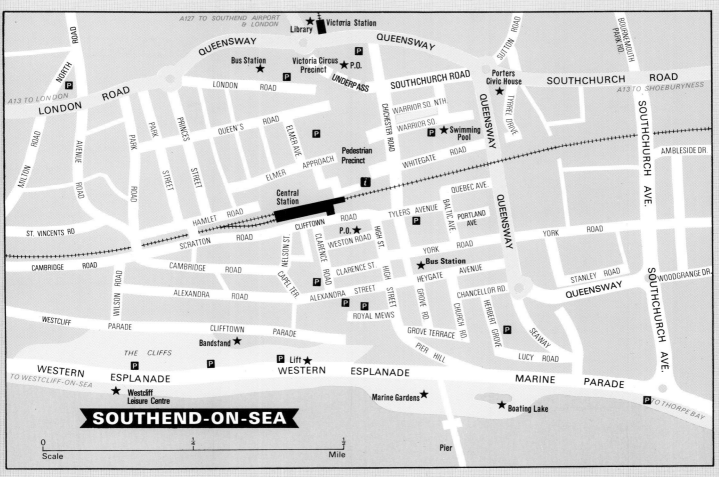

SOUTHEND-ON-SEA

A127 TO SOUTHEND AIRPORT & LONDON

Library — Victoria Station

QUEENSWAY — QUEENSWAY

Bus Station — Victoria Circus Precinct — P.O.

SOUTHCHURCH ROAD — Porters Civic House — SOUTHCHURCH ROAD — A13 TO SHOEBURYNESS

A13 TO LONDON — LONDON ROAD

NORTH ROAD

MILTON ROAD — AVENUE ROAD — PARK STREET — PRINCES STREET — LONDON ROAD — QUEEN'S ROAD

ELMER AVE. — CHICHESTER ROAD — WARRIOR SQ. NTH. — WARRIOR SQ. — Swimming Pool — SUTTON ROAD — BOURNEMOUTH PARK RD.

WHITEGATE ROAD — QUEENSWAY — TYRREL DRIVE

ST. VINCENTS RD. — ELMER APPROACH — Pedestrian Precinct — AMBLESIDE DR.

Central Station — CLIFFTOWN ROAD — P.O. — WESTON ROAD — TYLERS AVENUE — BALTIC AVE. — QUEBEC AVE. — QUEENSWAY

SCRATTON ROAD — NELSON ST. — CLARENCE ROAD — HIGH ST. — PORTLAND AVE. — YORK ROAD — WOODGRANGE DR.

CAMBRIDGE ROAD — CAMBRIDGE ROAD — CLARENCE ST. — YORK ROAD — Bus Station — STANLEY ROAD — SOUTHCHURCH AVE.

ALEXANDRA ROAD — CAPEL TER. — ALEXANDRA STREET — HEYGATE AVENUE — GROVE RD. — CHANCELLOR RD. — HERBERT GROVE — QUEENSWAY

WILSON ROAD — WESTCLIFF PARADE — CLIFFTOWN PARADE — Royal Mews — GROVE TERRACE — CHURCH RD. — SEAWAY — LUCY ROAD

Bandstand — PIER HILL

THE CLIFFS — Lift — WESTERN ESPLANADE — MARINE PARADE

WESTERN ESPLANADE — TO WESTCLIFF-ON-SEA — Westcliff Leisure Centre — Marine Gardens — Boating Lake — TO THORPE BAY

Pier

Scale 0 — 1/4 — 1/2 Mile

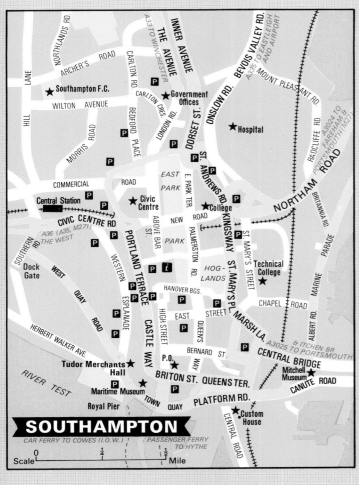

SOUTHAMPTON

NORTHLANDS RD. — INNER AVENUE — THE AVENUE — A33 TO WINCHESTER — BEVOIS VALLEY RD. — A335 TO EASTLEIGH AND AIRPORT — MOUNT PLEASANT RD.

HILL LANE — ARCHER'S ROAD — CARLTON RD. — Government Offices — CARLTON CRES. — ONSLOW RD. — RADCLIFFE RD. — A3024 TO FAREHAM & PORTSMOUTH (M27)

Southampton F.C. — WILTON AVENUE — LONDON RD. — DORSET ST. — Hospital — NORTHAM ROAD

MORRIS RD. — BEDFORD PLACE — EAST PARK — E. PARK TER. — BRITANNIA RD. — MARINE PARADE

COMMERCIAL ROAD — Central Station — Civic Centre — ST. ANDREWS RD. — NEW ROAD — College — KINGSWAY — ST. MARY'S PL. — ST. MARY'S STREET

CIVIC CENTRE RD. — ABOVE BAR ST. — NEW PARK — PALMERSTON RD.

A36 (A35, M271) — THE WEST — PORTLAND TERRACE — HOG-LANDS — Technical College — CHAPEL ROAD — ALBERT RD. — A3025 TO PORTSMOUTH & CENTRAL BRIDGE

SOUTHERN — WESTERN ESPLANADE — HANOVER BGS. — CENTRAL BRIDGE

Dock Gate — WEST QUAY ROAD — CASTLE WAY — HIGH STREET — EAST STREET — QUEENS WAY — MARSH LA. — CANUTE ROAD

HERBERT WALKER AVE. — Tudor Merchants Hall — P.O. — BERNARD ST. — Mitchell Museum

RIVER TEST — Maritime Museum — BRITON ST. QUEENS TER. — PLATFORM RD.

Royal Pier — TOWN QUAY — Custom House — CENTRAL ROAD

CAR FERRY TO COWES (I.O.W.) — PASSENGER FERRY TO HYTHE

Scale 0 — 1/4 — 1/2 Mile

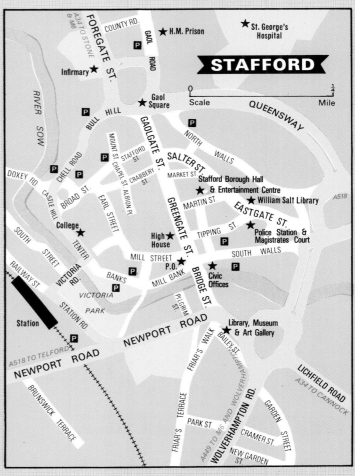

STAFFORD

A34 TO STONE & M6 — FOREGATE ST. — COUNTY RD. — GAOL — H.M. Prison — St. George's Hospital

Infirmary — Gaol Square — QUEENSWAY

RIVER SOW — Bull Hill — GAOLGATE ST. — SALTER ST. — NORTH WALLS

Scale 0 — 1/4 Mile

DOXEY RD. — Chell Road — MOUNT ST. — STAFFORD ST. — CHAPEL ST. — ALBION PL. — CRABBERY ST. — Market St. — Stafford Borough Hall & Entertainment Centre — William Salt Library — A518

CASTLE HILL — BROAD ST. — EARL STREET — MARTIN ST. — GREENGATE ST. — EASTGATE ST.

SOUTH STREET — College — High House — TENTER — TIPPING ST. — Police Station & Magistrates Court

RAILWAY ST. — VICTORIA RD. — MILL STREET — BANKS — P.O. — MILL BANK — SOUTH WALLS

Station — STATION RD. — VICTORIA PARK — BRIDGE ST. — Civic Offices — PILGRIM ST.

A518 TO TELFORD — NEWPORT ROAD — NEWPORT ROAD — Library, Museum & Art Gallery — BAILEY ST. — LICHFIELD ROAD — A34 TO CANNOCK

BRUNSWICK TERRACE — FRIAR'S TERRACE — PARK ST. — FRIAR'S WALK — WOLVERHAMPTON RD. — GARDEN STREET

A449 TO M6 AND WOLVERHAMPTON — WOLVERHAMPTON RD. — CRAMER ST. — NEW GARDEN ST.

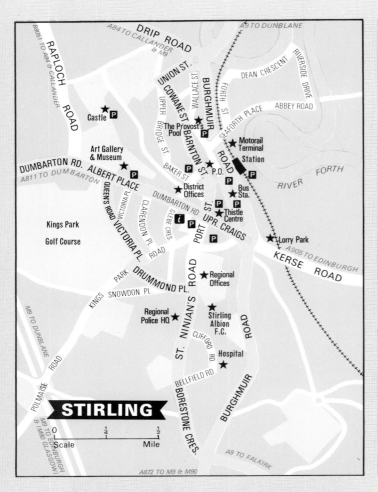

STIRLING

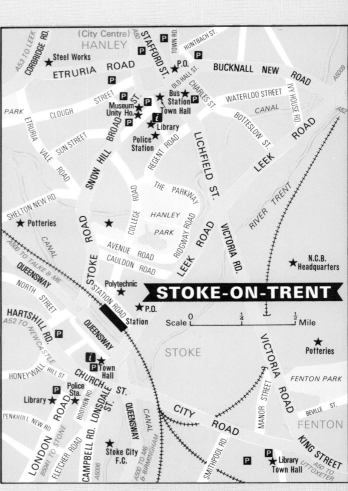

STOKE-ON-TRENT

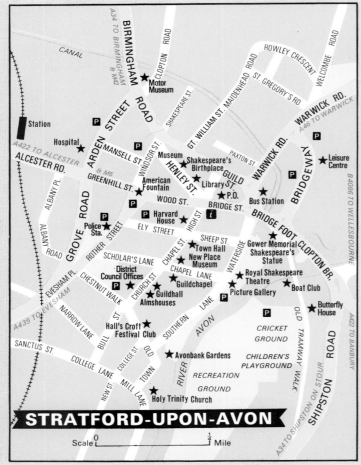

STRATFORD-UPON-AVON

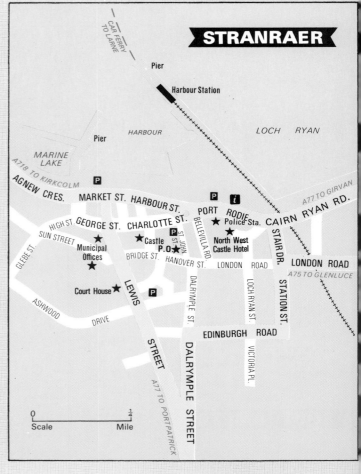

STRANRAER

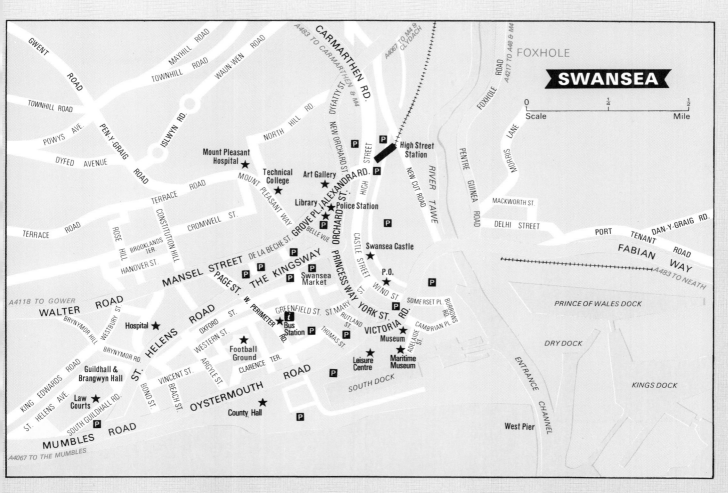

SWANSEA

FOXHOLE

Scale 0 — ¼ — ½ Mile

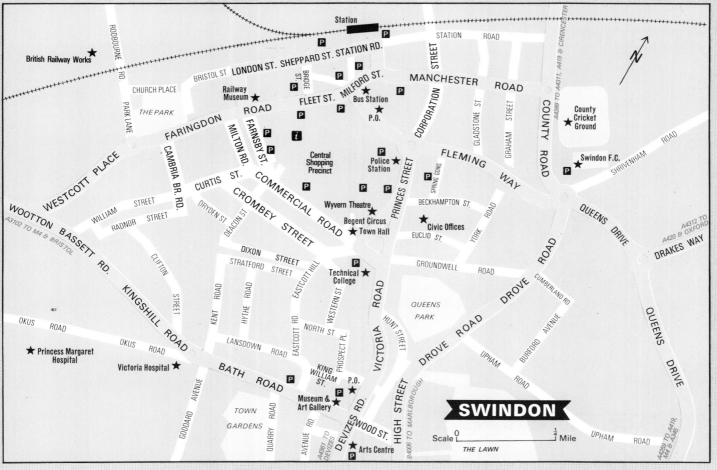

SWINDON

Scale 0 — ¼ Mile

THE LAWN

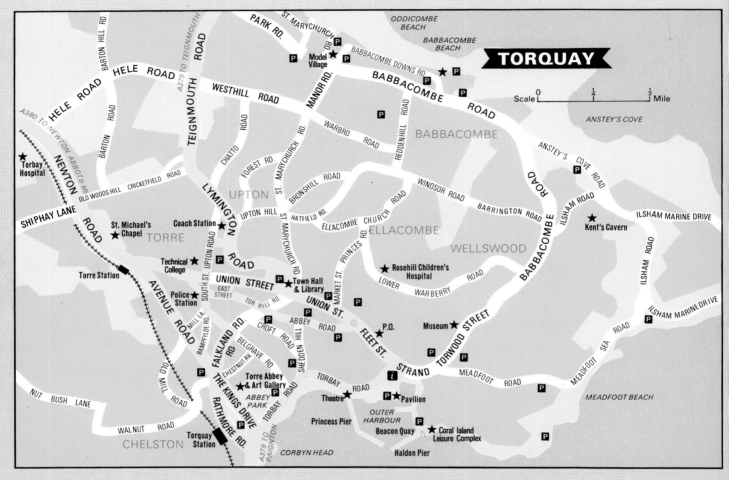

TORQUAY

Scale 0 — ¼ — ½ Mile

ODDICOMBE BEACH
BABBACOMBE BEACH
ANSTEY'S COVE
BABBACOMBE
WELLSWOOD
ELLACOMBE
UPTON
TORRE
Torbay Hospital
St. Michael's Chapel
Coach Station
Technical College
Torre Station
Police Station
Town Hall & Library
Rosehill Children's Hospital
Kent's Cavern
ILSHAM MARINE DRIVE
P.O.
Museum
Torre Abbey & Art Gallery
Abbey Park
Theatre
Pavilion
Princess Pier
OUTER HARBOUR
Beacon Quay
Coral Island Leisure Complex
Haldon Pier
CHELSTON
Torquay Station
CORBYN HEAD
MEADFOOT BEACH

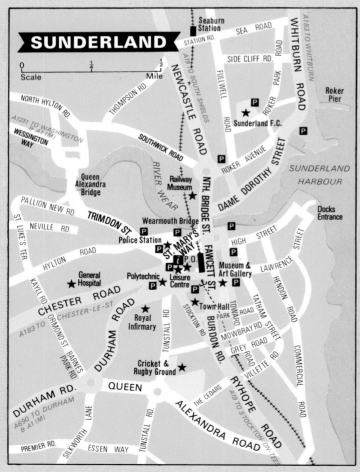

SUNDERLAND

Scale 0 — ¼ — ½ Mile

Seaburn Station
Sunderland F.C.
Roker Pier
SUNDERLAND HARBOUR
Docks Entrance
Queen Alexandra Bridge
Railway Museum
Wearmouth Bridge
Police Station
P.O.
General Hospital
Polytechnic
Leisure Centre
Museum & Art Gallery
Town Hall
Royal Infirmary
Cricket & Rugby Ground
QUEEN
ALEXANDRA ROAD

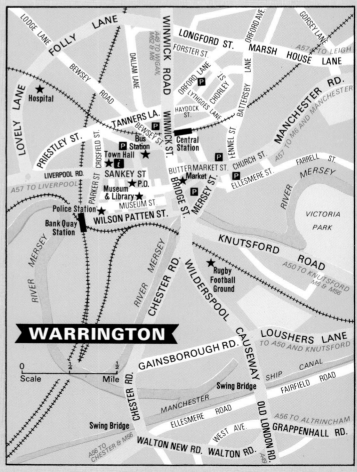

WARRINGTON

Scale 0 — ¼ — ½ Mile

Hospital
FOLLY LANE
LONGFORD ST.
MARSH HOUSE LANE
MANCHESTER RD.
Tanners La.
Bus Station
Central Station
Town Hall
Market
P.O.
Museum & Library
Police Station
Bank Quay Station
Wilson Patten St.
VICTORIA PARK
KNUTSFORD ROAD
Rugby Football Ground
WILDERSPOOL CAUSEWAY
LOUSHERS LANE
GAINSBOROUGH RD.
Swing Bridge
SHIP CANAL
Swing Bridge
GRAPPENHALL RD.
WALTON NEW RD. WALTON RD.

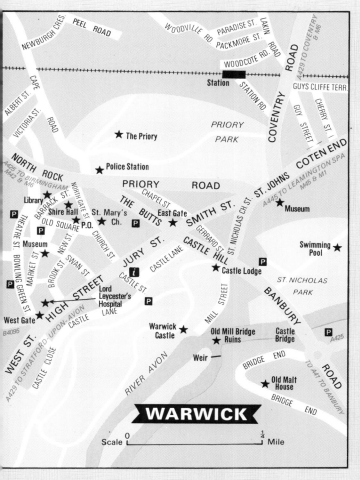

WARWICK

NEWBURGH CRES. PEEL ROAD
WOODVILLE RD. PARADISE ST. LAKIN
PACKMORE ST. WOODCOTE RD.
A429 TO COVENTRY M6
ALBERT ST.
Station STATION RD.
CAPE ROAD
GUYS CLIFFE TERR.
VICTORIA ST.
COVENTRY ROAD
★ The Priory
PRIORY PARK
GUY STREET
CHERRY ST.
COTEN END
NORTH ROCK
A425 TO BIRMINGHAM M42 & M6
★ Police Station
PRIORY ROAD
CHAPEL ST.
ST. JOHNS
A445 TO LEAMINGTON SPA M45 & M1
Library
NORTH GATE ST.
ST. NICHOLAS CH. ST.
SMITH ST.
★ Museum
BARRACK ST.
THE BUTTS
East Gate
Shire Hall ★ St. Mary's Ch.
GERRARD ST.
Swimming Pool ★
Old Square P.O.
CHURCH ST.
CASTLE HILL
THEATRE ST.
Museum
JURY ST.
Castle Lodge ★
ST. NICHOLAS PARK
BOWLING GREEN ST.
SWAN ST.
NEW ST.
HIGH STREET
Lord Leycester's Hospital
CASTLE LANE
CASTLE ST.
MILL STREET
BANBURY
BROOK ST.
MARKET ST.
Warwick Castle ★
Old Mill Bridge Ruins ★
Castle Bridge
A425
West Gate
CASTLE CLOSE
A429 TO STRATFORD-UPON-AVON
B4095
WEST ST.
CASTLE
River Avon
Weir
BRIDGE END
ROAD
A41 TO BANBURY
★ Old Malt House
BRIDGE END
Scale 0 ¼ Mile

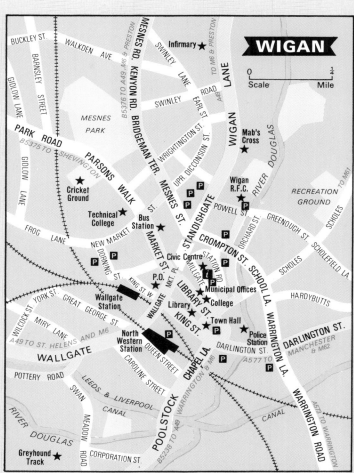

WIGAN

BUCKLEY ST.
WALKDEN AVE.
SWINLEY
★ Infirmary
TO M6 & PRESTON
0 ¼ Scale Mile
BARNSLEY STREET
GIDLOW LANE
PARK ROAD
B5375 TO SHEVINGTON
MESNES PARK
MESNES RD.
KENYON RD.
SWINLEY LANE
EARL ST.
WRIGHTINGTON ST.
B5376 TO A49, M6 & PRESTON
BRIDGEMAN TER.
A49 TO M6 & PRESTON
WIGAN LANE
Mab's Cross ★
RECREATION GROUND
PARSONS WALK
★ Cricket Ground
UPR. DICCONSON ST.
MESNES ST.
STANDISHGATE
Wigan R.F.C. ★
River Douglas
SCHOLES
Technical College ★
Bus Station ★
NEW MARKET ST.
Civic Centre
STATION RD.
Powell St.
SCHOOL LA.
GREENOUGH ST.
SCHOLEFIELD LA.
FROG LANE
DORNING ST.
P.O.
CROMPTON ST.
CRIBLE ST.
Municipal Offices
HARDYBUTTS
WILCOCK ST.
YORK ST.
GREAT GEORGE ST.
Wallgate Station
KING ST. W.
LIBRARY ST.
College
KING ST.
MARKET ST.
MKT. PL.
WALLGATE
Library
DARLINGTON ST.
A49 TO ST. HELENS AND M6
MIRY LANE
North Western Station
Queen Street
Town Hall ★
Police Station ★
DARLINGTON ST.
MANCHESTER & M62
WALLGATE
CAROLINE STREET
CHAPEL LA.
A577 TO
WARRINGTON LA.
POTTERY ROAD
LEEDS & LIVERPOOL CANAL
WARRINGTON & M6
A579 TO
SWAN MEADOW ROAD
RIVER DOUGLAS
B5238 TO A49
POOLSTOCK
WARRINGTON ROAD
CORPORATION ST.
Greyhound Track ★
CANAL

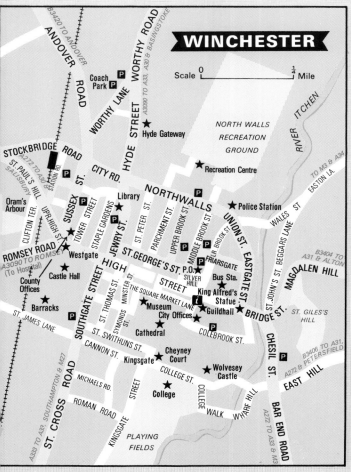

WINCHESTER

B3420 TO ANDOVER
WORTHY ROAD
ANDOVER ROAD
WORTHY LANE
A30 & BASINGSTOKE
Scale 0 ¼ Mile
Coach Park
A3090 TO A33, A30 & BASINGSTOKE
HYDE STREET
NORTH WALLS RECREATION GROUND
RIVER ITCHEN
★ Hyde Gateway
STOCKBRIDGE ROAD
CITY RD.
A272 TO A30
★ Recreation Centre
TO M3 & A34
ST. PAUL'S HILL
SALISBURY
STATION RD.
NORTHWALLS
EASTON LA.
Oram's Arbour
SUSSEX ST.
Library
ST. PETER ST.
PARCHMENT ST.
UPPER BROOK ST.
★ Police Station
CLIFTON TER.
UPHIGH ST.
TOWER STREET
STAPLE GARDENS
JEWRY ST.
MIDDLE BROOK ST.
LR. BROOK ST.
UNION ST.
WALES ST.
EASTGATE ST.
MAGDALEN HILL
ROMSEY ROAD
A3090 TO ROMSEY (To Hospital)
Westgate
ST. GEORGE'S ST.
FRIARSGATE
ST. JOHN'S ST.
BEGGARS LANE
B3404 TO A31 & ALTON
County Offices
Castle Hall
HIGH STREET
SILVER HILL
Bus Sta.
Barracks
ST. THOMAS ST.
ST. SWITHUNS ST.
King Alfred's Statue ★
SYMONDS ST.
MINSTER LA.
THE SQUARE MARKET LANE
Museum
City Offices
Guildhall
COLEBROOK ST.
ST. GILES'S HILL
SOUTHGATE STREET
CANNON ST.
Cathedral
CHESIL ST.
ST. JAMES LANE
Kingsgate
Cheyney Court
COLLEGE ST.
B3406 TO A31 & PETERSFIELD
A272 TO A33 & M3
EAST HILL
MICHAELS RD.
Wolvesey Castle ★
ST. CROSS ROAD
A333 TO A33, SOUTHAMPTON & M27
ROMAN ROAD
★ College
COLLEGE WALK
WHARF HILL
BAR END ROAD
KINGSGATE STREET
PLAYING FIELDS

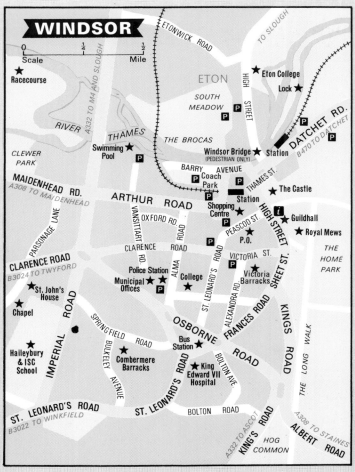

WINDSOR

ETONWICK ROAD
TO SLOUGH
0 ¼ ½ Scale Mile
★ Racecourse
ETON
★ Eton College
SOUTH MEADOW
HIGH STREET
Lock ★
A332 TO M4 AND SLOUGH
RIVER
THAMES
THE BROCAS
DATCHET RD.
CLEWER PARK
Swimming Pool ★
Windsor Bridge ★ Station
(PEDESTRIAN ONLY)
B470 TO DATCHET
MAIDENHEAD RD.
A308 TO MAIDENHEAD
BARRY AVENUE
Coach Park
THAMES ST.
Station
★ The Castle
ARTHUR ROAD
OXFORD RD.
Shopping Centre
HIGH STREET
Guildhall
PARSONAGE LANE
VANSITTART RD.
CLARENCE RD.
PEASCOD ST.
P.O.
★ Royal Mews
CLARENCE ROAD
B3024 TO TWYFORD
VICTORIA ST.
THE HOME PARK
Police Station
ALMA ROAD
College
Victoria Barracks
Municipal Offices
ST. LEONARD'S RD.
ALEXANDRA RD.
FRANCES ROAD
SHEET ST.
KINGS ROAD
St. John's House
IMPERIAL ROAD
SPRINGFIELD ROAD
BULKELEY AVENUE
Bus Station
OSBORNE ROAD
BOLTON AVE.
THE LONG WALK
Chapel
Haileybury & ISC School
Combermere Barracks
King Edward VII Hospital
ST. LEONARD'S ROAD
BOLTON ROAD
A308 TO STAINES
B3022 TO WINKFIELD
ST. LEONARD'S ROAD
A332 TO ASCOT
KING'S ROAD
HOG COMMON
ALBERT ROAD

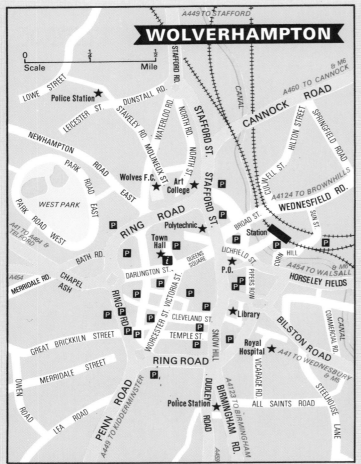

WOLVERHAMPTON

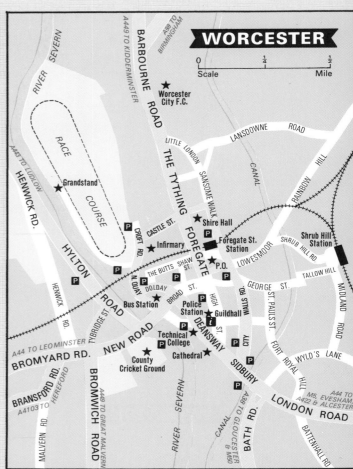

WORCESTER

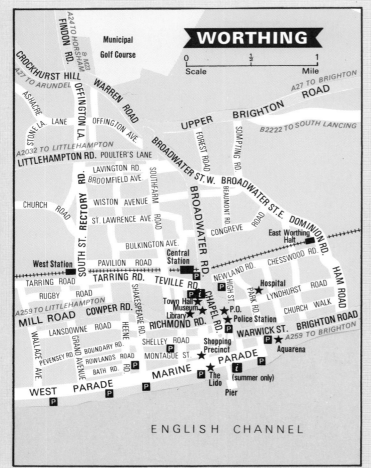

WORTHING

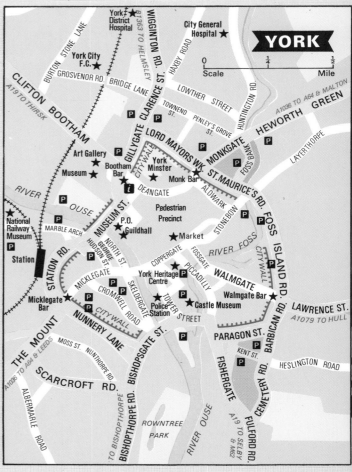

YORK

INDEX

This index refers to places in the main map section on pages 2-115
Listed below are the abbreviations used in the index.

Avon	Avn	Greater London	GL	Powys	Pwys
Bedfordshire	Beds	Greater Manchester	GM	Shetland	Shet
Berkshire	Berks	Gwynedd	Gynd	Shropshire	Salop
Borders	Bdrs	Hampshire	Hants	Somerset	Som
Buckinghamshire	Bucks	Hereford & Worcester	H & W	Staffordshire	Staffs
Cambridgeshire	Cambs	Hertfordshire	Herts	Strathclyde	Strath
Central	Cent	Highland	Hghld	Suffolk	Sflk
Cheshire	Ches	Humberside	Humb	Surrey	Sry
Cleveland	Clev	Isle of Man	IOM	Sussex, East	E Ssx
Cornwall	Corn	Isle of Wight	IOW	Sussex, West	W Ssx
Cumbria	Cumb	Lancashire	Lancs	Tayside	Tays
Derbyshire	Derbs	Leicestershire	Leics	Tyne and Wear	T & W
Dorset	Dors	Lincolnshire	Lincs	Warwickshire	Warks
Dumfries & Galloway	D & G	Lothian	Loth	Western Isles	W Is
Durham	Dur	Merseyside	Mers	West Midlands	W Mids
Essex	Esx	Norfolk	Nflk	Wiltshire	Wilts
Glamorgan, Mid	M Glam	Northamptonshire	Northants	Yorkshire, North	N Yorks
Glamorgan, South	S Glam	Northumberland	Northld	Yorkshire, South	S Yorks
Glamorgan, West	W Glam	Nottinghamshire	Notts	Yorkshire, West	W Yorks
Gloucestershire	Glos	Orkney	Ork		
Grampian	Gramp	Oxfordshire	Oxon		

A

Abbas Combe 9 D1
Abberley 29 B1
Abberton Esx 34 E7
Abberton H & W 29 D2
Abbess Roding 33 B7
Abbeycwmhir 27 E3
Abbey Dore 28 C4
Abbey Hulton 49 D7
Abbey St Bathans 83 C6
Abbeystead 54 E2
Abbeytown 68 E4
Abbey Wood 24 E5
Abbotrule 76 C4
Abbots Bickington 6 C5
Abbots Bromley 40 C2
Abbotsbury 9 B5
Abbotsford 76 B2
Abbotsham 6 D4
Abbotskerswell 5 D4
Abbots Langley 23 E1
Abbots Leigh 20 E3
Abbotsley 32 D3
Abbots Morton 30 A2
Abbots Ripton 32 D1
Abbot's Salford 30 A2
Abbotswood 10 E2
Abbotts Ann 22 C7
Abdon 38 E6
Aber Dyfed 26 D6
Aber Gynd 47 A3
Aber Gynd 46 B7
Aber S Glam 18 E5
Aberaeron 26 D4
Aberaman 19 A3
Aberangell 37 C5
Aberarad 26 C6
Aberarder Hghld 94 E3
Aberarder Tays 94 C7
Aberargie 88 C7
Aberargoed 19 B4
Aberarth 26 D4
Aberavon 18 C4
Aber-banc 26 C6
Aberbeeg 19 C3
Aber Bowlan 27 A7
Abercanaid 19 A3
Abercarn 19 C4
Abercastle 16 B2
Abercegir 37 C5
Aberchalder 94 D4
Aberchirder 104 E3
Abercorn 81 E4
Abercraf 18 D2
Abercrombie 83 A2
Abercrychan 27 B7
Abercwmboi 19 A3
Abercynon 19 A4
Abercywarch 37 C4
Aberdalgie 88 B6

Aberdare 19 A3
Aberdaron 36 A3
Aberdeen 97 E3
Aberdour 82 B4
Aberduhonw 27 E5
Aberdulais 18 C4
Aberdyfi 37 A6
Aberedw 27 E6
Abereiddy 16 A2
Abererch 46 C7
Aberfan 19 A3
Aberfeldy 87 E4
Aberffraw 46 C4
Aberffrwd 27 A3
Aberford 57 C4
Aberfoyle 80 E1
Abergarw 18 E5
Abergavenny 19 C2
Abergele 47 D3
Abergiar 26 E6
Abergorlech 17 D2
Abergwesyn 27 C5
Abergwili 17 C3
Abergwydol 37 B5
Abergwynant 37 A4
Abergwynfi 18 D4
Abergynolwyn 37 A5
Aberhafesp 37 E6
Aberhosan 37 C6
Aberkenfig 18 D5
Aberlady 82 E5
Aberlemno 89 B3
Aberllefenni 37 B5
Aber-Llia 18 E2
Abermad 27 A3
Abermeurig 26 E5
Abermule 38 A5
Aber-naint 38 A2
Abernant 17 B3
Aber-nant 19 A3
Abernethy 88 C7
Abernyte 88 D5
Aber-pergwm 18 D3
Aberporth 26 B5
Aberriw (Berriew) 38 A4
Aberscross 103 A1
Abersky 94 D3
Abersoch 36 C3
Abersychan 19 C3
Abertillery 19 C3
Abertridwr M Glam 19 B5
Abertridwr Pwys 37 E4
Abertysswg 19 B3
Aberuthven 88 A7
Aberyscir 18 E1
Aberystwyth 26 E2
Abingdon 22 D2
Abinger Common 12 D2
Abington Strath 74 E3
Abington Pigotts 32 E4
Ab Kettleby 41 E2
Ablington 30 D7
Abney 50 C3

Aboyne 97 A4
Abram 49 A1
Abriachan 94 D2
Abridge 24 E3
Abrigland 68 C4
Abson 21 B3
Abthorpe 31 B3
Aby 53 C4
Acarsaid 85 B1
Acaster Malbis 57 D3
Acaster Selby 57 D3
Accrington 55 B5
Accurrach 86 C6
Acha 84 C3
Achacha 86 A4
Achachuirn 93 A2
Achadacaie 79 C5
Achadh-chaorrunn 72 B2
Achadunan 86 C7
Achafour 80 A4
Achagavle 85 D3
Achaglass 72 B3
Achahoish 79 B4
Achalader 88 C4
Achallader 86 E4
Achaluachrach 102 E1
Achamore 78 E4
Achanacairn 86 A5
Achanamara 79 B3
Achandunie 102 E4
Achany 102 D1
Achaphubuil 86 B1
Acharacle 85 C2
Achargary 110 C3
Acharn Strath 86 C5
Acharn Tays 87 D4
Acharosson 79 D4
Achateny 85 B1
Achath 97 C2
Achavanich 111 B4
Achduart 101 C1
Achentoul 110 D5
Achfary 108 E5
Achgarve 101 A2
Achiemore Hghld 109 A2
Achiemore Hghld 110 D3
Achies 111 B3
A'Chill 91 C5
Achiltibuie 101 C1
Achina 110 C2
Achindown 103 B7
Achinduich Gramp 102 D2
Achinduich Hghld 102 D1
Achingills 111 B2
Achintee Hghld 101 B7
Achintee Hghld 86 C1
Achintraid 93 A1
Achlean 95 B6
Achleanan 85 B3
Achleek 85 D3
Achlian 86 C6
Achlyness 108 E3

Achmony 94 D2
Achmore Cent 87 B5
Achmore Hghld 93 A1
Achmore W Is 107 B5
Achnaba 79 D3
Achnabat 94 D2
Achnabourin 110 C3
Achnacarnin 108 C5
Achnacloich 86 A5
Achnaclyth 111 A5
Achnacraig 85 A4
Achnacroish 85 E4
Achnadrish 85 A3
Achnafalnich 86 D6
Achnafauld 87 E5
Achnagairn 102 D7
Achnagarron 102 E4
Achnaha Hghld 85 C4
Achnaha Hghld 85 A2
Achnahanat 102 D2
Achnahannet 95 C3
Achnairn 109 C7
Achnalea 85 E2
Achnaluachrach 102 E1
Achnanellan 85 D2
Achnasaul 93 D6
Achnasheen 101 D6
Achnashelloch 79 C2
Achnastank 104 A5
Achorn 111 B5
Achosnich Hghld 103 A2
Achosnich Hghld 85 A2
Achriabhach 86 C2
Achriesgill 108 E3
Achrimsdale 103 C1
A' Chrois 80 B1
Achronich 85 A5
Achscoriclate 111 A4
Achtoty 109 D2
Achurch 42 D1
Achuvoldrach 109 C3
Achvaich 103 A2
Achvlair 86 A3
Achvraie 101 C1
Ackergill 111 D3
Acklam Clev 64 B2
Acklam N Yorks 64 E7
Ackleton 39 B5
Acklington 77 D5
Ackton 57 C5
Ackworth Moor Top 57 C6
Acle 45 C4
Acock's Green 40 D6
Acol 15 D2
Acomb Northld 70 C2
Acomb N Yorks 57 D2
Aconbury 28 E4
Acre 55 B5
Acrefair 48 B7
Acrise Place 15 B4
Acton Ches 49 A6
Acton GL 24 C4

Acton H & W 29 C1
Acton Salop 38 C6
Acton Sflk 34 C4
Acton Beauchamp 29 A2
Acton Bridge 48 E4
Acton Burnell 38 E4
Acton Green 29 A2
Acton Pigott 38 E4
Acton Round 39 A5
Acton Scott 38 D6
Acton Trussell 40 B3
Acton Turville 21 C2
Adamhill 73 D4
Adbaston 39 B2
Adber 9 B1
Adderbury 30 E4
Adderley 39 A1
Adderstone 77 C2
Addiewell 81 D5
Addingham 56 D3
Addington Bucks 31 C5
Addington GL 24 D6
Addington Kent 13 D1
Addiscombe 24 D6
Addlestone 23 E5
Addlethorpe 53 D5
Adel 57 A3
Adeney 39 A3
Adfa 37 E5
Adforton 38 D7
Adisham 15 C3
Adlestrop 30 C5
Adlingfleet 58 D5
Adlington 55 A6
Admaston Salop 39 A3
Admaston Staffs 40 C2
Admington 30 B3
Adsborough 8 D1
Adstock 31 C5
Adstone 31 A2
Adversane 12 C4
Advie 95 E2
Adwalton 57 A5
Adwell 23 A2
Adwick le Street 57 D7
Adwick upon Dearne 57 C7
Ae Village 74 E7
Affleck Gramp 105 B6
Affleck Tays 89 A5
Affpuddle 9 E4
Afton Bridgend 74 B4
Agglethorpe 63 A6
Aigburth 48 C3
Aignish 107 C4
Aike 59 A3
Aikerness 112 D1
Aikers 113 D2
Aiketgate 69 C5
Aikshaw 68 E5
Aikton 69 A4
Ailey 28 C3
Ailsworth 42 E5
Aimster 111 B2

Ainderby Quernhow 63 D6
Ainderby Steeple 63 D5
Aingers Green 35 A6
Ainsdale 54 C6
Ainstable 69 D5
Ainsworth 55 B6
Ainthorpe 64 E3
Aintree 48 C2
Aird 98 B6
Aird Dell 107 C1
Airdrie Fife 83 A2
Airdrie Strath 81 B5
Aird Tunga 107 C4
Aird Uig 106 D4
Airieland 67 D5
Airies 66 A4
Airigh-drishaig 92 E1
Airmyn 58 C5
Airntully 88 B5
Airor 92 E4
Airriehassan 66 E6
Airth 81 C3
Airton 55 D2
Aisby Lincs 52 B2
Aisby Lincs 42 D1
Aiskew 63 D6
Aislaby Dur 64 B2
Aislaby N Yorks 65 A3
Aislaby N Yorks 64 E5
Aisthorpe 52 C4
Aith Fetlar 114 F3
Aith Ork 112 B5
Aith Ork 112 F4
Aith Shet 115 C2
Aitnoch 95 C2
Akeld 77 A3
Akeley 31 C4
Akenham 35 A4
Albaston 4 E3
Alberbury 38 C3
Albourne 12 E5
Albrighton Salop 40 A4
Albrighton Salop 38 D3
Alburgh 45 B7
Albury Herts 33 A6
Albury Sry 12 C2
Albury Heath 12 C2
Alby Hill 45 A2
Alcaig 102 D6
Alcaston 38 D6
Alcester 30 A2
Alciston 13 C6
Alcombe 7 D2
Alconbury 32 C1
Alconbury Weston 32 C1
Aldborough Nflk 45 A2
Aldborough N Yorks 57 C1
Aldbourne 22 B4
Aldbrough Humb 59 C4
Aldbrough St John 63 C3
Aldburgh 38 D6
Aldbury 31 E6
Aldclune 88 A2

Aldeburgh 35 D3
Aldeby 45 D6
Aldenham 24 B3
Alderbury 10 C2
Alderford 45 A4
Alderholt 10 C3
Alderley 21 B1
Alderley Edge 49 C4
Aldermans Green 41 A6
Aldermaston 22 E5
Aldermaston Soke 23 A5
Alderminster 30 C3
Aldersey Green 48 D6
Aldershot 23 C6
Alderton Glos 30 A4
Alderton Northants 31 C3
Alderton Salop 38 D2
Alderton Sflk 35 C4
Alderton Wilts 21 C2
Alderwasley 50 E5
Aldfield 57 A1
Aldford 48 D6
Aldham Esx 34 D6
Aldham Sflk 34 E4
Aldie Gramp 105 D5
Aldie Hghld 103 A3
Aldingbourne 12 B6
Aldingham 61 B6
Aldington H & W 30 A3
Aldington Kent 15 A5
Aldivalloch 104 B6
Aldochlay 80 C2
Aldons 66 C2
Aldreth 33 A1
Aldridge 40 C4
Aldringham 35 D2
Aldro 65 A7
Aldsworth 30 B7
Aldunie 104 B6
Aldville 88 A5
Aldwark Derbs 50 D5
Aldwark N Yorks 57 C1
Aldwick 12 B7
Aldwincle 42 D6
Aldworth 22 E4
Alexandria 80 C4
Alfardisworthy 6 B5
Alfington 8 C4
Alfold 12 C3
Alford Gramp 97 A2
Alford Lincs 53 C4
Alford Som 21 A7
Alford Crossways 12 C3
Alfreton 51 A5
Alfrick 29 B2
Alfriston 13 C6
Algakirk 43 A1
Alhampton 21 A7
Alkborough 58 D5
Alkerton 30 D3
Alkham 15 C4
Alkington 38 E1
Alkmonton 50 C7
Allaleigh 5 D5
Allanaquoich 96 B4
Allancreich 97 A4
Allangillfoot 75 C6
Allanton Bdrs 83 D7
Allanton D & G 74 E7
Allanton Strath 81 C6
Allardice 97 D6
Allasdale 90 B5
All Cannings 21 E4
Allendale Town 70 B3
Allenheads 70 B4
Allensford 70 D3
Allen's Green 33 A7
Allensmore 28 D4
Aller 9 A1
Allerby 68 D6
Allerford Devon 4 E2
Allerford Som 7 D2
Allerston 65 A5
Allerthorpe 58 C3
Allerton Mers 48 C3
Allerton W Yorks 56 E4
Allerton Bywater 57 C5
Allesley 40 E6
Allestree 50 E7
Allexton 42 B4
Allgreave 49 D5
Allhallows 14 D1
Alligin Shuas 101 A6
Allimore Green 40 A3
Allington Lincs 52 B7
Allington Wilts 10 D1
Allington Wilts 21 E4

Allithwaite 61 C6
Allnabad 109 B4
Alloa 81 C2
Allonby 68 D5
Alloway 73 C6
All Saints 32 E3
All Saints South Elmham 45 C7
Allscot 39 B5
All Stretton 38 D5
Alltachoanaich 85 D3
Alltbeithe 93 C2
Alltforgan 37 D3
Alltmawr 27 E6
Alltnacaillich 109 B4
Allt na h'Airbhe 101 D2
Alltsigh 94 C4
Alltwalis 17 C2
Alltwen 18 C3
Alltyblaca 26 E6
Allweston 9 C2
Almeley 28 C2
Almer 10 A5
Almington 39 B1
Almiston Cross 6 C4
Almondbank 88 B6
Almondbury 56 E6
Almondsbury 21 A2
Alne 57 C1
Alness 102 E5
Alnham 77 A4
Alnmouth 77 D4
Alnwick 77 C4
Alphamstone 34 C5
Alpheton 34 C3
Alphington 7 D7
Alpington 45 C5
Alport 50 D4
Alpraham 48 E6
Alresford 34 E6
Alrewas 40 D3
Alrick 88 C2
Alsager 49 B6
Alsagers Bank 49 C7
Alsop en le Dale 50 C5
Alston 70 A4
Alstone 29 D4
Alstonefield 50 C5
Alswear 7 B4
Altagalvash 79 D5
Altanduin 110 D6
Altarnun 4 C2
Altass 102 D1
Alterwall 111 C2
Altham 55 B4
Althorne 25 E3
Althorpe 58 D7
Alticry 66 D6
Altnafeadh 86 D3
Altnaharra 109 C5
Altofts 57 B5
Alton Derbs 50 E4
Alton Hants 11 D1
Alton Staffs 50 B6
Alton Pancras 9 C3
Alton Priors 22 A5
Altonside 104 A3
Altrincham 49 B3
Altura 93 E5
Alva 81 C2
Alvanley 48 D4
Alvaston 50 E7
Alvechurch 40 C7
Alvecote 40 E4
Alvediston 10 A2
Alveley 39 B6
Alverdiscott 6 E4
Alverstoke 11 B5
Alverstone 11 B6
Alverton 51 D6
Alvescot 30 C7
Alveston Avn 21 A2
Alveston Warks 30 C2
Alvie 95 B5
Alvingham 53 B2
Alvington 29 A7
Alwalton 42 E5
Alwinton 77 A5
Alwoodley Gates 57 B3
Alyth 88 D4
Amalebra 2 B5
Ambergate 50 E5
Amber Hill 53 A7
Amberley Glos 29 C7
Amberley W Ssx 12 C5
Amble 77 D5
Amblecote 40 A6

Ambleside 61 C3
Ambleston 16 D3
Ambrismore 72 E2
Ambrosden 31 B6
Amcotts 58 D6
Amersham 23 D2
Amhuinnsuidhe 106 D7
Amington 40 E4
Amisfield Town 75 A7
Amlwch 46 D1
Amlwch Port 46 D1
Ammanford 18 B2
Amotherby 64 E6
Ampfield 10 E2
Ampleforth 64 C6
Ampleforth College 64 C6
Ampney Crucis 30 A7
Ampney St Mary 30 A7
Ampney St Peter 30 A7
Amport 22 B7
Ampthill 32 B5
Ampton 34 C1
Amroth 16 E5
Amulree 87 E5
Anaboard 95 D2
Anaheilt 85 E2
Ancaster 52 C7
Anchor 38 A6
Ancroft 77 A1
Ancrum 76 C3
Ancton 12 B6
Anderby 53 D4
Anderson 9 E4
Anderton 49 A4
Andover 22 C7
Andover Down 22 C7
Andoversford 30 A6
Andreas 60 d2
Angarrack 2 C5
Angersleigh 8 C2
Angerton 69 A4
Angle 16 B5
Anglers Retreat 37 B6
Angmering 12 C6
Angram 57 D3
Anie 87 B7
Ankerville 103 B4
Anlaby 59 A5
Anmer 44 B3
Annan 68 E3
Annaside 60 E5
Annat Hghld 101 A6
Annat Strath 86 B6
Annbank 73 D5
Annesley 51 B5
Annesley Woodhouse 51 A5
Annfield Plain 70 E3
Annscroft 38 D4
Ansdell 54 C5
Ansford 21 A7
Ansley 40 E5
Anslow 40 E2
Anslow Gate 40 E2
Anstey Herts 33 A5
Anstey Leics 41 C4
Anston 51 B2
Anstruther 83 A2
Ansty Warks 41 A6
Ansty Wilts 10 A2
Ansty W Ssx 12 E4
Anthill Common 11 C3
Anthorn 68 E4
Antingham 45 B2
Antony 4 D5
Antrobus 49 A4
Anvil Corner 6 C6
Anwick 52 E6
Anwoth 67 B5
Aonach 85 C1
Aoradh 78 B5
Apethorpe 42 D5
Apley 52 E4
Apperknowle 50 E3
Apperley 29 C5
Appleby 58 E6
Appleby-in-Westmorland 69 E7
Appleby Magna 41 A3
Appleby Parva 41 A4
Appleby Street 24 D2
Applecross 100 E7
Appledore Devon 6 D3
Appledore Devon 8 B2
Appledore Kent 14 E6
Appledore Heath 14 E5

Appleford 22 E2
Appleshaw 22 C7
Applethwaite 69 A7
Appleton Ches 49 A3
Appleton Oxon 30 E7
Appleton-le-Moors 64 E5
Appleton-le-Street 64 E6
Appleton Roebuck 57 D3
Appleton Wiske 63 D4
Appletreehall 76 B4
Appletreewick 56 D1
Appley 8 B1
Appley Bridge 48 E1
Apse Heath 11 B6
Apsley 23 E1
Apsley End 32 C5
Apuldram 11 E4
Arbirlot 89 C4
Arborfield 23 B5
Arborfield Cross 23 B5
Arborfield Garrison 23 B5
Arbroath 89 C4
Arbuthnott 97 D6
Archdeacon Newton 63 C3
Archiestown 104 A4
Arclid Green 49 B5
Ard a'Chapuill 79 E4
Ardacheranbeg 79 E3
Ardacheranmor 79 E3
Ardachoil 85 D5
Ardachvie 93 D5
Ardaily 72 A2
Ardalanish 84 E7
Ardanaiseig 86 B6
Ardaneaskan 93 A1
Ardanstur 85 E7
Ardantiobairt 85 C3
Ardantrive 85 E5
Ardbeg Bute 79 E5
Ardbeg Islay 78 D7
Ardbeg Strath 80 A3
Ardblair 94 C2
Ardbrecknish 86 B6
Ardcharnich 101 D3
Ardchiavaig 84 E7
Ardchoirk 85 D5
Ardchonnel 86 A5
Ardchonnell 86 A7
Ardchrishnish 85 A6
Ardchuilk 93 E1
Ardchullarie More 87 B7
Ardchyle 87 B6
Ardd-lin 38 B3
Ardeley 32 E6
Ardelve 93 A2
Arden 80 C3
Ardencaple 85 D7
Ardens Grafton 30 B2
Ardentinny 80 A3
Ardeonaig 87 C5
Ardersier 103 A6
Ardery 85 D2
Ardessie 101 C3
Ardfad 85 D7
Ardfern 79 C1
Ardfin 78 D5
Ardgartan 80 B1
Ardgay 102 D2
Ardgenavan 86 C7
Ardgowan 80 B4
Ardgowse 97 B2
Ardgye 103 E5
Ardhallow 80 A4
Ardhasig 106 D7
Ardheslaig 100 E6
Ardiecow 104 D2
Ardinamar 85 D7
Ardindrean 101 D3
Ardingly 13 A4
Ardington 22 D3
Ardintoul 93 A2
Ardivachar 98 B7
Ardkinglas 86 C7
Ardlair 104 D6
Ardlamont 79 D5
Ardleigh 34 E6
Ardleish 86 E7
Ardler 88 D4
Ardley 31 A5
Ardlui 86 E7
Ardlussa 79 A3
Ardmaddy 86 B5
Ardmair 101 D2
Ardmaleish 79 E5
Ardmay 80 B1
Ardmenish 78 E4

Ardminish 72 A3
Ardmolich 85 D1
Ardmore Hghld 103 A3
Ardmore Islay 78 D6
Ardmore Strath 85 B6
Ardmore Strath 80 C4
Ardnackaig 79 B2
Ardnacross 85 B4
Ardnadam 80 A3
Ardnadrochit 85 D5
Ardnagowan 79 E1
Ardnagrask 102 D7
Ardnahein 80 A2
Ardnahoe 78 D4
Ardnastang 85 E2
Ardnave 78 B4
Ardo 80 A1
Ardo 105 B5
Ardoch D & G 74 D5
Ardoch Gramp 103 E6
Ardoch Tays 88 B5
Ardochrig 74 B1
Ardochu 102 E1
Ardoyne 104 E6
Ardpatrick 79 B5
Ardpeaton 80 B3
Ardradnaig 87 D4
Ardrishaig 79 C3
Ardroe 108 C6
Ardroil 106 D4
Ardrossan 73 B3
Ardscalpsie 72 E2
Ardshave 103 A2
Ardshealach 85 C2
Ardshellach 85 D7
Ardslave 99 A3
Ardsley 57 B7
Ardsley East 57 B5
Ardslignish 85 B2
Ardtalla 78 D6
Ardtalnaig 87 D5
Ardtaraig 79 E3
Ardteatle 86 C6
Ardtoe 85 C1
Ardtornish 85 D4
Ardtrostan 87 C6
Ardtur 86 A4
Arduaine 85 D7
Ardullie 102 E5
Ardura 85 C5
Ardvar 108 D5
Ardvasar 92 D4
Ardveich 87 C6
Ardverikie 94 D7
Ardvey Harris 99 A2
Ardvey Harris 98 E3
Ardvorlich Strath 86 E7
Ardvorlich Tays 87 C6
Ardvourlie 106 E6
Ardwall 67 B5
Ardwell D & G 66 C6
Ardwell Gramp 104 B5
Ardwell Strath 66 C1
Areley Kings 40 A7
Arevegaig 85 C2
Arford 11 E1
Argaty 81 B1
Argoed 19 B4
Argoed Mill 27 D4
Argrennan 67 D5
Arichamish 79 D1
Arichastlich 86 D5
Arichonan 79 B2
Aridhglas 84 E6
Arienskill 92 E6
Arileod 84 C3
Arinacrinachd 100 E6
Arinafad Beg 79 B3
Arinagour 84 D3
Arinambane 90 C3
Arinanuan 72 B4
Arinechan 79 D1
Arion 112 B5
Arisaig 92 D6
Arivruaich 107 A6
Arkendale 57 B1
Arkesden 33 A5
Arkholme 61 E6
Arkleby 68 E6
Arkleside 63 A6
Arkley 24 C3
Arksey 57 D7
Arkwright Town 51 A3
Arlary 82 B2
Arlecdon 60 E2
Arlesey 32 C5

Arleston 39 A3
Arley Ches 49 A3
Arley Warks 40 E5
Arlingham 29 B6
Arlington Devon 7 A2
Arlington E Ssx 13 C6
Arlington Glos 30 B7
Armadale Hghld 110 C2
Armadale Loth 81 D5
Armathwaite 69 D5
Arminghall 45 B5
Armitage 40 C3
Armscote 30 C3
Armston 42 D6
Armthorpe 57 E7
Arnabost 84 D3
Arnage 105 C5
Arncliffe 62 E7
Arncliffe Cote 62 E7
Arncott 31 B6
Arncroach 83 A2
Arne 10 A6
Arnesby 41 D5
Arngask 88 C7
Arngibbon 81 A2
Arngomery 81 A2
Arnhall 89 C2
Arnipol 92 E6
Arnisdale 93 A3
Arnish 100 C7
Arnisort 99 C6
Arniston Engine 82 D6
Arnol 107 B3
Arnold 51 B6
Arnprior 81 A2
Arnside 61 D6
Arowry 48 D7
Arrad Foot 61 C5
Arradoul 104 C2
Arram 59 A3
Arrat 89 C3
Arrathorne 63 C5
Arreton 11 B6
Arrington 32 E3
Arrivain 86 D5
Arrochar 80 B1
Arrow 30 A2
Arscaig 109 C7
Artafellie 102 E7
Arthington 57 A3
Arthingworth 41 E6
Arthog 37 A4
Arthrath 105 C5
Arthurstone 88 D4
Artrochie 105 D5
Aruadh 78 B5
Arundel 12 C6
Aryhoulan 86 B2
Asby 68 D7
Ascog 80 A5
Ascot 23 D5
Ascott 30 D4
Ascott-under-Wychwood 30 C6
Ascreavie 88 E3
Asenby 63 D7
Asfordby 41 E3
Asfordby Hill 41 E3
Asgarby Lincs 53 B5
Asgarby Lincs 52 E7
Ash Devon 6 E6
Ash Kent 15 C3
Ash Kent 25 A6
Ash Som 9 A1
Ash Sry 23 C6
Ashampstead 22 E4
Ashbocking 35 A3
Ashbourne Derbs 50 C6
Ashbrittle 8 B1
Ash Bullayne 7 B6
Ashburnham Place 13 D5
Ashburton 5 C4
Ashbury Devon 6 E7
Ashbury Oxon 22 B3
Ashby 58 E7
Ashby by Partney 53 C5
Ashby cum Fenby 59 C7
Ashby de la Launde 52 D6
Ashby de la Zouch 41 A3
Ashby Folville 41 E3
Ashby Magna 41 C5
Ashby Parva 41 C6
Ashby Puerorum 53 B4
Ashby St Ledgers 31 A1
Ashby St Mary 45 C5
Ashchurch 29 D4
Ashcombe 8 A6

Ashcott 20 D7
Ashdon 33 B4
Ashe 22 E6
Asheldham 25 E2
Ashen 33 D4
Ashenden 14 D5
Ashendon 31 C6
Ashens 79 C4
Ashfield Cent 81 B1
Ashfield Sflk 35 B2
Ashfield Strath 79 B3
Ashfield Green 35 B1
Ashfold Crossways 12 E4
Ashford Derbs 50 C4
Ashford Devon 5 B6
Ashford Devon 6 E3
Ashford Dorset 10 C3
Ashford Kent 15 A4
Ashford Sry 23 E4
Ashford Bowdler 38 E7
Ashford Carbonel 38 E7
Ashford Hill 22 E5
Ashiesteel 76 A2
Ashill Devon 8 B2
Ashill Nflk 44 C5
Ashill Som 8 E2
Ashingdon 25 D3
Ashington Northld 77 D7
Ashington Som 9 B1
Ashington W Ssx 12 D5
Ashkirk 76 A3
Ashleworth 29 C5
Ashley Cambs 33 C2
Ashley Ches 49 B3
Ashley Devon 7 A5
Ashley Glos 21 D1
Ashley Hants 10 E1
Ashley Hants 10 D5
Ashley Northants 41 E5
Ashley Staffs 39 B1
Ashley Wilts 21 C4
Ashley Green 23 D1
Ash Magna 38 E1
Ashmanhaugh 45 C3
Ashmansworth 22 D6
Ashmansworthy 6 C5
Ash Mill 7 B4
Ashmore Dors 10 A3
Ashmore Tays 88 C3
Ashorne 30 D2
Ashover 50 E4
Ashow 41 A7
Ashperton 29 A3
Ashprington 5 D5
Ash Priors 8 C1
Ashreigney 7 A5
Ashridge 31 E6
Ashtead 12 D1
Ash Thomas 8 B2
Ashton Ches 48 E5
Ashton Corn 2 D6
Ashton Devon 5 D2
Ashton H & W 28 E1
Ashton Northants 42 D6
Ashton Northants 31 C3
Ashton Common 21 C5
Ashton-in-Makerfield 48 E2
Ashton Keynes 21 E1
Ashton under Hill 29 D4
Ashton-Under -Lyne 49 D2
Ashton upon Mersey
   49 B2
Ashurst Hants 10 E3
Ashurst Kent 13 C3
Ashurst W Ssx 12 D5
Ashurstwood 13 B3
Ash Vale 23 C6
Ashwater 6 C7
Ashwell Herts 32 D5
Ashwell Leics 42 B3
Ashwellthorpe 45 A6
Ashwick 21 A6
Ashwicken 44 B4
Ashybank 76 B4
Askam In Furness 61 B6
Askern 57 D6
Askernish 90 C3
Askerswell 9 B4
Askett 31 D7
Askham Cumb 69 D7
Askham Notts 51 D3
Askham Bryan 57 D3
Askham Richard 57 D3
Asknish 79 D2
Askrigg 62 E5
Askwith 56 E3
Aslackby 42 D1

Aslacton 45 A6
Aslockton 51 D6
Aspall 35 A2
Aspatria 68 E5
Aspenden 32 E6
Aspley Guise 31 E4
Aspull 49 A1
Assary 85 D1
Asselby 58 C5
Assington 34 D5
Astbury 49 C5
Astcote 31 B2
Asterby 53 A4
Asterley 38 C4
Asterton 38 C5
Asthall 30 C6
Asthall Leigh 30 D6
Astley H & W 29 B1
Astley Salop 38 E3
Astley W Mids 41 A6
Astley Abbotts 39 B5
Astley Bridge 55 B6
Astley Cross 29 C1
Astley Green 49 B2
Aston Berks 23 B3
Aston Ches 49 A7
Aston Ches 48 E4
Aston Derbs 50 C2
Aston H & W 38 D7
Aston Herts 32 D6
Aston Oxon 30 D7
Aston Salop 39 A4
Aston Salop 38 E2
Aston Staffs 40 B1
Aston Staffs 49 B7
Aston S Yorks 51 A2
Aston W Mids 40 C6
Aston Abbotts 31 D5
Aston Botterell 39 A6
Aston Cantlow 30 B2
Aston Clinton 31 D6
Aston Crews 29 A5
Aston Cross 29 D4
Aston End 32 D6
Aston Eyre 39 A5
Aston Fields 29 D1
Aston Flamville 41 B5
Aston Ingham 29 A5
Aston juxta Mondrum
   49 A6
Aston le Walls 30 E2
Aston Magna 30 B4
Aston Munslow 38 E6
Aston on Clun 38 C6
Aston-on-Trent 41 B2
Aston Rogers 38 C4
Aston Rowant 23 B2
Aston Sandford 31 C7
Aston Somerville 30 A4
Aston Subedge 30 B3
Aston Tirrold 22 E3
Aston upon Trent 41 B2
Aston Upthorpe 22 E3
Astwick 32 D5
Astwood 31 E3
Astwood Bank 30 A1
Aswarby 42 D1
Aswardby 53 B4
Aswick Grange 43 B3
Atcham 38 E4
Atch Lench 30 A2
Athelington 35 B1
Athelney 8 E1
Athelstaneford 83 A5
Atherington 6 E4
Atherstone 41 A5
Atherstone on Stour 30 C2
Atherton 49 A1
Atlow 50 D6
Attadale 93 B1
Attenborough 51 B7
Atterby 52 C2
Attleborough Nflk 44 E6
Attleborough Warks 41 A5
Attlebridge 45 A4
Atwick 59 B2
Atworth 21 C4
Aubourn 52 C5
Auch 86 E5
Auchachenna 86 B6
Auchairne 66 C2
Auchallater 96 B5
Auchameanach 72 C2
Aucharnie 104 E4
Auchattie 97 B4
Auchavan 88 C2
Auchbraad 79 C3

Auchbreck 104 A6
Auchelie 95 D7
Auchenblae 97 C6
Auchenbothie 80 C4
Auchenbrack 67 D1
Auchenbreck 79 E3
Auchencairn 67 D5
Auchencrow 83 D6
Auchendinny 82 C6
Auchendolly 67 D4
Auchendrane 73 C6
Aucheneck 80 D3
Auchengray 81 D6
Auchenhalrig 104 B2
Auchenheath 74 D1
Auchenhessnane 74 D6
Auchenmalg 66 D5
Auchenrivock 75 D7
Auchentiber 73 C3
Auchentroig 80 E2
Auchernach 96 D2
Auchessan 87 A6
Auchgourish 95 C4
Auchinafaud 72 B2
Auchincruive 73 C5
Auchindarroch Hghld
   86 B3
Auchindarroch Hghld
   79 C3
Auchindrain 79 E1
Auchindrean 101 D3
Auchinleck Strath 73 E5
Auchinloch 81 A4
Auchinner 87 C7
Auchinroath 104 A3
Auchintoul Gramp 104 E3
Auchintoul Hghld 102 D2
Auchinvennal 80 B3
Auchiries 105 D5
Auchleven 104 E6
Auchlochan 74 D2
Auchlunies 97 A4
Auchlunkart 104 B4
Auchlyne 87 B6
Auchmacoy 105 C5
Auchmair 104 B6
Auchmankle 66 C4
Auchmithie 89 C4
Auchmuirbridge 82 C2
Auchmull 97 A6
Auchnabony 67 D6
Auchnabreac 79 E1
Auchnacloich 87 E5
Auchnacoshan 86 A5
Auchnacraig 85 D5
Auchnacree 89 A2
Auchnafree 87 E5
Auchnagallin 95 D2
Auchnagatt 105 C4
Auchnaha 79 D3
Auchnangoul 79 E1
Aucholzie 96 D4
Auchorrie 97 B3
Auchraw 87 B6
Auchreoch 86 E6
Auchronie 96 E5
Auchry 105 A3
Auchterarder 88 A7
Auchtercairn 101 A4
Auchterderran 82 C3
Auchterhouse 88 E5
Auchtermuchty 88 D7
Auchterneed 102 C6
Auchtertool 82 C3
Auchtertyre Cent 86 E6
Auchtertyre Gramp 103 E6
Auchtertyre Tays 88 D4
Auchtoo 87 B6
Auchuirgill 102 C1
Auckingill 111 D2
Auckley 57 E7
Audenshaw 49 D2
Audlem 49 A7
Audley 49 B6
Audley End 33 B5
Aughton Humb 58 C4
Aughton Lancs 48 C1
Aughton Lancs 54 E1
Aughton S Yorks 51 A2
Aughton Park 48 D1
Auldearn 103 C6
Aulden 28 D2
Auldhame 83 A4
Auldhouse 81 A6
Aulich 87 C3
Aultanrynie 109 A5

Aultbea 101 A3
Aultgrishan 101 A3
Ault Hucknall 51 A4
Aultibea 111 A6
Aultiphurst 110 D2
Aultmore 104 C3
Aultnagoire 94 D3
Aultnapaddock 104 B4
Aulton 104 E6
Aultvoulin 92 E4
Aundorach 95 C4
Aunk 8 B3
Aunsby 42 D1
Auquhorthies 105 B6
Aust 20 E2
Austerfield 51 C1
Austonley 56 E7
Austrey 40 E4
Austwick 55 B1
Authorpe 53 B3
Authorpe Row 53 D4
Avalon, Isle of 20 E7
Avebury 21 E4
Aveley 25 A4
Avening 21 C1
Averham 51 D5
Aveton Gifford 5 B6
Avielochan 95 C4
Aviemore 95 B4
Avington Berks 22 C5
Avington Hants 11 B1
Avoch 102 E6
Avon 10 C5
Avonbridge 81 D4
Avon Dassett 30 E2
Avonmouth 20 E3
Avonwick 5 C5
Awbridge 10 E2
Awhirk D & G 66 B5
Awkley 20 E2
Awliscombe 8 C3
Awre 29 B7
Awsworth 51 A6
Axbridge 20 D5
Axford Hants 23 A7
Axford Wilts 22 B5
Axminster 8 D4
Axmouth 8 D4
Aycliffe 71 A6
Aydon 70 D2
Aylburton 29 A7
Ayle 70 A4
Aylesbeare 8 B4
Aylesbury 31 D6
Aylesby 59 C7
Aylesford 13 E1
Aylesham 15 C3
Aylestone 41 C4
Aylmerton 45 A2
Aylsham 45 A3
Aylton 29 A4
Aymestrey 28 D1
Aynho 31 A4
Ayot St Lawrence 32 C7
Ayot St Peter 32 D7
Ayr 73 C5
Aysgarth 63 A6
Ayshford 8 B2
Ayside 61 C5
Ayston 42 B4
Aythorpe Roding 33 B7
Ayton Bdrs 83 E6
Ayton Tays 88 C7
Aywick 114 E4
Azerley 63 C7

B
Babbacombe 5 E4
Babbinswood 38 C2
Babcary 9 B1
Babel 27 C7
Babell 48 A4
Babeny 5 B3
Babraham 33 B3
Babworth 51 C2
Bachnagairn 96 C6
Back 107 C3
Backaland 112 E3
Backaskaill 112 D1
Backbarrow 61 C5
Backfolds 105 D3
Backford 48 C4
Backhill 105 D5
Backhill of Trustach 97 B4
Backies Gramp 104 C3
Backies Hghld 103 B1

Backlass 111 C3
Backmuir of New Gilston
   82 E2
Back of Keppoch 92 D6
Backside 104 C5
Backwell 20 D4
Backworth 71 A1
Bacon End 33 C7
Baconsthorpe 45 A2
Bacton H & W 28 C4
Bacton Nflk 45 C2
Bacton Sflk 34 E2
Bacup 55 C5
Badachro 100 E4
Badanloch 110 C5
Badavanich 101 D6
Badbea 111 A7
Badbury 22 A3
Badby 31 A2
Badcall 108 D4
Badcaul 101 C2
Baddeley Green 49 D6
Baddesley Ensor 40 E5
Baddidarach 108 C6
Badenscoth 105 A5
Badenyon 96 D2
Badger 39 B5
Badgerbank 49 C4
Badgers Mount 24 F6
Badgeworth 29 D6
Badgworth 20 C5
Badicaul 92 E2
Badingham 35 C2
Badintagairt 109 B7
Badlesmere 15 A3
Badley 34 E3
Badlibster 111 C4
Badluachrach 101 B2
Badminton 21 C2
Badnaban 108 C6
Badnabay 108 E4
Badnafrave 96 C2
Badnagie 111 B5
Badnambiast 87 D1
Badninish 103 A2
Badrallach 101 C2
Badsell 13 C2
Badsey 30 A3
Badshot Lea 23 C7
Badsworth 57 C6
Badwell Ash 34 D2
Badyo 88 A2
Bagby 64 B5
Bage, The 28 B3
Bag Enderby 53 B4
Bagendon 30 A7
Baggrow 68 E5
Bagh Gleann Speireig
   79 A2
Bagillt 48 B4
Baginton 41 A7
Baglan 18 C4
Bagley 38 D2
Bagmore 23 A7
Bagnall 49 D6
Bagnor 22 D5
Bagshot Sry 23 D5
Bagshot Wilts 22 C5
Bagstone 21 A2
Bagthorpe Nflk 44 B2
Bagthorpe Notts 51 A5
Baguley 49 C3
Bagworth 41 B4
Bagwy Llydiart 28 D5
Baildon 56 E4
Bailebeag 94 D4
Baile Boidheach 79 B4
Baileguish 95 B6
Bailemeonach 85 C4
BaHetonach 85 C1
Baileyhead 69 D2
Bailliemore 85 E6
Baillieward 104 C5
Bainbridge 62 E5
Bainshole 104 E5
Bainton Humb 58 E2
Bainton Northants 42 D4
Bairnkine 76 C4
Bakebare 104 B5
Baker's End 32 E7
Baker Street 25 B4
Bakewell 50 D7
Bala 47 D7
Balachuirn 100 C7
Balaglas 98 C6
Balaldie 103 B4

Balallan 107 A5
Balameanach 79 C2
Balarumindubh 78 C2
Balaruminmore 78 C2
Balbeg Hghld 94 C2
Balbeg Hghld 94 C3
Balbeggie 88 C6
Balbirnie 82 C2
Balbithan 97 C2
Balblair 103 A5
Balcharn 102 D1
Balcherry 103 B3
Balchers 105 A3
Balchladich 108 C5
Balchraggan 102 D7
Balchrick 108 D2
Balcombe 13 A3
Balcomie 83 B2
Balcurvie 82 D2
Baldernock 80 E4
Baldersby 63 D7
Balderstone 55 A4
Balderton 52 B6
Baldhu 2 E4
Baldinnie 89 A7
Baldock 32 D5
Baldovie 89 A5
Baldrine 60 d3
Baldslow 14 D7
Baldwin 60 c3
Baldwinholme 69 B4
Baldwin's Gate 39 B1
Bale 44 E2
Balelone 98 B4
Balemartine 84 A4
Balemore 98 B5
Balendoch 88 D4
Balephuil 84 A4
Balerno 82 B6
Balernock 80 B3
Balevulin 85 A6
Balfield 89 B2
Balfour Gramp 97 A4
Balfour Ork 112 D5
Balfron 80 E3
Balgarva 98 B7
Balgavies 89 B3
Balgedie 82 B2
Balgonar 81 E2
Balgove 105 B5
Balgowan 68 A7
Balgown 99 C5
Balgray 89 A5
Balgreen 105 A3
Balgreggan 66 B5
Balgy 101 A6
Balhaldie 81 C1
Balhary 88 D4
Balhelvie 88 E6
Balhousie 82 E2
Baliasta 114 F2
Baligill 110 D2
Baligoun 85 E6
Balindore 86 A5
Balintore Hghld 103 B4
Balintraid 103 A4
Balintyre 87 C4
Balivanich 98 B6
Balkeerie 88 E4
Balkholme 58 C5
Balkissock 66 C2
Ball 38 C2
Ballabeg 60 b4
Ballacannell 60 d3
Ballacarnane Beg 60 c3
Ballachulish 86 B3
Balladoole 60 b5
Ballafesson 60 b4
Ballagyr 60 b3
Ballajora 60 d2
Ballakilpheric 60 b4
Ballamodha 60 b4
Ballantrae 66 B2
Ballantrushal 107 B2
Ballasalla IOM 60 b4
Ballater 96 D4
Ballaterach 96 E4
Ballaugh 60 c2
Ballaveare 60 c4
Ballchraggan 103 A4
Ballechin 88 A3
Balleich 89 E1
Ballemeanoch 80 A1
Ballencrieff 82 E5
Ball Haye Green 49 D6
Ball Hill 22 D5
Ballidon 50 D5

Balliekine 72 C4
Balliemore *Strath* 80 A2
Balliemore *Tays* 87 D3
Ballig 60 b3
Ballimeanoch 86 B7
Ballimore *Cent* 87 B7
Ballimore *Strath* 79 D3
Ballinaby 78 B5
Ballindean 88 D6
Ballingdon 34 C4
Ballinger Common 23 D1
Ballingham 28 E4
Ballingry 82 B3
Ballinlick 88 A4
Ballinluig 88 A3
Ballintuim 88 C3
Ballivain 72 A5
Balloch *Hghld* 103 A7
Balloch *Strath* 80 C3
Balloch *Tays* 88 E3
Balloch *Tays* 87 E7
Ballochandrain 79 D3
Ballochford 104 B5
Ballochgair 72 B5
Ballochmorrie 66 D2
Ballochmyle 73 E5
Ballochroy 72 B2
Ballochyle 80 A3
Ballogie 97 A4
Balls Cross 12 B4
Ballyaurgan 79 B4
Ballygown 85 A4
Ballygrant 78 C5
Ballyhaugh 84 C3
Ballymichael 72 D4
Balmacara 93 A2
Balmaclellan 67 C3
Balmacneil 88 A3
Balmadies 89 B3
Balmae 67 C6
Balmaha 80 D2
Balmalcolm 82 D2
Balmartin 98 B4
Balmeanach 85 A5
Balmedie 89 B4
Balmerino 88 E6
Balmerlawn 10 E4
Balminnoch 66 D4
Balmore *Hghld* 103 B7
Balmore *Hghld* 94 B2
Balmore *Hghld* 99 B7
Balmore *Strath* 81 A4
Balmullo 89 A6
Balmungie 103 A6
Balmyle 88 C3
Balnaboth 88 E2
Balnabruaich 103 A5
Balnacra 101 B7
Balnafoich 94 E2
Balnagall 103 B3
Balnaguard 88 A3
Balnahard *Strath* 78 D2
Balnahard *Strath* 85 A5
Balnain 94 C2
Balnakeil 109 A2
Balnamoon 89 B2
Balnapaling 103 A5
Balnespick 95 B5
Balquhidder 87 B6
Balranald 98 B5
Balsall 40 E7
Balsall Common 40 E7
Balscote 30 D3
Balsham 33 B3
Baltasound 114 F2
Balterley 49 B6
Baltersan 67 A4
Balthangie 105 B3
Balthayock 88 C6
Baltonsborough 20 E7
Baluachraig 79 C2
Balulve 78 D5
Balure *Strath* 86 B5
Balure *Strath* 85 E5
Balvaird 102 D6
Balvarran 88 B2
Balvicar 85 D7
Balvraid *Hghld* 93 A3
Balvraid *Hghld* 95 B2
Balygrundle 85 E4
Bamber Bridge 54 E5
Bambers Green 33 B6
Bamburgh 77 C2
Bamff 88 D3
Bamford 50 D2
Bampton *Cumb* 61 E2
Bampton *Devon* 7 D4

Bampton *Oxon* 30 D7
Banavie 86 C1
Banbury 30 E3
Banchor 103 C7
Banchory 97 B4
Banchory-Devenick 97 E3
Bancyfelin 17 B4
Banc-y-ffordd 17 C2
Bandon 82 C2
Banff 104 E2
Bangor *Gynd* 46 E3
Bangor Is-coed 48 C7
Bangor Teifi 26 C6
Banham 44 E7
Bank 10 D4
Bank End 61 A5
Bankend *D & G* 68 D3
Bankend *Strath* 74 D2
Bankfoot 88 B5
Bankhead *D & G* 67 D6
Bankhead *Gramp* 97 B2
Bankhead *Gramp* 97 D2
Bankhead *Gramp* 97 B3
Bank Newton 55 D2
Banknock 81 B4
Banks *Cumb* 69 D3
Banks *Lancs* 54 C5
Bankshill 75 B7
Bank Street 29 A1
Banningham 45 B3
Bannister Green 33 C6
Bannockburn 81 C2
Banstead 12 E1
Bantham 5 B6
Banwell 20 C5
Bapchild 14 E2
Baptiston 80 E3
Barachander 86 B6
Baraer 66 E4
Barassie 73 C4
Barbaraville 103 A4
Barber Booth 50 C2
Barbon 62 B6
Barbrook 7 B2
Barby 41 C7
Barcaldine 86 A4
Barcaple 67 C5
Barcheston 30 C4
Barcloy 67 D5
Barcombe 13 B5
Barcombe Cross 13 B5
Barden 63 B5
Bardennoch 67 B1
Bardfield Saling 33 C6
Bardney 52 E5
Bardon *Gramp* 104 A3
Bardon *Leics* 41 B3
Bardon Mill 70 A2
Bardsea 61 C6
Bardsey 57 B3
Bardsley 49 D1
Bardwell 34 D1
Barewood 28 C2
Barfad 79 C5
Barford *Nflk* 45 A5
Barford *Warks* 30 C1
Barford St John 30 E4
Barford St Martin 10 B1
Barford St Michael 30 E4
Barfreston 15 C3
Bargaly 67 A4
Bargany 73 B7
Bargoed 19 B3
Bargrennan 66 E3
Bar Hall 33 D5
Barham *Cambs* 32 C1
Barham *Kent* 15 C3
Barham *Sflk* 35 A3
Barharrow 67 C5
Bar Hill 32 E2
Barholm *D & G* 67 A5
Barholm *Lincs* 42 D3
Barkby 41 D4
Barkby Thorpe 41 D4
Barkestone-le-Vale 51 D7
Barkham 23 B5
Barking *GL* 24 E4
Barking *Sflk* 34 E3
Barkingside 24 E4
Barkisland 56 D6
Barkston *Lincs* 52 C7
Barkston *N Yorks* 57 C4
Barkway 32 E5
Barkwith 52 E3
Barlae 66 D4
Barlaston 40 A1
Barlavington 12 B5

Barlay 67 B5
Barlborough 51 A3
Barlby 57 E4
Barlestone 41 B4
Barley *Herts* 33 A5
Barley *Lancs* 55 C3
Barleycroft End 33 A6
Barleyhill 70 D3
Barleythorpe 42 B4
Barling 25 E4
Barlings 52 D4
Barlow *Derbs* 50 E3
Barlow *N Yorks* 57 E5
Barlow *T & W* 70 E2
Barmby Moor 58 C3
Barmby on the Marsh
  57 E5
Barmer 44 C2
Barmolloch 79 C2
Barmoor Lane End 77 B2
Barmouth 37 A4
Barmpton 63 D3
Barmston 59 B2
Barnacabber 80 A3
Barnacarry *Strath* 85 E6
Barnacarry *Strath* 79 E2
Barnack 42 D4
Barnacle 41 A6
Barnamuc 86 B4
Barnard Castle 63 A3
Barnard Gate 30 E6
Barnardiston 33 D4
Barnard's Green 29 B3
Barnbarroch *D & G* 66 E5
Barnbarroch *D & G* 68 B4
Barnburgh 57 C7
Barnby 45 D7
Barnby Dun 57 E7
Barnby in the Willows
  52 B6
Barnby Moor 51 C2
Barndennoch 74 D7
Barnes 24 C5
Barnet 24 C3
Barnetby le Wold 59 A7
Barney 44 D2
Barnham *Sflk* 34 C1
Barnham *W Ssx* 12 B6
Barnham Broom 44 E5
Barnhead 89 C3
Barnhill 103 E6
Barnhills 66 A3
Barningham *Dur* 63 A3
Barningham *Sflk* 34 D1
Barnoldby le Beck 59 C7
Barnoldswick 55 C3
Barns 96 E2
Barns Green 12 D4
Barnsley *Glos* 30 A7
Barnsley *S Yorks* 57 B7
Barnstaple 6 E3
Barnston *Essx* 33 C7
Barnston *Mers* 48 B3
Barnt Green 40 C7
Barnton 49 A4
Barnwell All Saints 42 D6
Barnwell St Andrew 42 D6
Barnwood 29 C6
Barr *D & G* 68 D1
Barr *Hghld* 85 C3
Barr *Hghld* 78 C5
Barrachrail 85 E6
Barrackan 79 B1
Barraglom 106 E4
Barran 86 C6
Barrapoll 84 A4
Barras 97 D5
Barrasford 70 C1
Barravullin 79 B1
Barregarrow 60 c3
Barrhead 80 E6
Barrhill 66 D2
Barrington *Cambs* 32 E4
Barrington *Som* 8 E2
Barripper 2 D5
Barrisdale 93 A4
Barrmill 80 C6
Barrnacarry 85 E6
Barrock 111 C1
Barrow *Lancs* 55 B4
Barrow *Leics* 42 B3
Barrow *Salop* 39 A4
Barrow *Sflk* 33 D2
Barrow *Som* 21 B7
Barrowby 42 B1
Barrowden 42 C4

Barrowford 55 C4
Barrow Gurney 20 E4
Barrow Haven 59 A5
Barrow in Furness 61 A7
Barrow Nook 48 D1
Barrow Street 21 C7
Barrow upon Humber
  59 A5
Barrow upon Soar 41 C3
Barrow upon Trent 41 A2
Barry *S Glam* 19 B7
Barry *Tays* 89 B5
Barry Links Station 89 B5
Barsby 41 D3
Barsham 45 C7
Barskimming 73 D5
Barsloisnoch 79 C2
Barston 40 E7
Bartestree 28 E3
Barthol Chapel 105 B5
Bartholmey 49 B6
Bartley 10 E5
Bartlow 33 B4
Barton *Cambs* 33 A3
Barton *Ches* 48 D6
Barton *Devon* 5 E4
Barton *Glos* 30 A5
Barton *Lancs* 54 E4
Barton *Lancs* 48 C1
Barton *N Yorks* 63 C4
Barton *Warks* 30 B2
Barton Bendish 44 B5
Barton Common 45 C3
Barton End 21 C1
Barton Hartshorn 31 B4
Barton in Fabis 51 B7
Barton in the Beans 41 A4
Barton in the Clay 32 B5
Barton-le-Street 64 E6
Barton-le-Willows 64 E7
Barton Mills 33 D1
Barton on Sea 10 D5
Barton-on-the-Heath 30 C4
Barton St David 20 E7
Barton Seagrave 42 B7
Barton Stacey 22 D7
Barton Turf 45 C3
Barton-under-Needwood
  40 D3
Barton-upon-Humber
  59 A5
Barvas 107 B3
Barway 33 B1
Barwell 41 B5
Barwhillanty 67 D3
Barwhinnock 67 C5
Barwick 9 B2
Barwick in Elmet 57 B4
Barwinnock 66 E6
Baschurch 38 D2
Bascote 30 E1
Basford Green 49 D6
Bashall Eaves 55 A3
Bashall Town 55 B3
Bashley 10 D5
Basildon *Esx* 25 C4
Basing 23 A6
Basingstoke 23 A6
Baslow 50 D3
Bason Bridge 20 C6
Bassaleg 19 C5
Bassenthwaite 69 A6
Bassett 11 A3
Bassett's Cross 6 E6
Bassingbourn 32 E4
Bassingfield 51 C7
Bassingham 52 C6
Bassingthorpe 42 C2
Basta 114 E3
Baston 42 E3
Bastwick 45 D4
Batavaime 87 A5
Batchworth 23 E2
Batchworth Heath 23 E2
Batcombe *Dors* 9 C3
Batcombe *Som* 21 A7
Bate Heath 49 A4
Bath 21 B4
Bathampton 21 B4
Bathealton 8 B1
Batheaston 21 B4
Bathford 21 B4
Bathgate 81 D5
Bathley 51 D5
Bathpool *Corn* 4 C3
Bathpool *Som* 8 D1
Batley 57 A5

Batsford 30 B4
Battersby 64 C3
Battersea 24 C5
Battisborough Cross 5 A6
Battisford 34 E3
Battisford Tye 34 E3
Battle *E Ssx* 13 E5
Battle *Pwys* 27 E7
Battledown 30 A5
Battlefield 38 E3
Battlesbridge 25 C3
Battlesden 31 E5
Battleton 7 D4
Battramsley 10 E5
Batt's Corner 23 C7
Bauds of Cullen 104 C2
Baugh 84 B4
Baughton 29 C3
Baughurst 22 E6
Baulds 97 B4
Baulking *Lincs* 53 A4
Baulking *Oxon* 22 C2
Baumber 53 A4
Baunton 30 A7
Baveney Wood 39 A7
Baverstock 10 B1
Bawburgh 45 A5
Bawdeswell 44 E3
Bawdrip 20 C7
Bawdsey 35 C4
Bawtry 51 C1
Baxenden 55 B5
Baxterley 40 E5
Baycliff 61 B6
Baydon 22 B4
Bayford *Herts* 24 D2
Bayford *Som* 9 D1
Bayfordbury 32 E7
Bayham Abbey 13 D3
Bayhead 98 B5
Bayles 70 A4
Baylham 35 A3
Baynards Green 31 A5
Baysham 28 E5
Bayston Hill 38 D4
Bayston Hill 38 D4
Baythorn End 33 D4
Bayton 39 A7
Beach 85 D3
Beachampton 31 C4
Beachborough 15 B5
Beachley 20 E1
Beacon 8 C3
Beacon End 34 D6
Beacon's Bottom 23 B2
Beaconsfield 23 D2
Beadlam 64 D5
Beadnell 77 D3
Beaford 6 E5
Beal *Nthld* 77 B1
Beal *N Yorks* 57 D5
Bealach 86 A3
Bealbridge 49 A6
Beambrook 49 A6
Beamhurst 50 B7
Beaminster 9 A3
Beamish 71 A3
Beamsley 56 D2
Bean 25 A5
Beanacre 21 D4
Beanley 77 B4
Beaquoy 112 C4
Beardon 5 A2
Beare Green 12 D2
Bearley 30 B1
Bearnie 105 C5
Bearnock 94 C2
Bearnus 84 E4
Bearpark 71 A4
Bearsbridge 70 A3
Bearsden 80 E4
Bearsted 14 D3
Bearwood 10 B5
Beattock 75 A5
Beauchamp Roding 24 F2
Beauchief 50 E2
Beaudesert 30 B1
Beaufort *Gwent* 19 B2
Beaulieu 10 E4
Beauly 102 D7
Beaumaris 47 A3
Beaumont *Cumb* 69 B4
Beaumont *Esx* 35 A6
Beausale 40 E7
Beauworth 11 B2
Beaver Green 14 E4
Beaworthy 6 D7
Beazley End 33 D6
Bebington 48 C3
Bebside 77 D7

Beccles 45 D6
Becconsall 54 D5
Beckbury 39 B4
Beckenham 24 D6
Beckermet 60 E3
Beck Foot 62 B5
Beckfoot *Cumb* 61 A3
Beckfoot *Cumb* 68 D5
Beckford 29 D4
Beckhampton 21 E4
Beck Hole 65 A3
Beckingham *Lincs* 52 B6
Beckingham *Notts* 51 D1
Beckington 21 B5
Beckley *E Ssx* 14 D6
Beckley *Oxon* 31 A6
Beck Row 33 C1
Beck Side 61 B5
Beckton 24 E4
Beckwithshaw 57 A2
Becontree 24 E4
Bedale 63 C6
Bedburn 70 E5
Bedchester 9 E2
Beddau 19 A5
Beddgelert 46 E6
Beddingham 13 B6
Beddington 24 D6
Beddington Corner 24 C6
Bedell's End 25 B2
Bedfield 35 B2
Bedford 32 B4
Bedgebury Cross 13 E3
Bedhampton 11 C4
Bedingfield 35 A2
Bedlington 77 D7
Bedlinog 19 A3
Bedmond 23 E1
Bednall 40 B3
Bedol 48 B4
Bedrule 76 C4
Bedstone 38 C7
Bedwas 19 B5
Bedwellty 40 D5
Bedworth 41 A6
Beeby 41 D4
Beech *Hants* 11 C1
Beech *Staffs* 40 A1
Beechamwell 44 B5
Beechingstoke 21 E5
Beedon 22 D4
Beeford 59 B2
Beeley 50 D4
Beelsby 59 C7
Beenham 22 E5
Beer 8 D5
Beer Crocombe 8 E1
Beer Hackett 9 B2
Beesands 5 D6
Beesby 53 C3
Beeson 5 D6
Beeston *Beds* 32 C4
Beeston *Ches* 48 E6
Beeston *Nflk* 44 D4
Beeston *Notts* 51 B7
Beeston *W Yorks* 57 A4
Beeston Regis 45 A1
Beeston St Lawrence
  45 C3
Beeswing 68 B3
Beetham 61 D6
Beetley 44 D4
Began 19 C5
Begbroke 30 E6
Begelly 16 E5
Beggshill 104 D5
Beguildy 38 A7
Beighton *Derbs* 51 A2
Beighton *Nflk* 45 C5
Beith 80 C6
Bekesbourne 15 B3
Belaugh 45 B4
Belbroughton 40 B7
Belchamp Otten 34 C4
Belchamp St Paul 33 D4
Belchamp Walter 34 C4
Belchford 53 A4
Belford 77 C2
Belgrave 41 C4
Belhaven 83 B5
Belhelvie 97 E2
Belhinnie 104 C6
Bellabeg 96 D2
Belladrum 102 D7
Bellanoch 79 B2
Bellasize 58 D5

Bellaty 88 D3
Bell Bar 24 C2
Bell Busk 55 D2
Belleau 53 C4
Bell End 40 B7
Bellerby 63 B5
Bellever 5 B3
Bell Green 41 A6
Belliehill 89 B2
Bellingdon 23 D1
Bellingham 76 E7
Belloch 72 A4
Bellochantuy 72 A4
Bellsdyke 81 D3
Bellshill Northld 77 C2
Bellshill Strath 81 B5
Bellsquarry 81 E5
Bells Yew Green 13 D3
Belluton 21 A4
Belmaduthy 102 E6
Belmesthorpe 42 D3
Belmont GL 24 C6
Belmont Lancs 55 A6
Belmore 80 B3
Belowda 3 B2
Belper 50 E6
Belper Lane End 50 E6
Belsay 70 E1
Belses 76 B3
Belsford 5 C5
Belstead 35 A4
Belston 73 C5
Belstone 7 A7
Belsyde 81 D4
Belthorn 55 B5
Beltoft 58 D7
Belton Humb 58 C7
Belton Leics 41 B2
Belton Leics 42 B4
Belton Lincs 42 C1
Belton Nflk 45 D5
Beltring 13 D2
Belvedere 24 E5
Belvoir 42 B1
Bembridge 11 C6
Bemersyde 76 B2
Bempton 65 D6
Benacre 45 E7
Benbuie 67 D1
Bendish 32 C6
Benenden 14 D4
Benfield 66 E4
Bengate 45 C3
Bengeo 32 E7
Benholm 89 E2
Beningbrough 57 D2
Benington 32 E6
Benllech 46 E2
Benmore Cent 87 A6
Benmore Strath 80 A3
Bennacott 6 B7
Bennan 67 C3
Bennington 53 B7
Bennington Sea End 53 C7
Benniworth 53 A3
Benover 13 E2
Benson 23 A2
Benthall Northld 77 D3
Benthall Salop 39 A4
Bentham 29 D6
Bentley Hants 23 B7
Bentley Humb 59 A4
Bentley S Yorks 57 D7
Bentley Warks 40 E5
Bentley Heath 40 D7
Benton 7 A3
Benton Square 71 A1
Bentpath 75 D6
Bentworth 23 A7
Benvie 88 E5
Benville Lane 9 B3
Benwick 43 B5
Beoley 30 A1
Bepton 11 E3
Berbeth 73 D7
Berden 33 A6
Berea 16 A3
Bere Alston 4 E4
Bere Ferrers 4 E4
Berepper 2 D6
Bere Regis 9 E4
Bergh Apton 45 C5
Berinsfield 22 E2
Berkeley 21 A1
Berkhamsted 23 D1
Berkley 21 C6
Berkswell 40 E7

Bermondsey 24 D5
Bernera 93 A2
Berners Roding 25 B2
Berney Arms Station
  45 D5
Bernice 80 A2
Bernisdale 100 B6
Berrick Salome 23 A2
Berriedale 111 B6
Berrington Northld 77 B1
Berrington Salop 38 E4
Berrow 20 B5
Berrow Green 29 B2
Berry Hill Dyfed 16 D1
Berry Hill Glos 28 E6
Berryhillock 104 D2
Berrynarbor 6 E2
Berry Pomeroy 5 D4
Bersham 48 C7
Berstane 112 D5
Berth-ddu 47 B6
Berwick 13 C6
Berwick Bassett 21 E3
Berwick Hill 70 E1
Berwick St James 10 B1
Berwick St John 10 A2
Berwick St Leonard 10 A1
Berwick-upon-Tweed
  83 E7
Besford H & W 29 D3
Besford Salop 38 E2
Bessacarr 57 E7
Bessels Leigh 30 E7
Bessingby 65 D7
Bessingham 45 A2
Best Beech Hill 13 D3
Besthorpe Nflk 44 E6
Besthorpe Notts 52 B5
Beswick 59 A3
Betchworth 12 E2
Bethania Dyfed 26 E4
Bethania Gynd 47 B6
Bethel Gynd 46 E4
Bethel Gynd 46 C3
Bethersden 14 E4
Bethesda Dyfed 16 D4
Bethesda Gynd 47 A4
Bethlehem 18 B1
Bethnal Green 24 D4
Betley 49 B7
Betsham 25 B5
Betteshanger 15 D3
Bettiscombe 8 E4
Bettisfield 38 D1
Betton Salop 38 C4
Betton Salop 39 A1
Bettws 18 D5
Bettws Bledrws 26 E5
Bettws Cedewain 38 A5
Bettws Evan 26 C6
Bettws Gwerfil Goch
  47 E6
Bettws-Newydd 19 D3
Bettws-y-crwyn 38 B6
Bettyhill 110 C2
Betws 18 B2
Betws Disserth 28 A2
Betws Garmon 46 E5
Betws-y-coed 47 B5
Betws-yn-Rhos 47 D3
Beulah Dyfed 26 B6
Beulah Pwys 27 D5
Bevendean 13 A6
Bevercotes 51 C3
Beverley 59 A4
Beverstone 21 C1
Bevington 21 A1
Bewaldeth 69 A6
Bewcastle 69 D2
Bewdley 39 B7
Bewerley 56 E1
Bewholme 59 B2
Bewley Common 21 D4
Bexhill 13 E6
Bexley 24 E5
Bexleyheath 24 E5
Bexwell 44 A5
Beyton 34 D2
Bhalamus 107 A7
Biallaid 95 A6
Bibury 30 B7
Bicester 31 A5
Bickenhall 8 D2
Bickenhill 40 D6
Bicker 43 A1
Bickerstaffe 48 D1
Bickerton Ches 48 E6

Bickerton N Yorks 57 C2
Bickford 40 A3
Bickham Bridge 5 C5
Bickham House 8 A5
Bickington Devon 6 E3
Bickington Devon 5 C3
Bickleigh Devon 5 A4
Bickleigh Devon 7 D6
Bickleton 6 E3
Bickley 24 E6
Bickley Moss 48 E7
Bickley Town 48 E7
Bicknacre 25 C2
Bicknoller 20 A7
Bicknor 14 D3
Bickton 10 C3
Bicton Dors 8 B5
Bicton Salop 38 D3
Bicton Salop 38 B6
Bicton Heath 38 D3
Bidborough 15 A2
Biddenden 14 D5
Biddenham 32 B3
Biddisham 20 C5
Biddlesden 31 B3
Biddlestone 77 A5
Biddulph 49 C6
Biddulph Moor 49 D6
Bideford 6 D4
Bidford-on-Avon 30 B2
Bidston 48 B2
Bielby 58 C3
Bieldside 97 D3
Bierley IOW 11 B7
Bierley W Yorks 56 E4
Bierton 31 D6
Bigbury 5 B6
Bigbury-on-Sea 5 B6
Bigby 59 B7
Bigert Mire 61 A4
Biggar Cumb 61 A7
Biggar Strath 75 A2
Biggin 32 E5
Biggin Derbs 50 D6
Biggin Derbs 50 C5
Biggin N Yorks 57 D4
Biggings 115 A1
Biggin Hill 13 B1
Biggleswade 32 C4
Bigholms 75 D7
Bighouse 110 D2
Bighton 11 C1
Bignor 12 B5
Big Sand 100 E4
Bigton 115 C5
Bilberry 3 C3
Bilborough 51 B6
Bilbrook Som 7 E2
Bilbrook Staffs 40 A4
Bilbrough 57 D3
Bilbster 111 C3
Bildershaw 71 A6
Bildeston 34 D4
Billericay 25 B3
Billesdon 41 E4
Billesley 30 B2
Billingborough 42 E1
Billinge 48 E1
Billingford Nflk 35 A1
Billingford Nflk 44 E3
Billingham 64 B1
Billinghay 52 E6
Billingley 57 C7
Billingshurst 12 C4
Billingsley 39 B6
Billington Beds 31 E5
Billington Lancs 55 B4
Billockby 45 D4
Billy Row 70 E5
Bilsborrow 54 E3
Bilsby 53 C4
Bilsdean 83 C5
Bilsington 15 A5
Bilsthorpe 51 C4
Bilston Loth 82 C6
Bilston W Mids 40 B5
Bilstone 41 A4
Bilting 15 A4
Bilton Humb 59 B4
Bilton Northld 77 D4
Bilton N Yorks 57 C2
Bilton N Yorks 57 B2
Bilton Warks 41 B7
Bimbister 112 C5
Binbrook 53 A2

Bincombe 9 C5
Bindal 103 C3
Binegar 21 A6
Bines Green 12 D5
Binfield 23 C4
Binfield Heath 23 B4
Bingfield 70 C1
Bingham 51 D7
Bingham's Melcombe
  9 D3
Bingley 56 E4
Binham 44 D2
Binley Hants 22 D6
Binley W Mids 41 A7
Binniehill 81 C4
Binsness 103 D5
Binsoe 63 C7
Binstead 11 B5
Binsted Hants 23 B7
Binsted W Ssx 12 B6
Binton 30 B2
Bintree 44 E3
Binweston 38 C4
Birch Esx 34 D7
Birch GM 55 A6
Bircham Newton 44 B2
Bircham Tofts 44 B2
Birchanger 33 B6
Bircher 28 D1
Birchfield 102 C2
Birch Green 34 D7
Birchgrove S Glam 19 B6
Birchgrove W Glam 18 C4
Birch Heath 48 E5
Birchington 15 D2
Birchover 50 D4
Birch Vale 50 B2
Bircotes 51 C1
Birdbrook 33 D4
Bird End 40 C5
Birdfield 79 D2
Birdham 11 E4
Birdingbury 30 E1
Birdlip 29 D6
Birdsall 65 A7
Birdsgreen 39 B6
Birdsmoor Gate 8 E3
Birdwell 57 B7
Birdwood 29 B6
Birgham 76 D2
Birichen 103 A2
Birkby 63 D4
Birkdale Mers 54 C6
Birkdale N Yorks 62 D4
Birkenhead 48 C3
Birkenhills 105 A4
Birkenshaw W Yorks
  57 A5
Birkhall 96 D4
Birkhill Bdrs 76 B1
Birkhill D & G 75 C4
Birkin 57 D5
Birks 97 C3
Birkwood 74 D2
Birley 28 D2
Birley Carr 50 E1
Birling Kent 25 B6
Birling Northld 77 D5
Birling Gap 13 C7
Birlingham 29 D3
Birmingham 40 C6
Birnam 88 B4
Birsay 112 B4
Birse 97 A4
Birsemore 97 A4
Birstall 41 C4
Birstall Smithies 57 A5
Birstwith 57 A2
Birthorpe 42 E1
Birtley H & W 28 C1
Birtley Northld 70 B1
Birtley T & W 71 A3
Birts Street 29 B4
Bisbrooke 42 B5
Bisham 23 C3
Bishampton 29 D2
Bishop Auckland 71 A6
Bishopbridge 52 D2
Bishopbriggs 81 A4
Bishop Burton 58 E4
Bishop Loch 81 A5
Bishop Middleham 71 B5
Bishopmill 104 A2
Bishop Monkton 57 B1
Bishop Norton 52 C2
Bishopsbourne 15 B3
Bishops Cannings 21 E4

Bishop's Castle 38 C6
Bishop's Caundle 9 C2
Bishop's Cleeve 29 D5
Bishop's Frome 29 A3
Bishop's Green 33 C7
Bishop's Hull 8 D1
Bishop's Itchington 30 D2
Bishop's Lydeard 8 C1
Bishop's Nympton 7 B4
Bishop's Offley 39 B2
Bishop's Seat 80 A4
Bishop's Stortford 33 A6
Bishop's Sutton 11 C1
Bishop's Tachbrook 30 D1
Bishop's Tawton 6 E3
Bishopsteignton 8 A6
Bishopstoke 11 A3
Bishopston 17 D7
Bishopstone Bucks 31 D6
Bishopstone E Ssx 13 B6
Bishopstone H & W 28 D3
Bishopstone Wilts 22 B3
Bishopstone Wilts 10 B2
Bishopstrow 21 C6
Bishop Sutton 20 E5
Bishop's Waltham 11 B3
Bishopswood Som 8 D2
Bishop's Wood Staffs
  40 A4
Bishopsworth 20 E4
Bishop Thornton 57 A1
Bishopthorpe 57 D3
Bishopton Dur 71 B6
Bishopton Strath 80 D4
Bishop Wilton 58 C2
Bishton Glos 29 D7
Bisley Sry 12 B1
Bispham 54 C4
Bissoe 2 E4
Bisterne 10 C4
Bisterne Close 10 D4
Bitchfield 42 C2
Bittadon 6 E2
Bittaford 5 B5
Bittering 44 D4
Bitterley 38 E7
Bitterne 11 A3
Bitteswell 41 C6
Bitton 21 A4
Bix 23 B3
Bixter 115 C2
Blaby 41 C5
Blackacre 75 A6
Blackadder 83 D7
Blackawton 5 D5
Blackborough 8 B3
Blackborough End 44 A4
Black Bourton 30 C7
Blackboys 13 C4
Blackbraes Cent 81 D4
Blackbraes Gramp 97 D2
Blackbrook 39 B1
Blackburn Gramp 97 D2
Blackburn Lancs 55 A5
Blackburn Loth 81 D5
Black Callerton 70 E2
Blackcastle 103 B6
Blackchambers 97 C2
Black Clauchrie 66 D2
Black Corries 86 D3
Blackcraig D & G 67 A4
Blackcraig D & G 67 D2
Black Cross 3 B2
Blackden Heath 49 B4
Blackdog 97 E2
Black Dog 7 C6
Blackdown Devon 5 A2
Blackdown Dors 8 E3
Blackfield 11 A4
Blackford Cumb 69 B3
Blackford Som 9 C1
Blackford Som 20 D6
Blackford Tays 81 C1
Blackfordby 41 A3
Blackgang 11 A7
Blackhall 82 C5
Blackhall Colliery 71 C5
Blackham 13 B3
Blackheath Esx 34 E6
Blackheath Sry 12 C2
Blackheath W Mids 40 B6
Black Heddon 70 D1
Blackhill Gramp 105 D3
Blackhill Gramp 105 D4
Blackhillock Gramp 104 C4
Blackhillock Gramp 104 B3

Blackhills 104 A3
Blackland 21 E4
Blackley 49 C1
Blacklunans 88 C2
Black Marsh 38 C4
Blackmill 18 E5
Blackmoor Hants 11 D1
Blackmoor Som 8 C2
Blackmoor Gate 7 A2
Blackmore 25 B2
Blackmore End Esx 33 D5
Blackmore End Herts
  32 C7
Black Mount 86 D4
Blackness Cent 81 E4
Blackness Gramp 97 B4
Blackness Hghld 111 C5
Blacknest 23 B7
Black Notley 33 D6
Blacko 55 C3
Black Pill 18 B4
Blackpool 54 C4
Blackpool Gate 69 D2
Blackridge 81 C5
Blackrock Gwent 19 C2
Blackrock Islay 78 C5
Blackrod 55 A6
Blackshaw 68 D3
Blackshaw Head 55 D5
Blacksmith's Corner 34 E5
Blackstone 12 E5
Blackthorn 31 B6
Blackthorpe 34 D2
Blacktoft 58 D5
Blacktop 97 D3
Black Torrington 6 D6
Blacktown 19 C5
Blackwardine 28 E2
Blackwater Corn 2 E4
Blackwater Hants 23 C6
Blackwater IOW 11 B6
Blackwater Sflk 35 E1
Blackwaterfoot 72 C5
Blackwell Derbs 50 C3
Blackwell Dur 63 C3
Blackwell Notts 51 A5
Blackwell Warks 30 C3
Blackwell W Mids 40 B7
Blackwells End 29 B5
Blackwood D & G 74 E7
Blackwood Gwent 19 B4
Blackwood Strath 74 C1
Blackwood Hill 49 D6
Blacon 48 C5
Bladbean 15 B4
Blades 62 E5
Bladnoch 67 A5
Bladon 30 E6
Blaenannerch 26 B6
Blaenau Ffestiniog 47 B6
Blaenavon 19 C3
Blaenawey 19 C2
Blaen Dyryn 27 D7
Blaenffos 16 E2
Blaengarw 18 E4
Blaengwrach 18 D3
Blaengwynfi 18 D4
Blaenos 27 B7
Blaenplwyf 26 E3
Blaenporth 26 B6
Blaenrhondda 18 E3
Blaenwaun 17 A3
Blaen-y-coed 17 B3
Blagdon Avn 20 E5
Blagdon Devon 5 D4
Blagdon Som 8 D2
Blagdon Hill 20 E5
Blaich 86 B1
Blaina 19 C3
Blairannaich 80 C1
Blair Atholl 87 E2
Blairbuie 80 A4
Blair Drummond 81 B2
Blairgowrie 88 C4
Blairhall 81 E3
Blairhoyle 81 A1
Blairhullichan 80 D1
Blairingone 81 D2
Blairkip 73 E5
Blairlogie 81 C2
Blairmore Hghld 103 A1
Blairmore Hghld 108 D3
Blairmore Strath 80 A3
Blairnairn 80 B3
Blairnamarrow 96 C2
Blairpark 80 B6
Blairquhan 73 C7

Blairquhosh 80 E3
Blair's Ferry 79 D5
Blairshinnoch 104 E2
Blairuskinmore 80 D1
Blairvadach 80 B3
Blairdryne 97 C4
Blairythan 105 C6
Blaisdon 29 B6
Blakebrook 40 A7
Blakedown 40 A7
Blake Hall 24 F2
Blakelaw Bdrs 76 D2
Blakelaw T & W 71 A2
Blakemere 28 C3
Blakeney Glos 29 A7
Blakeney Nflk 44 E1
Blakenhall Ches 49 B7
Blakenhall W Mids 40 B5
Blakeshall 40 A6
Blakesley 31 B2
Blanchland 70 C3
Blandford Camp 10 A4
Blandford Forum 9 E3
Blandford St Mary 9 E3
Bland Hill 57 A2
Blanefield 80 E4
Blankney 52 D5
Blàr a'Chaoruinn 86 C2
Blargie 94 E6
Blarglas 80 C3
Blarmachfoldach 86 B2
Blarnalevoch 101 D2
Blashford 10 C4
Blaston 42 B5
Blatherwycke 42 C5
Blawith 61 B5
Blaxhall 35 C3
Blaxton 57 E7
Blaydon 70 E2
Bleadon 20 C5
Bleak Hey Nook 56 D7
Blean 15 B2
Bleasby 51 D6
Bleatarn 62 C3
Blebocraigs 89 A7
Bleddfa 28 B1
Bledington 30 C5
Bledlow 31 C7
Bledlow Ridge 23 B2
Blencarn 69 E6
Blencogo 68 E5
Blencow 69 C6
Blendworth 11 D3
Blennerhasset 68 E5
Blervie Castle 103 D6
Bletchingdon 31 A6
Bletchingley 13 A1
Bletchley Bucks 31 D4
Bletchley Salop 39 A1
Bletherston 16 D3
Bletsoe 32 B3
Blewbury 22 E3
Blickling 45 A3
Blidworth 51 B5
Blindburn Gramp 105 C5
Blindburn Northld 76 E4
Blindcrake 68 E6
Blindley Heath 13 A2
Blindman's Bay 79 D5
Blisland 4 A3
Blissford 10 C3
Bliss Gate 39 B7
Blisworth 31 C2
Blithbury 40 C2
Blitterlees 68 E4
Blockley 30 B4
Blofield 45 C5
Blo Norton 34 E1
Blore 50 C6
Blossomfield 40 D7
Blount's Green 50 B7
Bloxham 30 E4
Bloxholm 52 D6
Bloxwich 40 B4
Bloxworth 9 E4
Blubberhouses 56 E2
Blue Anchor Corn 3 B3
Blue Anchor Som 7 E2
Blue Bell Hill 14 C2
Bluemill 96 E2
Blundell Sands 19 D4
Blundeston 45 E6
Blunham 32 C3
Blunsdon St Andrew 22 A3
Bluntisham 32 E1
Blunts 4 D4
Blyborough 52 C2

Blyford 35 D1
Blymhill 40 A3
Blyth Northld 77 E7
Blyth Notts 51 C2
Blyth Bridge 75 B1
Blythburgh 35 D1
Blythe Bridge 49 D7
Blythe Marsh 49 D7
Blyton 52 B2
Boarhills 89 B7
Boarhunt 11 C4
Boarshead 13 C3
Boars Hill 30 E7
Boarstall 31 B6
Boarzell 13 E4
Boasley Cross 6 E7
Boath 102 D4
Boat o' Brig 104 B3
Boat of Garten 95 C4
Bobbing 14 D2
Bobbington 40 A5
Bobbingworth 24 F2
Bocaddon 3 D3
Bochastle 81 A1
Bockhampton 22 C4
Bocking 33 D6
Bocking Churchstreet 33 D6
Boconnoc 3 D2
Boddam Gramp 105 E4
Boddam Shet 115 C6
Boddington 29 C5
Bodedern 46 C2
Bodelwyddan 47 E3
Bodenham H & W 28 E2
Bodenham Wilts 10 C2
Bodenham Moor 28 E2
Bodesbeck 75 B4
Bodewryd 46 C1
Bodfach Hall 38 A2
Bodfari 47 E3
Bodffordd 46 D3
Bodfuan 46 C7
Bodham Street 45 A1
Bodiam 13 E4
Bodicote 30 E4
Bodieve 3 B1
Bodinnick 3 D3
Bodior 46 B3
Bodle Street Green 13 D5
Bodmin 3 C2
Bodney 44 C6
Bodorgan 46 C4
Bodsham Green 15 B4
Bog, The 73 C4
Bogallan 102 E6
Bogbain 103 A7
Bogbrae 105 D5
Bogbuie 102 D6
Bogend 73 C4
Bogfern 97 A3
Bogfields 97 A3
Bogfold 105 B3
Boghan 81 A2
Boghead Strath 74 C1
Boghead Strath 74 B3
Boghole 103 C6
Bogmuir 104 B2
Bogniebrae 104 D4
Bognor Regis 12 B7
Bogrie 74 D7
Bogroy 95 C3
Bogston 96 D3
Bogton 104 E3
Bogue 67 C2
Bohenie 93 E6
Bohortha 3 A5
Bojewyan 2 A5
Bolam 70 E6
Bolberry 5 B7
Bolderwood 10 D4
Bold Heath 48 E3
Boldon 71 B2
Boldre 10 E5
Boldron 63 A3
Bole 51 D2
Bolehill 50 D5
Boleigh 2 B6
Boleside 76 A2
Bolgoed 18 B3
Bolham 7 D5
Bolham Water 8 C2
Bolingey 2 E3
Bollington Ches 49 D4
Bollington Ches 49 B3
Bolney 12 E4
Bolnhurst 32 B3

Bolshan 89 C3
Bolsover 51 A3
Bolsterstone 50 D1
Bolstone 28 E4
Boltby 64 B5
Bolter End 23 B2
Bolton Cumb 69 E7
Bolton GM 49 B1
Bolton Humb 58 C2
Bolton Loth 83 A5
Bolton Northld 77 C4
Bolton Abbey 56 D2
Bolton Bridge 56 D2
Bolton by Bowland 55 B3
Boltonfellend 69 C3
Boltongate 69 A5
Bolton-le-Sands 54 D1
Bolton Low Houses 69 A5
Bolton-on-Swale 63 C5
Bolton Percy 57 D3
Bolton upon Dearne 57 C7
Bolventor 4 B3
Bombie 67 D5
Bomere Heath 38 D3
Bonar-Bridge 102 E2
Bonawe 86 B5
Bonawe Quarries 86 B5
Bonby 59 A6
Boncath 17 A2
Bonchester Bridge 76 B4
Bonchurch 11 B7
Bondleigh 7 A6
Bonehill 40 D4
Bo'ness 81 D3
Bonhill 80 C4
Boningale 40 A4
Bonjedward 76 C3
Bonkle 81 C6
Bonnington Kent 15 A5
Bonnington Tays 89 B5
Bonnybank 82 D2
Bonnybridge 81 C3
Bonnykelly 105 B3
Bonnyrigg 82 D6
Bonnyton Gramp 104 E5
Bonnyton Tays 89 C3
Bonnyton Tays 88 E5
Bonsall 50 D5
Bont 19 D2
Bontddu 37 A4
Bont-dolgadfan 37 C5
Bontgoch Elerch 27 A2
Bont Newydd 37 B3
Bontnewydd 46 D5
Bontuchel 47 E5
Bonvilston 19 A6
Bon-y-maen 18 B4
Boohay 5 E5
Booker 23 C2
Booley 38 E2
Boor 101 A3
Boosbeck 64 D2
Boot 61 A3
Boothby Graffoe 52 C6
Boothby Pagnell 42 C1
Boothstown 49 B1
Boothtown 56 D5
Boothville 31 C1
Booth Wood 56 D6
Bootle Cumb 61 A5
Bootle Mers 48 C2
Booton 45 A3
Boquhan 80 E3
Boraston 39 A7
Borden 14 D2
Bordley 55 D1
Bòrd Mór 72 B4
Bordon Camp 11 D1
Boreham Esx 25 C2
Boreham Wilts 21 D6
Boreham Street 13 D5
Borehamwood 24 B3
Boreland Cent 87 B5
Boreland D & G 75 B6
Boreland D & G 66 E4
Boreraig 99 A6
Borgie 109 D3
Borgue D & G 67 C6
Borgue Hghld 111 B6
Borley 34 C4
Borlum 94 B5
Borness 67 C6
Bornish 90 C3
Boroughbridge 57 B1
Borough Green 13 D1
Borras Head 48 C6
Borrowash 51 A7

Borrowby N Yorks 64 E2
Borrowby N Yorks 64 B5
Borrowdale 61 B2
Borrowston 106 E3
Borsham 98 E3
Borstal 14 C2
Borth 27 A2
Borthwick 82 D7
Borthwickbrae 76 A4
Borthwickshiels 76 A4
Borth-y-Gêst 46 E7
Borve Harris 100 B7
Borve W Is 98 D3
Borve W Is 90 B5
Borvemore 98 E2
Borwick 61 E6
Bosavern 2 A5
Bosbury 29 A3
Boscastle 4 A1
Boscombe Dors 10 C5
Boscombe Wilts 10 D1
Boscoppa 3 C3
Bosham 11 E4
Bosherston 16 C6
Bosley 49 D5
Bossall 64 E7
Bossiney 4 A2
Bossingham 15 B4
Bossington Hants 10 E1
Bossington Som 7 C2
Bostock Green 49 A5
Boston 53 B7
Boston Spa 57 C3
Boswinger 3 B4
Botallack 2 A5
Botarua 98 B4
Botcheston 41 B4
Botesdale 34 E1
Bothal 77 D7
Bothamsall 51 C3
Bothel 68 E6
Bothenhampton 9 A4
Botley Bucks 23 D1
Botley Hants 11 B3
Botley Oxon 30 E7
Botloe's Green 29 B5
Botolph 31 C5
Botolphs 12 D6
Bottacks 102 C5
Bottesford Humb 58 D7
Bottesford Leics 42 B1
Bottisham 33 B2
Bottisham Lode 33 B2
Bottomcraig 88 E6
Bottom Head 55 A1
Bottoms 55 D5
Botusfleming 4 E4
Botwnnog 46 B7
Bough Beech 13 B2
Boughrood 28 A4
Boughspring 20 E1
Boughton Nflk 44 B5
Boughton Northants 31 C1
Boughton Notts 51 C4
Boughton Aluph 15 A4
Boughton Green 13 E1
Boughton Lees 15 A4
Boughton Malherbe 14 D4
Boughton Monchelsea 13 E1
Boughton Street 15 A3
Boulby 64 E2
Bouldon 38 E6
Boulmer 77 D4
Boulston 16 C4
Boultenstone 96 E2
Boultham 52 C5
Bourn 32 E3
Bournbrook 40 C6
Bourne 42 D2
Bourne, The 23 C7
Bournebridge 24 F3
Bourne End Beds 31 E3
Bourne End Bucks 23 C3
Bourne End Herts 23 E1
Bournemouth 10 B5
Bournes Green 29 D7
Bournheath 40 B7
Bournmoor 71 B3
Bournville 40 C6
Bourton Avn 20 C4
Bourton Dors 21 B7
Bourton Oxon 22 B3
Bourton Salop 38 E5
Bourton on Dunsmore 41 B7
Bourton-on-the-Hill 30 B4

Bourton-on-the-Water 30 B5
Bousd 84 D2
Bouth 61 C5
Bouthwaite 63 B7
Bovain 87 B5
Boveney 23 D4
Boveridge 10 B3
Boverton 18 E7
Bovey Tracey 5 D3
Bovingdon 23 E1
Bovington Camp 9 E5
Bow Devon 7 B6
Bow Ork 113 C2
Bowbank 70 C6
Bow Brickhill 31 E4
Bowburn 71 B5
Bowcombe 11 A6
Bowd 8 C4
Bowden Bdrs 76 B2
Bowden Devon 5 D6
Bowden Hill 21 C4
Bowdon 49 B3
Bower 76 D7
Bowerchalke 10 B2
Bower Hinton 9 A2
Bowermadden 111 C2
Bowers Gifford 25 C4
Bowershall 81 E2
Bowertower 111 C2
Bowes 62 E3
Bowgreave 54 D3
Bowhill 76 A3
Bowland Bridge 61 D5
Bowley 28 E2
Bowlhead Green 12 B3
Bowling 80 D4
Bowling Bank 48 C7
Bowling Green 29 C2
Bowmanstead 38 C5
Bowmore 78 C6
Bowness-on-Solway 69 A3
Bowness-on-Windermere 61 D5
Bow of Fife 88 E7
Bowsden 77 A1
Bow Street 27 A2
Bowthorpe 45 A5
Bowtrees 81 D3
Box Glos 29 C7
Box Wilts 21 C4
Boxbush 29 B6
Box End 32 B4
Boxford Berks 22 D4
Boxford Sflk 34 D4
Boxgrove 12 B6
Boxley 13 E1
Boxmoor 23 E1
Boxted Esx 34 E5
Boxted Sflk 34 C3
Boxted Cross 34 E5
Boxworth 32 E2
Boxworth End 32 E2
Boyden Gate 15 C2
Boydston 73 D4
Boylestone 50 C7
Boyndie 104 E2
Boyndlie 105 C2
Boynton 65 D7
Boysack 89 C4
Boyton Corn 6 C7
Boyton Sflk 35 C4
Boyton Wilts 10 A1
Bozeat 31 E2
Brabling Green 35 B2
Brabourne 15 B4
Brabourne Lees 15 A4
Brabstermire 111 D2
Bracadale 92 A1
Braceborough 42 D3
Bracebridge 52 C5
Bracebridge Heath 52 C5
Braceby 42 D1
Bracewell 55 C3
Brachla 94 D2
Brackans 105 A3
Brackenber 62 C3
Brackenfield 50 E5
Bracklach 104 B6
Bracklamore 105 B3
Brackletter 93 D6
Brackley Hghld 103 B6
Brackley Northants 31 A4
Brackly 79 C3
Bracknell 23 C5

Braco 81 C1
Bracobrae 104 D3
Bracon Ash 45 A6
Bracora 92 E5
Bracorina 92 E5
Bradbourne 50 D5
Bradbury 71 B6
Bradda 60 a4
Bradden 31 B3
Bradenham 23 C2
Bradenstoke 21 E3
Bradfield Berks 23 A4
Bradfield Devon 8 B2
Bradfield Esx 35 A5
Bradfield Nflk 45 B2
Bradfield S Yorks 50 D1
Bradfield Combust 34 C3
Bradfield End Green 33 C5
Bradfield Green 49 A6
Bradfield Heath 35 A5
Bradfield St Clare 34 D3
Bradfield StGeorge 34 D3
Bradford Devon 6 D6
Bradford Northld 77 C2
Bradford W Yorks 56 E4
Bradford Abbas 9 B2
Bradford Leigh 21 C4
Bradford-on-Avon 21 C4
Bradford-on-Tone 8 C1
Bradford Peverell 9 C4
Brading 11 C6
Bradley Derbs 50 D6
Bradley H & W 59 C7
Bradley Hants 23 A7
Bradley Humb 59 C7
Bradley N Yorks 63 A6
Bradley Staffs 40 A3
Bradley W Mids 40 B5
Bradley Green 29 D1
Bradley in the Moors 50 B6
Bradmore Notts 51 B7
Bradmore W Mids 40 A5
Bradninch 7 D6
Bradnop 50 B5
Bradpole 9 A4
Bradshaw 56 B6
Bradstone 4 D2
Bradwell Bucks 31 D4
Bradwell Derbs 50 C2
Bradwell Esx 34 C6
Bradwell Nflk 45 E5
Bradwell Green 49 B5
Bradwell-on-Sea 25 F2
Bradwell Waterside 25 E2
Bradworthy 6 C5
Brae D & G 68 B2
Brae Hghld 102 E5
Brae Shet 115 C1
Braeantra 102 D4
Brae Doune 102 C1
Braedownie 96 C6
Braefoot 105 A4
Braegrum 88 B6
Braehead Gramp 104 B4
Braehead Ork 113 C1
Braehead Ork 112 D2
Braehead Strath 74 D2
Braehead Tays 89 C3
Braehoulland 114 B2
Braeleny 87 C7
Braemar 96 B4
Braemore Hghld 102 D1
Braemore Hghld 111 A5
Braemore Hghld 101 D4
Braenaloin 96 C4
Braes of Enzie 104 B3
Braes of Foss 87 D3
Braes of Ullapool 101 D2
Braeswick 112 F3
Braeval 80 E1
Brafferton Dur 71 A6
Brafferton N Yorks 64 B6
Brafield-on-the-Green 31 D2
Bragar 107 A3
Bragbury End 32 D6
Bragenham 31 E5
Braglenbeg 86 A6
Braichmelyn 47 A4
Braides 54 D2
Braidwood 74 D1
Brailes Hill 30 C4
Brailsford 50 D6
Braintree 33 D6
Braiseworth 10 E2
Braiseworth 35 A1

Braishfield 10 E2
Braithwaite *Cumb* 69 A7
Braithwaite *S Yorks* 57 E6
Braithwell 51 B1
Bramber 12 D5
Brambletye 13 B3
Bramcote 51 B7
Bramdean 11 C2
Bramerton 45 B5
Bramfield *Herts* 32 D7
Bramfield *Sflk* 35 D1
Bramford 35 A4
Bramhall 49 C3
Bramham 57 C3
Bramhope 57 A3
Bramley *Hants* 23 A6
Bramley *Sry* 12 C2
Bramley *S Yorks* 51 A1
Bramling 15 C3
Brampford Speke 7 D7
Brampton *Cambs* 32 D1
Brampton *Cumb* 69 D3
Brampton *Cumb* 69 E7
Brampton *Lincs* 52 B4
Brampton *Nflk* 45 B3
Brampton *Sflk* 45 D7
Brampton *S Yorks* 57 C7
Brampton Abbotts 29 A5
Brampton Ash 41 E6
Brampton Bryan 38 C7
Brampton-en-le-Morthen 51 A2
Bramshall 50 B7
Bramshaw 10 D3
Bramshill 23 B5
Bramshott 11 E1
Bramwell 9 A1
Branault 85 B2
Brancaster 44 B1
Branchill 103 D6
Branderburgh 104 A1
Brandesburton 59 B3
Brandeston 35 B2
Brand Green 29 B5
Brandis Corner 6 D6
Brandon *Dur* 71 A5
Brandon *Lincs* 52 C7
Brandon *Northld* 77 B4
Brandon *Sflk* 44 B7
Brandon *Warks* 41 B7
Brandon Bank 44 A7
Brandon Creek 44 A6
Brandon Parva 44 E5
Brandsby 64 C6
Brands Hatch 25 A6
Brandy Wharf 52 D2
Brane 2 B6
Bran End 33 C6
Branksome 10 B5
Branksome Park 10 B5
Branncewell 43 D4
Bransby 52 B4
Branscombe 8 C5
Bransford 29 B2
Bransford Bridge 29 C2
Bransgore 10 C5
Branson's Cross 40 C7
Branston *Leics* 42 B2
Branston *Lincs* 52 D5
Branston *Staffs* 40 E2
Branston Booths 52 D5
Branstone 11 B6
Brant Broughton 52 C6
Brantham 35 A5
Branthwaite 69 A6
Brantingham 58 E5
Branton *Northld* 77 B4
Branton *S Yorks* 57 E7
Brantwood 61 C5
Branxholm Bridgend 76 A4
Branxholme 76 A4
Branxton 76 E2
Brassington 50 D5
Brasted 13 B1
Brasted Chart 13 B1
Bratoft 53 C5
Brattleby 52 C3
Bratton 21 D5
Bratton Clovelly 6 D7
Bratton Fleming 7 A3
Bratton Seymour 9 C1
Braughing 32 E6
Braunston *Leics* 42 B4
Braunston *Northants* 31 A1
Braunstone 41 C4
Braunton 6 D3

Brawby 64 E6
Brawdy 16 B3
Brawl 110 D2
Brawlbin 111 A3
Bray *Berks* 23 D4
Braybrooke 41 E6
Braydon Manor 21 E2
Brayford 7 A3
Brayshaw 55 B2
Bray Shop 4 D3
Brayton 57 E4
Brazacott 6 B7
Breach 15 B4
Breachwood Green 32 C6
Breaclete 106 E4
Breadsall 50 E7
Breadstone 29 B7
Breage 2 D6
Breakachy 102 C7
Breakon 114 F1
Breakon 114 F1
Bream 29 A7
Breamore 10 C3
Brean 20 B5
Brearton 57 B1
Breasclete 107 A4
Breaston 51 A7
Brechfa 17 D2
Brechin 89 B2
Brecklate 72 A6
Breckles 44 D6
Breckonside 74 D5
Brecon 19 A1
Bredbury 49 D2
Brede 14 D7
Bredenbury 29 A2
Bredfield 35 B3
Bredgar 14 D2
Bredhurst 14 C2
Bredicot 29 D2
Bredon 29 D4
Bredon's Hardwick 29 D4
Bredon's Norton 29 D4
Bredwardine 28 C3
Breedon on the Hill 41 B2
Breighton 58 C4
Breihascro 107 C2
Breinton 28 D4
Breivig 107 C4
Bremhill 21 D3
Brenachoille 79 E1
Brenchley 13 D2
Brendon 7 B2
Brenish 106 C5
Brenkley 71 A1
Brent 24 C4
Brent Eleigh 34 D4
Brentford 24 B5
Brentingby 41 E3
Brent Knoll 20 C5
Brent Pelham 33 A5
Brentwood 25 A3
Brenzett 15 A6
Breoch 67 D5
Brereton 40 C3
Brereton Green 49 B5
Brereton Heath 49 C5
Bressingham 44 E7
Bretabister 115 D2
Bretby 40 E2
Bretford 41 B7
Bretforton 30 A3
Bretherdale Head 61 E3
Bretherton 54 D5
Brettenham *Nflk* 44 D7
Brettenham *Sflk* 34 D3
Bretton 48 C5
Brewham 21 B7
Brewood 40 A4
Briach 103 D6
Briantspuddle 9 E4
Bricket Wood 24 B2
Bricklehampton 29 D3
Brickwall 14 D6
Bride 60 d1
Bridekirk 68 E6
Bridell 26 A6
Bridestowe 5 A2
Brideswell *Gramp* 104 D5
Bridford 5 D2
Bridge 15 B3
Bridge End 115 C4
Bridge End *Beds* 32 B3
Bridge End *Lincs* 42 E1
Bridgefoot 33 A4
Bridgefoot *Cumb* 68 D7
Bridge Green 33 A5

Bridgehampton 9 B1
Bridge Hewick 63 D7
Bridgemary 11 B4
Bridgend *Corn* 3 D3
Bridgend *Cumb* 61 C2
Bridgend *D & G* 75 A5
Bridgend *Gramp* 104 D5
Bridgend *Gramp* 104 B5
Bridgend *Loth* 81 E4
Bridgend *M Glam* 18 E6
Bridgend *Strath* 78 C5
Bridgend *Strath* 79 C2
Bridgend *Tays* 88 E7
Bridgend *Tays* 89 B2
Bridgend *Tays* 88 C6
Bridgend of Lintrathen 88 D3
Bridge of Alford 97 A2
Bridge of Allan 81 B2
Bridge of Avon 95 E2
Bridge of Balgie 87 B4
Bridge of Bogendreip 97 B4
Bridge of Brewlands 88 C2
Bridge of Brown 95 E3
Bridge of Buchat 96 D2
Bridge of Cally 88 C3
Bridge of Canny 97 B4
Bridge of Coe 86 C3
Bridge of Craigisla 88 D3
Bridge of Dee *D & G* 67 D4
Bridge of Dee *Gramp* 96 B4
Bridge of Dee *Gramp* 97 B4
Bridge of Don 97 E3
Bridge of Dun 89 C3
Bridge of Dye 97 B5
Bridge of Earn 88 C7
Bridge of Ericht 87 B3
Bridge of Ess 97 A4
Bridge of Feugh 97 C4
Bridge of Forss 111 A2
Bridge of Gairn 96 D4
Bridge of Gaur 87 B3
Bridge of Muchalls 97 D4
Bridge of Muick 96 D4
Bridge of Oich 94 B5
Bridge of Orchy 86 D5
Bridge of Tilt 87 E2
Bridge of Tynet 104 B2
Bridge of Walls 115 B2
Bridge of Weir 80 C5
Bridgerule 6 B6
Bridges 38 C5
Bridge Sollers 28 D3
Bridge Street 34 C4
Bridgeton 97 A2
Bridgetown *Corn* 4 D2
Bridgetown *Som* 7 D3
Bridge Trafford 48 E4
Bridgeyate 21 A3
Bridgham 44 D7
Bridgnorth 39 B5
Bridgtown 40 B4
Bridgwater 20 C7
Bridlington 65 D7
Bridport 9 A4
Bridstow 28 E5
Brierfield 55 C4
Brierley *Glos* 29 A6
Brierley *H & W* 28 D2
Brierley *S Yorks* 57 C6
Brierley Hill 40 B6
Brierton 64 B1
Brigehaugh 104 B5
Brigg 59 A7
Brigham *Cumb* 68 D6
Brigham *Humb* 59 A2
Brighouse 56 E5
Brighstone 11 A6
Brightgate 50 D5
Brighthampton 30 D7
Brightling 13 D4
Brightlingsea 34 E7
Brighton *Corn* 3 B3
Brighton *E Ssx* 13 A6
Brightons 81 D4
Brightwalton 22 D4
Brightwell *Oxon* 22 E2
Brightwell Baldwin 23 A2
Brightwell-cum-Sotwell 22 E2
Brignall 63 A3
Brig o'Turk 80 E1
Brigsley 59 C7
Brigsteer 61 D5

Brigstock 42 C6
Brill *Bucks* 31 B6
Brill *Corn* 2 E6
Brilley 28 B3
Brilley Mountain 28 B3
Brimfield 28 E1
Brimington 51 A3
Brimington Common 51 A3
Brimley 5 C3
Brimpsfield 29 D6
Brimpton 22 E5
Brims 113 B3
Brimstage 48 C3
Brind 58 C4
Brindister *Shet* 115 B2
Brindle 54 E5
Brindley Ford 49 C6
Brineton 40 A3
Bringhurst 42 B5
Brington 32 B1
Briningham 44 E2
Brinkhill 53 B4
Brinkley 33 C3
Brinklow 41 B7
Brinkworth 21 E2
Brinmore 94 E3
Brinscall 55 A5
Brinsley 51 A6
Brinsop 28 D3
Brinsworth 51 A1
Brinton 44 E2
Brinyan 112 D4
Brisco 69 C4
Brisley 44 D3
Brislington 21 A3
Bristol 20 E3
Briston 44 E2
Britannia 55 C5
Britford 10 C2
Briton Ferry 18 C4
Britwell Salome 23 A2
Brixham 5 E5
Brixton 5 A5
Brixton Deverill 21 C7
Brixworth 41 E7
Brize Norton 30 C7
Broad Blunsdon 22 A2
Broadbottom 49 D2
Broadbridge 11 E4
Broadbridge Heath 12 D3
Broad Campden 30 B4
Broad Chalke 10 B2
Broad Clyst 7 D7
Broadford *Hghld* 92 D2
Broadford Bridge 12 C4
Broadgate 61 A5
Broad Green *Beds* 31 E3
Broad Green *Esx* 34 C6
Broad Green *H & W* 29 B2
Broadgroves 33 C6
Broadhaugh 76 A5
Broad Haven *Dyfed* 16 B4
Broadheath *GM* 49 B3
Broadheath *H & W* 29 A1
Broadhembury 8 C3
Broadhempston 5 D4
Broad Hill 33 B1
Broad Hinton 22 A4
Broadholme 52 B4
Broadland Row 14 D7
Broadlay 17 B5
Broad Laying 22 D5
Broadley *GM* 55 C6
Broadley *Gramp* 104 C2
Broadley Common 24 E2
Broad Marston 30 B3
Broadmere 23 A7
Broadnymet 7 B6
Broadoak 17 D3
Broad Oak *Cumb* 61 A4
Broadoak *Dors* 9 A4
Broadoak *E Ssx* 13 D4
Broad Oak *E Ssx* 14 D6
Broad Oak *H & W* 28 D5
Broadoak *Kent* 15 B2
Broadsea 105 C2
Broadstairs 15 D2
Broadstone *Dors* 10 B5
Broadstone *Salop* 38 E6
Broad Street 14 D3
Broadstreet Common 19 D5
Broad Street Green 25 D2
Broad Town 21 E3
Broadwas 29 B2
Broadwater *Herts* 32 D6
Broadwater *W Ssx* 12 D6

Broadway *Dyfed* 17 B5
Broadway *Dyfed* 17 A4
Broadway *H & W* 30 A4
Broadway *Sflk* 35 C1
Broadway *Som* 8 E2
Broadwell *Glos* 30 C5
Broadwell *Oxon* 30 C7
Broadwell *Warks* 30 E1
Broadwell Lane End 28 E6
Broadwey 9 C5
Broadwindsor 9 A3
Broadwood Kelly 7 A6
Broadwoodwidger 4 E2
Brobury 28 C3
Brochloch 67 B1
Brock 84 B4
Brockbridge 11 C3
Brockdam 77 C3
Brockdish 35 B1
Brockenhurst 10 D4
Brockfield 57 E2
Brockford Street 35 A2
Brockhall 31 B1
Brockham 12 E2
Brockhampton *Glos* 30 A5
Brockhampton *H & W* 28 E4
Brockholes 56 E6
Brockhurst 13 B3
Brocklebank 69 B5
Brocklesby 59 B6
Brockley 20 D4
Brockley Green 34 C3
Brockton *Salop* 38 E5
Brockton *Salop* 39 B4
Brockton *Salop* 38 C4
Brockton *Salop* 38 C6
Brockweir 28 E7
Brockwood Park 11 C2
Brockworth 29 C6
Brocton 40 B3
Brodick 72 E4
Brodsworth 57 D7
Brogborough 31 E4
Brogyntyn 38 B1
Brokenborough 21 D2
Broken Cross *Ches* 49 C4
Broken Cross *Ches* 49 A4
Bromborough 48 C3
Brome 35 A1
Brome Street 35 A1
Bromeswell 35 C3
Bromfield *Cumb* 68 E5
Bromfield *Salop* 38 D7
Bromham *Beds* 32 B3
Bromham *Wilts* 21 D4
Bromley 24 E6
Bromley 24 E6
Bromley Green 14 E5
Brompton *Kent* 14 C2
Brompton *N Yorks* 63 D5
Brompton *N Yorks* 65 B5
Brompton-on-Swale 63 C5
Brompton Ralph 7 E3
Brompton Regis 7 D3
Bromsash 29 A5
Bromsberrow Heath 29 B4
Bromsgrove 40 B7
Bromstead 39 B3
Bromyard 29 A2
Bromyard Downs 29 A2
Bronaber 47 B7
Bronant 27 A4
Brongest 26 C6
Bronington 38 D1
Bronllys 28 A4
Bron-y-Gaer 17 B4
Brongarth 38 B1
Bronydd 28 B3
Bron-y-Gaer 17 B4
Brook *Dyfed* 17 A5
Brook *Hants* 10 D3
Brook *Hants* 10 E2
Brook *IOW* 10 E6
Brook *Kent* 15 A4
Brook *Sry* 12 B3
Brooke *Leics* 42 B4
Brooke *Nflk* 45 B6
Brookend 20 E1
Brookhouse 54 E1
Brookhouse Green 49 C5
Brookland 14 E6
Brooklands 68 B2
Brookmans Park 24 C2
Brooks 38 A5
Brooks Green 12 D4
Brook Street 34 C4
Brook Street *Esx* 25 A3

Brook Street *Kent* 14 E5
Brook Street *W Ssx* 13 A4
Brookthorpe 29 C6
Brookwood 12 B1
Broom *Beds* 32 C4
Broom *Warks* 30 A2
Broomcroft 38 E4
Broome *H & W* 40 B7
Broome *Nflk* 45 C6
Broome *Salop* 38 C6
Broomedge 49 C3
Broomer's Corner 12 D4
Broome Wood 77 C4
Broomfield *Esx* 25 C2
Broomfield *Gramp* 105 C5
Broomfield *Kent* 15 C2
Broomfield *Kent* 14 D3
Broomfield *Som* 20 B7
Broomfleet 58 D5
Broomhaugh 70 D2
Broomhead 105 C2
Broom Hill 10 B4
Broomhill 77 D5
Broom of Dalreoch 88 B7
Broom's Green 29 B4
Brora 103 C1
Broseley 39 A4
Brothertoft 53 A7
Brotherton 57 C5
Brotton 64 D2
Broubster 111 A2
Brough *Bressay* 115 E3
Brough *Cumb* 62 C3
Brough *Derbs* 50 C2
Brough *Hghld* 111 C1
Brough *Humb* 58 E5
Brough *Notts* 52 B6
Brough *Ork* 112 C5
Brough *Shet* 114 D5
Brough *Whalsay* 115 E1
Brough *Yell* 114 E5
Broughall 48 E7
Brougham 69 D7
Brough Sowerby 62 C3
Broughton *Bdrs* 75 B2
Broughton *Bucks* 31 D3
Broughton *Cambs* 32 D1
Broughton *Clwyd* 48 C5
Broughton *GM* 49 C1
Broughton *Hants* 10 E1
Broughton *Humb* 58 E7
Broughton *Lancs* 54 E4
Broughton *Northants* 42 B7
Broughton *N Yorks* 64 E6
Broughton *N Yorks* 55 D2
Broughton *Ork* 112 D2
Broughton *Oxon* 30 E4
Broughton *S Glam* 18 E6
Broughton Astley 41 C5
Broughton Beck 61 B5
Broughton Gifford 21 C4
Broughton Hackett 29 D2
Broughton in Furness 61 B5
Broughton Mills 61 B5
Broughton Moor 68 D6
Broughton Poggs 30 C7
Broughtown 112 F2
Broughty Ferry 89 A5
Browland 115 B2
Brown Candover 11 B1
Brown Edge *Lancs* 54 C6
Brown Edge *Staffs* 49 D6
Brownhill 105 B4
Brownhills *Fife* 89 B7
Brownhills *W Mids* 40 C4
Brown Lees 49 C6
Brownlow Heath 49 C5
Brownshill Green 41 A6
Brownston 5 B5
Broxa 65 B4
Broxbourne 24 D2
Broxburn *Loth* 81 E4
Broxburn *Loth* 83 B5
Broxholme 52 C4
Broxted 33 B6
Broxwood 28 C2
Bruachmary 103 B7
Bruan 111 D5
Brucehill 80 E2
Brue 107 B3
Bruera 48 D5
Bruichladdich 78 B5
Bruisyard 35 C2
Bruisyard Street 35 C2
Brund 50 C4

Brundall 45 C5
Brundish 35 B2
Brundish Street 35 B1
Brunthill 105 B3
Bruntingthorpe 41 D5
Bruntland 104 C6
Brunton *Fife* 88 E6
Brunton *Northld* 77 D3
Brushford 7 D4
Brushford Barton 7 A6
Bruton 21 A7
Bryanston 9 E3
Brydekirk 68 E2
Brymbo 48 B6
Bryn *Dyfed* 17 D5
Bryn *GM* 48 E1
Bryn *Gynd* 37 C3
Bryn *Pwys* 38 B6
Bryn *W Glam* 18 D4
Bryn, The 19 D3
Brynamman 18 C2
Brynberian 16 E2
Bryncethin 18 E5
Bryncir 46 D6
Bryn-côch 18 C4
Bryncroes 46 B7
Bryncrug 37 A5
Bryneglwys 48 A7
Brynford 48 A4
Bryn Gates 48 E1
Bryngwran 46 C3
Bryngwyn *Gwent* 19 D3
Bryngwyn *Pwys* 28 A3
Bryn-henllan 16 D2
Brynhoffnant 26 C5
Brynmawr 19 B2
Brynmelyn 38 A7
Brynmenyn 18 E5
Brynna 18 E5
Brynog 26 E5
Brynrefail 46 D2
Brynsadler 19 A5
Brynsiencyn 46 D4
Brynteg 46 D2
Bryn-y-Cae 18 E5
Bryn-y-maen 47 C3
Bualintur 92 B2
Bualnaluib 101 A2
Buarthia 18 E5
Bubbenhall 41 A7
Bubwith 58 C4
Buccleuch 75 D4
Buchan 67 D4
Buchanhaven 105 E4
Buchanty 88 A6
Buchlyvie 80 E2
Buckabank 69 B5
Buckby Wharf 31 B1
Buckden *Cambs* 32 C2
Buckden *N Yorks* 62 E7
Buckenham 45 C5
Buckerell 8 C3
Buckfast 5 C4
Buckfastleigh 5 C4
Buckhaven 82 D3
Buckholm 76 A2
Buckhorn Weston 9 D1
Buckhurst Hill 24 E3
Buckie 104 C2
Buckies 111 B2
Buckingham 31 B4
Buckland *Bucks* 31 D6
Buckland *Devon,* 5 B6
Buckland *Glos* 30 A4
Buckland *Herts* 32 E5
Buckland *Kent* 15 C4
Buckland *Oxon* 22 C2
Buckland *Sry* 12 E1
Buckland Brewer 6 D4
Buckland Common 23 D1
Buckland Dinham 21 B5
Buckland Filleigh 6 D6
Buckland in the Moor 5 C3
Buckland Monachorum
  4 E4
Buckland Newton 9 C3
Buckland St Mary 8 D2
Buckland-tout-Saints 5 C6
Bucklebury 22 E4
Bucklerheads 89 A5
Bucklers Hard 11 A5
Bucklesham 35 B4
Buckley 48 B5
Buckman Corner 12 C4
Buckminster 42 B2
Bucknall *Lincs* 52 E5
Bucknall *Staffs* 49 D7

Bucknell *Oxon* 31 A5
Bucknell *Salop* 38 C7
Bucksburn 97 D3
Buck's Cross 6 C4
Bucks Green 12 C3
Bucks Hill 23 E1
Bucks Horn Oak 23 C7
Buck's Mills 6 C4
Buckspool 16 C6
Buckton *H & W* 38 C7
Buckton *Humb* 65 D6
Buckton *Northld* 77 B2
Buckworth 32 C1
Budbrooke 30 C1
Budby 51 C4
Buddon 89 B5
Bude 6 B6
Budlake 7 D6
Budle 77 C2
Budleigh Salterton 8 B5
Budock Water 2 E5
Buerton 49 A7
Bugbrooke 31 B2
Bugle 3 C3
Bugthorpe 58 C2
Buildwas 39 A4
Builth Road 27 E5
Builth Wells 27 E5
Bulby 42 D2
Buldoo 110 E2
Bulford 22 A7
Bulkeley 48 E6
Bulkington *Warks* 41 A6
Bulkington *Wilts* 21 D5
Bulkworthy 6 C5
Bull Bay 46 D1
Bullers of Buchan 105 E5
Bulley 29 B6
Bull Green 14 E5
Bullington 22 D7
Bullpot Farm 62 B6
Bull's Green 32 D7
Bullwood 80 A4
Bulmer *Esx* 34 C4
Bulmer *N Yorks* 57 E1
Bulmer Tye 34 C5
Bulphan 25 B4
Bulverhythe 13 E6
Bulwark 105 C4
Bulwell 51 B6
Bulwick 42 C5
Bumble's Green 24 E2
Bun-an-uillt 78 B5
Bunarkaig 93 D6
Bunbury 48 E6
Bundalloch 93 A2
Buness 114 F2
Bungay 45 C7
Bunlarie 72 B4
Bunloit 94 D3
Bun Loyne 93 E4
Bunnahakhainn 78 D4
Bunny 41 C2
Buntait 94 B2
Buntingford 32 E6
Bunwell 45 A6
Bunwell Street 45 A6
Burbage *Derbs* 50 B3
Burbage *Leics* 41 B5
Burbage *Wilts* 22 B5
Burchett's Green 23 C3
Burcombe 10 B1
Burcot 22 E2
Burcott 31 D5
Burdale 65 A7
Burdocks 12 C4
Bures 34 D5
Bures Green 34 D5
Burford 30 C6
Burgar 112 C4
Burgate 34 E1
Burgess Hill 13 A5
Burgh 35 B3
Burgh by Sands 69 B4
Burgh Castle 45 D5
Burghclere 22 D5
Burghead 103 E5
Burghfield 23 A5
Burghfield Common 23 A5
Burghfield Hill 23 A5
Burgh Heath 12 E1
Burghill 28 D3
Burgh le Marsh 53 D5
Burgh next Aylsham 45 B3
Burgh on Bain 53 A3
Burgh St Margaret 45 D4

Burgh St Peter 45 D6
Burghwallis 57 D6
Burham 14 C2
Buriton 11 D3
Burland 49 A6
Burlawn 3 B1
Burleigh 23 D5
Burlescombe 8 B2
Burleston 9 D4
Burley *Hants* 10 D4
Burley *Leics* 42 B3
Burleydam 49 A7
Burley Gate 28 E3
Burley in Wharfedale
  56 E3
Burley Street 10 D4
Burlingjobb 28 B2
Burlow 15 A5
Burlton 38 D2
Burmarsh 15 B5
Burmington 30 C4
Burn 57 D5
Burnage 49 C2
Burnaston 50 D7
Burnby 58 D3
Burndell 12 B6
Burnend 105 B4
Burneside 61 E5
Burness 112 F2
Burneston 63 D6
Burnett 21 A4
Burnfoot *Bdrs* 76 B4
Burnfoot *Bdrs* 76 A4
Burnfoot *Hghld* 110 D5
Burnfoot *Tays* 81 D1
Burnham *Bucks* 23 D3
Burnham *Humb* 59 A6
Burnham Deepdale 44 C1
Burnham Green 32 D7
Burnham Market 44 C1
Burnham Norton 44 C1
Burnham-on-Crouch 25 E3
Burnham Overy 44 C1
Burnham-on-Sea 20 C6
Burnham Overy 44 C1
Burnham Thorpe 44 C1
Burnhaven 105 E4
Burnhead *D & G* 67 B2
Burnhead *D & G* 74 D6
Burnhervie 97 C2
Burnhill Green 39 B4
Burnhope 70 E4
Burnhouse 80 C6
Burniston 65 C4
Burnley 55 C4
Burnmouth 83 E6
Burn Naze 54 C3
Burn of Cambus 81 B1
Burnopfield 70 E3
Burnsall 56 D1
Burnside *Fife* 82 B2
Burnside *Gramp* 97 C2
Burnside *Loth* 81 E4
Burnside *Shet* 114 B5
Burnside *Strath* 73 E6
Burnside *Tays* 89 B3
Burnside of Duntrune
  89 A5
Burnswark 68 E2
Burntcliff Top 49 D5
Burnthouse 2 E5
Burnt Houses 70 E6
Burntisland 82 C4
Burnton 73 D6
Burntwood 40 C4
Burntwood Green 40 C4
Burnt Yates 57 A1
Burpham *Sry* 12 C1
Burpham *W Ssx* 12 C6
Burradon *Northld* 77 A5
Burradon *T & W* 71 A1
Burrafirth 114 F1
Burraland 115 B3
Burravoe *Shet* 114 E4
Burravoe *Shet* 115 C1
Burrells 62 B3
Burrelton 88 C5
Burridge 11 B3
Burrill 63 C6
Burringham 58 D7
Burrington *Avn* 20 D5
Burrington *Devon* 7 A5
Burrington *H & W* 38 D7
Burrough End 33 C3
Burrough Green 33 C3
Burrough on the Hill 41 E3
Burrow Bridge 20 C7
Burrowhill 23 D5

Burry Port 17 C5
Burscough 54 D6
Burscough Bridge 54 D6
Bursea 58 D4
Burshill 59 A3
Bursledon 11 A4
Burslem 49 C7
Burstall 34 E4
Burstock 9 A3
Burston *Nflk* 45 A7
Burston *Staffs* 40 B1
Burstow 13 A2
Burstwick 59 C5
Burtersett 62 D6
Burton *Ches* 48 C4
Burton *Ches* 48 E5
Burton *Cumb* 61 E6
Burton *Dors* 10 C5
Burton *Dors* 9 C4
Burton *Dyfed* 16 C5
Burton *Lincs* 52 C4
Burton *Northld* 77 C2
Burton *Som* 20 A6
Burton *Wilts* 21 C3
Burton Agnes 65 D7
Burton Bradstock 9 A5
Burton Coggles 42 C2
Burton Constable 59 B4
Burton Fleming 65 C6
Burton Green *Clwyd* 48 C6
Burton Green *W Mids*
  40 E7
Burton Hastings 41 B6
Burton in Lonsdale 62 B7
Burton Joyce 51 C6
Burton Latimer 42 C7
Burton Lazars 41 E3
Burton Leonard 57 B1
Burton on the Wolds 41 C2
Burton Overy 41 D5
Burton Pedwardine 52 E7
Burton Pidsea 59 C4
Burton Salmon 57 C5
Burton upon Stather 58 D6
Burton upon Trent 40 E2
Burtonwood 48 E2
Burwardsley 48 E6
Burwarton 39 A6
Burwash 13 D4
Burwash Common 13 D4
Burwash Weald 13 D4
Burwell *Cambs* 33 B2
Burwell *Lincs* 53 B4
Burwen 46 D1
Burwick *Ork* 113 D3
Burwick *Shet* 115 C3
Bury *Cambs* 43 A6
Bury *GM* 55 C6
Bury *Som* 7 D4
Bury *W Ssx* 12 C5
Buryas Bridge 2 B6
Bury Green 33 A6
Bury St Edmunds 34 C2
Burythorpe 64 E7
Busbridge 12 B2
Busby *Strath* 80 E6
Busby *Tays* 88 B6
Buscot 22 B2
Bush Bank 28 D2
Bushbury 40 B4
Bushby 41 D4
Bush Crathie 96 C4
Bushey 24 B3
Bushey Heath 24 B3
Bush Green 45 B7
Bushley 29 C4
Bushton 21 E3
Bussage 29 C7
Busta 115 C1
Butcher's Cross 15 A4
Butcombe 20 E4
Buthill 103 E5
Butleigh 20 E7
Butleigh Wootton 20 E7
Butler's Hill 51 B6
Butlers Marston 30 D2
Butley 11 A4
Butsfield 70 E4
Butterburn 69 E2
Buttercrambe 58 C2
Butterknowle 70 E6
Butterleigh 7 D6
Butterley 51 A5
Buttermere *Cumb* 61 A2
Buttermere *Wilts* 22 C5
Butters Green 49 C6
Buttershaw 56 E5

Butterstone 88 B4
Butterton 50 B5
Butterwick *Lincs* 53 B7
Butterwick *N Yorks* 65 B6
Butterwick *N Yorks* 64 E6
Butt Green 49 A6
Buttington 38 B4
Butt Lane 49 C6
Buttonoak 39 B7
Buxhall 34 E3
Buxted 13 B4
Buxton *Derbs* 50 B3
Buxton *Nflk* 45 B3
Buxton Heath 45 A3
Bwlch 28 A5
Bwlch-clawdd 17 B2
Bwlchgwyn 48 B6
Bwlchllan 26 E5
Bwlchnewydd 17 B3
Bwlchtocyn 36 C3
Bwlch-y-cibau 38 A3
Bwlch-y-dolar 38 A2
Bwlch-y-ffridd 37 E6
Bwlch-y-groes 17 A2
Bwlch-y-Rhiw 36 B3
Bwlch-y-sarnau 27 E3
Byers Green 71 A5
Byfield 31 A2
Byfleet 23 E5
Byford 28 C3
Bygrave 32 D5
Byker 71 A2
Bylane End 4 C4
Bylchau 47 D4
Byley 49 B5
Bynea 17 D6
Byrness 76 D5
Bythorn 32 B1
Byton 28 C1
Byworth 12 B4

C
Cabourne 59 B7
Cabrach *Gramp* 104 B6
Cabrach *Jura* 78 D3
Cackle Street 14 D7
Cacrabank 75 D4
Cadboll 103 B4
Cadbury 7 D6
Cadbury Barton 7 A5
Cadder 81 A4
Cadderlie 86 B5
Caddington 32 B7
Caddletown 85 D7
Caddonfoot 76 A2
Cadeby *Leics* 41 B4
Cadeby *S Yorks* 57 D7
Cadeleigh 7 D6
Cade Street 13 D4
Cadgwith 2 E7
Cadham 82 C2
Cadishead 49 B2
Cadle 18 B4
Cadley 22 B5
Cadmore End 23 B2
Cadnam 10 D3
Cadney 52 A7
Cadole 48 B5
Cadover Bridge 5 A4
Cadoxton *S Glam* 19 B7
Cadoxton *W Glam* 18 C4
Caeathro 46 D4
Caehopkin 18 D2
Caen 111 A7
Caenby 52 D3
Caenby Corner 52 C3
Caeo 27 A7
Caerau *M Glam* 18 D4
Caerau *S Glam* 19 B6
Caerdeon 37 A4
Caer Farchell 16 A3
Caergeiliog 46 C3
Caergwrle 48 C6
Caerhun 47 B3
Caer-Lan 18 D2
Caerleon 19 D4
Caer Llan 28 D7
Caernarfon 46 D4
Caerphilly 19 B5
Caersws 37 E6
Caerwent 20 D1
Caerwys 48 A4
Caethle 37 A6
Caggan 96 C2
Cairnargat 104 C5
Cairnbaan 79 C2

Cairnbeathie 97 A3
Cairnbrogie 105 B6
Cairnbulg 105 D2
Cairncake 105 B4
Cairncross 83 D6
Cairndoon 66 E7
Cairndow 86 C7
Cairness 105 D2
Cairney 88 E7
Cairneyhill 81 E3
Cairngrassie 97 E4
Cairnhill *Gramp* 105 C6
Cairnhill *Gramp* 104 E5
Cairnie *Gramp* 97 D3
Cairnie *Gramp* 97 D3
Cairnorrie 105 B4
Cairnryan 66 B4
Cairnsmore 67 A4
Caister-on-Sea 45 E4
Caistor 59 B7
Caistor StEdmund 45 B5
Caistron 77 A5
Caitha 76 A1
Cake Street 44 E6
Calbost 107 C6
Calbourne 11 A6
Calcot 23 A4
Calcott 15 B2
Caldarvan 80 D3
Caldback 114 F2
Caldbeck 69 B6
Caldbergh 63 A6
Caldecote *Cambs* 32 E3
Caldecote *Cambs* 42 E6
Caldecote *Herts* 32 D5
Caldecote *Warks* 41 A5
Caldecott *Leics* 42 B5
Caldecott *Northants* 31 E1
Calderbank 81 B5
Calder Bridge 60 E3
Calderbrook 55 D6
Caldercruix 81 C5
Calderglen 81 A6
Calder Mains 111 A3
Caldermill 74 B1
Calder Vale 54 E3
Caldhame 89 A4
Caldicot 20 D2
Caldwell *Derbs* 40 E3
Caldwell *N Yorks* 63 B3
Caldwell *Strath* 80 D6
Caldy 48 B3
Caledrhydiau 26 D5
Calfsound 112 E3
Calgary 84 E3
Califer 103 D6
California *Cent* 81 D4
California *Nflk* 45 E4
Calke 41 A2
Callaly 77 B5
Callander 81 A1
Callanish 107 A4
Callerton Lane End 70 E2
Callestick 2 E3
Calligarry 92 D4
Callington 4 D4
Callisterhall 75 C7
Callow *H & W* 28 D4
Callow End 29 C3
Callow Hill *H & W* 39 B7
Callow Hill *Wilts* 21 E2
Callows Grave 28 E1
Callyburn 72 B5
Calmore 10 E3
Calmsden 30 A7
Calne 21 D3
Calow 51 A3
Calrossie 103 B4
Calshot 11 A4
Calstock 4 E4
Calstone Wellington 21 E4
Calthorpe 45 A2
Calthwaite 69 C5
Calton *N Yorks* 55 D2
Calton *Staffs* 50 C5
Calver 50 D3
Calverhall 39 A1
Calver Hill 28 C3
Calverleigh 7 D5
Calverley 57 A4
Calvert 31 B5
Calverton *Bucks* 31 C4
Calverton *Notts* 51 C6
Calvine 87 E2
Calvo 68 E4
Cam 21 B1

Camascross 92 D3
Camasdarach 92 D5
Camasnacróise 85 E3
Camasterach 100 E7
Camastianavaig 92 C1
Camasunary 92 C3
Camault Muir 102 D7
Camb 114 E3
Camber 14 E7
Camberley 23 C5
Camberwell 24 D5
Camblesforth 57 E5
Cambo 77 B7
Cambois 77 E7
Camborne 2 D4
Cambridge 33 A3
Cambus 81 C2
Cambusbarron 81 B2
Cambuskenneth 81 C2
Cambuslang 81 A6
Cambusnethan 81 C6
Cambus o'May 96 E4
Camchuart 79 D3
Camden 24 C4
Camelford 4 B2
Camelon 81 C3
Camelsdale 11 E1
Camer 25 B6
Cameron 80 C3
Camerory 95 D2
Camer's Green 29 B4
Camerton Avn 21 A5
Camerton Cumb 68 D6
Camfield Place 24 C2
Camghouran 87 B3
Cammachmore 97 E4
Cammeringham 52 C3
Campbelltown 103 A6
Campbeltown 72 B5
Camperdown 71 A1
Camphouse 85 B2
Campmuir 88 D5
Campsall 57 D6
Campsea Ashe 35 C3
Camps Heath 45 E6
Campton 32 C5
Camrose 16 C3
Camsail 80 B3
Camserney 87 E4
Camstraddan 80 C2
Camus-luinie 93 B2
Camusnagaul Hghld 86 B1
Camusnagaul Hghld
 101 C3
Camusteel 100 E7
Camusurich 87 C5
Camusvrachan 87 C4
Canada 10 D3
Canaston Bridge 16 D4
Candacraig 96 D4
Candlesby 53 C5
Candyburn 75 A1
Cane End 23 A4
Canewdon 25 D3
Canford Bottom 10 B4
Canford Cliffs 10 B6
Canford Magna 10 B5
Canisbay 111 D1
Cann 9 E1
Cannards Grave 21 A6
Cann Common 9 E1
Cannich 94 B2
Cannington 20 B7
Cannock 40 B3
Cannock Wood 40 C3
Canonbie 69 B2
Canon Bridge 28 D3
Canon Frome 29 A3
Canon Pyon 28 D3
Canons Ashby 31 A2
Canonstown 2 C5
Canterbury 15 B3
Cantley Nflk 45 C5
Cantley S Yorks 57 E7
Cantlop 38 E4
Canton 19 B6
Cantray 103 A7
Cantraydoune 103 A7
Cantraywood 103 A7
Cantsfield 62 B7
Canvey Island 25 C4
Canwell Hall 40 D4
Canwick 52 C5
Canworthy Water 6 B7
Caol 86 C1
Caolasnacon 86 C2
Caoles 84 B4

Capel Kent 13 D2
Capel Sry 12 D2
Capel Bangor 27 A2
Capel Betws Lleucu 27 A5
Capel Carmel 36 A3
Capel Coch 46 D2
Capel Curig 47 B5
Capel Cynon 26 C6
Capel Dewi Dyfed 27 A2
Capel Dewi Dyfed 26 D6
Capel Dewi Dyfed 17 C3
Capel Garmon 47 C5
Capel Gwyn Dyfed 17 C3
Capel Gwyn Gynd 46 C3
Capel Gwynfe 18 C1
Capel Hendre 17 D4
Capel Isaac 17 D3
Capel Iwan 17 A2
Capel le Ferne 15 C5
Capel Llanilterm 19 A6
Capel St Andrews 35 C4
Capel St Mary 35 A5
Capel St Silin 26 E5
Capel Seion 27 A3
Capel Tygwydd 26 B6
Capeluchaf 46 D6
Capelulo 47 B3
Capel-y-ffin 28 B4
Capenhurst 48 C4
Capernwray 61 E6
Capheaton 77 B7
Cappercleuch 75 C3
Capplegill 61 A3
Capstone 14 C2
Capton 5 D5
Caputh 88 B4
Carbellow 74 B3
Carbeth 80 E2
Carbis Bay 2 C5
Carbost Skye 100 B7
Carbost Skye 92 A1
Carbrooke 44 D5
Carburton 51 C3
Carcary 89 C3
Carclew 2 E5
Carco 74 C4
Car Colston 51 D6
Carcroft 57 D7
Cardenden 82 C3
Cardeston 38 C3
Cardiff 19 B6
Cardigan 26 A6
Cardington Beds 32 B4
Cardington Salop 38 E5
Cardinham 3 D2
Cardno 105 C2
Cardoness 67 B5
Cardow 103 E7
Cardrona 75 D2
Cardross 80 C4
Cardurnock 68 E4
Careby 42 D3
Careston 89 B2
Carew 86 D5
Carew Cheriton 16 D5
Carew Newton 16 D5
Carey 28 E4
Carfrae 83 A6
Cargen 68 C2
Cargill 88 C5
Cargo 69 B4
Cargo Fleet 64 C1
Cargreen 4 E4
Carham 76 D2
Carhampton 7 E2
Carharrack 2 E4
Carie Tays 87 C3
Carie Tays 87 C5
Carines 2 E3
Carinish 98 C6
Carisbrooke 11 A6
Cark 61 C6
Carkeel 4 E4
Carland Cross 3 A3
Carlby 42 D3
Carlecotes 56 E7
Carleton Cumb 69 C4
Carleton Lancs 54 C4
Carleton N Yorks 55 D3
Carleton W Yorks 57 C5
Carleton Fishery 66 C2
Carleton Forehoe 44 E5
Carleton Rode 45 A6
Carlingcott 21 A5
Carlisle 69 B4
Carlops 82 B7
Carloway 107 A3

Carlton Beds 31 E2
Carlton Cambs 33 C3
Carlton Clev 71 B6
Carlton Humb 57 E5
Carlton Leics 41 A4
Carlton Notts 51 C6
Carlton N Yorks 63 A6
Carlton N Yorks 64 D5
Carlton Sflk 35 C2
Carlton S Yorks 57 B6
Carlton W Yorks 57 B5
Carlton Colville 45 E6
Carlton Curlieu 41 D5
Carlton Husthwaite 64 B6
Carlton in Cleveland 64 C3
Carlton in Lindrick 51 B2
Carlton-le-Moorland 52 C6
Carlton Miniott 63 D6
Carlton-on-Trent 51 D4
Carlton Scroop 52 C7
Carluke 81 C6
Carlyon Bay 3 C3
Carmarthen 17 C3
Carmel Clwyd 38 D1
Carmel Clwyd 17 D4
Carmel Gynd 46 D5
Carmel Gynd 46 C2
Carminish 98 E3
Carmont 97 D5
Carmunnock 80 E6
Carmyle 81 A5
Carmyllie 89 B4
Carn Islay 78 B6
Carn Islay 78 A6
Carnaby 65 D7
Carnach 93 C2
Carnassarie 79 C1
Carnbee 83 A2
Carnbo 81 E1
Carn Brea 2 D4
Carndearg 85 A1
Carnduncan 78 B5
Carne 3 B5
Carnforth 61 D6
Carnhell Green 2 D5
Carnichal 105 C3
Carnmore 78 C7
Carno 37 D6
Carnoch Hghld 93 A5
Carnoch Hghld 94 B2
Carnoch Hghld 101 E6
Carnoch Hghld 103 B7
Carnock 81 E3
Carnon Downs 2 E4
Carnousie 104 E3
Carnoustie 89 B5
Carnwath 74 E1
Carnworth 2 A5
Carperby 63 A6
Carradale 72 C4
Carragrich 99 B2
Carrbridge 95 C3
Carreglefn 46 C2
Carrick Fife, 89 A6
Carrick Strath 80 A2
Carrick Strath 79 D3
Carriden 81 E3
Carrine 72 A7
Carrington GM 49 B2
Carrington Lincs 53 B6
Carrington Loth 82 D6
Carroch 67 C1
Carrog 48 A7
Carroglen 87 D6
Carrol 103 B1
Carron Cent 81 C3
Carron Gramp 104 A4
Carron Strath 79 D2
Carronbridge Cent 81 B3
Carronbridge D & G 74 D6
Carronshore 81 C3
Carrot 89 A4
Carr Shield 70 B4
Carruntherstown 68 E2
Carruthmuir 80 C5
Carr Vale 51 A4
Carrville 71 B4
Carry 79 D5
Carsaig 85 B6
Carscreugh 66 D4
Carse 79 B5
Carsegowan 67 A5
Carse Gray 89 A3
Carseriggan 66 E4
Carsethorn 68 C4
Carsgoe 111 B2
Carshalton 24 C6

Carsington 50 D5
Carsluith 67 A5
Carsphairn 67 B1
Carstairs 74 E1
Carswell Marsh 22 C2
Carter's Clay 10 E2
Carterton 30 C7
Carterway Heads 70 D3
Carthew 3 C3
Carthorpe 63 D6
Cartington 77 B5
Cartmel 61 C6
Cartmel Fell 61 D5
Carway 17 C5
Caryshader 106 D4
Cas 79 B5
Cascob 28 B1
Cashell 80 C2
Cashlie 87 A4
Cashmoor 10 A3
Cassington 30 E6
Cassop 71 B5
Casswell's Bridge 42 E2
Castellau 19 A5
Castell Gorfod 17 A3
Castell Howell 26 D6
Castell-y-bwch 19 C4
Casterton 62 B7
Castle Acre 44 C4
Castle Ashby 31 D2
Castle Bank 40 B2
Castlebay 90 B6
Castle Bolton 63 A5
Castle Bromwich 40 D6
Castle Bytham 42 C3
Castlebythe 16 D3
Castle Caereinion 38 A4
Castle Camps 33 C4
Castle Carrock 69 D4
Castlecary 81 B4
Castle Cary 21 A7
Castle Combe 21 C3
Castlecraig Bdrs 75 B1
Castlecraig Hghld 103 B5
Castle Donington 41 B2
Castle Douglas 67 D4
Castle Eaton 22 A2
Castle Eden 71 C5
Castle End 40 E7
Castlefairn 67 D2
Castleford 57 C5
Castle Frome 29 A3
Castle Gresley 40 E3
Castle Heaton 77 A1
Castle Hedingham 33 D5
Castle Hill Devon 7 A4
Castle Hill Sflk 35 A4
Castle Howard 64 E6
Castle Kennedy 66 C5
Castle Levan 80 B4
Castlemaddy 67 B2
Castle Madoc 27 E7
Castlemartin 16 C6
Castlemilk D & G 68 E2
Castlemilk Strath 81 A6
Castle Morris 16 C2
Castlemorton 29 B4
Castle O'er 75 C6
Castle Pulverbatch 38 D4
Castle Rising 44 A3
Castleside 70 D4
Castle Stuart 103 A7
Castlethorpe 31 C3
Castleton Bdrs 76 B6
Castleton Derbs 50 C2
Castleton Gramp 105 A3
Castleton Gwent 19 C5
Castleton Lancs 55 C6
Castleton N Yorks 64 D3
Castleton Strath 79 C3
Castleton Tays 88 E4
Castletown Hghld 111 B2
Castletown Hghld 103 A7
Castletown IOM 60 b5
Castletown T & W 71 B3
Castleweary 76 A5
Castlewigg 67 A6
Caston 44 D6
Castor 42 E5
Castramont 67 B4
Cat and Fiddle Inn 50 B3
Catbrain 20 E2
Catchall 2 B6
Catcleugh 76 D5
Catcliffe 51 A2
Catcott 20 C7

Catcott Burtle 20 D6
Caterham 13 A1
Catesby 31 A2
Catfield 45 C3
Catford 24 D5
Catforth 54 D4
Cathedine 28 A5
Catherington 11 C3
Catherton 39 A7
Catlow 55 C4
Catlowdy 69 C2
Catmore 22 D4
Caton Devon 5 C3
Caton Lancs 54 E1
Cator Court 5 B3
Catrine 73 E5
Cat's Ash 19 D4
Catsfield 13 E5
Catshill 40 B7
Cattadale 78 C5
Cattal 57 C2
Cattawade 35 A5
Catterall 54 D3
Catterick 63 C5
Catterick Bridge 63 C5
Catterick Camp 63 B5
Catterlen 69 C6
Catterline 97 D6
Catterton 57 D3
Catthorpe 41 C7
Cattistock 9 B4
Catton Nflk 45 B4
Catton Northld 70 B3
Catton N Yorks 63 D7
Catton Hall 40 E3
Catwick 59 B3
Catworth 32 B1
Caudle Green 29 C4
Caudworthy 4 C2
Cauldcoats 74 B1
Cauldcots 89 C4
Cauldhame Cent 81 A2
Cauldhame Cent 81 C1
Cauldon 50 B6
Cauldside 76 A7
Caulkerbush 68 C4
Caunsall 40 A6
Caunton 51 D4
Causeway End 67 A4
Causewayhead Cent
 81 C2
Causewayhead Cumb
 68 E4
Causeyend 97 E2
Causey Park 77 C6
Cautley 62 B5
Cavendish 34 C4
Cavenham 33 D2
Cavens 68 C4
Caversfield 31 A5
Caversham 23 B4
Caversta 107 B6
Caverswall 49 D7
Cawdor 103 B6
Cawkwell 53 A4
Cawood 57 D4
Cawsand 4 E5
Cawston 45 A3
Cawthorne 57 A7
Cawthorpe 42 D2
Cawton 64 D6
Caxton 32 E3
Caxton End 32 E3
Caxton Gibbet 32 D2
Caynham 38 E7
Caythorpe Lincs 52 C7
Caythorpe Notts 51 C6
Cayton 65 C5
Cedig 37 D3
Cefn-brîth 47 D5
Cefn-caer-Ferch 46 D6
Cefn Cantref 19 A1
Cefn Coch Clwyd 48 A6
Cefn Coch Pwys 38 A2
Cefn-coed-y-cymmer
 19 A3
Cefn Cribwr 18 D5
Cefn Cross 18 D5
Cefn-ddwysarn 47 D7
Cefndeuddwr 37 B3
Cefn-Einion 38 B6
Cefneithin 17 D4
Cefngorwydd 27 D6
Cefn-gwyn 38 A6
Cefn Hengoed 19 B4
Cefn Mably 19 C5

Cefn-Mawr 48 B7
Cefn-y-bedd 48 C6
Cefn-y-pant 16 E3
Ceidio 46 D2
Ceidio Fawr 46 B7
Ceint 46 D3
Cellan 27 A6
Cellardyke 83 A2
Cellarhead 49 D7
Cemaes Bay 46 C1
Cemmaes 37 C5
Cemmaes Road 37 C5
Cenarth 26 B6
Cennin 46 D6
Ceres 89 A7
Cerne Abbas 9 C3
Cerney Wick 21 E1
Cerrigceinwen 46 D3
Cerrigydrudion 47 D6
Cessford 76 D3
Chaceley 29 C4
Chacewater 2 E4
Chackmore 31 B4
Chacombe 30 E3
Chadderton 49 D1
Chaddesden 50 E7
Chaddesley Corbett 40 A7
Chaddleworth 22 D4
Chadlington 30 D5
Chadshunt 30 D2
Chad Valley 40 C6
Chadwell 41 E2
Chadwell St Mary 25 B5
Chadwick End 40 E7
Chaffcombe 8 E2
Chagford 5 C2
Chailey 13 A5
Chainhurst 13 E2
Chalbury Common 10 B4
Chaldon 13 A1
Chaldon Herring 9 D5
Chale 11 A7
Chale Green 11 A7
Chalfont Common 23 D2
Chalfont St Giles 23 D2
Chalfont St Peter 23 D2
Chalford 29 C7
Chalgrove 23 A2
Chalk 25 B5
Challacombe 7 A2
Challoch 66 E4
Challock Lees 15 A3
Chalmington 9 B3
Chalton Beds 32 B6
Chalton Hants 11 D3
Chalvington 13 C6
Champany 81 E4
Chandler's Cross 23 E2
Chandler's Ford 11 A2
Channerwick 115 D5
Chantry Sflk 35 A4
Chantry Som 21 B6
Chapel Fife 82 C3
Chapel Allerton Som 20 D5
Chapel Allerton W Yorks
 57 A4
Chapel Amble 3 B1
Chapelbank 88 B7
Chapel Brampton 31 C1
Chapel Chorlton 40 A1
Chapel Cross 13 D4
Chapeldonan 73 B7
Chapel End 41 A5
Chapelend Way 33 D5
Chapel-en-le-Frith 50 B2
Chapel Fields 41 A5
Chapelgate 43 C2
Chapel Haddlesey 57 D5
Chapel Hall 80 A5
Chapelhall 81 B5
Chapel Hill Gramp 105 D5
Chapel Hill Gwent 28 E7
Chapelhill Hghld 103 B4
Chapel Hill Lincs 53 A6
Chapelhill Tays 88 D6
Chapelhill Tays 88 B5
Chapelknowe 69 B2
Chapel Lawn 38 C7
Chapel le Dale 62 C7
Chapel of Garioch 105 A6
Chapel Rossan 66 C6
Chapel Row 22 E5
Chapel St Leonards 53 D4
Chapel Stile 61 C3
Chapelton Strath 74 B1
Chapelton Tays 89 C4
Chapel Town Corn 3 A3

Chapeltown *Cumb* 69 C2
Chapeltown *GM* 55 B6
Chapeltown *Gramp* 104 A6
Chapeltown *S Yorks* 50 E1
Chapmanslade 21 C6
Chapmore End 32 E7
Chappel 34 C6
Chard 8 E3
Chardstock 8 E3
Charfield 21 B1
Charing 14 E4
Charing Heath 14 E4
Charingworth 30 B4
Charlbury 30 D6
Charlcombe 21 B4
Charlcote 21 D3
Charlecote 30 C2
Charles 7 A3
Charleshill 23 C7
Charleston 88 E4
Charlestown *Corn* 3 C3
Charlestown *Dors* 9 C6
Charlestown *Fife* 81 E3
Charlestown *Gramp* 97 E3
Charlestown *Gramp*
105 D2
Charlestown *Hghld* 101 A4
Charlestown *Hghld* 102 E7
Charlestown of Aberlour
104 A4
Charles Tye 34 E3
Charlesworth 50 B1
Charleton 5 C6
Charlinch 20 D4
Charlton *GL* 24 E5
Charlton *H & W* 30 A3
Charlton *Hants* 22 C7
Charlton *Herts* 32 C6
Charlton *Northants* 31 A4
Charlton *Northld* 76 E7
Charlton *Oxon* 22 D3
Charlton *Som* 21 A5
Charlton *Wilts* 10 A2
Charlton *Wilts* 10 C2
Charlton *Wilts* 21 D2
Charlton *Wilts* 22 A6
Charlton *W Ssx* 11 E3
Charlton Abbots 30 A5
Charlton Adam 9 B1
Charlton Horethorne 9 C1
Charlton Kings 29 D5
Charlton Mackrell 9 B1
Charlton Marshall 9 E3
Charlton Musgrove 9 D1
Charlton-on-Otmoor 31 A6
Charlwood 12 E2
Charminster 9 C4
Charmouth 8 E4
Charndon 31 B5
Charney Bassett 22 C2
Charnock Richard 54 E6
Charsfield 35 B3
Chart Corner 14 D3
Charter Alley 22 B6
Charterhouse 20 D5
Charterstones 97 C6
Charterville Allotments
30 D6
Chartham 15 B3
Chartham Hatch 15 B3
Chartridge 23 D1
Chart Sutton 14 D4
Charwelton 31 A2
Chase End Street 29 B4
Chase Terrace 40 C4
Chasetown 40 C4
Chastleton 30 C5
Chasty 6 C6
Chatburn 55 B3
Chatcull 39 B1
Chatelherault 81 B6
Chatham 14 C2
Chathill 77 C3
Chattenden 14 C1
Chatteris 43 B6
Chattisham 34 E4
Chatto 76 D4
Chatton 77 B3
Chawleigh 7 B5
Chawley 30 E7
Chawston 32 C3
Chawton 11 D1
Cheadle *GM* 49 C3
Cheadle *Staffs* 50 B6
Cheadle Hulme 49 C3
Cheam 24 C6
Chearsley 31 C6

Chebsey 40 A2
Checkendon 23 A3
Checkley *Ches* 49 B7
Checkley *H & W* 28 E4
Checkley *Staffs* 50 B7
Chedburgh 33 D3
Cheddar 20 D5
Cheddington 31 E6
Cheddleton 49 D6
Cheddon Fitzpaine 8 D1
Chedglow 21 D1
Chedgrave 45 C6
Chedington 9 A3
Chediston 35 C1
Chedworth 30 A6
Chedzoy 20 C7
Cheeklaw 83 C7
Cheesden 55 C6
Cheeseman's Green 15 A5
Cheetham Hill 49 C1
Cheldon 7 B5
Chelford 49 C4
Chellaston 50 E7
Chellington 31 E2
Chelmarsh 39 B6
Chelmondiston 35 B5
Chelmorton 50 C4
Chelmsford 25 C2
Chelsfield 24 E6
Chelsham 13 A1
Chelsworth 34 D4
Cheltenham 29 D5
Chelveston 31 E1
Chelvey 20 D4
Chelwood 21 A4
Chelwood Gate 13 B3
Chelworth 21 D1
Cheney Longville 38 D6
Chenies 23 E2
Chepstow 20 E1
Chequers 15 B3
Cherhill 21 E3
Cherington *Glos* 21 D1
Cherington *Warks* 30 C4
Cheriton *Devon* 8 C3
Cheriton *Devon* 7 B2
Cheriton *Dyfed* 16 C6
Cheriton *Hants* 11 B2
Cheriton *Som* 9 C1
Cheriton *W Glam* 17 C6
Cheriton Bishop 7 B7
Cheriton Cross 7 B7
Cheriton Fitzpaine 7 C6
Cherrington 39 A3
Cherry Burton 58 E3
Cherry Hinton 33 A3
Cherry Willingham 52 D4
Chertsey 23 E5
Cheselbourne 9 D4
Chesham 23 D1
Chesham Bois 23 D2
Cheshunt 24 D2
Cheslyn Hay 40 B4
Chessington 24 B6
Chester 48 D5
Chesterblade 21 A6
Chesterfield *Derbs* 50 E3
Chesterfield *Staffs* 40 D4
Chester-le-Street 71 A3
Chesters *Bdrs* 76 C4
Chesters *Bdrs* 76 C3
Chesterton *Cambs* 33 A2
Chesterton *Cambs* 42 E5
Chesterton *Oxon* 31 A5
Chesterton *Salop* 39 B5
Chesterton *Staffs* 49 C7
Chesterton Green 30 D2
Chestfield 15 B2
Cheswardine 39 B2
Cheswick 77 B1
Chetnole 9 C3
Chettiscombe 7 D5
Chettisham 43 D6
Chettle 10 A3
Chetton 39 A5
Chetwode 31 B5
Chetwynd Aston 39 B3
Cheveley 33 C2
Chevening 13 B1
Cheverell's Green 32 B7
Chevington 33 D3
Chevington Drift 77 D6
Chevithorne 7 D5
Chew Magna 20 E4
Chew Stoke 20 E4
Chewton Keynsham 21 A4
Chewton Mendip 20 E5

Chicheley 31 E3
Chichester 11 E4
Chickerell 9 C5
Chickering 35 B1
Chicklade 10 A1
Chickney 33 B6
Chidden 11 C3
Chiddingfold 12 B3
Chiddingly 13 C5
Chiddingstone Causeway
13 C2
Chiddingstone Hoath
13 C2
Chideock 9 A4
Chidham 11 D4
Chidswick Green 33 C7
Chieveley 22 D4
Chignall St James 25 B2
Chignall Smealy 33 C7
Chigwell 24 E3
Chigwell Row 24 E3
Chilbolton 10 E1
Chilcomb 11 B2
Chilcombe 9 B4
Chilcompton 21 A5
Chilcote 40 E3
Childer Thornton 48 C4
Childrey 22 C3
Child's Ercall 39 A2
Childswickham 30 A4
Childwall 48 D3
Childwick Green 32 C7
Chilfrome 9 B4
Chilgrove 11 E3
Chilham 15 A3
Chillaton 4 E2
Chillenden 15 C3
Chillerton 11 A6
Chillesford 35 C3
Chillingham 77 B3
Chillington *Devon* 5 C6
Chillington *Som* 8 E2
Chilmark 10 A1
Chilson 10 D6
Chilsworthy *Corn* 4 E3
Chilsworthy *Devon* 6 C6
Chilthorne Domer 9 B2
Chilton *Bucks* 31 B6
Chilton *Dur* 71 B5
Chilton *Oxon* 22 D3
Chilton Candover 22 E7
Chilton Cantelo 9 B1
Chilton Foliat 22 C4
Chilton Polden 20 C7
Chilton Street 33 D4
Chilton Trinity 20 B7
Chilvers Cotton 41 A5
Chilworth *Hants* 11 A3
Chilworth *Sry* 12 C2
Chimney 30 D7
Chineham 23 A6
Chingford 24 D3
Chinley 50 B2
Chinley Head 50 B2
Chinnor 23 B2
Chipchase Castle 70 B1
Chipley Park 8 C1
Chipnall 39 B1
Chippenham *Cambs* 33 C2
Chippenham *Wilts* 21 D3
Chipperfield 23 E1
Chipping *Herts* 32 E5
Chipping *Lancs* 55 A3
Chipping Campden 30 B4
Chipping Hill 34 C7
Chipping Norton 30 D5
Chipping Ongar 24 F2
Chipping Sodbury 21 B2
Chipping Warden 30 E3
Chipstable 8 B1
Chipstead *Kent* 13 C1
Chipstead *Sry* 12 E1
Chirbury 38 B5
Chirk 38 B1
Chirmorie 66 D3
Chirnside 83 D7
Chirnsidebridge 83 D7
Chirton 21 E5
Chisbury 22 B5
Chiscan 72 A6
Chiseldon 22 A4
Chiselborough 9 A2
Chislehampton 22 E2
Chislehurst 24 E5
Chislet 15 C2

Chiswell Green 24 B2
Chiswick 24 C5
Chisworth 49 D2
Chithurst 11 E2
Chittering 33 A1
Chitterne 21 D6
Chitterne St Mary 21 D6
Chittlehamholt 7 A4
Chittlehampton 7 A4
Chittoe 21 D4
Chivelstone 5 C7
Chobham 23 D5
Choicelee 83 C7
Cholderton 22 B7
Cholesbury 23 D1
Cholesy 22 E3
Cholstrey 28 D2
Cholwell 21 A5
Chop Gate 64 C4
Chopwell 70 E3
Chorley *Ches* 48 E6
Chorley *Lancs* 54 E6
Chorley *Salop* 39 A6
Chorley *Staffs* 40 C3
Chorleywood 23 E2
Chorlton 49 B6
Chorlton-cum-Hardy 49 C2
Chorlton Lane 48 D7
Chowley 48 D6
Chrishall 33 A5
Chrishall Grange 33 A4
Christchurch *Cambs*
43 D5
Christchurch *Dors* 10 C5
Christchurch *Glos* 28 E6
Christchurch *Gwent* 19 D5
Christian Malford 21 D3
Christleton 48 D5
Christmas Common 23 B2
Christon 20 C5
Christon Bank 77 D3
Christow 5 D2
Chriswell 80 B4
Chryston 80 A3
Chudleigh 5 D3
Chudleigh Knighton 5 D3
Chulmleigh 7 A5
Chunal 50 B1
Church 55 B5
Churcham 29 B6
Church Aston 39 B3
Church Brampton 31 C1
Church Broughton 50 D7
Church Crookham 23 C6
Churchdown 29 C6
Church Eaton 40 A3
Church End *Beds* 32 C5
Church End *Beds* 31 E5
Church End *Cambs* 43 B4
Church End *Cambs* 33 A3
Church End *Esx* 33 B4
Church End *Esx* 33 D6
Churchend *Esx* 25 F3
Churchend *Esx* 33 C6
Church End *Hants* 23 A6
Church End *Herts* 32 B7
Church End *Humb* 59 A2
Church End *Lincs* 43 A1
Church End *Lincs* 53 C2
Church End *Warks* 40 E5
Church End *Wilts* 21 E3
Church Enstone 30 D5
Church Fenton 57 D4
Churchgate 24 D2
Churchgate Street 33 A7
Church Green 8 C4
Church Gresley 40 E3
Church Handborough
30 E6
Church Houses 64 D4
Churchill *Avn* 20 D5
Churchill *H & W* 29 D2
Churchill *H & W* 40 A7
Churchill *Oxon* 30 C5
Churchingford 8 D2
Church Knowle 10 A6
Church Langton 41 E5
Church Lawford 41 B7
Church Lawton 49 C6
Church Leigh 50 B7
Church Lench 30 A2
Church Minshull 49 A5
Church Norton 11 E5
Churchover 41 C6
Church Preen 38 E5
Church Pulverbatch 38 D4

Churchstanton 8 C2
Church Stoke 38 B5
Churchstow 5 C6
Church Stowe 31 B2
Church Street 14 C1
Church Stretton 38 D5
Churchthorpe 53 B2
Churchtown *Devon* 7 A2
Churchtown *IOM* 60 d2
Churchtown *Lancs* 54 D3
Churchtown *Mers* 54 C6
Church Village 19 A5
Church Warsop 51 B4
Churston Ferrers 5 E5
Churt 11 E1
Churton 70 C1
Churwell 57 A5
Chute Cadley 22 C6
Chute Standen 22 C6
Chwilog 46 D7
Chyandour 2 B5
Cilan Uchaf 36 B3
Cilcain 48 A5
Cilcennin 26 E4
Cilfrew 18 C3
Cilfynydd 19 A4
Cilgerran 26 A6
Cilgwyn *Dyfed* 16 D2
Cilgwyn *Dyfed* 27 B7
Ciliau-Aeron 26 E5
Cilmery 27 E5
Cilrhedyn 17 A2
Cilwendeg 17 A2
Cilybebyll 18 C3
Cilycwm 27 B6
Cinderford 29 A6
Cirencester 30 A7
City, The 23 B2
City Dulas 46 D2
City of London 24 D4
City of Westminster 24 C5
Clabhach 84 D4
Clachadow 86 A6
Clachaig 80 A3
Clachan *Hghld* 92 C1
Clachan *Strath* 86 C7
Clachan *Strath* 85 E4
Clachan *Strath* 72 B2
Clachan *Tays* 87 E2
Clachan *W Is* 98 B7
Clachandhu 85 A5
Clachan of Campsie 81 A4
Clachan of Glendaruel
79 D3
Clachan-Seil 85 D7
Clachanturn 96 C4
Clachbrech 79 B4
Clachnabrain 88 E2
Clachnaharry 102 E7
Clachtoll 108 C6
Clackmannan 81 D2
Clacton-on-Sea 35 A7
Claddach Kirkibost 98 B5
Claddach-kyles 98 B5
Cladich 86 B6
Claggan *Hghld* 86 C1
Claggan *Hghld* 85 D4
Claigan 99 B6
Claines 29 C2
Clandown 21 A5
Clanfield *Hants* 11 C3
Clanfield *Oxon* 30 C7
Clannaborough Barton
7 B6
Clanville 22 C7
Claonaig 72 C2
Claonairigh 79 E1
Claonel 102 D1
Clapgate 10 B4
Clap Gate 57 B3
Clapham *Beds* 32 B3
Clapham *GL* 24 C5
Clapham *N Yorks* 55 B1
Clapham *W Ssx* 12 C6
Clapham Hill 15 B2
Clappers 83 E7
Clappersgate 61 C3
Clapton *Glos* 30 B6
Clapton *Som* 9 A3
Clapton-in-Gordano 20 D3
Clapworthy 7 A4
Clarbeston 16 D3
Clarbeston Road 16 D3
Clarborough 51 D2
Clardon 111 B2
Clare *Sflk* 33 D4

Clarebrand 67 D4
Clarencefield 68 D3
Clareton 57 B2
Clarilaw 76 B4
Clarkston *Strath* 81 B5
Clarkston *Strath* 80 E6
Clashban 102 E2
Clashcoig 102 E2
Clashgour 86 D4
Clashindarroch 104 C5
Clashmore 103 A3
Clashnessie 108 C5
Clashnoir 104 A6
Clathy 88 A7
Clatt 104 D6
Clatter 37 D6
Clatterford End 24 F2
Clattering Bridge 97 B6
Clatteringshaws 67 B3
Clatworthy 7 E3
Clauchaneasy 66 E3
Claughton *Lancs* 54 E1
Claughton *Lancs* 54 E3
Claverdon 30 B1
Claverham 20 D4
Clavering 33 A5
Claverley 39 B5
Claverton 21 B4
Clawdd-newydd 47 E5
Clawfin 73 E7
Clawthorpe 61 E6
Clawton 6 C7
Claxby *Lincs* 53 C4
Claxby *Lincs* 52 E2
Claxby Pluckacre 53 B5
Claxton *Nflk* 45 C5
Claxton *N Yorks* 57 E1
Claybrooke Magna 41 B6
Claybrooke Parva 41 B6
Clay Common 45 D7
Clay Coton 41 C7
Clay Cross 50 E4
Claydene 13 B2
Claydon *Oxon* 30 E2
Claydon *Sflk* 35 A3
Claygate *Kent* 13 E2
Claygate *Sry* 24 B6
Claygate Cross 13 D1
Clayhanger *Devon* 8 C2
Clayhanger *W Mids* 40 C4
Clayhidon 8 C2
Claypits 29 B6
Claypole 52 B7
Clays of Allan 103 B4
Claythorpe 53 C4
Clayton *Staffs* 49 C7
Clayton *S Yorks* 57 C7
Clayton *W Ssx* 13 A5
Clayton *W Yorks* 56 E5
Clayton-le-Moors 55 B4
Clayton-le-Woods 54 E5
Clayton West 57 A6
Clayworth 51 D2
Cleadale 92 B6
Cleadon 71 B2
Clearbrook 5 A4
Clearwell 28 E7
Cleasby 63 C3
Cleat 113 C6
Cleatlam 63 B3
Cleatop 55 C1
Cleator 60 E2
Cleator Moor 60 E2
Cleckheaton 56 E5
Cleedownton 38 E6
Cleehill 38 E7
Clee St Margaret 38 E6
Cleethorpes 59 D7
Cleeton St Mary 39 A7
Cleeve *Avn* 20 D4
Cleeve *Oxon* 23 A3
Cleeve Hill 29 D5
Cleeve Prior 30 A3
Cleghorn 74 E1
Clehonger 28 D4
Cleigh 85 E6
Cleish 81 E2
Cleland 81 B6
Clemenstone 18 E6
Clench Common 22 A5
Clenchwarton 43 D2
Clent 40 B7
Cleobury Mortimer 39 A7
Cleobury North 39 A6
Clephanton 103 B6
Clerklands 76 B3
Clestrain 113 C1
Cleuchbrae 68 D2

Cleuch Head 76 B4
Clevancy 21 E3
Clevedon 20 D3
Cleveland Tontine 64 B4
Cleveleys 54 C3
Clevelode 29 C3
Cleverton 21 D2
Clewer Berks 23 D4
Clewer Som 20 D5
Cley next the Sea 44 E1
Cliburn 69 D7
Cliddesden 23 A7
Cliff Dyfed 17 B5
Cliff Hghld 85 C2
Cliffe Kent 14 C1
Cliffe N Yorks 57 E4
Cliff End 14 D7
Cliffe Woods 14 C1
Clifford H & W 28 B3
Clifford W Yorks 57 C3
Clifford Chambers 30 B2
Clifford's Mesne 29 B5
Cliffsend 15 D2
Clifton Avn 20 E3
Clifton Beds 32 C5
Clifton Cent 86 E5
Clifton Cumb 68 D7
Clifton Cumb 69 D7
Clifton Derbs 50 C6
Clifton H & W 29 C3
Clifton Lancs 54 D4
Clifton Northld 77 D7
Clifton Notts 51 B7
Clifton Oxon 30 E4
Clifton Campville 40 E3
Clifton Hampden 22 E2
Clifton Reynes 31 E2
Clifton upon Dunsmore
  41 C7
Clifton upon Teme 29 B1
Cliftonville 15 D1
Climping 12 C6
Climpy 81 D6
Clint 57 A2
Clinterty 97 D2
Clint Green 44 E4
Clintmains 76 C2
Clippesby 45 D4
Clipsham 42 C3
Clipston Northants 41 E6
Clipston Notts 51 C7
Clipstone 51 C4
Clipstone Village 51 B4
Clitheroe 55 B3
Clive 38 E2
Cliveden 40 B6
Clivocast 114 F2
Clocaenog 47 E5
Clochan 104 C2
Clochtow 105 D5
Clock Face 48 E2
Clockhill 105 B4
Cloddach 103 E6
Clodock 28 C5
Cloichran 87 C5
Cloichran 87 C5
Clola 105 D4
Clonrae 74 D6
Clophill 32 B5
Clopton 42 D6
Clopton Green 33 D3
Closeburn 74 D6
Close Clark 60 b4
Closworth 9 B2
Clothall 32 D5
Clothan 114 D4
Clotton 48 E5
Clough Cumb 62 C5
Clough GM 55 D6
Clough Foot 55 D5
Cloughton 65 C4
Cloughton Newlands
  65 C4
Clounlaid 85 D3
Clousta 115 C2
Clouston 112 C5
Clova Gramp 104 C6
Clova Tays 96 D6
Clovelly 6 C4
Clovelly Cross 6 C4
Clove Lodge 62 E3
Clovenfords 76 A2
Clovenstone 97 C2
Cloverhill 97 E2
Cloves 103 E5
Clovullin 86 B2
Clowne 51 A3

Clows Top 39 B7
Cloyntie 73 C7
Cluanach 78 C6
Clubworthy 6 B7
Cluer 99 A2
Clun 38 C6
Clunas 103 B7
Clunbury 38 C6
Clune Gramp 104 D2
Clune Hghld 95 A3
Clunes 93 E6
Clungunford 38 C7
Clunie Gramp 104 E3
Clunie Tays 88 C4
Clunton 38 C6
Cluny 82 C3
Clutton Avn 21 A5
Clutton Ches 48 D6
Clwt-y-bont 46 E4
Clydach Gwent 19 C2
Clydach W Glam 18 B3
Clydach Vale 18 E4
Clydebank 80 E5
Clydey 17 A2
Clyffe Pypard 21 E3
Clyn 16 E2
Clynder 80 B3
Clynderwen 16 E4
Clynelish 103 B1
Clyn-Fiew 17 A2
Clynnog-fawr 46 D6
Clyro 28 B3
Clyst Honiton 7 D7
Clyst Hydon 8 B3
Clyst St George 8 A5
Clyst St Lawrence 8 B3
Clyst St Mary 7 D7
Clyth Burn 111 C5
Cnewr 18 D1
Cnoc nan Sltheag 80 E1
Cnwch Coch 27 A3
Coachford 104 C4
Coad's Green 4 C3
Coal Aston 50 E3
Coalbrookdale 39 A4
Coalbrookvale 19 B3
Coalburn 74 D2
Coalburns 70 E2
Coalcleugh 70 B4
Coaley 29 B7
Coalpit Heath 21 A2
Coalpit Hill 49 C6
Coalport 39 A4
Coalsnaughton 81 D2
Coaltown of Balgonie
  82 C3
Coaltown of Wemyss
  82 D3
Coalville 41 B3
Coat 9 A1
Coatbridge 81 B5
Coate Wilts 22 A3
Coate Wilts 21 E4
Coates Cambs 43 B5
Coates Glos 29 D7
Coates W Ssx 12 C5
Coatham 64 C1
Coatham Mundeville 63 C3
Cobairdy 104 D4
Cobbaton 7 A4
Coberley 29 D6
Cobham Kent 25 B6
Cobham Sry 24 B6
Cobleland 80 E2
Cobnash 28 D1
Coburty 105 C2
Cochno 80 D4
Cock Alley 51 A3
Cockayne 64 D4
Cockayne Hatley 32 D4
Cock Bridge 96 C3
Cockburnspath 83 C5
Cock Clarks 25 D2
Cockenzie and Port Seton
  82 E5
Cockerham 54 D2
Cockerington 53 B3
Cockermouth 68 E6
Cockernhoe Green 32 C6
Cockett 18 B4
Cockfield Dur 70 E6
Cockfield Sflk 34 D3
Cockfosters 24 C3
Cocking 11 E3
Cockington 5 D4
Cocklake 20 D6

Cockley Beck 61 B3
Cockley Cley 44 B5
Cockpole Green 23 B3
Cockshutt 38 D2
Cockthorpe 44 D1
Cockwood 8 A5
Codda 4 B3
Coddenham 35 A3
Codford St Mary 10 A1
Codford St Peter 21 D6
Codicote 32 D7
Codmore Hill 12 C4
Codnor 51 A6
Codrington 21 B3
Codsall 40 A4
Codsall Wood 40 A4
Coedana 46 D2
Coedely 19 A5
Coedkernew 19 C5
Coed Morgan 19 D2
Coedpenmaen 19 A4
Coedpoeth 48 B6
Coed-y-paen Dyfed 18 D2
Coed-y-paen Gwent 19 D4
Coed-yr-ynys 28 A5
Coelbren 18 D2
Coffcott Green 6 C7
Coffinswell 5 D4
Cofton Hackett 40 C7
Cogan 19 B6
Cogenhoe 31 D1
Coggeshall 34 C6
Coggins Mill 13 B4
Coilacriech 96 D5
Coilantogle 80 E1
Coileitir 86 C4
Coilesan 80 B1
Coillaig 86 B6
Coille Mhorgil 93 D4
Coille -righ 93 B2
Coillore 92 A1
Coity 18 E5
Colaboll 109 C7
Colan 3 A2
Colaton Raleigh 8 B5
Colbost 99 B7
Colbury 10 E3
Colby Cumb 69 E7
Colby IOM 60 b4
Colby Nflk 45 B2
Colchester 34 E6
Colcot 19 B7
Cold Ash 22 E5
Cold Ashby 41 D7
Cold Ashton 21 B3
Cold Aston 30 B6
Coldbackie 109 D2
Cold Blow 16 E4
Coldblow 24 F5
Cold Brayfield 31 E2
Coldean 13 A6
Coldeast 5 D3
Colden Common 11 A2
Coldfair Green 35 D2
Coldham 43 C4
Cold Hanworth 52 D3
Coldharbour 12 D2
Coldhayes 11 D2
Cold Hesledon 71 C4
Cold Higham 31 B2
Coldingham 83 E6
Cold Kirby 64 C5
Cold Newton 41 E4
Cold Norton 25 D2
Cold Overton 42 B3
Coldrain 81 E1
Coldred 15 C4
Coldrey 23 B7
Coldridge 7 A6
Coldrife 77 B6
Coldstream 76 E2
Coldwaltham 12 C5
Coldwells 105 E5
Cole 21 A7
Colebatch 38 C6
Colebrook Devon 8 B3
Colebrook Devon 5 A5
Colebrooke 7 B7
Coleby Humb 58 D6
Coleby Lincs 52 C5
Coleford Devon 7 B6
Coleford Glos 28 E6
Coleford Som 21 A6
Cole Green 32 D7

Colehill Dors 10 B4
Coleman's Hatch 13 B3
Colemere 38 D1
Colemore 11 D1
Colenden 88 C6
Coleorton 41 A3
Colerne 21 C3
Cole's Cross 5 C5
Colesden 32 C3
Colesbourne 29 D6
Coleshill Bucks 23 D2
Coleshill Oxon 22 B2
Coleshill Warks 40 D6
Colestocks 8 B3
Colfin 66 B5
Colgate 12 E3
Colgrain 80 C2
Colinsburgh 82 E2
Colinton 82 C6
Colintraive 79 E4
Colkirk 44 D3
Coll 107 C4
Collace 88 D5
Collafirth Shet 115 D1
Collafirth Shet 114 C3
Collamoor Head 4 D3
Collaton St Mary 5 D4
Collessie 88 D7
Collier Row 24 E3
Collier's End 32 E6
Collier Street 13 E2
Colliery Row 71 B4
Collieston 105 D6
Collin 68 D2
Collingbourne Ducis 22 B6
Collingbourne Kingston
  22 B6
Collingham Notts 52 B5
Collingham W Yorks 57 B3
Collington 29 A1
Collingtree 31 C2
Collingwood 13 E4
Collins Green 48 E2
Colliston 89 C4
Collmuir 97 A3
Collycroft 41 A6
Collyweston 42 C4
Colmonell 66 C2
Colmworth 32 C3
Colnabaichin 96 C3
Colnbrook 23 E4
Colne Cambs 32 E1
Colne Lancs 55 C4
Colne Engaine 34 C5
Colney 45 A5
Colney Heath 24 C2
Colney Street 24 B2
Coln Rogers 30 A7
Coln St Aldwyns 30 B7
Coln St Dennis 96 B5
Colonsay 78 C2
Colpy 104 E5
Colquhar 75 D1
Colquirk 67 A5
Colsterdale 63 B6
Colsterworth 42 C2
Colston Bassett 51 D7
Coltfield 103 E5
Coltishall 45 B4
Colton Cumb 61 C5
Colton Nflk 45 A5
Colton N Yorks 57 D3
Colton Staffs 40 C2
Colva 28 B2
Colvend 68 B4
Colvister 114 E3
Colwall 29 B3
Colwall Green 29 B3
Colwall Stone 29 B3
Colwell 70 C1
Colwich 40 C2
Colwick 51 C7
Colwinston 18 E6
Colworth 12 B6
Colwyn Bay 47 C3
Colyford 8 D4
Colyton 8 D4
Combe Berks 22 C5
Combe Devon 5 C6
Combe Dors 5 D2
Combe H & W 28 C1
Combe Oxon 30 E6
Combe Down 21 B4
Combe Florey 20 A7
Combe Hay 21 B5
Combeinteignhead 8 A6
Combe Martin 6 E2

Combe Moor 28 C1
Combe Raleigh 8 C3
Comberbach 49 A4
Comberford 40 D4
Comberton Cambs 32 E3
Comberton H & W 28 D1
Combe St Nicholas 8 E2
Combpyne 8 D4
Combrook 30 D2
Combs Derbs 50 B3
Combs Sflk 34 E3
Combs Ford 34 E3
Combwich 20 B6
Comer 80 C1
Comers 97 B3
Commercial End 33 B2
Commins Coch 37 C5
Common, The Gwent
  19 D4
Common, The Northants
  31 C4
Commondale 64 D2
Common Edge 54 C4
Common Moor 4 C4
Commonside 50 D6
Common Side 50 E3
Compstall 49 D2
Compton Berks 22 E4
Compton Devon 5 D4
Compton Hants 11 D3
Compton Hants 11 A2
Compton Sry 12 B2
Compton Wilts 9 E2
Compton W Ssx 9 E2
Compton Abbas 9 E2
Compton Abdale 30 A6
Compton Bassett 21 E3
Compton Beauchamp
  22 B3
Compton Bishop 20 C5
Compton Chamberlayne
  10 B2
Compton Dando 21 A4
Compton Dundon 20 E5
Compton Martin 20 E5
Compton Pauncefoot 9 C1
Compton Valence 9 B4
Comra 94 D1
Comrie 87 D6
Conchra Hghld 93 A2
Conchra Strath 79 E3
Concraigie 88 C4
Conder Green 54 D2
Conderton 29 D4
Condicote 30 B5
Condorrat 81 B4
Condover 38 D4
Coneyhurst Common
  12 D4
Coneysthorpe 64 E6
Coneythorpe 57 B2
Coney Weston 34 D1
Conford 11 E1
Congash 95 D3
Congerstone 41 A4
Congham 44 B3
Congleton 49 C5
Congresbury 20 D4
Conicavel 103 C6
Coningsby 53 A6
Conington Cambs 42 E6
Conington Cambs 32 E2
Conisbrough 51 B1
Conisholme 53 B2
Coniston Cumb 61 C5
Coniston Humb 59 B4
Coniston Cold 55 D2
Conistone 55 D1
Conland 104 E4
Connah's Quay 48 B5
Connel 86 A5
Connel Park 74 B4
Connor Downs 2 C5
Conon Bridge 102 D6
Cononish 86 B6
Cononley 55 D3
Cononsyth 89 B4
Consall 49 D7
Consett 70 E3
Constable Burton 63 B5
Constantine 2 E6
Contin 102 C6
Contlaw 97 D3
Contullich 102 E4
Conwy 47 B3
Conyer 14 E2
Cooden 13 E6

Coodham 73 D4
Cookbury 6 D6
Cookham 23 C3
Cookham Dean 23 C3
Cookham Rise 23 C3
Cookhill 30 A2
Cookley H & W 40 A6
Cookley Sflk 35 C1
Cookley Green 23 A2
Cookney 97 D4
Cooksbridge 13 B5
Cookshill 49 D7
Cookston 105 C5
Cooksmill Green 25 B2
Coolham 12 D4
Cooling 14 C1
Coombe Corn 41 B6
Coombe Corn 41 B6
Coombe Bissett 10 C2
Coombe Hill 29 C5
Coombe Keynes 9 E5
Coombes 12 D6
Coopersale Common
  24 E2
Cooper's Corner 13 E4
Cooper's Hill 23 D4
Cootham 12 C5
Copdock 35 A4
Copford Green 34 D6
Copgrove 57 B1
Copister 114 D5
Cople 32 C4
Copley 70 D6
Coplow Dale 50 C3
Copmanthorpe 57 D3
Coppathorne 6 B6
Coppenhall 40 B3
Coppenhall Moss 49 B6
Coppingford 42 E6
Copperidge 9 E1
Copplestone 7 B6
Coppull 54 E6
Coppull Moor 54 E6
Copsale 12 D4
Copster Green 55 A4
Copston Magna 41 B6
Cop Street 15 D2
Copster Green 55 A4
Copt Heath 40 D7
Copt Hewick 63 D7
Copthorne 13 A3
Copt Oak 41 B3
Copy Lake 7 A5
Copythorne 10 E3
Coralhill 105 D2
Corbiegoe 111 D4
Corbridge 70 C2
Corby 42 B6
Corby Glen 42 C2
Cordach 97 B4
Coreley 39 A7
Corfe 8 D2
Corfe Mullen 10 A5
Corfton 38 D6
Corgarff 96 C3
Corhampton 11 C2
Corlarach Hill 80 A4
Corley 41 A6
Corley Ash 40 E6
Corley Moor 40 E6
Cornabus 78 C7
Corney 61 A4
Cornforth 71 B5
Cornhill 104 D3
Cornhill-on-Tweed 76 E2
Cornholme 55 D5
Cornish Hall End 33 C5
Cornquoy 113 E2
Cornriggs 70 B4
Cornsay 70 E4
Corntown Hghld 102 D6
Corntown M Glam 18 E6
Cornwell 30 C5
Cornwood 5 B5
Cornworthy 5 D5
Corpach 86 B1
Corpusty 45 A3
Corrachree 96 E3
Corran Hghld 93 A4
Corran Hghld 86 B2
Corran Strath 80 B2
Corranbuie 79 C5
Corranmore 79 B1
Corrany 60 d3
Corriclorne 85 E7
Corrie 72 E3
Corriechrevie 72 B2
Corrie Common 75 C7

Corriecravie 72 D5
Corriedoo 67 C2
Corrievorrie 95 A3
Corrimony 94 B2
Corringham Esx 25 C4
Corringham Lincs 52 B2
Corris Uchaf 37 B5
Corrlarach 86 A1
Corrow 80 A1
Corry 92 D2
Corrychurrachan 86 B2
Corrygills 72 E4
Corrykinloch 109 A6
Corrylach 72 B4
Corrymuckloch 87 E5
Corry of Ardnagrask 102 D7
Corsback 111 C1
Corscombe 9 B3
Corse 104 E4
Corsebank 74 D4
Corsehill 75 B7
Corse Lawn 29 C4
Corsemalzie 66 E5
Corse of Kinnoir 104 D4
Corsewall 66 B4
Corsham 21 C4
Corsley 21 C6
Corsley Heath 21 C6
Corsock 67 D3
Corston Avn 21 A4
Corston Wilts 21 D2
Corstorphine 82 B5
Cortachy 88 E3
Corton Sflk 45 E6
Corton Wilts 21 D6
Corton Denham 9 C1
Corunna 98 C5
Corwen 47 E6
Coryton Devon 4 E2
Coryton Esx 25 C4
Cosby 41 C5
Coseley 40 B5
Cosgrove 31 C3
Cosham 11 C4
Cosheston 16 D5
Coshieville 87 D4
Cossall 51 A6
Cossington Leics 41 D3
Cossington Som 20 C6
Costa 112 C4
Costessey 45 A4
Costock 41 C2
Coston Leics 42 B2
Coston Nflk 44 E5
Cote Oxon 30 D7
Cote Som 20 C6
Cotebrook 48 E5
Cotehill 69 C4
Cotes Cumb 61 D5
Cotes Leics 41 C2
Cotes Staffs 40 A1
Cotesbach 41 C6
Cotgrave 51 C7
Cothall 97 D2
Cotham 51 D6
Cothelstone 20 A7
Cothercott 38 D4
Cotherstone 63 A3
Cothill 22 D2
Cotleigh 8 D3
Coton Cambs 33 A3
Coton Northants 41 D7
Coton Staffs 40 B1
Coton Staffs 40 D4
Coton Clanford 40 A2
Coton in the Clay 40 D2
Coton in the Elms 40 E3
Cott 54 D4
Cottam Humb 65 B7
Cottam Lancs 54 D4
Cottam Notts 52 B4
Cottartown 95 D2
Cottenham 33 A2
Cotterdale 62 D5
Cottered 32 E6
Cotteridge 40 C6
Cotterstock 42 D5
Cottesbrooke 41 E7
Cottesmore 42 C3
Cottingham Humb 59 A4
Cottingham Northants 42 B5
Cottisford 31 A4
Cotton 34 E2
Cotton End 32 B4
Cottown 97 C2

Cot-town Gramp 104 D6
Cot-town Gramp 105 B4
Cotwalton 40 B1
Couchsmill 3 D3
Coughton H & W 28 E5
Coughton Warks 30 A1
Cougie 93 E2
Coulaghailtro 79 B5
Coulags 101 B7
Coull 97 A3
Coulport 80 B3
Coulsdon 13 A1
Coulter 75 A2
Coultershaw Bridge 12 B5
Coultings 20 B6
Coulton 64 D6
Coultra 38 E6
Cound 38 E4
Coundon 71 A6
Coundon Grange 71 A6
Countersett 62 E6
Countess Wear 8 A5
Countesthorpe 41 C5
Counthorpe 42 D2
Countisbury 7 B2
County Oak 12 E3
Coupar Angus 88 D5
Coupland Cumb 62 C3
Coupland Northld 77 A2
Cour 72 C3
Court-at-Street 15 A5
Court Barton 7 D7
Courteenhall 31 C2
Court Henry 17 D3
Courtsend 25 F3
Courtway 20 B7
Cousland 82 D6
Cousley Wood 13 D3
Coustonn 79 E4
Cove Devon 7 D5
Cove Hants 23 C6
Cove Hghld 101 A2
Cove Strath 80 B3
Cove Bay 97 E3
Covehithe 45 E7
Coven 40 B4
Coveney 43 C6
Covenham St Bartholomew 53 B2
Covenham St Mary 53 B2
Coventry 41 A7
Coverack 2 E7
Coverham 63 B6
Covesea 103 E4
Covington Cambs 32 B1
Covington Strath 74 E2
Cowan Bridge 62 B7
Cowbeech 13 D5
Cowbit 43 A3
Cowbridge 18 E6
Cowden 13 B2
Cowdenbeath 82 B3
Cowden Pound 13 B2
Cowes 11 A5
Cowesby 64 B5
Cowfold 12 E4
Cowgill 62 C6
Cowie Cent 81 C3
Cowie Gramp 97 D5
Cowlam Manor 65 B7
Cowley Bucks 31 B5
Cowley Devon 7 D7
Cowley GL 23 E3
Cowley Glos 29 D6
Cowley Oxon 31 A7
Cowling N Yorks 55 D3
Cowling N Yorks 63 C6
Cowlinge 33 D3
Cowmes 56 E6
Cowpen 77 D7
Cowpen Bewley 64 B1
Cowplain 11 D3
Cowshill 70 B4
Cowthorpe 57 C2
Coxbank 49 A7
Coxbench 50 E6
Cox Common 45 D7
Coxheath 13 E1
Coxhoe 71 B5
Coxley 20 E6
Coxtie Green 25 A3
Coxwold 64 C6
Coychurch 18 E6
Coylet 80 A3
Coylton 73 D6
Coylumbridge 95 C4
Coynach 96 E3

Coynachie 104 C5
Coytra-hen 18 D5
Crabadon 5 C5
Crabbs Cross 30 A1
Crabtree Devon 5 A5
Crabtree W Ssx 12 E4
Crackaig 78 E5
Crackenthorpe 69 E7
Crackington 6 A7
Crackington Haven 6 A7
Crackleybank 39 B3
Crackpot 62 E5
Cracoe 55 D1
Craddock 8 B2
Cradley H & W 29 B3
Cradley W Mids 40 B6
Crafthole 4 D5
Cragaig 85 A5
Cragg 56 D5
Craggan Gramp 95 E2
Craggan Hghld 95 D3
Craggan Strath 80 B2
Craggan Tays 87 E7
Cragganruar 87 C4
Craggie Hghld 95 A2
Craggie Hghld 110 D7
Craghead 71 A3
Craibstow 97 D2
Craichie 89 B4
Craig Clwyd 47 E3
Craig D & G 67 B4
Craig D & G 67 C4
Craig Hghld 100 E5
Craig Hghld 86 B5
Craig Hghld 85 B6
Craig S Glam 19 A6
Craig Strath 101 C7
Craig Strath 73 C7
Craigandale 79 E3
Craigans 79 D2
Craigbeg 94 C7
Craigcefnparc 18 B3
Craigcleuch 75 D7
Craigculter 105 C3
Craigdallie 88 D6
Craigdam 105 B5
Craigdarroch D & G 67 D1
Craigdarroch Strath 74 B5
Craigdhu D & G 66 E6
Craigdhu Hghld 102 C7
Craigearn 97 C2
Craigellachie 104 A4
Craigellie 105 D2
Craigencallie 67 B3
Craigend Gramp 103 E6
Craigend Tays 88 C6
Craigendoran 80 C3
Craigengillan 67 D2
Craigenputtock 67 D2
Craigens 78 B5
Craigentuie 80 C2
Craiggiecat 97 D4
Craigglass 79 C2
Craighall 89 A7
Craighead 103 A5
Craighlaw 66 E4
Craighouse 78 E5
Craigie Gramp 97 E2
Craigie Strath 73 D4
Craigie Tays 88 C4
Craigieburn 61 A3
Craigieholm 88 C5
Craigie Shethin 105 B5
Craiglockhart 82 C5
Craiglug 97 D4
Craigmaud 105 B3
Craigmillar 82 C5
Craigmore 80 A5
Craigmyle 97 B3
Craignafeich 79 D4
Craignant 38 B1
Craignavie 87 B5
Craigneil 66 C2
Craignure 85 D5
Craigo 89 C2
Craigoshina 97 A6
Craigow 81 E1
Craig Penllyn 18 E6
Craigpot 97 B2
Craigrothie 88 E7
Craigroy Gramp 103 E6
Craigroy Gramp 95 E2
Craigruie 87 B6
Craigsanquhar 88 E7
Craigton Cent 81 A3
Craigton Gramp 97 D3
Craigton Tays 89 B5

Craigton Tays 88 E3
Craigtown 110 D3
Craig-y-nos 18 D2
Craik Bdrs 75 D5
Craik Gramp 104 C6
Crail 83 B2
Crailing 76 C3
Crailinghall 76 C3
Craiselound 51 D1
Crakehall 63 C5
Crakehill 64 B6
Craleacain 79 E1
Crambe 64 E7
Cramlington 71 A1
Cramond 82 B5
Cranage 49 B5
Cranberry 40 A1
Cranborne 10 B3
Cranborne Common 10 C3
Cranbourne 23 D4
Cranbrook 13 E3
Cranbrook Common 13 E3
Cranfield 31 E3
Cranford Devon 6 C4
Cranford GL 24 B5
Cranford St Andrew 42 C7
Cranford St John 42 C7
Cranham Esx 25 A4
Cranham Glos 29 C6
Crank 48 E2
Cranleigh 12 C3
Cranmer Green 34 E1
Cranmore Hants 10 E5
Cranmore Som 21 A6
Cranna 104 E3
Crannach 104 C3
Cranoe 41 E5
Cransford 35 C2
Cranshaws 83 B6
Cranstal 60 d1
Crantock 2 E2
Cranwell 52 D6
Cranwich 44 B6
Cranworth 44 D5
Crapstone 5 A4
Crarae 79 D2
Crask Inn 109 C6
Craskins 97 A3
Crask of Aigas 102 C7
Craster 77 D4
Craswall 28 B4
Cratfield 35 C1
Crathes 97 C4
Crathie Gramp 96 C4
Crathie Hghld 94 D6
Crathorne 64 B3
Craven Arms 38 D6
Craw 72 C3
Crawcrook 70 E2
Crawford Lancs 48 E1
Crawford Strath 74 E3
Crawfordjohn 74 D3
Crawfordton 67 D1
Crawick 74 C4
Crawley Hants 11 A1
Crawley Oxon 30 D6
Crawley W Ssx 12 E3
Crawley Down 13 A3
Crawley Side 70 C4
Crawshawbooth 55 C5
Crawton 97 D6
Crawyn 60 c2
Cray N Yorks 62 E7
Cray Pwys 18 D1
Cray Tays 88 C2
Crayford 24 F5
Crayke 64 C6
Crays Hill 25 C3
Cray's Pond 23 A3
Crazies Hill 23 B3
Creacombe 7 C5
Creagbheitheachain 86 A2
Creagorry 98 B7
Creaton 41 E7
Creca 69 A2
Credenhill 28 D3
Crediton 7 C6
Creech St Michael 8 D1
Creed 3 B4
Creedy Park 7 C6
Creekmouth 24 E4
Creeting St Mary 34 E3
Creeton 42 D2
Creetown 67 A5
Creggans 79 E1
Cregneish 60 a5
Cregrina 28 A2

Creich 88 E6
Creigiau 19 A5
Crelevan 94 B2
Cremyll 4 E5
Cressage 38 E4
Cresselly 16 D5
Cressing 33 D6
Cresswell Dyfed 16 D5
Cresswell Northld 77 D6
Cresswell Staffs 40 B1
Cresswell Staffs 51 B3
Creswell 51 B3
Cretingham 35 B2
Cretshengan 79 B5
Crewe Ches 49 B6
Crewe Ches 48 D6
Crew Green 38 C3
Crewkerne 9 A3
Crewton 50 E7
Crianlarich 86 B6
Cribyn 26 E5
Criccieth 46 D7
Crich 50 E5
Crich Carr 50 E5
Crichie 105 C4
Crichton 82 D6
Crick Gwent 20 D1
Crick Northants 41 C7
Crickadarn 27 E6
Cricket Malherbie 8 E2
Cricket St Thomas 8 E3
Crickheath 38 B2
Crickhowell 19 C2
Cricklade 21 E1
Cricklewood 24 C3
Cridling Stubbs 57 D5
Crieff 87 E6
Criggion 38 B3
Crigglestone 57 B6
Crimdon Park 71 C5
Crimond 105 D3
Crimonmogate 105 D3
Crimplesham 44 A5
Crinan 79 B2
Cringleford 45 A5
Cringletie 75 C1
Crinow 16 E4
Cripplesease 2 C5
Cripp's Corner 13 E4
Crix 33 D7
Croachy 94 E3
Croalchapel 74 E6
Croasdale 60 E2
Crockenhill 24 F6
Crockernwell 7 B7
Crockerton 21 C6
Crocketford or Ninemile Bar 68 B2
Crockey Hill 57 E3
Crockham Hill 13 B1
Crockhurst Street 13 D2
Crockleford Heath 34 E6
Crock Street 8 E2
Croesau Bach 38 B2
Croeserw 18 D4
Croesgoch 16 B2
Croes Hywel 19 D2
Croesor 47 A6
Croesyceiliog Dyfed 17 C4
Croesyceiliog Gwent 19 D4
Croes-y-mwyalch 19 D4
Croes y pant 19 D3
Croft Ches 49 A2
Croft Leics 41 C5
Croft Lincs 53 D5
Crofthead 69 B2
Croftmore 87 E2
Crofton Wilts 22 B5
Crofton W Yorks 57 B6
Croft-on-Tees 63 C4
Crofts 67 D3
Crofts of Benachielt 111 B5
Crofts of Blackburn 104 D5
Crofts of Buinach 103 E6
Crofts of Haddo 105 B5
Crofts of Savoch 105 D3
Crofts of Shanquhar 104 D5
Crofty 17 D6
Crogen 47 E7
Croggan 85 D6
Croglin 69 D5
Croick Hghld 102 C2
Croick Hghld 110 D3
Croit-bheinn 85 E1

Croit e Caley 60 b5
Cromalt 101 E1
Cromarty 103 A5
Crombie Mill 89 B4
Cromblet 105 A5
Cromdale 95 D3
Cromer Herts 32 D6
Cromer Nflk 45 B1
Cromer Hyde 32 D7
Cromford 50 D5
Cromhall 21 A1
Cromhall Common 21 A2
Cromore 107 C5
Crompton Fold 49 D1
Cromra 94 D7
Cromwell 51 D4
Cronberry 74 B3
Crondall 23 B7
Cronk, The 60 c2
Cronk-y-Voddy 60 c3
Cronton 48 D3
Crook Cumb 61 D5
Crook Dur 70 E5
Crookedholm 73 D4
Crooked Oak 7 B4
Crookham Berks 22 E5
Crookham Northld 77 A2
Crookham Village 23 B6
Crooklands 61 E5
Crook of Alves 103 E5
Crook of Devon 81 E1
Cropredy 30 E3
Cropston 41 C3
Cropthorne 29 D3
Cropton 64 E5
Cropwell Bishop 51 C7
Cropwell Butler 51 C7
Crosby Cumb 68 D6
Crosby Humb 58 D6
Crosby IOM 60 c4
Crosby Mers 48 C2
Crosby Court 63 D5
Crosby Garrett 62 C4
Crosby Ravensworth 62 B3
Croscombe 20 E6
Cross Lewis 106 D7
Cross Som 20 D5
Cross W Is 107 D1
Crossal 92 B1
Crossapol 84 C3
Crossapoll 84 A4
Cross Ash 28 D6
Cross-at-Hand 13 E2
Crossbost 107 B5
Cross Bush 12 C6
Crosscanonby 68 D6
Crossdale Street 45 B2
Crossdougal 90 C3
Crossens 54 C6
Crossford D & G 74 D7
Crossford Fife 81 E3
Crossford Strath 74 D1
Cross Foxes 37 B4
Crossgate 43 A2
Crossgatehall 82 D6
Crossgates Fife 82 B4
Crossgates Pwys 27 E4
Crossgates Tays 88 B6
Cross Gates W Yorks 57 B4
Crossgill 54 E1
Cross Green Devon 4 D2
Cross Green Sflk 34 D3
Cross Hands Dyfed 17 D4
Crosshands Strath 73 D4
Cross Hill Derbs 51 A6
Crosshill Fife 82 B3
Crosshill Strath 73 C7
Crosshouse 73 C4
Cross Houses 38 E4
Crossings 50 B2
Cross in Hand 15 A4
Cross Inn Dyfed 26 C5
Cross Inn Dyfed 26 E5
Cross Inn S Glam 19 A5
Crosskeys Gwent 19 C4
Crosskeys Nflk 43 D3
Crosskirk 111 A1
Cross Lane Head 39 B5
Crosslanes Clwyd 48 C7
Cross Lanes Clwyd 48 C7
Cross Lanes N Yorks 57 D1
Crosslanes Powys 38 C3
Crosslee Bdrs 75 D4
Crosslee Strath 80 D5

Crosslet 80 D4
Crossmichael 67 D4
Crossmoor 54 D4
Cross of Jackson 105 A5
Cross o'the Hands 50 D6
Crossroads 97 C4
Cross Street 35 A1
Crossway 28 D6
Crossway Green 29 C1
Crossways 28 E6
Crosswell 16 E2
Crosthwaite 54 D6
Croston 54 D6
Crostwick 45 B4
Crostwight 45 C3
Crouch 13 D1
Crouch Hill 9 D2
Croughton 31 A4
Crovie 105 B2
Crowan 2 D5
Crowborough 13 C3
Crowcombe 20 A7
Crowdecote 50 C4
Crowdhill 11 A2
Crowfield Northants 31 B3
Crowfield Sflk 35 A3
Crow Hill 29 A5
Crowhurst E Ssx 13 E5
Crowhurst Sry 13 A2
Crowland Lincs 43 A3
Crowland Sflk 34 E1
Crowlas 2 C5
Crowle H & W 29 D2
Crowle Humb 58 C6
Crowle Green 29 D2
Crowlista 106 D4
Crownhill 4 E5
Crownthorpe 44 E5
Crowntown 2 D5
Crows-an-wra 2 A6
Crowthorne 23 C5
Crowton 48 E4
Croxall 40 D3
Croxdale 71 A5
Croxden 50 B7
Croxley Green 23 E2
Croxton Cambs 32 D3
Croxton Humb 59 A6
Croxton Nflk 44 C7
Croxton Staffs 39 B1
Croxtonbank 39 B1
Croxton Green 48 E6
Croxton Kerrial 42 B2
Croy Hghld 103 A7
Croy Strath 81 B4
Croyde 6 D3
Croydon Cambs 32 E4
Croydon GL 24 D6
Cruach 78 C6
Cruachan 86 A7
Cruchie 104 D4
Cruckmeole 38 D4
Cruckton 38 D3
Cruden Bay 105 D5
Crudgington 39 A3
Crudwell 21 D1
Crûg 38 A7
Crugmeer 3 B1
Crulivig 106 E4
Crumlin Gwent 19 C4
Crundale Dyfed 16 C4
Crundale Kent 15 A4
Crunwear 16 E4
Crutherland 81 A6
Cruwys Morchard 7 C5
Crux Easton 22 D6
Crwbin 17 C4
Cryers Hill 23 C2
Crymlyn 47 A3
Crymmych 16 E2
Crynant 18 C3
Crystal Palace 24 D5
Cuaig 100 E6
Cubbington 30 D1
Cubert 2 E3
Cublington 31 D5
Cuckfield 13 A4
Cucklington 9 D1
Cuckney 51 B3
Cuckoo's Nest 48 C5
Cuddesdon 31 A7
Cuddington Bucks 31 C6
Cuddington Ches 48 E4
Cuddington Heath 48 D7
Cuddy Hill 54 D4
Cudham 13 B1

Cudliptown 5 A3
Cudrish 94 D2
Cudworth Som 8 E2
Cudworth S Yorks 57 B7
Cuffley 24 D2
Cuidrach 99 C6
Cuier 90 B5
Cuilmuich 80 A2
Cuil-uaine 86 A5
Culagach 90 D3
Culbo 102 E5
Culbokie 102 E6
Culbone 7 C2
Culcabock 102 E7
Culcharan 86 A5
Culcharry 103 B6
Culcheth 49 A2
Culcreuch 81 A3
Culdrain 104 D5
Culduie 100 E7
Culford 34 C1
Culgaith 69 E7
Culgower 110 E7
Culham 22 E2
Culindrach 72 D2
Culkein 108 C5
Culkerton 21 D1
Cullachie 95 C3
Cullen Gramp 104 D2
Cullercoats 71 B1
Cullerlie 97 C3
Cullicudden 102 E5
Culligran 102 B7
Cullingworth 56 D4
Cullipool 85 D7
Cullivoe 114 E2
Culloch 87 D7
Cullompton 8 B3
Culmaily 103 B2
Culmington 38 D6
Culmstock 8 C2
Culnacraig 101 C1
Culnadalloch 86 A5
Culnaknock 100 C5
Culnamean 92 B2
Culpho 35 B4
Culrain 102 D2
Culross 81 D3
Culroy 73 C6
Culsh Gramp 96 D4
Culsh Gramp 105 B4
Culshabben 66 E5
Culswick 115 B3
Culterallers 75 A2
Cultercullen 105 C6
Cultoquhey 87 E6
Cults D & G 67 A6
Cults Gramp 97 D3
Cultybraggan Camp 87 D7
Culverstone Green 25 B6
Culverthorpe 52 D7
Culvie 104 D3
Culworth 31 A3
Cumbernauld 81 B4
Cumberworth 53 D4
Cuminestown 105 B3
Cumloden 67 A4
Cummersdale 69 B4
Cummertrees 68 E3
Cummingstown 103 E5
Cumnock 73 E6
Cumnor 30 E7
Cumrew 69 D4
Cumrue 75 A7
Cumstoun 67 C5
Cumwhinton 69 C4
Cumwhitton 69 D4
Cundall 64 B6
Cunninghamhead 73 C3
Cunningsburgh 115 D4
Cunnister 114 E3
Cunnoquhie 88 E7
Cunside 109 C3
Cupar 88 E7
Cupar Muir 88 E7
Curbar 50 D3
Curbridge Hants 11 B3
Curbridge Oxon 30 D7
Curdridge 11 B3
Curdworth 40 D5
Curland 8 D2
Curload 8 E1
Curridge 22 D4
Currie 82 B6
Currochfauld 74 B1
Curry Mallet 8 E1
Curry Rivel 8 E1

Curteis' Corner 14 D5
Curtisden Green 13 E2
Cury 2 D6
Cushnie 105 A2
Cushuish 20 A7
Cusop 28 B3
Cutcloy 67 A7
Cutcombe 7 D3
Cuthill 103 A3
Cutiau 37 A4
Cutnall Green 29 C1
Cutsdean 30 A4
Cutthorpe 50 E3
Cutts 115 D4
Cuttyhill 105 D3
Cuxham 23 A2
Cuxton 14 C2
Cuxwold 59 B7
Cwm Clwyd 47 E3
Cwm Gwent 19 B3
Cwm W Glam 18 B4
Cwmaman 19 A4
Cwmavon 18 C4
Cwmbach Dyfed 17 A3
Cwmbach M Glam 19 A3
Cwmbach Pwys 28 A4
Cwmbach Pwys 27 E5
Cwmbelan 27 D2
Cwmbran 19 C4
Cwmbrwyno 27 B2
Cwmcarn 19 C4
Cwmcarvan 28 D7
Cwm-Cewydd 37 C4
Cwmcoy 26 B6
Cwm Cynfelyn 27 A2
Cwmdare 18 E3
Cwmdu Dyfed 27 A7
Cwmdu Pwys 28 A5
Cwmduad 17 B2
Cwmdulas 27 D5
Cwmfelin Boeth 16 E4
Cwmfelinfach 19 B4
Cwmfelin Mynach 17 A3
Cwmffrwd 17 C4
Cwm Frrwd-oer 19 C3
Cwmgiedd 18 C2
Cwmgors 18 C2
Cwmgwrach 18 D3
Cwm Irfon 27 C6
Cwmisfael 17 C4
Cwm-Llinau 37 C5
Cwmllyfri 17 B4
Cwmllynfell 18 C2
Cwm Morgan 17 A2
Cwm Owen 27 E6
Cwm-parc 18 E4
Cwmpengraig 17 B2
Cwmsychpant 26 D6
Cwmsymlog 27 A2
Cwmtillery 19 C3
Cwm-y-glo 46 E4
Cwmyoy 28 B5
Cwmystwyth 27 B3
Cwrt 37 A5
Cwrt-newydd 26 D6
Cwrt-y-gollen 19 C2
Cydweli 17 C5
Cyffylliog 47 E5
Cymmer M Glam 8 B3
Cymmer M Glam 18 D4
Cynghordy 27 C7
Cynheidre 17 C5
Cynwyd 47 E6
Cynwyl Elfed 17 B3

D

Dabton 74 D6
Daccombe 5 E4
Dacre Cumb 69 C7
Dacre N Yorks 56 E1
Dacre Banks 56 E1
Daddry Shield 70 B5
Dadford 31 B4
Dadlington 41 B5
Dafen 17 D5
Daffy Green 44 D5
Dagenham 24 F4
Daggons 10 C3
Daglingworth 29 D7
Dagnall 31 E6
Dail 86 B5
Dailly 73 B7
Dailnamac 86 A5
Daimh-sgeir 78 D5
Dairsiemuir 89 A7
Dalavich 86 A7

Dalballoch 94 E6
Dalbeattie 68 B3
Dalbeg Hghld 94 E4
Dalbeg W Is 107 A3
Dalblair 74 B4
Dalbog 97 A6
Dalbreck 110 C7
Dalbury 50 D7
Dalby 60 b4
Dalchalloch 87 D2
Dalchalm 103 C1
Dalchenna 79 E1
Dalchork 109 C7
Dalchreichart 93 E3
Dalchruin 87 D7
Dalcross 103 A7
Dalderby 53 A5
Daldownie 96 C3
Dale Derbs 51 A7
Dale Dyfed 16 B5
Dale Shet 115 A2
Dale Head 61 D2
Dalehouse 64 E2
Dalelea 85 D2
Dale Park 12 B6
Daless 95 B2
Dalestie 96 B2
Dalfad 96 D3
Dalganachan 111 A5
Dalgarven 73 B3
Dalgety Bay 82 B4
Dalginross 87 D6
Dalgonar 74 C5
Dalguise 88 A4
Dalhalvaig 110 D3
Dalham 33 D2
Daliburgh 90 C3
Daligan 80 C3
Dalivaddy 72 A6
Daljarrock 66 C2
Dalkeith 82 D6
Dall 87 B3
Dallachoilish 86 A4
Dallas 97 D2
Dallaschyle 103 B7
Dallash 67 A4
Dallinghoo 35 B3
Dallington E Ssx 13 D5
Dallington Northants 31 C1
Dalmadilly 97 C2
Dalmally 86 C6
Dalmarnock 88 A4
Dalmellington 73 D7
Dalmeny 82 B5
Dalmichy 109 C7
Dalmore 102 E5
Dalnabreck 85 D2
Dalnacarn 88 B2
Dalnaha 85 C6
Dalnahaitnach 95 B4
Dalnamain 103 A2
Dalnatrat 86 A3
Dalnavie 102 E4
Dalness 86 C3
Dalnessie 109 D7
Dalnigap 66 C3
Dalqueich 81 E1
Dalreoch 66 C2
Dalriech 87 D5
Dalroy 103 A7
Dalrulzian 88 C3
Dalry D & G 67 C2
Dalry Strath 73 B3
Dalrymple 73 C6
Dalserf 81 B6
Dalshangan 67 B2
Dalskairth 68 C2
Dalston 69 B4
Dalswinton 74 E7
Daltomach 95 A3
Dalton D & G 68 E2
Dalton Lancs 48 D1
Dalton Northld 70 E1
Dalton Northld 70 C3
Dalton N Yorks 64 B6
Dalton N Yorks 63 B4
Dalton S Yorks 51 A1
Dalton-in-Furness 61 B6
Dalton-le-Dale 71 C4
Dalton-on-Tees 63 C4
Dalton Piercy 71 C5
Daltot 79 B3
Daltra 103 C7
Dalveich 87 C6
Dalvennan 73 C6
Dalvourn 94 E2
Dalwhinnie 94 E7

Dalwood 8 D3
Damerham 10 C3
Damgate 45 C5
Damnaglaur 66 C7
Damside 88 A7
Danbury 25 C2
Danby 64 E3
Danby Wiske 63 D5
Dandaleith 104 A4
Danderhall 80 C5
Dane End 32 E6
Danebridge 49 D5
Danehill 13 B4
Dane Hills 41 C4
Danesmoor 51 A4
Danestone 97 E2
Darby Green 29 C1
Darenth 25 C1
Daresbury 48 E3
Darfield 57 C7
Darlaston 40 B5
Darley 57 A2
Darlingscott 30 C3
Darlington 63 C3
Darliston 38 E1
Darlton 51 D3
Darnabo 105 A4
Darnall 50 E2
Darnford 97 C4
Darngarroch 67 C4
Darnick 76 B2
Darowen 37 C5
Darra 105 A4
Darras Hall 70 E1
Darrington 57 C6
Darsham 35 D1
Dartfield 105 D3
Dartford 24 F5
Dartington 5 C4
Dartmeet 5 B3
Dartmouth 5 D5
Darton 57 B6
Darvel 73 E5
Darwell 13 E4
Darwen 55 A5
Datchet 23 D4
Datchworth 32 D7
Datchworth Green 32 D7
Daubhill 49 B1
Daugh of Kinermony 104 A4
Dauntsey 21 D2
Dava 95 D2
Davaar 72 B6
Davan 96 E3
Davenham 49 A4
Daventry 31 A1
Davidson's Mains 82 C5
Davidstow 4 B2
Davington 75 C5
Daviot Gramp 105 A6
Daviot Hghld 95 A2
Davoch of Grange 104 C3
Dawley 39 A4
Dawlish 8 A6
Dawn 47 C3
Daws Heath 25 D4
Dawsmere 43 C1
Daylesford 30 C5
Ddol 48 A4
Deal 15 D3
Deal Hall 25 F3
Dean Cumb 68 D7
Dean Devon 5 C4
Dean Dors 10 A3
Dean Hants 11 B3
Dean Oxon 30 D5
Dean Som 21 A6
Dean Bank 71 A5
Deanburnhaugh 75 D4
Deane 22 E6
Deanland 10 A3
Dean Prior 5 C4
Dean Row 49 C3
Deanscales 68 D7
Deanshanger 31 C4
Deanston 81 B1
Dean Street 13 E1
Dearham 68 D6
Debach 35 B3
Debate 75 C7
Debden 33 B5
Debden Cross 33 B5
Debenham 35 A2

Dechmont 81 E4
Deddington 30 E4
Dedham 34 E5
Deecastle 96 E4
Deene 42 C5
Deenethorpe 42 C5
Deepcar 50 D1
Deepcut 12 B1
Deepdale Cumb 62 C6
Deepdale N Yorks 62 D7
Deeping St James 42 E4
Deeping St Nicholas 43 A3
Deeping Gate 42 E4
Deerhurst 29 C5
Defford 29 C5
Defynnog 18 E1
Deganwy 47 B3
Degnish 85 D7
Deighton N Yorks 63 D4
Deighton N Yorks 57 E3
Deiniolen 46 E4
Delabole 4 A2
Delamere 48 E5
Delavorar 96 B2
Delchirach 95 E2
Delfrigs 105 C6
Delliefure 95 D2
Delnabo 96 B2
Delny 103 A4
Delph 49 D1
Delphorie 96 E2
Delves 70 E4
Delvine 88 C4
Dembleby 42 D1
Denaby 51 A1
Denaby Main 51 A1
Denbigh 47 E4
Denbury 5 D4
Denby 50 E6
Denby Dale 57 A7
Denchworth 22 C2
Dendron 61 B6
Denford 42 C7
Dengie 25 E2
Denham Bucks 23 E3
Denham Sflk 35 A1
Denham Sflk 33 D2
Denham Green 23 E3
Denhead 97 C2
Denhead Fife 89 A7
Denhead Gramp 105 C3
Denhead Tays 88 E5
Denhead Tays 89 B4
Denholm 76 B4
Denholme 56 D4
Denholme Clough 56 D4
Denmead 11 C3
Denmill 97 D2
Denmoss 104 E4
Dennington 35 B2
Denny 81 C3
Dennyloanhead 81 C3
Denshaw 55 D6
Denside 97 D4
Densole 15 C4
Denston 33 D3
Denstone 50 B6
Dent 62 C6
Denton Cambs 42 E6
Denton Dur 63 C3
Denton E Ssx 13 B6
Denton GM 49 D2
Denton Kent 15 C4
Denton Lincs 42 B1
Denton Nflk 45 B7
Denton Northants 31 D2
Denton N Yorks 56 E3
Denton Oxon 31 A7
Denver 44 A5
Denvilles 11 D4
Denwick 77 D4
Deopham 44 E5
Deopham Green 44 E6
Depden 33 D3
Deptford GL 24 D5
Deptford Wilts 10 B1
Derby 50 E7
Derbyhaven 60 b5
Dererach 85 B6
Deri 19 B3
Derringstone 15 C4
Derrington 40 A2
Derry 87 C6
Derry Hill 21 D3
Derrynaculen 85 B6
Derrythorpe 58 D7
Dersingham 44 A2

Dervaig 85 A3
Derwen 47 E5
Derwenlas 37 B6
Derwydd 18 B2
Derybruich 79 D4
Desborough 42 B6
Desford 41 B4
Detchant 77 B2
Detling 13 E1
Deuddwr 38 B3
Deunant 47 D4
Deuxhill 39 A6
Devauden 20 D1
Devil's Bridge 27 B3
Devizes 21 E4
Devonport 4 E5
Devonside 81 D2
Devoran 2 E5
Dewar 75 D1
Dewlish 9 D4
Dewsall Court 28 D4
Dewsbury 57 A5
Dhoon 60 d3
Dhoor 60 d2
Dhowin 60 d1
Dhuhallow 94 D3
Dial Post 12 D5
Dibden 10 E4
Dibden Purlieu 11 A4
Dickleburgh 45 A7
Didbrook 30 A4
Didcot 22 E2
Diddington 32 C2
Diddlebury 38 E6
Didley 28 D4
Didling 11 E3
Didmarton 21 C2
Didsbury 49 C2
Didworthy 5 B4
Digby 52 D6
Diggle 56 D7
Digmoor 48 D1
Digswell 32 D7
Dihewyd 26 D5
Dildawn 67 D5
Dilham 45 C3
Dilhorne 49 D7
Dilston 70 C2
Dilton Marsh 21 C6
Dilwyn 28 D2
Dilwyn Common 28 D2
Dinas Dyfed 16 D2
Dinas Dyfed 17 A2
Dinas Gynd 46 D5
Dinas Gynd 46 B7
Dinas-Mawddwy 37 C4
Dinas Powys 19 B6
Dinchope 38 D6
Dinder 20 E6
Dinedor 28 E4
Dingestow 28 D6
Dingley 41 E6
Dingwall 102 D6
Dinlabyre 76 B6
Dinnet 96 E4
Dinnington Som 9 A2
Dinnington S Yorks 51 B2
Dinnington T & W 71 A1
Dinorwic 46 E4
Dinton Bucks 31 C6
Dinton Wilts 10 B1
Dinvin D & G 66 B5
Dinwoodie Mains 75 B6
Dinworthy 6 C5
Dippen 72 B4
Dippenhall 23 C7
Dippin 72 E5
Dipple Gramp 104 B3
Diptford 5 C5
Dipton 70 E3
Dirdhu 95 D3
Dirleton 83 A4
Discoed 28 B1
Diseworth 41 B2
Dishes 112 F4
Dishforth 63 D7
Dishig 85 A5
Disley 49 D3
Diss 35 A1
Disserth 27 E5
Distington 68 D7
Ditcheat 21 A7
Ditchingham 45 C6
Ditchley 30 D5
Ditchling 13 A5
Ditteridge 21 C4
Dittisham 5 D5

Ditton Ches 48 D3
Ditton Kent 13 E1
Ditton Green 33 C3
Ditton Priors 39 A6
Dixton Glos 29 D4
Dixton Gwent 28 E6
Dobwalls 4 C4
Doccombe 5 C2
Dochgarroch 102 E7
Docking 44 B2
Docklow 28 E2
Dockray 69 B7
Doddinghurst 25 A3
Doddington Cambs 43 C5
Doddington Kent 14 E3
Doddington Lincs 52 B4
Doddington Northld 77 B2
Doddington Salop 39 A7
Doddiscombsleigh 5 D2
Dodford H & W 40 B7
Dodford Northants 31 B1
Dodington Avn 21 B2
Dodington Som 20 A6
Dodleston 48 C5
Dodworth 57 B7
Doe Lea 51 A4
Dogdyke 53 A6
Dogmersfield 23 B6
Dog Village 7 D7
Doire na Guaile 100 D6
Doire-nam-bo 92 B3
Doirlinn 85 C3
Dolanog 37 E4
Dolau 28 A1
Dolbenmaen 46 E6
Dolfach 27 D3
Dôl Fawr 37 C5
Dolf'ôr 38 A6
Dolfor 38 A6
Dolgarreg Dyfed 27 B7
Dolgarreg Gynd 47 B4
Dolgellau 37 B4
Dolgoch 37 A5
Dol-gran 17 C2
Doll 103 B1
Dollar 81 D2
Dolleycanney 28 A3
Dolphinholme 54 E2
Dolphinton 75 B1
Dolton 6 E5
Dolwen Clwyd 47 C3
Dolwen Pwys 37 D5
Dolwyddelan 47 B5
Dolybont 27 A2
Dolyhir 28 B2
Dolyronen 37 C5
Dolywern 38 B1
Domgay 38 B3
Doncaster 57 D7
Donhead St Andrew 10 A2
Donhead St Mary 10 A2
Donibristle 82 B4
Donington 43 A1
Donington le Heath 41 B3
Donington on Bain 53 A3
Donisthorpe 41 A3
Donkey Town 23 D5
Donnington Berks 22 D5
Donnington Glos 30 B5
Donnington H & W 29 B4
Donnington Salop 38 E4
Donnington Salop 39 B3
Donnington W Ssx 11 E4
Donyatt 8 E2
Dorchester Dors 9 C4
Dorchester Oxon 22 E2
Dordon 40 E4
Dore 50 E2
Dores 94 D2
Dorket Head 51 B6
Dorking 12 D2
Dormansland 13 B2
Dormans Park 13 A2
Dormanstown 64 C1
Dormington 28 E3
Dorney 23 D4
Dornie 93 A2
Dornoch 103 A3
Dornock 69 A3
Dorrery 111 A3
Dorridge 40 D7
Dorrington Lincs 52 D6
Dorrington Salop 38 D4
Dorsell 97 A2
Dorsington 30 B3
Dorstone 28 C3
Dorton 31 B6

Dorusduain 93 B2
Dosthill 40 E5
Dotland 70 C3
Dottery 9 A4
Doublebois 3 D2
Dougalston 80 E4
Dougarie 72 C4
Doughton 21 C1
Douglas IOM 60 c4
Douglas Strath 74 D2
Douglas and Angus 89 A5
Douglas Hall 68 B4
Douglas Hill 47 A4
Douglastown 89 A4
Doulting 21 A6
Dounby 112 B4
Doune Cent 81 B1
Doune Hghld 95 B5
Doune Strath 80 C2
Doune Strath 86 E7
Doune Park 105 A2
Douneside 96 E3
Dounie Hghld 102 E3
Dounie Hghld 102 D2
Dounreay 110 E2
Dousland 5 A4
Dovaston 38 C2
Dove Holes 50 B3
Dovenby 68 D6
Dover 15 D4
Doverdale 29 C1
Doveridge 50 C7
Doversgreen 12 E2
Dowally 88 B4
Dowdeswell 29 D6
Dowhill 71 B3
Dowland 6 E5
Dowlands 8 D4
Dowlish Wake 8 E2
Down 13 D3
Down Ampney 22 A2
Downderry 4 D5
Downe 24 E6
Downend Avn 21 A3
Downend Berks 22 D4
Downend IOW 11 B6
Downfield 88 E5
Downgate 4 D3
Downham Cambs 43 D6
Downham Esx 25 C3
Downham Lancs 55 B3
Downham Northld 76 E2
Downham Market 44 A5
Down Hatherley 29 C5
Downhead Corn 4 C2
Downhead Som 21 A6
Downhill 63 B5
Downholland Cross 48 C1
Downholme 63 B5
Downiepark 89 A3
Downies 97 E4
Downing 48 A4
Downley 23 C2
Down St Mary 7 B6
Downside 20 E4
Downside Abbey 21 A5
Down Thomas 5 A5
Downton Devon 5 A2
Downton Dors 10 D5
Downton Wilts 10 C2
Downton on the Rock 38 D7
Dowsby 42 E2
Dowthwaitehead 69 B7
Doynton 21 B3
Draethen 19 C5
Draffan 74 C1
Drakeland Corner 5 A5
Drakes Broughton 29 D3
Drakes Cross 40 C7
Drambuie 74 C4
Draughton Northants 41 E7
Draughton N Yorks 56 D2
Drax 57 E5
Draycote 30 E1
Draycott Derbs 51 A7
Draycott Glos 30 B4
Draycott H & W 29 C3
Draycott Som 20 D5
Draycott in the Clay 40 D2
Draycott in the Moors 49 D7
Drayton H & W 40 B7
Drayton Hants 11 C4
Drayton Leics 42 B5
Drayton Lincs 43 A1

Drayton Nflk 45 A4
Drayton Oxon 30 E3
Drayton Oxon 22 D2
Drayton Som 9 A1
Drayton Bassett 40 D4
Drayton Beauchamp 31 E6
Drayton Camp 22 D7
Drayton Parslow 31 D5
Drayton St Leonard 22 E2
Drebley 56 D2
Dreemskerry 60 d2
Dreenhill 16 C4
Drefach Dyfed 26 E6
Drefach Dyfed 17 B2
Drefach Dyfed 17 D4
Dreghorn 73 C4
Drellingore 15 C4
Drem 83 A5
Drewsteignton 7 B7
Driby 53 B4
Driffield 21 E1
Drift 2 B6
Drigg 60 E4
Drighlington 57 A5
Drimfern 86 B7
Drimlee 86 C7
Drimore 98 B7
Drimpton 9 A3
Drimsynie 80 A1
Drimvore 79 C2
Drinkstone 34 D2
Drinkstone Green 34 D2
Drishaig Strath 86 C7
Drishaig Strath 86 C6
Drissaig 86 A7
Drointon 40 C2
Droitwich 29 C1
Dron 88 C7
Dronfield 50 E3
Dronfield Woodhouse 50 E3
Drongan 73 D6
Dronley 88 E5
Dropmore 23 D3
Droxford 11 C3
Droylsden 49 D2
Druid 47 E6
Druidston 16 B4
Drumarbin 86 B2
Druimavuic 86 B4
Druimbuidhe 85 C3
Druimdrishaig 79 B4
Druimindarroch 92 D6
Druimkinnerras 94 C2
Drum Gramp 105 B4
Drum Strath 79 D4
Drum Tays 81 E1
Drumachloy 79 E5
Drumbeg 108 D5
Drumblade 104 D4
Drumbuie Hghld 92 E1
Drumburgh 69 A4
Drumchapel 80 E4
Drumchardine 102 D7
Drumchork 101 A3
Drumcruilton 74 D5
Drumdelgie 104 C4
Drumderfit 102 E6
Drumeldrie 82 E2
Drumelzier 75 B2
Drumfearn 92 D3
Drumfern 86 A1
Drumgarve 72 B5
Drumgley 89 A3
Drumguish 95 A6
Drumhead 97 B4
Drumin 95 E2
Drumine 103 A6
Drumjohn 67 B1
Drumkilavie 72 B6
Drumlamford 66 D3
Drumlasie 97 B3
Drumlemble 72 A6
Drumlithie 97 C5
Drummond Cent 81 A1
Drummond Hghld 102 E5
Drummore 66 C7
Drumnadrochit 94 D3
Drumnagorrach 104 D3
Drumnatorran 85 E2
Drumore 72 B5
Drumour 88 A5
Drumrash 67 C3
Drums Gramp 105 C6
Drums Tays 88 E2
Drumsturdy 89 A5
Drumuie 100 B7
Drumuillie 95 C3

Drumvaich 81 A1
Drumwhindle 105 C5
Drumwhirn 67 D3
Drunkendub 89 C4
Drury 48 B5
Drybeck 62 B3
Drybridge Gramp 104 C2
Drybridge Strath 73 C4
Drybrook 29 A6
Dry Doddington 52 B7
Dry Drayton 32 E2
Drygrange 76 B2
Dry Harbour 100 D6
Dryhope 75 C3
Drymen 80 D3
Drymuir 105 C4
Drynoch 92 B1
Dry Sandford 30 E7
Dryslwyn 17 D3
Dry Street 25 B4
Dryton 38 E4
Duachy 85 E6
Dubford 105 A2
Dubhchladach 79 C5
Dubheads 88 A6
Dubton 89 B3
Duchal 80 C5
Duchally 109 A7
Duchray 80 D2
Duck End 33 C6
Duckington 48 D6
Ducklington 30 D7
Duck's Cross 32 C3
Duddington 82 C5
Duddington 42 C4
Duddleswell 13 B4
Duddo 77 A1
Duddon 48 E5
Duddon Bridge 61 A5
Dudleston Heath 38 C1
Dudley T & W 71 A1
Dudley W Mids 40 B5
Dudley Hill 56 E4
Dudley Port 40 B5
Dudsbury 10 B5
Dudwick 105 C5
Duffield 50 E6
Duffryn 18 D4
Dufftown 104 B4
Duffus 103 E5
Dufton 69 E7
Duggleby 65 A7
Duiar 95 E2
Duible 110 E7
Duiletter 86 C5
Duinish 87 C2
Duirinish 92 E1
Duisdalemor 92 D3
Duisky 86 B1
Dukestown 19 B2
Dukinfield 49 D2
Dulas 46 D2
Dulax 96 D2
Dulcote 20 E6
Dulford 8 B3
Dull 87 E4
Dullingham 33 C3
Dulnain Bridge 95 C3
Duloe Beds 32 C2
Duloe Corn 4 C5
Dulsie 103 C7
Dulverton 7 D4
Dulwich 24 D5
Dumbarton 80 D4
Dumbleton 30 A4
Dumcrieff 75 B5
Dumeath 104 C5
Dumfin 80 C3
Dumfries 68 C2
Dummer 22 E7
Dunach 85 E6
Dunalastair 87 D3
Dunan Hghld 92 C2
Dunan Strath 80 A4
Dunans 79 E2
Dunball 20 C6
Dunbar 83 B5
Dunbeath 111 B6
Dunbeg 85 E5
Dunblane 81 B1
Dunbog 88 D7
Duncanston Gramp 104 D6
Duncanston Hghld 102 D6
Dunchideock 5 D2
Dunchurch 41 B7
Duncombe 54 E4
Duncote 31 B2

Duncow 74 E7
Duncraggan 80 E1
Duncrievie 82 B2
Duncroist 87 B5
Duncrub 88 B7
Duncryne 80 D3
Duncton 12 B5
Dundee 89 A5
Dundon 20 D7
Dundonald Strath 73 C4
Dundonnell 101 C3
Dundraw 69 A5
Dundreggan 94 B4
Dundrennan 67 D6
Dundry 20 E4
Dunearn 82 C4
Dunecht 97 C3
Dunfermline 81 E3
Dunfield 22 A2
Dunford Bridge 56 E7
Dungavel 74 B2
Dunham 52 B4
Dunham-on-the-Hill 48 D4
Dunhampton 29 C1
Dunham Town 49 B3
Dunholme 52 D4
Dunino 89 B7
Dunipace 81 C3
Dunira 87 D6
Dunkeld 88 B4
Dunkerton 21 B5
Dunkeswell 8 C3
Dunkeswick 57 B3
Dunkirk 15 A3
Dunk's Green 13 D1
Dunlappie 89 B2
Dunley 29 B1
Dunlop 73 D3
Dunloskin 80 A4
Dunmere 3 C2
Dunmore Strath 79 B5
Dunn 111 B3
Dunnabie 75 C7
Dunnet 111 C1
Dunnichen 89 B4
Dunning 88 B7
Dunnington Humb 59 B2
Dunnington N Yorks 57 E2
Dunnington Warks 30 A2
Dunnockshaw 55 C5
Dunoon 80 A4
Dunragit 66 C5
Dunrostan 79 B3
Duns 83 C7
Dunsby 42 E2
Dunscore 74 D7
Dunscroft 57 E7
Dunsdale 64 D2
Dunsden Green 23 B4
Dunsfold 12 C3
Dunsford 5 D2
Dunshelt 88 D7
Dunshillock 105 C4
Dunsinnan 88 C5
Dunskeath Ness 103 A5
Dunsley 65 A2
Dunsmore 31 D7
Dunsop Bridge 55 A3
Dunstable 32 B6
Dunstall 40 D2
Dunstall Green 33 D2
Dunstan 77 D4
Dunster 7 D2
Duns Tew 30 E5
Dunston Lincs 52 D5
Dunston Nflk 45 B5
Dunston Staffs 40 B3
Dunston T & W 71 A2
Dunstone 5 C6
Dunsville 57 E7
Dunswell 59 A4
Dunsyre 75 A1
Dunterton 4 D3
Duntisbourne Abbots 29 D7
Duntisbourne Leer 29 D7
Duntish 9 C3
Duntocher 80 D4
Dunton Beds 32 D4
Dunton Bucks 31 D5
Dunton Nflk 44 C2
Dunton Bassett 41 C5
Dunton Green 13 C1
Dunton Wayletts 25 B3
Duntulm 100 B4
Dunure 73 B6
Dunure Mains 73 B6

Dunvant 17 D6
Dunvegan 99 B7
Dunvornie 102 D6
Dunwich 35 D1
Dura 89 A7
Durdar 69 C4
Durgates 13 D3
Durham 71 A4
Durinemast 85 C3
Durisdeer 74 D5
Durleigh 20 B7
Durley Hants 11 B3
Durley Wilts 22 B5
Durley Street 11 B3
Durnamuck 101 C2
Durness 109 B2
Durno 105 A6
Durran Hghld 111 B2
Durran Strath 79 D1
Durrington Wilts 22 A7
Durrington W Ssx 12 D6
Dursley 21 B1
Durston 8 D1
Durweston 9 E3
Dury 115 D1
Duston 31 C1
Duthil 95 C3
Dutlas 38 B7
Duton Hill 33 C6
Dutton 48 E4
Duxford 33 A4
Dwygyfylchi 47 B3
Dwyran 46 D4
Dyce 97 D2
Dyffryn 18 D4
Dyffryn Ardudwy 36 E3
Dyffryn Castell 27 B2
Dyffryn Ceidrych 18 C1
Dyffryn Cellwen 18 D3
Dyke Devon 6 C4
Dyke Gramp 103 C6
Dyke Hghld 110 D3
Dyke Lincs 42 E2
Dykehead Strath 81 C6
Dykehead Tays 88 E2
Dykelands 89 D2
Dykends 88 D3
Dykeside 105 A4
Dylife 37 C6
Dymchurch 15 B6
Dymock 29 A4
Dyrham 21 B3
Dysart Fife 82 D3
Dyserth 47 E3

E

Eagland Hill 54 D3
Eagle 52 B5
Eaglescliffe 64 B2
Eaglesfield Cumb 68 D7
Eaglesfield D & G 69 A2
Eaglesham 80 E6
Eagley 55 B6
Eairy 60 b4
Eakley 31 D2
Eakring 51 C4
Ealand 58 C6
Ealing 24 B4
Eamont Bridge 69 D7
Earby 55 D3
Earcroft 55 A5
Eardington 39 B5
Eardisland 28 D2
Eardisley 28 C3
Eardiston H & W 29 A1
Eardiston Salop 38 C2
Earith 32 E1
Earle 77 A3
Earlestown 48 E2
Earlham 45 A5
Earlish 99 C5
Earls Barton 31 D1
Earls Colne 34 C6
Earl's Common 29 D2
Earl's Croome 29 C3
Earlsdon 41 A7
Earlsferry 82 E2
Earlsford 105 B5
Earl's Green 34 E2
Earl Shilton 41 B5
Earl Soham 35 B2
Earl Sterndale 50 B4
Earlston Bdrs 76 B2
Earl Stonham 35 A3
Earlswood 40 D7
Earlswood Common 20 D1

Earnley 11 E5
Earsdon 71 B1
Earsdon Moor 77 C6
Earsham 45 C7
Earswick 57 E2
Eartham 12 B6
Earthcott Green 21 A2
Easby 64 C3
Easdale 85 D7
Easebourne 11 E2
Easenhall 41 B7
Eashing 12 B2
Easington Bucks 31 B6
Easington Clev 64 E2
Easington Dur 71 C4
Easington Humb 59 D6
Easington Northld 77 C2
Easington Oxon 23 A2
Easington Colliery 71 C4
Easington Lane 71 B4
Easingwold 57 D1
Easole Street 15 C3
Eason's Green 13 C5
East Aberthaw 19 A7
East Allington 5 C6
East Anstey 7 C4
East Appleton 63 C5
East Ashey 11 B6
East Ashling 11 E4
East Ayton 65 B5
East Barkwith 52 E3
East Barming 13 E1
East Barnby 65 A2
East Barnet 24 C3
East Barsham 44 D2
East Beckham 45 A1
East Bedfont 24 B5
East Bergholt 34 E5
East Bilney 44 D4
East Blatchington 13 B6
East Boldon 71 B2
East Boldre 10 E4
East Bolton 77 C4
Eastbourne Dur 63 D3
Eastbourne E Ssx 13 D7
East Bradenham 44 D5
East Brent 20 C5
East Bridge 35 D2
East Bridgford 51 C6
East Brora 103 C1
East Buckland 7 A3
East Budleigh 8 B5
Eastburn 58 E2
East Burrafirth 115 C2
East Burton 9 E5
Eastbury Berks 22 C4
Eastbury GL 23 E2
Eastby 56 D2
East Cairnbeg 97 C6
East Calder 81 E5
East Carleton 45 A5
East Carlton 42 B6
East Chaldon 9 D5
East Challow 22 C3
East Charleton 5 C6
East Chiltington 13 A5
East Chinnock 9 A2
East Chisenbury 22 A6
Eastchurch 14 E1
East Clandon 12 C1
East Claydon 31 C5
East Clyth 111 C5
East Coker 9 B2
Eastcombe Glos 29 C7
Eastcombe Som 20 A7
East Cornworthy 5 D5
Eastcote GL 24 B4
Eastcote Northants 31 B2
Eastcote W Mids 40 D7
Eastcott Corn 6 B5
Eastcott Wilts 21 E5
East Cottingwith 58 C3
East Coulston 21 D5
Eastcourt 21 D1
East Cowes 11 B5
East Cowick 57 E5
East Cowton 63 D4
East Creech 10 A6
East Croachy 94 E3
East Darlochan 72 A5
East Dean Hants 10 D2
East Dean W Ssx 12 B5
East Dereham 44 D4
East Down 6 E2
East Drayton 51 D3

East End Avn 20 D3
East End Dors 10 A5
East End Esx 34 E5
Eastend Esx 25 E3
East End Hants 22 D5
East End Hants 10 E5
East End Herts 33 A6
East End Kent 14 D5
East End Oxon 30 D6
Eastend Oxon 30 D5
Easter Ardross 102 E4
Easter Balmoral 96 C4
Easter Boleskine 94 D3
Easter Borland 81 A1
Easter Compton 20 E2
Easter Davoch 96 E3
Easter Drummond 94 C4
Easter Dullater 81 A1
Easter Ellisker 78 B6
Easter Fearn 102 E3
Easter Galcantray 103 B7
Eastergate 12 B6
Easter Kinkell 102 D6
Easter Knox 89 B5
Easter Lednathie 88 E2
Easter Moniack 102 D7
Easter Ord 97 D3
Easter Poldar 81 A2
Easter Skeld 115 C3
Easter Slumbay 93 A1
Easterton 21 E5
Eastertown 20 C5
Easter Whyntie 104 E2
East Farleigh 13 E1
East Farndon 41 E6
East Ferry 52 B2
Eastfield N Yorks 65 C5
Eastfield Hall 77 D5
East Fleet 9 C5
East Fortune 83 A5
East Garston 22 C4
Eastgate Dur 70 C5
Eastgate Lincs 42 E3
Eastgate Nflk 45 A3
East Ginge 22 D3
East Goscote 41 D3
East Grafton 22 B5
East Grimstead 10 D2
East Grinstead 13 A3
East Guldeford 14 E6
East Haddon 31 B1
East Hagbourne 22 E3
East Halton 59 B6
East Ham 24 E4
Eastham 48 C3
Easthampstead 23 C5
East Hanney 22 D2
East Hanningfield 25 C2
East Hardwick 57 C6
East Harling 44 D7
East Harlsey 64 B4
East Harptree 20 E5
East Hartford 71 A1
East Harting 11 D3
East Hatley 32 D3
East Hauxwell 63 B5
East Haven 89 B5
Eastheath 23 C5
East Heckington 52 E7
East Hedleyhope 70 E4
East Helmsdale 111 A7
East Hendred 22 D3
East Heslerton 65 B6
East Hoathly 13 C5
Easthope 38 E5
East Horndon 25 B4
Easthorpe Esx 34 D6
Easthorpe Lincs 42 B1
Easthorpe Notts 51 D5
Easthorpe Wold 58 D3
East Horrington 20 E6
East Horsley 12 C1
Easthouses 82 D6
East Huntspill 20 C6
East Hyde 32 C7
East Ilsley 22 D3
Eastington Devon 7 B6
Eastington Glos 30 B6
Eastington Glos 29 B7
East Keal 53 B5
East Kennett 22 A5
East Keswick 57 B3
East Kilbride 81 A6
East Kirkby 53 B5
East Knapton 65 A6

East Knighton 9 E5
East Knoyle 21 C7
East Lambrook 9 A2
East Langdon 15 D4
East Langton 41 E5
East Langwell 103 A1
East Lavant 11 E4
East Lavington 12 B5
East Layton 63 B4
Eastleach Martin 30 B7
Eastleach Turville 30 B7
East Leake 41 C2
East Learmouth 76 E2
East Leigh 7 A6
Eastleigh 6 D4
Eastleigh 11 A3
East Lexham 44 C4
East Lilburn 77 B3
Eastling 14 E3
East Linton 83 A5
East Liss 11 D2
East Lochussie 102 D6
East Looe 4 C5
East Lound 51 D1
East Lulworth 9 E5
East Lutton 65 B7
East Lydford 20 E7
East Mains 97 B4
East Malling 13 E1
East March 89 A5
East Marden 11 E3
East Markham 51 D3
East Marton 55 D2
East Meon 11 C2
East Mere 7 D5
East Mey 111 D1
East Molesey 24 B6
East Morden 10 A5
East Morton 56 E3
East Ness 64 D6
East Norton 41 E4
East Oakley 22 E7
Eastoft 58 D6
East Ogwell 5 D3
Eastoke 11 D5
East Ord 83 E7
East Panson 6 C7
East Peckham 13 D2
East Pennard 20 E7
East Poringland 45 B5
East Portlemouth 5 C7
East Prawle 5 C7
East Preston 12 C6
East Putford 6 C5
East Quantoxhead 20 A6
East Rainton 71 B4
East Ravendale 53 A2
East Raynham 44 C3
East Rigton 57 B3
East Rolstone 20 C3
East Rounton 64 B3
East Rudham 44 C3
East Runton 45 A1
East Ruston 45 C3
Eastry 15 D3
East Saltoun 82 E6
East Shefford 22 C4
East Sleekburn 77 D7
East Somerton 45 D4
East Stoke Dors 9 E5
East Stoke Notts 51 D6
East Stour 9 E1
East Stourmouth 15 C2
East Stratton 22 E7

East Studdal 15 D4
East Taphouse 3 D2
East Tarbet 66 C7
East-the-Water 6 D4
East Thirston 77 C6
East Tilbury 25 B5
East Tisted 11 D1
East Torrington 52 E3
East Tuddenham 44 E4
East Tytherley 10 D2
East Tytherton 21 D3
East Village 7 C6
Eastville 53 C6
East Wall 38 E5
East Walton 44 B4
Eastwell 41 E2
East Wellow 10 E2
East Wemyss 82 D3
East Whitburn 81 D5
East Wickham 24 E5
East Williamston 16 D5
East Winch 44 A4
East Wittering 11 D5
East Witton 63 B6
Eastwood Esx 25 D4
Eastwood Notts 51 A6
Eastwood W Yorks 55 D5
East Woodhay 22 D5
East Worldham 11 D1
East Worlington 7 B5
East Wretham 44 D6
East Yell 114 E4
Eathorpe 30 D1
Eaton Ches 49 C5
Eaton Ches 48 E5
Eaton Leics 41 E2
Eaton Nflk 45 B5
Eaton Notts 51 D3
Eaton Oxon 30 E7
Eaton Salop 38 D6
Eaton Salop 38 C6
Eaton Bishop 28 D4
Eaton Bray 31 E5
Eaton Constantine 38 E4
Eaton Ford 32 C3
Eaton Green 31 E5
Eaton Hall 48 D5
Eaton Hastings 22 B2
Eaton Socon 32 C3
Eaton upon Tern 39 A2
Eaval 98 C6
Eavestone 57 A1
Ebberston 65 A5
Ebbesborne Wake 10 A2
Ebbw Vale 19 B3
Ebchester 70 E3
Ebford 8 A5
Ebrington 30 B3
Ecchinswell 22 E5
Ecclaw 83 C6
Ecclefechan 68 E2
Eccles Bdrs 76 B1
Eccles D & G 74 D6
Eccles GM 49 B2
Eccles Kent 14 C2
Ecclesfield 50 E1
Eccleshall 40 A2
Ecclesmachan 81 E4
Eccles Road 44 E6
Eccleston Ches 48 D5
Eccleston Lancs 54 E6
Eccleston Mers 48 D2
Eccup 57 A3
Echt 97 C3
Eckford 76 D3
Eckington Derbs 51 A3
Eckington H & W 29 D3
Ecton Northants 31 D1
Ecton Staffs 50 B5
Edale 50 C2
Edburton 12 E5
Edderside 68 E5
Edderton 103 A3
Eddington 22 C5
Eddleston 75 C1
Eddlewood 81 B6
Edenbridge 13 B2
Edendonich 86 C6
Edenfield 55 C6
Edenhall 69 D6
Edenham 42 D2
Eden Park 24 D6
Edensor 50 D4
Edentaggart 80 C2

Edenthorpe 57 E7
Edern 46 B7
Edgarley 20 E7
Edgbaston 40 C6
Edgcott 31 B5
Edgcumbe 2 E5
Edge Glos 29 C7
Edge Salop 38 C4
Edgebolton 38 E2
Edge End 28 E6
Edgefield 44 E2
Edgeley 48 E7
Edgerley 38 C3
Edgeworth 29 D7
Edginswell 5 D4
Edgmond 39 B3
Edgmond Marsh 39 B2
Edgton 38 C6
Edgware 24 C3
Edgworth 55 B6
Edial 40 C4
Edinample 87 C6
Edinbain 99 C6
Edinbanchory 96 E2
Edinbarnet 80 E4
Edinburgh 82 C5
Edinchip 87 B6
Edingale 40 E3
Edingley 51 C5
Edingthorpe 45 C2
Edington Som 20 C7
Edington Wilts 21 D5
Edintore 104 C4
Edinvale 103 E6
Edistone 6 B4
Edithmead 20 C6
Edith Weston 42 C4
Edlaston 50 C6
Edlesborough 31 E6
Edlingham 77 C5
Edlington 53 A4
Edmondsham 10 B3
Edmondsley 71 A4
Edmondthorpe 42 B3
Edmonstone 112 E4
Edmonton 24 D3
Edmundbyers 72 E2
Ednam 76 D2
Ednaston 50 D6
Edney Common 25 B2
Edra 87 A7
Edradynate 87 E3
Edrom 83 D7
Edstaston 38 E1
Edstone 30 B1
Edvin Loach 29 A2
Edwalton 51 B7
Edwardstone 34 D4
Edwinsford 27 A7
Edwinstowe 51 C4
Edworth 32 D4
Edwyn Ralph 29 A2
Edzell 89 B2
Efail-Isaf 19 A5
Efailnewydd 46 C7
Efenechtyd 48 A6
Effingham 12 D1
Effirth 115 C2
Efford 7 C6
Egbury 22 D6
Egdean 12 B4
Egerton GM 55 B6
Egerton Kent 14 E4
Egerton Green 48 E6
Egg Buckland 4 E5
Eggerness 67 A6
Eggesford Barton 7 A5
Eggington 31 E5
Egginton Beds 40 E2
Egglescliffe 64 B2
Eggleston 70 D6
Egham 23 E4
Egleton 42 B4
Eglingham 77 C4
Egloshayle 4 A3
Egloskerry 4 C2
Eglwysbach 47 C3
Eglwys-Brewis 19 A7
Eglwys Cross 48 D7
Eglwysfach 37 A6
Eglwyswrw 16 E2
Egmanton 51 D4
Egmere 44 D2
Egremont 60 E2
Egton 65 A3
Egton Bridge 65 A3
Egypt 22 D7

Eight Ash Green 34 D6
Eignaig 85 D4
Eil 95 B4
Eilanreach 93 A3
Eilean Darach 101 D3
Eishken 107 B6
Eisingrug 47 A7
Eisteddfa Gurig 27 B2
Elan Village 27 D4
Elberton 21 A2
Elburton 5 A5
Elcho 88 C6
Elcombe 22 A3
Eldernell 43 B5
Eldersfield 29 B4
Elderslie 80 D5
Eldrick 66 D2
Eldroth 55 B1
Eldwick 56 E3
Elerch 27 A2
Elford Northld 77 C2
Elford Staffs 40 D3
Elgin 104 A2
Elgol 92 C3
Elham 15 B4
Elie 82 E2
Elilaw 77 A5
Elim 10 E3
Eling 10 E3
Eliock 74 C5
Elishaw 76 E6
Elkesley 51 C3
Elkstone 29 D6
Elland 56 E5
Ellary 79 B4
Ellastone 50 C6
Ellemford 83 C6
Ellenborough 68 D6
Ellenhall 40 A2
Ellen's Green 12 D3
Ellerbeck 64 B4
Ellerby Humb 59 B4
Ellerdine Heath 39 A2
Elleric 86 B4
Ellerker 58 E5
Ellerton Humb 58 C4
Ellerton N Yorks 63 C5
Ellerton Salop 39 B2
Ellesborough 31 D7
Ellesmere 38 C1
Ellesmere Port 48 D4
Ellingham Hants 10 C4
Ellingham Nflk 45 C6
Ellingham Northld 77 C3
Ellingstring 63 B6
Ellington Cambs 32 C1
Ellington Northld 77 D6
Ellisfield 23 A7
Ellistown 41 B3
Ellon 105 C5
Ellonby 69 C6
Ellough 45 D7
Elloughton 58 E5
Ellwood 28 E7
Elm 43 C4
Elmbridge 29 C1
Elmdon Esx 33 A5
Elmdon W Mids 40 D6
Elmdon Heath 40 D6
Elmesthorpe 41 B5
Elmhurst 40 D3
Elmley Lovett 29 C1
Elmore 29 B6
Elmore Back 29 B6
Elm Park 24 F4
Elmscott 6 B4
Elmsett 34 E4
Elmstead Market 34 E6
Elmstone 15 C2
Elmstone Hardwicke 29 D5
Elmswell 34 D2
Elmswell 58 E2
Elmton 51 B3
Elphin Hghld 108 E7
Elphinstone 82 D5
Elrick Gramp 97 D3
Elrick Gramp 104 C6
Elrick Mill 105 C4
Elrig 66 E6
Elrigbeag 86 C7
Elsdon 77 A6
Elsecar 57 B7
Elsenham 33 B6
Elsfield 31 A7
Elsham 59 A6
Elsing 44 E4

Elslack 55 D3
Elsrickle 75 A1
Elstead 12 B2
Elsted 11 E3
Elsthorpe 42 D2
Elstob 71 B6
Elston Lancs 55 A4
Elston Notts 51 D6
Elstone 7 A5
Elstow 32 B4
Elstree 24 B3
Elstronwick 59 C4
Elswick 54 D4
Elsworth 32 E2
Elterwater 61 C3
Eltham 24 E5
Eltisley 32 D3
Elton Cambs 42 D5
Elton Ches 48 D4
Elton Clev 64 B2
Elton Derbs 50 D4
Elton Glos 29 A6
Elton H & W 38 D7
Elton Notts 51 D7
Elvanfoot 74 E4
Elvaston 51 A7
Elveden 34 C1
Elvingston 82 E5
Elvington Kent 15 C3
Elvington N Yorks 57 E3
Elwick Clev 71 C5
Elwick Northld 77 C2
Elworth 49 B5
Elworthy 7 E3
Ely Cambs 43 D6
Ely S Glam 19 B6
Emberton 31 D3
Embleton Cumb 68 E6
Embleton Northld 77 D3
Embo 103 B2
Emborough 21 A5
Embo Street 103 B2
Embsay 56 D2
Emerald Bank 69 A7
Emery Down 10 D4
Emley 57 A6
Emley Moor 57 A6
Emmer Green 23 B4
Emmington 31 C7
Emneth 43 C4
Emneth Hungate 43 D4
Empingham 42 C4
Empshott 11 D1
Emsworth 11 D4
Enaclete 106 E5
Enborne 22 D5
Enchmarsh 38 D5
Enderby 41 C5
Endmoor 61 E5
Endon 49 D6
Enfield 24 D3
Enford 22 A6
Engine Common 21 A2
Englefield 23 A4
Englefield Green 23 D4
Englesea-brook 49 B6
English Bicknor 28 E6
Englishcombe 21 B4
English Frankton 38 D2
Enham-Alamein 22 C7
Enmore 20 B7
Ennerdale Bridge 60 E2
Enoch 88 B2
Enochdu 88 B2
Ensay 84 E4
Ensdon 38 D3
Ensis 6 E4
Enstone 30 D5
Enterkinfoot 74 D5
Enterpen 64 B3
Enville 40 A6
Eoligarry 90 C5
Eorabus 84 E6
Eorodale 107 D1
Eoropie 107 D1
Epperstone 51 C6
Epping 24 E2
Epping Green Esx 24 E2
Epping Green Herts 24 C2
Epping Upland 24 E2
Eppleby 63 B3
Eppleworth 59 A4
Epsom 24 C6
Epwell 30 D3
Epworth 58 C7
Erbistock 48 C7
Erbusaig 92 E2

Erdington 40 D5
Eredine 79 D1
Eriboll 109 B3
Ericstane 75 A4
Eridge Green 15 A3
Erines 79 C4
Eriswell 33 D1
Erith 24 F5
Erlestoke 21 D5
Ermington 5 B5
Ermington 45 A2
Errogie 94 D3
Errol 88 D6
Errollston 105 D5
Ersary 90 C5
Ervie 66 B4
Erwarton 35 B5
Erwood 27 E6
Eryholme 63 D4
Eryrys 48 B6
Escairt 72 C2
Escart 79 C5
Escrick 57 E3
Esgair 17 B3
Esgairgeiliog 37 B5
Esh 70 E4
Esher 24 B6
Eshott 77 D6
Eshton 55 D2
Esh Winning 70 E4
Eskadale 94 C2
Eskbank 82 D6
Eskdale Green 61 A3
Eskdalemuir 75 C6
Eskham 53 B2
Esknish 78 C5
Esprick 54 D4
Essendine 42 D3
Essendon 24 C2
Essich 94 E2
Essington 40 B4
Esslemont 105 C6
Eston 64 C2
Etal 77 A2
Etchilhampton 21 E4
Etchingham 13 E4
Etchinghill Kent 15 B5
Etchinghill Staffs 40 C3
Ethie Mains 89 C4
Eton 23 D4
Eton Wick 23 D4
Etteridge 94 E6
Ettingshall 40 B5
Ettington 30 C3
Etton Humb 58 E3
Etton Northants 42 E4
Ettrick 75 C4
Ettrickbridge 75 D3
Etwall 50 D7
Eurach 79 C1
Euston 34 C1
Euxton 54 E6
Evanton 102 E5
Evedon 52 D7
Evelix 103 A2
Evenjobb 28 B1
Evenley 31 A4
Evenlode 30 C5
Evenwood 70 E6
Everbay 112 F4
Evercreech 21 A7
Everdon 31 A2
Everingham 58 D3
Everleigh 22 A6
Everley Hghld 111 D2
Everley N Yorks 65 B5
Eversholt 31 E4
Evershot 9 B3
Eversley 23 B5
Eversley Cross 23 B5
Everthorpe 58 E4
Everton Beds 32 D3
Everton Hants 10 D5
Everton Notts 51 C1
Evertown 69 B2
Evesbatch 29 A3
Evesham 30 A3
Evington 41 D4
Ewden Village 50 D1
Ewell 24 C6
Ewell Minnis 15 C4
Ewelme 23 A2
Ewen 21 E1
Ewenny 18 E6
Ewerby 52 E7
Ewerby Thorpe 52 E7
Ewhurst E Ssx 13 E4

Ewhurst Sry 12 C2
Ewhurst Green 12 C3
Ewloe 48 C5
Ewood 55 A5
Eworthy 6 D7
Ewshot 23 C7
Ewyas Harold 28 C5
Exbourne 7 A6
Exbury 11 A4
Exebridge 7 D4
Exelby 63 C6
Exeter 7 D7
Exford 7 C3
Exfords Green 38 D4
Exhall 30 B2
Exlade Street 23 A3
Exminster 8 A5
Exmouth 8 B5
Exnaboe 115 C6
Exning 33 C2
Exton Devon 8 A5
Exton Hants 11 C2
Exton Leics 42 C3
Exton Som 7 D3
Exwick 7 D7
Eyam 50 D3
Eydon 31 A2
Eye H & W 28 D1
Eye Northants 43 A4
Eye Sfik 35 A1
Eye Green 43 A4
Eyemouth 83 E6
Eyeworth 32 D4
Eyhorne Street 14 D3
Eyke 35 C3
Eynesbury 32 C3
Eynsford 24 F6
Eynsham 30 E7
Eype 9 A4
Eyre 100 B6
Eythorne 15 C4
Eyton Clwyd 48 C7
Eyton Clwyd 28 D1
Eyton Salop 38 C6
Eyton upon the Weald Moors 39 A3
Eywood 28 C1

F
Faccombe 22 C6
Faceby 64 B3
Faddiley 48 E6
Faddoch 93 B2
Fadmoor 64 D5
Faebait 102 C6
Faifley 80 E4
Faifax 35 C2
Failand 20 E3
Failford 73 D5
Failsworth 49 D1
Fain 101 D4
Fairbourne 37 A4
Fairburn 57 C5
Fairfield Derbs 50 B3
Fairfield H & W 40 B7
Fairford 30 B7
Fairgirth 68 B4
Fairholm 81 B6
Fairholme 63 D6
Fairley 97 D3
Fairlie 80 B6
Fairlight 14 D7
Fairmile 8 B4
Fairmilehead 82 C6
Fair Oak 11 A3
Fairoak 39 B1
Fair Oak Green 23 A5
Fairseat 25 B6
Fairstead Esx 33 D7
Fairstead Nflk 45 B3
Fairwarp 13 B4
Fairy Cross 6 D4
Fairyhill 17 C6
Fakenham 44 D3
Fakenham Magna 34 C1
Fala 82 E6
Fala Dam 82 E6
Faldingworth 52 D3
Falfield Avn 21 A1
Falfield Fife 82 E2
Falkenham 35 B5
Falkirk 81 C3
Falkland 82 C2
Falla 76 D4
Fallgate 50 E4
Fallin 81 C2
Falmer 13 A6
Falmouth 3 A5

Falsgrave 65 C5
Falstone 76 D7
Fanagmore 108 D3
Fanans 86 B6
Fancott 32 B6
Fangdale Beck 64 C4
Fangfoss 58 C2
Fanmore 85 A4
Fans 76 C1
Farcet 43 A5
Far Cotton 31 C2
Farden 38 E7
Fareham 11 B4
Farewell 40 C3
Far Forest 39 B7
Far Gearstones 62 C6
Faringdon 22 B2
Farington 54 E5
Farlam 69 D4
Farlary 103 A1
Farleigh Avn 20 D4
Farleigh Sry 24 D6
Farleigh Hungerford 21 B5
Farleigh Wallop 23 A7
Farlesthorpe 53 C4
Farleton 61 E5
Farleton Fell 61 E5
Farley Salop 38 C4
Farley Staffs 50 B6
Farley Wilts 10 D2
Farley Green 12 C2
Farley Hill 23 B5
Farleys End 29 B6
Farlington 57 E1
Farlow 39 A6
Farmborough 21 A4
Farmcote 30 A5
Farmers 27 A6
Farmington 30 B6
Farmoor 30 E7
Farnachty 104 C2
Farnborough Berks 22 D3
Farnborough GL 24 E6
Farnborough Hants 23 C6
Farnborough Warks 30 E3
Farnborough Green 23 C6
Farncombe 12 B1
Farndish 31 E1
Farndon Ches 48 D6
Farndon Notts 51 D5
Farnell 89 C3
Farnham Dors 10 A3
Farnham Esx 33 A6
Farnham N Yorks 57 B1
Farnham Sfik 35 C2
Farnham Sry 23 C7
Farnham Common 23 D3
Farnham Green 33 A6
Farnham Royal 23 D3
Farningham 25 A6
Farnley 57 A3
Farnley Tyas 56 E6
Farnsfield 51 C5
Farnworth Ches 48 E3
Farnworth GM 49 B1
Farr Hghld 110 C3
Farr Hghld 94 E2
Farr Hghld 95 B5
Farraline 94 D3
Farringdon 8 B4
Farrington Gurney 21 A5
Farsley 57 A4
Farthing Street 31 A4
Farthingloe 15 C4
Farthingstone 31 B2
Farway 8 C4
Fasag 101 A6
Fasagrianach 101 D4
Faskadale 85 B1
Fasnacloich 86 B4
Fasnakyle 94 B3
Fasque 97 B6
Fassfern 86 B1
Fatfield 71 B3
Fattahead 104 E3
Faugh 69 D4
Fauldhouse 81 D5
Faulkbourne 33 D7
Faulkland 21 B5
Fauls 38 E1
Faversham 15 A2
Favillar 104 A5
Fawdington 64 B6
Fawdon 71 A2
Fawfieldhead 50 B4

Fawkham Green 25 A6
Fawler 30 D6
Fawley Berks 22 C3
Fawley Bucks 23 B3
Fawley Hants 11 A4
Fawley Chapel 28 E5
Fawsyde 97 D6
Faxfleet 58 D5
Faygate 12 E3
Fazeley 40 E4
Fearby 63 B6
Fearn 103 B4
Fearnach 79 E4
Fearnan 87 D4
Fearnbeg 100 E6
Fearnhead 49 A2
Fearnmore 100 E5
Fearnoch 79 D4
Featherstone Staffs 40 B4
Featherstone W Yorks 57 C5
Feckenham 30 A1
Feering 34 C6
Feetham 62 E5
Feith-hill 104 E4
Feizor 29 B1
Felbridge 13 A3
Felbrigg 45 B2
Felcourt 13 A2
Felden 23 E1
Felindre Dyfed 18 C1
Felindre Dyfed 17 D3
Felindre Pwys 38 A6
Felindre W Glam 18 B3
Felinfach 27 E7
Felingwm Uchaf 17 D3
Felixkirk 64 B5
Felixstowe 35 C5
Felixstoweferry 35 C5
Felkington 77 A1
Felldownhead 4 D2
Felling 71 A2
Fellonmore 85 C6
Felmersham 31 E2
Felmingham 45 B3
Felpham 12 B7
Felsham 34 D3
Felsted 33 C6
Feltham 24 B5
Felthorpe 45 A4
Felton Avn 20 E4
Felton H & W 28 E3
Felton Northld 77 C5
Felton Butler 38 C3
Feltwell 44 B6
Fence 55 C4
Fence Houses 71 B3
Fencott 31 A6
Fendike Corner 53 C5
Fen Ditton 33 A2
Fen Drayton 32 E2
Fen End 40 E7
Fenhouses 53 A7
Feniscowles 55 A5
Feniton 8 C4
Fenny Bentley 50 C5
Fenny Bridges 8 C4
Fenny Compton 30 E2
Fenny Drayton 41 A5
Fenny Stratford 31 D4
Fenrother 77 C6
Fenstanton 32 E2
Fen Street 44 D6
Fenton Cambs 32 E1
Fenton Lincs 52 B4
Fenton Lincs 52 B6
Fenton Staffs 49 C7
Fenton Town 77 A2
Fenwick Northld 70 D1
Fenwick Northld 77 B2
Fenwick Strath 73 D3
Fenwick S Yorks 57 D6
Feochaig 72 B6
Feoirlinn 79 E4
Feock 3 A5
Feolin 78 E5
Feolin Ferry 78 D5
Feorlan 72 A7
Feriniquarrie 99 A6
Fern 89 A2
Ferndale 18 E4
Ferndown 10 B4
Ferness 103 C7
Fernham 22 B2
Fernhill 29 B3
Fernhill Heath 29 C2

Fernhurst 12 B4
Fernie 88 E7
Fernilea 92 A1
Fernilee 50 B3
Fernybank 97 A6
Ferrensby 57 B1
Ferring 12 C6
Ferrybridge 57 C5
Ferry Bridge 9 C6
Ferryden 89 D3
Ferryhill 71 A5
Ferryside 17 B4
Fersfield 44 E7
Fersit 86 E1
Feshiebridge 95 B5
Fetcham 12 D1
Fetterangus 105 C3
Fettercairn 97 B6
Feus of Caldhame 89 C2
Fewcott 31 A4
Fewston 56 E2
Ffairfach 18 B1
Ffair Rhos 27 B4
Ffawyddog 19 C2
Ffestiniog 47 B6
Ffordd-las 48 A5
Fforest 17 D5
Fforest-fach 18 B4
Ffostrasol 26 C6
Ffridd Uchaf 46 E5
Ffrith 48 B6
Ffrwdgrech 19 A1
Ffynnon-ddrain 17 C3
Ffynnongroyw 48 A3
Fichlie 96 E2
Fidden 84 E6
Fiddington Glos 29 D4
Fiddington Som 20 B6
Fiddler's Green 28 E4
Fiddlers Hamlet 24 E2
Field 50 B7
Field Broughton 61 C5
Field Dalling 44 E2
Field Head 41 B4
Fifehead Magdalen 9 D1
Fifehead Neville 9 D2
Fife Keith 104 C3
Fifield Berks 23 D4
Fifield Oxon 30 C6
Fifield Bavant 10 B4
Figheldean 22 A7
Filby 45 D4
Filey 65 D5
Filgrave 31 D3
Filkins 30 C7
Filleigh Devon 7 A4
Filleigh Devon 7 B5
Fillingham 52 C3
Fillongley 40 E6
Filmore Hill 11 C2
Filton 21 A3
Fimber 65 A7
Finavon 89 A3
Fincham 44 A5
Finchampstead 23 B5
Finchdean 11 D3
Finchingfield 33 C5
Finchley 24 C3
Findern 50 E7
Findhorn 103 D5
Findhuglen 87 D7
Findochty 104 C2
Findo Gask 88 B6
Findon Gramp 97 E4
Findon W Ssx 12 D6
Findon Mains 102 E5
Findrassie 103 E5
Findron 96 E3
Finedon 42 C7
Fingal Street 35 B2
Fingask 105 A6
Fingerpost 39 B7
Fingest 23 B2
Finghall 63 B6
Fingland Cumb 69 A4
Fingland D & G 75 C5
Finglesham 15 D3
Fingringhoe 34 E6
Finiskaig 93 A5
Finlarig 87 B5
Finmere 31 B4
Finnart Strath 80 B2
Finnart Tays 87 B3
Finningham 34 E2
Finningley 51 C1
Finnygaud 104 E3

Finsbury 24 D4
Finstall 29 D1
Finsthwaite 61 C5
Finstock 30 D6
Finstown 112 C5
Fintry Cent 81 A3
Fintry Gramp 105 A3
Finzean 97 A4
Fionnphort 84 D6
Firbank 62 B5
Firbeck 51 B2
Firgrove 55 D6
Firsby 53 C5
First Coast 101 B2
Firth 114 D5
Fir Tree 70 E5
Fir Vale 50 E1
Fishbourne IOW 11 B5
Fishbourne W Ssx 11 E4
Fishburn 71 B4
Fisherford 104 E5
Fisher's Pond 11 A2
Fisher's Row 54 D3
Fisherstreet 12 B3
Fisherton Hghld 103 A6
Fisherton de la Mere
   10 B1
Fishguard 16 C2
Fishlake 57 E6
Fishley Barton 6 E4
Fishpond Bottom 8 E4
Fishpool 49 C1
Fishtoft 53 B7
Fishtoft Drove 53 B7
Fishtown of Usan 89 D3
Fishwick Bdrs 83 E7
Fishwick Lancs 54 E5
Fiskavaig 92 A1
Fiskerton Lincs 52 D4
Fiskerton Notts 51 D5
Fittleton 22 A7
Fittleworth 12 C5
Fitton End 43 C3
Fitz 38 D3
Fitzhead 8 C1
Fitzwilliam 57 C6
Fiunary 85 C4
Five Ash Down 13 B4
Five Ashes 15 A4
Five Bridges 29 A3
Fivehead 8 E1
Fivelanes 4 C2
Five Oak Green 13 D2
Five Oaks 12 C4
Five Penny Borve 107 C2
Five Penny Ness 107 D1
Five Roads 17 C5
Five Turnings 38 B7
Fivig 107 A3
Flackwell Heath 23 C2
Fladbury 29 D3
Fladdabister 115 D4
Flagg 50 C4
Flamborough 65 E6
Flamstead 32 B7
Flamstead End 24 D2
Flansham 12 B6
Flasby 55 D2
Flash 50 B4
Flask Inn 65 B3
Flatford Mill 34 E5
Flatt, The 69 D2
Flaunden 23 E1
Flawborough 51 D6
Flawith 57 C1
Flax Bourton 20 E4
Flaxby 57 B2
Flaxley 29 A6
Flaxpool 20 A7
Flaxton 57 E1
Fleckney 41 D5
Flecknoe 31 A1
Fleet Hants 23 C6
Fleet Lincs 43 B2
Fleetham 77 C3
Fleet Hargate 43 B2
Fleetwood 54 C3
Flemingston 19 A6
Flemington 81 A6
Flempton 34 C2
Fletchertown 69 A5
Fletching 13 B4
Flete 5 B5
Fleuchats 96 D3
Fleur-de-Lis 19 B4
Flexbury 6 B6
Flexford 12 B1

Flimby 68 D6
Flimwell 13 E3
Flint 48 B4
Flintham 51 D6
Flint Mountain 48 B5
Flinton 59 C4
Flishinghurst 13 E3
Flitcham 44 B3
Flitton 32 B5
Flitwick 32 B5
Flixborough 58 D6
Flixton GM 49 B2
Flixton N Yorks 65 C6
Flixton Sflk 45 C7
Flobbets 105 A5
Flockton 57 A6
Flockton Green 57 A6
Flodabay 98 E3
Flodden 77 A2
Flodigarry 100 B4
Flookburgh 61 C6
Floors 104 C3
Flordon 45 A6
Flore 31 B1
Flotterton 77 A5
Flowton 34 E4
Flushing Corn 3 A5
Flushing Gramp 105 D4
Flyford Flavell 29 D2
Fobbing 25 C4
Fochabers 104 B3
Fochriw 19 B3
Fockerby 58 D6
Fodderletter 95 E3
Fodderty 102 D6
Foel 37 D4
Foffarty 89 A4
Fogo 76 D1
Fogorig 76 D1
Foindle 108 D4
Folda 88 C2
Fole 50 B7
Foleshill 41 A6
Folke 9 C2
Folkestone 15 C5
Folkingham 42 D1
Folkington 15 A6
Folksworth 42 E5
Folkton 65 C6
Folla Rule 105 A5
Follifoot 57 B2
Folly Dors 9 D3
Folly Dyfed 16 C3
Folly Gate 6 E7
Fonthill Bishop 10 A1
Fonthill Gifford 10 A1
Fontmell Magna 9 E2
Fontwell 12 B6
Foolow 50 C3
Foots Cray 24 E5
Forbestown 96 D2
Force Forge 61 C5
Forcett 63 B3
Forches Cross 7 B5
Ford Bucks 31 C7
Ford Devon 5 B5
Ford Devon 6 D4
Ford Dyfed 16 C3
Ford Glos 30 A5
Ford Loth 82 D6
Ford Mers 48 C2
Ford Northld 77 A2
Ford Salop 38 D3
Ford Som 8 B1
Ford Som 8 B1
Ford Staffs 50 B5
Ford Strath 79 C1
Ford Wilts 21 C3
Ford W Ssx 12 C6
Fordcombe 13 C2
Fordell 82 B4
Forden 38 B4
Ford End 33 C7
Forder Green 5 C4
Fordham Cambs 33 C1
Fordham Esx 34 D6
Fordham Nflk 44 A6
Fordham Abbey 33 C2
Fordingbridge 10 C3
Fordon 65 C6
Fordoun 97 C6
Fordstreet 34 D6
Ford Street 8 C2
Fordwells 30 D6
Fordwich 15 B3
Fordyce 104 D2

Forebrae 88 A6
Foreland 78 B5
Foremark 41 A2
Forest 70 B6
Forestburn Gate 77 B6
Forest Gate 24 E4
Forest Green 12 D2
Forest Hall Cumb 61 E3
Forest Hall T & W 71 A2
Forest Head 69 D4
Forest Hill 31 A7
Forest Mill 81 D2
Forest Row 13 B3
Forestside 11 D3
Forest Town 51 B4
Forfar 89 A3
Forgandenny 88 B7
Forgie 104 B3
Forgieside 104 C3
Formby 48 B1
Forncett End 45 A6
Forncett St Mary 45 A6
Forncett St Peter 45 A6
Forneth 88 B4
Fornham All Saints 34 C2
Fornham St Martin 34 C2
Fornighty 103 C6
Forres 103 D6
Forrest 81 C5
Forrest Field 67 B2
Forsbrook 49 D7
Forse 111 C5
Forsie 111 A2
Forsinain 110 E4
Forsinard 110 D4
Forstal, The 14 D4
Forston 9 C4
Forteviot 88 B7
Forth 81 D6
Forthampton 29 C4
Fortingall 87 D4
Forton Hants 22 D7
Forton Lancs 54 D2
Forton Salop 38 D3
Forton Som 8 E3
Forton Staffs 39 B2
Fortrie 104 E4
Fortrose 103 A6
Fortuneswell 9 C6
Fort William 86 C1
Forty Green 23 D2
Forty Hill 24 D3
Forward Green 35 A3
Fosbury 22 C6
Foscot 30 C5
Fosdyke 43 B1
Foss 87 D3
Fossdale 62 D5
Fossebridge 30 A6
Foss-y-ffin 26 D4
Foster's Booth 31 B2
Foster Street 24 E2
Foston Derbs 50 C7
Foston Lincs 52 B7
Foston N Yorks 57 E1
Foston on the Wolds
   59 B2
Fotherby 53 B2
Fotheringhay 42 D5
Foubister 113 E1
Foulbog 75 C5
Foulden Bdrs 83 E7
Foulden Nflk 44 B6
Foul Mile 13 D5
Foulridge 55 C3
Foulsham 44 E3
Foulzie 105 A3
Fountainhall 76 A1
Four Ashes Sflk 34 E1
Four Ashes Staffs 40 B4
Four Crosses Clwyd 47 E6
Fourcrosses Gynd 46 C7
Four Crosses Pwys 38 B3
Four Crosses Pwys 37 E5
Four Crosses Staffs 40 B4
Four Elms 13 B2
Four Forks 20 B7
Four Gotes 43 C3
Fourlane Ends 50 E5
Four Lanes 2 D5
Fourlanes End 49 C6
Four Marks 11 C1
Four Mile Bridge 46 B3
Four Oaks E Ssx 14 D6

Four Oaks W Mids 40 E6
Four Oaks W Mids 40 D5
Fourpenny 103 B2
Fourstones 70 B2
Four Throws 13 E4
Fovant 10 B2
Foveran 105 C6
Fowey 3 D3
Fowlis 88 E5
Fowlis Wester 88 A6
Fowlmere 33 A4
Fownhope 28 E4
Foxcote 30 A6
Foxdale 60 b4
Foxearth 34 C4
Foxfield 61 B5
Foxham 21 D3
Foxhole Corn 3 B3
Foxhole Hghld 94 D2
Foxholes 65 C6
Foxhunt Green 13 C5
Fox Lane 23 C6
Foxley H & W 30 E3
Foxley Nflk 44 E3
Foxley Northants 31 B2
Foxley Wilts 21 C2
Foxlydiate 31 B7
Fox Street 34 E6
Foxt 50 B6
Foxton Cambs 33 A4
Foxton Dur 71 B6
Foxton Leics 41 E5
Foxup 62 D7
Foxwist Green 49 A5
Foy 28 E5
Foyers 94 C3
Frachadil 84 E3
Fraddon 3 B3
Fradley 40 D3
Fradswell 40 B1
Fraisthorpe 65 D7
Framfield 13 B4
Framingham Earl 45 B5
Framingham Pigot 45 B5
Framlingham 35 B2
Frampton Dors 9 C4
Frampton Lincs 43 B1
Frampton Cotterell 21 A2
Frampton Mansell 29 D7
Frampton on Severn 29 B7
Frampton West End 53 B7
Framsden 35 A3
Framwellgate Moor 71 A4
Franche 40 A7
Frankby 48 B3
Frankley 40 B6
Frankton 41 B7
Frant 15 A3
Fraserburgh 105 C2
Frating Green 34 E6
Fratton 11 C4
Freathy 4 D5
Freckenham 33 C1
Freckleton 54 D5
Freeby 42 B2
Freefolk 22 D7
Freeland 30 E6
Freemantle 11 A3
Freester 115 D2
Freethorpe 45 D5
Freethorpe Common
   45 D5
Freiston Lincs 53 B7
Freiston Lincs 52 C7
Freiston Shore 43 C1
Fremington Devon 6 E3
Fremington N Yorks 63 A5
Frenchay 21 A3
Frenchbeer 5 B2
Frendraught 104 E4
Frenich 80 D1
Frensham 23 C7
Fresgoe 110 E2
Freshfield 48 B1
Freshford Avn 21 B4
Freshwater 10 E6
Fressingfield 35 B1
Freston 35 A5
Freswick 111 D2
Frettenham 45 B4
Freuchie 82 C2
Freystrop Cross 16 C4
Friars Carse 74 E7
Friar's Gate 13 B3
Friarton 88 C6
Friday Bridge 43 C4
Friday Street E Ssx 13 D6

Friday Street Sry 12 D2
Fridaythorpe 58 D2
Friern Barnet 24 C3
Friesthorpe 52 D3
Frieth 23 B2
Frilford 22 D2
Frilsham 22 E4
Frimley 23 C6
Frimley Green 23 C6
Frindsbury 14 C2
Fring 44 B2
Fringford 31 B5
Frinsted 14 D3
Frinton-on-Sea 35 B7
Friockheim 89 B4
Friog 37 A4
Frisby on the Wreake
   41 D3
Friskney 53 C6
Friskney Eaudike 53 C6
Friston Sflk 35 D2
Friston W Ssx 13 C7
Fritchley 50 E5
Frith 14 E3
Fritham 10 D3
Frith Bank 53 B7
Frith Common 29 A1
Frithelstock 6 D5
Frithville 53 B6
Frittenden 14 D4
Fritton Nflk 45 B6
Fritton Nflk 45 D5
Fritwell 31 A5
Frizington 60 E2
Frocester 29 B7
Frochas 38 B3
Frodesley 38 E4
Frodingham 58 D6
Frodsham 48 E4
Frogden 76 D3
Frog End 33 A3
Froggatt 50 D3
Froghall 50 B6
Frogham 10 C3
Frogmore Hants 23 C5
Frogmore Herts 24 B2
Frogmore Sry 23 C5
Frog Pool 29 B1
Frolesworth 41 C5
Frome 21 B6
Frome St Quintin 9 B3
Fromes Hill 29 A3
Fron Gynd 46 C7
Fron Pwys 38 B4
Fron Pwys 27 E4
Froncysyllte 48 B7
Fron-goch 47 D7
Frostenden 45 D7
Frosterley 70 D5
Froxfield 22 B5
Froxfield Green 11 D2
Fryerning 25 B2
Fryton 64 D6
Fugglestone St Peter
   10 C1
Fulbeck 52 C6
Fulbourn 33 B3
Fulbrook 30 C6
Fulford N Yorks 57 E3
Fulford Som 8 D1
Fulford Staffs 40 B1
Fulham 24 C5
Fulking 12 E5
Fuller Street 33 D7
Fullerton 10 E1
Fulletby 53 A4
Fullready 30 C3
Full Sutton 58 C2
Fulmer 23 D3
Fulmodeston 44 D2
Fulnetby 52 D4
Fulstow 53 B2
Fulwell Oxon 30 D5
Fulwell T & W 71 B3
Fulwood Lancs 54 E4
Fulwood S Yorks 50 E2
Fundenhall 45 A6
Funtington 11 D4
Funtley 11 B4
Funzie 114 E4
Furley 8 D3
Furnace Dyfed 37 A6
Furnace Hghld 101 B4
Furnace Strath 79 E1
Furneux Pelham 33 A6
Furzehill 7 B2
Furze Platt 23 C3

Fyfett 8 D2
Fyfield *Esx* 24 F2
Fyfield *Glos* 30 C7
Fyfield *Hants* 22 B7
Fyfield *Oxon* 22 D2
Fyfield *Wilts* 22 A5
Fylingthorpe 65 B3
Fyvie 105 A5

G

Gablon 103 A2
Gaddesby 41 D3
Gaddesden Row 32 B7
Gaer 28 A5
Gaer llwyd 20 D4
Gaerwen 46 D3
Gagingwell 30 E5
Gaick 94 E2
Gailey 40 B3
Gainford 63 B3
Gainsborough 52 B3
Gairloch 101 A4
Gairlochy 93 D6
Gairneybank 82 B3
Gaitsgill 69 B5
Gala Bank 76 A1
Galashiels 76 A2
Galby 41 D4
Galdenoch 66 C4
Galgate 54 D2
Galhampton 9 C1
Gall 88 B5
Gallanach 85 E6
Gallantry Bank 48 E6
Gallatown 82 C3
Gallchoille 79 B2
Gallery 89 C2
Galley Common 41 A5
Galleyend 25 C2
Galleywood 25 C2
Gallowfauld 89 A4
Gallowstree Common
  23 A3
Gallowstree Elm 40 A6
Galltair 93 A2
Galmisdale 92 B6
Galmpton *Devon* 5 D5
Galmpton *Devon* 5 B6
Galphay 63 C7
Galston 73 E5
Galtrigill 99 A6
Gamblesby 69 E6
Gamble's Green 33 D7
Gamlingay 32 D3
Gammaton Cross 6 D4
Gammersgill 63 A6
Gamrie 105 A2
Gamston *Notts* 51 D3
Gamston *Notts* 51 C7
Ganarew 28 E6
Gangsdown Hill 23 A3
Ganllwyd 37 B3
Gannochy 97 A6
Ganstead 59 B4
Ganthorpe 64 D6
Ganton 65 B6
Gaodhail 85 C5
Garabal 86 E7
Gara Bridge 5 B2
Garadheancal 101 B1
Garbat 102 C5
Garboldisham 44 E7
Garden 80 E2
Gardenstown 105 A2
Garderhouse 115 C3
Gardham 58 E3
Gare Hill 21 B6
Garelochhead 80 B2
Garenin 106 E3
Garford 22 D2
Garforth 57 C4
Gargrave 55 D2
Gargunnock 81 B2
Gariob 79 B3
Garlieston 67 A6
Garlogie 97 C3
Garmond 105 B3
Garmony 85 C4
Garmouth 104 B2
Garn 46 B7
Garnant 18 B2
Garn-Dolbenmaen 46 D6
Garneddwen 37 B4
Garnett Bridge 61 E5
Garrabost 107 D4
Garrachra 79 E3

Garralburn 104 C3
Garras 2 E6
Garreg 47 A6
Garreg Bank 38 B3
Garrick 87 E7
Garrison, The 2 b2
Garroch 67 B2
Garrochty 72 E2
Garros 100 B5
Garrow 87 E4
Garryhorn 67 B1
Garrynamonie 90 C4
Garsdale Head 62 C5
Garsdon 21 D2
Garshall Green 40 B1
Garsington 31 A7
Garstang 54 D3
Garston 48 D3
Garswood 48 E2
Gartachoil 80 E2
Gartally 94 C2
Gartavaich 72 C2
Gartbreck 78 B6
Garth *Clwyd* 48 B7
Garth *Gynd* 46 E3
Garth *IOM* 60 c4
Garth *M Glam* 18 D4
Garth *Pwys* 27 D6
Garth *Shet* 115 B2
Garthbrengy 27 E7
Gartheli 26 E5
Garthmyl 38 A5
Garthorpe *Humb* 58 D6
Garthorpe *Leics* 42 B2
Garths 61 E5
Garthynty 27 B6
Gartincaber 81 A1
Gartly 104 D5
Gartmore 80 E2
Gartnagrenach 72 B2
Gartnatra 78 C5
Gartness *Cent* 80 E3
Gartocharn 80 D3
Garton 59 C4
Garton-on-the-Wolds 58 E2
Gartshore 81 A4
Gartymore 111 A7
Garvald 83 A5
Garvamore 94 D6
Garvan 86 A1
Garvard 78 C2
Garve 102 B5
Garveld 72 A7
Garvestone 44 E5
Garvie 79 E2
Garvock *Gramp* 97 C6
Garvock *Tays* 88 B7
Garwald 75 C5
Garwaldwaterfoot 75 C5
Garway 28 D5
Garway Hill 28 D5
Gary-aloteger 107 A7
Garynahine 107 A4
Gask *Gramp* 105 D4
Gask *Gramp* 105 A4
Gask *Tays* 88 A7
Gaskan 85 E1
Gass 73 D7
Gastard 21 C4
Gasthorpe 44 D7
Gatcombe 11 A6
Gateacre 48 D3
Gatebeck 61 E5
Gate Burton 52 B3
Gateford 51 B2
Gateforth 57 D5
Gatehead 73 C4
Gate Helmsley 57 E2
Gatehouse *Strath* 78 E4
Gatehouse *Tays* 87 E4
Gatehouse of Fleet 67 B5
Gatelawbridge 74 E6
Gateley 44 D3
Gatenby 63 D6
Gateshaw 76 D3
Gateshead 71 A2
Gatesheath 48 D5
Gateside *Fife* 82 B2
Gateside *Gramp* 97 B2
Gateside *Strath* 80 C6
Gateside *Tays* 88 E4
Gateside *Tays* 89 A4
Gatherdam 97 A2
Gathurst 48 E1
Gatley 49 C3
Gattonside 76 B2
Gaufron 27 E4

Gauldry 88 E6
Gaunt's Common 10 B4
Gautby 52 E4
Gavinton 83 C7
Gawber 57 B7
Gawcott 31 B4
Gawsworth 49 C5
Gawthrop 62 B6
Gawthwaite 61 B5
Gaydon 30 D2
Gayhurst 31 D3
Gayles 63 B4
Gay Street 12 C4
Gayton *Mers* 48 B3
Gayton *Nflk* 44 B4
Gayton *Northants* 31 C2
Gayton *Staffs* 40 B2
Gayton le Marsh 53 C3
Gayton le Wold 53 A3
Gayton Thorpe 44 B4
Gaywood 44 A3
Gazeley 33 D2
Geanies 103 B4
Gearach 78 B6
Gearnsary 110 C5
Gearradh 86 A2
Gèarraidh Euscleit 107 C3
Geary 99 B5
Gearymore 99 C7
Gedding 34 D3
Geddington 42 B6
Gedling 51 C6
Gedney 43 C2
Gedney Broadgate 43 C2
Gedney Drove End 43 C2
Gedney Dyke 43 C2
Gedney Hill 43 B3
Gedrave 35 D4
Gee Cross 49 D2
Gelder Shiel 96 C4
Geldeston 45 C6
Gell *Clwyd* 47 C4
Gell *Gynd* 46 D7
Gelligaer 19 B4
Gelli Gynan 48 A6
Gellilydan 47 A7
Gellioedd 47 D6
Gelly 16 D4
Gellyburn 88 B5
Gellywen 17 A3
Gelston 67 D5
Gembling 59 B2
Gemmil 79 B1
Genoch 66 C5
Genoch Square 66 C5
Gentleshaw 40 C3
Georgeham 6 D3
George Nympton 7 B4
Georgetown 80 D5
Georth 112 C4
Gerlan 47 A4
Germansweek 6 D7
Germoe 2 C6
Gerrans 3 A5
Gerrards Cross 23 E3
Gerston 111 B3
Gestingthorpe 34 C5
Geuffordd 38 B3
Geufron 27 C2
Gibbshill 67 D3
Gibraltar 53 D6
Gidea Park 24 F3
Gidleigh 5 B2
Gifford 83 A6
Giffordland 73 B3
Giggleswick 55 C1
Gilberdyke 58 D5
Gilchriston 82 E6
Gilcrux 68 E6
Gildersome 57 A5
Gildingwells 51 B2
Gileston 19 A7
Gilfach *M Glam* 19 B4
Gilfach *M Glam* 19 B4
Gilfach Goch 18 E4
Gilfachrheda 26 D5
Gill 73 B3
Gillamoor 64 D4
Gillenbie 75 B7
Gillfoot 68 C2
Gillgarran 68 D7
Gilling East 64 D6
Gillingham *Dors* 9 E1
Gillingham *Kent* 14 C2
Gillingham *Nflk* 45 D6

Gilling West 63 B4
Gillivoan 111 B5
Gillock 111 C3
Gillow Heath 49 C6
Gills 111 D1
Gill's Green 13 E3
Gilmanscleuch 75 D3
Gilmerton *Loth* 82 C6
Gilmerton *Tays* 87 E6
Gilmilnscroft 73 E5
Gilmonby 62 E3
Gilmorton 41 C6
Gilsland 69 E3
Gilsland Spa 69 E3
Gilstead Moor 56 E4
Gilston 82 E7
Gilston Park 33 A7
Gilwern 19 C2
Gimingham 45 B2
Gindiscol 115 D4
Giortein Driseach 85 A6
Gipping 34 E2
Gipsey Bridge 53 A6
Girlsta 115 D2
Girsby 63 D4
Girthon 67 C5
Girton *Cambs* 33 A2
Girton *Notts* 52 B5
Girvan 66 C1
Gisburn 55 C3
Gisla 106 E5
Gisleham 45 E7
Gislingham 34 E1
Gissing 45 A7
Gittisham 8 C4
Givons Grove 12 D1
Glack 105 A6
Glackour 101 D3
Gladestry 28 B2
Gladsmuir 82 E5
Glaic 79 E4
Glais 18 C3
Glaisdale 64 E3
Glaister 72 D4
Glame 100 C7
Glamis 88 E4
Glanaber Terrace 47 B6
Glan Adda 46 E3
Glanaman 18 B2
Glan Bran 27 B7
Glan-Conwy 47 C5
Glanderston 104 D6
Glandford 44 E1
Glandwr *Dyfed* 16 E3
Glandwr *Gwent* 19 C3
Glangrwyne 19 C2
Glan Honddu 27 E7
Glan-llynfi 18 D4
Glan-Mule 38 A5
Glanrhyd 26 A6
Glan-Sefin 18 C1
Glanton 77 B4
Glanvilles Wootton 9 C3
Glan-y-don 48 A4
Glanyllyn 19 B5
Glan-yr-afon *Gynd* 47 D6
Glan-yr-afon *Gynd* 47 E6
Glapthorn 42 D5
Glapwell 51 A4
Glasahoile 80 D1
Glas-allt Shiel 96 C5
Glasbury 28 A4
Glaschoil 95 D2
Glascoed 19 D3
Glascote 40 E4
Glascwm 28 A2
Glasdrum 86 B4
Glasfryn 47 D5
Glasgow 80 E5
Glashmore 97 C3
Glasinfryn 46 E4
Glasnacardoch 92 D5
Glaspant 17 A2
Glaspwll 37 B6
Glassaugh 104 D2
Glassburn 94 B2
Glassel 97 B4
Glassenbury 13 E3
Glasserton 67 A7
Glassford 74 C1
Glasshouse Hill 29 B5
Glasshouses 56 E1
Glassingall 81 B1
Glasslie 82 C2
Glasson *Cumb* 69 A3
Glasson *Lancs* 54 D2

Glassonby 69 D6
Glasterlaw 89 C3
Glaston 42 B4
Glastonbury 20 D7
Glatton 42 E6
Glazebury 49 A2
Glazeley 39 B6
Gleadless Townend 50 E2
Gleadsmoss 49 C5
Gleaston 61 B6
Glecknabae 79 E5
Gledhow 57 B4
Gledrid 38 B1
Glemsford 34 C4
Glen *D & G* 68 B2
Glen *D & G* 67 B5
Glenae 74 E7
Glenaladale 85 E1
Glenald 80 B2
Glenarm 88 E2
Glen Auldyn 60 d2
Glenbarr 72 A4
Glenbatrick 78 E3
Glenbeg *Hghld* 102 B3
Glenbeg *Hghld* 95 D3
Glenbeg *Hghld* 85 B2
Glenbeich 87 C6
Glenbervie *Cent* 81 C3
Glenbervie *Gramp* 97 C5
Glenboig 81 B5
Glenborrodale 85 C2
Glenbranter 80 A2
Glenbreck 75 A3
Glenbrittle 92 B2
Glenbuck 74 C3
Glenbyre 85 B6
Glencaird 66 E3
Glencaple 68 C3
Glencarse 88 C6
Glencat 97 A4
Glenceitlein 86 C4
Glencloy 72 E4
Glencoe 86 C3
Glenconglass 95 E3
Glencoul 108 E5
Glencraig 82 B3
Glencripesdale 85 C3
Glencrosh 67 D2
Glencruittein 85 E5
Glencuie 96 E2
Glendearg *Bdrs* 76 B2
Glendearg *D & G* 75 C5
Glendessary 93 B5
Glendevon 81 D1
Glendhu 108 E5
Glendoebeg 94 C5
Glendoick 88 D6
Glendoune 66 C1
Glendrissaig 66 C1
Glenduckie 88 D7
Glenduisk 66 D2
Gleneagles 81 D1
Glenearn 88 C7
Glenegedale 78 C6
Glenelg 93 A3
Glenfarg 88 C7
Glenfeochan 85 E6
Glenfield 41 C4
Glenfinnan 93 B6
Glenfoot 88 C7
Glengalmadale 85 E3
Glengap 67 C5
Glengarnock 80 C6
Glengarrisdale 79 A2
Glengennet 66 D1
Glengolly 111 B2
Glengrasco 100 B7
Glengyle 86 E7
Glenhead 74 D7
Glenhead Farm 88 D2
Glenhurrich 85 E2
Glenkerry 75 C4
Glenkiln Reservoir 68 B2
Glenkin 80 A3
Glenkindie 96 E2
Glenlair 67 D3
Glenlatterach 103 E6
Glenlean 79 E3
Glenlee *D & G* 67 C2
Glenlee *Tays* 96 E6
Glenlichorn 87 D7
Glenlochar 67 D4
Glenluce 66 C5
Glenmallan 80 B2
Glen Mark 96 E5
Glenmarksie 102 B6
Glenmaye 60 b3

Glenmeanie 101 E6
Glenmore *Bute* 79 E5
Glenmore *Skye* 100 B7
Glenmoy 89 A2
Glenmuick 109 A7
Glennoe 86 B5
Glenochar 74 E4
Glenogil 89 A2
Glen Parva 41 C5
Glenquiech 89 A2
Glenramskill 72 B6
Glenrazle 66 E4
Glenridding 61 C2
Glenrisdell 72 C2
Glenrossal 102 C1
Glenrothes 82 C2
Glensanda 85 E4
Glensaugh 97 B6
Glensgaich 102 C5
Glenshalg 97 A3
Glenshee 88 A5
Glenshellish 80 A2
Glensluan 79 E2
Glentham 52 D2
Glenton 104 E6
Glentress 75 C2
Glentruan 60 d1
Glentworth 52 C3
Glenuachdarach 100 B6
Glenure 86 B4
Glenurquhart 103 A5
Glen Vine 60 c4
Glenwhilly 66 C3
Glespin 74 D3
Gletness 115 D2
Glewstone 28 E5
Glinton 42 E4
Glooston 41 E5
Glororum 77 C2
Glossop 50 B1
Gloster Hill 77 D5
Gloucester 29 C6
Gloup 114 E2
Glusburn 56 D3
Gluss 114 C5
Glympton 30 E5
Glyn 47 B5
Glynarthen 26 C6
Glyn Ceiriog 38 B1
Glyncorrwg 18 D4
Glyn-Cywarch 47 A7
Glynde 13 B6
Glyndebourne 13 B5
Glyndyfrdwy 48 A7
Glyn-Neath 18 D3
Glynogwr 18 E5
Glyntaff 19 A5
Glynteg 17 B2
Gnosall 40 A2
Gnosall Heath 40 A2
Goadby 41 E5
Goadby Marwood 41 E2
Goatacre 21 E3
Goatfield 79 E1
Goathill 9 C2
Goathland 65 A3
Goathurst 20 B7
Gobernuisgeach 110 E5
Gobowen 38 C1
Godalming 12 B2
Godmanchester 32 D1
Godmanstone 9 C4
Godmersham 15 A3
Godolphin Cross 2 D5
Godor 38 B3
Godre'r-graig 18 C3
Godshill *Hants* 10 C3
Godshill *IOW* 11 B6
Godstone 13 A1
Goetre 19 D3
Goff's Oak 24 D2
Gogar 82 B5
Gogarth 47 B2
Goginan 27 A2
Goirtean a'Chladaich
  86 B1
Goirtein 79 D3
Golan 46 E6
Golant 3 D3
Golberdon 4 D3
Golborne 49 A2
Golcar 56 D6
Goldcliff 19 D5
Golden Cross 13 C5
Golden Green 13 D2
Golden Grove 17 D4
Goldenhill 49 C6

Golden Pot 23 B7
Golden Valley 29 D5
Golders Green 24 C4
Goldhanger 25 E2
Goldielea 68 C2
Golding 38 E4
Goldsborough N Yorks 65 A2
Goldsborough N Yorks 57 B2
Goldsithney 2 C5
Goldthorpe 57 C7
Goldworthy 6 C4
Golspie 103 B2
Golval 110 D2
Gomersal 57 A5
Gometra 84 E4
Gomshall 12 C2
Gonalston 51 C6
Gonfirth Shet 115 C1
Good Easter 33 C7
Gooderstone 44 B5
Goodleigh 6 E3
Goodmanham 58 D3
Goodnestone Kent 15 C3
Goodnestone Kent 15 A2
Goodrich 28 E6
Goodrington 5 D5
Goodwick 16 C2
Goodwood House 11 E4
Goodworth Clatford 22 C7
Goodyers End 41 A6
Goole 58 C5
Goonbell 2 E4
Goonhavern 2 E3
Goose Green 13 D1
Gooseham 6 B5
Goosewell 5 A5
Goosey 22 C2
Goosnargh 54 E4
Goostrey 49 B5
Gorcott Hill 30 A1
Gordon 76 C1
Gordonbush 103 B1
Gordonstoun 103 E5
Gordonstown Gramp 104 D3
Gordonstown Gramp 105 A5
Gore 15 D2
Gorebridge 82 D6
Gorefield 43 C3
Goring 23 A3
Goring-by-Sea 12 D6
Gorleston on Sea 45 E5
Gorrley 10 C3
Gorllwyn 17 B2
Gornalwood 40 B5
Gorrachie 105 A3
Gorran Churchtown 3 B4
Gorran Haven 3 C4
Gors 27 A3
Gorsedd 48 A4
Gorseinon 17 D6
Gorseness 112 D5
Gorslas 17 D4
Gorsley 29 A5
Gorsley Common 29 A5
Gorstan 102 B5
Gorstanvorran 85 E1
Gorsty Common 28 D4
Gortantaoid 78 C4
Gorten 85 D5
Gortenanrue 85 D6
Gortenbuie 85 B5
Gortenfern 85 C2
Gorton Coll 84 C3
Gorton GM 49 C2
Gosbeck 35 A3
Gosberton 43 A1
Goseley Dale 41 A2
Gosfield 33 D6
Gosforth Cumb 60 E3
Gosforth T & W 71 A2
Gosmore 26 D5
Gossmore 32 C6
Gospel End 40 B5
Gosport 11 C5
Gossabrough 114 E4
Goswick 77 B1
Gotham 51 B7
Gotherington 29 D5
Gott 115 D3
Goudhurst 13 E3
Goulaby 98 C4
Goulceby 53 A4
Gourdas 105 A4

Gourdon 97 D6
Gourock 80 B4
Govan 80 E5
Goveton 5 C6
Gowdall 57 E5
Gowerton 17 D6
Gowkhall 81 E3
Gowthorpe 58 C2
Goxhill Humb 59 B3
Goxhill Humb 59 B5
Grabbet Park 13 A3
Gradbach 49 D5
Grade 2 E7
Graffham 12 B5
Grafham 32 C2
Grafton H & W 28 D4
Grafton H & W 28 E1
Grafton N Yorks 57 C1
Grafton Oxon 30 C7
Grafton Salop 38 D3
Grafton Flyford 29 D2
Grafton Regis 31 C3
Grafton Underwood 42 C6
Grafty Green 14 D4
Graianrhyd 48 B6
Graig Clwyd 18 B3
Graig Gynd 47 C3
Graig-fechan 48 A6
Grain 14 D1
Grainel 78 B5
Grainhow 105 B4
Grainsby 53 A2
Grainthorpe 53 B2
Grampound 3 B4
Grampound Road 3 B3
Granborough 31 C5
Granby 51 D7
Grandborough 30 E1
Grandtully 88 A3
Grange Cumb 61 B2
Grange Hghld 94 B2
Grange Kent 14 D2
Grange Mers 48 B3
Grange N Yorks 64 C4
Grange Tays 88 D6
Grange, The Mers 48 B3
Grange Crossroads 104 C3
Grange Hill 24 E3
Grangemill 50 D5
Grange Moor 57 A6
Grangemouth 81 D3
Grangemuir 83 A2
Grange of Lindores 88 D7
Grange-over-Sands 61 D6
Grangepans 11 B1
Grangetown Clev 64 C1
Grangetown S Glam 19 B6
Grange Villa 71 A3
Granish 95 B4
Gransmoor 59 B2
Granston 16 B2
Grantchester 33 A3
Grantham 42 C1
Grantham 12 C2
Grantlodge 97 C2
Granton Loth 82 C5
Grantown-on-Spey 95 D3
Grantshouse 83 D6
Grappenhall 49 A3
Grasby 59 A7
Grasmere 61 C3
Grasscroft 49 D1
Grassendale 48 C3
Grassholme 70 C6
Grassington 56 D1
Grassmoor 51 A4
Grassthorpe 51 D4
Grateley 22 B7
Gratwich 50 B7
Graveley Cambs 32 D2
Graveley Herts 32 D6
Gravelly Hill 40 D5
Gravels 38 C4
Graven 114 D3
Graveney 15 A2
Gravesend 25 B5
Gravir 107 B6
Grayingham 52 C2
Grayrigg 61 E5
Grays 25 B5
Grayshott 11 E1
Grayswood 12 B3
Grazeley 23 A5
Greasbrough 51 A1
Greasby 48 B3
Great Abington 33 B4

Great Addington 42 C7
Great Alne 30 B2
Great Altcar 48 C1
Great Amwell 32 E7
Great Asby 62 B3
Great Ashfield 34 D2
Great Ayton 64 C2
Great Baddow 25 C2
Great Badminton 21 C2
Great Bardfield 33 C5
Great Barford 32 C3
Great Barr 40 C5
Great Barrington 30 C6
Great Barrow 48 D5
Great Barton 34 C2
Great Barugh 64 E6
Great Bavington 77 A7
Great Bealings 35 B4
Great Bedwyn 22 B5
Great Bentley 35 A6
Great Billing 31 D1
Great Bircham 44 B2
Great Blakenham 35 A3
Great Bolas 39 A2
Great Bookham 12 D1
Great Bourton 30 E3
Great Bowden 41 E6
Great Bradley 33 C3
Great Braxted 34 C7
Great Bricett 34 E3
Great Brickhill 31 E4
Great Bridgeford 40 A2
Great Brington 31 B1
Great Bromley 34 E6
Great Broughton Cumb 68 D6
Great Broughton N Yorks 64 C3
Great Budworth 49 A4
Great Burdon 63 D3
Great Burstead 25 B3
Great Busby 64 C3
Great Canfield 33 B7
Great Canney 25 D2
Great Carlton 53 C3
Great Casterton 42 D4
Great Chart 14 E4
Great Chatwell 39 B3
Great Chesterford 33 B4
Great Cheverell 21 D5
Great Chishill 33 A5
Great Clacton 35 A7
Great Coates 59 C6
Great Comberton 29 D3
Great Corby 69 C4
Great Cornard 34 C4
Great Cowden 59 C3
Great Coxwell 22 B2
Great Cransley 42 B7
Great Cressingham 44 C5
Great Crosby 48 C2
Great Cubley 50 C7
Great Dalby 41 E3
Great Doddington 31 D1
Great Driffield 59 A2
Great Dunham 44 C4
Great Dunmow 33 C6
Great Durnford 10 C1
Great Easton Esx 33 C6
Great Easton Leics 42 B5
Great Eccleston 54 D3
Great Edstone 64 E5
Great Ellingham 44 E6
Great Elm 21 B6
Great Eversden 32 E3
Great Fencote 63 C5
Great Finborough 34 E3
Greatford 42 D3
Great Fransham 44 C4
Great Gaddesden 32 B7
Greatgate 50 B6
Great Gidding 42 E6
Great Givendale 58 D2
Great Glemham 35 C2
Great Glen 41 D5
Great Gonerby 42 B1
Great Gransden 32 D3
Great Green Nflk 45 B7
Great Green Sflk 34 D3
Great Habton 64 E6
Great Hale 52 E7
Great Hallingbury 33 B7
Greatham Clev 64 B1
Greatham Hants 11 D1
Greatham W Ssx 12 C5
Great Hampden 31 D7
Great Hanwood 38 D4

Great Harrowden 42 B7
Great Harwood 55 B4
Great Haseley 31 B7
Great Hatfield 59 B3
Great Haywood 63 A7
Great Heath 41 A6
Great Heck 57 D5
Great Henny 34 C5
Great Hinton 21 D5
Great Hockham 44 D6
Great Holland 35 B7
Great Horkesley 34 D5
Great Hormead 33 A5
Great Horwood 31 C4
Great Houghton Northants 31 C2
Great Houghton S Yorks 57 C7
Great Hucklow 50 C3
Great Kelk 59 B2
Great Kimble 31 D7
Great Kingshill 23 C2
Great Langton 63 C5
Great Leighs 33 D7
Great Limber 59 B7
Great Linford 31 D3
Great Livermere 34 C1
Great Longstone 50 C3
Great Lumley 71 A4
Great Lyth 38 D4
Great Malvern 29 B3
Great Maplestead 34 C5
Great Marton 54 C4
Great Massingham 44 B3
Great Melton 45 A5
Great Milton 31 B7
Great Missenden 31 D7
Great Mitton 55 B4
Great Mongeham 15 D3
Great Moulton 45 A6
Great Musgrave 62 C3
Great Ness 38 C3
Great Oak 19 D3
Great Oakley Esx 35 A6
Great Oakley Northants 42 B6
Great Offley 32 C6
Great Ormside 62 C3
Great Orton 69 B4
Great Oxendon 41 E6
Great Palgrave 44 C4
Great Parndon 24 E2
Great Paxton 32 D2
Great Plumpton 54 C4
Great Plumstead 45 B4
Great Ponton 42 C1
Great Preston 57 C5
Great Raveley 43 A6
Great Rissington 30 B6
Great Rollright 30 D4
Great Rudbaxton 16 C3
Great Ryburgh 44 D3
Great Ryle 77 B4
Great Ryton 38 D4
Great Saling 33 D6
Great Salkeld 69 D6
Great Sampford 33 C5
Great Sankey 48 E3
Great Saughall 48 C5
Great Saxham 33 D2
Great Shefford 22 C4
Great Shelford 33 A3
Great Smeaton 63 D4
Great Snoring 44 D2
Great Somerford 21 D2
Great Soudley 39 B2
Great Stainton 71 B6
Great Stambridge 25 D3
Great Staughton 32 C2
Great Steeping 53 C5
Great Stonar 15 D3
Greatstone-on-Sea 15 A6
Great Strickland 69 D7
Great Stukeley 32 D1
Great Sturton 53 A4
Great Sutton 48 C4
Great Swinburne 70 C1
Great Tew 30 D5
Great Tey 34 C6
Great Thurlow 33 C3
Great Torrington 6 D5
Great Tosson 77 B5
Great Totham Esx 34 C7
Great Totham Esx 34 C7
Great Urswick 61 B6
Great Wakering 25 E4
Great Waldingfield 34 D4

Great Walsingham 44 D2
Great Waltham 33 C7
Great Warley 25 A3
Great Washbourne 29 D4
Great Welnetham 34 C3
Great Wenham 34 E5
Great Whittington 70 D1
Great Wigborough 34 D7
Great Wilbraham 33 B3
Great Wishford 10 B1
Great Witcombe 29 D6
Great Witley 29 B1
Great Wolford 30 C4
Great Woolstone 31 D4
Greatworth 31 A3
Great Wratting 33 C4
Great Wymondley 32 D6
Great Wyrley 40 B4
Great Wytheford 38 E3
Great Yarmouth 45 E5
Great Yeldham 33 D5
Green, The 86 A4
Greenbank Gramp 96 C3
Greenbank Lancs 54 E2
Greenburn 89 A5
Greendams 97 B4
Greendikes 77 B3
Green End Beds 32 C3
Green End Herts 32 E6
Greenfield Beds 32 B5
Greenfield Clwyd 48 A4
Greenfield GM 49 D1
Greenfield Hghld 93 E4
Greenfield Oxon 23 B2
Greenford 24 B4
Greengairs 81 B4
Greenhalgh 54 D4
Greenhall 104 E6
Greenham Berks 22 D5
Greenham Som 8 B1
Green Hammerton 57 C2
Greenhaugh 76 D7
Greenhead 69 E3
Greenheads 105 D5
Greenhill E Ssx 15 A4
Greenhill GL 24 B4
Greenhill Hghld 103 C1
Greenhill S Yorks 50 E2
Green Hill Wilts 50 E2
Greenhithe 25 A5
Greenholm 73 E5
Greenholme 61 E3
Greenhow Hill 56 E1
Greenigo 113 D1
Greenland 111 C2
Greenlands 23 B3
Greenlaw Bdrs 76 D1
Greenlaw Gramp 104 E3
Greenloaning 81 C1
Greenmount 55 B6
Greenmyre 105 B5
Greenock 80 B4
Greenodd 61 C5
Green Ore 20 E6
Greenscares 87 E7
Greenside 70 E2
Greenskairs 105 A2
Greens Norton 31 B3
Greenstead Green 34 C6
Greensted 24 F2
Green Street 24 B3
Green Street Green GL 24 E6
Green Street Green Kent 25 A5
Green Tye 33 A7
Greenwich 24 E5
Greet 30 A4
Greete 38 E7
Greetham Leics 42 C3
Greetham Lincs 53 B4
Greetland 56 D5
Greinton 20 D7
Grenaby 60 b4
Grenach 79 E5
Grendon Northants 31 D1
Grendon Warks 38 B5
Grendon Common 40 E5
Grendon Green 28 E2
Grendon Underwood 31 B5
Grenetote 98 C4
Grenoside 50 E1
Gresford 48 C6
Gresham 45 A2
Greshornish 99 C6
Gress 107 C3

Gressenhall 44 D4
Gressenhall Green 44 D4
Gressingham 54 E1
Greta Bridge 63 A3
Gretna 69 B3
Gretna Green 69 B3
Gretton Glos 30 A4
Gretton Northants 42 C5
Gretton Salop 38 E5
Grewelthorpe 63 C7
Greygarth 63 B7
Greylake 20 C7
Greys Green 23 B3
Greysouthen 68 D7
Greystoke 69 C6
Greystone Gramp 96 C4
Greystone Lancs 55 C3
Greystone Tays 89 B4
Greywell 23 B6
Gribthorpe 58 C4
Gribton 74 E7
Griff 41 A6
Griffithstown 19 C4
Grigadale 85 A2
Grigghall 61 D5
Grimeford Village 55 A6
Grimersta 107 A4
Grimethorpe 57 C7
Griminish 98 B6
Grimister 114 D3
Grimley 29 C1
Grimmet 73 C6
Grimness 113 D2
Grimoldby 53 B3
Grimpo 38 C2
Grimsargh 54 E4
Grimsbury 30 E3
Grimsby 59 C6
Grimscote 31 B2
Grimscott 6 B6
Grimshader 107 C5
Grimsthorpe 42 D2
Grimston Leics 41 D2
Grimston Nflk 44 B3
Grimstone 9 C4
Grindale 65 D6
Grindle 39 B4
Grindleford 50 D3
Grindleton 55 B3
Grindley 40 C2
Grindlow 50 C3
Grindon Northld 77 A1
Grindon Staffs 50 B5
Gringley on the Hill 51 D1
Grinsdale 69 B4
Grinshill 38 E2
Grinton 63 A5
Grishipoll 84 C3
Gristhorpe 65 C5
Griston 44 D6
Gritley 113 E1
Grittenham 21 E2
Grittleton 21 C3
Grizebeck 61 B5
Grizedale 61 C5
Grobister 112 F4
Groby 41 C4
Groes W Glam 47 E4
Groes-faen 19 A5
Groesffordd 46 D5
Groesffordd Marli 47 E3
Groesllwyd 38 B3
Groeslon 46 D5
Grogarry 90 C2
Grogport 72 C3
Gronant 47 E2
Groombridge 13 C3
Grosebay 99 A2
Grosmont Gwent 28 D5
Grosmont N Yorks 65 A3
Grotaig 94 C3
Groton 34 D4
Grove Dors 9 C6
Grove Kent 15 C2
Grove Notts 51 D3
Grove Oxon 22 D2
Grove Park 24 E5
Grovesend 17 D5
Gruids 102 D1
Gruinard Flats 78 B5
Gruline 85 B4
Grundcruie 88 B6
Grundisburgh 35 B3
Gruting 115 B3
Grutness 115 D7
Gualachulain 86 C4
Guardbridge 89 A7

Guarlford 29 C3
Guay 88 B4
Gubbergill 60 E4
Guestling Green 14 D7
Guestwick 44 E3
Guide Post 77 D7
Guilden Morden 32 D4
Guilden Sutton 48 D5
Guildford 12 C2
Guildtown 88 C5
Guilsborough 41 D7
Guilsfield 38 B3
Guisborough 64 D2
Guiseley 56 E3
Guist 44 D3
Guith 112 E3
Guiting Power 30 A5
Gulberwick 115 D4
Gullane 82 E4
Gulval 2 B5
Gumfreston 16 E5
Gumley 41 D6
Gunby Humb 58 C4
Gunby Lincs 42 C2
Gundleton 11 C1
Gunn 7 A3
Gunnerside 62 E5
Gunnerton 70 C1
Gunness 58 D6
Gunnislake 4 E3
Gunnista 115 E3
Gunter's Bridge 12 B4
Gunthorpe Nflk 44 E2
Gunthorpe Notts 51 C6
Gunton Halt 45 B2
Gunville 11 A6
Gunwalloe 2 D6
Gurnard 11 A5
Gurney Slade 21 A6
Gurnos 18 C3
Gussage All Saints 10 B3
Gussage St Michael 10 A3
Guston 15 D4
Gutcher 114 E3
Guthrie 89 B3
Gutters Hill 25 C2
Guyhirn 43 B4
Guynd 89 B4
Guy's Head 43 C2
Guy's Marsh 9 E1
Guyzance 77 D5
Gwaelod-y-garth 19 B5
Gwaenysgor 47 E2
Gwaithla 28 B2
Gwalchmai 46 C3
Gwaun-Cae-Gurwen 18 C2
Gwaun-leision 18 C2
Gwaynynog 47 E4
Gwbert-on-Sea 26 A6
Gweek 2 E6
Gwehelog 19 D3
Gwenddwr 27 E6
Gwennap 2 E4
Gwenter 2 E7
Gwernaffield 48 B5
Gwernesney 28 D7
Gwernogle 17 D2
Gwernymynydd 48 B5
Gwespyr 48 A3
Gwinear 2 C5
Gwithian 2 C4
Gwyddelwern 47 E6
Gwyddgrug 17 C2
Gwystre 27 E4
Gwytherin 47 C4
Gyfelia 48 C7
Gyffin 47 B3
Gyffylliog 47 E5
Gylen 85 E6

H

Habberley H & W 76 E7
Habberley Salop 38 C4
Habost Lewis 107 B6
Habost Lewis 107 D1
Habrough 59 B6
Haccombe 5 D3
Hacconby 42 E2
Haceby 42 D1
Hacheston 35 C3
Hackenthorpe 51 A2
Hackford 44 E5
Hackforth 63 C5
Hackland 112 C4
Hacklete 106 E4
Hackleton 31 D2

Hacklinge 15 D3
Hackness N Yorks 65 B4
Hackness Ork 113 C2
Hackney 24 D4
Hackthorn 52 C3
Hackthorpe 69 D7
Hacombe 5 B3
Hadden 76 D2
Haddenham Bucks 31 C7
Haddenham Cambs 33 A1
Haddington Lincs 52 C5
Haddington Loth 83 A5
Haddiscoe 45 D6
Haddon 42 E5
Hademore 40 D4
Hadfield 50 B1
Hadham Cross 33 A7
Hadham Ford 33 A6
Hadleigh Esx 25 D4
Hadleigh Sflk 34 E4
Hadleigh Heath 34 D4
Hadley 39 A3
Hadley End 40 D2
Hadlow 13 D2
Hadlow Down 13 C4
Hadnall 38 E2
Hadstock 33 B4
Hadzor 29 D1
Haffenden Quarter 14 D4
Hafod-Dinbych 47 C5
Hafodunos 47 C4
Haggate 55 C4
Haggbeck 69 C2
Haggs 81 B4
Hagley H & W 28 E3
Hagley H & W 40 B6
Hagnaby 53 B5
Hagworthingham 53 B5
Haigh 49 A1
Haighton Green 54 E4
Haile 60 E3
Hailes 30 A4
Hailey Herts 32 E7
Hailey Oxon 23 A3
Hailey Oxon 30 D6
Hailsham 15 A6
Hail Weston 32 C2
Haimer 111 B2
Hainault 24 E3
Hainford 45 B4
Hainton 52 E3
Haisthorpe 65 D7
Halam 51 C5
Halbeath 82 B4
Halberton 8 B2
Halcro 111 C2
Hale Ches 49 B3
Hale GM 49 B3
Hale Hants 10 C3
Hale Bank 48 D3
Halebarns 49 B3
Hales Nflk 45 C6
Hales Staffs 39 B1
Halesowen 40 B6
Hales Place 15 B3
Hale Street 13 D2
Halesworth 35 C1
Halewood 48 D3
Halford Salop 38 D6
Halford Warks 30 C3
Halfpenny Green 40 A5
Halfway Berks 22 D5
Halfway Dyfed 27 A7
Halfway Pwys 27 C7
Halfway S Yorks 51 A2
Halfway House Salop 38 C3
Halfway Houses 14 E1
Halghton Mill 48 D7
Halifax 56 D5
Halistra 99 B6
Halkirk 111 B3
Halkyn 48 B4
Hall 80 D6
Halland 13 C5
Hallaton 41 E5
Hallatrow 21 A5
Hallbankgate 69 D4
Hallcrofts 75 D7
Hall Dunnerdale 61 B5
Hallen 20 E3
Hall Green 40 D6
Hallin 99 B6
Halling 14 C2
Hallington Lincs 53 B3
Hallington Northld 70 C1
Hall of the Forest 38 B6

Halloughton 51 C5
Hallow 29 C2
Hallow Heath 29 C2
Hallrule 76 B4
Halls 83 B5
Hallsands 5 D7
Hall's Green 32 D6
Hall's Tenement 69 D4
Halltoft End 53 B7
Hallworthy 4 B2
Halmer End 49 B7
Halmore 29 A7
Halmyre Mains 75 B1
Halnaker 12 B6
Halsall 54 C6
Halse Northants 31 A3
Halse Som 8 C1
Halsetown 2 C5
Halsham 59 C5
Halsinger 6 E3
Halstead Esx 34 C5
Halstead Kent 24 E6
Halstead Leics 41 E4
Halstock 9 B3
Haltham 53 A5
Halton Bucks 31 D6
Halton Ches 48 E3
Halton Clwyd 38 C1
Halton Lancs 54 E1
Halton Northld 70 D2
Halton East 56 D2
Halton Gill 62 D7
Halton Holegate 53 C5
Halton Lea Gate 69 E4
Halton West 55 C2
Haltwhistle 70 A2
Halvergate 45 D5
Halwell 5 C5
Halwill 6 D7
Ham Dors 9 E2
Ham GL 24 B5
Ham Glos 21 A1
Ham Kent 15 D3
Ham Som 8 D1
Ham Wilts 22 C5
Hamble 11 A4
Hambleden 23 B3
Hambledon Hants 11 C3
Hambledon Sry 12 B3
Hambleton Lancs 54 C3
Hambleton N Yorks 57 D4
Hambleton Mosside 54 C3
Hambridge 8 E1
Hambrook Avn 21 A3
Hambrook W Ssx 11 D4
Hameringham 53 B5
Hamerton 32 C1
Hametoun 115 b1
Ham Green Avn 20 E3
Ham Green H & W 30 A1
Ham Hill 14 C2
Hamilton 81 B6
Hamlet 3 A2
Hammerpot 12 C6
Hammersmith 24 C5
Hammerwich 40 C4
Hammerwood 13 B3
Hammond Street 24 D2
Hammoon 9 E2
Hamnavoe Shet 115 C4
Hamnavoe Shet 114 D4
Hamnavoe Shet 114 B4
Hamnavoe Shet 114 D5
Hampden Park 13 D6
Hampden Row 31 D7
Hampnett 30 A6
Hampole 57 D6
Hampreston 10 B5
Hampstead GL 24 C4
Hampstead Nflk 45 A2
Hampstead Norris 22 E4
Hampsthwaite 57 A2
Hampton GL 24 B6
Hampton Gloucs 30 A7
Hampton Salop 39 B6
Hampton Bishop 28 E4
Hampton Heath 48 D7
Hampton in Arden 40 E6
Hampton Lovett 29 C1
Hampton Lucy 30 C2
Hampton on the Hill 30 C1
Hampton Poyle 31 A6
Hamptworth 10 D3
Hamsey 13 B5
Hamstall Ridware 40 D3
Hamstead IOW 10 E5
Hamstead W Mids 40 C5

Hamstead Marshall 22 D5
Hamsterley Dur 70 E5
Hamsterley Dur 70 E3
Hamstreet Kent 15 A5
Ham Street Som 20 E7
Hamworthy 10 A5
Hanbury H & W 29 D1
Hanbury Staffs 40 D2
Hanbury Woodend 40 D2
Hanchurch 49 C7
Handbridge 48 D5
Handcross 12 E3
Handforth 49 C3
Handley 48 D6
Handsacre 40 C3
Handsworth S Yorks 51 A2
Handsworth W Mids 40 C5
Hanford 49 C7
Hanging Bridge 50 C6
Hanging Langford 10 B1
Hangingshaw 75 B7
Hangleton 12 E6
Hanham 21 A3
Hankelow 49 A7
Hankerton 21 D1
Hankham 13 D6
Hanley 49 C7
Hanley Castle 29 C3
Hanley Childe 29 A1
Hanley Swan 29 C3
Hanley William 29 A1
Hanlith 55 D1
Hanmer 48 D7
Hannah 53 D4
Hannington Hants 22 E6
Hannington Northants 42 B7
Hannington Wilts 22 A2
Hannington Wick 22 A2
Hanslope 31 D3
Hanthorpe 42 D2
Hanwell GL 12 D3
Hanwell Oxon 30 E3
Hanworth GL 24 B5
Hanworth Nflk 45 A2
Happisburgh 45 C2
Happisburgh Common 45 C3
Hapsford 48 D4
Hapton Lancs 55 B4
Hapton Nflk 45 A6
Harberton 5 C5
Harbertonford 5 C5
Harbledown 15 B3
Harborne 40 C6
Harborough Magna 41 B7
Harbottle 77 A5
Harbourneford 5 C4
Harbridge 10 C3
Harbury 30 D2
Harby Leics 51 D7
Harby Notts 52 B4
Harcombe 8 C4
Harden 56 D4
Hardenhuish 21 D3
Hardham 12 C5
Hardingham 44 E5
Hardingstone 31 C2
Hardings Wood 49 C6
Hardington 21 B5
Hardington Mandeville 9 B2
Hardington Marsh 9 B3
Hardley 11 A4
Hardley Street 45 C5
Hardmead 31 E3
Hardraw 62 D5
Hardstoft 51 A4
Hardway Hants 11 C4
Hardway Som 21 B7
Hardwick Bucks 31 D6
Hardwick Cambs 32 E3
Hardwick Nflk 45 B6
Hardwick Northants 31 D1
Hardwick Oxon 30 D7
Hardwick Oxon 31 A5
Hardwicke Glos 29 D5
Hardwicke Glos 29 B6
Hardwicke H & W 28 B3
Hardy's Green 34 D6
Hareby 53 B5
Hareden 53 A2
Harefield 23 E2
Hare Hatch 23 C4
Harehills 57 B4
Harelaw 74 E1

Haresceugh 69 E5
Harescombe 29 C6
Haresfield 29 C6
Hareshaw 74 B1
Hare Street Beds 32 E6
Hare Street Herts 32 E6
Harewood Devon 4 E4
Harewood W Yorks 57 B3
Harewood End 28 E5
Hargate 45 A6
Hargham 44 E6
Hargrave Ches 48 D5
Hargrave Northants 32 B1
Hargrave Sflk 33 D3
Hargrave Green 33 D3
Haringey 24 D3
Harker 69 B3
Harkstead 35 A5
Harlaston 40 E3
Harlaxton 42 B1
Harlech 46 E7
Harlesden 24 C4
Harleston Nflk 45 B7
Harleston Sflk 34 E2
Harlestone 31 C1
Harle Syke 55 C4
Harley 38 E4
Harlington 32 B5
Harlosh 99 B7
Harlow 33 A7
Harlow Hill 70 D2
Harlthorpe 58 C4
Harlton 32 E3
Harman's Cross 10 A6
Harmby 63 B6
Harmer Green 32 D7
Harmer Hill 38 D2
Harmondsworth 23 E4
Harmston 52 C5
Harnham 10 C2
Harnhill 30 A7
Harold Hill 24 F3
Haroldston West 16 B4
Haroldswick 114 F1
Harold Wood 25 A3
Harome 64 D5
Harpenden 32 C7
Harpford 8 B4
Harpham 65 C7
Harpley H & W 29 A1
Harpley Nflk 44 B3
Harpole 31 B1
Harprigg 62 B6
Harpsdale 111 B3
Harpsden 23 B3
Harpswell 52 C3
Harpurhey 49 C1
Harpur Hill 50 B3
Harrapool 92 D2
Harrier 115 b1
Harrietfield 88 A6
Harrietsham 14 D3
Harrington Lincs 53 B4
Harrington Northants 41 E6
Harringworth 42 C5
Harris 92 A5
Harriseahead 49 C6
Harrogate 57 B2
Harrold 31 E2
Harrow GL 24 B4
Harrow Hghld 111 C1
Harrowbarrow 4 D4
Harrowden 32 B4
Harrow on the Hill 24 B4
Harston Cambs 33 A3
Harston Leics 42 B1
Hart 71 C5
Hartburn Clev 64 B2
Hartburn Northld 77 B7
Hartest 34 C3
Hartfield E Ssx 13 B3
Hartfield Hghld 100 E3
Hartfield Strath 80 B3
Hartford Cambs 32 D1
Hartford Ches 49 A4
Hartfordbridge 23 B6
Hartford End 33 C7
Harthill Ches 48 D6
Harthill Loth 81 D5
Harthill S Yorks 51 A2
Hartington 50 C4
Hartland 6 B4
Hartlebury 40 A7
Hartlepool 71 D5

Hartley Cumb 62 C4
Hartley Kent 25 B6
Hartley Kent 25 E3
Hartley Northld 71 B1
Hartley Wespall 23 A6
Hartley Wintney 23 B6
Hartlip 14 D2
Harton N Yorks 64 E7
Harton Salop 38 D6
Harton T & W 71 B2
Hartpury 29 B5
Hartrigge 76 C3
Hartshill 41 A5
Hart's Hill 40 B6
Hartshorne 41 A2
Hartsop 61 D2
Hartwell Bucks 31 C6
Hartwell Esx 13 B3
Hartwell Northants 31 C2
Harvel 25 B6
Harvington H & W 30 A3
Harvington H & W 40 A7
Harvington Cross 30 A3
Harwell 22 D3
Harwich 35 B5
Harwood Dur 70 B5
Harwood GM 55 B6
Harwood Dale 65 B4
Harwood on Teviot 76 A5
Harworth 51 C1
Hasbury 40 B6
Hascombe 12 C3
Haselbech 41 E7
Haselbury Plucknett 9 A2
Haseley 30 C1
Haselor 30 B2
Hasfield 29 C5
Hasguard 16 B5
Haskayne 48 C1
Hasketon 35 B3
Hasland 50 E4
Haslemere 12 B3
Haslingden 55 B5
Haslingden Grane 55 B5
Haslingfield 33 A3
Haslington 49 B6
Hassall 49 B6
Hassall Green 49 B6
Hassell Street 15 A4
Hassendean 76 B3
Hassingham 45 C5
Hassocks 13 A5
Hassop 50 D3
Haster 111 D3
Hastigrow 111 C2
Hastingleigh 15 A4
Hastings 13 E6
Hastingwood 24 E2
Hastoe 23 D1
Haswell 71 B4
Hatch Beds 32 C4
Hatch Hants 23 A6
Hatch Wilts 10 A2
Hatch Beauchamp 8 E1
Hatch End 24 B3
Hatching Green 32 C7
Hatchmere 48 E4
Hatcliffe 59 C7
Hatfield H & W 28 E2
Hatfield Herts 24 C2
Hatfield S Yorks 57 E7
Hatfield Broad Oak 33 B7
Hatfield Heath 33 B7
Hatfield Hyde 32 D7
Hatfield Peverel 33 D7
Hatfield Woodhouse 57 E7
Hatford 22 C2
Hatherden 22 C6
Hatherleigh 6 E6
Hathern 41 C2
Hatherop 30 B7
Hathersage 50 D2
Hatherton Ches 49 A7
Hatherton Staffs 40 B3
Hatley St George 32 D3
Hatt 4 D4
Hattingley 11 C1
Hatton Ches 48 E3
Hatton Derbs 50 D7
Hatton GL 24 B5
Hatton Gramp 105 D5
Hatton Lincs 52 E4
Hatton Salop 38 D5
Hatton Warks 30 C1
Hattoncrook 105 B6
Hatton Heath 48 D5
Hatton of Fintray 97 D2

Haugham 53 B3
Haughhead 81 A4
Haugh Head 77 B3
Haughley 34 E2
Haughley Green 34 E2
Haughley New Street 34 E2
Haugh of Glass 104 C5
Haugh of Urr 68 B3
Haughs 104 D4
Haughton Notts 51 C3
Haughton Salop 39 A5
Haughton Salop 38 E3
Haughton Salop 38 C2
Haughton Staffs 40 A2
Haughton Green 49 D2
Haughton Le Skerne 63 D3
Haughton Moss 48 E6
Haultwick 32 E6
Haun 90 D4
Haunton 40 E3
Hauxley 77 D5
Hauxton 33 A3
Havant 11 D4
Haven 28 D2
Haven Side 59 D5
Havenstreet 11 B5
Haverfordwest 16 C4
Haverhill 33 C4
Haverigg 61 A6
Havering 25 A4
Havering-atte-Bower 24 F3
Haversham 31 D3
Haverthwaite 61 C5
Haverton Hill 64 B1
Hawarden 48 C5
Hawbridge 29 D3
Hawcoat 61 B6
Hawen 26 C6
Hawes 62 D6
Hawford 29 C2
Hawick 76 B4
Hawkchurch 8 E3
Hawkedon 33 D3
Hawkenbury 15 A3
Hawkeridge 21 C5
Hawkerland 8 B5
Hawkesbury 21 B2
Hawkesbury Upton 21 B2
Hawkes End 40 E6
Hawkhill 77 D4
Hawkhillock 105 C5
Hawkhurst 13 E3
Hawkinge 15 C5
Hawkley 11 D2
Hawkridge 7 C3
Hawkshead 61 C5
Hawksland 74 D2
Hawkswick 62 E7
Hawksworth Notts 51 D6
Hawksworth W Yorks 56 E3
Hawkwell Esx 25 D3
Hawkwell Northld 70 D1
Hawley Hants 23 C6
Hawley Kent 25 A5
Hawling 30 A5
Hawnby 64 C5
Haworth 56 D4
Hawsker 65 B3
Hawstead 34 C3
Hawthorn Dur 71 C4
Hawthorn Wilts 21 C4
Hawthorn Hill Berks 23 C4
Hawthorn Hill Lincs 53 A6
Hawthorpe 42 D2
Hawton 51 D5
Haxby 57 E2
Haxey 51 D1
Haxted 13 B2
Haydock 48 E2
Haydon 9 C2
Haydon Bridge 70 B2
Haydon Wick 22 A3
Haye 4 D3
Hayes GL 23 E3
Hayes GL 24 E6
Hayfield Derbs 50 B2
Hayfield Hghld 86 B6
Hayfield Hghld 111 B2
Hayhillock 89 B4
Haylands 11 B5
Hayle 2 C5
Hay Mills 40 D6
Haynes 32 B4
Hay-on-Wye 28 B3
Hayscastle 16 B3

Hayscastle Cross 16 C3
Hay Street 32 E6
Hayton Cumb 69 D4
Hayton Cumb 68 E5
Hayton Humb 58 D3
Hayton Notts 51 D2
Hayton's Bent 38 E6
Haytor Vale 5 C3
Haywards Heath 13 A4
Haywood Oaks 51 C5
Hazelbank Hghld 79 E1
Hazelbank Strath 74 D1
Hazelbury Bryan 9 D3
Hazeleigh 25 D2
Hazelend 33 A6
Hazeley 23 B6
Hazelfield 67 D6
Hazel Grove 49 D3
Hazelhead 97 D3
Hazelside 74 D3
Hazelslade 40 C3
Hazelton Walls 88 E6
Hazelwood 50 E6
Hazlemere 23 C2
Hazlerigg 71 A1
Hazleton 30 A6
Heacham 44 A2
Headbourne Worthy 11 A1
Head Bridge 7 A5
Headcorn 14 D4
Headington 31 A7
Headlam 63 B3
Headless Cross 30 A1
Headley Hants 11 E1
Headley Hants 22 E5
Headley Sry 12 E1
Headon 51 D3
Heads Nook 69 C4
Heage 50 E5
Healaugh N Yorks 63 A5
Healaugh N Yorks 57 C3
Heald Green 49 C3
Heale 7 A2
Healey GM 55 C6
Healey Northld 70 D3
Healey N Yorks 63 B6
Healeyfield 70 D4
Healing 59 C6
Heamoor 2 B5
Heanish 84 B4
Heanor 51 A6
Heanton Punchardon 6 E3
Heanton Satchville 6 E5
Heapey 55 A5
Heapham 52 B3
Hearthstane 75 B3
Heasley Mill 7 B3
Heaste 92 D3
Heath 51 A4
Heath, The 34 D4
Heath and Reach 31 E5
Heathcot 97 D3
Heathcote Derbs 50 C4
Heathcote Salop 39 A2
Heath End Hants 23 C6
Heath End Hants 22 E5
Heather 41 A3
Heathfield Devon 5 D3
Heathfield E Ssx 15 A4
Heathfield Som 8 C1
Heath Hayes 40 C3
Heath Hill 39 B3
Heath House 20 D6
Heathton 40 A5
Heath Town 40 B5
Heatley 49 A3
Heaton Lancs 54 D1
Heaton Staffs 49 D5
Heaton T & W 71 A2
Heaton Moor 49 C2
Heaverham 15 A1
Heaviley 49 D3
Hebburn 71 B2
Hebden 56 D1
Hebden Bridge 55 D5
Hebden Green 49 A5
Hebing End 32 E6
Hebron Dyfed 16 E3
Hebron Northld 77 C7
Heck 75 A7
Heckfield 23 B5
Heckfield Green 35 A1
Heckfordbridge 34 D6
Heckingham 45 C6
Heckington 52 E7
Heckmondwike 57 A5
Heddington 21 D4

Heddle 112 C5
Heddon-on-the-Wall 70 E2
Hedenham 45 C6
Hedge End 11 A3
Hedgerley 23 D3
Hedging 8 E1
Hedley on the Hill 70 D3
Hednesford 40 C3
Hedon 59 B5
Heeley 50 E2
Heglibister 115 C2
Heighington Dur 71 A6
Heighington Lincs 52 D5
Heilam 109 B3
Heithat 75 B7
Heiton 76 D2
Hele Devon 6 E2
Hele Devon 7 D6
Hele Bridge 6 E6
Helebridge 6 B6
Hele Lane 7 B5
Helensburgh 80 B3
Helford 2 E6
Helhoughton 44 C3
Helions Bumpstead 33 C4
Helland 4 A3
Hellesdon 45 A4
Hellidon 31 A2
Hellifield 55 C2
Hellingly 15 A5
Hellington 45 C5
Hellister 115 C3
Helmdon 31 A3
Helmingham 35 A3
Helmsdale 111 A7
Helmshore 55 B5
Helmsley 64 D5
Helperby 57 C1
Helperthorpe 65 B6
Helpringham 52 E7
Helpston 42 E4
Helsby 48 D4
Helston 2 D6
Helstone 4 A2
Helton 69 D7
Helwith 63 A4
Helwith Bridge 55 C1
Hemblington 45 C4
Hemborough Post 5 D5
Hemel Hempstead 23 E1
Hemingbrough 57 E4
Hemingby 53 A4
Hemingford Abbots 32 D1
Hemingford Grey 32 D1
Hemingstone 35 A3
Hemington Leics 41 B2
Hemington Northants 42 D6
Hemington Som 21 B5
Hemley 35 B4
Hemlington 64 B2
Hempholme 59 A2
Hempnall 45 B6
Hempnall Green 45 B6
Hempriggs 103 E5
Hempriggs House 111 D4
Hempstead Esx 33 C5
Hempstead Nflk 45 D3
Hempstead Nflk 45 A2
Hempsted Glos 29 C6
Hempton Nflk 44 D3
Hempton Oxon 30 E4
Hemsby 45 D4
Hemswell 52 C2
Hemsworth 57 C6
Hemyock 8 C2
Henbury Avn 20 E3
Henbury Ches 49 C4
Henderland 68 B2
Hendersyde Park 76 D2
Hendon GL 24 C4
Hendon T & W 71 C3
Hendy 17 D5
Heneglwys 46 D3
Henfield 12 E5
Henford 6 C7
Hengherst 14 E5
Hengoed M Glam 19 B4
Hengoed Pwys 28 B2
Hengoed Salop 38 B1
Hengrave 34 C2
Henham 33 B6
Heniarth 38 A4
Henlade 8 D1
Henley Salop 38 E7
Henley Sflk 35 A3

Henley Som 20 D7
Henley W Ssx 11 E2
Henley Corner 20 D7
Henley-in-Arden 30 B1
Henley on Thames 23 B3
Henley Park 12 B1
Henley's Down 13 E5
Henllan Clwyd 47 E4
Henllan Dyfed 26 C6
Henllan Amgoed 16 E3
Henllys Dyfed 27 B7
Henllys S Glam 19 C4
Henlow 32 C5
Hennock 5 D2
Henny Street 34 C5
Henryd 47 B3
Hensall 57 D5
Henshaw 70 A2
Hensingham 60 D2
Henstead 45 D7
Hensting 11 A2
Henstridge 9 D2
Henstridge Marsh 9 D1
Henton Oxon 31 C7
Henton Som 20 D6
Henwick 29 C2
Henwood 4 C3
Heogan 115 D3
Heol-ddu 17 D4
Heol-llygoden 28 A5
Heol Senni 18 E1
Heol-y-Cyw 18 E5
Hepburn 77 B3
Hepple 77 B6
Hepscott 77 D7
Heptonstall 55 D5
Hepworth Sflk 34 D1
Hepworth W Yorks 56 E7
Herbrandston 16 B5
Herdicott 6 C7
Hereford 28 E3
Hergest 28 B2
Heriot 82 D7
Hermitage Bdrs 76 B6
Hermitage Berks 22 E4
Hermitage D & G 68 B3
Hermitage Dors 9 C3
Hermitage Hants 11 D4
Hermitage, The 12 E1
Hermon Dyfed 17 B2
Hermon Dyfed 17 A2
Hermon Gynd 46 C4
Herne 15 B2
Herne Bay 15 B2
Herner 6 E4
Hernhill 15 A2
Herodsfoot 4 C4
Herongate 25 B3
Heronsgate 23 E2
Herriard 23 A7
Herringfleet 45 D6
Herrings Green 32 B4
Herringswell 33 D1
Herrington 71 B3
Hersden 15 B2
Hersham 24 B6
Herstmonceux 13 D5
Herston Dors 10 B7
Herston Hghld 113 D2
Hertford 32 E7
Hertford Heath 32 E7
Hertingfordbury 32 E7
Hesketh Bank 54 D5
Hesketh Lane 55 A3
Hesket Newmarket 69 B6
Heskin Green 54 E6
Hesleden 71 C5
Hesleyside 76 E7
Heslington 57 E2
Hessay 57 D2
Hessenford 4 D5
Hessett 34 D2
Hessle 59 A5
Hest Bank 54 D1
Heston 24 B5
Heswall 48 B3
Hethe 31 A5
Hetherington 70 B1
Hethersett 45 A5
Hethersgill 69 C3
Hethfelton 9 E5
Hethpool 76 E3
Hett 71 A5
Hetton 55 D2
Hetton-le-Hole 71 B4
Heugh 70 D1
Heugh-head Gramp 96 D2

Heugh-head Gramp 97 A4
Heveningham 35 C1
Hever 13 B2
Heversham 61 D5
Hevingham 45 B3
Hewas Water 3 B4
Hewell Grange 30 A1
Hewell Lane 29 D1
Hewelsfield 28 E7
Hewelsfield Common 28 E7
Hewish Avn 20 D4
Hewish Som 9 A3
Hewton 6 E7
Hexham 70 C2
Hextable 24 F5
Hexton 32 C5
Hexworthy 5 B3
Heybridge Esx 25 B3
Heybridge Esx 25 D2
Heybridge Basin 25 D2
Heybrook Bay 4 E6
Heydon Cambs 33 A4
Heydon Nflk 45 A3
Heydour 42 D1
Heyford 31 B2
Heylipoll 84 A4
Heylor 114 B4
Heysham 54 D1
Heyshaw 56 E1
Heyshott 11 E3
Heyside 49 D1
Heytesbury 21 D6
Heythrop 30 D5
Heywood GM 55 C6
Heywood Wilts 21 C5
Hibaldstow 58 E7
Hickleton 57 C7
Hickling Nflk 45 D3
Hickling Notts 41 D2
Hickling Broad 45 D3
Hickling Green 45 D3
Hickling Heath 45 D3
Hickstead 12 E4
Hidcote Boyce 30 B3
High Ackworth 57 C6
Higham Derbs 50 E5
Higham Kent 14 C1
Higham Kent 14 C1
Higham Lancs 55 C4
Higham Sflk 33 D2
Higham Sflk 34 E5
Higham Dykes 70 E1
Higham Ferrers 31 E1
Higham Gobion 32 C5
Higham on the Hill 41 A5
Highampton 6 D6
Higham Wood 13 D2
High Balantyre 86 B7
High Beach 24 E3
High Bentham 55 A1
High Bickington 6 E4
High Birkwith 62 D7
High Blantyre 81 A6
High Borgue 67 C5
High Bray 7 A3
Highbridge 20 C6
Highbrook 13 A3
High Brooms 15 A2
High Bullen 6 E4
Highburton 56 E6
High Burton 63 C6
Highbury 21 A6
Highbury Vale 51 B6
High Buston 77 D5
High Callerton 70 E1
High Catton 58 C2
Highclere 22 D5
Highclere Castle 22 D6
Highcliffe 10 D5
High Cogges 30 D7
High Coniscliffe 63 C3
High Cross Hants 11 D2
High Cross Herts 32 E7
High Cross Bank 41 A3
High Easter 33 C7
High Ellington 63 B6
High Entercommon 63 D4
Higher Ansty 9 D3
Higher Ashton 5 D2
Higher Ballam 54 C4
Higher Brixham 5 E5
High Ercall 38 E3
Higher Grange 38 C1
Higher Green 49 B1
Higher Kingcombe 9 B4
Higher Penwortham 54 E5

Higher Tale 4 E3
Higher Town 2 b2
Higher Walreddon 4 E3
Higher Walton Ches 48 E3
Higher Walton Lancs 54 E5
Higher Whitley 49 A3
Higher Wych 48 D7
High Etherley 70 E6
Highfield Humb 58 C4
Highfield Strath 80 C6
Highfield T & W 70 E3
Highfields 32 E3
High Garrett 33 D6
High Gate 55 D5
High Grange 70 E5
High Grantley 57 A1
High Green H & W 29 C3
High Green Nflk 45 A5
High Green S Yorks 50 E1
Highgreen Manor 76 E6
High Halden 14 E5
High Halstow 14 C1
High Ham 20 D7
High Harrington 68 D7
High Harrogate 57 B2
High Hartington 77 B7
High Hatton 39 A2
High Hawsker 65 B3
High Heath 39 A2
High Hesket 69 C5
High Hoyland 57 A6
High Hunsley 58 E4
High Hurstwood 13 B4
High Hutton 64 E7
High Ireby 69 A6
High Kilburn 64 C6
High Kilphin 66 C2
High Lane 51 A6
Highlane Ches 49 C5
Highlane Derbs 51 A2
High Lane H & W 29 A1
High Laver 24 F2
Highlaws 68 E5
Highleadon 29 B5
High Legh 49 A3
Highleigh 11 E5
High Leven 64 B2
Highley 39 B6
High Littleton 21 A5
High Lorton 68 E7
Highmead 26 E6
High Melton 57 D7
Highmoor Cross 23 B3
Highmoor Hill 20 D2
Highnam 29 B6
High Newton 61 D5
High Newton-by-the-Sea 77 D3
High Nibthwaite 61 B5
High Offley 39 B2
High Ongar 24 F2
High Onn 40 A3
High Risby 58 E6
High Roding 33 C7
High Salvington 12 D6
High Shaw 62 D5
High Spen 70 E3
Highstead 15 C2
Highsted 14 E2
High Street Corn 3 B3
High Street Kent 13 E3
High Street Sflk 35 D3
High Street Green 34 E3
Highstreet Green Esx 33 D5
Highstreet Green Herts 23 E1
Hightae 68 D2
High Throston 71 C5
Hightown Ches 49 C5
Hightown Mers 48 B1
High Toynton 53 A5
High Trewhitt 77 B5
Highway 21 E3
Highweek 5 D3
Highwood 25 B2
Highworth 22 B2
High Wray 61 C5
High Wych 33 A7
High Wycombe 23 C2
Hilborough 44 C5
Hilcott 22 A6
Hildenborough 15 A2
Hildersham 33 B4
Hilderstone 40 B1
Hilderthorpe 65 D7

Hilfield 9 C3
Hilgay 44 A6
Hill 21 A1
Hill, The 57 D5
Hillam 57 D5
Hillbeck 62 C3
Hillberry 60 c4
Hillborough Kent 15 C2
Hillbrae Gramp 104 E4
Hillbrae Gramp 105 A6
Hillbrae Gramp 105 B5
Hill Brow 11 D2
Hill Chorlton 39 B1
Hill Dyke 53 B7
Hill End Dur 70 D5
Hill End Fife 81 E2
Hillend Fife 82 B4
Hillend Gramp 104 C4
Hillend Loth 82 C6
Hill End N Yorks 56 D2
Hillesden 31 B5
Hillesley 21 B2
Hillfarrance 8 C1
Hill Head 11 B4
Hillhead Devon 11 B4
Hillhead of Auchentumb
  105 C3
Hillhead of Cocklaw
  105 D4
Hilliard's Cross 40 D3
Hilliclay 111 B2
Hillingdon 23 E3
Hillington 44 B3
Hillmorton 41 C7
Hillockhead Gramp 96 D3
Hillockhead Gramp 96 E2
Hill of Beath 82 B3
Hill of Fearn 103 B4
Hill of Maud Crofts 104 C2
Hillowton 67 D4
Hillpound 11 B3
Hill Ridware 40 C3
Hill Row 33 A1
Hillsford Bridge 7 B2
Hillside Gramp 97 E4
Hillside Gramp 103 E5
Hillside Shet 115 D1
Hillside Tays 89 D2
Hills Town 51 A4
Hillswick 114 B5
Hill Top Hants 11 A4
Hill Top W Yorks 57 B6
Hill Top Oxnop Ghyll 62 E5
Hill View 10 A5
Hillway 11 C6
Hillwell 115 C6
Hilmarton 21 E3
Hilperton 21 C5
Hilsea 11 C4
Hilton Cambs 32 D2
Hilton Clev 64 B2
Hilton Cumb 70 A6
Hilton Derbs 50 D7
Hilton Dors 9 D3
Hilton Dur 70 E6
Hilton Gramp 105 C5
Hilton Hghld 103 C3
Hilton Salop 39 B5
Hilton of Cadboll 103 B4
Hilton of Delnies 103 B6
Himbleton 29 D2
Himley 40 A5
Hincaster 61 E5
Hinckley 41 B5
Hinderclay 34 E1
Hinderwell 64 E2
Hindford 38 C1
Hindhead 11 E1
Hindley 49 A1
Hindley Green 49 A1
Hindlip 29 C2
Hindolveston 44 E3
Hindon 10 A1
Hindringham 44 D2
Hingham 44 E5
Hinstock 39 A2
Hintlesham 34 E4
Hinton Avn 21 B3
Hinton H & W 28 C4
Hinton Hants 10 D5
Hinton Northants 31 A2
Hinton Salop 38 D4
Hinton Admiral 10 D5
Hinton Ampner 11 B2
Hinton Blewett 20 E5
Hinton-in-the-Hedges
  31 A4

Hinton Marsh 11 B2
Hinton Martell 10 B4
Hinton on the Green 30 A3
Hinton Parva 22 B3
Hinton St George 9 A2
Hinton St Mary 9 D2
Hinton Waldrist 22 C2
Hints Salop 39 A7
Hints Staffs 40 D4
Hinwick 31 E1
Hinxhill 15 A4
Hinxton 33 A4
Hinxworth 32 D4
Hipperholme 56 E5
Hirn 97 C3
Hirnant 37 E3
Hirst 77 D7
Hirst Courtney 57 E5
Hirwaen 48 A5
Hirwaun 18 E3
Hiscott 6 E4
Histon 33 A2
Hitcham Bucks 23 D3
Hitcham Sflk 34 D3
Hitchin 32 C6
Hither Green 24 D5
Hittisleigh 7 B7
Hixon 40 C2
Hoaden 15 C3
Hoaldalbert 28 C5
Hoar Cross 40 D2
Hoarwithy 28 E5
Hoath 15 C2
Hobarris 38 C7
Hobbister 113 C1
Hobbs Lots Bridge 43 B4
Hobkirk 76 B4
Hobland Hall 45 E5
Hobson 70 E3
Hoby 41 D3
Hockering 44 E4
Hockerton 51 D5
Hockley 25 D3
Hockley Heath 40 D7
Hockliffe 31 E5
Hockwold cum Wilton
  44 B7
Hockworthy 8 B2
Hoddesdon 24 C2
Hoddlesden 55 B5
Hodgeston 16 D6
Hodnet 39 A2
Hodthorpe 51 B3
Hoe 44 D4
Hoe Gate 11 C3
Hoff 62 B3
Hoffleet Stow 43 A1
Hoggeston 31 D5
Hoggie 104 D2
Hoghton 55 A5
Hognaston 50 D5
Hogsthorpe 53 D4
Holbeach 43 B2
Holbeach Bank 43 B2
Holbeach Clough 43 B2
Holbeach Drove 43 B3
Holbeach Hurn 43 B2
Holbeach St Johns 43 B3
Holbeach St Marks 43 B1
Holbeach St Matthew
  43 C1
Holbeck 51 B3
Holberrow Green 30 A2
Holbeton 5 B5
Holborn 24 D4
Holborough 14 C2
Holbrook Derbs 50 E6
Holbrook Sflk 35 A5
Holburn 77 B2
Holbury 11 A4
Holcombe Devon 8 A6
Holcombe Som 21 A6
Holcombe Rogus 8 B2
Holcot 31 C1
Holden 55 B3
Holdenby 31 B1
Holdenhurst 10 C5
Holdgate 38 E6
Holdingham 52 D7
Holditch 8 E3
Hole-in-the-Wall 29 A5
Hole Park 14 D5
Hole Street 12 D5
Holford 20 A6
Holgate 63 A4
Holker 61 C6
Holkham 44 C1

Hollacombe 6 C6
Holland Ork 112 D1
Holland Ork 112 F4
Holland Sry 13 B1
Holland-on-Sea 35 B7
Hollandstoun 112 G1
Hollee 69 A3
Hollesley 35 C4
Hollingbourne 14 D3
Hollingbury 13 A6
Hollington Derbs 50 D7
Hollington E Ssx 13 E5
Hollington Staffs 50 B7
Hollingworth 50 B1
Hollins 49 C1
Hollinsclough 50 B4
Hollins Green 49 A2
Hollinswood 39 A4
Hollinwood 38 E1
Hollocombe 7 A5
Holloway 50 E5
Hollowell 41 D7
Hollybush Gwent 19 B3
Hollybush H & W 29 B4
Holly End 43 C4
Holly Green 29 C3
Hollym 59 D5
Holm D & G 74 D6
Holm D & G 75 C6
Holmbury St Mary 12 D2
Holmbush Corn 3 C3
Holmbush W Ssx 12 E3
Holme Cambs 42 E6
Holme Cumb 61 E6
Holme D & G 67 C3
Holme Notts 52 B6
Holme W Yorks 56 E7
Holme Chapel 55 C5
Holme Hale 44 C5
Holme Lacy 28 E4
Holme Marsh 28 C2
Holme next the Sea 44 B1
Holme-on-Spalding-Moor
  58 D4
Holme on the Wolds 58 E3
Holme Pierrepoint 51 C7
Holmer 28 E3
Holmer Green 23 D2
Holme Rose 103 B7
Holmes Chapel 49 B5
Holmesfield 50 E3
Holmes Hill 13 C5
Holmeswood 54 D6
Holmewood 51 A4
Holmfield 56 D5
Holmfirth 56 E7
Holmhead D & G 67 D2
Holmhead Strath 73 E5
Holmpton 59 D5
Holmrook 60 E4
Holmsey Green 33 C1
Holmsgarth 115 D3
Holmside 71 A4
Holmston 73 C5
Holne 5 C4
Holnest 9 C3
Holsworthy 6 C6
Holsworthy Beacon 6 C6
Holt Clwyd 48 D6
Holt Dors 10 B4
Holt H & W 29 C1
Holt Nflk 44 E2
Holt Wilts 21 C4
Holtby 57 E2
Holt End H & W 30 A1
Holt End Hants 11 C1
Holt Fleet 29 C1
Holt Heath Dors 10 B4
Holt Heath H & W 29 C1
Holton Lincs 52 E3
Holton Oxon 31 B7
Holton Sflk 35 D1
Holton Som 9 C1
Holton Heath 10 A5
Holton le Clay 59 C7
Holton le Moor 52 D2
Holton St Mary 34 E5
Holtspur 23 D3
Holtye Common 13 B3
Holwell Dors 9 D3
Holwell Herts 32 C5
Holwell Leics 41 E2
Holwell Oxon 30 C7
Holwick 70 C6
Holworth 9 D5
Holybourne 23 B7
Holy Cross 40 B7

Holyhead 46 B2
Holymoorside 50 E4
Holyport 23 C4
Holystone 77 A5
Holytown 81 B5
Holywell Cambs 32 E1
Holywell Clwyd 48 A4
Holywell Corn 2 E3
Holywell Dors 9 B3
Holywell E Ssx 13 D7
Holywell Green 56 D6
Holywell Lake 8 C1
Holywell Row 33 D1
Holywood D & G 74 E7
Homer 39 A4
Homersfield 45 B7
Hom Green 28 E5
Homington 10 C2
Honeyborough 16 C5
Honeybourne 30 B3
Honeychurch 7 A6
Honey Hill 15 B2
Honey Tye 34 D5
Honiley 40 E7
Honing 45 C3
Honingham 45 A4
Honington Lincs 52 C7
Honington Sflk 34 D1
Honington Warks 30 C3
Honiton 8 C3
Honley 56 E6
Hoo 14 C1
Hooe Devon 5 A5
Hooe E Ssx 13 D6
Hooe Common 13 D5
Hoo Green 35 B3
Hook Dyfed 16 C4
Hook Hants 23 B6
Hook Humb 58 C5
Hook Sry 24 B6
Hook Wilts 21 E2
Hook-a-Gate 38 D4
Hooke 9 B3
Hookgate 39 B1
Hook Green Kent 13 D3
Hook Green Kent 25 B6
Hook Green Kent 25 B5
Hook Norton 30 D4
Hookway 7 C7
Hookwood 12 E2
Hoole 48 D5
Hooley 12 E1
Hooton 48 C4
Hooton Levitt 51 B1
Hooton Pagnell 57 C7
Hooton Roberts 51 A1
Hopcrofts Holt 30 E5
Hope Clwyd 48 C6
Hope Derbs 50 C2
Hope Devon 5 B6
Hope Pwys 38 B4
Hope Salop 38 C4
Hope Bagot 38 E7
Hope Bowdler 38 D5
Hope End Green 33 B6
Hopehouse 75 C4
Hopeman 103 E5
Hope Mansell 29 A6
Hopesay 38 C6
Hope's Green 25 C4
Hope under Dinmore 28 E2
Hopkinstown 19 A4
Hopton Derbs 50 D5
Hopton Nflk 45 E6
Hopton Salop 38 E2
Hopton Sflk 34 D1
Hopton Staffs 40 B2
Hopton Cangeford 38 E6
Hopton Castle 38 C7
Hopton Wafers 39 A7
Hopwas 40 D4
Hopwood 40 C7
Horam 15 A5
Horbling 42 E1
Horbury 57 A6
Horden 71 C4
Horderley 38 D6
Hordle 10 D5
Hordley 38 C1
Horeb Dyfed 17 C5
Horeb Dyfed 26 C6
Horfield 20 E3
Horham 35 B1
Horkesley Heath 34 D6
Horkstow 58 E6
Horley Oxon 30 E3
Horley W Ssx 12 E2

Hornblotton Green 20 E7
Hornby Lancs 54 E1
Hornby N Yorks 63 C5
Hornby N Yorks 63 D4
Horncastle 53 A5
Hornchurch 24 F4
Horncliffe 77 A1
Horndean Bdrs 76 E1
Horndean Hants 11 D3
Horndon 5 A2
Horndon on the Hill 25 B4
Horne 13 A2
Horn Hill 23 E2
Horniehaugh 89 A2
Horning 45 C4
Horninghold 42 B5
Horninglow 40 E2
Horningsea 33 A2
Horningsham 21 C6
Horningtoft 44 D3
Horningtops 4 C4
Hornsby 69 D4
Horns Cross 6 C4
Hornsea 59 C3
Hornsey 24 D4
Hornton 30 D3
Horrabridge 5 A4
Horridge 5 C3
Horringer 34 C2
Horsebridge Devon 4 E3
Horsebridge E Ssx 15 A5
Horsebridge Hants 10 E1
Horse Bridge Staffs 49 D6
Horsebrook 40 A3
Horsehay 39 A4
Horseheath 33 C4
Horsehouse 63 A6
Horsell 12 B1
Horseman's Green 48 D7
Horseway 43 C6
Horsey 45 D3
Horsford 45 A4
Horsforth 57 A4
Horsham H & W 29 B2
Horsham W Ssx 12 D3
Horsham St Faith 45 B4
Horsington Lincs 52 E5
Horsington Som 9 D1
Horsley Derbs 50 E6
Horsley Glos 21 C1
Horsley Northld 70 D2
Horsley Northld 76 E6
Horsley Cross 35 A6
Horsleycross Street 35 A6
Horsleyhill 76 B4
Horsley Woodhouse 50 E6
Horsmonden 13 E2
Horspath 31 A7
Horstead 45 B4
Horsted Keynes 13 A4
Horton Avn 21 B2
Horton Berks 23 E4
Horton Bucks 31 E6
Horton Dors 10 B4
Horton Northants 31 D2
Horton Northld 77 B2
Horton N Yorks 55 C2
Horton Som 8 E2
Horton Staffs 49 D6
Horton W Glam 17 C7
Horton Wilts 21 E4
Horton Common 10 B4
Horton Green 48 D7
Horton Heath 11 A3
Horton in Ribblesdale
  62 D7
Horton Kirby 25 A6
Horwich 55 A6
Horwood 6 E4
Hose 41 E2
Hoses 61 B5
Hosh 87 E6
Hosta 98 B4
Hoswick 115 D5
Hotham 58 D4
Hothfield 14 E4
Hoton 41 C2
Houbie 114 F3
Hough Ches 49 B6
Hougham 52 B7
Hougharry 98 B4
Hough Green 48 D3
Hough-on-the-Hill 52 C7
Horkesley Heath 34 D6
Houghton Cambs 32 D1
Houghton Cumb 69 C4
Houghton Devon 5 B6
Houghton Devon 8 B5

Houghton Dyfed 16 C5
Houghton Hants 10 E1
Houghton W Ssx 12 C5
Houghton Bank 71 A6
Houghton Conquest 32 B4
Houghton-le-Side 71 A6
Houghton le Spring 71 B3
Houghton on the Hill 41 D4
Houghton Regis 32 B6
Houghton St Giles 44 D2
Houlsyke 64 E3
Hound Green 23 B6
Houndslow 76 C1
Houndwood 83 D6
Hounsdown 10 E3
Hounslow 24 B5
Hounslow Green 33 C7
Househill 103 B6
Housetter 114 C4
Houston 80 D5
Houstry 111 B5
Houstry of Dunn 111 C3
Hove 12 E6
Hoveringham 51 C6
Hoveton 45 C4
Hovingham 64 D6
How 69 D4
How Caple 29 A4
Howden 58 C5
Howden-le-Wear 70 E5
Howe Cumb 61 D5
Howe Hghld 111 D2
Howe Nflk 45 B6
Howe N Yorks 63 D6
Howe, The 60 b5
Howe Green 25 C2
Howell 52 E7
How End 32 B4
Howe of Teuchar 105 A4
Howe Street Esx 33 C7
Howe Street Esx 33 C5
Howey 27 E5
Howgate 82 C7
Howgill 56 D2
Howick 77 D4
Howle 39 A2
Howlett End 33 B5
Howley 8 D3
How Man 60 D2
Howmore 90 C2
Hownam 76 D4
Hownam Mains 76 D3
Howpasley 75 D5
Howsgarth 112 F3
Howsham Lincs 59 A7
Howsham N Yorks 64 E7
Howtel 76 E2
Howton 28 D5
Howwood 80 C5
Hoxa 113 D2
Hoxne 35 A1
Hoy 111 C2
Hoylake 48 B3
Hoyland Nether 57 B7
Hoyland Swaine 57 A7
Hubbert's Bridge 53 A7
Huby 57 D1
Hucclecote 29 C6
Hucking 14 D3
Hucknall 51 B6
Huckworthy Bridge 5 A3
Huddersfield 56 E6
Huddington 29 D2
Hudscott 7 A4
Hudswell 63 B4
Huggate 58 D2
Hugglescote 41 B3
Hughenden Valley 23 C2
Hughley 38 E5
Hugh Town 2 b2
Hugmore 48 C6
Huish Devon 6 E5
Huish Wilts 22 A5
Huish Champflower 8 B1
Huish Episcopi 9 A1
Hulcott 31 D6
Hulland 50 D6
Hullavington 21 C2
Hullbridge 25 D3
Hulme End 50 C5
Hulme Walfield 49 C5
Hulver Street 45 D7
Humber Court 28 E2
Humberston 59 D7
Humberstone 41 D4
Humbie 82 E6

Humbleton *Humb* 59 C4
Humbleton *Northld* 77 A3
Humby 42 D1
Hume 76 D1
Humehall 76 D1
Humshaugh 70 C1
Huna 111 D1
Huncoat 55 B4
Huncote 41 C5
Hundalee 76 C4
Hunderthwaite 70 C6
Hundleby 53 B5
Hundleton 16 C5
Hundon 33 D4
Hundred, The 11 B3
Hundred Acres 11 B3
Hundred End 54 D5
Hungarton 41 D4
Hungerford *Berks* 22 C5
Hungerford *Hants* 10 C3
Hungerford Newtown
  22 C4
Hunglader 99 C4
Hunmanby 65 C6
Hunningham 30 D1
Hunny Hill 11 A6
Hunsdon 33 A4
Hunsingore 57 C2
Hunsonby 69 D6
Hunspow 111 C1
Hunstanton 44 A1
Hunstanworth 70 C4
Hunston *Sflk* 34 D2
Hunston *W Ssx* 11 E4
Hunstrete 21 A4
Hunt End 30 A1
Hunter's Quay 80 A4
Hunterston 80 A6
Huntford 76 C5
Hunt House 65 A4
Huntingdon 32 D1
Huntingfield 35 C1
Huntingford 21 C7
Huntington *H & W* 28 B2
Huntington *N Yorks* 57 E2
Huntington *Staffs* 40 B3
Huntingtower 88 B6
Huntley 29 B6
Huntly 104 D5
Huntlywood 76 C1
Hunton *Hants* 11 A1
Hunton *Kent* 13 E2
Hunton *N Yorks* 63 B5
Huntonbridge 23 E1
Huntsham 8 B1
Huntshaw Cross 6 E4
Huntspill 20 C6
Huntworth 20 C7
Hunwick 70 E5
Hunworth 44 E2
Hurdsfield 49 D4
Hurley *Berks* 23 C3
Hurley *Warks* 40 E5
Hurley Bottom 23 C3
Hurlford 73 D4
Hurliness 113 B3
Hurn 10 C5
Hursley 11 A2
Hurst *Berks* 23 B4
Hurst *GM* 49 D1
Hurst *N Yorks* 63 A4
Hurstbourne Priors 22 D7
Hurstbourne Tarrant 22 C6
Hurst Green *E Ssx* 13 E4
Hurst Green *Lancs* 55 A4
Hurst Green *Sry* 13 A1
Hurstpierpoint 12 E5
Hurstway Common 28 B3
Hurstwood 55 C4
Hurtmore 12 B2
Hurworth-on-Tees 63 D3
Hury 62 E3
Husabost 99 B6
Husbands Bosworth 41 D6
Husborne Crawley 31 E4
Husthwaite 64 C6
Huthwaite 51 A5
Huttoft 53 D4
Hutton *Avn* 20 C5
Hutton *Bdrs* 83 E7
Hutton *Cumb* 69 C7
Hutton *Esx* 25 B3
Hutton *Lancs* 54 D5
Hutton Bonville 63 D4
Hutton Buscel 65 B5
Hutton Conyers 63 D7

Hutton Cranswick 59 A2
Hutton End 69 C6
Hutton Henry 71 C5
Hutton-le-Hole 64 E4
Hutton Magna 63 B3
Hutton Roof *Cumb* 61 E6
Hutton Roof *Cumb* 69 B6
Hutton Rudby 64 B3
Hutton Sessay 64 B6
Hutton Wandesley 57 D2
Huxley 48 E5
Huxter *Shet* 115 C2
Huxter *Whalsay* 115 E1
Huyton 48 D2
Hycemoor 60 E5
Hyde *Glos* 29 D3
Hyde *GM* 49 D2
Hyde Heath 23 D1
Hyde Lea 40 B2
Hydestile 12 B2
Hydro 60 d2
Hyndford Bridge 74 E1
Hyndlee 76 B5
Hynish 84 A5
Hyssington 38 C5
Hythe *Hants* 11 A4
Hythe *Kent* 15 B5
Hythe End 23 E4
Hythie 105 D3
Hyton 60 E5

I

Ianstown 104 C2
Ibberton 9 D3
Ible 50 D5
Ibsley 10 C4
Ibstock 41 B3
Ibstone 23 B2
Ibthorpe 22 C6
Ibworth 22 E6
Ickburgh 44 C6
Ickenham 23 E3
Ickford 31 B7
Ickham 15 C3
Ickleford 32 C5
Icklesham 14 D7
Ickleton 33 A4
Icklingham 33 D1
Ickwell Green 32 C4
Icomb 30 C5
Idbury 30 C5
Iddesleigh 6 E6
Ide 7 C7
Ideford 5 D3
Ide Hill 13 B1
Iden 14 E6
Iden Green *Kent* 13 E3
Iden Green *Kent* 14 D5
Idlicote 30 C3
Idmiston 10 C1
Idoch 105 A4
Idridgehay 50 D6
Idrigil 99 C5
Idstone 22 B3
Idvies 89 B4
Iffley 31 A7
Ifield *Kent* 25 B5
Ifield *W Ssx* 12 E3
Ifieldwood 12 E3
Ifold 12 C3
Iford 13 B6
Ifton Heath 38 C1
Ightfield 38 E1
Ightham 15 A1
Iken 35 D3
Ilam 50 C5
Ilchester 9 B1
Ilderton 77 B3
Ilford 24 E4
Ilfracombe 6 E2
Ilkeston 51 A6
Ilketshall St Andrew 45 C7
Ilketshall St John 45 C7
Ilketshall St Lawrence
  45 C7
Ilketshall St Margaret
  45 C7
Ilkley 56 E3
Illey 40 B6
Illington 44 D6
Illingworth 56 D5
Illogan 2 D4
Illston on the Hill 41 E5
Ilmer 31 C7
Ilmington 30 C3
Ilminster 8 E2

Ilsington 5 C3
Ilston 17 D6
Ilton *N Yorks* 63 B7
Ilton *Som* 8 E2
Imachar 72 C3
Immeroin 87 B7
Immingham 59 B6
Immingham Dock 59 B6
Impington 33 A2
Ince 48 D4
Ince Blundell 48 C1
Ince-in-Makerfield 48 E1
Inch 97 B6
Inchbare 89 C2
Inchberry 104 B3
Inchbraoch 89 D3
Inchgrundle 96 E6
Inchindown 102 E4
Inchinnan 80 D5
Inchkinloch 109 C4
Inchlaggan 93 D4
Inchlumpie 102 D4
Inchmarlo 97 B4
Inchmore 93 D4
Inchnabobart 96 D5
Inchnacardoch 94 B4
Inchnadamph 108 E6
Inchory 96 B3
Inchrory 95 D5
Inchture 88 D6
Inchvuilt 93 E1
Inchyra 88 C6
Indian Queens 3 B3
Inerval 78 C7
Ingarve Green 25 B3
Ingatestone 25 B3
Ingbirchworth 57 A7
Ingerthorpe 57 A1
Ingestre 40 B2
Ingham *Lincs* 52 C3
Ingham *Nflk* 45 C3
Ingham *Sflk* 34 C1
Ingleby 41 A2
Ingleby Arncliffe 64 B3
Ingleby Cross 64 B3
Ingleby Greenhow 64 C3
Inglesbatch 21 B4
Inglesham 22 B2
Ingleton *Dur* 70 E6
Ingleton *N Yorks* 62 B7
Inglewhite 54 E4
Ingmire Hall 62 B5
Ingoe 70 D1
Ingoldisthorpe 44 A2
Ingoldmells 53 D5
Ingoldsby 42 D1
Ingon 30 C2
Ingram 77 B4
Ingrave 25 B3
Ingrow 56 D4
Ings 61 D5
Ingst 20 E2
Ingworth 45 A3
Inistrynich 86 C6
Injebreck 60 c3
Inkberrow 30 A2
Inkhorn 105 C5
Inkpen 22 C5
Inkstack 111 C1
Innellan 80 A5
Innergellie 83 A2
Innerleithen 75 D2
Innerleven 82 D2
Innermessan 66 B4
Innerwick *Loth* 83 C5
Innerwick *Tays* 87 B4
Inninbeg 85 C4
Insch 104 E6
Insh 95 B5
Inshaig 86 A3
Inshore 109 A2
Inskip 54 D4
Instow 6 D3
Intake 50 E2
Intwood 45 A5
Inver *Gramp* 96 C4
Inver *Hghld* 103 B3
Inver *Hghld* 111 B6
Inver *Strath* 86 A4
Inver *Tays* 88 B4
Inverailort 92 E6
Inver Alligin 101 A6
Inverallochy 105 D2
Inveran *Down* 102 D2
Inverarnan *Tays* 87 C4
Inveraray 79 E1
Inverardoch Mains 81 B1

Inverardran 86 E6
Inverarish 92 C1
Inverarity 89 A4
Inverarnan 86 E7
Inverasdale 101 A3
Inverbain 100 E6
Inverbeg 80 C2
Inverbervie 97 D6
Inverbroom 101 D3
Inverbrough 95 B2
Invercassley 102 C1
Invercharnan 86 C4
Inverchaolain 79 E4
Inverchorachan 86 D7
Inverchoran 101 E6
Invercreran 86 B4
Inverdruie 95 C4
Invereen 95 A2
Invererne 103 D5
Inveresk 82 D5
Inverey 95 D7
Inverfarigaig 94 D3
Invergarry 94 B5
Invergelder 96 C4
Invergeldie 87 D6
Invergloy 93 E6
Invergordon 103 A5
Invergowrie 88 E5
Inverguseran 92 E4
Inverhadden 87 C3
Inverherive 86 E6
Inverhope 109 B2
Inverie 92 E4
Inverinan 86 A7
Inverinate 93 B2
Inverkeilor 89 C4
Inverkeithing 82 B4
Inverkeithny 104 E4
Inverkip 80 B4
Inverkirkaig 108 C7
Inverlael 101 D3
Inverlauren 80 C3
Inverliever 79 C1
Inverliver 86 B5
Inverlochlarig 87 A7
Inverlochy 86 C6
Inver Mallie 93 D6
Invermay 88 B7
Invermoriston 94 C4
Invernaver 110 C2
Inverneil 79 C3
Inverness 102 E7
Invernettie 105 E4
Invernoaden 80 A2
Inverquharity 89 A3
Inverquhomery 105 D4
Inverroy 93 E6
Inversanda 86 A3
Invershiel 93 B3
Invertrossachs 80 E1
Inverugie 105 D4
Inveruglas 80 C1
Inveruglass 95 B5
Inverurie 105 A6
Invervar 87 C4
Invervegain 79 E4
Inverythan 105 A4
Inwardleigh 6 E7
Inworth 34 C7
Iping 11 E2
Ipplepen 5 D4
Ippollitts 32 C6
Ipsden 23 A3
Ipstones 50 B6
Ipswich 35 A4
Irby 48 B3
Irby in the Marsh 53 C5
Irby upon Humber 59 B7
Irchester 31 E1
Ireby *Cumb* 69 A6
Ireby *Lancs* 62 B7
Ireland 115 C5
Ireland *Ork* 113 C1
Ireleth 61 B6
Ireshopeburn 70 B5
Irlam 49 B2
Irnham 42 D2
Iron Acton 21 A2
Iron-Bridge 39 A4
Iron Cross 30 A2
Ironside 105 B3
Ironville 51 A5
Irstead 45 C3
Irthington 69 C3
Irthlingborough 42 C7
Irton 65 C5

Irvine 73 C4
Isauld 110 E2
Isbister *Ork* 112 D5
Isbister *Ork* 112 B4
Isbister *Shet* 115 E1
Isbister *Shet* 114 C3
Isfield 13 B5
Isham 42 B7
Ishriff 85 C5
Islay 78 C5
Isle, The 38 D3
Isle Abbotts 8 E1
Isle Brewers 8 E1
Isleham 33 C1
Isle of Dogs 24 D5
Isle of Whithorn 67 A7
Islesburgh 115 C1
Isleworth 24 B5
Isley Walton 41 B2
Islington 24 D4
Islip *Northants* 42 C7
Islip *Oxon* 31 A6
Islivig 106 C5
Isombridge 39 A3
Istead Rise 25 B6
Itchen Abbas 11 B1
Itchen Stoke 11 B1
Itchingfield 12 D4
Itchington 21 A2
Itteringham 45 A2
Itton 7 A7
Itton Common 20 D1
Ivegill 69 C5
Ivelet 62 E5
Iver 23 E3
Iver Heath 23 E3
Iveston 70 E3
Ivinghoe 31 E6
Ivinghoe Aston 31 E6
Ivington 28 D2
Ivington Green 28 D2
Ivybridge 5 B5
Ivychurch 15 A6
Ivyend 38 C3
Ivy Hatch 15 A1
Ivy Todd 44 C5
Iwade 14 E2
Iwerne Courtney 9 E2
Iwerne Minster 9 E2
Ixworth 34 D1
Ixworth Thorpe 34 D1

J

Jack Hill 56 E2
Jackton 80 E6
Jacobstow 6 A7
Jacobstowe 6 E6
Jameston 16 D6
Jamestown *D & G* 75 D6
Jamestown *Hghld* 102 C6
Jamestown *Strath* 80 C3
Janefield 103 A6
Janetstown *Hghld* 111 B5
Janetstown *Hghld* 111 A2
Jarrow 71 B2
Jarvis Brook 13 C4
Jaspers Greens 33 D6
Jawcraig 81 C4
Jayes Park 12 D2
Jaywick 35 A7
Jedburgh 76 C3
Jeffreyston 16 D5
Jemimaville 103 A5
Jersay 81 C5
Jerviswood 74 D1
Jesmond 71 A2
Jevington 15 A6
Jodrell Bank 49 B4
Johnby 69 C6
John's Cross 13 E4
Johnshaven 89 D2
Johnston *Clwyd* 48 C7
Johnston *Dyfed* 16 C4
Johnstone 80 D5
Johnstonebridge 75 B6
Johnstone Castle 80 D5
Johnstown 17 B4
Joppa *Loth* 82 D5
Joppa *Strath* 73 D6
Jordans 23 D2
Jordanston 16 C2
Jordanstone 88 D4
Jordons 23 D2
Jump 57 B7
Juniper Green 82 C6
Jura 78 D5

Jurby East 60 c2

K

Kaber 62 C3
Kaimes *Loth* 82 C6
Kallin 98 C6
Kames *Strath* 79 D4
Kames *Strath* 74 B3
Kames *Strath* 85 E7
Kates Cabin 42 E5
Kea 3 A4
Keadby 58 D6
Keal Coates 53 B5
Kearsley 49 B1
Kearstwick 62 B7
Kearton 62 E5
Kearvaig 108 E1
Keasden 55 B1
Kebholes 104 E3
Keckwick 48 E3
Keddington 53 B3
Kedington 33 D4
Kedleston 50 D6
Keelby 59 B6
Keele 49 C7
Keeley Green 32 B4
Keenie 97 A6
Keeres Green 33 B7
Keeston 16 C4
Keevil 21 D5
Kegworth 41 B2
Kehelland 2 D4
Keig 97 B2
Keighley 56 D3
Keil *Hghld* 86 A3
Keil *Strath* 72 A7
Keilhill 105 A3
Keillmore 79 A3
Keillor 88 D4
Keillour 88 A6
Keills 78 D5
Keils 78 E5
Keinton Mandeville 20 E7
Keir 81 B2
Keir Mill 74 D6
Keisby 42 D2
Keisley 70 A6
Keiss 111 D2
Keith 104 C3
Keithick 88 D5
Keithmore 104 B5
Keithock 89 C2
Kelbrook 55 D3
Kelby 52 D7
Keld *Cumb* 61 E6
Keld *N Yorks* 62 D4
Keldholme 64 E5
Keldy Castle 64 E4
Kelfield *Humb* 58 D7
Kelfield *N Yorks* 57 D4
Kelham 51 D5
Kellan 85 B4
Kellas *Gramp* 103 E6
Kellas *Tays* 89 A5
Kellaton 5 D7
Kelleth 62 B4
Kelleythorpe 59 A2
Kelling 44 E1
Kellington 57 D5
Kelloe 71 B5
Kelly 4 D2
Kelly Bray 4 D3
Kelmarsh 41 E7
Kelmscot 22 B2
Kelsale 35 C2
Kelsall 48 E5
Kelsay 78 A6
Kelshall 32 E5
Kelsick 68 E4
Kelso 76 D2
Kelstedge 50 E4
Kelstern 53 A2
Kelston 21 A4
Keltneyburn 87 D4
Kelton 68 C2
Kelton Hill 67 D5
Kelty 82 B3
Kelvedon 34 C7
Kelvedon Hatch 25 A3
Kelynack 2 A6
Kemback 89 A7
Kemberton 39 B4
Kemble 21 D1
Kemerton 29 D4
Kemeys Commander
  19 D3

Kemeys Inferior 19 D4
Kemnay 97 C2
Kempley 29 A5
Kempley Green 29 A5
Kempsey 29 C3
Kempsford 22 A2
Kempston 32 B4
Kempston Hardwick 32 B4
Kempton 38 C6
Kemp Town 13 A6
Kemsing 15 A1
Kenardington 14 E5
Kenchester 28 D3
Kencot 30 C7
Kendal 61 E5
Kenderchurch 28 D5
Kenfig 18 D5
Kenfig Hill 18 D5
Kenilworth 40 E7
Kenknock Cent 87 A5
Kenknock Tays 87 B4
Kenley GL 13 A1
Kenley Salop 38 E4
Kenmore Hghld 100 E6
Kenmore Strath 79 E1
Kenmore Tays 87 D4
Kenmore W Is 107 A7
Kenn Avn 20 D4
Kenn Devon 8 A5
Kennavay 99 B2
Kennerleigh 7 C6
Kennerty 97 B4
Kennet Camb 33 D2
Kennet Strath 81 D2
Kennethmont 104 B6
Kennett 33 C2
Kennford 8 A5
Kenninghall 44 E7
Kennington Kent 15 A4
Kennington Oxon 31 A7
Kennoway 82 D2
Kennyhill 44 A4
Kennythorpe 64 E7
Kensaleyre 100 B6
Kensary 111 C4
Kensington and Chelsea 24 C5
Kensworth 32 B7
Kensworth Common 32 B7
Kentallen 86 B3
Kentchurch 28 D5
Kentford 33 D2
Kentisbeare 8 B3
Kentisbury 7 A2
Kentisbury Ford 7 A2
Kentmere 61 D3
Kenton Devon 8 A5
Kenton Sflk 35 A2
Kenton T & W 71 A2
Kentra 85 C2
Kents Bank 61 C6
Kent's Green 29 B5
Kent's Oak 10 E2
Kent Street E Ssx 13 E5
Kent Street Kent 13 D1
Kenwick 38 D1
Kenwyn 3 A4
Kenyon 49 A2
Keoldale 109 A2
Keose 107 B5
Keppanach 86 B2
Keppoch Hghld 93 B2
Keppoch Strath 80 C4
Keprigan 72 A6
Kepwick 64 B4
Keresley 41 A6
Kerne Bridge 28 E6
Kerridge 49 D4
Kerris 2 B6
Kerry 38 A5
Kerrycroy 80 A5
Kerrysdale 101 A4
Kerry's Gate 28 C4
Kersall 51 D4
Kersey 34 E4
Kershader 107 B6
Kershopefoot 76 A7
Kersoe 29 D4
Kerswell 8 B3
Kerswell Green 29 C3
Kesgrave 35 B4
Kessingland 45 E7
Kessingland Beach 45 E7
Kestle Mill 3 A3
Keston 24 E6
Keswick Cumb 69 A7
Keswick Nflk 45 B5

Keswick Nflk 45 C2
Ketsby 53 B4
Kettering 42 B7
Ketteringham 45 A5
Kettins 88 D5
Kettlebaston 34 D3
Kettlebridge 82 D2
Kettlebrook 40 E4
Kettleburgh 35 B2
Kettleholm 68 E2
Kettleness 65 A2
Kettleshulme 49 D4
Kettlesing 57 A2
Kettlesing Bottom 57 A2
Kettlestone 44 D2
Kettlethorpe 52 B4
Kettletoft 112 F3
Kettlewell 62 E7
Ketton 42 C4
Kew 24 B5
Kewstoke 20 C4
Kexbrough 57 B7
Kexby Lincs 52 B3
Kexby N Yorks 58 C2
Key Green 49 C5
Keyham 41 D4
Keyhaven 10 E5
Keyingham 59 C5
Keymer 13 A5
Keynsham 21 A4
Keysoe 32 B2
Keysoe Row 32 B2
Key's Toft 53 C6
Keyston 32 B1
Keyworth 51 C7
Kibblesworth 71 A3
Kibworth Beauchamp 41 D5
Kibworth Harcourt 41 D5
Kidbrooke 24 E5
Kiddal Lane End 57 C4
Kiddemore Green 40 A4
Kidderminster 40 A7
Kiddington 30 E5
Kidlington 30 E6
Kidmore End 23 A4
Kidsdale 67 A7
Kidsgrove 49 C6
Kidstones 62 E6
Kidwelly 17 C5
Kiel Crofts 85 E5
Kielder 76 C6
Kilbady 104 C3
Kilbarchan 80 D5
Kilbeg 92 D4
Kilberry Strath 79 B5
Kilbirnie 80 C6
Kilblaan 86 C7
Kilbraur 110 D7
Kilbrenan 85 A4
Kilbride Strath 85 E6
Kilbride Strath 79 E5
Kilbride Strath 79 D5
Kilbridemore 79 E2
Kilburn Derbs 50 E6
Kilburn N Yorks 64 C6
Kilby 41 D5
Kilcadzow 74 D1
Kilchattan 80 A6
Kilchenzie 72 A5
Kilchiaran 78 B5
Kilchoan Hghld 85 A2
Kilchoan Strath 85 D7
Kilchoman 78 B5
Kilchrenan 86 B6
Kilchrist 72 A6
Kilconquhar 82 E2
Kilcot 29 A5
Kilcoy 102 D6
Kilcreggan 80 B3
Kildale 64 D3
Kildonan Hghld 110 E6
Kildonan Strath 72 E5
Kildonnan 92 B6
Kildrochet 66 B5
Kildrummy 96 E2
Kildwick 56 D3
Kilenan 78 C6
Kilfinan 79 D4
Kilfinnan 93 E5
Kilgetty 16 E5
Kilgwrrwg Common 20 D1
Kilham Humb 65 C7
Kilham Northld 76 E2
Kilkenneth 84 A4
Kilkenny 30 A6
Kilkerran Strath 72 B6

Kilkerran Strath 73 C7
Kilkhampton 6 B5
Killamarsh 51 A2
Killay 18 B4
Killbeg 85 C4
Killean Strath 72 A3
Killean Strath 79 E1
Killearn 80 E3
Killellan 72 A6
Killen Hghld 102 E6
Killerby 63 B3
Killichonan 87 B3
Killichronan 85 B4
Killiechanate 93 E6
Killiecrankie 88 A2
Killiehuntly 95 A5
Killiemor 85 A5
Killilan 93 B1
Killin Cent 87 B5
Killin Hghld 103 B1
Killimster 111 D3
Killin 87 B5
Killinaig 85 A6
Killinallan 78 C4
Killinghall 57 A2
Killington 62 B6
Killingworth 71 A1
Killochyett 76 A1
Killocraw 72 A4
Killundine 85 B4
Killypole 72 A6
Kilmacolm 80 C5
Kilmaha 79 D1
Kilmahog 81 A1
Kilmalieu 85 E3
Kilmaluag 100 B4
Kilmany 88 E6
Kilmarie 92 C3
Kilmarnock 73 D4
Kilmartin 79 C2
Kilmaurs 73 D3
Kilmelford 85 E7
Kilmersdon 21 A5
Kilmeston 11 B2
Kilmichael 72 A5
Kilmichael Glassary 79 C2
Kilmichael of Inverlussa 79 B3
Kilmington Devon 8 D4
Kilmington Wilts 21 B7
Kilmorack 102 C7
Kilmore 85 E6
Kilmory Hghld 92 A4
Kilmory Hghld 85 B1
Kilmory Strath 79 B3
Kilmory Strath 79 B4
Kilmote 110 E7
Kilmuir Hghld 99 B7
Kilmuir Hghld 102 E7
Kilmuir Hghld 103 A4
Kilmun 80 A3
Kilmux 82 D2
Kilnave 78 B4
Kilndown 13 E3
Kiln Green 23 C4
Kilnhurst 51 A1
Kilninian 84 E4
Kilninver 85 E6
Kiln Pit Hill 70 D3
Kilnsea 59 E6
Kilnsey 55 D1
Kilnwick 58 E3
Kiloran 78 C2
Kilpatrick 72 D5
Kilpeck 28 D4
Kilpheder 90 C4
Kilphedir 110 E7
Kilpin 58 C5
Kilrenny 83 A2
Kilsby 41 C7
Kilspindie 88 D6
Kilstay 66 C7
Kilsyth 81 B4
Kiltarlity 102 D7
Kilton Clev 64 E2
Kilton Som 20 A6
Kiltyre 87 C5
Kilvaxter 99 C5
Kilve 20 A6
Kilverston 44 C7
Kilvington 51 D6
Kilwinning 73 C3
Kimberley Nflk 44 E5
Kimberley Notts 51 A6
Kimblesworth 71 A4
Kimble Wick 31 D7
Kimbolton Cambs 32 B2
Kimbolton H & W 28 E1

Kimcote 41 C6
Kimmeridge 10 A7
Kimmerston 77 A2
Kimpton Hants 22 B7
Kimpton Herts 32 C7
Kinaldy 89 B7
Kinbeachie 102 E5
Kinblethmont 89 C4
Kinbrace 110 D5
Kinbreack 93 C5
Kinbuck 81 B1
Kincaldrum 89 A4
Kincaple 89 A7
Kincardine Fife 81 D3
Kincardine Hghld 102 E3
Kincardine O'Neil 97 A4
Kinclaven 88 C5
Kincorth 97 E3
Kincraig Gramp 105 C6
Kincraig Hghld 95 B5
Kincraigie 88 A3
Kindallachan 88 A3
Kinellar 97 D2
Kineton Glos 30 A5
Kineton Warks 30 D2
Kineton Green 40 D6
Kinfauns 88 C6
Kingarth 72 E2
Kingcoed 28 D7
Kingerby 52 D2
Kingham 30 C5
Kingholm Quay 68 C2
Kinghorn 82 C4
Kinglassie 82 C3
Kingoodie Gramp 105 B6
Kingoodie Tays 88 E6
Kingsand 4 E5
Kingsbarns 89 B7
Kingsbridge Devon 5 C6
Kingsbridge Som 7 D3
King's Bromley 40 D3
Kingsburgh 99 C6
Kingsbury GL 24 B4
Kingsbury Warks 40 E5
Kingsbury Episcopi 9 A1
Kings Caple 28 E5
Kingscavil 81 E4
Kingsclere 22 E6
King's Cliffe 42 D5
Kingscote 21 C1
Kingscott 6 E5
King's Coughton 30 A2
Kingscross 72 E5
Kingsdale 82 D2
Kingsdon 9 B1
Kingsdown 15 D4
Kingseat 82 B3
Kingsey 31 C7
Kingsfold Dyfed 16 C6
Kingsfold W Ssx 12 D3
Kingsford Gramp 97 D3
Kingsford Gramp 105 A4
Kingsford Gramp 97 A2
Kingsford H & W 40 A6
Kingsford Strath 73 D3
Kingsforth 59 A6
King's Green 29 B4
Kings Head 13 A4
Kingsheanton 6 E3
King's Heath 40 C6
King's Hill 40 B5
Kingshouse 87 B6
Kingskerswell 5 D4
Kingskettle 82 D2
Kingsland Gynd 46 B2
Kingsland H & W 28 D1
Kings Langley 23 E1
Kingsley Ches 48 E4
Kingsley Hants 11 D1
Kingsley Staffs 50 B6
Kingsley Green 11 E1
King's Lynn 44 A3
Kings Meaburn 69 E7
King's Moor 20 D6
Kings Muir Bdrs 75 C2
Kingsmuir Tays 89 A4
King's Newton 41 A2
Kingsnorth Kent 14 D1
Kingsnorth Kent 15 A5
King's Norton Leics 41 D4
King's Norton W Mids 40 C7
King's Nympton 7 A5
King's Pyon 28 D2
Kings Ripton 32 D1
King's Somborne 10 E1
King's Stag 9 D2

King's Stanley 29 C7
King's Sutton 30 E4
Kingstanding 40 C5
Kingsteignton 5 D3
Kingsteps 103 C6
King Sterndale 50 B3
Kingsthorne 28 D4
Kingsthorpe 31 C1
Kingston Cambs 32 E3
Kingston Devon 5 B6
Kingston Dors 9 D3
Kingston Dors 10 A7
Kingston Gramp 104 B2
Kingston Hants 10 C4
Kingston IOW 11 A6
Kingston Kent 15 B3
Kingston Loth 83 A4
Kingston Som 8 D1
Kingston W Ssx 12 C6
Kingston Bagpuize 22 D2
Kingston Blount 23 B2
Kingston by Sea 12 E6
Kingston Deverill 21 C7
Kingstone H & W 28 D4
Kingstone Som 8 E2
Kingstone Staffs 40 C2
Kingston Lisle 22 C3
Kingston near Lewes 13 A6
Kingston on Soar 41 C2
Kingston Russell 9 B4
Kingston Seymour 20 C4
Kingston Upon Hull 59 A5
Kingston Upon Thames 24 B6
Kingstown 69 B4
King's Walden 32 C6
Kingswear 5 D5
Kingswells Gramp 97 D3
Kingswells Strath 73 E3
Kingswinford 40 A6
Kingswood Avn 21 A3
Kingswood Bucks 31 B6
Kingswood Glos 21 B1
Kingswood Kent 12 E1
Kingswood Pwys 38 B4
Kingswood Sry 14 D3
Kingswood Warks 40 D7
Kingswood Common 28 B2
Kings Worthy 11 A1
Kingthorpe 52 E4
Kington H & W 29 D2
Kington H & W 28 B2
Kington Langley 21 D3
Kington Magna 9 D1
Kington St Michael 21 D3
Kingussie 95 A5
Kingweston 20 E7
Kinharrachie 105 C5
Kinharvie 68 C3
Kinkell 81 A4
Kinkell Bridge 88 A7
Kinknockie 105 D4
Kinloch Fife 88 D7
Kinloch Hghld 109 A5
Kinloch Hghld 102 D4
Kinloch Hghld 85 C3
Kinloch Rum 92 B5
Kinloch Tays 88 D4
Kinloch Tays 88 C4
Kinlochan 85 E2
Kinlochard 80 D1
Kinlocharkaig 93 B5
Kinlochbeoraid 93 A6
Kinlochbervie 108 E3
Kinlocheil 86 A1
Kinlochetive 86 C4
Kinlochewe 101 C5
Kinloch Hourn 93 B4
Kinloch Laggan 94 D7
Kinlochlaich 86 A4
Kinlochleven 86 C2
Kinlochmoidart 85 D1
Kinlochmorar 93 A5
Kinlochmore 86 C2
Kinloch Rannoch 87 C3
Kinlochspelve 85 C6
Kinloss 103 D5
Kinmel Bay 47 D2
Kinmuck 97 D2
Kinnadie 105 C4
Kinnaird 88 D6
Kinneff 97 D6
Kinnelhead 75 A5
Kinnell Cent 87 B5
Kinnell Tays 89 C3
Kinnerley 38 C2

Kinnersley H & W 28 C3
Kinnersley H & W 29 C3
Kinnerton Pwys 28 B1
Kinnesswood 82 B2
Kinnettles 89 A4
Kinninvie 70 D6
Kinnordy 88 E3
Kinoulton 51 C7
Kinrara 95 B5
Kinross 82 B2
Kinrossie 88 C5
Kinsbourne Green 32 C7
Kinsham 28 C1
Kinsley 57 C6
Kinson 10 B5
Kintarvie 107 A6
Kintbury 22 C5
Kintessack 103 C5
Kintillo 88 C7
Kintocher 97 A3
Kinton H & W 38 D7
Kinton H & W 29 C3
Kinton Salop 38 C3
Kintore 97 C2
Kintour 78 C5
Kintra Islay 78 C7
Kintra Mull 84 E6
Kintradwell 103 C1
Kintraw 79 C1
Kinuachdrach 79 B2
Kinveachy 95 C4
Kinver 40 A6
Kiplaw Croft 105 D5
Kiplin 63 C5
Kipp 87 B7
Kippax 57 C4
Kippen Cent 81 A2
Kippen Tays 88 B7
Kippford 68 B4
Kipping's Cross 13 D2
Kirbister Ork 113 C1
Kirbister Ork 112 F4
Kirbuster 112 B4
Kirby Bedon 45 B5
Kirby Cane 45 C6
Kirby Corner 40 E7
Kirby Cross 35 B6
Kirby Grindalythe 65 B7
Kirby Hill N Yorks 63 B4
Kirby Hill N Yorks 57 B1
Kirby Knowle 64 B5
Kirby le Soken 35 B6
Kirby Misperton 64 E6
Kirby Muxloe 41 C4
Kirby Overblow 45 C6
Kirby Row 45 C6
Kirby Sigston 64 B4
Kirby Underdale 58 D2
Kirby Wiske 63 D6
Kirdford 12 C4
Kirivick 107 A3
Kirk 111 C3
Kirkabister 115 D4
Kirkandrews 67 C6
Kirkandrews upon Eden 69 B4
Kirkbampton 69 B4
Kirkbean 68 C4
Kirk Bramwith 57 E6
Kirkbride 69 A4
Kirkbridge 63 C5
Kirkbuddo 89 B4
Kirkburn Bdrs 75 C2
Kirkburn Humb 58 E2
Kirkburton 56 E6
Kirkby Lincs 52 D2
Kirkby Mers 48 D2
Kirkby N Yorks 64 C3
Kirkby Bellars 41 E3
Kirkby Fleetham 63 C5
Kirkby Green 52 D6
Kirkby in Ashfield 51 A5
Kirkby la Thorpe 52 D7
Kirkby Lonsdale 62 B7
Kirkby Malham 55 C1
Kirkby Mallory 41 B4
Kirkby Malzeard 63 C7
Kirkby Mills 64 E5
Kirkbymoorside 64 D5
Kirkby on Bain 53 A5
Kirkby Stephen 62 C4
Kirkby Thore 69 E7
Kirkby Underwood 42 D2
Kirkby Wharfe 57 D3
Kirkcaldy 82 C3
Kirkcambeck 69 D3
Kirkcolm 66 B4
Kirkconnel D & G 74 C4

Kirkconnell *D & G* 68 C3
Kirkcowan 66 E4
Kirkcudbright 67 C5
Kirkdale 67 B5
Kirkdean 75 B1
Kirk Deighton 57 B2
Kirk Ella 59 A5
Kirkfieldbank 74 D1
Kirkgunzeon 68 B3
Kirk Hallam 51 A6
Kirkham *Lancs* 54 D4
Kirkham *N Yorks* 64 E7
Kirkhamgate 57 A5
Kirk Hammerton 57 C2
Kirkharle 77 B7
Kirkhaugh 69 E5
Kirkheaton *Northld* 70 D1
Kirkheaton *W Yorks* 56 E6
Kirkhill *Gramp* 104 B3
Kirkhill *Hghld* 102 D7
Kirkhill *Tays* 89 C2
Kirkhill of Kennethmont
104 D6
Kirkhope 75 D3
Kirkibost 106 E4
Kirkinch 88 E4
Kirkinner 67 A5
Kirkintilloch 81 A4
Kirk Ireton 50 D5
Kirkland *Cumb* 69 E6
Kirkland *D & G* 60 E2
Kirkland *D & G* 74 D6
Kirkland *D & G* 74 C4
Kirk Langley 50 D7
Kirkleatham 64 C1
Kirklevington 64 B3
Kirkley 45 E6
Kirkleyditch 49 C4
Kirklington *Notts* 51 C5
Kirklington *N Yorks* 63 D6
Kirklinton 69 C3
Kirkliston 82 B5
Kirkmaiden 66 C7
Kirk Merrington 71 A5
Kirk Michael 60 c2
Kirkmichael *Strath* 73 C7
Kirkmichael *Tays* 88 B2
Kirkmond le Mire 52 E2
Kirkmuirhill 74 C1
Kirknewton *Loth* 82 B6
Kirknewton *Northld* 77 A2
Kirkney 104 D5
Kirk of Shotts 81 C5
Kirkoswald *Cumb* 69 D5
Kirkoswald *Strath* 73 B7
Kirkpatrick Durham 67 D3
Kirkpatrick-Fleming 69 A2
Kirk Sandall 57 E7
Kirksanton 61 A5
Kirk Smeaton 57 D6
Kirkstall 57 A4
Kirkstead 52 E5
Kirkstile *D & G* 75 D6
Kirkstile *Gramp* 104 D5
Kirkton *Bdrs* 76 B4
Kirkton *D & G* 74 E7
Kirkton *Fife* 88 E6
Kirkton *Gramp* 104 E6
Kirkton *Gramp* 104 E3
Kirkton *Gramp* 105 B4
Kirkton *Gramp* 97 B2
Kirkton *Hghld* 94 E2
Kirkton *Hghld* 103 A2
Kirkton *Hghld* 103 A6
Kirkton *Hghld* 79 B1
Kirkton *Hghld* 110 D2
Kirkton *Hghld* 93 A2
Kirkton *Tays* 89 A4
Kirkton *Tays* 88 A7
Kirktonhill 89 C2
Kirkton Manor 75 C2
Kirkton of Airlie 88 E3
Kirkton of Auchterhouse
88 E5
Kirkton of Barevan 103 B7
Kirkton of Bourtie 105 B6
Kirkton of Collace 88 C5
Kirkton of Craig 89 D3
Kirkton of Culsalmond
104 E5
Kirkton of Durris 97 C4
Kirkton of Glenbuchat
96 D2
Kirkton of Glenisla 88 D2
Kirkton of Kingoldrum
88 E3
Kirkton of Lethendy 88 C4

Kirkton of Logie Buchan
105 C6
Kirkton of Maryculter
97 D4
Kirkton of Menmuir 89 B2
Kirkton of Monikie 89 B5
Kirkton of Skene 97 D3
Kirkton of Strathmartine
88 E5
Kirkton of Tealing 89 A5
Kirktown 105 D3
Kirktown of Alvah 104 E2
Kirktown of Auchterless
105 A4
Kirktown of Deskford
104 D2
Kirktown of Fetteresso
97 D5
Kirktown of Rayne 104 E5
Kirktown of Slains 105 D6
Kirkwall 112 D5
Kirkwhelpington 77 A7
Kirk Yetholm 76 E3
Kirmington 59 B6
Kirn 80 A4
Kirriemuir 88 E3
Kirstead Green 45 B6
Kirtlebridge 69 A2
Kirtling 33 C3
Kirtling Green 33 C3
Kirtlington 30 E6
Kirtomy 110 C2
Kirton *Lincs* 43 B1
Kirton *Notts* 51 C4
Kirton *Sflk* 35 B5
Kirton End 53 A7
Kirton Holme 53 A7
Kirton in Lindsey 52 C2
Kiscadle 72 E5
Kishorn 101 A7
Kislingbury 31 B2
Kismeblon Bridge 6 E6
Kites Hardwick 30 E1
Kitley 5 A5
Kitwood 11 C1
Kiveton Park 51 A2
Klibreck 109 C5
Knabbygates 104 D3
Knaith 52 B3
Knap Corner 9 E1
Knaphill 12 B1
Knapp *Som* 8 E1
Knapp *Tays* 88 D5
Knapton *Nflk* 45 C2
Knapton *N Yorks* 57 D2
Knapwell 32 E2
Knaresborough 57 B2
Knarsdale 69 E4
Knaven 105 B4
Knayton 64 B5
Knebworth 32 D6
Knedlington 58 C5
Kneesall 51 D4
Kneesworth 32 E4
Kneeton 51 D6
Knelston 17 C7
Knettishall 44 D7
Knightacott 7 A3
Knightcote 30 D2
Knighton *Devon* 5 A6
Knighton *Leics* 41 D4
Knighton *Pwys* 38 B7
Knighton *Som* 20 A6
Knighton *Staffs* 39 B2
Knighton *Staffs* 49 B7
Knightshayes Court 7 D5
Knightwick 29 B2
Knill 28 B1
Knipoch 85 E6
Knipton 42 B1
Knitsley 70 E4
Kniveton 50 D5
Knock *Cumb* 69 E7
Knock *Hghld* 104 D3
Knock *Strath* 85 B5
Knock *W Is* 107 C4
Knockalava 79 D2
Knockaloe Moar 60 b3
Knockan 108 E7
Knockandhu 104 A6
Knockando 103 E7
Knockbain 102 E6
Knockban 101 E5
Knockbreck 103 A3
Knockbrex 67 B6
Knockdamph 101 E2

Knockdee 111 B2
Knockdow 80 A4
Knockdown 21 C2
Knockenkelly 72 E5
Knockentiber 73 C4
Knockfin 93 E2
Knockgray 67 B1
Knockholt 13 B1
Knockholt Pound 13 B1
Knockin 38 C2
Knockintorran 98 B5
Knocklearn 67 D3
Knocknaha 72 A6
Knocknain 66 A4
Knocknalling 67 B2
Knock of Auchnahannet
95 D2
Knocksharry 60 b3
Knockville 66 E3
Knockvologan 84 E7
Knodishall 35 D2
Knolls Green 49 C4
Knolton 38 C1
Knook 21 D6
Knopton Green 28 D2
Knossington 42 B4
Knott End-on-Sea 54 C3
Knotting 32 B2
Knotting Green 32 B2
Knottingley 57 D5
Knotty Ash 48 D2
Knotty Green 23 D2
Knowbury 38 E7
Knowe 66 E3
Knowesgate 77 A7
Knoweside 73 B6
Knowes of Elrick 104 E3
Knowetownhead 76 B4
Knowhead 105 C3
Knowle *Avn* 21 A3
Knowle *Devon* 7 B6
Knowle *Devon* 6 D3
Knowle *Dorset* 8 B5
Knowle *Salop* 38 E7
Knowle *W Mids* 40 D7
Knowle Green 55 A4
Knowle Hall 20 C6
Knowl Hill 23 C4
Knowlton *Dorset* 10 B4
Knowlton *Kent* 15 C3
Knowl Wall 40 A1
Knowsley 48 D2
Knowstone 7 C4
Knucklas 38 B7
Knutsford 49 B4
Knypersley 49 C6
Kyleakin 92 E2
Kyle of Lochalsh 92 E2
Kylerhea 92 E2
Kylesbeg 85 C1
Kylesknoydart 93 A5
Kylesmorar 93 A5
Kyles Scalpay 99 B2
Kylestrome 108 E5
Kyloag 102 E2
Kyloe 77 B1
Kynnersley 39 A3
Kyre Park 29 A1

L
Labost 107 A3
Laceby 59 C7
Lacey Green 31 D7
Lach Dennis 49 B4
Lackalee 99 A2
Lackford 33 D1
Lacock 21 D4
Ladbroke 30 E2
Laddingford 13 D2
Lade Bank 53 B6
Ladock 3 A3
Ladybank *Fife* 82 D2
Ladycross 4 D2
Ladyfield 86 B7
Lady Hall 61 A5
Ladykirk 76 E1
Ladysford 105 C2
Lady's Green 33 D3
Lagalochan 85 E7
Lagavulin 78 D7
Lagg *Hghld* 85 C2
Lagg *Strath* 72 D5
Lagg *Strath* 78 E4
Lagg *Strath* 73 B6
Laggan *Cent* 87 B7
Laggan *Gramp* 104 B5

Laggan *Hghld* 93 E5
Laggan *Hghld* 94 E6
Laggan *Strath* 78 B6
Laggan Bridge 78 C6
Lagganulva 85 A4
Lagganvoulin 96 B2
Laglingarten 80 A1
Lagnalean 102 E7
Lagrae 74 C4
Laguna 88 C5
Lahill 82 E2
Laid 109 B4
Laide 101 A2
Laig 92 B6
Laight 74 B4
Laimhrig 107 D2
Lainchoil 95 D4
Laindon 25 B4
Lair 88 C2
Lairg 102 D1
Lairigmór 86 C2
Laithers 104 E4
Laithes 69 C6
Lake 10 C1
Lakenham 45 B5
Lakenheath 44 B7
Lakesend 43 D5
Lakeside 61 C5
Laleham 23 E5
Laleston 18 D6
Lamarsh 34 C5
Lamas 45 B2
Lamb Corner 34 E5
Lamberhurst 13 D3
Lamberhurst Quarter
13 D3
Lamberton 83 E7
Lambeth 24 D5
Lambfell Moar 60 b3
Lambley *Northld* 69 E4
Lambley *Notts* 51 C6
Lambourn 22 C4
Lambourne 24 E3
Lambourne End 24 E3
Lambourn Woodlands
22 C4
Lambs Green 12 E3
Lambston 16 C4
Lamerton 4 E3
Lamesley 71 A3
Lamington *Hghld* 103 A4
Lamington *Strath* 74 E2
Lamlash 72 E4
Lamloch 67 B1
Lamonby 69 C6
Lamorran 3 A4
Lampert 69 E2
Lampeter 26 E6
Lampeter-Velfrey 16 E4
Lamphey 16 D5
Lamplugh 68 D7
Lamport 41 E7
Lamyatt 21 A7
Lana 6 C7
Lanark 74 D1
Lancaster 54 D1
Lanchester 70 E4
Landbeach 33 A2
Landcross 6 D4
Landerberry 97 C3
Landewednack 2 E7
Landford 10 D3
Landford Manor 10 D2
Landimore 17 C6
Landkey 6 E3
Landore 18 B4
Landrake 4 E4
Landscove 5 C4
Landshipping 16 D4
Landulph 4 E4
Landwade 33 C2
Landywood 40 B4
Laneast 4 C2
Lane End *Bucks* 23 C2
Lane-end *Corn* 3 C2
Lane End *Cumb* 61 A4
Lane End *Derbs* 51 A4
Lane End *Dors* 9 E4
Lane Green 40 A4
Laneham 52 B4
Lane Head *GM* 49 A2
Lane Head *W Yorks* 56 E7
Laneshaw Bridge 55 D3
Langamull 84 E3
Langar 51 D7
Langass 98 C5
Langbank 80 C4
Langbar 56 D2

Langcliffe 55 C1
Langdale End 65 B4
Langdon 4 D2
Langdon Beck 70 B5
Langdon Hills 25 B4
Langdon House 8 A6
Langdyke 82 D2
Langenhoe 34 E7
Langford *Beds* 32 C4
Langford *Devon* 8 B3
Langford *Esx* 25 D2
Langford *Nflk* 44 C6
Langford *Notts* 52 B6
Langford *Oxon* 30 C7
Langford Budville 8 C1
Langford End 32 C3
Langham *Esx* 34 E5
Langham *Leics* 42 B3
Langham *Nflk* 44 E1
Langham *Sflk* 34 D2
Langham Moor 34 E5
Langho 55 B4
Langholm 75 D7
Langlands 67 C5
Langlee 76 C4
Langleeford 77 A3
Langley *Berks* 23 E4
Langley *Ches* 49 D4
Langley *Esx* 33 A5
Langley *Hants* 11 A4
Langley *Herts* 32 D6
Langley *Kent* 14 D3
Langley *Notts* 51 A6
Langley *Warks* 30 B1
Langley *W Ssx* 11 E2
Langley Burrell 21 D3
Langley Green 50 D7
Langley Marsh 8 B1
Langley Mill 51 A6
Langley Moor 71 A4
Langley Park 71 A4
Langley Street 45 C5
Langney 13 D6
Langold 51 B2
Langore 4 D2
Langport 9 A1
Langrick 53 A7
Langridge *Avn* 21 B4
Langridge *Devon* 6 E4
Langridgeford 6 E4
Langrigg 68 E5
Langrish 11 D2
Langriville 53 A7
Langsett 57 A7
Langshaw 76 B2
Langshawburn 75 C5
Langside 87 D7
Langskaill 112 D2
Langstone 11 D4
Langthorne 63 C5
Langthorpe 57 B1
Langthwaite 63 A4
Langtoft *Humb* 65 C7
Langtoft *Lincs* 42 E3
Langton *Dur* 63 B3
Langton *Lincs* 53 B4
Langton *Lincs* 53 A5
Langton *N Yorks* 64 E7
Langton by Wragby 52 E4
Langton Green 13 C3
Langton Herring 9 C5
Langton Long Blandford
9 E3
Langton Matravers 10 A7
Langtree 6 D5
Langwathby 69 D6
Langwell 102 C1
Langworth 52 D4
Lanivet 3 C2
Lanlivery 3 C3
Lanner 2 E5
Lanreath 3 D3
Lansallos 3 D3
Lansdown 21 B4
Lanteglos 4 A2
Lanton *Bdrs* 76 C3
Lanton *Northld* 77 A2
Lapford 7 B6
Lapley 40 A3
Lapworth 40 D7
Larachbeg 85 C4
Larach na Gaibhre 79 B5
Larbert 81 C3
Larden Green 48 E6
Larg 66 E3
Largie 104 E5

Largiemore 79 D3
Largoward 82 E2
Largs 80 B6
Largue 104 E4
Largybaan 72 A6
Largybeg 72 E5
Largymore 72 E5
Larkhall 81 B6
Lark Hall 33 B3
Larkhill 22 A7
Larling 44 D7
Laroch 86 B3
Larriston 76 B6
Lartington 63 A3
Lary 96 D3
Lasborough 21 C1
Lasham 23 A7
Lassington 29 B5
Lassintullich 87 C3
Lassodie 82 B3
Lasswade 82 D6
Lastingham 64 E4
Latchford 49 A3
Latchingdon 25 D2
Latchley 4 E3
Lately Common 49 A2
Lathallan Mill 82 E2
Lathbury 31 D3
Latheron 111 B5
Lathockar Mains 82 E2
Lathones 82 E2
Lathrisk 82 C2
Latimer 23 E2
Latteridge 21 A2
Lattiford 9 C1
Lattinford 34 E5
Latton 21 E1
Lauchentyre 67 B5
Lauchintilly 97 C2
Lauder 76 B1
Laugharne 17 B4
Laughterton 52 B4
Laughton *E Ssx* 13 B5
Laughton *Leics* 41 D6
Laughton *Lincs* 42 D1
Laughton *Lincs* 52 B2
Laughton en le Morthen
51 B2
Launcells 6 B6
Launcells Cross 6 B6
Launceston 4 D2
Launton 31 B5
Laurencekirk 97 C6
Laurieston 67 C4
Lavendon 31 E2
Lavenham 34 D4
Laverhay 75 B6
Lavernock 19 B7
Laversdale 69 C3
Laverstok 10 C1
Laverstoke *Hants* 22 D7
Laverton *Glos* 30 A4
Laverton *N Yorks* 63 C7
Laverton *Som* 21 B5
Lavister 48 C6
Law 81 C6
Lawers *Tays* 87 D6
Lawers *Tays* 87 C5
Lawford 34 E5
Lawhitton 4 D2
Lawkland 55 B1
Lawley 39 A4
Lawnhead 40 A2
Lawrenny 16 D5
Laws 89 A5
Lawshall 34 C3
Lawton 28 D2
Laxay 107 B5
Laxdale 107 C4
Laxey 60 d3
Laxfield 35 B1
Laxfirth *Shet* 115 D2
Laxfirth *Shet* 115 D3
Laxford Bridge 108 E4
Laxo 115 D1
Laxton *Humb* 58 C5
Laxton *Northants* 42 C5
Laxton *Notts* 51 D4
Laycock 56 D3
Layer Breton 34 D7
Layer de la Haye 34 D6
Layer Marney 34 D7
Layham 34 E4
Laysters Pole 28 E1
Laytham 58 C4
Lazenby 64 C2
Lazonby 69 D6

Lea Derbs 50 E5
Lea H & W 29 A5
Lea Lincs 52 B3
Lea Salop 38 C6
Lea Salop 38 D4
Lea Wilts 21 D2
Leachkin 102 E7
Leack 79 E2
Leadburn 82 C7
Leadenham 52 C6
Leaden Roding 33 B7
Leadgate Cumb 70 A4
Leadgate Dur 70 E3
Leadgate T & W 70 E3
Leadhills 74 D4
Leafield 30 D6
Leake Common Side
  53 B6
Leake Hurn's End 53 C7
Lealands 15 A5
Lealholm 64 E3
Lealt Jura 79 A2
Lealt Skye 100 C5
Lea Marston 40 E5
Leamington Hastings
  30 E1
Leanach Hghld 79 E2
Leanach Hghld 103 B7
Leanaig 102 D6
Leanoch 103 E6
Leargybreck 78 E4
Learney 97 B3
Leasgill 61 D5
Leasingham 52 D7
Leask 105 D5
Leatherhead 12 D1
Leathley 57 A3
Leaton 38 D3
Lea Town 54 D4
Leaveland 14 E3
Leavening 64 E7
Leaves Green 24 E6
Lea Yeat 62 C6
Lebberston 65 C5
Lechlade 22 B2
Lechuary 79 C2
Leck 62 B7
Leckford 10 E1
Leckfurin 110 C3
Leckgruinart 78 B5
Leckhampstead Berks
  22 D4
Leckhampstead Bucks
  31 C4
Leckhampton 29 D6
Leckie 101 C5
Leckmelm 101 D2
Leckroy 94 B6
Leckwith 19 B6
Leconfield 59 A3
Ledaig Strath 86 A5
Ledaig W Is 90 B6
Ledard 80 D1
Ledbeg 108 E7
Ledburn 31 E5
Ledbury 29 B4
Ledcharrie 87 B6
Ledgemoor 28 D2
Ledgowan 101 D6
Ledicot 28 D1
Ledmore Hghld 108 E7
Ledmore Strath 85 B4
Lednagullin 110 D2
Ledsham Ches 48 C4
Ledsham W Yorks 57 C5
Ledston 57 C5
Ledwell 30 E5
Lee Devon 6 D2
Lee Hants 10 E3
Lee Lancs 54 E2
Lee Salop 38 D1
Lee Strath 85 A6
Lee, The 31 D7
Leebotten 115 D5
Leebotwood 38 D5
Lee Brockhurst 38 E2
Leece 61 B7
Lee Clump 23 D1
Leeds Kent 14 D3
Leeds W Yorks 57 B4
Leedstown 2 D5
Leeford 7 B2
Leegomery 39 A3
Lee Green 49 A5
Leek 49 D6
Leek Wootton 30 C1
Lee Mill Bridge 5 A5

Leeming N Yorks 63 C6
Leeming W Yorks 56 D4
Leeming Bar 63 C6
Lee Moor 5 A4
Lee-on-the-Solent 11 B4
Lees Derbs 50 D7
Lees GM 49 D1
Leeswood 48 B6
Legars 76 D1
Legbourne 53 B3
Legerwood 76 B1
Legsby 52 E3
Leicester 41 C4
Leicester Forest East
  41 C4
Leigh Dors 9 C3
Leigh Glos 29 C5
Leigh GM 49 A1
Leigh H & W 29 B2
Leigh Kent 15 A2
Leigh Salop 38 C4
Leigh Sry 12 E2
Leigh Wilts 21 E1
Leigh Beck 25 D4
Leigh Common 9 D1
Leigh Delamere 21 C3
Leigh Green 14 D5
Leigh-on-Sea 25 D4
Leigh Sinton 29 B2
Leighterton 21 C1
Leighton N Yorks 63 B7
Leighton Pwys 38 B4
Leighton Salop 39 A4
Leighton Som 21 B6
Leighton Bromswold
  32 C1
Leighton Buzzard 31 E5
Leigh upon Mendip 21 A6
Leigh Woods 20 E3
Leinthall Earls 28 D1
Leinthall Starkes 28 D1
Leintwardine 38 D7
Leire 41 C5
Leirinmore 109 B2
Leishmore 102 B7
Leiston 35 D2
Leitfie 88 D4
Leith 82 C5
Leitholm 76 D1
Lelant 2 C5
Lelley 59 C4
Lem Hill 39 B7
Lemington 70 E2
Lemnas 105 B2
Lempitlaw 76 D2
Lemsford 32 D7
Lenchwick 30 A3
Lendalfoot 66 C1
Lendrick 80 E1
Lenham 14 D3
Lenham Heath 14 E4
Lenie 94 D3
Lenimore 72 C3
Lennel 76 E1
Lennoxlove Ho 83 A5
Lennox Plunton 67 C5
Lennoxtown 81 A4
Lenton 42 D1
Lenwade 44 E4
Lenzie 81 A4
Leoch 88 E5
Leochel-Cushnie 97 A2
Leominster 28 D2
Leonard Stanley 29 C7
Leorin 78 C7
Lepe 11 A5
Lephinchapel 79 D2
Lephinmore 79 D2
Leppington 64 E7
Lepton 57 A6
Lerags 85 E6
Lergiechoniemore 79 C1
Lerryn 3 D3
Lerwick 115 D3
Lesbury 77 D4
Leschangie 97 C2
Lescrow 3 D3
Leslie Fife 82 C2
Leslie Gramp 104 D6
Lesmahagow 74 D2
Lesnewth 6 A7
Lessendrum 104 D4
Lessingham 45 C3
Lessonhall 69 A4
Leswalt 66 B4
Letchmore Heath 24 B3
Letchworth 32 D5

Letcombe Bassett 22 C3
Letcombe Regis 22 C3
Letham Fife 88 E7
Letham Tays 89 B4
Lethanhill 73 D6
Lethendy 88 C6
Lethenty 105 B4
Letheringham 35 B3
Letheringsett 44 E2
Letterewe 101 B4
Letterfearn 93 A2
Lettermorar 92 E6
Lettermore Hghld 85 A4
Lettermore Hghld 109 D4
Letters 101 D3
Letterston 16 C3
Lettoch Hghld 95 D4
Lettoch Hghld 95 D2
Letton H & W 38 C7
Letton H & W 28 C3
Letty Green 32 D7
Letwell 51 B2
Leuchars 89 A6
Leurbost 107 B5
Levedale 40 A3
Leven Fife 82 D2
Leven Humb 59 B3
Levenhall 82 D5
Levens 61 D5
Levenshulme 49 C2
Levenwick 115 D5
Leverburgh 98 E3
Leverington 43 C3
Leverstock Green 23 E1
Leverton 53 B7
Leverton Outgate 53 C7
Levington 35 B5
Levisham 65 A4
Levishie 94 C4
Lew 30 D7
Lewannick 4 C2
Lewdown 4 E2
Lewes 13 B5
Leweston 16 C3
Lewis Burn 76 B7
Lewisham 24 D5
Lewiston 94 D3
Lewknor 23 B2
Leworthy 7 A3
Lewtrenchard 4 E2
Ley 3 D2
Leybourne 13 D1
Leyburn 63 B5
Leycett 49 B7
Ley Green 32 C6
Leyland 54 E2
Leylodge 97 C2
Leys Gramp 105 D3
Leys Gramp 96 E3
Leys Tays 88 D5
Leysdown-on-Sea 15 A1
Leysmill 89 C4
Leys of Cossans 88 E4
Leyton 24 D4
Lezant 4 D3
Lfaithddu 27 E2
Lhanbryde 104 A2
Lhen, The 60 c1
Liatrie 93 E1
Libanus 18 E1
Libberton 74 E1
Liberton 82 C6
Lichfield 40 D4
Lickey 40 B7
Lickey End 40 B7
Lickfold 12 B4
Liddel 113 D3
Liddesdale 85 D3
Liddington 22 B3
Lidgate Derbs 50 E3
Lidgate Sfk 33 D3
Lidlington 31 E4
Lidsing 14 C2
Lidstone 30 D5
Lienassie 93 B2
Lieurary dist 111 A2
Liff 88 E5
Lifton 4 D2
Liftondown 4 D2
Lighthorne 30 D2
Lightwater 23 D5
Lightwood 49 D7
Lightwood Green Ches
  49 A7
Lightwood Green Clwyd
  48 C7

Likisto 99 A2
Lilbourne 41 C7
Lilburn Tower 77 B3
Lilleshall 39 B3
Lilley Berks 22 D4
Lilley Herts 32 C6
Lilliesleaf 76 B3
Lillingstone Dayrell 31 C4
Lillingstone Lovell 31 C3
Lillington 9 C2
Lilliput 10 B6
Lilstock 20 A6
Limbrick 55 A6
Limefield 55 C6
Limehillock 104 D3
Limekilnburn 81 B6
Limekilns 81 E3
Limerstone 11 A6
Limington 9 B1
Limpenhoe 45 C5
Limpley Stoke 21 B4
Limpsfield 13 B1
Linbriggs 76 E5
Linby 51 B5
Linchmere 11 E1
Lincoln 52 C4
Lincomb 29 C1
Lincombe 5 C5
Lindale 61 D5
Lindal in Furness 61 B6
Lindean 76 A2
Lindertis 88 E3
Lindfield 13 A4
Lindford 11 E1
Lindifferon 88 E7
Lindley 56 E6
Lindores 88 D7
Lindridge 29 A1
Lindsaig 79 D4
Lindsell 33 C6
Lindsey 34 D4
Linford Esx 25 B5
Linford Hants 10 C4
Lingague 60 b4
Lingay Fen 33 A3
Lingdale 64 D2
Lingen 28 C1
Lingfield 13 A2
Lingwood 45 C5
Linhead 10 E3
Linhope 76 A5
Liniclett 98 B7
Linkenholt 22 C6
Linkhill 14 D6
Linkinhorne 4 D3
Linklater 113 D3
Linksness 113 B1
Linktown 82 C3
Linley 38 C5
Linley Green 29 A2
Linlithgow 81 D4
Linlithgow Bridge 81 D4
Linnburn 80 B3
Linnels 70 C2
Linneraineach 101 D1
Linney 16 B6
Linn of Muick Cott 96 D5
Linshader 107 A4
Linshiels 76 E5
Linsidemore 102 D2
Linslade 31 E5
Linstead Parva 35 C1
Linstock 69 C4
Linthwaite 56 D6
Lintlaw 83 D7
Lintmill 104 D2
Linton Bdrs 76 D3
Linton Cambs 33 B4
Linton Derbs 40 E3
Linton Gramp 97 C2
Linton H & W 29 A5
Linton Kent 13 E1
Linton Kent 13 E2
Linton N Yorks 55 D1
Linton-on-Ouse 57 C1
Lintzford 70 E3
Linwood Hants 10 C4
Linwood Lincs 52 E3
Linwood Strath 80 D5
Lionel 107 D1
Liphook 11 E1
Liscombe 7 C3
Liskeard 4 C4
Liss 11 D2
Lissett 59 B2
Lissington 52 E3
Liston 34 C4

Lisvane 19 B5
Liswerry 19 D5
Litcham 44 C4
Litchborough 31 B2
Litchfield 22 D6
Litherland 48 C2
Litlington Cambs 32 E4
Litlington E Ssx 13 C6
Little Abington 33 B4
Little Addington 42 C7
Little Alne 30 C1
Little Amwell 32 E7
Little Assynt 108 D6
Little Aston 40 C4
Little Atherfield 11 A6
Little Ayton 64 C2
Little Baddow 25 C2
Little Badminton 21 C2
Little Ballinluig 88 A3
Little Bampton 69 A4
Little Bardfield 33 C5
Little Barford 32 C3
Little Barningham 45 A2
Little Barrington 30 C6
Little Barugh 64 E6
Little Bealings 35 B4
Littlebeck 65 A3
Little Bedwyn 22 B5
Little Bentley 35 A6
Little Berkhamsted 24 C2
Little Billing 31 D1
Little Birch 28 E4
Little Bispham 54 C3
Little Blakenham 35 A4
Little Bookham 12 D1
Littleborough GM 55 D6
Littleborough Notts 52 B3
Littlebourne 15 C3
Little Bowden 41 E6
Little Bradley 33 C3
Little Brampton 38 C6
Little Braxted 34 C7
Little Brechin 89 B2
Littlebredy 9 B5
Little Brickhill 31 E4
Little Bridgeford 40 A2
Little Brington 31 B1
Little Bromley 34 E6
Little Broughton 68 D6
Little Budworth 48 E5
Little Burstead 25 B3
Little Burton 59 B3
Littlebury 33 B5
Littlebury Green 33 A5
Little Bytham 42 D3
Little Carlton 53 B5
Little Casterton 42 D4
Little Catwick 59 B3
Little Cawthorpe 53 B3
Little Chalfont 23 D2
Little Chart 14 E4
Little Chesterford 33 B4
Little Cheverell 21 D5
Little Chishill 33 A5
Little Clacton 35 A7
Little Clifton 68 D7
Little Coggeshall 34 C6
Little Comberton 29 D3
Little Common 13 E6
Little Compton 30 C4
Little Cowarne 29 A2
Little Coxwell 22 B2
Little Creich 102 E3
Little Cressingham 44 C5
Little Crosby 48 C1
Little Cubleys 50 C7
Little Dalby 41 E3
Littledean 29 A6
Little Dens 105 D4
Little Dewchurch 28 E4
Little Driffield 59 A2
Little Dunham 44 C4
Little Dunkeld 88 B4
Little Dunmow 33 C6
Little Easton 33 C6
Little Eaton 50 E6
Little Ellingham 44 E6
Little End 24 F2
Little Eversden 32 E3
Little Fakenham 34 D1
Little Faringdon 30 C7
Little Fencote 63 C5
Little Fenton 57 D4
Littleferry 103 B2
Little Finborough 34 E3
Little Fransham 44 D4
Little Gaddesden 31 E6

Little Garway 28 D5
Little Gidding 42 E6
Little Glemham 35 C3
Little Gorsley 29 A5
Little Gransden 32 D3
Little Grimsby 53 B2
Little Gruinard 101 B3
Little Habton 64 E6
Little Hadham 33 A6
Little Hale 52 E7
Little Hallingbury 33 B7
Littleham Devon 6 D4
Littleham Devon 8 B5
Little Hampden 31 D7
Littlehampton 12 C6
Little Harrowden 42 B7
Little Haseley 31 B7
Little Hautbois 45 B3
Little Haven 16 B4
Little Hay 40 D4
Little Hayfield 50 B2
Little Haywood 40 C2
Little Heath 41 A6
Littlehempston 5 D4
Little Hereford 28 E1
Little Holtby 63 C5
Little Horkesley 34 D5
Little Hormead 33 A6
Little Horsted 13 B5
Little Horwood 31 C4
Little Houghton Northants
  31 D2
Littlehoughton Northld
  77 D4
Little Hucklow 50 C3
Little Hulton 49 B1
Little Hungerford 22 E4
Little Kimble 31 D7
Little Kineton 30 D2
Little Kingshill 23 C2
Little Langford 10 B1
Little Laver 24 F2
Little Lawford 41 B7
Little Leigh 49 A4
Little Leighs 33 D7
Little Lever 49 B1
Little Ley 97 B2
Little Linford 31 D3
Little London E Ssx 13 C4
Little London Hants 22 C7
Little London Hants 23 A6
Little London IOM 60 c3
Little London Lincs 43 C2
Little London Lincs 43 A2
Little London Lincs 53 B4
Little London Nflk 43 D2
Little London Nflk 44 A4
Little Longstone 50 C3
Little Malvern 29 B3
Little Maplestead 34 C5
Little Marcle 29 A4
Little Marlow 23 C3
Little Massingham 44 B3
Little Melton 45 A5
Little Mill Gwent 19 D3
Littlemill Hghld 103 C6
Littlemill Strath 73 D6
Little Milton 31 B7
Little Missenden 23 D2
Littlemore 31 A7
Little Musgrave 62 C3
Little Ness 38 D3
Little Neston 48 B4
Little Newcastle 16 C3
Little Newsham 63 B3
Little Oakley Esx 35 B6
Little Oakley Northants
  42 B6
Little Orton 69 B4
Little Ouseburn 57 C1
Littleover 50 E7
Little Parndon 33 A7
Little Paxton 32 C2
Little Petherick 3 B1
Little Plumstead 45 C4
Little Ponton 42 C1
Littleport 43 D6
Little Raveley 32 D1
Little Ribston 57 B2
Little Rissington 30 B6
Little Rogart 103 A1
Little Ryburgh 44 D3
Little Salkeld 69 D6
Little Sampford 33 C5
Little Saxham 33 D2
Little Scatwell 102 B6
Little Shelford 33 A3

Little Smeaton 57 D6
Little Snoring 44 D2
Little Sodbury 21 B2
Little Somborne 10 E1
Little Somerford 21 D2
Little Stainton 71 B6
Little Stanney 48 D4
Little Staughton 32 C2
Little Steeping 53 C5
Littlestone-on-Sea 15 A6
Little Stonham 35 A2
Little Stretton Leics 41 D4
Little Stretton Salop 38 D5
Little Strickland 61 E2
Little Stukeley 32 D1
Little Sutton 48 C4
Little Tew 30 D5
Little Tey 34 C6
Little Thetford 33 B1
Little Thirkleby 64 B6
Little Thorpe Dur 71 C4
Littlethorpe N Yorks 57 B1
Little Thurlow 33 C3
Little Thurrock 25 B5
Littleton Ches 48 D5
Littleton Hants 11 A1
Littleton Som 20 D7
Littleton Sry 23 E5
Littleton Tays 88 D5
Littleton Drew 21 C2
Littleton-on-Severn 20 E1
Littleton Pannell 21 D5
Little Torboll 103 A2
Little Torrington 6 D5
Little Totham 34 C7
Little Town 61 B2
Littletown 71 B4
Little Urswick 61 B6
Little Wakering 25 E4
Little Walden 33 B4
Little Waldingfield 34 D4
Little Walsingham 44 D2
Little Waltham 33 D7
Little Warley 25 B3
Little Weighton 58 E4
Little Welland 29 C4
Little Welnetham 34 C3
Little Wenham 34 E5
Little Wenlock 39 A4
Little Whittingham Green 35 B1
Little Whittington 70 C2
Littlewick Green 23 C4
Little Wilbraham 33 B3
Little Witcombe 29 D6
Little Witley 29 B1
Little Wittenham 22 E2
Little Wolford 30 C4
Littleworth H & W 29 C2
Littleworth Oxon 22 C2
Littleworth Staffs 40 C3
Little Wratting 33 C4
Little Wymondley 32 D6
Little Wyrley 40 C4
Little Yeldham 33 D5
Littley Green 33 C7
Litton Derbs 50 C3
Litton N Yorks 62 E7
Litton Som 20 E5
Litton Cheney 9 B4
Liverpool 48 C2
Liversedge 57 A5
Liverton Clev 64 E2
Liverton Devon 5 D3
Liverton Street 14 D3
Livingston 81 E5
Livingston Village 81 E5
Lixwm 48 A4
Lizard 2 D7
Llaingoch 46 B2
Llan 37 C5
Llanaber 37 A4
Llanaelhaearn 46 C6
Llanafan 27 A3
Llanafan-fawr 27 D5
Llanafan-fechan 27 D5
Llanallgo 46 E2
Llanarmon 46 D7
Llanarmon Dyffryn Ceiriog 38 A1
Llanarmon-yn-Ial 48 A6
Llanarth Dyfed 26 D5
Llanarth Gwent 19 D2
Llanarthney 17 D3
Llanasa 48 A3
Llanayron 26 D4

Llanbabo 46 C2
Llanbadarn Fawr 27 A2
Llanbadarn Fynydd 27 E3
Llanbadarn-y-garreg 28 A3
Llanbadoc 19 D4
Llanbadrig 46 C1
Llanbeder 19 D4
Llanbedr Gynd 36 E3
Llanbedr Pwys 28 B5
Llanbedr Pwys 28 A3
Llanbedr-Dyffryn-Clwyd 48 A6
Llanbedrgoch 46 E2
Llanbedrog 46 C7
Llanbedr-y-cennin 47 B4
Llanberis 46 E4
Llanbethery 19 A7
Llanbister 38 A7
Llanbister Road Station 38 A7
Llanblethian 18 E6
Llanboidy 17 A3
Llanbradach 19 B4
Llanbrynmair 37 D5
Llancarfan 19 A6
Llancayo 19 D3
Llancynfelyn 37 A6
Llandafal 19 B3
Llandaff 19 B6
Llandaff North 19 B6
Llandanwg 36 E3
Llandawke 17 A4
Llanddaniel Fab 46 D3
Llanddarog 17 D4
Llanddeiniol 26 E3
Llanddeiniolen 46 E4
Llandderfel 47 D7
Llanddeusant Dyfed 18 C1
Llanddeusant Gynd 46 C2
Llanddew 27 E7
Llanddewi 17 C7
Llanddewi Brefi 27 A5
Llanddewi'r Cwm 27 E6
Llanddewi Rhydderch 19 D2
Llanddewi Velfrey 16 E4
Llanddoged 47 C4
Llanddona 46 E3
Llanddowror 17 A4
Llanddulas 47 D3
Llanddwywe 36 E3
Llanddyfnan 46 E3
Llandefaelog 17 C4
Llandefaelog Fach 27 E7
Llandefaelog-tre'r-graig 28 A4
Llandefalle 28 A4
Llandegai 46 E3
Llandegfan 46 E3
Llandegla 48 A6
Llandegley 28 A1
Llandegveth 19 D4
Llandegwning 46 B7
Llandeilo 18 B1
Llandeilo Abercywyn 17 B4
Llandeilo Graban 27 E6
Llandeilo'r Fan 27 C7
Llandeloy 16 B3
Llandenny 28 D7
Llandevenny 20 D2
Llandewi Ystradenny 28 A1
Llandinabo 28 E5
Llandinam 27 E2
Llandissilio 16 E3
Llandogo 28 E7
Llandough S Glam 19 B6
Llandough S Glam 18 E6
Llandovery 27 B7
Llandow 18 E6
Llandre Dyfed 27 A6
Llandre Dyfed 16 E3
Llandre Dyfed 27 A2
Llandrillo 47 E7
Llandrillo-yn-Rhos 47 C2
Llandrindod Wells 27 E4
Llandrinio 38 B3
Llandudno 47 B2
Llandwrog 46 D5
Llandybie 18 B2
Llandyfan 18 B2
Llandyfriog 26 C6
Llandyfrydog 46 D2
Llandygwydd 26 B6
Llandyrnog 48 A5
Llandyry 17 C5

Llandysilio 38 B3
Llandyssil 38 A5
Llandyssul 26 D6
Llanedeyrn 19 C5
Llanegryn 36 E5
Llanegwad 17 D3
Llaneilian 46 D1
Llanelian-yn-Rhos 47 C3
Llanelidan 48 A6
Llanelieu 28 A4
Llanellen 19 D2
Llanelli 17 D5
Llanelltyd 37 B4
Llanelly 19 C2
Llanelwedd 27 E5
Llanenddwyn 36 E3
Llanengan 36 B3
Llanerchymedd 46 D2
Llanerch-yrfa 27 C5
Llanerfyl 37 E5
Llanfabon 19 B4
Llanfachraeth 46 C2
Llanfachreth 37 B3
Llanfaelog 46 C3
Llanfaelrhys 36 B3
Llanfaes Gynd 47 A3
Llanfaes Pwys 19 A1
Llanfaethlu 46 C2
Llanfaglan 46 D4
Llanfair 36 E3
Llanfair Caereinion 38 A4
Llanfair Clydogau 27 A5
Llanfair Dyffryn Clwyd 48 A6
Llanfairfechan 47 A3
Llanfair-green 19 D2
Llanfair-Nant-Gwyn 16 E2
Llanfair-Orllwyn 26 C6
Llanfairpwllgwyngyll 46 E3
Llanfair Talhaiarn 47 D4
Llanfair Waterdine 38 B7
Llanfairynghornwy 46 C1
Llanfair-yn-Neubwll 46 C3
Llanfallteg 16 E3
Llanfallteg West 16 E4
Llanfaredd 27 E5
Llanfarian 26 E3
Llanfechain 38 A2
Llanfechell 46 C1
Llanfendigaid 36 E5
Llanferres 48 A5
Llanfflewyn 46 C2
Llanfigael 46 C2
Llanfihangel 37 E4
Llanfihangel ar-Arth 17 C2
Llanfihangel Crucorney 28 C5
Llanfihangel Glyn Myfyr 47 D6
Llanfihangel Nant Bran 27 D7
Llanfihangel-nant-Melan 28 A2
Llanfihangel Rhydithon 28 A1
Llanfihangel Rogiet 28 A5
Llanfihangel-Tal-y-llyn 28 A5
Llanfihangel uwch-gwili 17 C3
Llanfihangel-y-Creuddyn 27 A3
Llanfihangel-y-pennant Gynd 46 E6
Llanfihangel-y-pennant Gynd 37 A5
Llanfihangel-y-traethau 46 E7
Llanfilo 28 A4
Llanfoist 19 C2
Llanfor 47 D7
Llanfrechfa 19 D4
Llanfrothen 47 A6
Llanfrynach 19 A1
Llanfwrog Clwyd 48 A6
Llanfwrog Gynd 46 C2
Llanfyllin 38 A3
Llanfynydd Clwyd 48 B6
Llanfynydd Dyfed 17 D3
Llanfyrnach 17 A2
Llangadfan 37 E4
Llangadog 18 C1
Llangadwaladr Clwyd 38 A1
Llangadwaladr Gynd 46 C4
Llangaffo 46 D4

Llangain 17 B4
Llangammarch Wells 27 D6
Llangan 18 E6
Llangarron 28 E5
Llangasty-Talyllyn 28 A5
Llangathen 17 D3
Llangattock 19 C2
Llangattock Lingoed 28 C5
Llangattock nigh Usk 19 D2
Llangattock-Vibon-Avel 28 D6
Llangedwyn 38 A2
Llangefni 46 D3
Llangeinor 18 E5
Llangeinwen 46 D4
Llangeitho 27 A5
Llangeler 17 B5
Llangelynin 36 E5
Llangendeirne 17 C4
Llangennech 17 D5
Llangennith 17 C6
Llangenny 19 C2
Llangernyw 47 C4
Llangian 36 B3
Llangiwg 18 C3
Llanglydwen 16 E3
Llangoed 47 A3
Llangoedmor 26 B6
Llangollen 48 B7
Llangolman 16 E3
Llangorse 28 A5
Llangorwen 27 A2
Llangovan 28 D7
Llangower 47 D7
Llangranog 26 C5
Llangristiolus 46 D3
Llangrove 28 E6
Llangua 28 C5
Llangunllo 38 B7
Llangunnor 17 C4
Llangurig 27 D2
Llangwm Clwyd 47 D6
Llangwm Dyfed 16 C5
Llangwm Gwent 20 D1
Llangwm-isaf 28 D7
Llangwnnadl 46 B7
Llangwyfan 48 A5
Llangwyllog 46 D3
Llangwyryfon 26 E3
Llangybi Dyfed 27 A5
Llangybi Gwent 19 D4
Llangybi Gynd 46 D6
Llangyfelach 18 B4
Llangynhafal 48 A5
Llangynidr 19 B2
Llangynin 17 A4
Llangynmyd 18 D5
Llangynog Dyfed 17 B4
Llangynog Pwys 37 E3
Llanhamlach 19 A1
Llanharan 19 A5
Llanharry 19 A5
Llanharry 19 A5
Llanhennock 19 D4
Llanhilleth 19 C3
Llanidloes 27 D2
Llaniestyn 46 B7
Llanigon 28 B4
Llanilar 27 A3
Llanilid 18 E5
Llanishen Gwent 28 D7
Llanishen S Glam 19 B5
Llanllawddog 17 C3
Llanllechid 47 A4
Llanlleonfel 27 D5
Llanllowel 8 B3
Llanllugan 37 E5
Llanllwch 17 B4
Llanllwchaiarn 38 A5
Llanllwni 26 D6
Llanllyfni 46 D5
Llanllywel 19 D4
Llanllywel 19 D4
Llanmadoc 17 C6
Llanmaes 18 E7
Llanmartin 19 D5
Llanmerewig 38 A5
Llanmihangel 18 E6
Llanmorlais 17 D6
Llannefydd 47 D3
Llannerch 47 E3
Llannerch-y-mor 48 A4
Llannon 17 D5
Llannor 46 C7
Llanon 26 E4

Llanover 19 D3
Llanpumsaint 17 C3
Llanreithan 16 B3
Llanrhaeadr-ym-Mochnant 38 A2
Llanrhaiadr 47 E4
Llanrhian 16 B2
Llanrhidian 17 C6
Llanrhos 47 B2
Llanrhyddlad 46 C2
Llanrhystud 26 E4
Llanrothal 28 D6
Llanrug 46 E4
Llanrumney 19 C5
Llanrwst 47 B4
Llansadurnen 17 A4
Llansadwrn Dyfed 27 A7
Llansadwrn Gynd 46 E3
Llansaint 17 B5
Llansamlet 18 B4
Llansannan 47 D4
Llansannor 18 E6
Llansantffraed 28 A5
Llansantffraed-Cwmdeuddwr 27 D4
Llansantffraed-in-Elvel 27 E5
Llansantffraid 26 E4
Llansantffraid Glan Conwy 47 C3
Llansantffraid-ym-Mechain 38 B2
Llansawel 27 A7
Llansilin 38 B2
Llansoy 28 D7
Llanspyddid 19 A1
Llanstadwell 16 C5
Llanstephan Dyfed 17 B4
Llanstephan Pwys 28 A3
Llantarnam 19 D4
Llanteg 19 E4
Llanthony 28 B5
Llantilio-Crossenny 19 D2
Llantilio Pertholey 19 D2
Llantood 26 A6
Llantrisant Gwent 19 D4
Llantrisant M Glam 19 A5
Llantrithyd 19 A6
Llantwit Fardre 19 A5
Llantwit Major 18 E7
Llantysilio 48 A7
Llanuwchllyn 47 C7
Llanvaches 20 D1
Llanvair-Discoed 20 D1
Llanvapley 19 D2
Llanvetherine 19 D2
Llanveynoe 28 C4
Llanvihangel Gobion 19 D3
Llanvihangel Rogiet 20 D2
Llanvihangel-Ystern-Llewern 28 D6
Llanwarne 28 E5
Llanwddyn 37 E4
Llanwenog 26 D6
Llanwern 19 D5
Llanwinio 17 A3
Llanwnda Dyfed 16 C2
Llanwnda Gynd 46 D5
Llanwnen 26 E6
Llanwnog 37 E6
Llanwonno 19 A4
Llanwrda 28 B7
Llanwrin 37 B5
Llanwrthwl 27 D4
Llanwrtyd 27 C6
Llanwrtyd Wells 27 C6
Llanwyddelan 37 E5
Llanyblodwel 38 B2
Llanybri 17 B4
Llanybyther 26 E6
Llanycefn 16 D3
Llanychaer Bridge 16 C2
Llanycil 27 D7
Llanycrwys 27 A6
Llanymawddwy 37 D4
Llanymynech 38 B2
Llanynghenedl 46 C2
Llanynys 48 A5
Llan-y-pwll 48 C6
Llanyre 27 E4
Llanystumdwy 46 D7
Llanywern 28 A5
Llawhaden 16 D4
Llawnt 38 B1
Llawr-y-dref 36 B3
Llawryglyn 37 D6
Llay 48 C6

Llechcynfarwy 46 C2
Llechfaen 19 A1
Llechryd Dyfed 26 B6
Llechryd Gwent 19 B3
Llechrydau 38 B1
Lledrod Clwyd 38 B2
Lledrod Dyfed 27 A3
Llethr 16 B3
Llidiadnenog 17 D2
Llidiardau 36 A3
Llithfaen 46 C6
Lloc 48 A4
Llong 48 B5
Llowes 28 A3
Lloyney 38 B7
Llwydcoed 18 E3
Llwydiarth 37 E4
Llwyn 38 B6
Llwyncelyn 26 D5
Llwyndafydd 26 C5
Llwynderw 38 B4
Llwyndyrys 46 C6
Llwyngwril 36 E5
Llwynhendy 17 D6
Llwyn Madoc 27 D5
Llwynmawr 38 B1
Llwyn-onn 26 D5
Llwyn-y-brain Dyfed 16 E4
Llwyn-y-brain Dyfed 27 B7
Llwynypia 18 E4
Llynclys 38 B2
Llynfaes 46 D3
Llysfaen 47 C3
Llyswen 28 A4
Llysworney 18 E6
Llys-y-frân 16 D3
Llywel 27 C7
Loandhu 103 B4
Loanhead 82 C6
Loans 73 C4
Lochailort 92 E6
Lochaline 85 C4
Lochans 66 B5
Locharbriggs 74 E7
Lochawe 86 C6
Lochboisdale 90 C3
Lochbuie 85 C6
Lochdhu Hotel 111 A4
Lochdonhead 85 D5
Lochdrum 101 E4
Lochearnhead 87 B6
Lochee 88 E5
Loch Eil Centre 86 B1
Lochend Hghld 111 C2
Lochend Hghld 94 D2
Lochfoot 68 B2
Lochgair 79 D2
Lochgarthside 94 D4
Lochgelly 82 B3
Lochgilphead 79 C3
Lochgoilhead 80 A1
Lochgoin 73 E3
Loch Head D & G 66 E6
Loch Head D & G 67 A1
Loch-hill 104 E4
Lochinver 108 C6
Lochlair 89 B4
Lochlane 87 E6
Lochlea 73 D4
Lochmaben 75 A7
Lochmaddy 98 D5
Lochore 82 B3
Lochranza 72 D2
Lochs Crofts 104 B2
Lochside Gramp 89 D2
Lochside Hghld 109 B3
Lochside Hghld 110 D5
Lochside Hghld 111 C2
Lochton 66 D2
Lochty 83 A2
Lochuisge 85 D3
Lochurr 67 D2
Lochwinnoch 80 C6
Lockengate 3 C2
Lockerbie 75 B7
Lockeridge 22 A5
Lockerley 10 D2
Locking 20 C5
Lockington Humb 58 E3
Lockington Leics 41 B2
Lockleywood 39 A2
Locksbottom 24 E6
Locks Heath 11 B4
Lockton 65 A5
Loddington Leics 41 E4
Loddington Northants 42 B7

Loddiswell 5 C6
Loddon 45 C6
Lode 33 B2
Loders 9 A4
Lodsworth 12 B4
Lofthouse *N Yorks* 63 B7
Lofthouse *W Yorks* 57 B5
Loftus 64 E2
Logan *D & G* 66 B6
Logan *Strath* 73 E5
Loggerheads 39 B1
Loggie 101 D2
Logie *Fife* 89 A6
Logie *Gramp* 103 D6
Logie *Gramp* 105 D3
Logie *Tays* 89 C2
Logie *Tays* 88 E3
Logie Coldstone 96 E3
Logie Newton 104 E5
Logie Pert 89 C2
Logierait 88 A3
Login 16 E3
Lolworth 32 E2
Lonbain 100 D6
Londesborough 58 D3
London 24 D5
London Colney 24 B2
Londonderry *N Yorks*
63 D6
Londonthorpe 42 C1
Londubh 101 A3
Lonemore 103 A3
Long Ashton 20 E3
Long Bennington 52 B7
Longbenton 71 A2
Longborough 30 B5
Long Bredy 9 B4
Longbridge *Warks* 30 C1
Longbridge *W Mids* 40 C7
Longbridge Deverill 21 C6
Long Buckby 31 B1
Longburgh 69 B4
Longburton 9 C2
Longcastle 66 E6
Long Clawson 41 E2
Longcliffe 50 D5
Long Common 11 B3
Long Compton *Staffs*
40 A2
Long Compton *Warks*
30 C4
Longcot 22 B2
Long Craig 89 D3
Long Crendon 31 B7
Long Crichel 10 A3
Longcross *Devon* 4 E3
Longcross *Sry* 23 D5
Longden 38 D4
Long Ditton 24 B6
Longdon *H & W* 29 C4
Longdon *Staffs* 40 C3
Longdon upon Tern 39 A3
Longdown 7 C7
Long Downs 2 E5
Long Drax 57 E5
Longdrum *Gramp* 97 E2
Longdrum *Tays* 88 D2
Long Duckmanton 51 A3
Long Eaton 51 A7
Longfield 25 B6
Longfleet 10 B5
Longford *Derbs* 50 D7
Longford *GL* 23 E4
Longford *Glos* 29 C5
Longford *Salop* 39 B3
Longford *Salop* 39 A1
Longford *W Mids* 41 A6
Longforgan 88 E6
Longformacus 83 B7
Longframlington 77 C5
Long Gill 55 B2
Longham *Dors* 10 B5
Longham *Nflk* 44 D4
Long Hanborough 30 E6
Long Hermiston 82 B5
Longhill 105 C3
Longhirst 77 D7
Longhope 29 A6
Longhope 113 C2
Longhorsley 77 C6
Longhoughton 77 D4
Long Itchington 30 E1
Longlands 104 C6
Longlane *Berks* 22 E4
Longlane *Derbs* 50 D7
Long Lawford 41 B7
Longley Green 29 B2

Long Load 9 A1
Longmanhill 105 A2
Long Marston *Herts* 31 D6
Long Marston *N Yorks*
57 C2
Long Marston *Warks*
30 B3
Long Marton 69 E7
Long Melford 34 C4
Longmorn 104 A3
Long Newnton 21 D1
Longnewton *Dur* 76 B3
Longnewton *Northld* 76 B3
Longney 29 B6
Longniddry 82 E5
Longnor *Salop* 38 D4
Longnor *Staffs* 50 B4
Longparish 22 D7
Long Preston 55 C2
Longridge *Lancs* 55 A4
Longridge *Loth* 81 D5
Longridge Towers 77 A1
Longriggend 81 C4
Long Riston 59 B3
Longrock 2 C5
Longsdon 49 D6
Longside 105 D4
Longslow 39 A1
Longstanton All Saints
32 E2
Longstanton St Michael
33 A2
Longstock 10 E1
Long Stowe 32 E3
Long Stratton 45 A6
Long Street *Bucks* 31 C3
Longstreet *Wilts* 22 A6
Long Sutton *Hants* 23 B7
Long Sutton *Lincs* 43 C2
Long Sutton *Som* 9 A1
Longthorpe 42 E5
Long Thurlow 34 E2
Longton *Lancs* 54 D5
Longton *Staffs* 49 D7
Longtown *Cumb* 69 B3
Longtown *H & W* 28 C5
Longville in the Dale 38 E5
Long Waste 39 A3
Long Whatton 41 B2
Longwick 31 C7
Long Wittenham 22 E2
Longwitton 77 B7
Longwood *Salop* 39 A4
Longwood House 11 B2
Longworth 22 C2
Longyester 83 A6
Lonmore 99 B7
Loose 13 E1
Loosegate 43 B2
Loosley Row 31 D7
Lootcherbrae 104 E3
Lopcombe Corner 10 D1
Lopen 9 A2
Loppington 38 D2
Lorbottle 77 B5
Lords Hill 21 C6
Lorgill 99 A7
Lorn 80 C3
Lornty 88 C4
Loscoe 51 A6
Lossiemouth 104 A1
Lossit 78 A6
Lostock Gralam 49 A4
Lostock Green 49 A4
Lostwithiel 3 D3
Lothbeg 110 E7
Lothersdale 55 D3
Lothmore 110 E7
Loudwater 23 C2
Loughborough 41 C3
Loughor 17 D6
Loughton *Bucks* 31 D4
Loughton *Esx* 24 E3
Loughton *Salop* 39 A6
Lound *Lincs* 42 D3
Lound *Notts* 51 C2
Lound *Sflk* 45 E6
Lount 41 A3
Lour 89 A4
Louth *Lincs* 53 B3
Loveacott 6 E4
Love Clough 55 C5
Lovedean 11 C3
Lover 10 D2
Loversall 51 B1
Loves Green 25 B2
Lovesome Hill 63 D5

Loveston 16 D5
Lovington 20 E7
Low 61 D5
Low Bolton 63 A5
Low Bradfield 50 D1
Low Bradley 56 D3
Low Braithwaite 69 C5
Low Brunton 70 C2
Low Burnham 58 C7
Low Burton 63 C6
Low Catton 58 C2
Low Coniscliffe 63 C3
Low Crosby 69 C4
Lowdham 51 C6
Low Dinsdale 63 D3
Low Eggborough 57 D5
Low Entercommon 63 D4
Lower Aisholt 20 B7
Lower Apperley 29 C5
Lower Ashton 5 D2
Lower Assendon 23 B3
Lower Auchalick 79 D4
Lower Barewood 28 C2
Lower Basildon 23 A4
Lower Bayble 107 D4
Lower Beeding 12 E4
Lower Benefield 42 C6
Lower Bentham 55 A1
Lower Berry Hill 28 E6
Lower Boddington 30 E2
Lower Boscaswell 2 A5
Lower Bourne 23 C7
Lower Brailes 30 D4
Lower Breakish 92 D2
Lower Broad Heath 29 C2
Lower Brockhampton
9 D4
Lower Brynamman 18 C2
Lower Bullingham 28 E4
Lower Cam 29 B7
Lower Camster 88 D4
Lower Chapel 27 E7
Lower Chute 22 C6
Lower Cwmtwrch 18 C2
Lower Darwen 55 A5
Lower Dean 32 B2
Lower Diabaig 101 A5
Lower Dicker 15 A5
Lower Down 38 C6
Lower Dunsforth 57 C1
Lower Egleton 29 A3
Lower End 31 D1
Lower Failand 20 E3
Lower Farringdon 11 D1
Lower Fernoch 86 B7
Lower Frankton 38 B7
Lower Freystrop 16 C4
Lower Froyle 23 B7
Lower Gledfield 102 D2
Lower Godney 20 D6
Lower Green *Kent* 13 D2
Lower Green *Nflk* 44 D2
Lower Green *Staffs* 40 B4
Lower Halstow 14 D2
Lower Hardres 15 B3
Lower Hawthwaite 61 B5
Lower Hayton 38 E6
Lower Hergest 28 B2
Lower Heyford 30 E5
Lower Higham 14 C1
Lower Holbrook 35 A5
Lower Hordley 38 C2
Lower Kilchattan 78 C2
Lower Killeyan 78 B7
Lower Kingcombe 9 B4
Lower Kinnerton 48 C5
Lower Langford 20 D4
Lower Largo 82 E2
Lower Lemington 30 C4
Lower Lydbrook 29 A6
Lower Lye 28 D1
Lower Machen 19 C5
Lower Maes-coed 28 C4
Lower Mayland 25 E2
Lower Moor 29 D3
Lower Nazeing 24 D2
Lower Oakfield 82 B3
Lower Ollach 92 C1
Lower Penarth 19 B7
Lower Penn 40 A5
Lower Pennington 10 E5
Lower Peover 49 B4
Lower Quinton 30 B3
Lower Shader 107 B2
Lower Shelton 31 E3
Lower Shiplake 23 B4
Lower Shuckburgh 30 E1

Lower Slaughter 30 B5
Lower Stanton St Quintin
21 D2
Lower Stoke 14 D1
Lower Street 13 E5
Lower Sundon 32 B6
Lower Swanwick 11 A4
Lower Swell 30 B5
Lower Tean 50 B7
Lower Thurnam 54 D2
Lower Tysoe 30 D3
Lower Upham 11 B3
Lower Vexford 20 A7
Lower Wallop 38 C4
Lower Walton 49 A3
Lower Weare 20 D5
Lower Welson 28 B2
Lower Whitley 49 A4
Lower Wield 23 A7
Lower Winchendon 31 C6
Lower Woodend 23 C3
Lower Woodford 10 C1
Lower Wraxall 9 B3
Lowesby 41 E4
Lowestoft 45 E6
Lowestoft End 45 E6
Loweswater 68 E7
Low Etherley 70 E6
Low Gate 70 C2
Lowgill *Cumb* 62 B5
Lowgill *Lancs* 55 A1
Low Habberley 40 A7
Low Ham 9 A1
Low Hawkser 65 B3
Low Haygarth 62 B5
Low Hesket 69 C5
Low Hesleyhurst 77 B6
Low Hutton 64 E7
Lowick *Cumb* 61 B5
Lowick *Northants* 42 C6
Lowick *Northld* 77 B2
Low Kilphin 66 C2
Low Laithe 56 E1
Low Leighton 50 B2
Lowick *Northld* 77 B2
Low Marishes 65 A6
Low Mill 64 D4
Low Moor 55 B3
Low Newton-by-the-Sea
77 D3
Lownie Moor 89 A4
Low Redford 70 D5
Low Row *Cumb* 69 D3
Low Row *N Yorks* 62 E5
Low Santon 58 E6
Lowsonford 30 B1
Low Stillaig 79 D5
Low Street 45 C3
Lowther 69 D7
Lowther College 47 D3
Lowthorpe 65 C7
Low Thurlton 45 D6
Lowton 49 A2
Lowton Common 49 A2
Low Torry 81 E3
Low Toynton 53 A4
Low Waters 81 B6
Low Wood 61 C5
Low Worsall 63 D4
Loxbeare 7 D5
Loxhill 12 C3
Loxhore 7 A3
Loxley 30 C2
Loxton 20 C5
Loxwood 12 C3
Lubachoinnich 102 C2
Lubcroy 102 B1
Lubenham 41 E6
Lubfearn 102 B4
Lubmore 101 C6
Lubnaclach 86 E2
Lubreoch 87 A4
Luccombe 7 D2
Luccombe Village 11 B6
Luccumbe 7 D2
Lucker 77 C2
Luckett 4 D3
Luckington 21 C2
Lucklawhill 89 A6
Lucknam 21 C3
Luckwell Bridge 7 D3
Lucott Cross 7 C2
Lucton 28 D1
Ludag 90 C4
Ludborough 53 A2
Ludchurch 16 E4
Luddenden 56 D5
Luddenham Court 14 E2

Luddesdown 25 B6
Luddington *Humb* 58 D6
Luddington *Warks* 30 B2
Luddington in the Brook
42 E6
Ludford *Lincs* 52 E3
Ludford *Salop* 38 E7
Ludgershall *Bucks* 31 B6
Ludgershall *Wilts* 22 B6
Ludgvan 2 C5
Ludham 45 C4
Ludlow 38 E7
Ludney 53 B2
Ludstock 29 A4
Ludwell 10 A2
Ludworth 71 B4
Luffincott 6 C7
Luffness 82 E4
Lugar 73 E5
Luggiebank 81 B4
Lugton 80 D6
Lugwardine 28 E3
Luib 92 C2
Luib-chonnal 94 B6
Lùibeilt 86 D2
Lulham 28 D3
Lullington *Derbs* 40 E3
Lullington *Som* 21 B5
Lulsgate Bottom 20 E4
Lulsley 29 B2
Lumb 56 D5
Lumbutts 55 D5
Lumby 57 C4
Lumphanan 97 A3
Lumphinnans 82 B3
Lumsdaine 83 D6
Lumsden 104 C6
Lunan 89 C3
Lunanhead 89 A3
Luncarty 88 B6
Lund *Humb* 58 E3
Lund *N Yorks* 57 E4
Lund *Shet* 114 E2
Lundavra 86 B2
Lunderton 105 E4
Lundie *Hghld* 93 D3
Lundie *Tays* 88 D5
Lundin Links 82 E2
Lunga 79 B1
Lunna 115 D1
Lunning 115 E1
Lunsford's Cross 13 E5
Lunt 48 C1
Luntley 28 C2
Luppitt 8 C3
Lupton 61 E5
Lurgashall 12 B4
Lurignich 86 A3
Lusby 53 B5
Luskentyre 98 E2
Luss 80 C2
Lussagiven 79 B4
Lustleigh 5 C2
Luston 28 D1
Luthermuir 89 C2
Luthrie 88 E7
Luton *Beds* 32 B6
Luton *Devon* 8 B3
Luton *Devon* 8 A6
Luton *Kent* 14 C2
Lutterworth 41 C6
Lutton *Devon* 5 A5
Lutton *Lincs* 43 C2
Lutton *Northants* 42 E6
Luxborough 7 D3
Luxulyan 3 C3
Lybster *Hghld* 111 A2
Lybster *Hghld* 111 C5
Lydacott 6 D5
Lydbury North 38 C6
Lydcott 7 A3
Lydd 15 A6
Lydden 15 C4
Lyddington 42 B5
Lydeard St Lawrence
20 A7
Lydford *Devon* 5 A2
Lydgate 55 D5
Lydham 38 C5
Lydiard Millicent 21 E2
Lydiate 48 C1
Lydlinch 9 D2
Lydney 29 A7
Lydstep 16 D6
Lye 40 B6
Lye Green 23 D1
Lyford 22 C2

Lymbridge Green 15 B4
Lymekilns 81 A6
Lyme Regis 8 E4
Lyminge 15 B4
Lymington 10 E5
Lyminster 12 C6
Lymm 49 A3
Lymore 10 D5
Lympne 15 B5
Lympsham 20 C5
Lympstone 8 A5
Lynaberack 95 A6
Lynchat 95 A5
Lyndhurst 10 D4
Lyndon 42 C4
Lyne *Gramp* 97 C3
Lyne *Sry* 23 E5
Lyneal 38 D1
Lynedale 99 C6
Lynegar 111 C3
Lyneham *Oxon* 30 C5
Lyneham *Wilts* 21 E3
Lyneholmeford 69 D2
Lyne House 12 D3
Lynemore *Gramp* 95 E2
Lynemore *Hghld* 95 D3
Lynemouth 77 D6
Lyne of Gorthleck 94 D3
Lyne of Skene 97 C2
Lyness 113 C2
Lynford 44 C6
Lyng *Nflk* 44 E4
Lyng *Som* 8 E1
Lynmore 95 D2
Lynmouth 7 B2
Lynsted 14 E2
Lynton 7 B2
Lyon's Gate 9 C3
Lyonshall 28 C2
Lyrabus 78 B5
Lytchett Matravers 10 A5
Lytchett Minster 10 A5
Lyth 111 C2
Lytham 54 C5
Lytham St Anne's 54 C5
Lythe 65 A2
Lythe Hill 29 D4
Lythes 113 D3
Lythmore 111 A2

M
Mabie 68 C2
Mablethorpe 53 D3
Mabws 27 A5
Macclesfield 49 D4
Macclesfield Forest 49 D4
Macduff 105 A2
Machan 81 B6
Machany 88 A7
Macharioch 72 B7
Machen 19 C5
Machir 78 B5
Machrie *Arran* 72 C4
Machrie *Islay* 78 C7
Machrihanish 72 A5
Machrins 78 C2
Machynlleth 37 B5
Mackworth 50 E7
Macmerry 82 E5
Macterry 105 A4
Madderty 88 A6
Maddiston 81 D4
Madehurst 12 B5
Madeley *Salop* 39 A4
Madeley *Staffs* 49 B7
Madeley Heath 49 B7
Madford 8 C2
Madingley 32 E2
Madjeston 9 E1
Madley 28 D4
Madresfield 29 C3
Madron 2 B5
Maenaddwyn 46 D2
Maenclochog 16 D3
Maendy 19 A6
Maentwrog 47 A6
Maer 39 B1
Maerdy *Clwyd* 47 E6
Maerdy *Dyfed* 18 B1
Maerdy *M Glam* 18 E4
Maerdy *Powys* 27 D7
Maesbrook 38 B2
Maesbury Marsh 38 C2
Maes-glas 19 C5
Maesgwynne 17 A3
Maeshafn 48 B5

Maesllyn 26 C6
Maesmynis 27 E6
Maesteg 18 D4
Maes-Treylow 28 B1
Maesybont 17 D4
Maesycrugiau 26 D6
Maesycwmmer 19 B4
Magdalen Laver 24 F2
Maggieknockater 104 B4
Magham Down 13 D5
Maghull 48 C1
Magor 20 D2
Magreig 68 B2
Maiden Bradley 21 C7
Maidencombe 5 E4
Maidenhead 23 C3
Maiden Law 70 E4
Maiden Newton 9 B4
Maidens 73 B7
Maidenwell Corn 4 B3
Maidenwell Lincs 53 B4
Maiden Wells 16 C6
Maidford 31 B2
Maids' Moreton 31 C4
Maidstone 13 E1
Maidwell 41 E7
Mail 115 D5
Mains of Ardestie 89 B5
Mains of Balhall 89 B2
Mains of Ballindarg 89 A3
Mains of Burgie 103 D6
Mains of Dillavaird 97 C5
Mains of Drimnin 85 B3
Mains of Drum 97 D4
Mains of Faillie 95 A2
Mains of Melgund 89 B3
Mains of Sluie 103 D6
Mains of Tannachy 104 B2
Mains of Tig 66 C2
Mains of Watten 111 C3
Mainsriddle 68 C4
Mainstone 38 B6
Maisemore 29 C5
Makendon 76 E5
Malaclete 98 B4
Malborough 5 C7
Malden 24 C6
Maldon 25 D2
Malham 55 D1
Maligar 100 B5
Mallaig 92 D5
Mallaigmore 92 D5
Mallaigvaig 92 D5
Malleny Mills 82 B6
Malletsheugh 80 E6
Malling 80 E1
Malltraeth 46 D4
Mallwyd 37 C4
Malmesbury 21 D2
Malmsmead 7 B2
Malpas Ches 48 D7
Malpas Corn 3 A4
Malpas Gwent 19 D4
Maltby Clev 64 B2
Maltby S Yorks 51 B1
Maltby le Marsh 53 C3
Malting Green 34 D6
Maltman's Hill 14 E4
Malton 64 E6
Malvern Link 29 B3
Malvern Wells 29 B3
Mambeg 80 B3
Mamble 39 A7
Mamhead 8 A5
Manaccan 2 E6
Manafon 38 A4
Manaton 5 C2
Manby 53 B3
Mancetter 41 A5
Manchester 49 C2
Mancot 48 C5
Mandally 93 E4
Manea 43 C6
Maneight 73 E7
Manfield 63 C3
Mangaster 114 C5
Mangersta 106 D4
Mangotsfield 21 A3
Manish 99 A3
Mankinholes 55 D5
Manley 48 E4
Manmoel 19 B3
Mannel 84 A4
Manningford Bohune 22 A6
Manningford Bruce 22 A6
Mannings Heath 12 E4
Mannington 10 B4

Manningtree 35 A5
Mannofield 97 E3
Manorbier 16 D6
Manordeifi 26 B6
Manordeilo 18 B1
Manorowen 16 C2
Mansell Gamage 28 C3
Mansell Lacy 28 D3
Mansergh 62 B6
Mansfield Notts 51 B4
Mansfield Woodhouse 51 B4
Mansriggs 61 B5
Manston 9 E2
Manswood 10 A4
Manthorpe Lincs 42 D3
Manthorpe Lincs 42 C1
Manton Leics 42 B4
Manton Lincs 58 E7
Manton Wilts 22 A5
Manuden 33 A6
Maoim 107 D2
Maolachy 85 E7
Maplebeck 51 D4
Maple Cross 23 E2
Mapledurham 23 A4
Mapledurwell 23 A6
Maplehurst 12 D4
Mapleton 50 C6
Mapperley 51 A6
Mapperton 9 B4
Mappleborough Green 30 A1
Mappleton 59 C3
Mapplewell 57 B7
Mappowder 9 D3
Marazion 2 C5
Marbury 48 E7
March 43 C5
Marcham 22 D2
Marchamley 38 E2
Marchington 50 C7
Marchington Woodlands 40 D2
Marchwiel 48 C7
Marchwood 10 E4
Marcross 18 E7
Marcus 89 B3
Marden H & W 28 E3
Marden Kent 13 E2
Marden T & W 71 B1
Marden Wilts 21 E5
Marden Beech 13 E2
Marden Thorn 13 E2
Mardy 19 D2
Marefield 41 E4
Mareham le Fen 53 A5
Mareham on the Hill 53 A5
Maresfield 13 B4
Marfleet 59 B5
Margam 18 C5
Margaret Marsh 9 E2
Margaret Roding 33 B7
Margaretting 25 B2
Margate 15 D1
Margnaheglish 72 E4
Marham 44 B4
Marholm 42 E4
Marian Cwm 47 E3
Marian-glas 46 E2
Mariansleigh 7 B4
Marishader 100 B5
Maristow 4 E4
Marivig 107 C6
Mark 20 C6
Markbeech 13 B2
Markby 53 C4
Mark Causeway 20 C6
Mark Cross 15 A3
Markdow 66 C3
Market Bosworth 41 B4
Market Deeping 42 E3
Market Drayton 39 A1
Market Harborough 41 E6
Markethill Tays 88 D5
Market Lavington 21 E5
Market Overton 42 B3
Market Rasen 52 E3
Market Stainton 53 A4
Market Street 45 B3
Market Warsop 51 B4
Market Weighton 58 D3
Markfield 41 B3
Markham 19 B3

Markham Clinton 51 D3
Markham Moor 51 D3
Markinch 82 C2
Markington 57 A1
Marksbury 21 A4
Marks Gate 24 E3
Markshall 34 C6
Marks Tey 34 D6
Markwell 4 D5
Markyate 32 B7
Marlborough 22 A5
Marldon 5 D4
Marlesford 35 C3
Marley Green 48 E7
Marley Hill 71 A3
Marli 47 E3
Marlingford 45 A5
Marloes 16 A5
Marlow 23 C3
Marlpit Hill 13 B2
Marlpool 51 A6
Marnhull 9 D2
Marnoch 104 D3
Marple 49 D3
Marr 57 D7
Marrel 111 A7
Marrick 63 A5
Marrister 115 E1
Marros 17 E5
Marsden T & W 71 C2
Marsden W Yorks 56 D6
Marsett 62 E6
Marsh 8 D2
Marsh, The 38 C5
Marshall Hill 51 C6
Marshall's Heath 32 C7
Marshalsea 7 E3
Marsham 45 A3
Marshaw 54 E2
Marsh Baldon 22 E2
Marshborough 15 C3
Marshbrook 38 D6
Marsh Chapel 53 B2
Marshfield Avn 21 B3
Marshfield Gwent 19 C5
Marshgate 6 A7
Marsh Gibbon 31 B5
Marsh Green Devon 8 B4
Marsh Green Kent 13 B2
Marsh Green Salop 39 A3
Marshland St James 43 D4
Marsh Lane 51 A3
Marshside 54 C6
Marsh Street 7 D2
Marshwood 8 E4
Marske 63 B4
Marske-by-the-Sea 64 D1
Marston Ches 49 A4
Marston H & W 28 C2
Marston Lincs 52 B7
Marston Oxon 31 A7
Marston Staffs 40 B2
Marston Staffs 40 A3
Marston Warks 40 E5
Marston Wilts 21 D5
Marston Green 40 D6
Marston Magna 9 B1
Marston Meysey 22 A2
Marston Montgomery 50 C7
Marston Moretaine 31 E3
Marston on Dove 40 E2
Marston St Lawrence 31 A3
Marston Stannett 28 E2
Marston Trussell 41 D6
Marstow 28 E6
Marsworth 31 E6
Marten 22 B5
Marthall 49 C4
Martham 45 D4
Martin Hants 10 B3
Martin Lincs 52 E6
Martin Drove End 10 B2
Martinhoe 7 A2
Martin Hussingtree 29 C1
Martinscroft 49 A3
Martinstown Dors 9 C5
Martlesham 35 B4
Martletwy 16 D4
Martley 29 B2
Martock 9 A2
Marton Ches 49 C5
Marton Clev 64 C2
Marton Cumb 61 B6
Marton Humb 59 B4

Marton Lincs 52 B3
Marton N Yorks 57 C1
Marton N Yorks 64 E5
Marton Salop 38 B4
Marton Warks 30 E1
Marton Abbey 57 D1
Marton-le-Moor 63 D7
Martyr's Green 12 C1
Martyr Worthy 11 B1
Marwick 112 B4
Marwood 6 E3
Marybank 102 C6
Maryburgh 102 D6
Maryfield 115 D3
Marygold 83 D6
Maryhill Gramp 105 B4
Maryhill Strath 80 E5
Marykirk 89 C2
Marylebone 48 E1
Marypark 95 E2
Maryport Cumb 68 D6
Maryport D & G 66 C7
Marystow 4 E2
Mary Tavy 5 A3
Maryton 89 C3
Marywell Gramp 97 E4
Marywell Gramp 97 A4
Marywell Tays 89 C4
Masham 63 C6
Mashbury 33 C7
Mastrick 97 E3
Matching 33 B7
Matching Green 33 B7
Matching Tye 33 B7
Matfen 70 D1
Matfield 13 D2
Mathern 20 E1
Mathon 29 B3
Mathry 16 B2
Matlaske 45 A2
Matlock 50 E4
Matlock Bank 50 E4
Matlock Bath 50 D5
Matson 29 C6
Matterdale End 69 B7
Mattersey 51 C2
Mattingley 23 B6
Mattishall 44 E4
Mattishall Burgh 44 E4
Mauchline 73 D5
Maud 105 C4
Maugersbury 30 B5
Maughold 60 d2
Mauld 94 B2
Maulden 32 B5
Maulds Meaburn 62 B3
Maunby 63 D6
Maund Bryan 28 E2
Maundown 8 B1
Mautby 45 D4
Mavesyn Ridware 40 C3
Mavis Enderby 53 B5
Mawbray 68 D5
Mawdesley 54 D6
Mawdlam 18 D5
Mawgan 2 E6
Maw Green 40 C5
Mawla 2 D4
Mawnan 2 E6
Mawnan Smith 2 E6
Maxey 42 E4
Maxstoke 40 E6
Maxton Bdrs 76 C3
Maxton Kent 15 D4
Maxwellheugh 76 D2
Maxwelton 74 D7
Maxweltown 68 C2
Maxworthy 6 B7
Maybole 73 C7
Mayen 104 D4
Mayfield E Ssx 15 A4
Mayfield Staffs 50 C6
Mayford 12 B1
Maynard's Green 15 A5
Maypole 13 C2
Maypole Green 45 D6
Maywick 115 C5
Mead End 10 B2
Meadle 31 D7
Meadowmill 82 E5
Meadowtown 38 C4
Meal Bank 61 E5
Meals 52 C2
Mealsgate 69 A5
Meanley 55 B3
Mearbeck 55 C1
Meare 20 D6

Meare Green 8 E1
Mearns 80 E6
Mears Ashby 31 D1
Measham 41 A3
Meathop 61 D5
Meaux 59 A4
Meavag 99 A2
Meavy 5 A4
Medbourne 41 E5
Meddon 6 B5
Meden Vale 51 B4
Medmenham 23 C3
Medomsley 70 E3
Medstead 11 C1
Meerbrook 49 D5
Meer End 40 E7
Meesden 33 A5
Meeth 6 E6
Meggethead 75 B3
Meidrim 17 A3
Meifod Clwyd 47 E5
Meifod Pwys 38 A3
Meigle 88 D4
Meikle Earnock 81 B6
Meikleour 88 C5
Meikle Rahane 80 B3
Meikle Strath 97 B6
Meikle Tarty 105 C6
Meikle Wartle 105 A5
Meinciau 17 C4
Meir 49 D7
Meirheath 40 B1
Melbost 107 C4
Melbost Borve 107 C2
Melbourn Cambs 32 E4
Melbourne Derbs 41 A2
Melbourne Humb 58 C3
Melbury 6 C5
Melbury Abbas 9 E1
Melbury Bubb 9 B3
Melbury Osmond 9 B3
Melbury Sampford 9 B3
Melchbourne 32 B2
Melchet Court 10 D2
Melcombe Bingham 9 D3
Melcombe Regis 9 C5
Meldon Devon 6 E7
Meldon Northld 77 C7
Meldreth 32 E4
Melgarve 94 C6
Melgum 96 E3
Meliden 47 E2
Melincourt 18 D3
Melincryddan 18 C4
Melin-y-coed 47 C4
Melin-y-ddôl 37 E5
Melin-y-grug 37 E5
Melin-y-wîg 47 E6
Melkinthorpe 69 D7
Melkridge 70 A2
Melksham 21 D4
Mellangaun 101 A3
Melldalloch 79 D4
Melling Lancs 61 E6
Melling Mers 48 C1
Mellis 34 E1
Mellon Charles 101 A2
Mellon Udrigle 101 A2
Mellor Ches 49 D3
Mellor Lancs 55 A4
Mellor Brook 55 A4
Mells 21 B6
Melmerby Cumb 69 E6
Melmerby N Yorks 63 A6
Melmerby N Yorks 63 D7
Melplash 9 A4
Melrose Bdrs 76 B2
Melrose Gramp 105 A2
Melsonby 63 B4
Meltham 56 D6
Melton 35 B3
Meltonby 58 C2
Melton Constable 44 E2
Melton Mowbray 41 E3
Melton Ross 59 A6
Melvaig 100 E3
Melverley 38 C3
Melverley Green 38 C3
Melvich 110 D2
Membury 8 D3
Memsie 105 C2
Memus 89 A3
Menabilly 3 C3
Menai Bridge 46 E3
Mendham 45 B7
Mendlesham 35 A2
Mendlesham Green 34 E2

Menethorpe 64 E7
Menheniot 4 C4
Menie 105 C6
Mennock 74 D5
Menston 56 E3
Menstrie 81 C2
Mentmore 31 E6
Meoble 92 E6
Meole Brace 38 D3
Meon 11 B4
Meonstoke 11 C3
Meopham 25 B6
Meopham Green 25 B6
Mepal 43 C6
Meppershall 32 C5
Merbach 28 C3
Mercaston 50 D6
Mere Ches 49 B3
Mere Wilts 21 C7
Mere Brow 54 D6
Mere Clough 55 C4
Mere Green 40 D5
Mereworth 13 D1
Meriden 40 E6
Merkland D & G 67 D3
Merlin's Bridge 16 C4
Merridge 20 B7
Merrifield 5 D6
Merrington 38 D2
Merrion 16 C6
Merriott 9 A2
Merrivale 5 A3
Merrow 12 C1
Merry Hill 24 B3
Merrymeet 4 C4
Mersham 15 A5
Merstham 12 E1
Merston 11 E4
Merstone 11 B6
Merther 3 A4
Merthyr 17 B3
Merthyr Cynog 27 D7
Merthyr Dyfan 19 B7
Merthyr-mawr 18 D6
Merthyr Tydfil 19 A3
Merthyr Vale 19 A4
Merton Devon 6 E5
Merton GL 24 C6
Merton Nflk 44 D6
Merton Oxon 31 A6
Mertyn 48 A4
Mervinslaw 76 C4
Meshaw 7 B5
Messing 34 C7
Messingham 58 D7
Metfield 45 B7
Metheringham 52 D5
Methil 82 D3
Methlem 46 A7
Methley 57 B5
Methlick 105 B5
Methven 88 B6
Methwold 44 B6
Methwold Hithe 44 B6
Mettingham 45 C7
Metton 45 B2
Mevagissey 3 C4
Mexborough 51 A1
Mey 111 C1
Meysey Hampton 22 A2
Mial 100 E4
Miavaig 106 D4
Michaelchurch 28 E5
Michaelchurch Escley 28 C4
Michaelchurch-on-Arrow 28 B2
Michaelstone-y-Fedw 19 C5
Michaelston-le-Pit 19 B6
Michaelstow 4 A3
Micheldever 11 B1
Michelmersh 10 E2
Mickfield 35 A2
Mickleby 65 A2
Mickleham 12 D1
Micklehurst 49 D1
Mickleover 50 E7
Micklethwaite 69 A4
Mickleton Glos 30 B3
Mickleton N Yorks 70 C6
Mickletown 57 B5
Mickle Trafford 48 D5
Mickley 63 C7
Mickley Square 70 D2
Mid Ardlaw 105 C2
Midbea 112 D2

Mid Moul

Mid Beltie 97 B3
Mid Cairncross 96 E6
Mid Calder 81 E5
Mid Clyth 111 C5
Middle Assendon 23 B3
Middle Aston 30 E5
Middle Barton 30 E5
Middlebie 69 A2
Middle Claydon 31 C5
Middle Drums 89 B3
Middleham 63 B6
Middle Handley 51 A3
Middle Harling 44 D7
Middlehill *Corn* 4 C4
Middlehill *Gramp* 105 B4
Middlehope 38 D6
Middle Kames 79 D3
Middle Littleton 30 A3
Middle Maes-coed 28 C4
Middlemarsh 9 C3
Middle Mill 16 B3
Middle Rasen 52 D3
Middle Rigg 81 E1
Middlesbrough 64 B1
Middleshaw 61 E5
Middlesmoor 63 A7
Middlestone Moor 71 A5
Middlestown 57 A6
Middle Street 24 E2
Middleton *Cumb* 62 B6
Middleton *Derbs* 50 D5
Middleton *Derbs* 50 C4
Middleton *Esx* 34 C5
Middleton *GM* 49 C1
Middleton *Gramp* 97 D2
Middleton *H & W* 82 B2
Middleton *Hants* 22 D7
Middleton *Lancs* 54 D2
Middleton *Loth* 82 D7
Middleton *Nflk* 44 A4
Middleton *Northants* 42 B6
Middleton *Northld* 77 B7
Middleton *Northld* 77 C2
Middleton *N Yorks* 64 E5
Middleton *Salop* 38 B5
Middleton *Salop* 38 E7
Middleton *Salop* 38 C2
Middleton *Sflk* 35 D2
Middleton *Tays* 82 B2
Middleton *Tays* 88 C4
Middleton *Tays* 89 B4
Middleton *Warks* 40 D5
Middleton *W Glam* 17 C6
Middleton *W Yorks* 56 E3
Middleton *W Yorks* 57 B5
Middleton Bank Top 77 B7
Middleton Cheney 30 E3
Middleton Green 40 B1
Middleton Hall 77 A3
Middleton in Teesdale 70 C6
Middleton One Row 63 D3
Middleton-on-Leven 64 B3
Middleton-on-Sea 12 B6
Middleton on the Hill 28 E1
Middleton-on-the-Wolds 58 E3
Middleton Priors 39 A5
Middleton Quernhow 63 D7
Middleton St George 63 D3
Middleton Scriven 39 A6
Middleton Stoney 31 A5
Middleton Tyas 63 C4
Middletown *Cumb* 60 D3
Middletown *Pwys* 38 C3
Middle Tysoe 30 D3
Middle Wallop 10 D1
Middlewich 49 B5
Middle Winterslow 10 D1
Middle Witchyburn 104 E3
Middlewood 49 D3
Middle Woodford 10 C1
Middlewood Green 34 E2
Middleyard 73 E5
Middlezoy 20 C7
Middridge 71 A6
Midfield 109 C2
Midge Hall 54 E5
Midgeholme 69 E4
Midgham 22 E5
Midgley *W Yorks* 57 A6
Midgley *W Yorks* 56 D5
Midhopestones 50 D1
Midhurst 11 E2
Mid Lavant 11 E4
Midlem 76 B3
Mid Letter 79 E1
Mid Lix 87 B5
Mid Mossdale 62 D5
Midmuir 86 A6
Midpark 72 E2
Mid Sannox 72 E3
Midsomer Norton 21 A5
Mid Strome 93 A1
Mid Thundergay 72 C3
Midtown 109 C2
Midtown Brae 101 A3
Midville 53 B6
Mid Yell 114 D3
Migdale 102 E2
Migvie 96 E3
Milarrochy 80 D2
Milber 5 D3
Milbethill 104 E3
Milborne Port 9 C2
Milborne St Andrew 9 D4
Milborne Wick 9 C1
Milbourne 70 E1
Milburn 69 E7
Milbury Heath 21 A1
Milcombe 30 E4
Milden 34 D4
Mildenhall *Sflk* 33 D1
Mildenhall *Wilts* 22 B5
Milebrook 38 C7
Milebush *Kent* 13 E2
Mile Elm 21 D4
Mile End *Esx* 34 D6
Mile End *Glos* 28 E6
Mile End *Nflk* 44 B7
Mileham 44 D4
Milesmark 81 E3
Milfield 77 A2
Milford *Corn* 6 B4
Milford *Derbs* 50 E6
Milford *Salop* 38 D2
Milford *Sry* 12 B2
Milford *Staffs* 40 B2
Milford Haven 16 C5
Milford on Sea 10 D5
Milkwall 28 E7
Milland 11 E2
Milland Marsh 11 E2
Mill Bank 56 D5
Millbank 105 D4
Millbeck 69 A7
Millbounds 112 E3
Millbreck 105 D4
Millbridge 23 C7
Millbrook *Beds* 32 B5
Millbrook *Corn* 4 E5
Millbrook *Hants* 11 A3
Millburn *Gramp* 104 D6
Millburn *Gramp* 104 E5
Millcombe 5 D6
Millcorner 14 D6
Millden 97 E2
Milldens 89 B3
Millearn 88 A7
Mill End *Bucks* 23 B3
Mill End *Herts* 32 E5
Millend Green 33 C6
Millenheath 38 E1
Millerhill 82 D6
Miller's Dale 50 C3
Mill Green *Esx* 25 B2
Millgreen *Salop* 39 A2
Mill Hill 24 C3
Millholme 61 E5
Millhouse *Cumb* 69 B6
Millhouse *Hghld* 79 D4
Millhousebridge 75 B7
Mill Houses 55 A1
Millikenpark 80 D5
Millington 58 D2
Mill Lane 23 B6
Millmeece 40 A1
Millness 94 B2
Mill of Colp 105 A4
Mill of Fortune 87 D6
Mill of Monquich 97 D4
Mill of Uras 97 D5
Millom 61 A5
Millport 80 A6
Mill Street 44 E4
Millthorpe 42 E1
Millthrop 62 B5
Milltimber 97 D3
Millton 88 E4
Millton of Noth 104 D6
Milltown *D & G* 69 B2
Milltown *Derbs* 50 E4
Milltown *Devon* 6 E3
Milltown *Gramp* 96 E2
Milltown *Gramp* 104 D4
Milltown *Gramp* 97 B3
Milltown *Hghld* 103 C7
Milltown *Hghld* 102 B6
Milltown of Aberdalgie 88 B6
Milltown of Auchindown 104 B4
Milltown of Campfield 97 B3
Milltown of Craigston 105 A3
Milltown of Edinvillie 104 A5
Milltown of Minnes 105 C6
Milltown of Towie 96 E2
Milnathort 82 B2
Milngavie 80 E4
Milnrow 55 D6
Milnsbridge 56 E6
Milnthorpe 61 D5
Milovaig 99 A6
Milrig 73 E5
Milson 39 A7
Milsted 14 E3
Milston 22 A7
Milton *Cambs* 33 A2
Milton *Cent* 80 E1
Milton *Cent* 80 D2
Milton *Cumb* 69 D3
Milton *D & G* 74 D7
Milton *D & G* 68 B2
Milton *Derbs* 41 A2
Milton *Dyfed* 16 D5
Milton *Gramp* 104 D2
Milton *Gwent* 19 D5
Milton *Hghld* 103 A4
Milton *Hghld* 103 C6
Milton *Hghld* 100 E7
Milton *Hghld* 90 C3
Milton *Hghld* 102 D7
Milton *Hghld* 111 D3
Milton *Hghld* 94 C2
Milton *Notts* 51 D3
Milton *Oxon* 30 E4
Milton *Oxon* 22 D2
Milton *Oxon* 23 A2
Milton *Staffs* 49 D6
Milton *Strath* 80 D4
Milton *Strath* 80 E1
Milton *Tays* 88 A5
Milton Abbas 9 E3
Milton Abbot 4 E3
Milton Bridge 82 C6
Milton Bryan 31 E4
Milton Clevedon 21 A7
Milton Coldwells 105 C5
Milton Combe 4 E4
Milton Damerel 6 C5
Miltonduff 103 E5
Milton Ernest 32 B3
Milton Green 48 D6
Milton Hill 22 D2
Miltonhill 103 D5
Miltonise 66 C3
Milton Keynes 31 D4
Milton Lilbourne 22 A5
Milton Lockhart 74 D1
Milton Malsor 31 C2
Milton Morenish 87 C5
Milton of Auchinhove 97 A3
Milton of Balgonie 82 D2
Milton of Cairnborrow 104 C4
Milton of Campsie 81 A4
Milton of Cushnie 97 A2
Milton of Dalcapon 88 A3
Milton of Tullich 96 D4
Milton on Stour 9 D1
Milton Regis 14 E2
Milton-under-Wychwood 30 C6
Milverton 8 C1
Milwich 40 B1
Minard 79 D2
Minchington 10 A3
Minchinhampton 29 C7
Mindrum 76 E2
Minehead 7 D2
Minera 48 B6
Minety *Glos* 21 D1
Minety *Wilts* 21 E1
Minffordd *Gynd* 37 B4
Minffordd *Gynd* 46 E7
Mingary *Hghld* 85 A3
Mingary *Hghld* 90 C3
Miningsby 53 B5
Minions 4 C3
Minishant 73 C6
Minley Manor 23 C6
Minllyn 37 C4
Minnigaff 67 A4
Minnonie 105 A2
Minskip 57 B1
Minstead 10 D3
Minster *Kent* 14 E1
Minster *Kent* 15 D2
Minsterley 38 C4
Minster Lovell 30 D6
Minsterworth 29 B6
Minterne Magna 9 C3
Minting 52 E4
Mintlaw 105 D4
Minto 76 B3
Minton 38 D5
Minwear 16 D4
Minworth 40 D5
Miodar 84 B4
Mirbister 112 C5
Mireland 111 D2
Mirfield 57 A6
Miserden 29 D7
Miskin 19 A5
Misson 51 C1
Misterton *Leics* 41 C6
Misterton *Notts* 51 D1
Misterton *Som* 9 A3
Mistley 35 A5
Mitcham 24 C6
Mitcheldean 29 A6
Mitchell 3 A3
Mitchelland 61 D5
Mitchel Troy 28 D6
Mitcheltroy Common 28 D7
Mitford 77 C7
Mithian 2 E3
Mitton 40 A3
Mixbury 31 B4
Mixon 50 B5
Moar 87 B4
Moat 69 C2
Mobberley 49 B3
Moccas 28 C3
Mochdre *Clwyd* 47 C3
Mochdre *Pwys* 27 E2
Mochrum 66 E6
Mockbeggar 13 E2
Mockerkin 68 D7
Modbury 5 B5
Moddershall 40 B1
Modsarie 109 D2
Moelfre *Clwyd* 38 A2
Moelfre *Gynd* 46 E2
Moffat 75 A5
Mogerhanger 32 C4
Moin' a' choire 78 C5
Moira *Leics* 41 A3
Molash 15 A3
Mol-chlach *mt* 92 B3
Mold 48 B5
Molehill Green 33 B6
Molescroft 59 A3
Molesworth 32 B1
Mollance 67 D4
Molland 7 C4
Mollington *Ches* 48 C4
Mollington *Northants* 30 E3
Mollinsburn 81 B4
Monachty 26 E4
Monachylemore 87 A7
Moncreiffe 88 C7
Monevechadan 80 A1
Monewden 35 B3
Moneydie 88 B6
Moniaive 67 D1
Monifieth 89 A5
Monikie 89 A5
Monimail 88 D7
Monington 26 A6
Monken Hadley 24 C3
Monk Fryston 57 D5
Monkhopton 39 A5
Monkland 28 D2
Monkleigh 6 D4
Monknash 18 E6
Monkokehampton 6 E6
Monk's Common 12 E4
Monkseaton 71 B1
Monks Eleigh 34 D4
Monks' Heath 49 C4
Monk Sherborne 23 A6
Monkshill 105 A4
Monksilver 7 E3
Monks Kirby 41 B6
Monk Soham 35 B2
Monkstadt 99 C5
Monk Street 33 C6
Monkswood 19 D3
Monkton *Devon* 8 C3
Monkton *Kent* 15 C2
Monkton *Strath* 73 C5
Monkton *T & W* 71 B2
Monkton Combe 21 B4
Monkton Deverill 21 C7
Monkton Farleigh 21 C4
Monkton Heathfield 8 D1
Monkton Up Wimborne 10 B3
Monkwearmouth 71 B3
Monkwood 11 C1
Monmore Green 40 B5
Monmouth 28 E6
Monnington on Wye 28 C3
Monreith 66 E6
Montacute 9 A2
Monteach 105 B4
Montford 38 D3
Montgarrie 97 A2
Montgomery (Trefaldwyn) 38 B5
Montgreenan 73 C3
Montrave 82 D2
Montrose 89 D3
Monxton 22 C7
Monyash 50 C4
Monymusk 97 B2
Monzie 87 E6
Moodiesburn 81 A4
Moonzie 88 E7
Moor, The 13 E4
Moor Allerton 57 B4
Moorby 53 A5
Moor Cock 55 A1
Moorcot 28 C2
Moor Crichel 10 A4
Moordown 10 B5
Moore 48 E3
Moor End *Cumb* 61 E6
Moor End *Humb* 58 D4
Moorends 57 E6
Moorgate 54 E1
Moorgreen 51 A6
Moorhall 50 E3
Moorhampton 28 C3
Moorhouse *Cumb* 69 B4
Moorhouse *Notts* 51 D4
Moorlinch 20 C7
Moor Monkton 57 D2
Moor Nook 55 A4
Moorsholm 64 D2
Moor Side 53 A6
Moorside 49 D1
Moortown *IOW* 11 A6
Moortown *Lincs* 52 D2
Morangie 103 A3
Morborne 42 E5
Morchard Bishop 7 B6
Morcombelake 9 A4
Morcott 42 C4
Morda 38 B2
Morden *Dors* 10 A5
Morden *GL* 24 C6
Mordiford 28 E4
Mordon 71 B6
More 38 C5
Morebath 7 D4
Morebattle 76 D3
Morecambe 54 D1
Morefield 101 D2
Moreleigh 5 C5
Morenish 87 C5
Moresby 68 C7
Morestead 11 B2
Moreton *Dors* 9 E5
Moreton *Esx* 24 F2
Moreton *H & W* 28 E1
Moreton *Mers* 48 B3
Moreton *Oxon* 31 B7
Moreton Corbet 38 E2
Moreton End 32 C7
Moretonhampstead 5 C2
Moreton-in-Marsh 30 C4
Moreton Jeffries 29 A3
Moreton Morrell 30 D2
Moreton on Lugg 28 E3
Moreton Pinkney 31 A3
Moreton Say 39 A1
Moreton Valence 29 B7
Morfa Bychan 46 E7
Morfa Glas 18 D3
Morfa Nefyn 46 B6
Morgan's Vale 10 C2
Mork 28 E7
Morland 69 E7
Morley *Derbs* 50 E6
Morley *Dur* 70 E6
Morley *W Yorks* 57 A5
Morley Green 49 C3
Morley St Botolph 44 E6
Morningside *Loth* 82 C5
Morningside *Strath* 81 C6
Morningthorpe 45 B6
Morpeth 77 D7
Morphie 89 D2
Morrey 40 D3
Morriston 18 B4
Morroch 92 D6
Morston 44 E1
Mortehoe 6 D2
Mortimer 23 A5
Mortimer's Cross 28 D1
Mortimer West End 23 A5
Mortlake 24 C5
Morton *Avn* 21 A1
Morton *Derbs* 51 A4
Morton *Lincs* 42 D2
Morton *Lincs* 52 B2
Morton *Nflk* 45 A4
Morton *Notts* 51 D5
Morton *Salop* 38 B2
Morton Bagot 30 B1
Morton-on-Swale 63 D5
Morvah 2 B5
Morval 4 C5
Morvich 93 B2
Morvil 16 D2
Morville 39 A5
Morwenstow 6 B5
Morwick Hall 77 D5
Mosbrough 51 A2
Moscow 73 D3
Mosedale 69 B6
Moselden Height 56 D6
Moseley *H & W* 29 C2
Moseley *W Mids* 40 C6
Moss *Clwyd* 48 C6
Moss *Hghld* 84 A4
Moss *Strath* 80 E3
Moss *S Yorks* 57 D6
Mossat 96 E2
Moss Bank 48 E2
Mossbank 114 D5
Mossblown 73 C5
Mossburnford 76 C4
Mossend 81 B5
Mossgiel 73 D5
Mosshead 104 D5
Mosside 89 A3
Mossley 49 D1
Mossley Hill 48 C3
Moss Nook 49 C3
Moss of Barmuckity 104 A2
Moss-side *Gramp* 104 D3
Moss-side *Hghld* 103 B6
Moss Side *Lancs* 54 C4
Mosstodloch 104 B2
Mosston 89 B4
Mosterton 9 A3
Mostyn 48 A3
Mostyn Quay 48 A3
Motcombe 9 E1
Mote House 13 E1
Motherby 69 C7
Motherwell 81 B6
Mottingham 24 E5
Mottisfont 10 E2
Mottistone 11 A6
Mottram in Longdendale 49 D2
Mouldsworth 48 E4
Moulin 88 A3
Moulsecoomb 13 A6
Moulsford 22 E3
Moulsham 25 C2
Moulsoe 31 E3
Moulton *Ches* 49 A5
Moulton *Lincs* 43 B2
Moulton *Northants* 31 C1
Moulton *N Yorks* 63 C4
Moulton *Sflk* 33 C2
Moulton Chapel 43 A3
Moulton St Mary 45 D5
Moulton Seas End 43 B2

Mount *Corn* 2 E3
Mount *Corn* 3 D2
Mount *Hghld* 103 C7
Mountain Ash 19 A4
Mountain Cross 75 B1
Mountain Water 16 C3
Mountbenger 75 D3
Mountblairy 104 E3
Mount Bures 34 D5
Mount Edgcumbe 4 E5
Mountgerald 102 D5
Mount Hawke 2 E4
Mountjoy 3 A2
Mount Manisty 48 C4
Mountnessing 25 B3
Mount Oliphant 73 C6
Mounton 20 E1
Mount Pleasant *Derbs* 50 E6
Mount Pleasant *Sflk* 35 E1
Mountsorrel 41 C3
Mountstuart 80 A6
Mount Tabor 56 D5
Mousehole 2 B6
Mouswald 68 D2
Mow Cop 49 C6
Mowden 63 C3
Mowhaugh 76 E3
Mowsley 41 D6
Mowtie 97 D5
Moxley 40 B5
Moy *Gramp* 103 D5
Moy *Hghld* 93 D6
Moy *Hghld* 95 A2
Moy *Hghld* 94 C7
Moyles Court 10 C4
Moylgrove 26 A6
Muasdale 72 A3
Muchalls 97 E4
Much Birch 28 E4
Much Cowarne 29 A3
Much Dewchurch 28 D4
Muchelney 9 A1
Much Hadham 33 A7
Much Hoole 54 D5
Muchlarnick 4 C5
Much Marcle 29 A4
Muchra 75 C4
Muchrachd 93 E1
Much Wenlock 39 A5
Mucking 25 B4
Mucklestone 39 B1
Muckleton 38 E2
Muckletown 104 D6
Muckton 53 B3
Mudale 109 C5
Muddiford 6 E3
Muddles Green 13 C5
Muddleswood 12 E5
Mudeford 10 C5
Mudford 9 B2
Mudgley 20 D6
Mugeary 92 B1
Mugginton 50 D6
Muggleswick 70 D3
Muie 102 E1
Muir 95 D7
Muirden 105 A3
Muirdrum 89 B5
Muirhead *Fife* 82 C2
Muirhead *Gramp* 103 D5
Muirhead *Gramp* 97 A2
Muirhead *Strath* 81 A5
Muirhead *Tays* 88 E5
Muirhouses 81 E3
Muirkirk 74 B3
Muir of Fowlis 97 A2
Muir of Highfield 102 D6
Muir of Ord 102 D6
Muirshearlich 93 D6
Muirskie 97 D4
Muirtack 105 C5
Muirton *Tays* 89 C2
Muirton *Tays* 89 D2
Muirton of Ardblair 88 C4
Muirton of Ballochy 89 C2
Muirtown 88 A7
Muiryfold 105 A3
Muker 62 E4
Mulbarton 45 A5
Mulben 104 B3
Mulhagery 107 B7
Mullion 2 D7
Mumbles, The 18 B5
Mumby 53 D4
Munderfield Row 29 A2

Munderfield Stocks 29 A2
Mundesley 45 C2
Mundford 44 C6
Mundham *Nflk* 45 C6
Mundham *W Ssx* 45 C6
Mundon Hill 25 D2
Mundurno 97 E2
Munerigie 93 E4
Mungasdale 101 B2
Mungoswells 82 E5
Mungrisdale 69 B6
Munlochy 102 E6
Munsley 29 A3
Munslow 38 E6
Murchington 5 B2
Murcott 31 A6
Murdostoun 81 C6
Murkle 111 B2
Murlaganmore 87 B5
Murlaggan *Hghld* 93 C5
Murlaggan *Hghld* 94 B7
Murra 113 B1
Murroes 89 A5
Murrow 43 B4
Mursley 31 D5
Murston 14 E2
Murthill 89 A3
Murthly 88 B5
Murton *Cumb* 70 A6
Murton *Dur* 71 B4
Murton *Northld* 77 A1
Murton *N Yorks* 57 E2
Musbury 8 D4
Muscoates 64 D5
Musdale 86 A6
Musselburgh 82 D5
Muston *Leics* 42 B1
Muston *N Yorks* 65 C6
Mustow Green 40 A7
Mutford 45 D7
Muthill 87 E7
Mutterton 8 B3
Mybster 111 B3
Myddfai 27 B7
Myddle 38 D2
Myddlewood 38 D2
Mydroilyn 26 D5
Mylor 3 A5
Mylor Bridge 3 A5
Mynachlog-ddu 16 E2
Myndtown 38 C6
Mynydd-bach 20 D1
Mynydd-y-Glyn 19 A5
Mynytho 46 C7
Myrebird 97 C4
Mytchett 23 C6
Mytholm 55 D5
Mytholmroyd 56 D5
Myton-on-Swale 57 C1

N

Naburn 57 D3
Nackington 15 B3
Nacton 35 B4
Nafferton 59 A2
Naiad 81 B2
Nailbridge 29 A6
Nailsea 20 D3
Nailstone 41 B4
Nailsworth 21 C1
Nairn 103 B6
Nancegollan 2 D5
Nanhoron 46 B7
Nannau 37 B3
Nannerch 48 A5
Nanpantan 41 C3
Nanpean 3 B3
Nantclwyd Hall 48 A6
Nant-ddu 19 A2
Nanteos 27 A3
Nanternis 26 C5
Nantgaredig 17 C3
Nantgarw 19 B5
Nant-glâs 27 D4
Nantglyn 47 E4
Nantlle 46 E5
Nantmawr 38 B2
Nantmel 27 E4
Nantmor 47 A6
Nant Peris 47 A5
Nant-y-caws 17 C4
Nant-y-derry 19 D3
Nantyffyllon 18 D4
Nantyglo 19 B2
Nant-y-groes 27 E4

Nant-y-moel 18 E4
Naphill 23 C2
Nappa 55 C2
Napton on the Hill 30 E1
Narberth 16 E4
Narborough *Leics* 41 C5
Narborough *Nflk* 44 B4
Narrachan 86 A7
Nasareth 46 D6
Naseby 41 D7
Nash *Bucks* 31 C4
Nash *Gwent* 19 D5
Nash *H & W* 28 C1
Nash *Salop* 39 A7
Nash *Som* 18 E6
Nash Lee 31 D7
Nassington 42 D5
Nasty 32 E6
Nateby *Cumb* 62 C4
Nateby *Lancs* 54 D3
Nately 23 B6
Natland 61 E5
Naughton 34 E4
Naunton *Glos* 30 B5
Naunton *H & W* 29 C4
Naunton Beauchamp 29 D2
Naust 101 A3
Navenby 52 C6
Navestock 24 F3
Navestock Side 25 A3
Navidale 111 A7
Navity 103 A5
Nawton 64 D5
Nayland 34 D5
Nazeing 24 E2
Neacroft 10 C5
Neal's Green 41 A6
Neap 115 E1
Near Cotton 50 B6
Near Sawrey 61 C5
Neasham 63 C3
Neath 18 C4
Neatham 23 B7
Neatishead 45 C3
Nebo *Dyfed* 26 E4
Nebo *Gynd* 46 D5
Nebo *Gynd* 47 C5
Necton 44 C5
Nedd 108 D5
Nedderton 77 D7
Nedging Tye 34 E4
Needham 45 B7
Needham Market 34 E3
Needingworth 32 E1
Neen Savage 39 A7
Neen Sollars 39 A7
Neenton 39 A6
Nefyn 46 C6
Neilston 80 D6
Nelson *Lancs* 55 C4
Nelson *M Glam* 19 B4
Nelson Village 71 A1
Nemphlar 74 D1
Nempnett Thrubwell 20 E4
Nenthall 70 A4
Nenthead 70 A4
Nenthorn 76 C2
Nercwys 48 B5
Nereabolls 78 B6
Neriby 78 C5
Nerston 81 A6
Nesbit 77 A2
Ness *Ches* 48 C4
Ness *N Yorks* 64 D6
Nesscliffe 38 C3
Neston *Ches* 48 B4
Neston *Wilts* 21 C4
Nether Alderley 49 C4
Netheravon 22 A7
Nether Barr 67 A4
Nether Blainslie 76 B1
Netherbrae 105 A3
Netherbrough 112 C5
Nether Broughton 41 D2
Netherburn 74 C1
Nether Burrow 62 B7
Netherbury 9 A4
Netherby *Cumb* 69 B2
Netherby *N Yorks* 57 B3
Nether Cerne 9 A4
Nether Compton 9 B3
Nethercott 30 E5
Nether Crimond 105 B6
Nether Dalgliesh 75 C5
Nether Dallachy 104 B2
Nether End 50 D3

Netherend 28 E7
Nether Exe 7 D6
Netherfield *E Ssx* 13 E5
Netherfield *Notts* 51 C6
Netherfield *Strath* 74 C1
Nether Glasslaw 105 B3
Netherhall 80 B5
Netherhampton 10 C2
Nether Handwick 88 E4
Nether Haugh 51 A1
Nether Headon 51 D3
Nether Hesleden 62 D7
Nether Kellet 54 E1
Nether Kinmundy 105 D4
Nether Knock 75 D6
Nether Langwith 51 B3
Nether Lenshie 104 E4
Netherley 97 D4
Nethermill 75 A7
Nether Moor 50 E4
Nethermuir 105 C4
Nether Padley 50 D3
Nether Pitforthie 97 D6
Nether Poppleton 57 D2
Netherseal 40 E3
Nethershield 73 E5
Nether Silton 64 B4
Nether Stowey 20 A7
Netherstreet 21 D4
Netherthird 67 D5
Netherthong 56 E7
Netherthorpe 51 B2
Netherton *Ches* 48 E4
Netherton *Devon* 5 D3
Netherton *H & W* 29 D3
Netherton *Mers* 48 C1
Netherton *Northld* 77 A5
Netherton *Oxon* 22 D2
Netherton *Strath* 81 D6
Netherton *Tays* 89 B3
Netherton *Tays* 88 C3
Netherton *W Mids* 40 B6
Netherton *W Yorks* 57 A6
Nethertown *Cumb* 60 D3
Nethertown *Hghld* 111 D1
Nether Urquhart 82 B2
Nether Wallop 10 E1
Nether Wellwood 74 B3
Nether Whitacre 40 E5
Netherwitton 77 C6
Netherwood 68 C2
Nether Woodburn 7 C4
Nether Worton 30 E4
Nethy Bridge 95 D3
Netley 11 A4
Netley Marsh 10 E3
Nettlebed 23 B3
Nettlebridge 21 A6
Nettlecombe 7 E3
Nettleden 32 B7
Nettleham 52 D4
Nettlestead *Kent* 13 D1
Nettlestead *Sflk* 34 E4
Nettlestead Green 13 D1
Nettlestone 11 C5
Nettleton *Lincs* 59 B7
Nettleton *Wilts* 21 C3
Netton *Devon* 5 A6
Netton *Wilts* 10 C1
Neuadd *Gynd* 46 C1
Neuadd *Powys* 27 D6
Neuadd-fawr 27 B6
Nevendon 25 C3
Nevern 16 D1
Nevill Holt 42 B5
New Abbey 68 C3
New Aberdour 105 B2
New Addington 24 D6
New Alresford 11 B1
New Alyth 88 D4
New Annesley 51 B5
Newark *Cambs* 43 A4
Newark *Ork* 112 G2
Newark-on-Trent 51 D5
Newarthill 81 B6
New Ash Green 25 B6
Newbald 58 E4
Newbarn 15 B5
New Barnet 24 C3
Newbarns 61 B6
Newbattle 82 D6
New Beaupre 19 A6
New Bewick 77 B3
Newbiggin *Cumb* 69 C7
Newbiggin *Cumb* 69 E7
Newbiggin *Cumb* 69 D5
Newbiggin *Cumb* 61 B7

Newbiggin *Dur* 70 C6
Newbiggin *Northld* 70 C2
Newbiggin *N Yorks* 62 E6
Newbiggin *N Yorks* 62 E5
Newbiggin-by-the-Sea 77 E7
Newbigging *Gramp* 97 D4
Newbigging *Gramp* 105 A5
Newbigging *Gramp* 96 B5
Newbigging *Strath* 75 A1
Newbigging *Tays* 89 A5
Newbigging *Tays* 88 D4
Newbiggin-on-Lune 62 C4
Newbold *Derbs* 50 E3
Newbold *Leics* 41 B3
Newbold on Avon 41 B7
Newbold on Stour 30 C3
Newbold Pacey 30 C2
Newbold Verdon 41 B4
Newborough *Gynd* 46 D4
Newborough *Northants* 43 A4
Newborough *Staffs* 40 D2
Newbottle 31 A4
Newbourn 35 B4
New Bradwell 31 D3
New Brampton 50 E3
New Bridge 68 C2
Newbridge *Clwyd* 48 B7
Newbridge *Corn* 2 B5
Newbridge *Devon* 4 D4
Newbridge *Dyfed* 16 C2
Newbridge *Gwent* 19 C4
Newbridge *Hants* 10 D3
Newbridge *IOW* 11 A6
Newbridge *Loth* 82 B5
Newbridge *Oxon* 30 E7
Newbridge-on-Usk 19 D4
Newbridge on Wye 27 E5
New Brighton *Hants* 11 D4
New Brighton *Mers* 48 C2
New Brinsley 51 A5
Newbrough 70 B2
New Broughton 48 C6
New Buckenham 44 E6
Newburgh *Bdrs* 75 D3
Newburgh *Fife* 88 D7
Newburgh *Gramp* 105 C3
Newburgh *Gramp* 105 C6
Newburgh *Lancs* 54 D6
Newburn 70 E2
Newbury 22 D5
Newby *Clev* 64 C2
Newby *Cumb* 69 D7
Newby *Lancs* 55 C3
Newby *N Yorks* 55 B1
Newby Bridge 61 C5
Newby East 69 C4
New Byth 105 B3
Newby West 69 B4
Newby Wiske 63 D6
Newcastle *Gwent* 28 D6
Newcastle *M Glam* 18 E5
Newcastle *Salop* 38 B6
Newcastle Emlyn 26 C6
Newcastleton 76 A7
Newcastle-Under-Lyme 49 C7
Newcastle upon Tyne 71 A2
Newchapel *Dyfed* 17 A2
Newchapel *Sry* 13 A2
Newchapel *Staffs* 49 C6
Newchurch *Dyfed* 17 B3
Newchurch *Gwent* 20 D1
Newchurch *IOW* 11 B6
Newchurch *Kent* 15 A5
Newchurch *Lancs* 55 C5
Newchurch *Lancs* 55 C4
Newchurch *Pwys* 28 B2
New Clipstone 51 B4
New Costessey 45 A4
Newcott 8 D3
Newcraighall 82 D5
New Cross 29 A3
New Cumnock 74 B4
New Deer 105 B4
Newdigate 12 E2
New Duston 31 C1
New Earswick 57 E2
New Edlington 51 B1
New Elgin 104 A2
New Ellerby 59 B4
Newell Green 23 C4
New Eltham 24 E5
New End 30 A1

Newenden 14 D6
New England 42 E4
Newent 29 B5
Newerne 29 A7
New Farnley 57 A4
New Ferry 48 C3
Newfield *Dur* 71 A5
Newfield *Hghld* 103 A4
New Forest 104 C6
New Fryston 57 C5
Newgale 16 B3
New Galloway 67 C3
Newgate 44 E1
Newgate Street 24 D2
New Gilston 82 E2
Newgord 114 E2
Newhall *Ches* 49 A7
Newhall *Derbs* 40 E2
Newham *GL* 24 E4
Newham *Northld* 77 C3
Newham Hall 77 C3
New Hartley 71 B1
Newhaven 13 B6
New Haw 23 E5
Newhay 55 D6
New Hedges 16 E5
New Holland 59 A5
Newholm 65 A2
New Horton Grange 70 E1
New Houghton *Derbs* 51 A4
New Houghton *Nflk* 44 B3
Newhouse 81 B5
New Houses 62 D7
New Hutton 61 E5
New Hythe 13 E1
Newick 13 B4
Newington *Kent* 15 B5
Newington *Kent* 14 D2
Newington *Oxon* 23 A2
Newington Bagpath 21 C1
New Inn *Dyfed* 17 C2
New Inn *Fife* 82 C2
New Inn *Gwent* 28 D7
New Inn *Gwent* 28 D7
New Invention *Salop* 38 B7
New Invention *W Mids* 40 B4
New Lanark 74 D1
Newland *Glos* 28 E7
Newland *H & W* 29 B3
Newland *N Yorks* 57 E5
Newlandrig 82 D6
Newlands *Bdrs* 76 B6
Newlands *Northld* 70 D3
Newlands of Geise 111 A2
New Lane 54 D6
New Leake 53 C6
New Leeds 105 C3
New Leslie 104 D6
New Longton 54 E5
New Luce 66 C4
Newlyn 2 B6
Newlyn East 3 A3
Newmachar 97 D2
Newmains 81 C6
New Mains of Ury 97 D5
New Malden 24 C6
Newmarket *Sflk* 33 C2
Newmarket *W Is* 107 C4
New Marske 64 D1
New Marton 38 C1
Newmill *Bdrs* 76 A4
Newmill *Corn* 2 B5
Newmill *Gramp* 104 C3
New Mill *Gramp* 97 C5
Newmill *Gramp* 105 B4
Newmill *Gramp* 105 B6
New Mill *Herts* 31 E6
New Mill *W Yorks* 56 E7
Newmill End 32 C7
Newmill of Inshewan 89 A2
New Mills *Corn* 3 A3
New Mills *Derbs* 50 B2
New Mills *Gwent* 28 E7
Newmills *Hghld* 102 E5
New Mills *Pwys* 37 E5
Newmiln *Tays* 88 C5
Newmiln *Tays* 88 B6
Newmilns 73 E5
New Milton 10 D5
New Moat 16 D3
New Monkland 81 B5
Newnham *Glos* 29 A6
Newnham *Hants* 23 B6
Newnham *Herts* 32 D5
Newnham *Kent* 14 E3

Newnham *Northants* 31 A2
Newnham Bridge 29 A1
Newnham Paddox 41 B6
Newnoth 104 D5
New Orleans 72 B6
New Oscott 40 C5
New Park *Corn* 4 B2
New Park *Hants* 10 D4
New Pitsligo 105 B3
New Polzeath 3 B1
Newport *Corn* 4 D2
Newport *Devon* 6 E3
Newport *Dyfed* 16 D2
Newport *Esx* 33 B5
Newport *Glos* 21 B1
Newport *Gwent* 19 D5
Newport *Hghld* 111 B6
Newport *Humb* 58 D4
Newport *IOW* 11 A6
Newport *Nflk* 45 E4
Newport *Salop* 39 B3
Newport-on-Tay 89 A6
Newport Pagnell 31 D3
Newpound Common 12 C4
New Prestwick 73 C5
Newquay 3 A2
New Quay 26 C5
New Rackheath 45 B4
New Radnor 28 B1
New Rent 69 C6
New Road 19 A5
New Road Side 55 D3
New Romney 15 A6
New Rossington 51 C1
New Row 55 A4
New Sauchie 81 C2
New Sawley 51 A7
New Scone 88 C6
Newseat 105 A5
Newsham *Lancs* 54 E4
Newsham *Northld* 71 B1
Newsham *N Yorks* 63 B3
Newsham *N Yorks* 63 D6
Newsholme *Humb* 58 C5
Newsholme *Lancs* 55 C2
New Silksworth 71 B3
Newstead *Bdrs* 76 B2
Newstead *Northld* 77 C3
Newstead *Notts* 51 B5
Newthorpe 57 C4
Newtimber Place 12 E5
Newton *Bdrs* 76 C3
Newton *Cambs* 43 C3
Newton *Cambs* 33 A4
Newton *Ches* 48 E6
Newton *Ches* 48 E4
Newton *Cumb* 61 B6
Newton *D & G* 75 B6
Newton *Dyfed* 16 C3
Newton *GM* 49 D2
Newton *Gramp* 104 C4
Newton *Gramp* 10 D2
Newton *Gramp* 104 B2
Newton *H & W* 103 A7
Newton *H & W* 28 C1
Newton *H & W* 103 A7
Newton *Hants* 10 D2
Newton *Hghld* 111 D4
Newton *Hghld* 103 A7
Newton *Hghld* 111 C3
Newton *Hghld* 108 D5
Newton *Hghld* 102 D6
Newton *Lancs* 55 A2
Newton *Lancs* 61 E6
Newton *Lincs* 42 D1
Newton *Loth* 81 E4
Newton *M Glam* 18 D6
Newton *Nflk* 44 C4
Newton *Northants* 42 B6
Newton *Northld* 70 D2
Newton *Notts* 51 C6
Newton *Sflk* 34 D4
Newton *Staffs* 40 C2
Newton *Strath* 79 E2
Newton *Tays* 87 E5
Newton *Warks* 41 C7
Newton *W Glam* 18 B5
Newton *W Is* 98 C4
Newton *W Yorks* 57 C5
Newton Abbot 5 D3
Newtonairds 74 D7
Newton Arlosh 68 E4
Newton Aycliffe 71 A6
Newton Bay 79 E1
Newton Bewley 64 B1
Newton Blossomville
  31 E2

Newton Bromshold 31 E1
Newton Burgoland 41 A4
Newton by Toft 52 D3
Newton Ferrers 5 A6
Newton Ferry 98 C4
Newton Flotman 45 B6
Newtongrange 82 D6
Newton Harcourt 41 D5
Newtonhill 97 E4
Newton Kyme 57 C3
Newton-le-Willows *Lancs*
  48 E2
Newton-le-Willows *N Yorks*
  63 C6
Newton Longville 31 D4
Newton Mearns 80 E6
Newtonmill 89 C2
Newtonmore 95 A6
Newton Morrell 63 C4
Newton Mountain 16 C5
Newton Mulgrave 64 E2
Newton of Ardtoe 85 C1
Newton of Balcanquhal
  88 C7
Newton of Dalvey 103 D6
Newton of Falkland 82 C2
Newton of Leys 94 E2
Newton-on-Ouse 57 D2
Newton-on-Rawcliffe 65 A4
Newton-on-the-Moor 77 C5
Newton on Trent 52 B4
Newton Poppleford 8 B5
Newton Purcell 31 B4
Newton Regis 40 E4
Newton Reigny 69 C6
Newton St Cyres 7 C7
Newton St Faith 45 B4
Newton St Loe 21 B4
Newton St Petrock 6 D5
Newton Solney 40 E2
Newton Stacey 22 D7
Newton Stewart 67 A4
Newton Toney 22 B7
Newton Tracey 6 E4
Newton under Roseberry
  64 C2
Newton upon Derwent
  58 C3
Newton Valence 11 D1
New Town *Beds* 32 D4
New Town *Bucks* 23 D1
Newtown *Ches* 49 A7
Newtown *Ches* 48 E6
Newtown *Ches* 49 D3
Newtown *Corn* 2 E6
Newtown *Cumb* 69 D3
Newtown *Dors* 10 B5
New Town *Esx* 13 B4
New Town *Glos* 30 A4
Newtown *Gramp* 103 E5
Newtown *Gramp* 105 D4
Newtown *Gramp* 105 A2
Newtown *Gwent* 19 B2
Newtown *H & W* 94 B5
Newtown *H & W* 29 B4
Newtown *Hants* 11 C3
Newtown *Hants* 22 D5
Newtown *Hants* 10 D3
Newtown *Hants* 10 E2
Newtown *Hants* 11 B3
Newtown *Hghld* 94 B5
Newtown *IOM* 60 c4
Newtown *IOW* 11 A5
New Town *Loth* 82 E5
Newtown *Northld* 77 B5
Newtown *Northld* 77 A2
Newtown *Northld* 77 B3
Newtown *Pwys* 38 A5
Newtown *Salop* 38 D1
Newtown *Staffs* 49 D5
Newtown *Staffs* 50 B4
Newtown *Wilts* 10 A2
Newtown Linford 41 C3
Newtown St Boswells
  76 B2
Newtown Unthank 41 B4
Newtown (Y Drenewydd)
  38 A5
New Tredegar 19 B3
New Tupton 50 E4
Newtyle 88 D4
New Ulva 79 B3
New Walsoken 43 C4
New Waltham 59 C7
New Wimpole 32 E3
New Winton 82 E5
New Yatt 30 D6

New York *Lincs* 53 A6
New York *T & W* 71 B1
Neyland 16 C5
Nibley *Avn* 21 A2
Nibley *Glos* 29 A7
Nicholashayne 8 C2
Nicholaston 17 D7
Nidd 57 B1
Niddrie 82 D5
Nigg *Gramp* 97 E3
Nigg *Hghld* 103 B4
Nightcott 7 C4
Nilig 47 E5
Nine Ashes 24 F2
Ninebanks 70 A3
Nine Elms 22 A3
Nine Mile Burn 82 B7
Ninfield 13 E5
Ningwood 10 E6
Nisbet 76 C3
Niton 11 B7
Nitshill 80 E5
Nizels 13 C1
Noak Hill 24 F3
Noblehill 68 C2
Nobottle 31 B1
Nocton 52 D5
Noddsdale 80 B5
Noke 31 A6
Nolton 16 B4
No Man's Heath *Ches*
  48 E7
No Man's Heath *Warks*
  40 E4
Nomansland *Devon* 7 C5
Nomansland *Wilts* 10 D3
Noneley 38 D2
Nonington 15 C3
Nook 69 C2
Nook 61 E5
Noonsbrough 115 B2
Noranside 89 A2
Norbiton 24 B6
Norbreck 54 C3
Norbury *Ches* 48 E7
Norbury *Derbs* 50 C6
Norbury *Salop* 38 C5
Norbury *Staffs* 39 B2
Norchard 29 C1
Nordelph 43 D4
Norden *Dors* 10 A6
Nordley 39 A5
Nordley Common 39 A5
Norham 77 A1
Norland Town 56 D5
Norley 48 E4
Norleywood 10 E5
Normanby *Clev* 64 C2
Normanby *Humb* 58 D6
Normanby *Lincs* 52 D5
Normanby *N Yorks* 64 E5
Normanby le Wold 52 E2
Norman Cross 42 E5
Normandy 18 B1
Normann's Ruh 85 A4
Norman on the Wolds
  51 C7
Norman's Green 8 B3
Normanton *Derbs* 50 E7
Normanton *Lincs* 52 B7
Normanton *Lincs* 52 C7
Normanton *Notts* 51 D5
Normanton *W Yorks* 57 B5
Normanton le Heath 41 A3
Normanton on Soar 41 C2
Normanton on the Wolds
  51 D4
Normanton on Trent 51 D4
Normoss 54 C4
Norrington Common 21 C4
Norris Hill 41 A3
North Acre 44 D6
Northallerton 63 D5
Northall Green 44 E4
Northam *Devon* 6 D4
Northam *Hants* 11 A3
Northampton 31 C1
North Anston 51 B2
North Aston 30 E5

North Berwick 83 A4
North Boarhunt 11 C3
North Bogbain 104 B3
North Boisdale 90 C4
Northborough 42 E4
North Bourne 15 D3
North Bovey 5 C2
North Bradley 21 C5
North Brentor 4 E2
North Brewham 21 B7
Northbrook 30 E5
North Buckland 6 D2
North Burlingham 45 C4
North Cadbury 9 C1
North Cairn 66 A3
North Carlton *Lincs* 52 C4
North Carlton *Notts* 51 B2
North Cave 58 D4
North Cerney 30 A7
Northchapel 12 B4
North Charford 10 C3
North Charlton 77 C3
Northchurch 23 D1
North Cliffe 58 D4
North Clifton 52 B4
North Cockerington 53 B2
North Coker 9 B2
North Coles 59 D7
North Cornelly 18 D5
Northcote Manor 7 A5
Northcott 6 C7
North Cove 45 D7
North Cowton 63 C4
North Crawley 31 E3
North Cray 24 E5
North Creake 44 C2
North Crossaig 72 C2
North Curry 8 E1
North Dallens 86 A4
North Dalton 58 E2
North Dawn 113 D1
North Deighton 57 B2
North Dell 107 C1
North Duffield 57 E4
Northdyke 112 B4
North Elkington 53 A2
North Elmham 44 D3
North Elmsall 57 C6
North End *Avn* 20 D4
Northend *Avn* 21 B4
North End *Beds* 32 E4
North End *Berks* 22 D5
North End *Bucks* 31 D5
Northend *Bucks* 23 B2
North End *Esx* 33 C7
North End *Hants* 11 C4
North End *Nflk* 44 E6
Northend *Warks* 30 D2
North End *W Ssx* 12 D6
North Erradale 100 E3
North Essie 105 D3
North Ferriby 58 E5
Northfield *Bdrs* 83 E6
Northfield *Gramp* 105 B2
Northfield *Gramp* 111 D4
Northfield *Gramp* 97 E3
Northfield *W Mids* 40 C7
Northfleet 25 B5
North Frodingham 59 B2
North Galson 107 C2
North Gate 42 E2
North Green 45 B7
North Grimston 65 A7
North Hayling 11 D4
North Heasley 7 B3
North Heath 12 C4
North Hill 4 C3
North Hinksey 30 E7
North Holmwood 12 D2
Northhouse 76 A5
North Huish 5 C5
North Hykeham 52 C5
Northiam 14 D6
Northill 32 C4
Northington 11 B1
North Kelsey 59 A7
North Kessock 102 E7
North Killingholme 59 B6
North Kilvington 64 B5
North Kilworth 41 D6
North Kyme 52 E6
North Lancing 12 D6
Northlands 53 B6
Northleach 30 B6
North Lee 31 D7
North Leigh 30 D6

North Wick 20 E4
Northwick 20 E2
North Widcombe 20 E5
North Willingham 52 E3
North Wingfield 51 A4
North Witham 42 C2
Northwold 44 B6
Northwood *GL* 24 B3
Northwood *IOW* 11 A5
Northwood *Salop* 38 D1
Northwood End 32 B4
Northwood Green 29 B6
North Wootton *Dors* 9 C2
North Wootton *Nflk* 44 A3
North Wootton *Som* 20 E6
North Wraxall 21 C3
North Wroughton 22 A3
North Yardhope 77 A5
Norton *Ches* 48 E3
Norton *Clev* 64 B1
Norton *Glos* 29 C5
Norton *H & W* 29 C2
Norton *H & W* 40 A6
Norton *H & W* 30 A3
Norton *Herts* 32 D5
Norton *IOW* 10 E6
Norton *Northants* 31 B1
Norton *Notts* 51 B3
Norton *N Yorks* 64 E6
Norton *Pwys* 28 C1
Norton *Salop* 38 E4
Norton *Salop* 39 B4
Norton *Salop* 38 D6
Norton *Sflk* 34 D2
Norton *S Yorks* 57 D6
Norton *S Yorks* 50 E2
Norton *Wilts* 21 C2
Norton *W Ssx* 12 B6
Norton Bavant 21 D6
Norton Bridge 40 A1
Norton Canes 40 C4
Norton Canon 28 C3
Norton Disney 52 B6
Norton Ferris 21 B7
Norton Fitzwarren 8 C1
Norton Green 10 E6
Norton Hawkfield 20 E4
Norton Heath 25 B2
Norton in Hales 39 B1
Norton in the Moors 49 C6
Norton-Juxta-Twycross
  41 A4
Norton-le-Clay 64 B6
Norton Lindsey 30 C1
Norton Malreward 21 A4
Norton Mandeville 24 F2
Norton St Philip 21 B5
Norton Subcourse 45 D6
Norton sub Hamdon 9 A2
Norton Wood 28 C3
Norwell 51 D4
Norwell Woodhouse 51 D4
Norwich 45 B5
Norwick 114 F1
Norwood Green 24 B5
Norwood Hill 12 E2
Noseley 41 E5
Noss Mayo 5 A6
Nosterfield 63 C6
Nostie 93 A2
Note o' the Gate 76 B5
Notgrove 30 B5
Nottage 18 D6
Nottingham *Hghld* 111 C5
Nottingham *Notts* 51 B6
Notton *Wilts* 21 D4
Notton *W Yorks* 57 B6
Nounsley 33 D7
Noutard's Green 29 B1
Nowton 34 C2
Nox 38 D3
Noyadd Sharman 27 E6
Noyadd Trefawr 26 B6
Nuffield 23 A3
Nunburnholme 58 D3
Nuneaton 41 A5
Nuneham Courtenay 22 E2
Nun Monkton 57 D2
Nunney 21 B6
Nunnington 64 D6
Nunnington Park 8 B1
Nunstallon 5 D2
Nunthorpe 64 C2
Nunton *Wilts* 10 C2
Nunton *W Is* 98 B6
Nunwick *Northld* 70 B1
Nunwick *N Yorks* 63 D7

Nupdown 9 C3
Nup End *Bucks* 31 D6
Nup End *Glos* 29 C5
Nursling 10 E3
Nursted 11 D2
Nurton 40 A5
Nutbourne *W Ssx* 12 C5
Nutbourne *W Ssx* 11 D4
Nutfield 13 A1
Nuthall 51 B6
Nuthampstead 33 A5
Nuthurst *Warks* 40 D7
Nuthurst *W Ssx* 12 D4
Nutwell 57 E7
Nutley *E Ssx* 13 B4
Nutley *Hants* 23 A7
Nybster 111 D2
Nyetimber 11 E5
Nyewood 11 E2
Nymet Rowland 7 B6
Nymet Tracey 7 B6
Nympsfield 29 C7
Nynehead 8 C1
Nythe 20 D7
Nyton 12 B6

O

Oadby 41 D4
Oad Street 14 D2
Oak 6 E7
Oakamoor 50 B6
Oakbank *Hghld* 85 D5
Oakbank *Loth* 81 E5
Oakdale 19 B4
Oake 8 C1
Oakenclough 54 E3
Oakengates 39 B3
Oakenshaw *Dur* 71 A5
Oakenshaw *W Yorks* 56 E5
Oakford *Devon* 7 D4
Oakford *Dyfed* 26 D5
Oakgrove 49 D5
Oakham 42 B4
Oakhanger 11 D1
Oakhill 21 A6
Oakington 33 A2
Oaklands 47 C5
Oakle Street 29 B6
Oakley *Beds* 32 B3
Oakley *Bucks* 31 B6
Oakley *Fife* 81 E3
Oakley *Hants* 22 E6
Oakley *Sflk* 35 A1
Oakley Green 23 D4
Oakleypark 27 D2
Oakridge 29 D7
Oaks 38 D4
Oaksey 21 D1
Oakshaw Ford 69 D2
Oakthorpe 41 A3
Oaktree Hill 63 D5
Oakwoodhill 12 D3
Oakworth 56 D4
Oare *Kent* 15 A2
Oare *Som* 7 C2
Oare *Wilts* 22 A5
Oare Hill 22 A5
Oasby 42 D1
Oatfield 72 A6
Oath 8 E1
Oathlaw 89 A3
Oban 85 E5
Obinan 101 A2
Obley 38 C7
Oborne 9 C2
Occlestone Green 49 A5
Occold 35 A1
Occumster 111 C5
Ochertyre 87 E6
Ochiltree 73 E5
Ochr-y-mynydd 19 A3
Ochtermuthill 87 E7
Ochtertyre 81 B2
Ockbrook 51 A7
Ockham 12 C1
Ockle 85 B1
Ockley 12 D2
Ocle Pychard 28 E3
Octon 65 C7
Odcombe 9 B2
Oddingley 29 D2
Oddington *Glos* 30 C5
Oddington *Oxon* 31 A6
Oddsta 114 E3

Odell 31 E2
Odie 112 F4
Odiham 23 B6
Odstock 10 C2
Odstone 41 A4
Offchurch 30 D1
Offenham 30 A3
Offerton 49 D3
Offham *E Ssx* 13 B5
Offham *Kent* 13 D1
Offton 34 E4
Offwell 8 C4
Ogbourne Maizey 22 A4
Ogbourne St Andrew 22 A4
Ogbourne St George 22 B4
Ogden 56 D4
Ogil 89 A2
Ogle 70 E1
Ogmore 18 D6
Ogmore-by-Sea 18 D6
Ogmore Vale 18 E4
Okeford Fitzpaine 9 E2
Okehampton 6 E7
Okraquoy 115 D4
Olantigh 15 A4
Old 41 E7
Old Aberdeen 97 E3
Old Alresford 11 B1
Old Basford 51 B6
Oldberrow 30 B1
Old Bewick 77 B3
Old Bolingbroke 53 B5
Oldborough 7 B6
Old Brampton 50 E3
Old Bridge of Urr 67 D4
Old Buckenham 44 E6
Old Burghclere 22 D6
Oldbury *H & W* 40 B6
Oldbury *Kent* 15 A1
Oldbury *Salop* 39 B5
Oldbury *Warks* 41 A5
Oldbury-on-Severn 21 A1
Oldbury on the Hill 21 C2
Old Byland 64 C5
Oldcastle *Gwent* 28 C5
Oldcastle Heath 48 D7
Old Cleeve 7 E2
Old Colwyn 47 C3
Oldcotes 51 B2
Old Craig 105 C6
Old Craighall 82 D5
Old Crombie 104 D3
Old Dailly 66 E1
Old Dalby 41 D2
Old Deer 105 C4
Old Ellerby 59 B4
Old Felixstowe 35 C5
Oldfield *H & W* 29 C1
Oldfield *W Yorks* 56 D4
Old Fletton 42 E5
Oldford 21 B6
Old Glossop 50 B1
Old Goginan 27 A2
Old Goole 58 C5
Old Gore 29 A5
Oldhall 96 E4
Old Hall *Hghld* 111 C3
Old Hall *Humb* 59 C6
Oldham 49 D1
Oldhamstocks 83 C5
Old Heath 34 E6
Old Hill 40 B6
Oldhurst 32 E1
Old Hutton 61 E5
Old Kea 14 C4
Old Kilpatrick 80 D4
Old Kinnernie 97 C3
Old Knebworth 32 D6
Oldland 21 A3
Oldland Common 21 A3
Old Leake 53 C6
Old Malton 64 E6
Oldmeldrum 105 B6
Old Micklefield 57 C4
Oldmill 97 A3
Old Milverton 30 C1
Old Montsale 25 F3
Old Netley 11 A3
Old Newton 34 E2
Oldpark 39 A4
Old Philpstoun 81 E4
Old Poltalloch 79 C1
Old Radnor 28 B2

Old Rattray 105 D3
Old Rayne 104 E6
Oldridge 7 C7
Old Romney 15 A6
Old Scone 88 C6
Old Shields 81 C4
Oldshore 108 E3
Old Sodbury 21 B2
Old Somerby 42 C1
Oldstead 64 C5
Old Stratford 31 C3
Old Sunderlandwick 59 A2
Old Swinford 40 B6
Old Town *Cumb* 61 E5
Old Town *Cumb* 61 E5
Old Town *Northld* 76 E6
Oldtown of Aigas 102 C7
Oldtown of Ord 104 E3
Oldwalls 17 C6
Old Warden 32 C4
Oldways End 7 C4
Old Weston 32 B1
Oldwhat 105 B3
Old Windsor 23 D4
Old Wives Lees 15 A3
Old Woking 12 C1
Old Wolverton 31 D3
Oldwood 38 D2
Olgrinmore 111 A3
Oliclett 111 C4
Oliver 75 A3
Oliver's Battery 11 A2
Ollaberry 114 C4
Ollerton *Ches* 49 B4
Ollerton *Notts* 51 C4
Ollerton *Salop* 39 A2
Olney *Bucks* 31 B3
Olney *Northants* 31 D2
Olton 40 D6
Olveston 21 A2
Ombersley 29 C1
Ompton 51 C4
Onchan 60 d4
Onecote 50 B5
Ongar Hill 43 D2
Ongar Street 28 C1
Onibury 38 D7
Onich 86 B2
Onllwyn 18 D2
Onneley 49 B7
Onslow Village 12 B2
Opinan *Hghld* 100 E4
Orange Lane 76 D1
Orbliston 104 B3
Orbost 99 B7
Orby 53 C5
Orcadia 80 A5
Orchard 9 E2
Orchard Portman 8 D1
Orchard Wyndham 7 E2
Orcheston 21 E6
Orcop 28 D5
Orcop Hill 28 D5
Ord 92 D3
Ordhead 97 B2
Ordie 96 E3
Ordiequish 104 B3
Ordsall 51 C2
Ore 14 D7
Oreham Common 12 E5
Oreston 5 A5
Oreton 39 A6
Orford *Lancs* 49 A2
Orford *Sflk* 35 D3
Orgreave 40 D3
Orielton 16 C6
Orlestone 15 A5
Orleton *H & W* 28 D1
Orleton *H & W* 29 A1
Orleton Common 28 D1
Orlingbury 42 B7
Ormelie 111 B2
Ormesby 64 C2
Ormesby St Margaret 45 D4
Ormesby St Michael 45 D4
Ormiscaig 101 A2
Ormiston 82 E6
Ormsaigmore 85 A2
Ormskirk 48 D1
Orpington 24 E6
Orrell 48 E1
Orrisdale 60 c2
Orrok 97 E2
Orroland 67 D6
Orsett 25 B4
Orslow 40 A3

Orston 51 D6
Orton *Cumb* 62 B4
Orton *Northants* 42 B7
Orton Longueville 42 E5
Orton-on-the-Hill 41 A4
Orton Waterville 42 E5
Orwell 32 E3
Osbaldeston 55 A4
Osbaldwick 57 E2
Osbaston *Salop* 38 E3
Osbaston *Warks* 41 B4
Osborne 11 B5
Osbournby 42 D1
Oscroft 48 E5
Osdale 99 C7
Osgathorpe 41 B3
Osgodby *Lincs* 52 D2
Osgodby *N Yorks* 57 E4
Osgodby *N Yorks* 65 C5
Oskaig 92 C1
Osmaston *Derbs* 50 C6
Osmington 9 D5
Osmington Mills 9 D5
Osmotherley 64 B4
Osnaburgh 89 A7
Osney 30 E7
Ospringe 14 E2
Ossett 57 A5
Ossington 51 D4
Ostend 25 E3
Osterley Park 24 B5
Oswaldkirk 64 D6
Oswaldtwistle 55 B5
Oswestry 38 B2
Otford 13 C1
Otham 13 E1
Othery 20 C7
Otley *Sflk* 35 B3
Otley *W Yorks* 57 A3
Otter 79 D4
Otterbourne 11 A2
Otterburn *Northld* 76 E6
Otterburn *N Yorks* 55 C2
Otterburn Camp 76 E6
Otterden Place 14 E3
Otter Ferry 79 D3
Otterford 8 D2
Otterham 6 A7
Otterhampton 20 B6
Ottershaw 23 E5
Otterswick 114 E4
Otterton 8 B5
Ottery St Mary 8 B4
Ottinge 15 B4
Ottringham 59 C5
Oughterby 69 A4
Oughtershaw 62 D6
Oughtibridge 50 E1
Oulston 64 C6
Oulton *Cumb* 69 A4
Oulton *Nflk* 45 A3
Oulton *Sflk* 45 E6
Oulton *Staffs* 40 B1
Oulton *W Yorks* 57 B5
Oulton Broad 45 E6
Oulton Street 45 A3
Oundle 42 D6
Ousby 69 E6
Ousdale 111 A6
Ousden 33 D3
Ousefleet 58 D7
Ouston *Dur* 71 A3
Ouston *Northld* 70 D1
Outertown 112 B5
Outgate 61 C5
Outhgill 62 C4
Outlands 39 B1
Outlane 56 D6
Out Newton 59 D5
Out Rawcliffe 54 D3
Outwell 43 D4
Outwood *Sry* 13 A2
Outwood *W Yorks* 57 B5
Oval, The 21 B4
Ovenden 56 D5
Over *Avn* 20 E2
Over *Cambs* 32 E1
Over *Ches* 49 A5
Overbister *dist* 112 F2
Overbrae 105 B3
Overbury 29 D4
Over Compton 9 B2
Over End 50 D3
Over Haddon 50 D4
Over Kellet 54 E1
Over Kiddington 30 E5
Overleigh 20 D7

Over Norton 30 D5
Overpool 48 C4
Over Rankeilour 88 E7
Overseal 40 E3
Over Silton 64 B4
Oversland 15 A3
Oversley Green 30 A2
Overstone 31 D1
Over Stowey 20 A7
Overstrand 45 B1
Over Stratton 9 A2
Over Tabley 49 B4
Overton *Clwyd* 48 C7
Overton *Gramp* 97 D2
Overton *Gramp* 97 C2
Overton *Hants* 22 E7
Overton *Lancs* 54 D2
Overton *N Yorks* 57 D2
Overton *Salop* 38 D7
Overton *W Glam* 17 C7
Overtown 81 C6
Over Wallop 10 D1
Over Whitacre 40 E5
Over Worton 30 E5
Overy Staithe 44 C1
Oving *Bucks* 31 C5
Oving *W Ssx* 12 B6
Ovingdean 13 A6
Ovingham 70 D2
Ovington *Dur* 33 D4
Ovington *Esx* 33 D4
Ovington *Hants* 11 B1
Ovington *Nflk* 44 D5
Ovington *Northld* 70 D2
Ovington *N Yorks* 63 B3
Ower *Hants* 10 E3
Owermoigne 9 D5
Owlswick 31 C7
Owmby *Lincs* 59 A7
Owmby *Lincs* 52 C3
Owslebury 11 B2
Owston 41 E4
Owston Ferry 58 D7
Owstwick 59 C4
Owthorpe 51 C7
Oxborough 44 B5
Oxcliffe Hill 54 D1
Oxcombe 53 B4
Oxen End 33 C6
Oxenfoord Castle 82 D6
Oxenholme 61 E5
Oxenhope 56 D4
Oxen Park 61 C5
Oxenton 29 D4
Oxenwood 22 C6
Oxford 31 A7
Oxhill 30 D3
Oxley 40 B4
Oxley's Green 13 D4
Oxnam 76 D4
Oxnead 45 B3
Oxney Green 25 B2
Oxshott 24 B6
Oxspring 57 A7
Oxted 13 A1
Oxton *Bdrs* 82 E7
Oxton *Mers* 48 B3
Oxton *Notts* 51 C5
Oxwich 17 C7
Oxwichgreen 17 C7
Oxwick 44 D3
Oykel Bridge 102 B1
Oyne 104 E6
Ozleworth 21 B1

P

Packington 41 A3
Padanaram 89 A3
Padbury 31 C4
Paddington 24 C4
Paddlesworth 15 B5
Paddockhaugh 104 A3
Paddockhole 75 C7
Paddock Wood 13 D2
Paddolgreen 38 E1
Padeswood 48 B5
Padiham 55 B4
Padside 56 E2
Padstow 3 B1
Pagham 11 E5
Paglesham 25 E3
Paible 98 E2
Paignton 5 D4
Pailton 41 B6
Painscastle 28 A3
Painswick 29 C7

Paisley 80 D5
Pakefield 45 E6
Pakenham 34 D2
Pale 47 D7
Palestine 22 B7
Paley Street 23 C4
Palgowan 66 E2
Palgrave 35 A1
Pallinsburn House 76 E2
Palmerscross 104 A2
Palmerston 19 B7
Palnackie 68 B4
Palnure 67 A4
Palterton 51 A4
Pamber End 23 A6
Pamber Green 23 A6
Pamber Heath 23 A5
Pamington 29 D4
Pamphill 10 A4
Pampisford 33 A4
Pan 113 C2
Panborough 20 D6
Panbride 89 B5
Pancrasweek 6 B6
Pandy *Clwyd* 38 A1
Pandy *Gwent* 28 C5
Pandy *Gynd* 37 A5
Pandy *Pwys* 37 D5
Pandy Tudur 47 C4
Panfield 33 D6
Pangbourne 23 A4
Pangdean 12 E5
Pannal 57 B2
Pannanich 96 D4
Panpunton 38 B7
Pant 38 B2
Pantasaph 48 A4
Pant-glas 46 D6
Pantglas 37 B6
Pant-gwyn 37 C3
Pantgwyn 26 B6
Pant-Issau 18 B3
Pant Mawr 27 C2
Panton 52 E4
Pant-pastynog 47 E4
Pantperthog 37 B5
Pant-y-dŵr 27 D3
Pant-y-ffordd 48 B6
Pant-y-ffridd 38 A4
Pantyffynnon 18 B2
Panxworth 45 C4
Papcastle 68 E6
Papley 113 D2
Papple 83 A5
Papplewick 51 B5
Papworth Everard 32 D2
Papworth St Agnes 32 D2
Par 3 C3
Parbold 54 D6
Parbrook 20 E7
Parcllyn 26 B5
Parcrhydderch 27 A5
Pardshaw 68 D7
Parham 35 C2
Parishholm 74 C3
Park *Gramp* 105 D3
Park *Gramp* 97 C4
Park Corner 23 A3
Park End 70 B1
Parkend *Cumb* 69 B6
Parkend *Glos* 29 A7
Parkeston 35 B5
Parkford 89 A3
Parkgate *Ches* 48 B4
Parkgate *Ches* 49 B4
Park Gate *Hants* 11 B4
Parkgate *Sry* 12 E2
Park Gate *S Yorks* 51 A1
Parkham 6 C4
Parkham Ash 6 C4
Parkhill *Tays* 88 C4
Parkhill *Tays* 89 C4
Parkhouse 28 E7
Parkhurst 11 A5
Park Lane 38 D1
Parkmill 17 D7
Parkmore 104 B4
Parkneuk 97 C6
Parkstone 10 B5
Park Street 24 B2
Parley Common 10 B5
Parley Cross 10 B5
Parracombe 7 A2
Parrah Green 49 B7
Parrog 16 D2
Parsonby 68 E6
Parson Drove 43 B4

Partington 49 B2
Partney 53 C5
Parton *Cumb* 68 C7
Parton *D & G* 67 C3
Parton *Glos* 29 C5
Partridge Green 12 D5
Partrishaw 28 B5
Parwich 50 C5
Passenham 31 C4
Passfield 11 E1
Passingford Bridge 24 F3
Paston 45 C2
Patcham 13 A6
Patching 12 C6
Patchole 7 A2
Patchway 21 A2
Pateley Bridge 56 E1
Pathe 20 C7
Pathhead *Fife* 82 C3
Pathhead *Gramp* 89 D2
Pathhead *Loth* 82 D6
Pathhead *Strath* 74 B4
Path of Condie 88 B7
Patmore Heath 33 A6
Patna 73 D6
Patney 21 E5
Patrick 60 b3
Patrick Brompton 63 C5
Patrington 59 D5
Patrixbourne 15 B3
Patterdale 61 C2
Pattingham 40 A5
Pattishall 31 B2
Pattiswick 34 C6
Paul 2 B6
Paulerspury 31 C3
Paull 59 B5
Paulton 21 A5
Pauperhaugh 77 C6
Pavenham 31 E2
Pawlett 20 B6
Pawston 76 E2
Paxford 30 B4
Paxhill Park 13 A4
Paxton 83 E7
Payhembury 8 B3
Paythorne 55 C2
Peacehaven 13 B6
Peacemarsh 9 E1
Peachley 29 C2
Peak Dale 50 B3
Peak Forest 50 C3
Peakirk 42 E4
Pean Hill 15 B2
Pearsie 88 E3
Pease Cottage 12 E3
Peasedown St John 21 B5
Peasemore 22 D4
Peasenhall 35 C2
Peaslake 12 C2
Peasmarsh 14 D6
Peaston 82 E6
Peaston Bank 82 E6
Peat Inn 82 E2
Peatling Magna 41 C5
Peatling Parva 41 C6
Peaton 38 E6
Pebble Coombe 12 E1
Pebmarsh 34 C5
Pebworth 30 B3
Pecket Well 55 D5
Peckforton 48 E6
Peckleton 41 B4
Pedmore 40 B6
Pedwell 20 D7
Peebles 75 C1
Peel 60 b3
Peesweep, The 80 D6
Pegswood 77 D7
Peinchorran 92 C1
Peinlich 100 B6
Pelaw 71 A2
Pelcomb Bridge 16 C4
Pelcomb Cross 16 C4
Peldon 34 D7
Pelsall 40 C4
Pelton 71 A3
Pelutho 68 E5
Pelynt 4 C5
Pembrey 17 C5
Pembridge 28 C2
Pembroke 16 C5
Pembroke Dock 16 C5
Pembroke Ferry 16 C5
Pembury 13 D2
Penallt 28 E6
Penally 16 E6

Penalt 28 E5
Penant 26 E4
Penare 3 B4
Penarth 19 B6
Pen-bont Rhydybeddau 27 A2
Penboyr 17 B2
Penbryn 26 B5
Pencader 17 C2
Pencaitland 82 E6
Pencarreg 26 E6
Pencelli 19 A1
Pen-clawdd 17 D6
Pencoed 18 E5
Pencombe 28 E2
Pencoyd 28 E5
Pencraig *Dyfed* 27 A4
Pencraig *H & W* 28 E5
Pencraig *Pwys* 37 E3
Pendeen 2 A5
Penderyn 18 E3
Pendine 17 A5
Pendlebury 49 B1
Pendleton 55 B4
Pendock 29 B4
Pendoggett 4 A3
Pendomer 9 B2
Pendoylan 19 A6
Penegoes 37 B5
Pen-ffordd 16 D3
Pen-filia 18 B4
Pengam 19 B4
Penge 24 D5
Pengenffordd 28 A4
Pengorffwysfa 46 D1
Pengover Green 4 C4
Pen-groes-oped 19 D3
Pengwern 47 E3
Penhallow 2 E3
Penhalvean 2 E5
Penhow 20 D1
Penhurst 13 D5
Peniarth 37 A5
Penicuik 82 C7
Peninerine 90 C2
Peninver 72 B5
Pen-isa'r-cwm 37 E4
Penisar Waun 46 E4
Penistone 57 A7
Penjerrick 2 E5
Penketh 48 E3
Penkill 66 D1
Penkridge 40 B3
Penley 38 D1
Penllech 46 B7
Penllergaer 18 B4
Pen-llyn 46 C2
Penllyn 18 E6
Penmachno 47 B5
Penmaen *Gwent* 19 B4
Penmaen *W Glam* 17 D7
Penmaenmawr 47 B3
Penmaenpool 37 A4
Penmark 19 A7
Penmon 47 A2
Penmorfa 46 E6
Penmynydd 46 E3
Penn *Bucks* 23 D2
Penn *W Mids* 40 A5
Pennal 37 A5
Pennan 105 B2
Pennant 37 C6
Pennant-Melangell 37 E3
Pennard 17 D7
Pennerley 38 C5
Penninghame 66 E4
Pennington 61 B6
Penn Street 23 D2
Penny Bridge 61 C5
Pennyfuir 85 E5
Pennyghael 85 B6
Pennygown 85 C4
Pennymoor 7 C5
Penparc 26 B6
Penparcau 26 E2
Penperlleni 19 D3
Penpillick 3 C3
Penpol 3 D3
Penpoll 3 A5
Penpont *D & G* 74 D6
Penpont *Pwys* 18 E1
Penrherber 17 A2
Penrhiwceiber 19 A4
Penrhiwgoch 17 D4
Penrhiwllan 26 C6
Penrhiwpal 26 C6
Pen-rhos 17 C4

Penrhôs *Gwent* 28 D6
Penrhôs *Gynd* 46 C7
Penrhos *Gynd* 46 B2
Penrhos *Pwys* 18 D2
Penrhos-garnedd 46 E3
Penrhyn Bay 47 C2
Penrhyncoch 27 A2
Penrhyndeudraeth 47 A7
Penrhyn-side 47 C2
Penrhys 19 A4
Penrice 17 C7
Penrith 69 D6
Penrose 3 A1
Penruddock 69 C7
Penryn 2 E5
Pensarn *Clwyd* 47 D3
Pensarn *Dyfed* 17 C4
Pen-sarn *Gynd* 36 E3
Pen-sarn *Gynd* 46 D6
Pensax 29 B1
Pensby 48 B3
Penselwood 21 B7
Pensford 21 A4
Pensham 29 D3
Penshaw 71 B3
Penshurst 13 C2
Pensilva 4 C4
Pensnett 40 B6
Pentewan 3 C4
Pentir 46 E4
Pentire 2 E2
Pentireglaze 3 B1
Pentlepoir 16 E5
Pentney 44 B4
Penton Mewsey 22 C7
Pentraeth 46 E3
Pentre *Clwyd* 47 E4
Pentre *Clwyd* 48 B7
Pentre *Clwyd* 47 C4
Pentre *Gwent* 28 D6
Pentre *M Glam* 18 E4
Pentre *Pwys* 37 E3
Pentre *Pwys* 27 E2
Pentre *Pwys* 28 B1
Pentre *Salop* 38 C3
Pentre-b'âch 27 D7
Pentrebach 18 B3
Pentre-bach 19 A3
Pentrebeirdd 38 A3
Pentre Berw 46 D3
Pentre-bwlch 48 A7
Pentre-cagal 26 C6
Pentre-celyn *Clwyd* 48 A6
Pentre-celyn *Pwys* 37 C5
Pentre-chwyth 18 B4
Pentreclwydau 18 D3
Pentre-cwrt 17 B2
Pentre-Dolau-Honddu 27 D6
Pentre-dwfr 48 A7
Pentredwr 18 B4
Pentrefelin *Clwyd* 38 A2
Pentrefelin *Dyfed* 17 D3
Pentrefelin *Gwynd* 46 E7
Pentrefelin *Gwynd* 47 C3
Pentrefoelas 47 C5
Pentre-galar 16 E2
Pentregat 26 C5
Pentre Gwynfryn 36 E3
Pentre Halkyn 48 B4
Pentreheyling 38 B5
Pentre-llwyn-llŵyd 27 D5
Pentre Maelor 48 C7
Pentre-poeth 19 C5
Pentre'r-felin 27 D7
Pentre-tafarn-y-fedw 47 C4
Pentre ty gwyn 27 C7
Pentrich 50 E5
Pentridge 10 B3
Pen-twyn 28 E7
Pentyrch 19 B5
Penuwch 26 E4
Penwenham 6 A7
Penwithick 3 C3
Penwyllt 18 D2
Penybanc 18 B1
Penybont 28 A1
Pen-y-bont *Dyfed* 27 B7
Pen-y-bont *Powys* 37 E4
Pen-y-Bont *Powys* 38 B2
Penybontfawr 37 E3
Penybryn 19 B4
Pen-y-bryn 37 A4
Penycae 48 B7
Pen-y-Cae 18 D2
Pen-y-cae-mawr 20 D1
Pen-y-cefn 48 A4

Pen-y-clawdd 28 D7
Pen-y-coedcae 19 A5
Penycwm 16 B3
Penyffordd 48 C5
Pen-y-garn 17 D2
Penygarnedd 38 A2
Penygraig 18 E4
Penygroes *Clwyd* 46 D5
Penygroes *Dyfed* 17 D4
Pen-y-Park 28 B3
Pen-yr-hoel 28 D6
Penysarn 46 D1
Pen-y-stryt 48 A6
Penywaun 18 E3
Penzance 2 B5
Peopleton 29 D2
Peover Heath 49 B4
Peper Harow 12 B2
Peplow 39 A2
Perceton 73 C3
Perivale 24 B4
Perkhill 97 A3
Perkins Beach 38 C4
Perlethorpe 51 C3
Perranarworthal 2 E5
Perranporth 2 E3
Perranuthnoe 2 C6
Perranzabuloe 2 E3
Perry 32 C2
Perry Barr 40 C5
Perry Green 33 A7
Perry Street 25 B5
Persey 88 C3
Pershall 40 A2
Pershore 29 D3
Pert 89 C2
Pertenhall 32 B2
Perth 88 C6
Perthy 38 C1
Perton 40 A5
Pertwood 21 C7
Peterborough 42 E5
Peterburn 100 E3
Peterchurch 28 C4
Peterculter 97 D3
Peterhead 105 E4
Peterlee 71 C4
Petersfield 11 D2
Peter's Green 32 C7
Peters Marland 6 D5
Peterstone Wentlooge 19 C5
Peterston-super-Ely 19 A6
Peterstow 28 E5
Peter Tavy 5 A3
Petertown 113 C1
Petham 15 B3
Petrockstow 6 E6
Pett 14 D7
Pettaugh 35 A3
Pettinain 74 E1
Pettistree 35 B3
Petton *Devon* 8 B1
Petton *Salop* 38 D2
Petty 105 A5
Pettycur 82 C4
Pettymuick 105 C6
Petworth 12 B4
Pevensey 13 D6
Pewsey 22 A5
Phesdo 97 B6
Philham 6 B4
Philiphaugh 76 A3
Phillack 2 C5
Philleigh 3 A5
Philpstoun 81 E4
Phoenix Green 23 B6
Phoines 95 A6
Phorp 103 D6
Pibsbury 9 A1
Pica 68 D7
Piccadilly Corner 45 B7
Piccotts End 23 E1
Pickerells 24 F2
Pickering 64 E5
Picket Piece 22 C7
Picket Post 10 C4
Pickford Green 40 E6
Pickhill 63 D6
Picklescott 38 D5
Pickletillem 89 A6
Pickmere 49 A4
Pickstock 39 B2
Pickston 88 A6
Pickwell *Devon* 6 D2
Pickwell *Leics* 41 E3
Pickworth *Leics* 42 C3

Pickworth *Lincs* 42 D1
Picton *Ches* 48 D4
Picton *N Yorks* 64 B3
Piddinghoe 13 B6
Piddington *Northants* 31 D2
Piddington *Oxon* 31 B6
Piddlehinton 9 D4
Piddletrenthide 9 D4
Pidley 32 E1
Piercebridge 63 C3
Pierowall 112 D2
Pigdon 77 C7
Pikehall 50 C5
Pilgrims Hatch 25 A3
Pilham 52 B2
Pill 20 E3
Pillaton 4 D4
Pillerton Hersey 30 C3
Pillerton Priors 30 C3
Pilleth 28 B1
Pilley *Glos* 29 D6
Pilley *S Yorks* 57 B7
Pilley Bailey 10 E5
Pilling 54 D3
Pilling Lane 54 C3
Pillowell 29 A7
Pilning 20 E2
Pilsbury 50 C4
Pilsdon 9 A4
Pilsgate 42 D4
Pilsley *Derbs* 51 A4
Pilsley *Derbs* 50 D3
Pilton *Leics* 42 C4
Pilton *Northants* 42 D6
Pilton *Som* 20 E6
Pimperne 10 A4
Pinchbeck 43 A2
Pinchbeck Bars 43 A2
Pinchbeck West 43 A2
Pinchinthorpe 64 C2
Pinfold 54 C6
Pinhay 8 E4
Pinhoe 7 D7
Pinkneys Green 23 C3
Pinley Green 30 C1
Pinminnoch 66 C1
Pinmore 66 D1
Pinn 8 C5
Pinner 24 B4
Pinner Green 24 B3
Pinvin 29 D3
Pinwherry 66 C2
Pinxton 51 A5
Pipe and Lyde 28 E3
Pipe Gate 49 B7
Piperhall 72 E2
Piperhill 103 B6
Pipe Ridware 40 C3
Piperspool 4 C2
Pipewell 42 B6
Pippacott 6 E3
Pipton 28 A4
Pirbright 12 B1
Pirnmill 72 C3
Pirton *H & W* 29 C3
Pirton *Herts* 32 C5
Pisgah 81 B1
Pishill 23 B3
Pistyll 46 C6
Pit 8 B2
Pitagowan 87 E2
Pitcairngreen 88 B6
Pitcairns 88 B7
Pitcaple 105 A6
Pitchcombe 29 C7
Pitchcott 31 C5
Pitchford 38 E4
Pitch Green 31 C7
Pitch Place 12 B1
Pitcombe 21 A7
Pitcot 18 D6
Pitcox 83 B5
Pitcur 88 D5
Pitfichie 97 B2
Pitfour 105 C4
Pitgrudy 103 A2
Pitinnan 105 A5
Pitkennedy 89 B3
Pitkevy 82 C2
Pitlessie 82 D2
Pitlochry 88 A3
Pitmedden 105 B6
Pitminster 8 D2
Pitmuies 89 B4
Pitmunie 97 B2

Pitnacree 88 A3
Pitney 9 A1
Pitroddie 88 D6
Pitscottie 89 A7
Pitsea 25 C4
Pitsford 31 C1
Pitsford Hill 20 A7
Pitstone 31 E6
Pitstone Green 31 E6
Pitt Down 13 B4
Pittendreich 103 E5
Pittentrail 103 A1
Pittenweem 83 A2
Pittington 71 B4
Pittodrie 104 E6
Pitton 10 D1
Pittrichie 105 B6
Pity Me 71 A4
Pityme 3 B1
Pixey Green 35 B1
Place Newton 65 A6
Plaidy 105 A3
Plains 81 B5
Plaish 38 E5
Plaistow 12 C3
Plaitford 10 D3
Plâs 17 C3
Plas Gogerddan 27 A2
Plas Gwynant 47 A5
Plas Isaf 47 E6
Plasisaf 47 A8
Plâs Llwyd 47 D3
Plas Llwyngwern 37 B5
Plas Llysyn 37 D6
Plas Nantyr 38 A1
Plas-rhiw-Saeson 37 D5
Plastow Green 22 E5
Plas-yn-Cefn 47 E3
Platt *Kent* 15 A3
Platt *Kent* 13 D1
Platt Lane 38 E1
Plawsworth 71 A4
Plaxtol 13 D1
Playden 14 E6
Playford 35 B4
Play Hatch 23 B4
Playing Place 3 A4
Plealey 38 D4
Plean 81 C3
Pleasance 88 D7
Pleasington 55 A5
Pleasley 51 B4
Plenmeller 70 A2
Pleshey 33 C7
Plocaig 85 A2
Plockton 93 A1
Ploughfield 28 C3
Plowden 38 C6
Ploxgreen 38 C4
Pluckley 14 E4
Pluckley Thorne 14 E4
Plumbland 68 E6
Plumley 49 B4
Plumpton *E Ssx* 13 A5
Plumpton End 31 C3
Plumpton Green 13 A5
Plumpton Hall 69 C6
Plumpton Head 69 D6
Plumstead *GL* 24 E5
Plumstead *Nflk* 45 A2
Plumtree 51 C7
Plungar 51 D7
Plush 9 D3
Plwmp 26 C5
Plym Bridge 4 E5
Plymouth 4 E5
Plympton 5 A5
Plymstock 5 A5
Plymtree 8 B3
Pockley 64 D5
Pocklington 58 D3
Pocombe Bridge 7 D7
Pode Hole 43 A2
Podimore 9 B1
Podington 31 E1
Podmore 39 B1
Poffley End 30 D6
Pointon 42 E1
Pokesdown 10 C5
Polanach 86 A3
Polapit Tamar 4 D2
Polbae 66 D3
Polbain 108 B7
Polbathic 4 D5
Polbeth 81 E5
Polchar 95 B5
Poldean 75 B5

Polebrook 42 D6
Polegate 15 A6
Pole of Itlaw, The 104 E3
Poles 103 A2
Polesworth 40 E4
Polglass 101 C1
Polgooth 3 B3
Polgown 74 C5
Polin 108 D3
Polla 109 A3
Pollachar 90 C4
Polldubh 86 C2
Pollie 110 C7
Pollington 57 E6
Polloch 85 D2
Pollokshaws 80 E5
Pollyroy 111 A5
Polmassick 3 B4
Polmont 81 D4
Polnoon 80 E6
Polperro 4 C5
Polruan 3 D3
Polsham 20 E6
Polstead 34 D5
Poltalloch 79 C2
Poltimore 7 D7
Polton 82 C6
Polwarth 83 C7
Polyphant 4 C2
Polzeath 3 B1
Pondersbridge 43 A5
Ponders End 24 D3
Ponsanooth 2 E5
Ponsonby 60 E3
Ponsworthy 5 C3
Pont Aber 18 C1
Pont Aber Glaslyn 46 E6
Pontamman 18 B2
Pontantwn 17 C4
Pontardawe 18 C3
Pontardulais 17 D5
Pontarsais 17 C3
Pontblyddyn 48 B5
Pontbren llwyd 18 E3
Pont Ceri 26 B6
Pont Clydach 18 C2
Pont Crugnant 37 C6
Pont Cyfyng 47 B5
Pont Dolgarrog 47 B4
Pontefract 57 C5
Ponteland 70 E1
Ponterwyd 27 B2
Pontesbury 38 C4
Pontesford 38 D4
Pontfadog 38 B1
Pontfaen 16 D2
Pont-faen Dyfed 27 A6
Pont-faen Powys 27 D7
Ponthenri 17 C5
Pont-hir 19 D4
Ponthirwaun 26 B6
Pontllanfraith 19 B4
Pontlliw 18 B3
Pont-Llogel 37 E4
Pontlottyn 19 B3
Pontlyfni 46 D5
Pont Nedd Fechan 18 E3
Pont Newydd 28 B5
Pontnewydd 19 C4
Pontnewynydd 19 C3
Pont Pen-y-benglog 47 A4
Pont Petryal 47 E5
Pontrhydfendigaid 27 B4
Pont Rhyd-sarn 37 C3
Pont Rhyd-y-cyff 18 D5
Pontrhyd-y-fen 18 C4
Pontrhydygroes 27 B3
Pont-rhydyrun 19 D4
Pontrilas 28 C5
Pontrobert 38 A3
Pont-rug 46 E4
Ponts Green 13 D5
Pontshaen 26 D6
Pontshill 29 A5
Pontsticill 19 A2
Pont Walby 18 D3
Pontwelly 26 D6
Pontwyn 19 C5
Pontyates 17 C5
Pontyberem 17 C4
Pontybodkin 48 B6
Pontyclun 19 A5
Pontycymer 18 E4
Pontymister 19 C4
Pont-y-pant 47 B5

Pontypool 19 C3
Pontypool Road 19 D3
Pontypridd 19 A4
Pont yr Alwen 47 D5
Pontywaun 19 C4
Pooksgreen 10 E3
Pool 57 A3
Pool Bank 61 D5
Poole 10 B5
Poole Keynes 21 D1
Poolewe 101 A3
Pooley Bridge 69 C7
Poolhill 29 B5
Pool of Muckhart 81 E1
Pool Quay 38 B3
Pool Street 33 D5
Pope Hill 16 C4
Popeswood 23 C5
Popham 22 E7
Poplar 24 D4
Porchfield 11 A5
Porin 102 B6
Porkellis 2 D5
Porlock 7 C2
Porlock Weir 7 C2
Portachoillan 72 B2
Port Allen 81 B6
Port Appin 86 A4
Port Askaig 78 D5
Portavadie 79 D5
Port Bannatyne 79 E5
Portbury 20 D3
Port Carlisle 69 A3
Port Charlotte 78 B6
Portchester 11 C4
Port Clarence 64 C1
Port Dinorwic 46 E4
Port Ellen 78 C7
Port Elphinstone 97 C2
Portencross 73 A3
Port Erin 60 a5
Port Erroll 105 D5
Portesham 5 C5
Portessie 104 C2
Port e Vullen 60 d2
Port Eynon 17 C7
Portfield 85 D6
Portfield Gate 16 C4
Portgate 4 E2
Port Gaverne 4 A2
Port Glasgow 80 C4
Portgordon 104 B2
Portgower 111 A7
Porth Corn 3 A2
Porth M Glam 19 A4
Porthallow 2 E6
Porthcawl 18 D6
Porthceri 19 A7
Porth Colmon 46 A7
Porthcurno 2 A6
Port Henderson 100 E4
Porthgain 16 B2
Porthleven 2 D6
Porthmadog 46 E7
Porth Mellin 2 D7
Porthmeor 2 B5
Porth Navas 2 E6
Portholland 3 B4
Porthoustock 3 A6
Porthpean 3 C3
Porthtowan 2 D4
Porthyrhyd Dyfed 27 B7
Porthyrhyd Dyfed 17 D4
Porth y waen 38 B2
Portincaple 80 B2
Portington 58 C4
Portinnisherrich 86 A7
Portinscale 69 A7
Port Isaac 3 B1
Portishead 20 D3
Portknockie 104 C2
Portland Bridge 9 C6
Portlethen 97 E4
Portloe 3 B5
Port Logan 66 B6
Portmahomack 103 C3
Portmeirion 46 E7
Portmore 10 E5
Port Mulgrave 64 E2
Port na Craig 88 A3
Portnacroish 86 A4
Portnaguiran 107 D4
Portnahaven 78 A6
Portnaluchaig 92 D6
Portnancon 109 B2
Portobello 82 D5
Port of Menteith 80 E1

Port of Ness 107 D1
Porton 10 C1
Port o' Warren 68 B4
Portpatrick 66 B5
Port Penrhyn 46 E3
Portquin 3 B1
Port Ramsay 85 E4
Port St Mary 60 b5
Portscatho 3 A5
Portsea 11 C4
Portskerra 110 D2
Portskewett 20 D2
Portslade 12 E6
Portslade-by-Sea 12 E6
Portslogan 66 A5
Portsmouth 11 C4
Portsonachan 86 B6
Portsoy 104 D2
Port Sunlight 48 C3
Portswood 11 A3
Port Talbot 18 C4
Portuairk 85 A2
Portway H & W 40 C7
Portway H & W 28 C3
Port Wemyss 78 A6
Port William 66 E6
Portwrinkle 4 D5
Portyerrock 67 A7
Poslingford 33 D4
Postbridge 5 B3
Postcombe 23 B2
Postling 15 B5
Postwick 45 B5
Potarch 97 B4
Potsgrove 31 E5
Potten End 23 E1
Potterhamworth Booths
52 D5
Potterhanworth 52 D5
Potter Heigham 45 D4
Potterne 21 D5
Potterne Wick 21 D5
Potters Bar 24 C2
Potter's Cross 40 A6
Potters Crouch 24 B2
Potterspury 31 C3
Potter Street 24 E2
Potto 64 B3
Potton 32 D4
Pott Row 44 B3
Pott Shrigley 49 D4
Poughill Corn 6 B6
Poughill Devon 7 C6
Poulner 10 C4
Poulshot 21 D5
Poulton 30 B7
Poulton-le-Fylde 54 C4
Pound Bank 39 B7
Pound-ffald 17 D6
Poundgate 13 B4
Pound Green 13 C4
Pound Hill 12 E3
Poundland 66 C2
Poundon 31 B5
Poundsbridge 13 C2
Poundsgate 5 C3
Poundstock 6 B7
Powburn 77 B4
Powderham 8 A5
Powerstock 9 B4
Powfoot 68 E3
Pow Green 29 B3
Powick 29 C2
Powler's Piece 7 B5
Powmill 81 E2
Poxwell 9 D5
Poyle 23 E4
Poynings 12 E5
Poyntington 9 C2
Poynton Ches 49 D3
Poynton Salop 38 E3
Poynton Green 38 E3
Poyntzfield 103 A5
Poys Street 35 C1
Poyston Cross 16 C4
Poystreet Green 34 D3
Praa Sands 2 C6
Pratis 82 D2
Pratt's Bottom 24 E6
Praze-an-Beeble 2 D5
Predannack Wollas 2 D7
Predergast 16 C4
Prees 38 E1
Preesall 54 C3
Prees Green 38 E1

Preesgweene 38 C1
Prees Higher Heath 38 E1
Prenbrigog 48 B5
Prendwick 77 B4
Pren-gwyn 26 D6
Prenteg 46 E6
Prenton 48 C3
Prescot 48 D2
Prescott 38 D2
Presley 103 D6
Pressen 76 E2
Prestatyn 47 E2
Prestbury Glos 29 D5
Presteigne 28 C1
Presthope 38 E5
Prestleigh 21 A6
Prestolee 49 B1
Preston Bdrs 83 C7
Preston Devon 5 D3
Preston Dors 9 D5
Preston E Ssx 13 A6
Preston Glos 29 A4
Preston Glos 30 A7
Preston Herts 32 C6
Preston Humb 59 B4
Preston Kent 15 A2
Preston Kent 15 C2
Preston Lancs 54 E5
Preston Leics 42 B4
Preston Loth 83 A5
Preston Northld 77 C3
Preston Northld 71 B2
Preston Sflk 34 D3
Preston Wilts 21 E3
Preston Bagot 30 B1
Preston Bissett 31 B4
Preston Brockhurst 38 E2
Preston Brook 48 E3
Preston Candover 23 A7
Preston Capes 31 A2
Preston Deanery 31 C2
Preston Gubbals 38 D3
Preston on Stour 30 C3
Preston on the Hill 48 E3
Preston on Wye 28 C3
Prestonpans 82 D5
Preston Plucknett 9 B2
Preston-under-Scar 63 A5
Preston upon the Weald
Moors 39 A3
Preston Wynne 28 E3
Prestwich 49 C1
Prestwick Northld 70 E1
Prestwick Strath 73 C5
Prestwold 41 C2
Prestwood 31 D7
Price Town 18 E4
Prickwillow 43 D6
Priddy 20 E5
Priestfield 103 E7
Priest Hill 55 A4
Priest Hutton 61 E6
Priestland 73 E5
Priestweston 38 B5
Primethorpe 41 C5
Primrose Green 44 E4
Primrose Hill 43 B6
Princes End 40 B5
Princes Gate 16 E4
Princes Risborough 31 D7
Princethorpe 41 A7
Princetown Devon 5 A3
Princetown M Glam 19 B3
Prior Muir 89 B7
Prior's Frome 28 E4
Priors Hardwick 30 E2
Priors Marston 30 E2
Priory, The 11 C5
Priory Wood 28 B3
Priston 21 A4
Prittlewell 25 D4
Privett 11 C2
Prixford 6 E3
Proaig 78 D6
Probus 3 A4
Proncy 103 A2
Protsonhill 105 B2
Prudhoe 70 D2
Pubil 87 A4
Puckeridge 32 E6
Puckington 8 E2
Pucklechurch 21 A3
Puddinglake 49 B5
Puddington Ches 48 C4
Puddington Devon 7 C5
Puddlebrook 29 A6
Puddledock 44 E6

Puddletown 9 D4
Pudleston 28 E2
Pudsey 57 A4
Pulborough 12 C5
Puldagon 111 D4
Puleston 39 B2
Pulford 48 C6
Pulham 9 D3
Pulham Market 45 A7
Pulham St Mary 45 B7
Pulloxhill 32 B5
Pulrossie 103 A3
Pumpherston 81 E5
Pumsaint 27 A6
Puncheston 16 D3
Puncknowle 9 B5
Punnett's Town 13 D4
Purbrook 11 C4
Puriton 20 C6
Purleigh 25 D2
Purley Berks 23 A4
Purley GL 24 D6
Purlogue 38 B7
Purls Bridge 43 C6
Purse Caundle 9 C2
Purslow 38 C6
Purston Jaglin 57 C6
Purton Glos 21 E2
Purton Glos 29 A7
Purton Wilts 21 E2
Purton Stoke 21 E1
Purves Hall 76 D1
Pury End 31 C3
Pusey 22 C2
Putley 29 A4
Putloe 29 B7
Putney 24 C5
Puttenham Herts 31 D6
Puttenham Sry 12 B2
Puttock End 34 C4
Puxton 20 D4
Pwll 17 C5
Pwllcrochan 16 C5
Pwlldefaid 36 A3
Pwllgloyw 27 E7
Pwllheli 46 C7
Pwllmeyric 20 E1
Pwll Trap 17 A4
Pwll-y-glaw 18 C4
Pyecombe 12 E5
Pye Corner 19 D5
Pye Green 40 B3
Pyle IOW 11 A7
Pyle M Glam 18 D5
Pylle 21 A7
Pymore 43 C6
Pyrford 12 C1
Pyrton 23 A2
Pytchley 42 B7
Pyworthy 6 C6

Q
Quabbs 38 B6
Quadring 43 A1
Quadring Eaudike 43 A1
Quainton 31 C6
Quarff 115 D4
Quarley 22 B7
Quarndon 50 E6
Quarr Hill 11 B5
Quarrington 52 D7
Quarrington Hill 71 B5
Quarry Bank 40 B6
Quarrybank 48 E5
Quarrywood 103 E5
Quarter 81 B6
Quarters Spit 34 D7
Quatford 39 B5
Quatt 39 B6
Quebec 70 E4
Quedgeley 29 C6
Queen Adelaide 43 D6
Queen Camel 9 B1
Queen Charlton 21 A4
Queensbury 56 E4
Queensferry Clwyd 48 C5
Queen's Head 38 C2
Queen Street 13 D2
Queenzieburn 81 A4
Quemerford 21 E4
Quendale 115 C6
Quendon 33 B5
Queniborough 41 D3

Quenington 30 B7
Quernmore 54 E1
Queslett 40 C5
Quethiock 4 D4
Quholm 112 B5
Quicksands 32 C5
Quidenham 44 E7
Quidhampton Hants 22 E6
Quidhampton Wilts 10 C1
Quidnish 98 C4
Quina Brook 38 E1
Quindry 113 D2
Quine's Hill 60 c4
Quinhill 72 B2
Quinton Northants 31 C2
Quinton W Mids 40 B6
Quintrell Downs 3 A2
Quoditch 6 D7
Quoig 87 E6
Quoigs 81 C1
Quorn 41 C3
Quothquan 74 E2
Quoyloo 112 B4
Quoys 114 F1
Quoys of Reiss 111 D3

R
Raby 48 C4
Rachub 47 A4
Rackenford 7 C5
Rackham 12 C5
Rackheath 45 B4
Racks 68 D2
Rackwick Hoy 113 A2
Rackwick Westray 112 D2
Radbourne 50 D7
Radcliffe GM 49 B1
Radcliffe Northld 77 D5
Radcliffe on Trent 51 C7
Radclive 31 B4
Radcot 22 B2
Raddicombe 4 E3
Radford Oxon 30 E5
Radford W Mids 41 A6
Radford Semele 30 D1
Radipole 9 C5
Radlett 24 B2
Radley 22 E2
Radnage 23 B2
Radstock 21 A5
Radstone 31 A3
Radway 30 D3
Radway Green 49 B6
Radwell Beds 32 B3
Radwell Herts 32 D5
Radwinter 33 C5
Radyr 19 B5
Raechester 77 A7
Raemoir 97 B4
Raffin 108 C5
Rafford 103 D6
Ragdale 41 D3
Raglan 28 D7
Ragnall 52 B4
Rahoy 85 C3
Rainford 48 D1
Rainham GL 24 F4
Rainham Kent 14 D2
Rainhill 48 D2
Rainhill Stoops 48 E2
Rainigadale 107 A7
Rainow 49 D4
Rainton 63 D7
Rainworth 51 B5
Raisbeck 62 B4
Rait 88 D6
Raithby Lincs 53 B5
Raithby Lincs 53 B3
Rake 11 E2
Ram 26 E6
Ramasaig 99 A7
Rame Corn 2 E5
Rame Corn 4 E6
Ram Lane 14 E4
Rampisham 9 B3
Rampside 61 B7
Rampton Cambs 33 A2
Rampton Notts 51 D3
Ramsbottom 55 B6
Ramsbury 22 B4
Ramscraigs 111 B6
Ramsdean 11 D2
Ramsdell 22 E6
Ramsden 30 D6
Ramsden Bellhouse 25 C3

Ramsden Heath 25 C3
Ramsey *Cambs* 43 A6
Ramsey *Esx* 35 B5
Ramsey *IOM* 60 d2
Ramseycleuch 75 C4
Ramsey Forty Foot 43 B6
Ramsey Heights 43 A6
Ramsey Mereside 43 A6
Ramsey St Mary's 43 A6
Ramsgate 15 D2
Ramsgate Street 44 E2
Ramsgill 63 B7
Ramsholt 35 C4
Ramshorn 50 B6
Ramsnest Common 12 B3
Ranachan 85 D2
Ranby *Lincs* 53 A4
Ranby *Notts* 51 C2
Rand 52 E4
Randwick 29 C7
Rangemore 40 D2
Rangeworthy 21 A2
Rankinston 73 D6
Ranks Green 33 D7
Ranochan 93 A6
Ranskill 51 C2
Ranton 40 A2
Ranworth 45 C4
Rapness 112 E2
Rarey 85 E6
Rascarrel 67 D6
Raskelf 64 B6
Rassau 19 B2
Rastrick 56 E5
Ratby 41 C4
Ratcliffe Culey 41 A5
Ratcliffe on Soar 41 B2
Ratcliffe on the Wreake 41 D3
Ratford Bridge 16 C4
Rathen 105 D2
Rathillet 88 E6
Rathliesbeag 93 E6
Rathmell 55 C2
Ratho 88 E6
Rathven 104 C2
Ratley 30 D3
Ratlinghope 38 D5
Rattar 111 C1
Ratten Row 54 D3
Rattery 5 C4
Rattlesden 34 D3
Rattray 88 C4
Rauceby 52 D7
Raughton Head 69 B5
Raunds 42 C7
Ravenfield 51 A1
Ravenglass 60 E4
Raveningham 45 C6
Ravenscar 65 B3
Ravensdale 60 c2
Ravensden 32 B3
Ravenshaw 55 D3
Ravenshayes 7 D6
Ravenshead 51 B5
Ravensmoor 49 A6
Ravensthorpe *Northants* 41 D7
Ravensthorpe *W Yorks* 57 A5
Ravenstone *Bucks* 31 D2
Ravenstone *Leics* 41 B3
Ravenstonedale 62 C4
Ravenstruther 74 E1
Ravensworth 63 B4
Raw 65 B3
Rawcliffe *Humb* 57 E5
Rawcliffe *N Yorks* 57 D2
Rawcliffe Bridge 57 E5
Rawdon 57 A4
Rawmarsh 51 A1
Rawreth 25 C3
Rawridge 8 D3
Rawtenstall 55 C5
Rawyards 81 B5
Raxton 105 B5
Raydon 34 E5
Raylees 77 A6
Rayleigh 25 D3
Rayne 33 D6
Reach 33 B2
Read 55 B4
Reading 23 B4
Reading Street 14 E5
Reagill 62 B3
Rearquhar 103 A2
Rearsby 41 D3

Rease Heath 49 A6
Reaster 111 C2
Reawick 115 C3
Reay 110 E2
Reculver 15 C2
Redberth 16 D5
Redbourn 32 C7
Redbourne 52 C2
Redbridge 24 E4
Redbrook 28 E6
Redbrook Street 14 E5
Redburn *Hghld* 102 D7
Redburn *Hghld* 103 C7
Redcar 64 D1
Redcastle *Hghld* 102 D7
Redcastle *Tays* 89 C3
Redcliff Bay 20 D3
Redcloak 97 D5
Red Dial 69 A5
Reddish 49 C2
Redditch 30 A1
Rede 34 C3
Redenhall 45 B7
Redesmouth 76 E7
Redford *Gramp* 97 C6
Redford *Tays* 89 B4
Redford *W Ssx* 11 E2
Redgrave 34 E1
Redheugh 89 A2
Redhill *Avn* 20 D5
Redhill *Gramp* 104 D4
Redhill *Gramp* 104 E5
Redhill *Gramp* 97 C3
Redhill *Notts* 51 B6
Redhill *Salop* 39 B3
Redhill *Sry* 12 E1
Red Hill *Warks* 30 B2
Redhouse *Gramp* 104 D6
Redhouse *Hghld* 79 C5
Redhouses 78 C5
Redisham 45 D7
Redland *Avn* 20 E3
Redland *Ork* 112 C4
Redlingfield 35 A1
Redlynch *Som* 21 A7
Redlynch *Wilts* 10 D2
Redmarley D'Abitot 29 B4
Redmarshall 71 B6
Redmile 51 D7
Redmire 63 A5
Redmoor 3 C2
Rednal *Salop* 38 C2
Rednal *W Mids* 40 C7
Red Oaks Hill 33 C5
Redpath 76 B2
Redpoint 100 E5
Red Post *Corn* 6 B6
Red Post *Devon* 5 D4
Red Rock 48 E1
Red Roses 17 A4
Red Row 77 D6
Redruth 2 D4
Redscarhead 75 C1
Redshaw 74 D3
Redstone Bank 16 E4
Red Street 49 C6
Red Wharf Bay 46 E2
Redwick *Avn* 20 E2
Redwick *Gwent* 20 D2
Redworth 71 A6
Reed 32 E5
Reedham 45 D5
Reedness 58 C5
Reepham *Lincs* 52 D4
Reepham *Nflk* 45 A3
Reeth 63 A5
Regaby 60 d2
Reiff 108 B7
Reigate 12 E1
Reighton 65 D6
Reisgill 111 C5
Reiss 111 D3
Rejerrah 3 A3
Relubbus 2 C5
Relugas 103 C7
Remenham 23 B3
Remenham Hill 23 B3
Remony 87 D4
Rempstone 41 C2
Rendcomb 30 A7
Rendham 35 C2
Rendlesham 35 C3
Renfrew 80 D5
Renhold 32 B4
Renishaw 51 A3
Rennington 77 D4

Renton 80 C4
Renwick 69 D5
Repps 45 D4
Repton 41 A2
Rescobie 89 B3
Resipole 85 D2
Resolis 102 E5
Resolven 18 D3
Resourie 85 E1
Reswallie 89 B3
Retew 3 B3
Retford 51 D2
Rettendon 25 C3
Rettendon Place 25 C3
Retyn 3 A3
Reudle 84 E4
Revesby 53 A5
Rew 7 C7
Rewe 7 D7
Reydon 35 D1
Reymerston 44 E5
Reynalton 16 D5
Reynoldston 17 C6
Rezare 4 D3
Rhandirmwyn 27 B6
Rhaoine 102 E1
Rhayader 27 D4
Rhedyn 46 C7
Rhegreanoch 108 C7
Rhelonie 102 D2
Rhemore 85 B3
Rhes-y-cae 48 A4
Rhewl *Clwyd* 48 A7
Rhewl *Clwyd* 48 A5
Rhewl *Salop* 38 C1
Rhian 109 C7
Rhicarn 108 C6
Rhiconich 108 E3
Rhicullen 102 E4
Rhidorroch 101 D2
Rhifail 110 C4
Rhigos 18 E3
Rhilochan 103 A1
Rhinduie 102 D7
Rhireavach 101 C2
Rhiroy 101 D3
Rhives 103 B1
Rhiwargor 37 D3
Rhiwbryfdir 47 A6
Rhiwderin 19 C5
Rhiwlas *Clwyd* 38 A1
Rhiwlas *Gynd* 46 E4
Rhiwlas *Gynd* 47 D7
Rhodesia 51 B2
Rhodes Minnis 15 B4
Rhodiad 16 A3
Rhôd-mâd 26 E3
Rhonadale 72 B4
Rhonehouse or Kelton Hill 67 D5
Rh'ôs *Dyfed* 17 B2
Rhos *W Glam* 18 C3
Rhos Berse 48 B6
Rhoscolyn 46 B3
Rhoscrowther 16 C5
Rhosddu 48 C6
Rhôse 19 A7
Rhosesmor 48 B5
Rhos-fawr 46 C7
Rhosgadfan 46 E5
Rhosgoch *Gynd* 46 D2
Rhosgoch *Pwys* 28 A3
Rhos Hill 26 A6
Rhoslan 46 D6
Rhoslefain 36 E5
Rhosllanerchrugog 48 B7
Rhosmaen 18 B1
Rhosmeirch 46 D3
Rhosneigr 46 C3
Rhosnesni 48 C6
Rhos-on-Sea 47 C2
Rhossili 17 C7
Rhosson 16 A3
Rhostryfan 46 D5
Rhostyllen 48 C7
Rhosybol 46 D2
Rhos-y-brwyner 48 B5
Rhos-y-Foel 27 C2
Rhos-y-gwaliau 47 D7
Rhos-y-llan 46 B7
Rhos-y-mawn 47 C4
Rho3s-y-meirch 28 B1
Rhu *Strath* 80 B3
Rhuallt 47 E3
Rhubodach 79 E4
Rhuddlan 47 E3

Rhude Cross 7 A4
Rhue 101 C2
Rhulen 28 A2
Rhumach 92 D6
Rhyd *Gynd* 47 A6
Rhyd *Pwys* 37 D5
Rhydargaeau 17 C3
Rhydcymerau 17 D2
Rhydd 29 C3
Rhyd-Ddu 46 E5
Rhydding 18 C4
Rhydlewis 26 C6
Rhydlios 46 A7
Rhyd-lydan *Clwyd* 47 C5
Rhyd-lydan *Pwys* 37 E6
Rhydolion 36 B3
Rhydowen 26 D6
Rhydrosser 26 E4
Rhydspence 28 B3
Rhydtalog 48 B6
Rhydwyn 46 C2
Rhŷd-y-clafdy 46 C7
Rhydycroesau 38 B1
Rhydyfelin *Dyfed* 26 E3
Rhydyfelin *M Glam* 19 A5
Rhyd-y-foel 47 D3
Rhyd-y-fro 18 C3
Rhydymain 37 B3
Rhyd-y-meirch 19 D3
Rhydymwyn 48 B5
Rhyd-yr-onnen 37 A5
Rhyl 47 E2
Rhymney 19 B3
Rhyn 38 C1
Rhynd 88 C6
Rhynie *Gramp* 104 C6
Rhynie *Hghld* 103 B4
Ribbesford 39 B7
Ribbleton 54 E4
Ribchester 55 A4
Ribigill 109 C3
Riby 59 B7
Riccall 57 E4
Riccarton 73 D4
Richings Park 23 E4
Richmond 63 B4
Richmond upon Thames 24 B5
Rickarton 97 D5
Rickford 20 D5
Rickinghall Inferior 34 E1
Rickinghall Superior 34 E1
Rickling 33 A5
Rickling Green 33 B6
Rickmansworth 23 E2
Riddell 76 B3
Riddings *Cumb* 69 C2
Riddings *Derbs* 51 A5
Riddlecombe 7 A5
Riddlesden 56 D3
Riddlesworth 44 D7
Ridge *Dors* 10 A6
Ridge *Herts* 24 C2
Ridge *Wilts* 10 A1
Ridgebourne 27 E4
Ridge Green 13 A2
Ridgehill 20 E4
Ridge Lane 40 E5
Ridgeway 51 A2
Ridge Way 30 A1
Ridgeway Cross 29 B3
Ridgewell 33 D4
Ridgewood 13 B5
Ridgmont 31 E4
Riding Mill 70 D2
Ridley 25 B6
Ridleywood 48 D6
Ridlington *Leics* 42 B4
Ridlington *Nflk* 45 C2
Ridsdale 77 A7
Riechip 88 C4
Rigg *D & G* 69 A3
Rigg *Hghld* 100 C6
Riggend 81 B4
Righoul 103 B6
Rigmaden Park 62 B6
Rigsby 53 C4
Rigside 74 D2
Rileyhill 40 D3
Rilla Mill 4 C3
Rillington 65 A6
Rimington 55 C3
Rimpton 9 C1
Rimswell 59 D5
Rinaston 16 C3
Ringford 67 C5

Ringland 45 A4
Ringles Cross 13 B4
Ringmer 13 B5
Ringmore 5 B6
Ringorm 104 A4
Ring's End 43 B4
Ringsfield 45 D7
Ringsfield Corner 45 D7
Ringshall *Bucks* 31 E6
Ringshall *Sflk* 34 E3
Ringshall Stocks 34 E3
Ringstead *Nflk* 44 B1
Ringstead *Northants* 42 C7
Ringwood 10 C4
Ringwould 15 D4
Rinloan 96 C3
Rinmore 96 E2
Rinnigill 113 C2
Rinsey 2 C6
Ripe 13 C5
Ripley *Derbs* 50 E5
Ripley *Hants* 10 C5
Ripley *N Yorks* 57 A1
Ripley *Sry* 12 C1
Riplingham 58 E4
Ripon 63 D7
Rippingale 42 D2
Ripple *H & W* 29 C4
Ripple *Kent* 15 D3
Ripponden 56 D6
Risbury 28 E2
Risby *Humb* 58 E6
Risby *Sflk* 33 D2
Risca 19 C4
Rise 59 B3
Risegate 43 A2
Riseley *Beds* 32 B2
Riseley *Berks* 23 B5
Rishangles 35 A2
Rishton 55 B5
Rishworth 56 D6
Risley 51 A7
Risplith 57 A1
Rispond 109 B2
Rivar 22 C5
Rivenhall 34 C7
Rivenhall End 34 C7
River 12 B4
River Bank 33 B2
River Bridge 20 C6
Riverford Bridge 5 C4
Riverhead 13 C1
Rivington 55 A6
Road Ashton 21 C5
Roade 31 C2
Roadside 111 B2
Roadside of Kinneff 97 D6
Roadwater 7 E3
Roag 99 B7
Roa Island 61 B7
Roath 19 B6
Roberton *Bdrs* 76 A4
Roberton *Strath* 74 E3
Robertsbridge 13 E4
Robertstown 104 A4
Roberttown 56 E5
Robeston Cross 16 B5
Robeston Wathen 16 D4
Robin Hood *Derbs* 50 D3
Robin Hood *W Yorks* 57 B5
Robin Hood's Bay 65 B3
Robins 11 E2
Roborough 5 A4
Roborough 6 E5
Roby 48 D2
Roby Mill 48 E1
Rocester 50 C7
Roch 16 B3
Rochallie 88 C3
Rochdale 55 C6
Roche 3 B2
Rochester *Kent* 14 C2
Rochester *Northld* 76 E6
Rochford *Esx* 25 D3
Rochford *H & W* 29 A1
Rock *Corn* 3 B1
Rock *Gwent* 19 B4
Rock *H & W* 39 B7
Rock *Northld* 77 D3
Rockbeare 8 B4
Rockbourne 10 C3
Rockcliffe *Cumb* 69 B3
Rockcliffe *D & G* 68 B4
Rock Ferry 48 C3

Rockfield *Gwent* 28 D6
Rockfield *Hghld* 103 C3
Rockfield *Strath* 72 B2
Rockhampton 21 A1
Rockhead 4 A2
Rockingham 42 B5
Rockland All Saints 44 D6
Rockland St Mary 45 C5
Rockland St Peter 44 D6
Rockley 22 A4
Rockside 78 B5
Rockwell End 23 B3
Rockwell Green 8 C1
Rodborough 29 C7
Rodbourne 21 D2
Rodd 28 C1
Roddam 77 B3
Rodden 9 C5
Rode 21 C5
Rodeheath 49 C5
Rode Heath 49 C6
Rodel 98 E3
Roden 38 E3
Rodhuish 7 E3
Rodington 38 E3
Rodley 29 B6
Rodmarton 21 D1
Rodmell 13 B6
Rodmersham 14 E2
Rodney Stoke 20 D6
Rodsley 50 D6
Rodway 20 B6
Roecliffe 57 B1
Roe Green 32 E5
Roehampton 24 C5
Roesound 115 C1
Roffey 12 D3
Rogart 103 A1
Rogart Halt 103 A1
Rogate 11 E2
Rogerstone 19 C5
Rogiet 20 D2
Rois-bheinn 85 D1
Roker 71 C3
Rollesby 45 D4
Rolleston *Leics* 42 C7
Rolleston *Notts* 51 D5
Rolleston *Staffs* 40 E2
Rolster 3 D2
Rolston 59 C3
Rolvenden 14 D5
Rolvenden Layne 14 D5
Romaldkirk 70 C6
Romanby 63 D5
Romannobridge 75 B1
Romansleigh 7 B4
Romford 10 B4
Romford 24 F4
Romiley 49 D2
Romney Street 25 A6
Romsey 10 E2
Romsley *H & W* 40 B7
Romsley *Salop* 39 B6
Ronague 60 b4
Ronnachmore 78 C6
Rookhope 70 C4
Rookley 11 B6
Rooks Bridge 20 C5
Rookwith 63 C6
Roos 59 C4
Roosecote 61 B7
Ropley 11 C1
Ropley Dean 11 C1
Ropley Soke 11 C1
Ropsley 42 C1
Rora 105 D3
Rorrington 38 C4
Rosarie 104 B3
Rose 2 E3
Roseacre 54 D4
Rose Ash 7 B4
Rosebank 74 D1
Rosebrough 77 C3
Rosebush 16 D3
Rosedale Abbey 64 E4
Roseden 77 B3
Rose Green 34 D6
Rosehall 102 C1
Rosehearty 105 C2
Rosehill *Gramp* 97 A4
Rosehill *Salop* 39 A1
Roseisle 103 E5
Rosemarket 16 C5
Rosemarkie 103 A6
Rosemary Lane 8 C2
Rosemount *Tays* 88 D4
Rosepool 16 B4

Rosewarne **2 D5**
Rosewell **82 C6**
Roseworthy **2 D5**
Rosgill **61 E2**
Roshven **85 D1**
Roskhill **99 B7**
Rosley **69 B5**
Roslin **82 C6**
Rosliston **40 E3**
Rosneath **80 B3**
Ross *D & G* **67 C6**
Ross *Northld* **77 C2**
Ross *Tays* **87 D6**
Rossett **48 C6**
Rossie Ochill **88 B7**
Rossie Priory **88 D5**
Rossington **51 C1**
Rosskeen **102 E5**
Ross-on-Wye **29 A5**
Ross Priory **80 D3**
Roster **111 C3**
Rostherne **49 B3**
Rosthwaite *Cumb* **61 B2**
Rosthwaite *Cumb* **61 B5**
Roston **50 C6**
Rosyth **82 B4**
Rothbury **77 B5**
Rotherby **41 D3**
Rotherfield **15 A4**
Rotherfield Greys **23 B3**
Rotherfield Peppard **23 B3**
Rotherham **51 A1**
Rothersthorpe **31 C2**
Rotherwick **23 B6**
Rothes **104 A4**
Rothesay **79 E5**
Rothienorman **105 A5**
Rothiesholm **112 F4**
Rothley *Leics* **41 C3**
Rothley *Northld* **77 B7**
Rothwell *Lincs* **52 E2**
Rothwell *Northants* **42 B6**
Rothwell *W Yorks* **57 B5**
Rotsea **59 A2**
Rottal **88 E2**
Rottingdean **13 A6**
Rottington **60 D2**
Roud **11 B6**
Roudham **44 D7**
Rougham *Nflk* **44 C3**
Rougham *Nflk* **34 D2**
Rougham Green **34 D2**
Roughburn **94 B7**
Rough Close **40 B1**
Rough Common **15 B3**
Rough Heath **35 A7**
Roughlee **55 C3**
Roughley **40 D5**
Roughsike **69 D2**
Roughton *Lincs* **53 A5**
Roughton *Nflk* **45 B2**
Roughton *Salop* **39 B5**
Roundhay **57 B4**
Roundstreet Common **12 C4**
Roundway **21 E4**
Rousdon **8 D4**
Rousham **30 E5**
Rousham Gap **30 E5**
Rous Lench **30 A2**
Routh **59 A3**
Row *Corn* **4 A3**
Row *Cumb* **61 D5**
Rowanburn **69 C2**
Rowberrow **20 D5**
Rowchoish **80 C1**
Rowde **21 E4**
Rowen **47 B3**
Rowfoot **69 E3**
Rowhedge **34 E6**
Rowhook **12 D3**
Rowington **30 C1**
Rowington Green **40 E7**
Rowland **50 D3**
Rowlands Gill **70 E3**
Rowledge **23 C7**
Rowley *Devon* **7 B5**
Rowley *Dur* **70 D4**
Rowley *Humb* **58 E4**
Rowley *Salop* **38 C4**
Rowley Regis **40 B6**
Rowlstone **28 C5**
Rowly **12 C2**
Rowney Green **40 C7**
Rownhams **10 E3**
Rowrah **60 E2**
Rowsham **31 D6**

Rowsley **50 D4**
Rowston **52 D6**
Rowthorne **51 A4**
Rowton *Ches* **48 D5**
Rowton *Salop* **39 A3**
Rowton Castle **38 C3**
Rowton Moor **48 D5**
Roxburgh **76 C2**
Roxby *Humb* **58 E6**
Roxby *N Yorks* **64 E2**
Roxton **32 C3**
Roxwell **25 B2**
Royal British Legion Village **13 E1**
Royal Leamington Spa **30 D1**
Royal Tunbridge Wells **15 A3**
Roybridge **93 E6**
Roydon *Esx* **24 E2**
Roydon *Nflk* **44 E7**
Roydon *Nflk* **44 B3**
Royston *Herts* **32 E4**
Royston *S Yorks* **57 B6**
Royton **49 D1**
Ruabon **48 C7**
Ruaig **84 B4**
Ruanaich **84 A4**
Ruan Lanihorne **3 A4**
Ruan Major **2 E7**
Ruan Minor **2 E7**
Ruardean **29 A6**
Ruardean Woodside **29 A6**
Rubery **40 B7**
Ruckcroft **69 D5**
Ruckinge **15 A5**
Ruckland **53 B4**
Ruckley **38 E4**
Rudby **64 B3**
Rudchester **70 E2**
Ruddington **51 B7**
Rudford **29 B5**
Rudge **21 C5**
Rudgeway **21 A2**
Rudgwick **12 C3**
Rudhall **29 A5**
Rudley Green **25 D2**
Rudry **19 B5**
Rudston **65 C7**
Rudyard **49 D6**
Rufford *Lancs* **54 D6**
Rufford *Notts* **51 C4**
Rufforth **57 D2**
Ruffside **70 C3**
Rugby **41 C7**
Rugeley **40 C3**
Ruilick **102 D7**
Ruishton **8 D1**
Ruislip **23 E3**
Rumbling Bridge **81 E2**
Rumburgh **45 C7**
Rumford **3 A1**
Rumney **19 C6**
Runacraig **87 B7**
Runcorn **48 E3**
Runcton **11 E4**
Runcton Holme **44 A5**
Runfold **23 C7**
Runhall **44 E5**
Runham **45 D4**
Runival **93 B4**
Runnington **8 C1**
Runsell Green **25 C2**
Runswick **65 A2**
Runtaleave **88 D2**
Runwell **25 C3**
Ruscombe **23 C4**
Rushall *H & W* **29 A4**
Rushall *Nflk* **45 A7**
Rushall *Staffs* **40 C4**
Rushall *Wilts* **22 A5**
Rushbrooke **34 C2**
Rushbury **38 E5**
Rushden *Herts* **32 E5**
Rushden *Northants* **31 E1**
Rushford **44 D7**
Rush Green **24 F4**
Rushlake Green **13 D5**
Rushmere **45 D7**
Rushmere St Andrew **35 B4**
Rushmoor *Salop* **39 A3**
Rushmoor *Sry* **23 C7**
Rushmore **10 A3**
Rushock **40 A7**
Rusholme **49 C2**
Rushton *Ches* **48 E5**

Rushton *Northants* **42 B6**
Rushton *Salop* **39 A4**
Rushton Spencer **49 D5**
Rushwick **29 C2**
Rushyford **71 A6**
Ruskie **81 A1**
Ruskington **52 D6**
Rusko **67 B5**
Rusland **61 C5**
Rusper **12 E3**
Ruspidge **29 A6**
Russel **101 A7**
Russell's Water **23 B3**
Rusthall **15 A3**
Rustington **12 C6**
Ruston **65 B5**
Ruston Parva **65 C7**
Ruswarp **65 A3**
Rutherend **74 B1**
Rutherford **76 C2**
Rutherglen **81 A5**
Ruthernbridge **3 C2**
Ruthin **48 A6**
Ruthrieston **97 E3**
Ruthven *Gramp* **104 D4**
Ruthven *Hghld* **95 B2**
Ruthven *Hghld* **95 A6**
Ruthven *Tays* **88 D4**
Ruthvoes **3 B2**
Ruthwell **68 E3**
Ruyton-XI-Towns **38 C2**
Ryal **70 D1**
Ryal Fold **55 A5**
Ryall **22 D2**
Ryarsh **13 D1**
Rydal **61 C3**
Ryde **11 B5**
Rydon **6 C6**
Rye **14 E6**
Ryefield **102 D6**
Rye Foreign **14 D6**
Rye Harbour **14 E7**
Rye Park **24 D2**
Ryhall **22 E3**
Ryhill **57 B6**
Ryhope **71 C3**
Ryland **52 D3**
Rylstone **55 D2**
Ryme Intrinseca **9 B2**
Ryther **57 D4**
Ryton *Glos* **29 B4**
Ryton *N Yorks* **64 E6**
Ryton *Salop* **39 B4**
Ryton *IOW* **11 C6**
Ryton *T & W* **70 E2**
Ryton-on-Dunsmore **41 A7**

S
Sabden **55 B4**
Sackers Green **34 D5**
Sacombe **32 E7**
Sacriston **71 A4**
Sadberge **63 D3**
Saddell **72 B4**
Saddington **41 D5**
Saddle Bow **44 A4**
Sadgill **61 D3**
Saffron Walden **33 B5**
Sageston **16 D5**
Saham Toney **44 D5**
Saighton **48 D5**
Sailean **85 E4**
St Abbs **83 E6**
St Agnes **2 E3**
St Albans **24 B2**
St Allen **3 A3**
St Andrews **89 B7**
St Andrews Major **19 B6**
St Anne's **54 C5**
St Ann's **75 A6**
St Ann's Chapel **4 E3**
St Anthony **2 E6**
St Arvans **20 E1**
St Asaph **47 E3**
St Athan **19 A7**
St Audries **20 A6**
St Austell **3 C3**
St Bees **60 D2**
St Blazey Gate **3 C3**
St Boswells **76 B2**
St Breock **3 B1**
St Breward **4 A3**
St Briavels **28 E7**
St Brides **16 B4**
St Brides Major **18 D6**
St Brides Netherwent **20 D2**

St Brides-super-Ely **19 B6**
St Bride's Wentlooge **19 C5**
St Budeaux **4 E5**
Saintbury **30 B4**
St Buryan **2 B6**
St Catherine **7 E2**
St Catherines **80 A1**
St Clears **17 A4**
St Cleer **4 C4**
St Clement **3 A4**
St Clether **4 C2**
St Columb Major **3 B2**
St Columb Minor **3 A2**
St Combs **105 D2**
St Cross South Elmham **45 B7**
St Cyrus **89 D2**
St David's *Dyfed* **16 A3**
St Davids *Fife* **82 B4**
St David's *Tays* **88 A6**
St Day **2 E4**
St Decumans **9 C2**
St Dennis **3 B3**
St Devereux **28 D4**
St Dogmaels **26 A6**
St Dogwells **16 C3**
St Dominick **4 D4**
St Donats **18 E7**
St Edith's Marsh **21 D4**
St Endellion **3 B1**
St Enoder **3 A3**
St Erme **3 A4**
St Erth **2 C5**
St Erth Praze **2 C5**
St Ervan **3 A1**
St Eval **3 A2**
St Ewe **3 B4**
St Fagans **19 B6**
St Fergus **105 D3**
St Fillans **87 C6**
St Florence **16 D5**
St Gennys **6 A7**
St George **47 D3**
St George's **19 A6**
St Germans **4 D5**
St Giles-in-the-Heath **6 C7**
St Giles in the Wood **6 E5**
St Giles-on-the-Heath **16 C6**
St Harmon **27 D3**
St Helena **45 A4**
St Helen Auckland **70 E6**
St Helens *IOW* **11 C6**
St Helens *Mers* **48 E2**
St Hilary *Corn* **2 C5**
St Hilary *S Glam* **19 A6**
Saint Hill **13 A3**
St Illtyd **19 C3**
St Ippollitts **32 C6**
St Ishmael **17 B5**
St Ishmael's **16 B5**
St Issey **3 B1**
St Ive **4 D4**
St Ives *Cambs* **32 E1**
St Ives *Corn* **2 C4**
St Ives *Dors* **10 C4**
St James South Elmham **45 C7**
St John *Corn* **4 E5**
St John's *Dur* **70 D5**
St John's *H & W* **29 C2**
St John's *IOM* **60 b3**
St John's *Sry* **12 B1**
St John's Chapel *Devon* **6 E4**
St John's Chapel *Dur* **70 B5**
St John's Fen End **43 D3**
St John's Highway **43 D3**
St John's Kirk **74 E2**
St Judes **60 c2**
St Just *Corn* **2 A5**
St Just in Roseland **3 A5**
St Katherines **105 A5**
St Keverne **2 E6**
St Kew **4 A3**
St Kew Highway **4 A3**
St Keyne **4 C4**
St Lawrence *Corn* **3 C2**
St Lawrence *Esx* **25 E2**
St Lawrence *IOW* **11 B7**
St Leonards *Bucks* **23 D1**
St Leonards *Dors* **10 C4**
St Leonards *E Ssx* **13 E6**
St Leonards *Hants* **11 A5**
St Leonards Street **13 D1**

St Levan **2 A6**
St Lythans **19 B6**
St Mabyn **4 A3**
St Margarets **28 C4**
St Margaret's at Cliffe **15 D4**
St Margaret's Hope **113 D2**
St Margaret South Elmham **45 C7**
St Mark's **60 b4**
St Martin *Corn* **4 C5**
St Martin's *Salop* **38 C1**
St Martins *Tays* **88 C5**
St Martin's Green **2 E6**
St Mary Bourne **22 D6**
St Marychurch **5 E4**
St Mary Church **19 A6**
St Mary Cray **24 E6**
St Mary Hill **18 E6**
St Mary in the Marsh **15 A6**
St Marylebone **24 C4**
St Mary's *Ork* **113 D1**
St Mary's Bay **15 A6**
St Mary's Croft **66 B4**
St Mary's Grove **20 D4**
St Mary's Hoo **14 D1**
St Mawes **3 A5**
St Mawgan **3 A2**
St Mellion **4 D4**
St Mellons **19 C5**
St Merryn **3 A1**
St Mewan **3 B3**
St Michael Caerhays **3 B4**
St Michael Penkevil **3 A4**
St Michaels *H & W* **28 E1**
St Michaels *Kent* **14 D5**
St Michael's on Wyre **54 D3**
St Michael South Elmham **45 C7**
St Minver **3 B1**
St Monance **83 A2**
St Neot **3 D2**
St Neots **32 C2**
St Nicholas *Dyfed* **16 C2**
St Nicholas *S Glam* **19 A6**
St Nicholas at Wade **15 C2**
St Ninians **81 B2**
St Osyth **35 A7**
St Owen's Cross **28 E5**
St Paul's Cray **24 E6**
St Paul's Walden **32 C6**
St Peter's **15 D2**
St Petrox **16 C6**
St Pinnock **4 C4**
St Quivox **73 C5**
St Stephen **3 B3**
St Stephen's *Corn* **4 E5**
St Stephens *Corn* **4 D2**
St Stephens *Herts* **24 B2**
St Stephen's Coombe **3 B3**
St Teath **4 A2**
St Tudy **4 A3**
St Twynnells **16 C6**
St Veep **3 D3**
St Vigeans **89 C4**
St Vincents Cross **24 C2**
St Wenn **3 B2**
St Weonards **28 D5**
Salachail **86 B3**
Salcombe **5 C7**
Salcombe Regis **8 C5**
Salcott **34 D7**
Sale **49 B2**
Saleby **53 C4**
Sale Green **29 D2**
Salehurst **13 E4**
Salem *Dyfed* **18 B1**
Salem *Dyfed* **27 A2**
Salem *Gynd* **46 E5**
Salen *Hghld* **85 C2**
Salen *Strath* **85 B4**
Salesbury **55 A4**
Salford *Beds* **31 E4**
Salford *GM* **49 C2**
Salford *Oxon* **30 C5**
Salford Priors **30 A2**
Salfords **12 E2**
Salhouse **45 C4**
Saline **81 E2**
Salisbury **10 C2**
Salkeld Dykes **69 D6**
Sall **45 A3**

Sallachan **86 A2**
Sallachy **86 B7**
Sallachy *Hghld* **102 D1**
Sallachy *Hghld* **93 B1**
Salmonby **53 B4**
Salmond's Muir **89 B5**
Salperton **30 A5**
Salph End **32 B3**
Salsburgh **81 C5**
Salt **40 B2**
Saltash **4 E5**
Saltburn **103 A5**
Saltburn-by-the-Sea **64 D1**
Saltby **42 B2**
Saltcoats **73 B3**
Saltcotes **54 C5**
Saltdean **13 A6**
Salter **55 A1**
Salterforth **55 C3**
Salterhill **104 A2**
Salterswall **49 A5**
Saltfleet **53 C2**
Saltfleetby All Saints **53 C2**
Saltfleetby St Clement **53 C2**
Saltfleetby St Peter **53 C3**
Salford **21 A4**
Salthaugh Grange **59 C5**
Salt Hill **23 D3**
Salthouse **44 E1**
Saltley **40 C6**
Saltmarshe **58 C5**
Saltney **48 C5**
Salton **64 E5**
Saltram **5 A5**
Saltwick **77 C7**
Saltwood **15 B5**
Salvington **12 D6**
Salwarpe **29 C1**
Salwayash **9 A4**
Samala **98 B5**
Sambourne **30 A1**
Sambrook **39 B2**
Samlesbury **54 E5**
Samlesbury Bottoms **55 A5**
Sampford Arundel **8 C2**
Sampford Brett **7 E2**
Sampford Courtenay **7 A6**
Sampford Peverell **8 B2**
Sampford Spiney **5 A3**
Samuelston **82 E5**
Sanaigmore **78 B4**
Sancreed **2 B6**
Sancton **58 D4**
Sand **115 C3**
Sandaig *Hghld* **92 E4**
Sandaig *Hghld* **92 E3**
Sandbach **49 B5**
Sandbank **80 A3**
Sandbanks **10 B6**
Sandend **104 D2**
Sanderstead **24 D6**
Sandford *Avn* **20 D5**
Sandford *Cumb* **62 C3**
Sandford *Devon* **7 C6**
Sandford *Dors* **10 A6**
Sandford *IoW* **11 B6**
Sandford *Strath* **74 C1**
Sandford-on-Thames **31 A7**
Sandford Orcas **9 C1**
Sandford St Martin **30 E5**
Sandgarth **112 E5**
Sandgate **15 C5**
Sandhaven **105 C2**
Sandhead **66 B6**
Sandhills **9 B3**
Sandhoe **70 C2**
Sand Hole **58 D4**
Sandholme *Humb* **58 D4**
Sandholme *Lincs* **43 B1**
Sandhurst *Berks* **23 C6**
Sandhurst *Glos* **29 C5**
Sandhurst *Kent* **14 D6**
Sandhutton **63 D6**
Sand Hutton **57 E2**
Sandiacre **51 A7**
Sandilands **53 D3**
Sandiway **49 A4**
Sandleheath **10 C3**
Sandleigh **30 E7**
Sandling **13 E1**
Sandness **115 A2**
Sandon *Esx* **25 C2**

Sandon *Herts* 32 E5
Sandon *Staffs* 40 B2
Sandown 11 B6
Sandplace 4 C5
Sandridge *Herts* 32 C7
Sandridge *Wilts* 21 D4
Sandringham 44 A3
Sandrocks 13 A4
Sandsend 65 A2
Sand Side 61 B5
Sandside Head 110 E2
Sandsound 115 C3
Sandtoft 58 C7
Sanduck 5 C2
Sandway 14 D3
Sandwich 15 D3
Sandwick *Cumb* 61 D2
Sandwick *Ork* 113 D3
Sandwick *Shet* 115 D5
Sandwick *W Is* 107 C4
Sandwith 60 D2
Sandwood 108 E2
Sandy 32 C4
Sandycroft 48 C5
Sandygate *Devon* 5 D3
Sandygate *IOM* 60 c2
Sandy Haven 16 B5
Sandylands 54 D1
Sandy Lane *Wilts* 21 D4
Sandy Lane *W Yorks* 56 E4
Sandyway 28 D5
Sangobeg 109 B2
Sanna 85 A2
Sannaig 78 E5
Sanquhar 74 C5
Santon Bridge 61 A3
Santon Downham 44 C7
Sapcote 41 B5
Sapey Common 29 B1
Sapiston 34 D1
Sapperton *Glos* 29 D7
Sapperton *Lincs* 42 D1
Saracen's Head 43 B2
Sarclet 111 D4
Sardis 16 C5
Sarisbury 11 B4
Sarn *M Glam* 18 E5
Sarn *Pwys* 38 B5
Sarnau *Dyfed* 26 C5
Sarnau *Dyfed* 17 B4
Sarnau *Gynd* 47 D7
Sarnau *Pwys* 38 B3
Sarn-bâch 36 C3
Sarnesfield 28 C2
Sarn-Meyllteyrn 46 B7
Saron *Dyfed* 18 B2
Saron *Dyfed* 17 B2
Saron *Gynd* 46 E4
Sarratt 23 E2
Sarre 15 C2
Sarsden 30 C5
Sarsgrum 109 A2
Sartfield 60 c2
Satley 70 E4
Satterleigh 7 A4
Satterthwaite 61 C5
Sauchen 97 C2
Saucher 88 C5
Sauchieburn 89 C2
Sauchrie 73 C6
Saughall *Clwyd* 48 C4
Saughall *Corn* 66 D1
Saughall Massie 48 B3
Saughtree 76 B6
Saul 29 B2
Saundaig 86 A4
Saundby 51 D2
Saundersfoot 16 E5
Saunderton 31 C7
Saunton 6 D3
Sausthorpe 53 B5
Savalbeg 102 D1
Savalmore 102 D1
Sawbridgeworth 33 A7
Sawdon 65 B5
Sawley *Derbs* 51 A7
Sawley *Lancs* 55 B3
Sawley *N Yorks* 57 A1
Sawn Street 33 D5
Sawston 33 A4
Sawtry 42 E6
Saxby *Leics* 42 B2
Saxby *Lincs* 52 D3
Saxby All Saints 58 E6
Saxelbye 41 D2
Saxilby 52 B4

Saxlingham 44 E2
Saxlingham Green 45 B6
Saxlingham Nethergate 45 B6
Saxlingham Thorpe 45 B6
Saxmundham 35 C2
Saxondale 51 C7
Saxon Street 33 C3
Saxtead 35 B2
Saxtead Green 35 B2
Saxthorpe 45 A2
Saxton 57 C4
Sayers Common 12 E5
Scackleton 64 D6
Scadabay 99 A2
Scaftworth 51 C1
Scagglethorpe 65 A6
Scalasaig 78 C2
Scalby *Humb* 58 D5
Scalby *N Yorks* 65 C4
Scaldwell 41 E7
Scaleby 69 C3
Scalebyhill 69 C3
Scale Houses 69 D5
Scales *Cumb* 69 B7
Scales *Cumb* 61 B6
Scalford 41 E2
Scaling 64 E2
Scaliscro 106 E5
Scallasaig 93 A2
Scallastle 85 C5
Scalloway 115 D4
Scamadale 85 E6
Scamblesby 53 A4
Scamodale 85 E1
Scampston 65 A6
Scampton 52 C4
Scaniport 94 E2
Scapa 113 D1
Scar 112 F2
Scarastavore 98 E2
Scarborough 65 C5
Scarcewater 3 B3
Scarcliffe 51 A4
Scarcroft 57 B3
Scardroy 101 E6
Scarff 114 B5
Scarfskerry 111 C1
Scargill 63 A3
Scarinish 84 B4
Scarisbrick 54 C6
Scarning 44 D4
Scarrington 51 D6
Scarth Hill 48 D1
Scartho 59 C7
Scatraig 95 A2
Scaur *D & G* 68 B2
Scawby 58 E7
Scawton 64 C5
Scayne's Hill 13 A4
Scethrog 28 A5
Schaw 73 D5
Scholar Green 49 C6
Scholes *W Yorks* 57 B4
Scholes *W Yorks* 56 E7
Sciberscross 110 C7
Scleddau 16 C2
Scofton 51 C2
Scole 35 A1
Scolpaig 98 B4
Scolton 16 C3
Sconser 19 C4
Scoor 85 A7
Scopwick 52 D6
Scoraig 101 C2
Scorborough 59 A3
Scorrier 2 E4
Scorton *Lancs* 54 E3
Scorton *N Yorks* 63 C4
Sco Ruston 45 B3
Scotby 69 C4
Scotch Corner 63 C4
Scotforth 54 D2
Scothern 52 D4
Scotland Gate 77 D7
Scotlandwell 82 B2
Scotnish 79 B3
Scotsburn 103 A4
Scots' Gap 77 B7
Scotston *Gramp* 97 C6
Scotston *Tays* 88 A4
Scotstown *Hghld* 85 E2
Scotter 58 D7
Scotterthorpe 58 D7
Scottlethorpe 42 D2
Scotton *Lincs* 52 B2
Scotton *N Yorks* 63 B5

Scotton *N Yorks* 57 B2
Scottow 45 B3
Scoulton 44 D5
Scoulton Mere 44 D5
Scourie 108 D4
Scourie More 108 D4
Scousburgh 115 C6
Scrabster 111 A1
Scrainwood 77 A5
Scrane End 53 B7
Scraptoft 41 D4
Scratby 45 E4
Scrayingham 64 E7
Scredington 52 D7
Scremby 53 C5
Scremerston 77 B1
Screveton 51 D6
Scriven 57 B2
Scrooby 51 C1
Scropton 50 C7
Scrub Hill 53 A6
Scruton 63 C5
Sculthorpe 44 C2
Scunthorpe 58 D6
Seabank 86 A4
Seaborough 9 A3
Seacombe 48 C2
Seacroft *Lincs* 53 D5
Seacroft *W Yorks* 57 B4
Seafield *Hghld* 79 B3
Seafield *Strath* 73 C5
Seafield *Strath* 81 E5
Seaford 13 B7
Seaforth 48 C2
Seaforth Head 107 A6
Seagrave 41 D3
Seagry 21 D2
Seaham 71 C4
Seahouses 77 D2
Seal 15 A1
Sealand 48 C5
Seale 12 B2
Seamer *N Yorks* 64 B2
Seamer *N Yorks* 65 C5
Seamill 73 B3
Sea Palling 45 D3
Searby 59 A7
Seasalter 15 A2
Seascale 60 E3
Seathwaite 61 B2
Seatoller 61 B2
Seaton *Corn* 4 D5
Seaton *Cumb* 68 D6
Seaton *Devon* 8 D4
Seaton *Devon* 8 D4
Seaton *Dur* 71 C4
Seaton *Humb* 59 B3
Seaton *Leics* 42 C5
Seaton *Northld* 71 B1
Seaton Burn 71 A1
Seaton Carew 64 C1
Seaton Delaval 71 B1
Seaton Junction 8 D4
Seaton Ross 58 C3
Seatown *Gramp* 104 C2
Seatown *Gramp* 104 D2
Seatown *Gramp* 105 E3
Seave Green 64 C3
Seaview 11 C5
Seaville 68 E4
Seavington 9 A2
Sebastopol 19 C4
Sebergham 69 B5
Seckington 40 E4
Second Coast 101 B2
Sedbergh 62 B5
Sedbusk 62 D5
Sedgeberrow 30 A4
Sedgebrook 42 B1
Sedgefield 71 B6
Sedgeford 44 B2
Sedgehill 9 E1
Sedgley 40 B5
Sedgwick 61 E5
Sedlescombe 13 E5
Sedlescombe Street 13 E5
Seend 21 D4
Seend Cleeve 21 D4
Seer Green 23 D2
Seething 45 C6
Sefton 48 C1
Seghill 71 A1
Seighford 40 A2
Seilastotar 107 D1
Seilebost 98 E2
Seion 46 E4
Seisdon 40 A5

Selattyn 38 B1
Selborne 11 D1
Selby 57 E4
Selham 12 B4
Selkirk 76 A3
Sellack 28 E5
Sellafirth 114 E3
Sellindge 15 A5
Selling 15 A3
Sells Green 21 D4
Selly Oak 40 C6
Selmeston 13 C6
Selsdon 24 D6
Selsey 11 E5
Selsfield Common 13 A3
Selside 62 C7
Selstead 15 C4
Selston 51 A5
Selworthy 7 D2
Semblister 115 C2
Semer 34 D4
Semington 21 C4
Semley 9 E1
Send 12 C1
Sendmarsh 12 C1
Senghenydd 19 B4
Sennen 2 A6
Sennen Cove 2 A6
Sennybridge 18 E1
Senwick 67 C6
Sequer's Bridge 5 B5
Sessay 64 B6
Setchey 44 A4
Setley 10 E4
Setter *Shet* 115 E3
Setter *Shet* 115 B2
Setter *Shet* 115 C2
Settle 55 C1
Settrington 65 A6
Sevenhampton *Glos* 30 A5
Sevenhampton *Wilts* 22 B2
Seven Kings 24 E4
Sevenoaks 13 C1
Sevenoaks Weald 13 C1
Seven Sisters 18 D3
Seven Sorings 29 D6
Severn Beach 20 E2
Severn Stoke 29 C3
Sevington 15 A4
Sewards End 33 B5
Sewardstone 24 D3
Sewerby 65 E7
Seworgan 2 E5
Sewstern 42 B2
Sexhow 64 B3
Sezincote 30 B4
Sgodachail 102 C2
Shabbington 31 B7
Shackerley 40 A4
Shackerstone 41 A4
Shackleford 12 B2
Shadfen 77 D7
Shadforth 71 B4
Shadingfield 45 D7
Shadoxhurst 14 E5
Shadwell 44 D7
Shaftesbury 9 E1
Shafton 57 B6
Shalbourne 22 C5
Shalcombe 10 E6
Shalden 23 A7
Shaldon 8 A6
Shalfleet 11 A6
Shalford *Esx* 33 D6
Shalford *Sry* 12 C2
Shalford Green 33 D6
Shalloch Well 66 D2
Shallowford 7 B2
Shalmstry 111 B2
Shalstone 31 B4
Shalunt 79 E4
Shambellie 68 C3
Shamley Green 12 C2
Shandon 80 B3
Shandwick 103 B4
Shangton 41 E5
Shankhouse 71 A1
Shanklin 11 B6
Shannochie 72 D5
Shantron 80 C3
Shantullich 102 E6
Shanzie 88 D3
Shap 61 E2
Shapwick *Dors* 10 A4
Shapwick *Som* 20 D7
Shardlow 51 A7
Shareshill 40 B4

Sharlston 57 B6
Sharnbrook 31 E2
Sharnford 41 B5
Sharoe Green 54 E4
Sharow 63 D7
Sharpenhoe 32 B5
Sharperton 77 A5
Sharpham House 5 D5
Sharpness 29 A7
Sharpthorne 13 A3
Sharrington 44 E2
Shatterford 39 B6
Shaugh Bridge 5 A4
Shaughlaige-e-Quiggin 60 c3
Shaugh Prior 5 A4
Shavington 49 A6
Shaw *Berks* 22 D5
Shaw *GM* 49 D1
Shaw *Wilts* 21 C4
Shaw *Wilts* 22 A3
Shawbost 107 A3
Shawbury 38 E2
Shawclough 55 C6
Shawell 41 C6
Shawfoot 75 A7
Shawford 11 A2
Shawforth 55 C5
Shawhead 68 B2
Shaw Mills 57 A1
Sheader 100 B5
Sheanachie 72 B6
Sheandow 104 A5
Shear Cross 21 C6
Shearington 68 D3
Shearsby 41 D5
Shebbear 6 D6
Shebdon 39 B2
Shebster 111 A2
Shedfield 11 B3
Sheen 50 C4
Sheepscombe 29 C6
Sheepstor 5 A4
Sheepwash *Devon* 6 D6
Sheepwash *Northld* 77 D7
Sheepway 20 D3
Sheepy Magna 41 A4
Sheepy Parva 41 A4
Sheering 33 B7
Sheerness 14 E1
Sheet 11 D2
Sheffield 50 E2
Sheffield Bottom 23 A5
Sheffield Green 13 B4
Shefford 32 C5
Sheigra 108 D2
Sheinton 39 A4
Shelderton 38 D7
Sheldon *Derbs* 50 C4
Sheldon *Devon* 8 C3
Sheldon *W Mids* 40 D6
Sheldwich 15 A3
Shelf 56 E5
Shelfanger 45 A7
Shelfield 40 C4
Shelford 51 C6
Shellachan *Strath* 85 E6
Shellachan *Strath* 86 B6
Shellbrook Hill 38 C1
Shelley *Sflk* 34 E5
Shelley *W Yorks* 57 A6
Shellingford 22 C2
Shellow Bowells 25 B2
Shelsley Beauchamp 29 B1
Shelsley Walsh 29 B1
Shelton *Beds* 32 B2
Shelton *Nflk* 45 B6
Shelton *Notts* 51 D6
Shelton *Salop* 38 D3
Shelton Green 45 B6
Shelve 38 C5
Shelwick 28 E3
Shenfield 25 B3
Shenington 30 D3
Shenley 24 B2
Shenley Brook End 31 D4
Shenleybury 24 B2
Shenley Church End 31 D4
Shenmore 28 C4
Shennanton 66 E4
Shenstone *H & W* 40 A7
Shenstone *Staffs* 40 D4
Shenstone Woodend 40 D4
Shenton 41 A4
Shenval 104 A6

Shepeau Stow 43 B3
Sheperdine 21 A1
Shepherd's Green 23 B3
Shepherdswell 15 C4
Shepley 56 E7
Sheppardstown 111 C5
Shepperdine 21 A1
Shepperton 23 E5
Shepreth 32 E4
Shepshed 41 B3
Shepton 21 A7
Shepton Beauchamp 9 A2
Shepton Mallet 21 A6
Shepton Montague 21 A7
Shepway 13 E1
Sheraton 71 C5
Sherborne *Dors* 9 C2
Sherborne *Glos* 30 B6
Sherborne St John 23 A6
Sherbourne 30 C1
Sherburn *Dur* 71 B4
Sherburn *N Yorks* 65 B6
Sherburn in Elmet 57 C4
Shere 12 C2
Shereford 44 C3
Sherfield English 10 D2
Sherfield on Loddon 23 A6
Sherford 5 D6
Sheriffhales 39 B3
Sheriff Hutton 57 E1
Sheringham 45 A1
Sherington 31 D3
Shernborne 44 B2
Sherramore 94 D6
Sherrington 10 A1
Sherston 21 C2
Sherwood Green 6 E4
Sheshader 107 D4
Shettleston 81 A5
Shevington 48 E1
Shevington Moor 54 E6
Sheviock 4 D5
Shiel Bridge 93 B3
Shieldaig *Hghld* 101 A6
Shieldaig *Hghld* 101 A4
Shieldhill *Cent* 81 C4
Shieldhill *D & G* 67 C4
Shielfoot 85 C2
Shielhill 89 A3
Shiels 97 B3
Shifford 30 D7
Shifnal 39 B4
Shilbottle 77 C5
Shildon 71 A6
Shillingford *Devon* 7 D4
Shillingford *Oxon* 22 E2
Shillingford St George 8 A5
Shillingstone 9 E2
Shillington 32 C5
Shillmoor 76 E5
Shilstone 7 A6
Shilton *Oxon* 30 C7
Shilton *Warks* 41 B6
Shimpling *Nflk* 45 A7
Shimpling *Sflk* 34 C3
Shimpling Street 34 C3
Shincliffe 71 A4
Shiney Row 71 B3
Shinfield 23 B5
Shingay 32 E4
Shinglehead Point 34 D7
Shingle Street 35 C4
Shinner's Bridge 5 C4
Shinness 109 C7
Shipbourne 15 A1
Shipdham 44 D5
Shipham 20 D5
Shiphay 5 D4
Shiplake 23 B4
Shiplate 21 B4
Shipley *Northld* 77 C4
Shipley *Salop* 40 A5
Shipley *W Ssx* 12 D4
Shipley *W Yorks* 56 E6
Shipley Bridge *Devon* 5 B4
Shipley Bridge *Sry* 13 A2
Shipmeadow 45 C7
Shippon 22 D2
Shipston on Stour 30 C3
Shipton *Glos* 30 A6
Shipton *N Yorks* 57 D2
Shipton *Salop* 38 E5
Shipton Bellinger 22 B7
Shipton Gorge 9 A4
Shipton Green 11 E4

Shipton Moyne 21 C2
Shipton-on-Cherwell 30 E6
Shiptonthorpe 58 D3
Shipton-under-Wychwood 30 C6
Shira 86 C7
Shirburn 23 A2
Shirdley Hill 54 C6
Shirebrook 51 B4
Shirehampton 20 E3
Shiremoor 71 B1
Shirenewton 20 D1
Shire Oak 40 C4
Shireoaks 51 B2
Shirland 50 E5
Shirley Derbs 50 D6
Shirley Dors 10 C5
Shirley GL 24 D6
Shirley Hants 11 A3
Shirley W Mids 40 D7
Shirl Heath 28 D2
Shirrell Heath 11 B3
Shirwell 6 E3
Shirwell Cross 6 E3
Shiskine 72 D5
Shobdon 28 C1
Shobrooke 7 C6
Shocklach 48 D7
Shoeburyness 25 E4
Sholden 15 D3
Sholing 11 A3
Shooter's Hill 24 E5
Shoot Hill 38 D3
Shop Corn 3 A1
Shop Corn 6 B5
Shop Corner 35 B5
Shopland Hall 25 D4
Shoreditch 24 D4
Shoreham 24 F6
Shoreham-by-Sea 12 E6
Shoremill 103 A5
Shoresdean 77 A1
Shoreswood 77 A1
Shoretown 102 E5
Shorncote 21 E1
Shorne 25 B5
Shortacombe 5 A2
Short Cross 38 B4
Shortgate 13 B5
Shortgrave 33 B5
Short Green 45 A7
Short Heath Leics 41 A3
Short Heath W Mids 40 C5
Shortlanesend 3 A4
Shorwell 11 A6
Shoscombe 21 B5
Shotesham 45 B6
Shotgate 25 C3
Shotley 35 B5
Shotley Bridge 70 D3
Shotleyfield 70 D3
Shotley Gate 35 B5
Shotley Street 35 B5
Shottenden 15 A3
Shottermill 11 E1
Shottery 30 B2
Shotteswell 30 E3
Shottisham 35 C4
Shottle 50 E6
Shottlegate 50 E6
Shotton Clwyd 48 C5
Shotton Dur 71 C5
Shotton Northld 76 E2
Shotts 81 C5
Shotwick 48 C4
Shouldham 44 A5
Shouldham Thorpe 44 A5
Shoulton 29 C2
Shover's Green 13 D3
Shrawardine 38 D3
Shrawley 29 C1
Shrewley 30 C1
Shrewsbury 38 D3
Shrewton 21 E6
Shripney 12 B6
Shrivenham 22 B3
Shropham 44 D6
Shroton 9 E2
Shucknall 28 E3
Shudy Camps 33 C4
Shulishader 107 D4
Shurdington 29 D6
Shurlock Row 23 C4
Shurrery 111 A3
Shurton 20 B6
Shustoke 40 E5
Shute 8 D4

Shut End 40 B6
Shutford 30 D3
Shut Heath 40 A2
Shuthonger 29 C4
Shutlanger 31 C3
Shuttington 40 E4
Shuttlewood 51 A3
Shuttleworth 55 C6
Sibbaldbie 75 B7
Sibbertoft 41 D6
Sibdon Carwood 38 D6
Sibertswold 15 C4
Sibford Ferris 30 D4
Sibford Gower 30 D4
Sible Hedingham 33 D5
Sibsey 53 B6
Sibson Cambs 42 D5
Sibson Leics 41 A4
Sibster 111 D3
Sibthorpe 51 D6
Sibton 35 C2
Sicklesmere 34 C2
Sicklinghall 57 B3
Sidbury Devon 8 C4
Sidbury Salop 39 A6
Sidcot 20 D5
Sidcup 24 E5
Siddington Ches 49 C4
Siddington Glos 21 E1
Sidemoor 40 B7
Sidestrand 45 B2
Sidford 8 C4
Sidlesham 11 E5
Sidley 13 E6
Sidlowbridge 12 E2
Sidmouth 8 C5
Siefton 38 D6
Sigford 5 C3
Sigglesthorne 59 B3
Sigingstone 18 E6
Silchester 23 A5
Sileby 41 D3
Silecroft 61 A5
Silfield 45 A6
Silian 26 E5
Silkstone 57 A7
Silkstone Common 57 A7
Silksworth 71 B3
Silk Willoughby 52 D7
Silloth 68 E4
Sills 76 E5
Silpho 65 B4
Silsden 56 D3
Silsoe 32 B5
Silverburn 82 C6
Silvercraigs 79 C3
Silverdale Lancs 61 D6
Silverdale Staffs 49 C7
Silver End Beds 32 B4
Silver End Esx 34 C7
Silver Hill 13 E4
Silverley's Green 35 B1
Silvermoss 105 B5
Silverstone 31 B3
Silverton 7 D6
Silvington 39 A7
Silwick 115 B3
Simonburn 70 B1
Simonsbath 7 B3
Simonstone 55 B4
Simprim 76 E1
Simpson 31 B4
Sinclairston 73 D6
Sinderby 63 D6
Sinderhope 70 B3
Sindlesham 23 B5
Singdean 76 B5
Singleton Lancs 54 C4
Singleton W Ssx 11 E3
Singlewell 25 B5
Sinnahard 96 E2
Sinnington 64 E5
Sinton Green 29 C1
Sipson 23 E4
Sirhowy 19 B2
Sisland 45 C6
Sissinghurst 13 E3
Siston 21 A3
Sithney 2 D6
Sittenham 102 E4
Sittingbourne 14 E2
Six Ashes 39 B6
Sixhills 52 E3
Six Mile Bottom 33 B3
Six Mile Cottages 15 B4
Sixpenny Handley 10 A3
Sizewell 35 D2

Skail 110 C4
Skaill Ork 112 B5
Skaill Ork 113 E1
Skallary 90 B6
Skares Gramp 104 E5
Skares Strath 73 E6
Skarpigarth 115 B3
Skateraw Gramp 97 E4
Skateraw Loth 83 C5
Skaw Unst 114 F1
Skaw Whalsay 115 E1
Skeabost 100 B7
Skeabrae 112 B4
Skeeby 63 B4
Skeffington 41 E4
Skeffling 59 D6
Skegby 51 A4
Skegness 53 D5
Skelberry 115 C6
Skelbo 103 A2
Skeldon 73 C6
Skeldyke 43 B1
Skellingthorpe 52 C4
Skellister 115 D2
Skellow 57 D6
Skelmanthorpe 57 A6
Skelmersdale 48 D1
Skelmonae 105 B5
Skelmorlie 80 A5
Skelmuir 105 C4
Skelton Cumb 69 C6
Skelton Humb 58 C5
Skelton N Yorks 64 D2
Skelton N Yorks 63 A4
Skelton N Yorks 57 B1
Skelton N Yorks 57 D2
Skelton Green 64 D2
Skelwick 112 D2
Skendleby 53 C5
Skenfrith 28 D5
Skerne 59 A2
Skeroblingarry 72 B5
Skerray 109 D2
Sketty 18 B4
Skewen 18 C4
Skewsby 64 D6
Skeyton 45 B3
Skiag Bridge 108 E6
Skiary 93 B4
Skidbrooke 53 C2
Skidby 59 A4
Skigersta 107 D1
Skilgate 7 D4
Skillington 42 B2
Skinburness 68 E4
Skinidin 99 B7
Skinnet 111 B2
Skinningrove 64 E2
Skipness 72 C2
Skipsea 59 B2
Skipton 55 D2
Skipton-on-Swale 63 D7
Skipwith 57 E4
Skirbeck 53 B7
Skirbeck Quarter 53 B7
Skirling 75 A2
Skirmett 23 B3
Skirpenbeck 58 C2
Skirwith Cumb 69 E6
Skirwith N Yorks 62 C7
Skirza 111 D2
Skullomie 109 D2
Skye of Curr 95 C3
Slack 104 D5
Slackhall 50 B2
Slackhead 104 C2
Slad 29 C7
Slade 6 E2
Slade Green 24 F5
Slaggyford 69 E4
Slaidburn 55 B2
Slains Park 97 D6
Slaithwaite 56 D6
Slaley 70 C3
Slamannan 81 C4
Slapton Bucks 31 E5
Slapton Devon 5 D6
Slapton Northants 31 B3
Slatenber 62 C7
Slattadale 101 A4
Slattocks 49 C1
Slaugham 12 E4
Slaughden 35 D3
Slaughterford 21 C3
Slawston 41 E5
Sleaford Hants 11 E1
Sleaford Lincs 52 D7

Sleagill 61 E2
Sleapford 39 A3
Sledge Green 29 C4
Sledmere 65 B7
Sleeping Green 8 B4
Sleight 9 C5
Sleights 65 A3
Sleivemore 78 D5
Slepe 10 A5
Slickly 111 C2
Sliddery 72 D5
Sliemore 95 D3
Sligrachan 80 A2
Slimbridge 29 B7
Slindon Staffs 40 A1
Slindon W Ssx 12 B6
Slinfold 12 D3
Slingsby 64 D6
Slioch 104 D5
Slip End 32 B7
Slipton 42 C7
Slochd 95 B3
Slockavullin 79 C2
Slogarie 67 C4
Sloley 45 B3
Slongaber 68 B2
Sloothby 53 C4
Slough 23 D4
Sluggan 95 B3
Slyne 54 D1
Smailholm 76 C2
Smallbridge 55 D6
Smallburgh 45 C3
Smallburn Gramp 105 D4
Small Dole 12 E5
Smalley 51 A6
Smallfield 13 A2
Small Hythe 14 D5
Smallridge 8 E3
Smallthorne 49 C6
Smannell 22 C7
Smardale 62 C4
Smarden 14 D4
Smaull 78 B5
Smeale 60 d1
Smearisary 85 C1
Smeatharpe 8 C2
Smeeth 15 A5
Smeeton Westerby 41 D5
Smelthouses 56 E1
Smerral 111 B5
Smethwick 40 C6
Smisby 41 A3
Smith End Green 29 B2
Smithfield 69 C3
Smithincott 8 B2
Smiths Green 33 B6
Smithtown 103 A7
Smithy Green 49 B4
Smug Oak 24 B2
Smyths Green 34 D7
Snailbeach 38 C4
Snailwell 33 C2
Snainton 65 B5
Snaith 57 E5
Snape N Yorks 63 C6
Snape Sflk 35 C3
Snape Green 54 C6
Snape Street 35 C3
Snarestone 41 A4
Snarford 52 D3
Snargate 14 E6
Snave 15 A5
Sneachill 29 D2
Snead 38 C5
Sneaton 65 A3
Sneatonthorpe 65 B3
Snelland 52 D3
Snellings 60 D3
Snelston 50 C6
Snetterton 44 D6
Snettisham 44 A2
Snibston 41 B3
Snigs End 29 B5
Snishival 90 C2
Snitter 77 B5
Snitterby 52 C2
Snitterfield 30 C2
Snittlegarth 69 A6
Snitton 38 E7
Snodhill 28 C3
Snodland 14 C2
Snowshill 30 A4
Soar 5 C7
Soberton 11 C3
Soberton Heath 11 C3
Sockburn 63 D4

Sodylt Bank 38 C1
Soham 33 B1
Solam 78 D7
Soldon Cross 6 C5
Soldridge 11 C1
Sole Street Kent 15 A4
Sole Street Kent 25 B6
Solihull 40 D7
Sollas 98 C4
Sollers Dilwyn 28 D2
Sollers Hope 29 A4
Sollom 54 D6
Solva 16 B3
Solwaybank 69 B2
Somerby 41 E3
Somercotes 51 A5
Somerford Keynes 21 E1
Somerley 11 E5
Somerleyton 45 D6
Somersal Herbert 50 C7
Somersby 53 B4
Somersham Cambs 32 E1
Somersham Sflk 34 E4
Somerton Oxon 30 E5
Somerton Sflk 34 C3
Somerton Som 9 A1
Sompting 12 D6
Sonning 23 B4
Sonning Common 23 B3
Sopley 10 C5
Sopworth 21 C2
Sorbie 67 A6
Sordale 111 B2
Sorisdale 84 D2
Sorn 73 E5
Soroba 85 E6
Sortat 111 C2
Sotby 53 A4
Sots Hole 52 E5
Sotterly 45 D7
Soughton 48 B5
Soulbury 31 D5
Soulby 62 C3
Souldern 31 A4
Souldrop 31 E1
Sound Shet 115 D3
Sound Shet 115 C2
Soundwell 21 A3
Sourhope 76 E3
Sourlies 93 A5
Sourton 6 E7
Soutergate 61 B5
South Acre 44 C4
Southall 24 B4
South Alloa 81 C2
Southam Glos 29 D5
Southam Warks 30 E1
South Ambersham 12 B4
Southampton 11 A3
South Balloch 66 E1
South Bank 64 C1
Southbar 80 D5
South Barrow 9 C1
South Beddington 24 C6
South Benfleet 25 C4
South Bersted 12 B6
South Blackbog 105 A5
South Boisdale 90 C4
Southborough 15 A2
Southbourne Dors 10 C5
Southbourne W Ssx 11 D4
South Bowood 9 A4
South Brent 5 B4
South Brentor 4 E2
South Brewham 21 B7
South Broomhill 77 D6
Southburgh 44 E5
South Burlingham 45 C5
Southburn 58 E2
South Cadbury 9 C1
South Cairn 66 A4
South Carlton 52 C4
South Cave 58 E4
South Cerney 21 E1
South Chard 8 E3
South Charlton 77 C3
Southchurch 25 E4
South Cliffe 58 D4
South Clifton 52 B4
South Cockerington 53 B3
South Cornelly 18 D5
Southcott 6 E7
South Cove 45 E7
South Cowbog 105 B3
South Creake 44 C2
South Crosland 53 B3
South Croxton 41 D3

South Dalton 58 E3
South Darenth 25 A6
Southdean 76 C5
South Dell 107 C1
South Duffield 57 E4
Southease 13 B6
South Elkington 53 A3
South Elmsall 57 C6
South End Berks 22 E4
South End Bucks 31 D5
South End Cumb 61 B7
Southend Gramp 105 A4
South End Humb 59 B5
Southend Strath 72 A7
Southend-on-Sea 25 D4
Southerndown 18 D6
Southerness 68 C4
Southery 44 A6
South Fambridge 25 D3
South Fawley 22 C4
South Ferriby 58 E5
Southfleet 25 B5
South Galson 107 C2
South Garth 114 E3
Southgate GL 24 D3
Southgate Nflk 45 A3
Southgate Nflk 44 A2
South Glen Dale 90 C4
South Godstone 13 A2
South Green Esx 25 B3
South Green Nflk 44 E4
South Hall 79 E4
South Hanningfield 25 C3
South Harting 11 D3
South Hayling 11 D5
South Heath 23 D1
South Heighton 13 B6
South Hetton 71 B4
South Hiendley 57 B6
South Hill 4 D3
South Hole 6 B5
South Holmwood 12 D2
South Hornchurch 24 F4
South Howrat 80 B6
South Huish 5 B6
South Hykeham 52 C5
South Hylton 71 B3
Southill 32 C4
Southington 22 E7
South Kelsey 52 D2
South Kessock 102 E7
South Killingholme 59 B6
South Kilvington 64 B5
South Kilworth 41 D6
South Kirkby 57 C6
South Kirkton 97 C3
South Kyme 52 E7
South Lancing 12 D6
South Ledaig 86 A5
Southleigh 8 D4
South Leigh 30 D7
South Leverton 51 D2
South Littleton 30 A3
South Lochboisdale 90 C4
South Lopham 44 E7
South Luffenham 42 C4
South Lyncombe 21 B4
South Malling 13 B5
South Marston 22 A3
South Milford 57 C4
South Milton 5 C6
South Mimms 24 C2
Southminster 25 E3
South Molton 7 B4
South Moor 70 E3
South Moreton 22 E3
Southmuir 88 E3
South Muskham 51 D5
South Newbald 58 E4
South Newington 30 E4
South Newton Strath 72 D2
South Newton Wilts 10 B1
South Normanton 51 A5
South Norwood 24 D6
South Nutfield 13 A2
South Ockendon 25 A4
Southoe 32 C2
Southolt 35 A2
South Ormsby 53 B4
Southorpe 42 D4
South Otterington 63 D6
Southowram 56 E5
South Oxhey 24 B3
South Park 12 E2
South Perrott 9 A3
South Petherton 9 A2

South Petherwin 4 D2
South Pickenham 44 C5
South Pool 5 C6
Southport 54 C6
South Queensferry 82 B5
South Radworthy 7 B3
South Rauceby 52 D7
South Raynham 44 C3
South Redbriggs 105 A4
Southrepps 45 B2
South Reston 53 C3
Southrey 52 E5
Southrop 30 B7
Southrope 23 A7
South Runcton 44 A5
South Scarle 52 B5
Southsea *Clwyd* 48 C6
Southsea *Hants* 11 C5
South Shian 86 A4
South Shields 71 B2
South Skirlaugh 59 B4
South Somercotes 53 C2
South Stainley 57 B1
South Stoke *Avn* 21 B4
South Stoke *Oxon* 23 A3
South Stoke *W Ssx* 12 C5
South Street *E Ssx* 13 A5
South Street *Kent* 25 B6
South Tawton 7 A7
South Thoresby 53 C4
South Thundergay 72 C3
South Tidworth 22 B7
South Town 11 C1
Southtown *Nflk* 45 E5
Southtown *Ork* 115 C3
South View 115 C3
Southwaite *Cumb* 62 C4
Southwaite *Cumb* 69 C5
South Walsham 45 C4
Southwark 24 D5
South Warnborough 23 B7
Southwater 12 D4
Southway 20 E6
South Weald 25 A3
Southwell *Dors* 9 C6
Southwell *Notts* 51 D5
South Weston 23 B2
South Wheatley 6 B7
Southwick *Hants* 11 C4
Southwick *Northants* 42 D5
Southwick *T & W* 71 B3
Southwick *Wilts* 21 C5
Southwick *W Ssx* 12 E6
South Widcombe 20 E5
South Wigston 41 C5
South Willesborough 15 A4
South Willingham 52 E3
South Wingate 71 C5
South Wingfield 50 E5
South Witham 42 C3
Southwold 35 E1
South Wonston 11 A1
Southwood *Nflk* 45 C5
Southwood *Som* 20 E7
South Woodham Ferrers 25 D3
South Wootton 44 A3
South Wraxall 21 C4
South Yardley 40 D6
South Zeal 7 A7
Sowerby *N Yorks* 64 B5
Sowerby *W Yorks* 56 D5
Sowerby Bridge 56 D5
Sowerby Row 69 B5
Sowton 7 D7
Soyal 102 D2
Spa Common 45 B2
Spadeadam 69 D2
Spalding 43 A2
Spaldington 58 C4
Spaldwick 32 C1
Spalefield 83 A2
Spalford 52 B5
Spanby 42 D1
Sparham 44 E4
Spark Bridge 61 C5
Sparkford 9 C1
Sparkwell 5 A5
Sparrowpit 50 B2
Sparsholt *Hants* 11 A1
Sparsholt *Oxon* 22 C3
Spartylea 70 B4
Spaunton 64 E5
Spaxton 20 B7
Spean Bridge 93 E6

Speddoch 74 D7
Speen *Berks* 22 D5
Speen *Bucks* 23 C2
Speeton 65 D6
Speke 48 D3
Speldhurst 15 A2
Spelsbury 30 D5
Spellbrook 33 A7
Spencers Wood 23 B5
Spennithorne 63 B6
Spennymoor 71 A5
Spetchley 29 C2
Spetisbury 10 A4
Spexhall 45 C7
Spey Bay 104 B2
Speybridge 95 D3
Speyview 104 A4
Spilsby 53 C5
Spindlestone 77 C2
Spinkhill 51 A3
Spinningdale 102 E3
Spirthill 21 D3
Spital *Berks* 23 D4
Spital *Hghld* 111 B3
Spitalbrook 24 D2
Spital in the Street 52 C2
Spithurst 13 B5
Spittal *D & G* 67 A4
Spittal *D & G* 66 E5
Spittal *Dyfed* 16 C3
Spittal *Loth* 82 E5
Spittal *Northld* 83 E7
Spittalfield 88 C4
Spittal of Glenmuick 96 D5
Spittal of Glenshee 96 B6
Spixworth 45 B4
Spofforth 57 B2
Spondon 50 E7
Spooner Row 44 E6
Spoonley 39 A1
Sporle 44 C4
Spott 83 B5
Spratton 41 E7
Spreakley 23 C7
Spreyton 7 A7
Spridlington 52 D3
Springburn 80 E5
Springfield *D & G* 69 B3
Springfield *Fife* 88 E7
Springfield *Gramp* 103 D5
Springfield *Strath* 79 E4
Springfield *Tays* 88 C5
Springfield *W Mids* 40 D6
Springholm 68 B2
Springkell 69 A2
Springleys 105 A5
Springside 73 C4
Springthorpe 52 B3
Springwell 71 A3
Sproatley 59 B4
Sproston Green 49 B5
Sprotbrough 57 D7
Sproughton 35 A4
Sprouston 76 D2
Sprowston 45 B4
Sproxton *Leics* 42 B2
Sproxton *N Yorks* 64 D5
Spurstow 48 E6
Square Point 67 D3
Squires Gate 54 C4
Srondoire 79 C4
Sròndubh 101 A3
Sronphadruig Lodge 87 D1
Stableford 40 A1
Stackhouse 55 C1
Stackpole 16 C6
Stacksteads 55 C5
Staddiscombe 5 A5
Staddlethorpe 58 D5
Stadhampton 23 A2
Staffield 69 D5
Staffin 100 B5
Stafford 40 B2
Stagden Green 33 C7
Stagsden 31 E3
Stain 111 D2
Stainburn 57 A3
Stainby 42 C2
Staincross 57 B6
Staindrop 70 E6
Staines 23 E4
Stainfield *Lincs* 42 D2
Stainfield *Lincs* 52 E4
Stainforth *N Yorks* 55 C1
Stainforth *S Yorks* 57 E6
Staining 54 C4

Stainland 56 D6
Stainsacre 65 B3
Stainton *Clev* 64 B2
Stainton *Cumb* 61 E5
Stainton *Cumb* 69 C7
Stainton *Dur* 63 A3
Stainton *N Yorks* 63 B5
Stainton *S Yorks* 51 B1
Stainton by Langworth 52 D4
Staintondale 65 B4
Stainton le Vale 52 E2
Stainton with Adgarley 61 B6
Stair *Cumb* 69 A7
Stair *Strath* 73 D5
Staithes 64 E2
Stakeford 77 D7
Stake Pool 54 D3
Stalbridge 9 D2
Stalbridge Weston 9 D2
Stalham 45 C3
Stalham Green 45 C3
Stalisfield Green 14 E3
Stallingborough 59 C6
Stalling Busk 62 E6
Stalmine 54 C3
Stalybridge 49 D2
Stambourne 33 D5
Stamford *Lincs* 42 D4
Stamford *Northld* 77 D4
Stamford Bridge 58 C2
Stamfordham 70 D1
Stanborough 32 D7
Stanbridge *Beds* 31 E5
Stanbridge *Dors* 10 B4
Stanbridge Earls 10 E2
Stanbury 56 D4
Stand 81 B5
Standburn 81 D4
Standeford 40 B4
Standen 14 D5
Standford 11 E1
Standish 48 E1
Standlake 30 D7
Standon *Hants* 11 A2
Standon *Herts* 32 E6
Standon *Staffs* 40 A1
Stane 81 C6
Stanfield 44 D3
Stanford *Beds* 32 C4
Stanford *Kent* 15 B5
Stanford *Nflk* 44 C6
Stanford Bishop 29 A2
Stanford Bridge 29 B1
Stanford Dingley 22 E4
Stanford in the Vale 22 C2
Stanford le Hope 25 B4
Stanford on Avon 41 C7
Stanford on Soar 41 C2
Stanford on Teme 29 B1
Stanford Rivers 24 F2
Stanghow 64 D2
Stanground 43 A5
Stanhoe 44 C2
Stanhope *Bdrs* 75 B3
Stanhope *Dur* 70 C5
Stanion 42 C6
Stanley *Derbs* 51 A6
Stanley *Dur* 70 E3
Stanley *Staffs* 49 D6
Stanley *Tays* 88 C5
Stanley *W Yorks* 57 B5
Stanley Common 51 A6
Stanmer 13 A6
Stanmore *Berks* 22 D4
Stanmore *GL* 24 B3
Stannersburn 76 D7
Stanningfield 34 C3
Stannington *Northld* 71 A1
Stannington *S Yorks* 50 D2
Stansbatch 28 C1
Stansfield 33 D3
Stanstead 34 C4
Stanstead Abbots 32 E7
Stansted 25 B6
Stansted House 11 D3
Stansted Mountfitchet 33 B6
Stanton *Glos* 30 A4
Stanton *Northld* 77 C6
Stanton *Sflk* 34 D1
Stanton *Staffs* 40 E2
Stanton *Staffs* 50 C6
Stanton by Bridge 41 A2
Stanton by Dale 51 A7
Stanton Drew 20 E4

Stanton Fitzwarren 22 A2
Stanton Harcourt 30 E7
Stanton Hill 51 A4
Stanton in Peak 50 D4
Stanton Lacy 38 D7
Stanton Long 38 E5
Stanton on the Wolds 51 C7
Stanton Prior 21 A4
Stanton St Bernard 21 E4
Stanton St John 31 A7
Stanton St Quintin 21 D3
Stanton Street 34 D2
Stanton under Bardon 41 B3
Stanton upon Hine Heath 38 E2
Stanton Wick 21 A4
Stanwardine in the Fields 38 D2
Stanway *Esx* 34 D6
Stanway *Glos* 30 A4
Stanwell 23 E4
Stanwell Moor 23 E4
Stanwick 42 C7
Stanwix 69 B4
Stanydale 115 B2
Stape 64 E4
Stapehill 10 B4
Stapeley 49 A7
Staple 15 C3
Staple Cross 13 E4
Staplefield 12 E4
Staple Fitzpaine 8 D2
Stapleford *Cambs* 33 A3
Stapleford *Herts* 32 E7
Stapleford *Leics* 42 B3
Stapleford *Lincs* 52 B6
Stapleford *Notts* 51 A7
Stapleford *Wilts* 10 B1
Stapleford Abbotts 24 F3
Stapleford Tawney 24 F3
Staplegrove 8 D1
Staplehurst 13 E2
Staplers 11 B6
Stapleton *Avn* 21 A3
Stapleton *Cumb* 69 D2
Stapleton *H & W* 28 C1
Stapleton *Leics* 41 B5
Stapleton *N Yorks* 63 C3
Stapleton *Salop* 38 D4
Stapleton *Som* 9 A1
Stapley 8 C2
Staploe 32 C2
Staplow 29 A3
Star *Avn* 20 D5
Star *Dyfed* 17 A2
Starbotton 62 E7
Starcross 8 A5
Starlings Green 33 A5
Starr 67 A1
Starston 45 B7
Startforth 63 A3
Startley 21 D2
Statham 49 A3
Stathe 8 E1
Stathern 51 D7
Station Town 71 C5
Staughton Highway 32 C2
Staunton *Glos* 28 E6
Staunton *Glos* 29 B5
Staunton Harold Hall 41 A2
Staunton on Arrow 28 C1
Staunton on Wye 28 C3
Staveley *Cumb* 61 C5
Staveley *Cumb* 61 D5
Staveley *Derbs* 51 A3
Staveley *N Yorks* 57 B1
Staverton *Devon* 5 C4
Staverton *Glos* 29 C5
Staverton *Northants* 31 A1
Staverton *Wilts* 21 C4
Staverton Bridge 29 C5
Stawell 20 C7
Stawley 8 B1
Staxigoe 111 D3
Staxton 65 C6
Staylittle 37 C6
Staynall 54 C3
Staythorpe 51 D5
Stean 63 A7
Steane 31 A4
Stearsby 64 D6
Steart 20 B6
Stebbing 33 C6
Stebbing Green 33 C6
Stede Hill 14 D3

Steel Cross 13 C3
Steele Road 76 B6
Steen's Bridge 28 E2
Steep 11 D2
Steeple *Dors* 10 A6
Steeple *Esx* 25 E2
Steeple Ashton 21 D5
Steeple Aston 30 E5
Steeple Barton 30 E5
Steeple Bumpstead 33 C4
Steeple Claydon 31 C5
Steeple Gidding 42 E6
Steeple Langford 10 B1
Steeple Morden 32 D4
Steepleton Iwern 9 E2
Steeton 56 D3
Steinmanhill 105 A4
Stella 70 E2
Stelling Minnis 15 B4
Stemster *Hghld* 111 B2
Stemster *Hghld* 111 B4
Stenalees 3 C3
Stenhousemuir 81 C3
Stenigot 53 A3
Stenness 114 B5
Stenscholl 100 B5
Stenton *Loth* 83 B5
Stenton *Tays* 88 B4
Stepaside 16 E5
Steppingley 32 B5
Stepps 81 A5
Sternfield 35 C2
Sterridge 6 E2
Stert 21 E5
Stetchworth 33 C3
Stetla 70 E2
Stevenage 32 D6
Stevenston 73 B3
Steventon *Hants* 22 E7
Steventon *Oxon* 22 D2
Stevington 31 E2
Stewartby 32 B4
Stewarton *D & G* 67 A6
Stewarton *Strath* 73 D3
Stewkley 31 D5
Stewton 53 B3
Steyning 12 D5
Steynton 16 C5
Stibb 6 B5
Stibbard 44 D3
Stibb Cross 6 D5
Stibb Green 22 B5
Stibbington 42 D5
Stichill 76 D2
Sticker 3 B3
Stickford 53 B5
Sticklepath 7 A7
Stickney 53 B6
Stiffkey 44 D1
Stifford's Bridge 29 B3
Stilligarry 90 C2
Stillingfleet 57 D3
Stillington *Clev* 71 B6
Stillington *N Yorks* 57 D1
Stilton 42 E6
Stinchcombe 21 B1
Stinsford 9 D4
Stirchley *Salop* 39 A4
Stirchley *W Mids* 40 C6
Stirling *Cent* 81 B2
Stirling *Gramp* 105 E4
Stisted 34 C6
Stithians 2 E5
Stitley 111 B2
Stittenham 102 E4
Stivichall 41 A7
Stix 87 E4
Stixwould 52 E5
Stoak 48 D4
Stobo 75 B2
Stoborough 10 A6
Stoborough Green 10 A6
Stobwood 81 D6
Stock 25 B3
Stockbridge *Cent* 81 B1
Stockbridge *Hants* 10 E1
Stockbury 14 D2
Stockcross 22 D5
Stockdalewath 69 B5
Stockerston 42 B5
Stock Green 29 D2
Stockingford 41 A5
Stocking Pelham 33 A6
Stockland 8 D3
Stockland Bristol 20 B6
Stock Lane 22 B4
Stockleigh English 7 C6

Stockleigh Pomeroy 7 C6
Stockley 21 E4
Stocklinch 8 E2
Stockport 49 C3
Stocksbridge 50 D1
Stocksfield 70 D2
Stockton *H & W* 28 E1
Stockton *Nflk* 45 C6
Stockton *Salop* 39 B5
Stockton *Warks* 30 E1
Stockton *Wilts* 10 A1
Stockton Heath 49 A3
Stockton-on-Tees 64 B2
Stockton on Teme 29 B1
Stockton on the Forest 57 E2
Stockwith 51 D1
Stock Wood 30 A2
Stodday 54 D2
Stodmarsh 15 C2
Stody 44 E2
Stoer 108 C6
Stoford *Som* 9 B2
Stoford *Wilts* 10 B1
Stogumber 7 E3
Stogursey 20 B6
Stoke *Devon* 6 B4
Stoke *Hants* 22 D6
Stoke *Hants* 11 D4
Stoke *Kent* 14 D1
Stoke *W Mids* 41 A7
Stoke Abbott 9 A3
Stoke Albany 42 B6
Stoke Ash 35 A1
Stoke Bardolph 51 C6
Stoke Bliss 29 A1
Stoke Bruerne 31 C2
Stoke by Clare 33 D4
Stoke-by-Nayland 34 D5
Stoke Canon 7 D7
Stoke Charity 11 A1
Stoke Climsland 4 D3
Stoke D'Abernon 12 D1
Stoke Doyle 42 D6
Stoke Dry 42 B5
Stoke Ferry 44 B6
Stoke Fleming 5 D6
Stokeford 9 E5
Stoke Gabriel 5 D5
Stoke Gifford 21 A2
Stoke Golding 41 A5
Stoke Goldington 31 D3
Stokeham 51 D3
Stoke Hammond 31 D5
Stoke Heath 39 A2
Stoke Holy Cross 45 B5
Stokeinteignhead 8 A6
Stoke Lacy 29 A3
Stoke Lane 21 A6
Stoke Lyne 31 A5
Stoke Mandeville 31 D6
Stokenchurch 23 B2
Stoke Newington 24 D4
Stokenham 5 D6
Stoke-on-Trent 49 C6
Stoke Orchard 29 D5
Stoke Poges 23 D3
Stoke Prior *H & W* 29 D1
Stoke Prior *H & W* 28 E2
Stoke Rivers 7 A3
Stoke Rochford 42 C2
Stoke Row 23 A3
Stoke St Gregory 8 E1
Stoke St Mary 8 D1
Stoke St Milborough 38 E6
Stokesay 38 D6
Stokesby 45 D4
Stokesley 64 C3
Stoke sub Hamdon 9 A2
Stoke Talmage 23 A2
Stoke Trister 9 D1
Stoke upon Tern 39 A2
Stolford 20 B6
Stondon Massey 24 F2
Stone *Bucks* 31 C6
Stone *Glos* 21 A1
Stone *H & W* 40 A7
Stone *Kent* 25 A5
Stone *Kent* 14 E6
Stone *Staffs* 40 B1
Stone Allerton 20 C5
Ston Easton 21 A5
Stonebridge *E Ssx* 13 C4
Stonebridge *Warks* 40 E6
Stonebroom 51 A5
Stone Cross *E Ssx* 13 D6

Stone Cross *Kent* 15 A5
Stone Cross *Kent* 13 C3
Stoneferry 59 B4
Stonefield *Strath* 79 C4
Stonefield *Strath* 81 A6
Stonegate 13 D4
Stonegrave 64 D6
Stonehaugh 70 A1
Stonehaven 97 D5
Stonehouse *D & G* 68 B3
Stonehouse *Devon* 4 C5
Stonehouse *Glos* 29 C7
Stonehouse *Northld* 69 E4
Stonehouse *Strath* 74 C1
Stoneleigh 41 A7
Stonely 32 C2
Stoner Hill 11 D2
Stonesby 42 B2
Stonesfield 30 D6
Stones Green 35 A6
Stone Street *Kent* 15 A1
Stone Street *Nflk* 45 C7
Stonestreet Green 15 A5
Stoneybridge 90 C2
Stoney Cross 10 D3
Stoneygate 41 D4
Stoneyhills 25 E3
Stoney Houghton 51 A4
Stoneykirk 66 B5
Stoney Middleton 50 D3
Stoney Stanton 41 B5
Stoney Stoke 21 B7
Stoney Stratton 21 A7
Stoney Stretton 38 C4
Stoneywood 97 D2
Stonganess 114 E2
Stonham Aspal 35 A3
Stonnall 40 C4
Stonor 23 B3
Stonton Wyville 41 E5
Stonybreck 115 a1
Stonyhurst College 55 A4
Stony Middleton 50 D3
Stony Stratford 31 C3
Stoodleigh 7 D5
Stopham 12 C5
Stopsley 32 C6
Stoptide 3 B1
Storeton 48 C3
Stormore 21 C6
Stornoway 107 C4
Storridge 29 B3
Storrington 12 C5
Storth 61 D5
Storwood 58 C3
Stotfield 104 A1
Stotfold 32 D5
Stottesdon 39 A6
Stoughton *Leics* 41 D4
Stoughton *Sry* 12 B1
Stoughton *W Ssx* 11 E3
Stoul 92 E5
Stoulton 29 D3
Stourbridge 40 A6
Stourhead 21 B7
Stourpaine 9 E3
Stourport-on-Severn 40 A7
Stour Provost 9 D1
Stour Row 9 D1
Stourton *H & W* 40 A6
Stourton *Warks* 30 C4
Stourton *Wilts* 21 B7
Stourton Caundle 9 D2
Stove 112 F3
Stoven 45 D7
Stow *Bdrs* 76 A1
Stow *Lincs* 52 B3
Stow Bardolph 44 A5
Stow Bedon 44 D6
Stowbridge 44 A5
Stow cum Quy 33 B2
Stowe *Glos* 28 E7
Stowe *Salop* 38 C7
Stowe *Staffs* 40 C2
Stowell *Glos* 30 A6
Stowell *Som* 9 C1
Stowey 20 E5
Stowford 4 E2
Stowlangtoft 34 D2
Stow Longa 32 C1
Stow Maries 25 D3
Stowmarket 34 E3
Stow-on-the-Wold 30 B5
Stowting 15 B4
Stowupland 34 E3
Stracathro 89 C2
Strachan 97 B4

Strachur 79 E1
Stradbroke 35 B1
Stradishall 33 D3
Stradsett 44 A5
Stragglethorpe 52 C6
Straiton *Loth* 82 C6
Straiton *Strath* 73 C7
Straloch *Gramp* 105 B6
Straloch *Tays* 88 B2
Stramshall 50 B7
Strands 61 A3
Strang 60 c4
Stranraer 66 B4
Strata Florida 27 B4
Stratfield Mortimer 23 A5
Stratfield Saye 23 A5
Stratfield Turgis 23 A6
Stratford 29 C4
Stratford St Andrew 35 C2
Stratford St Mary 34 E5
Stratford Tony 10 B2
Stratford-upon-Avon 30 C2
Strath *Hghld* 111 C3
Strath *Hghld* 100 E4
Strathan *Hghld* 108 C6
Strathaven 74 C1
Strathblane 80 E4
Strathcanaird 101 D1
Strathcroy 108 C5
Strathdon 96 D2
Strathgirnock 96 D4
Strathkinness 89 A7
Strathmiglo 82 C2
Strathmore 79 C2
Strathpeffer 102 C6
Strathrannoch 102 B4
Strathrory 102 E4
Strathwhillan 72 E4
Strathy 110 D2
Strathyre 87 B7
Stratton *Corn* 6 B6
Stratton *Dors* 9 C4
Stratton *Glos* 30 A7
Stratton Audley 31 B5
Stratton-on-the-Fosse 21 A5
Stratton St Margaret 22 A3
Stratton St Michael 45 B6
Stratton Strawless 45 B3
Stravanan 72 E2
Stravithie 89 B7
Streat 13 A5
Streatham 24 C5
Streatley *Beds* 32 B6
Streatley *Berks* 22 E3
Street *Lancs* 54 E2
Street *N Yorks* 64 E3
Street *Som* 20 D7
Street Dinas 38 C1
Street End *Kent* 15 B3
Street End *W Ssx* 11 E5
Streethay 40 D3
Streetlam 63 D5
Streetly 40 C5
Strefford 38 D6
Strensall 57 E1
Strensham 29 D3
Stretcholt 20 B6
Strete 5 D6
Stretford 49 B2
Stretford Court 28 D2
Strethall 33 A5
Stretham 33 B1
Strettington 11 E4
Stretton *Ches* 49 A3
Stretton *Ches* 48 D6
Stretton *Derbs* 50 E4
Stretton *Leics* 42 C3
Stretton *Staffs* 40 A3
Stretton *Staffs* 40 E2
Stretton en le Field 41 A3
Stretton Grandison 29 A3
Stretton Heath 38 C3
Stretton-on-Dunsmore 41 B7
Stretton on Fosse 30 C4
Stretton under Fosse 41 B6
Stretton Westwood 38 E5
Stribers 61 C5
Strichen 105 C3
Stringston 20 A6
Strixton 31 E1
Stroat 20 E1
Stromeferry 93 A1

Stromemore 93 A1
Stromness 113 B1
Stronachlachar 87 A7
Strond 98 E3
Strone *Cent* 87 A7
Strone *Hghld* 94 D3
Strone *Hghld* 93 D6
Strone *Strath* 79 E2
Strone *Strath* 80 A3
Stronechrubie 108 E7
Stronenaba 93 E6
Stronfine 86 A5
Stronlag 80 A3
Stronmilchan 86 C6
Strontian 85 E2
Strontoiller 86 A6
Stronvar 87 B6
Strood 14 C2
Strood Green 12 C4
Stroquhan 74 D7
Stroud *Glos* 29 C7
Stroud *Hants* 11 D2
Stroud Common 12 C2
Stroud Green 29 C7
Stroul 80 B3
Stroxton 42 C1
Struanmore 92 A1
Strubby 53 C3
Strumpshaw 45 C5
Struthers 82 D2
Struy 94 C2
Stryt-issa 48 B7
Stryt-yr-hwch 48 C7
Stuartfield 105 C4
Stubbington 11 B4
Stubbins 55 B6
Stubhampton 10 A3
Stubley 50 E3
Stublick 70 B2
Stub Place 60 E4
Stubton 52 B7
Stuck *Bute* 79 E4
Stuck *Strath* 80 A2
Stuckgowan 80 C1
Stuckindroin 86 E7
Stuckton 10 C3
Stucreoch 79 E2
Studdon 70 B3
Studfold 62 D7
Stud Green 23 C4
Studham 32 B7
Studholme 69 A4
Studland 10 B6
Studley *Oxon* 31 A6
Studley *Warks* 30 A1
Studley Wilts 21 D3
Studley Common 30 A1
Studley Roger 63 C7
Stuggadhoo 60 c4
Stump Cross 33 B4
Stuntney 33 B1
Stunts Green 13 D5
Sturbridge 40 A1
Sturmer 33 C4
Sturminster Common 9 D2
Sturminster Marshall 10 A5
Sturminster Newton 9 D2
Sturry 15 B2
Sturton by Stow 52 B3
Sturton le Steeple 51 D2
Stuston 35 A1
Stutton *N Yorks* 57 C3
Stutton *Sflk* 35 A5
Styal 49 C3
Styrrup 51 C1
Succoth 80 B1
Succothmore 80 A1
Suckley 29 B2
Sudborough 42 C6
Sudbourne 35 D3
Sudbrook *Gwent* 20 E2
Sudbrook *Lincs* 52 C7
Sudbrooke 52 D4
Sudbury *Derbs* 50 C7
Sudbury *GL* 24 B4
Sudbury *Sflk* 34 C4
Suddie 102 E6
Sudgrove 29 D7
Suffield *Nflk* 45 B2
Suffield *N Yorks* 65 B4
Sugarloaf 14 E5
Sugnall 39 B1
Suie 87 A6
Suisnish 92 C1
Sulby 60 c2
Sulgrave 31 A3

Sulham 23 A4
Sulhamstead 23 A5
Sullington 12 C5
Sullom 114 C5
Sullom Voe Oil Terminal 114 C5
Sully 19 B7
Sumburgh 115 D7
Summer Bridge 56 E1
Summercourt 3 A3
Summerfield 44 B2
Summer Hill 48 C6
Summer-house 63 C3
Summerleaze 20 D2
Summerseat 55 B6
Summertown 31 A7
Summit 55 D6
Sunadale 72 C3
Sundaywell 74 D7
Sunderland *Cumb* 68 E6
Sunderland *T & W* 71 B3
Sunderland Bridge 71 A5
Sundhope 75 D3
Sundon Park 32 B6
Sundridge 13 B1
Sunhill 30 B7
Sunipol 84 E3
Sunken Island 34 D7
Sunk Island 59 C6
Sunningdale 23 D5
Sunninghill 23 D5
Sunningwell 30 E7
Sunniside *Dur* 70 E5
Sunniside *T & W* 71 A3
Sunny Bank 61 B5
Sunnylaw 81 B2
Sunnymead 31 A7
Sunnyside *Gramp* 97 D4
Sunnyside *Northld* 70 C2
Sunnyside *W Ssx* 13 A3
Sunwick 83 D7
Surbiton 24 B6
Surfleet 43 A2
Surfleet Seas End 43 A2
Surlingham 45 C5
Sustead 45 A2
Susworth 58 D7
Sutcombe 6 C5
Suton 44 E6
Sutterton 43 A1
Sutton *Beds* 32 D4
Sutton *Cambs* 33 A1
Sutton *Ches* 49 C6
Sutton *Ches* 48 C4
Sutton *GL* 24 C6
Sutton *Kent* 15 D4
Sutton *Lincs* 52 B6
Sutton *Nflk* 45 C3
Sutton *Northants* 42 D5
Sutton *Notts* 51 D7
Sutton *Notts* 51 C2
Sutton *Oxon* 30 E7
Sutton *Salop* 39 B6
Sutton *Salop* 39 A1
Sutton *Salop* 38 E6
Sutton *Salop* 38 E3
Sutton *Sflk* 35 C4
Sutton *Sry* 12 D2
Sutton *Staffs* 39 B2
Sutton *S Yorks* 57 D6
Sutton *W Ssx* 12 B5
Sutton at Hone 25 A5
Sutton Bassett 41 E5
Sutton Benger 21 D3
Sutton Bonington 41 C2
Sutton Bridge 43 C2
Sutton Cheney 41 B4
Sutton Coldfield 40 D5
Sutton Courtenay 22 E2
Sutton Crosses 43 C2
Sutton Downs 15 D4
Sutton Grange 63 C7
Sutton Green 12 C1
Sutton Holms 10 B4
Sutton Howgrave 63 D7
Sutton in Ashfield 51 B5
Sutton-in-Craven 56 D3
Sutton in the Elms 41 C5
Sutton Lane Ends 49 C6
Sutton Leach 48 E2
Sutton le Marsh 53 D3
Sutton Maddock 39 B4
Sutton Mallet 20 C7
Sutton Mandeville 10 A2
Sutton Montis 9 C1
Sutton-on-Hull 59 B4
Sutton on Sea 53 D3

Sutton-on-the-Forest 57 D1
Sutton on the Hill 50 D7
Sutton on Trent 51 D4
Sutton Poyntz 9 D5
Sutton St Edmund 43 B3
Sutton St James 43 B3
Sutton St Nicholas 28 E3
Sutton Scotney 11 A1
Sutton-under-Brailes 30 C4
Sutton-under-Whitestonecliffe 64 B5
Sutton upon Derwent 58 C3
Sutton Valence 14 D4
Sutton Veny 21 D6
Sutton Waldron 9 E2
Sutton Weaver 48 E4
Sutton Wick 22 D2
Swaby 53 B4
Swadlincote 41 A3
Swaffham 44 C5
Swaffham Bulbeck 33 B2
Swaffham Prior 33 B2
Swafield 45 B2
Swainbost 107 D1
Swainby 64 B3
Swainshill 28 D3
Swainsthorpe 45 B5
Swainswick 21 B4
Swalcliffe 30 D4
Swalecliffe 15 B2
Swallow 45 B7
Swallow Beck 52 C5
Swallowcliffe 10 A2
Swallowfield 23 B5
Swalwell 71 A2
Swampton 22 D6
Swanage 10 B7
Swanbach 49 A7
Swanbourne 31 D5
Swancote 39 B5
Swanland 58 E5
Swanlaws 76 D4
Swanley 24 F6
Swanmore 11 B3
Swannington *Leics* 41 B3
Swannington *Nflk* 45 A4
Swanscombe 25 B5
Swansea 18 B4
Swan Street 34 C6
Swanton Abbot 45 B3
Swanton Morley 44 E4
Swanton Novers 44 E2
Swanwick *Derbs* 51 A5
Swanwick *Hants* 11 B4
Swarby 52 D7
Swardeston 45 B5
Swarkestone 41 A2
Swarland 77 C5
Swarland Estate 77 C5
Swaton 42 E1
Swavesey 32 E2
Sway 10 D5
Swayfield 42 C2
Swaythling 11 A3
Swaythorpe 65 C7
Swefling 35 C2
Swell 8 E1
Swepstone 41 A3
Swerford 30 D4
Swettenham 49 C5
Swiftsden 13 E4
Swilland 35 A3
Swillbrook 54 D4
Swillington 57 B4
Swimbridge Newland 7 A3
Swinbrook 30 C6
Swincliffe 57 A2
Swinderby 52 B5
Swindon *Glos* 29 D5
Swindon *Staffs* 40 A5
Swindon *Wilts* 22 A3
Swine 59 B4
Swinefleet 58 C5
Swineshead *Beds* 32 B2
Swineshead *Lincs* 53 A7
Swineshead Bridge 53 A7
Swiney 111 C5
Swinford *Leics* 41 C7
Swinford *Oxon* 30 E7
Swingfield Minnis 15 C4
Swinhoe 77 D3
Swinhope 53 A2
Swining 115 D1
Swinithwaite 63 A6
Swinscoe 50 C6
Swinstead 42 D2

Swinton *Bdrs* 76 E1
Swinton *GM* 49 B1
Swinton *N Yorks* 64 E6
Swinton *N Yorks* 63 C7
Swinton *S Yorks* 51 A1
Swintonmill 76 E1
Swithland 41 C3
Swordale *Hghld* 102 D5
Swordale *W Is* 107 C4
Swordle 85 B1
Sworton Heath 49 A3
Swyddffynnon 27 A4
Swyncombe 23 A2
Swynnerton 40 A1
Swyre 9 B5
Syde 29 D6
Sydenham *GL* 24 D5
Sydenham *Oxon* 31 C7
Sydenham Damerel 4 E3
Syderstone 44 C2
Sydling St Nicholas 9 C4
Sydmonton 22 D6
Syerston 51 D6
Syke 55 C6
Sykehouse 57 E6
Sykes 55 A2
Sylen 17 D5
Symbister 115 E1
Symington *Strath* 74 E2
Symington *Strath* 73 C4
Symondsbury 9 A4
Symonds Yat 28 E6
Syre 109 D4
Syreford 30 A5
Syresham 31 B3
Syston *Leics* 41 D3
Syston *Lincs* 52 C7
Sytchampton 29 C1
Sywell 31 D1

T
Taagan 101 C5
Tacher 111 B4
Tackley 30 E5
Tacolneston 45 A6
Tadcaster 57 C3
Tadden 10 A4
Taddiford 6 D5
Taddington 50 C3
Tadley 23 A5
Tadlow 32 D4
Tadmarton 30 D4
Tadworth 12 E1
Tafarnaubach 19 B2
Tafarn-y-bwlch 16 D2
Tafarn-y-Gelyn 48 A5
Taff's Well 19 B5
Tafolwern 37 C5
Taibach 18 C5
Tai-bach 38 A2
Tain *Hghld* 111 C2
Tain *Hghld* 103 A3
Tai'r Bull 18 E1
Tairlaw 73 D7
Tai'r-lon 46 D5
Takeley 33 B6
Takeley Street 33 B6
Talachddu 27 E7
Talacre 48 A3
Talatoll 72 B2
Talaton 8 B4
Talbenny 16 B4
Talerddig 37 D5
Talgarreg 26 D5
Talgarth 28 A4
Taliesin 37 A6
Talisker 92 A1
Talke 49 C6
Talkin 69 D4
Talla Bheith 87 B3
Talladale 101 B4
Talla Linnfoots 75 B3
Tallarn Green 48 D7
Tallentire 68 E6
Talley 27 A7
Tallington 42 D4
Talmine 109 C2
Talog 17 B3
Talsarn 26 E5
Talsarnau 47 A7
Talskiddy 3 D2
Talwrn *Clwyd* 48 B7
Talwrn *Gynd* 46 D3
Talybont *Dyfed* 27 A2
Tal-y-bont *Gynd* 36 E3
Tal-y-bont *Gynd* 47 A3

Tal-y-bont *Gynd* 47 B4
Talybont *Pwys* 28 A5
Tal-y-cafn 47 B3
Talyllyn 28 A5
Tal-y-llyn 37 B4
Tal-y-Meryn 37 C4
Talysarn 46 D5
Talywern 37 C5
Tamavoid 80 E2
Tamerton Foliot 4 E4
Tamworth 40 E4
Tandridge 13 A1
Tanerdy 17 C3
Tanfield 70 E3
Tangiers 16 C4
Tanglandford 105 B5
Tangley 22 C6
Tangmere 12 B6
Tangwick 114 B5
Tangy 72 A5
Tankersley 50 E1
Tan-lan 47 A6
Tannach 111 D4
Tannachie 97 C5
Tannachy 103 A1
Tannadice 89 A3
Tannington 35 B2
Tannochside 81 B5
Tansley 50 E5
Tansor 42 D5
Tantobie 70 E3
Tanton 64 C2
Tanworth in Arden 40 D7
Tan-y-fron 47 D4
Tangyrisiau 47 A6
Tan-y-groes 26 B6
Tan-y-pistyll 37 E3
Tapeley 6 D4
Taplow 23 B3
Taravocan 86 B4
Tarbert *Hghld* 85 C2
Tarbert *Strath* 79 C5
Tarbert *Strath* 72 A2
Tarbert *Strath* 79 A3
Tarbert *W Is* 106 E7
Tarbet *Hghld* 92 E5
Tarbet *Strath* 80 C1
Tarbock Green 48 D3
Tarbolton 73 D5
Tarbothill 97 E2
Tarbrax 81 E6
Tardebigge 29 D1
Tardy Gate 54 E5
Tarfside 96 E6
Tarland 96 E3
Tarleton 54 D5
Tarlscough 54 D6
Tarlton 21 D1
Tarnbrook 54 E2
Tarnock 20 C5
Tarporley 48 E5
Tarr 20 A7
Tarrant Crawford 10 A4
Tarrant Gunville 10 A3
Tarrant Hinton 10 A3
Tarrant Keyneston 10 A4
Tarrant Launceston 10 A4
Tarrant Monkton 10 A4
Tarrant Rawston 10 A4
Tarrant Rushton 10 A4
Tarrel 103 B3
Tarring Neville 13 B6
Tarrington 29 A3
Tarrnacraig 72 D4
Tarsappie 88 C6
Tarskavaig 92 C3
Tarves 105 B5
Tarvie *Hghld* 102 C6
Tarvie *Tays* 88 B2
Tarvin 48 D5
Tarvin Sands 48 D5
Tasburgh 45 B6
Tasley 39 A5
Taston 30 D5
Tatenhill 40 E2
Tatham 55 A1
Tathwell 53 B3
Tatsfield 13 B1
Tattenhall 48 D6
Tatterford 44 C3
Tattersett 44 C3
Tattershall 53 A6
Tattershall Bridge 52 E6
Tattershall Thorpe 53 A6
Tattingstone 35 A5
Tatworth 8 E3
Taunton 8 D1

Tavelty 97 C2
Taverham 45 A4
Tavernspite 16 E4
Tavistock 4 E3
Taw Green 7 A6
Taw Green 7 A7
Tawstock 6 E4
Taxal 50 B3
Tayinloan 72 A3
Taylors Cross 6 D5
Taynafead 86 B7
Taynish 79 B3
Taynton *Glos* 29 B5
Taynton *Oxon* 30 C6
Taynuilt 86 B5
Tayock 89 C3
Tayovullin 78 B4
Tayport 89 A6
Tayvallich 79 B3
Tealby 52 E2
Team Valley 71 A2
Teanamachar 98 B5
Teangue 92 D4
Teasses 82 E2
Tebay 62 B4
Tebworth 31 E5
Tedburn St Mary 7 C7
Teddington *GL* 24 B5
Teddington *Glos* 29 D4
Tedstone Delamere 29 A2
Tedstone Wafre 29 A2
Teeton 41 D7
Teffont Evias 10 A1
Teffont Magna 10 A1
Tegryn 17 A2
Teigh 42 B3
Teigngrace 5 D3
Teignmouth 8 A6
Teindland 104 A3
Telford 39 A3
Telham 13 E5
Tellisford 21 C5
Telscombe Cliffs 13 B6
Tempar 87 C3
Templand 75 A7
Temple *Corn* 4 B3
Temple *Loth* 82 D7
Temple Bar 26 E5
Temple Cloud 21 A5
Temple Combe 9 D1
Temple Ewell 15 C4
Temple Grafton 30 B2
Temple Guiting 30 A5
Temple Hirst 57 E5
Temple Normanton 51 A4
Temple Sowerby 69 E7
Templeton *Devon* 7 C5
Templeton *Dyfed* 16 E4
Templeton Bridge 7 C5
Templewood 89 C2
Tempsford 32 C3
Tenbury Wells 28 E1
Tenby 16 E5
Tendring 35 A6
Tenga 85 B4
Ten Mile Bank 44 A6
Tenston 112 B5
Tenterden 14 D5
Terally 66 C6
Terling 33 D7
Ternhill 39 A1
Terregles 68 C2
Terrington 64 D6
Terrington St Clement
   43 D2
Terrington St John 43 D3
Tertowie 97 D2
Tervieside 104 A5
Teston 13 E1
Testwood 10 E3
Tetbury 21 C1
Tetbury Upton 21 C1
Tetchill 38 C1
Tetcott 6 C7
Tetford 53 B4
Tetney 59 D7
Tetney Lock 59 D7
Tetsworth 31 B7
Tettenhall 40 A5
Tettenhall Wood 40 A5
Tetworth 32 D3
Teuchan 105 D5
Teversal 51 A4
Teversham 33 A3
Teviothead 76 A5
Tewel 97 D5
Tewin 32 D7

Tewkesbury 29 C4
Teynham 14 E2
Thainstone 97 C2
Thakeham 12 D5
Thame 31 C7
Thames Ditton 24 B6
Thamesmead 24 E4
Thaneston 97 B6
Thanington 15 B3
Thankerton 74 E2
Tharston 45 A6
Thatcham 22 E5
Thatto Heath 48 E2
Thaxted 33 C5
Theakston 63 D6
Thealby 58 D6
Theale *Berks* 23 A4
Theale *Som* 20 D6
Thearne 59 A4
The Banking 105 A5
The Bar 12 D4
Theberton 35 D2
The Bratch 40 A5
The Burf 29 C1
The Chequer 48 D7
Thedden Grange 11 C1
Theddingworth 41 D6
Theddlethorpe All Saints
   53 C3
Theddlethorpe St Helen
   53 C3
The Den 102 E5
The Dicker 15 A6
The Folly 32 C7
The Haven 12 C3
The Knowle 13 D2
The Laurels 45 C6
The Leacon 14 E5
Thelbridge 7 B5
Thelbridge Barton 7 B5
The Leacon 14 E5
Thelnetham 34 E1
Thelveton 45 A7
Thelwall 49 A3
Themelthorpe 44 E3
The Mythe 29 C4
Thenford 31 A3
The Nobe 32 D7
Therfield 32 E5
The Rhos 16 D4
The Rowe 40 A1
The Stocks 14 E6
The Strid 56 D2
The Study 86 C3
The Stumble 43 B5
Thetford 44 C7
Theydon Bois 24 E3
Thickwood 21 C4
Thimbleby *Lincs* 53 A5
Thimbleby *N Yorks* 64 B4
Thirkleby 64 B6
Thirlby 64 B5
Thirlestane 76 B1
Thirn 63 C6
Thirsk 64 B5
Thistleton *Lancs* 54 D4
Thistleton *Leics* 42 C3
Thistley Green 33 C1
Thixendale 65 A7
Thockrington 70 C1
Tholomas Drove 43 C4
Tholthorpe 57 C1
Thomas Chapel 16 E5
Thompson 44 D6
Thomshill 104 A3
Thong 25 B5
Thoralby 63 A6
Thoresby 51 C3
Thoresway 52 E2
Thorganby *Lincs* 53 A2
Thorganby *N Yorks* 57 E3
Thorgill 64 E4
Thorington 35 D1
Thorington Street 34 E5
Thorlby 55 D2
Thorley 33 A7
Thorley Street *Cambs*
   33 A7
Thorley Street *IoW* 10 E6
Thormanby 64 B6
Thornaby-on-Tees 64 B2
Thornage 44 E2
Thornborough *Bucks*
   31 C4
Thornborough *N Yorks*
   63 C7
Thornbury *Avn* 21 A1
Thornbury *Devon* 6 D6

Thornbury *H & W* 29 A2
Thornby 41 D7
Thorncliff 50 B5
Thorncombe 8 E3
Thorncombe Street 12 C2
Thorncote Green 32 C4
Thorndon 35 A2
Thorne *Som* 9 B2
Thorne *S Yorks* 57 E6
Thorner 57 B3
Thornes 40 C4
Thorne St Margaret 8 B1
Thorney *Cambs* 43 A4
Thorney *GL* 23 E4
Thorney *Notts* 52 B4
Thorney *Som* 9 A1
Thorney Hill 10 D5
Thorn Falcon 8 D1
Thornford 9 C2
Thorngumbald 59 C5
Thornham 44 B1
Thornham Magna 35 A1
Thornham Parva 35 A1
Thornhaugh 42 D4
Thornhill *D & G* 74 D6
Thornhill *Derbs* 50 C2
Thornhill *Hants* 11 A3
Thornhill *S Glam* 19 B5
Thornhill *W Yorks* 57 A6
Thornholme *Cumb* 60 E3
Thornholme *Humb* 65 D7
Thornicombe 9 E3
Thornley *Dur* 71 B5
Thornley *Dur* 70 E5
Thornliebank 80 E6
Thorns 33 B3
Thornsett 50 B2
Thornthwaite *Cumb* 69 A7
Thornthwaite *N Yorks*
   56 E2
Thornton *Bucks* 31 C4
Thornton *Clev* 64 B2
Thornton *Fife* 82 C3
Thornton *Humb* 58 C3
Thornton *Lancs* 54 C3
Thornton *Leics* 41 B4
Thornton *Lincs* 53 A5
Thornton *Mers* 48 C1
Thornton *Northld* 77 A1
Thornton *Tays* 88 B4
Thornton *Tays* 88 E4
Thornton *W Yorks* 56 E4
Thornton Curtis 59 A6
Thornton Dale 65 A5
Thornton Hough 48 C3
Thornton-in-Craven 55 D3
Thornton-le-Beans 63 D5
Thornton-le-Clay 57 E1
Thornton le Moor *Lincs*
   52 D2
Thornton-le-Moor *N Yorks*
   63 D6
Thornton-le-Moors 48 D4
Thornton-le-Street 64 B5
Thorntonloch 83 C5
Thorntonpark 77 A1
Thornton Rust 62 E6
Thornton Steward 63 B6
Thornton Watlass 63 C6
Thornwood Common
   24 E2
Thornyhill 97 B6
Thornylee 76 A2
Thoroton 51 D6
Thorp Arch 57 C3
Thorpe *Derbs* 50 C5
Thorpe *Humb* 58 E3
Thorpe *Lincs* 53 C3
Thorpe *Nflk* 45 D6
Thorpe *Notts* 51 D6
Thorpe *N Yorks* 56 D1
Thorpe *Sry* 23 E5
Thorpe Abbotts 35 A1
Thorpe Acre 41 C2
Thorpe Arnold 41 E2
Thorpe Audlin 57 C6
Thorpe Bassett 65 A6
Thorpe Bay 25 E4
Thorpe by Water 42 B5
Thorpe Constantine 40 E4
Thorpe Culvert 53 C5
Thorpe End Garden Village
   45 B4
Thorpe Green 34 D3
Thorpe Hall 64 C6
Thorpe Hesley 50 E1
Thorpe in Balne 57 D6

Thorpe in the Fallows
   52 C3
Thorpe Langton 41 E5
Thorpe Larches 71 B6
Thorpe-le-Soken 35 A6
Thorpe le Street 58 D3
Thorpe Malsor 42 B7
Thorpe Mandeville 31 A3
Thorpe Market 45 B2
Thorpe Morieux 34 D3
Thorpeness 35 D3
Thorpe on the Hill *Lincs*
   52 C5
Thorpe on The Hill *W Yorks*
   57 B5
Thorpe St Andrew 45 B5
Thorpe St Peter 53 C5
Thorpe Salvin 51 B2
Thorpe Satchville 41 E3
Thorpe Thewles 64 B1
Thorpe Tilney Dales 52 E6
Thorpe Underwood 57 C2
Thorpe Waterville 42 D6
Thorpe Willoughby 57 D4
Thorpland 44 A5
Thorrington 34 E6
Thorverton 7 D6
Thrandeston 35 A1
Thrapston 42 C7
Thraxton 28 D4
Threapland 55 D1
Threapwood 48 D7
Three Bridges 12 E3
Three Chimneys 14 D5
Three Cocks 28 A4
Three Crosses 17 D6
Three Cups Corner 13 D4
Three Holes 43 D4
Three Legged Cross *Dors*
   10 B4
Three Legged Cross *Kent*
   13 D3
Three Mile Cross 23 B5
Threlkeld 69 B7
Threshers Bush 24 F2
Threshfield 55 D1
Threxton Hill 44 C6
Thriepley 88 E5
Thrigby 45 D4
Thringarth 70 C6
Thringstone 41 B3
Thrintoft 63 D5
Thriplow 33 A4
Throcking 32 E5
Throckley 70 E2
Throckmorton 29 D3
Throphill 77 C7
Thropton 77 B5
Throwleigh 7 A7
Throwley 14 E3
Thrumpton 51 B7
Thrumster 111 D4
Thrupp *Glos* 29 C7
Thrupp *Oxon* 30 E6
Thrushelton 4 E2
Thrushgill 55 A1
Thrussington 41 D3
Thruxton *H & W* 22 B7
Thruxton *Hants* 22 B7
Thrybergh 51 A1
Thulston 51 A7
Thundersley 25 C4
Thunderton 105 D4
Thundridge 32 E7
Thurcaston 41 C3
Thurcroft 51 A2
Thurdistoft 111 C2
Thurgarton *Nflk* 45 A2
Thurgarton *Notts* 51 C6
Thurgoland 57 A7
Thurlaston *Leics* 41 C5
Thurlaston *Warks* 41 B7
Thurlbear 8 D1
Thurlby *Lincs* 42 E3
Thurlby *Lincs* 52 C5
Thurleigh 32 B3
Thurlestone 5 B6
Thurloxton 8 D1
Thurlstone 57 A7
Thurlton 45 D6
Thurlwood 49 C5
Thurmaston 41 D4
Thurnby 41 D4
Thurne 45 D4
Thurnham *Kent* 14 D3
Thurning *Nflk* 44 E3
Thurning *Northants* 42 D6

Thurnscoe 57 C7
Thursby 69 B4
Thursford 44 D2
Thursley 12 B3
Thurso 111 B2
Thurstaston 48 B3
Thurston 34 D2
Thurstonfield 69 B4
Thurstonland 56 E6
Thurton 45 C5
Thurvaston 50 D7
Thuster 111 C3
Thuxton 44 E5
Thwaite *N Yorks* 62 D5
Thwaite *Sflk* 35 A2
Thwaite Head 61 C5
Thwaite St Mary 45 C6
Thwing 65 C6
Tibbermore 88 B6
Tibberton *Glos* 29 B5
Tibberton *H & W* 29 D2
Tibberton *Salop* 39 A2
Tibenham 45 A7
Tibertich 79 C1
Tibshelf 51 A4
Tibthorpe 58 E2
Ticehurst 13 D3
Tichborne 11 B1
Tickencote 42 C4
Tickenham 20 D3
Tickhill 51 B1
Ticklerton 38 D5
Ticknall 41 A2
Tickton 59 A3
Tidcombe 22 B6
Tiddington *Oxon* 31 B7
Tiddington *Warks* 30 C2
Tidebrook 13 D3
Tideford 4 D5
Tidenham 20 E1
Tidenham Chase 20 E1
Tideswell 50 C3
Tidmarsh 23 A4
Tidmington 30 C4
Tidpit 10 B3
Tiers Cross 16 C4
Tiffield 31 B2
Tifty 105 A4
Tigerton 89 B2
Tighachnoic 85 C4
Tigharry 98 B4
Tighcreag 102 E1
Tigh Ghlinnegabhar 86 A2
Tighnab_lair 87 D7
Tighnabruaich 79 D4
Tighnacomaire 86 A2
Tigley 5 C4
Tilbrook 32 B2
Tilbury 25 B5
Tile Cross 40 D6
Tile Hill 40 E7
Tilehurst 23 A4
Tilford 23 C7
Tillathrowie 104 C5
Tillers' Green 29 A4
Tillery 105 C6
Tilley 38 E2
Tillicoultry 81 D2
Tillingham 25 E2
Tillington *H & W* 28 D3
Tillington *W Ssx* 12 B4
Tillington Common 28 D3
Tillyarblet 89 B2
Tillybirloch 97 B3
Tillycairn 97 B2
Tillyfar 105 B4
Tillyfour 97 A2
Tillygreig 105 B6
Tillypronie 96 E3
Tilmanstone 15 D3
Tilney All Saints 43 D3
Tilney High End 43 D3
Tilney St Lawrence 43 D3
Tilshead 21 E6
Tilstock 38 E1
Tilston 48 D6
Tilstone Fearnall 48 E5
Tilsworth 31 E5
Tilton on the Hill 41 E4
Tiltups End 21 C1
Timberland 52 E5
Timberland Dales 52 E5
Timbersbrook 49 C5
Timberscombe 7 D2
Timble 56 E2
Timperley 49 B3
Timsbury *Avn* 21 A5

msbury *Hants* 10 E2
msgarry 106 D4
mworth Green 34 C2
ncleton 9 D4
ndale 69 E4
ngewick 31 B4
ngley 57 A5
ngrith 32 B5
nhay 4 E2
nhead 21 D5
nney 6 C7
nshill 57 A3
nsley 50 E1
nsley Green 12 E3
ntagel 4 A2
ntern Parva 28 E7
ntinhull 9 B2
ntwistle 50 B1
nwald 75 A7
nwell 42 D4
pperty *Gramp* 97 C5
pperty *Gramp* 105 C6
ptoe 10 D5
pton 40 B5
pton St John 8 B4
ptree 34 C7
ptree Heath 34 C7
rabad 27 C6
r-deunaw 18 B4
rindrish 93 E6
rley 29 C5
rphil 19 B3
ril 69 D7
r-y-dail 18 B2
rbury 10 A2
rsington 50 C5
ster 111 B2
chberry 6 B4
chfield 11 B4
chmarsh 32 B1
chwell 44 B1
rhby 51 C7
rley 28 C1
rsey 13 B1
rson 6 B6
rtensor 40 A1
rtleshall 44 C3
erton *Ches* 48 E5
erton *Devon* 7 D5
etshall St Margaret
r5 A7
etshall St Mary 45 A7
rall 40 B2
rover 42 C4
rab 113 E1
rbermory 85 B3
rbson 106 E4
rcher 104 E5
ckenham 21 E3
ckenham Wick 21 E2
ckholes 55 A5
ckington 21 A2
ckwith 57 C2
dber 9 D2
ddington *Beds* 32 B6
ddington *Glos* 30 A4
ddington *W Ssx* 12 C6
denham 30 C4
dhills *Cumb* 69 B3
dhills *Tays* 89 A5
dlachie 97 B2
dmorden 55 D5
dwick 51 A2
rt *Cambs* 32 E3
rt *Ches* 49 B4
rt *Lincs* 42 D3
rtcarl 111 D4
rt Hill 70 E6
rt Monks 45 D6
rt next Newton 52 D3
rtrees 44 C3
rts 111 D2
rts 114 D5
rtwood 44 D4
gston 77 D5
rkers Green 23 B4
rland 20 A7
rlard Royal 10 A3
rl Bar 93 D2
rler Down Gate 9 B3
rler Fratrum 9 B4
rler Porcorum 9 B4
rlerton *Notts* 51 C7
rlerton *N Yorks* 57 D1
rler Whelme 9 B3
rlesbury 34 D7
rlesby 64 C2

Tolleshunt D'Arcy 34 D7
Tolleshunt Knights 34 D7
Tolleshunt Major 34 D7
Toll of Birness 105 D5
Tolmachan 106 D7
Tolob 115 C6
Tolpuddle 9 D4
Tolstachaolais 106 E4
Tolvah 95 B6
Tolworth 24 B6
Tom an Fhuadain 107 B6
Tomatin 95 B3
Tombreck 94 E2
Tomchrasky 93 E3
Tomdoun 93 D4
Tomdow 103 D7
Tomich *Hghld* 102 D7
Tomich *Hghld* 94 B3
Tomintoul *Gramp* 96 B4
Tomintoul *Gramp* 96 B2
Tomnacross 102 D7
Tomnamoon 103 D6
Tomnaven 104 C5
Tomnavoulin 104 A6
Tomvaich 95 D2
Ton 19 D3
Tonbridge 15 A2
Tondu 18 D5
Tong 39 B4
Tonge 41 B2
Tongham 23 C7
Tongland 67 C5
Tong Norton 39 B4
Tong Street 56 E4
Tongue 19 C3
Tongwynlais 19 B5
Tonna 18 C4
Ton-Pentre 18 E4
Ton-teg 19 A5
Tonwell 32 E7
Tonypandy 18 E4
Tonyrefail 19 A5
Toot Baldon 31 A7
Toot Hill *Esx* 24 F2
Toot Hill *Hants* 10 E3
Topcliffe 63 D7
Topcroft 45 B6
Topcroft Street 45 B6
Top End 32 B2
Toppesfield 33 D5
Toppings 55 B6
Topsham 8 A5
Topsham Bridge 5 C5
Torastan 84 D2
Torbain 96 B2
Torbay 5 E4
Torbeg *Gramp* 96 D3
Torbeg *Strath* 72 C5
Torbryan 5 D4
Torcastle 86 C1
Torcross 5 D6
Tordarroch 94 E2
Tore 102 E6
Toreduff 103 E5
Toremore *Hghld* 95 E2
Toremore *Hghld* 111 B5
Torgyle 94 B4
Torksey 52 B4
Torlum 98 B6
Torlundy 86 C1
Tormarton 21 B3
Tormore 72 C4
Tormsdale 111 B3
Tornagrain 103 A7
Tornahaish 96 C3
Tornapress 101 A7
Tornaveen 97 B3
Torness 94 D3
Torpenhow 69 A6
Torphichen 81 D4
Torphins 97 B3
Torpoint 4 E5
Torquay 5 E4
Torquhan 76 A1
Torr-a-chlachan 85 A3
Torran *Hghld* 103 A4
Torran *Strath* 79 C1
Torrance *Strath* 81 A4
Torrance *Strath* 81 A6
Torrancroy 96 D2
Torraneidhinn 85 C3
Torr Fada 84 D4
Torrich 103 B6
Torridon 101 B6
Torrin 92 C2
Torrisdale 72 B4
Torrish 110 E7

Torrisholme 54 D1
Torrlaoighseach 93 B3
Torroble 102 D1
Torry *Gramp* 104 C4
Torry *Gramp* 97 E3
Torryburn 81 E3
Torsonce 76 A1
Torterston 105 D4
Torthorwald 68 D2
Tortington 12 C6
Tortworth 21 A1
Torver 61 B5
Torwood 81 C3
Torworth 51 C2
Tosberry 6 B4
Toscaig 92 E1
Toseland 32 D2
Tosside 55 B2
Tostarie 84 E4
Tostock 34 D2
Totaig 99 B6
Totamore 84 C3
Tote 100 B7
Totegan 110 D2
Totford 11 B1
Tothill 53 C3
Totland 10 E6
Totley 50 E3
Totnes 5 D4
Toton 51 B7
Tottenham 24 D3
Tottenhill 44 A4
Totteridge 24 C3
Totternhoe 31 E5
Tottington *GM* 55 B6
Tottington *Nflk* 44 C6
Totton 10 E3
Touchen-End 23 C4
Toulton 20 A7
Tovil 13 E1
Towcester 31 B3
Towednack 2 B5
Tower Hamlets 24 D4
Towersey 31 C7
Towie *Gramp* 105 B2
Towie *Gramp* 104 D6
Towie *Gramp* 96 E2
Tow Law 70 E5
Town End *Cumb* 61 D5
Town End *Cumb* 80 D4
Town Green 48 D1
Townhead 67 C6
Townhead of Greenlaw
67 D4
Townhill 82 B4
Town Row 15 A3
Townshend 2 C5
Town Street 44 B7
Town Yetholm 76 E3
Towthorpe *Humb* 65 B7
Towthorpe *N Yorks* 57 E2
Towton 57 C4
Towyn 47 D3
Toynton All Saints 53 B5
Toynton Fen Side 53 B5
Toynton St Peter 53 C5
Toy's Hill 13 B1
Trabboch 73 D5
Traboe 2 E6
Tradespark *Hghld* 103 B6
Tradespark *Ork* 113 D1
Trafford Park 49 B2
Trallong 18 E1
Tranch 19 C3
Tranent 82 E5
Trantlebeg 110 D3
Trantlemore 110 D3
Tranwell 77 C7
Trapp 18 B2
Traprain 83 A5
Traquair 75 D2
Trawden 55 D4
Trawsfynydd 47 B7
Trealaw 18 E4
Treales 54 D4
Trearddur Bay 46 B3
Treaslane 99 C6
Trebanos 18 C3
Trebarrow 6 B7
Trebartha 4 C3
Trebarwith 4 A2
Trebetherick 3 B1
Treborough 7 E3
Trebudannon 3 A2
Trebullett 4 D3
Treburley 4 D3
Trebyan 3 C2

Trecastle 18 D1
Trecwn 16 C2
Trecynon 18 E3
Tredavoe 2 B6
Tre-ddiog 16 B3
Tredegar 19 B3
Tredington *Glos* 29 D5
Tredington *Warks* 30 C3
Tredinnick *Corn* 3 B1
Tredinnick *Corn* 4 C5
Tredomen 28 A4
Tredrissi 16 D1
Tredunnock 19 D4
Treen 2 A6
Treeton 51 A2
Trefasser 16 B2
Trefdraeth 46 D3
Trefecca 28 A4
Trefeglwys 37 D6
Trefenter 27 A4
Treffgarne 16 C3
Treffynnon 16 B3
Trefil 19 B2
Trefilan 26 E5
Treflach 38 B2
Trefnanney 38 B3
Trefnant 47 E3
Trefonen 38 B2
Trefor 46 C3
Treforest 19 A5
Trefriw 47 B4
Tregadillett 4 C2
Tregaian 46 D3
Tregare 28 D6
Tregaron 27 A5
Tregarth 47 A4
Tregavethan 2 E4
Tregear 3 A4
Tregeare 4 C2
Tregeiriog 38 A1
Tregele 46 C1
Tregidden 2 E6
Treglemais 16 B3
Tregolds 3 A1
Tregole 6 A7
Tregonetha 3 B2
Tregony 3 B4
Tregoyd 28 A4
Tre-groes *Dyfed* 26 D6
Tre-groes *M Glam* 18 E5
Tre-guff 19 A6
Tregurrian 3 A2
Tregynon 37 E6
Trehafod 19 A4
Treharris 19 B4
Treherbert 18 E4
Trelassick 3 A3
Trelawnyd 47 E3
Trelech 17 A2
Trelech a'r Betws 17 B3
Treleddyd-fawr 16 A3
Trelewis 19 B4
Trelights 3 B1
Trelill 4 A3
Trelissick 3 A5
Trelleck 28 E7
Trelleck Grange 28 D7
Trelogan 48 E1
Trelystan 38 B4
Tremadog 46 E7
Tremail 4 B2
Tremain 26 B6
Tremaine 4 C2
Tremar 4 C4
Trematon 4 D5
Tremeirchion 47 E3
Tremethick Cross 2 B5
Trenance 3 A2
Trench 39 A3
Treneglos 4 C2
Trenewan 3 D3
Trent 9 B2
Trentham 49 C7
Trentishoe 7 A2
Treoes 18 E6
Treorchy 18 E4
Tre'r-dd'ôl 37 A6
Tre-Rhys 26 A6
Trerule Foot 4 D5
Tresaith 26 B5
Trescott 40 A5
Trescowe 2 C5
Tresham 21 B1
Treshnish 84 E4
Tresillian 3 A4
Tresinney 4 B2
Tresinwen 16 C1

Tresmeer 4 C2
Tresparrett Posts 6 A7
Tressait 87 E2
Tresta *Fetlar* 114 F3
Tresta *Shet* 115 C2
Treswell 51 D3
Trethurgy 3 C3
Tretio 16 A3
Tretire 28 E5
Tretower 28 A5
Treuddyn 48 B6
Trevalga 4 A2
Trevanson 3 B1
Trevarren 3 B2
Trevarrick 3 B4
Tre-vaughan 17 B3
Trevaughan 17 A4
Trevellas 2 E3
Treverva 2 E5
Trevethin 19 C3
Trevigro 4 D4
Trevine *Dyfed* 16 B2
Trevine *Strath* 86 B6
Treviscoe 3 B3
Trevone 3 A1
Trevor 46 C6
Trevose 3 A1
Trewalder 4 A2
Trewarmett 4 A2
Trewarthenick 3 B4
Trewassa 4 B2
Trewellard 2 A5
Trewen 4 C2
Trewern 38 B3
Trewidland 4 C4
Trewilym 26 A6
Trewint 6 A7
Trewithian 3 A5
Trewoon 3 B3
Treyarnon 3 A1
Treyford 11 E3
Triangle 56 D5
Trickett's Cross 10 B4
Trimdon 71 B5
Trimdon Grange 71 B5
Trimingham 45 B2
Trimley Marshes 34 E7
Trimley St Martin 35 B5
Trimley St Mary 35 B5
Trimpley 39 B7
Trimsaran 17 C5
Trimstone 6 E2
Trinafour 87 D2
Trinant 19 C3
Tring 31 E6
Trinity 89 C2
Trislaig 86 B1
Trispen 3 A3
Tritlington 77 D6
Trochrague 73 B7
Trochry 88 A4
Troedyraur 26 C6
Troedyrhiw 19 A3
Trofarth 86 D7
Troon *Corn* 2 D5
Troon *Strath* 73 C4
Trossary 90 C4
Troston 34 C1
Trostre 19 D3
Troswell 6 B7
Trottiscliffe 25 B6
Trotton 11 E2
Troughend 76 E6
Troustan 79 E4
Troutbeck 61 D3
Troutbeck Bridge 61 D3
Trowbridge 21 C5
Trow Green 28 E7
Trowle Common 21 C5
Trowley Bottom 32 B7
Trows 76 C2
Trowse Newton 45 B5
Trudernish 78 D6
Trudoxhill 21 B6
Trull 8 D1
Trumisgarry 98 C4
Trumpan 99 B5
Trumpet 29 A4
Trumpington 33 A3
Trunch 45 B2
Trunnah 54 C3
Truro 3 A4
Trusham 5 D2
Trusley 50 D7
Trusthorpe 53 D3
Truthan 3 A4
Trysull 40 A5

Tubney 22 D2
Tuckenhay 5 D5
Tuckingmill 2 D4
Tuddenham *Sflk* 35 A4
Tuddenham *Sflk* 33 D1
Tudeley 13 D2
Tudhoe 71 A5
Tudweiliog 46 B7
Tuffley 29 C6
Tufton *Dyfed* 16 D3
Tufton *Hants* 22 D7
Tugby 41 E4
Tugford 38 E6
Tughall 77 D3
Tuirnaig 101 A3
Tulchan 88 A6
Tullibody 81 C2
Tullich *Cent* 87 B5
Tullich *Gramp* 104 B4
Tullich *Hghld* 103 B4
Tullich *Hghld* 94 E3
Tullich *Strath* 86 B7
Tullich *Strath* 85 E7
Tullich Muir 103 A4
Tulliemet 88 A3
Tulloch *Gramp* 105 A5
Tulloch *Gramp* 103 D6
Tulloch *Hghld* 102 E2
Tullochgorm 79 D2
Tullochgribban 95 C3
Tullochvenus 97 A3
Tulloes 89 B4
Tullybannocher 87 D6
Tullybelton 88 B5
Tullyfergus 88 D4
Tullymurdoch 88 C3
Tullynessle 97 A2
Tumble 17 D4
Tumby 53 A6
Tumby Woodside 53 A6
Tummel Bridge 87 D3
Tunbridge Wells 61 A7
Tundergarth Mains 75 B7
Tunstall *Humb* 59 D4
Tunstall *Kent* 14 D2
Tunstall *Lancs* 62 B7
Tunstall *Nflk* 45 D5
Tunstall *N Yorks* 63 C5
Tunstall *Sflk* 35 C3
Tunstall *Staffs* 49 C6
Tunstead 45 C3
Tunworth 23 A7
Tun-y-cefn 47 E6
Tupsley 28 E3
Turbiskill 79 B3
Turclossie 105 B3
Turgis Green 23 A6
Turin 89 B3
Turkdean 30 B6
Tur Langton 41 E5
Turnastone 28 C4
Turnberry 73 B7
Turnchapel 4 E5
Turnditch 50 D6
Turner's Green 30 B1
Turners Hill 13 A3
Turners Puddle 9 E4
Turnford 24 D2
Turnworth 9 E3
Turret Bridge 94 B6
Turriff 105 A4
Turton Bottoms 55 B6
Turvey 31 E2
Turville 23 B2
Turville Heath 23 B2
Turweston 31 B4
Tutbury 40 E2
Tutnall 40 B7
Tutshill 20 E1
Tuttington 45 B3
Tuxford 51 D3
Twatt *Ork* 112 B4
Twatt *Shet* 115 C2
Twechar 81 A4
Tweedmouth 83 E7
Tweedsmuir 75 B3
Twelveheads 2 E4
Twenty 42 E7
Twerton 21 B4
Twickenham 24 B5
Twigworth 29 C5
Twineham 12 E5
Twinhoe 21 B5
Twinstead 34 C5
Twiss Green 49 A2
Twitchen *Devon* 7 B3
Twitchen *Salop* 38 C7

Twizell House 77 C3
Two Bridges 5 B3
Two Dales 50 D4
Two Gates 40 E4
Twycross 41 A4
Twyford Berks 23 B4
Twyford Bucks 31 B5
Twyford Derbs 41 A2
Twyford Dors 9 E2
Twyford Hants 11 A2
Twyford Leics 41 E4
Twyford Leics 41 E3
Twyford Nflk 44 E3
Twyford Common 28 E4
Twynholm 67 C5
Twyning 29 C4
Twyning Green 29 D4
Twynllanan 18 C1
Twyn-yr-odyn 19 B6
Twyn-y-Sheriff 28 D7
Twywell 42 C7
Tyberton 28 C4
Tycroes 18 B2
Tycrwyn 38 A3
Tydd Gote 43 C3
Tydd St Giles 43 C3
Tydd St Mary 43 C3
Tye Common 25 B3
Tye Green 33 D6
Tŷ-hen 46 A7
Tyldesley 49 A1
Tylegarw 19 A5
Tyler Hill 15 B2
Tylers Green Bucks 23 D2
Tylers Green Esx 24 F2
Tylorstown 19 A4
Tylwch 27 D2
Ty-mawr Clwyd 48 A7
Ty-mawr Clwyd 47 D6
Ty-nant Clwyd 47 D6
Ty-nant Gynd 37 D3
Tyndrum 86 E5
Tyneham 9 E5
Tynehead 82 D7
Tynemouth 71 B2
Tynewydd 18 E4
Tyninghame 83 B5
Tynribbie 86 A4
Tynron 74 D6
Tyn-y-Cym 27 C2
Tyn-y-ffridd 38 A1
Tyn-y-graig 27 E6
Ty'n-y-groes 47 B3
Tyringham 31 D3
Tythegston 18 D6
Tytherington Avn 21 A2
Tytherington Ches 49 D4
Tytherington Som 21 B6
Tytherington Wilts 21 D6
Tytherleigh 8 E3
T'y-uchaf 37 E3
Tywardreath 3 C3
Tywardreath Highway
 3 C3
Tywyn Gynd 47 B3
Tywyn Gynd 36 E5

U

Uachdar 98 B6
Ubbeston Green 35 C1
Ubley 20 E5
Uckerby 63 C4
Uckfield 13 B4
Uckinghall 29 C4
Uckington 29 D5
Uddingston 81 A5
Uddington 74 D2
Udimore 14 D7
Udny Green 105 B6
Udstonhead 74 C1
Uffcott 22 A4
Uffculme 8 B2
Uffington Lincs 42 D4
Uffington Oxon 22 C3
Uffington Salop 38 E3
Ufford Northants 42 D4
Ufford Sflk 35 B3
Ufton 30 D1
Ufton Nervet 23 A5
Ugborough 5 B5
Ugbrooke House 5 D3
Uggeshall 45 D7
Ugglebarnby 65 A3
Ugley 33 B6
Ugley Green 33 B6

Ugthorpe 64 E2
Uig Coll 84 C3
Uig Skye 99 C5
Uig Skye 99 A6
Uig Strath 80 A3
Uiginish 99 B7
Uigshader 100 B7
Uisken 84 E7
Ulbster 111 D4
Ulcat Row 69 C7
Ulceby Humb 59 B6
Ulceby Lincs 53 C4
Ulceby Cross 53 C4
Ulcombe 14 D4
Uldale 69 A6
Uldale House 62 C5
Uley 21 B1
Ulgham 77 D6
Ullapool 101 D2
Ullenhall 30 B1
Ullenwood 29 D6
Ulleskelf 57 D3
Ullesthorpe 41 C6
Ulley 51 A2
Ullingswick 28 E2
Ullinish 92 A1
Ullock 68 D7
Ulpha 61 A4
Ulrome 59 B2
Ulsta 114 D4
Ulting 25 D2
Uluvalt 85 B6
Ulverston 61 B6
Ulwell 10 B6
Ulzieside 74 C5
Umachan 100 D6
Unapool 108 E5
Underbarrow 61 D5
Underhoull 114 E2
Under River 15 A1
Underwood Derbs 51 A5
Underwood Gwent 19 D5
Undy 20 D2
Unifirth 115 B2
Union Croft 97 D4
Union Mills 60 c4
Unish 99 B5
Unstone 50 E3
Unthank 69 C6
Upavon 9 C3
Up Cerne 9 C3
Upchurch 14 D2
Upcott 28 C2
Upend 33 D3
Up Exe 7 D6
Uphall Dors 9 B3
Uphall Loth 81 E4
Upham Devon 7 C6
Upham Hants 11 B2
Uphampton 29 C1
Up Hatherley 29 D5
Uphill 20 C5
Up Hill Kent 15 C4
Up Holland 48 E1
Upleadon 29 B5
Upleatham 64 D2
Uplees 14 E2
Uploaders 20 E7
Uploders 9 B4
Uplowman 8 B2
Uplyme 8 E4
Up Marden 11 D3
Upminster 25 A4
Up Nately 23 A6
Upnor 14 C1
Upottery 8 D3
Uppark 11 D3
Upper Affcot 38 D6
Upper Ardchronie 102 E3
Upper Ardroscadale 79 E5
Upper Arley 39 B6
Upper Aston 40 A5
Upper Astrop 31 A4
Upper Barrack 105 C4
Upper Basildon 22 E4
Upper Bayble 107 D4
Upper Beeding 12 D5
Upper Benefield 42 C6
Upper Bighouse 110 D3
Upper Boat 19 B5
Upper Boddington 30 E2
Upper Borth 27 A2
Upper Brailes 30 D4
Upper Breakish 92 D2
Upper Breinton 28 D3
Upper Broughton 41 D2
Upper Bucklebury 22 E5

Upper Burgate 10 C3
Upper Burnhaugh 97 D4
Upper Caldecote 32 C4
Upper Camster 111 C4
Upper Catshill 40 B7
Upper Chapel 27 E6
Upper Chute 22 B6
Upper Clatford 22 C7
Upper Clynnog 46 D6
Upper Coberley 29 D6
Upper Coedcae 19 C3
Upper Colwall 29 B3
Upper Corris 37 B5
Upper Cwmbran 19 C4
Upper Cwmtwrch 18 C2
Upper Dallachy 104 B2
Upper Dean 32 B2
Upper Denby 57 A7
Upper Derraid 95 D2
Upper Diabaig 101 A5
Upper Dicker 15 A5
Upper Dunsforth 57 C1
Upper Elkstone 50 B5
Upper End 50 B3
Upper Farringdon 11 D1
Upper Framilode 29 B6
Upper Froyle 23 B7
Upper Glendessarry 93 B5
Upper Godney 20 D6
Upper Gornal 40 B5
Upper Gravenhurst 32 C5
Upper Green Berks 22 C5
Upper Green Esx 33 C4
Upper Hackney 50 D4
Upper Hale 23 C7
Upper Halliford 23 E5
Upper Halling 25 B6
Upper Hambleton 42 B4
Upper Hardres Court
 15 B3
Upper Hartfield 13 B3
Upper Hayton 38 E6
Upper Heath 38 E6
Upper Helmsley 57 E2
Upper Hergest 28 B2
Upper Heyford 30 E5
Upper Hill 28 D2
Upper Hopton 56 E6
Upper Hulme 50 B4
Upper Inglesham 22 B2
Upper Kilchattan 78 C2
Upper Killay 17 D6
Upper Kirkhill 97 E3
Upper Knockando 103 E7
Upper Lambourn 22 C3
Upper Langwith 51 B4
Upper Largo 82 E2
Upper Lochton 97 B4
Upper Longdon 40 C3
Upper Ludstone 40 A5
Upper Lybster 111 C5
Upper Lybrook 29 A6
Upper Maes-coed 28 C4
Upper Midhope 50 D1
Uppermill 49 D1
Upper Minety 21 E1
Upper Mitton 40 A7
Upper North Dean 23 C2
Upper Norwood 24 D5
Upper Obney 88 B5
Upper Ollach 92 C1
Upper Pond Street 33 A5
Upper Poppleton 57 D2
Upper Quinton 30 B3
Upper Ridinghill 105 D3
Upper Sanday 113 E1
Upper Sapey 29 A1
Upper Seagry 21 D2
Upper Shader 107 B2
Upper Shelton 31 E3
Upper Sheringham 45 A1
Upper Slaughter 30 B5
Upper Soudley 29 A6
Upper Stoke 41 A6
Upper Stondon 32 C5
Upper Stowe 31 B2
Upper Street Hants 10 C3
Upper Street Nflk 45 C4
Upper Street Sflk 35 A5
Upper Studley 21 D3
Upper Sundon 32 B6
Upper Swell 30 B5
Upper Tean 50 B7
Upperthong 56 E7
Upper Thurnam 28 D2
Upper Tillyrie 82 B2
Upperton 12 B4

Upper Tooting 24 C5
Upper Town 20 E4
Uppertown 111 D1
Upper Tysoe 30 D3
Upper Upham 22 B4
Upper Victoria 89 B5
Upper Wardington 30 E3
Upper Weald 31 D4
Upper Weedon 31 B2
Upper Welson 28 B2
Upper Wield 11 C1
Upper Winchendon 31 C6
Upper Woodford 10 C1
Upper Wootton 22 E6
Upper Wraxall 21 A7
Uppingham 42 B5
Uppington Dors 10 B4
Uppington Salop 38 E4
Upsall 64 B5
Upsettlington 76 E1
Upshire 24 E2
Up Somborne 10 E1
Upstreet 15 C2
Up Sydling 9 C3
Upton Berks 23 D4
Upton Bucks 31 C6
Upton Cambs 32 C1
Upton Ches 48 D5
Upton Corn 4 C3
Upton Devon 8 B3
Upton Dors 10 A5
Upton Hants 22 C6
Upton Hants 10 E3
Upton Lincs 52 B3
Upton Mers 48 B3
Upton Nflk 45 C4
Upton Northants 42 E4
Upton Northants 31 C1
Upton Notts 51 D3
Upton Notts 51 D5
Upton Oxon 22 E3
Upton Som 7 D4
Upton W Yorks 57 C6
Upton Bishop 29 A5
Upton Cheyney 21 A4
Upton Cressett 39 A5
Upton Cross 4 C3
Upton Green 45 C4
Upton Grey 23 A7
Upton Hellions 7 C6
Upton Lovell 21 D6
Upton Magna 38 E3
Upton Noble 21 B7
Upton Pyne 7 D7
Upton St Leonards 29 C6
Upton Scudamore 21 C6
Upton Snodsbury 29 D2
Upton upon Severn 29 C3
Upton Warren 29 D1
Upwaltham 12 B5
Upware 33 B1
Upwell 43 D4
Upwey 9 C5
Upwood 43 A6
Uradale 115 D4
Urafirth 114 C5
Uray 80 C2
Urchany 103 B7
Urchfont 21 E5
Urdimarsh 28 E3
Ure 114 B4
Urgha 99 A2
Urlay Nook 64 B2
Urmston 49 B2
Urquhart Gramp 104 A2
Urquhart Hghld 102 D6
Urra 64 C3
Urray 102 D6
Ushaw Moor 71 A4
Usk 19 D3
Uskavagh 98 C6
Usselby 52 D2
Utley 56 D3
Uton 7 C7
Utterby 53 B2
Uttoxeter 50 B7
Uwchmynydd 36 A3
Uxbridge 23 E3
Uyeasound 114 E2
Uzmaston 16 C4

V

Valley 46 B3
Valleyfield D & G 67 C5
Valleyfield Fife 81 E3
Valsgarth 114 F1

Valtos W Is 106 D4
Vange 25 C4
Vardre 18 B3
Varteg 19 C3
Vatten 99 B7
Vauld, The 28 E3
Vaynor 19 A2
Vaynor Park 38 A4
Veensgarth 115 D3
Velindre Dyfed 16 E2
Velindre Dyfed 17 B2
Velindre Pwys 28 A4
Vellow 7 E3
Venn 5 C6
Vennington 38 C4
Venn Ottery 8 B4
Ventnor 11 B7
Vernham Dean 22 C6
Vernham Street 22 C6
Vernolds Common 38 D6
Verwig 26 A6
Verwood 10 B4
Veryan 3 B5
Vicarage 8 D5
Vickerstown 61 A7
Victoria 3 B2
Vidlin 115 D1
Viewfield 111 A2
Viewpark 81 B5
Vigo 40 C4
Villavin 6 E5
Vinehall Street 13 E4
Vine's Cross 15 A5
Viney Hill 29 A7
Virginia Water 23 D5
Virginstow 6 C7
Virley 34 D7
Vobster 21 B6
Voe Shet 115 D1
Voe Shet 114 C4
Vowchurch 28 C4
Voxter 115 C1
Voy 112 B5

W

Wackerfield 70 E6
Wacton 45 A6
Wadborough 29 C3
Waddesdon 31 C6
Waddingham 52 C2
Waddington Lancs 55 B3
Waddington Lincs 52 C5
Waddingworth 52 E4
Wadebridge 3 B1
Wadeford 8 E2
Wadenhoe 42 D6
Wadesmill 32 E7
Wadhurst 13 D3
Wadshelf 50 E3
Wadsley Bridge 50 E1
Wadworth 51 B1
Wadworth Hill 59 C5
Waen 48 A5
Waen Fach 38 B3
Waen-wen 46 E4
Wag 111 A6
Wainfleet All Saints 53 C6
Wainfleet Bank 53 C6
Wainhouse Corner 6 A7
Wainscott 14 C1
Wainstalls 56 D5
Waitby 62 C4
Wakefield 57 B5
Wakerley 42 C5
Wakes Colne 34 C6
Walberswick 35 D1
Walberton 12 B6
Walcot Humb 58 D5
Walcot Lincs 42 D1
Walcot Lincs 52 E6
Walcot Salop 38 E3
Walcot Salop 38 C6
Walcot Warks 30 B2
Walcot Dales 52 E6
Walcote 41 C6
Walcott 45 C2
Walden 63 A6
Walden Head 62 E6
Walden Stubbs 57 D6
Waldershare Park 15 C4
Walderslade 14 C2
Walderton 11 D3
Walditch 9 A4
Waldley 50 C7
Waldridge 71 A4
Waldringfield 35 B4

Waldron 13 C5
Wales 51 A2
Walesby Lincs 52 E2
Walesby Notts 51 C3
Walford H & W 38 C7
Walford H & W 28 E5
Walford Salop 38 D2
Walgherton 49 A7
Walgrave 42 B7
Walhampton 10 E5
Walkden 49 B1
Walker 71 A2
Walkerburn 75 D2
Walker Fold 55 A3
Walkeringham 51 D1
Walkerith 51 D1
Walkern 32 D6
Walker's Green 28 E3
Walkerton 82 C2
Walkhampton 5 A4
Walkington 58 E4
Walk Mill 55 C5
Walkwood 30 A1
Wall Northld 70 C2
Wall Staffs 40 C4
Wallacehall 69 A2
Wallacetown 73 B7
Wallasey 48 B2
Wall Bank 38 E5
Wallbottle 70 E2
Wallend 14 D1
Waller's Green 29 A4
Wall Heath 40 A6
Wallingford 23 A3
Wallington GL 24 C6
Wallington Hants 11 B4
Wallington Herts 32 D5
Wallis 16 D3
Wallisdown 10 B5
Walliswood 12 D3
Walls 115 B3
Wallsend 71 A2
Wall under Haywood
 38 E5
Wallyford 82 D5
Walmer 15 D3
Walmer Bridge 54 D5
Walmersley 55 C6
Walmley 40 D5
Walpole 35 C1
Walpole Cross Keys
 43 D3
Walpole Highway 43 D3
Walpole St Andrew 43 D3
Walpole St Peter 43 D3
Walsall 40 C4
Walsall Wood 40 C4
Walsden 55 D5
Walsgrave on Sowe 41 A6
Walsham le Willows 34 E1
Walsoken 43 C3
Walston 75 A1
Walsworth 32 C5
Walterstone 28 C5
Waltham Humb 59 C7
Waltham Kent 15 B4
Waltham Abbey 24 D2
Waltham Chase 11 B3
Waltham Forest 24 D3
Waltham on the Wolds
 42 B2
Waltham St Lawrence
 23 C4
Walthamstow 24 D4
Walton Bucks 31 D6
Walton Bucks 31 D4
Walton Cambs 42 E4
Walton Cumb 69 D3
Walton Derbs 50 E4
Walton Leics 41 C6
Walton Pwys 28 B2
Walton Salop 38 E3
Walton Sflk 35 B5
Walton Som 20 D7
Walton Staffs 40 A1
Walton Warks 30 C2
Walton W Yorks 57 B6
Walton W Yorks 57 C3
Walton Cardiff 29 D4
Walton East 16 D3
Walton-in-Gordano 20 D3
Walton-le-Dale 54 E5
Walton-on-Thames 24 B6
Walton on the Hill Mers
 48 C2
Walton on the Hill Sry
 12 E1

Walton-on-the-Hill *Staffs* 40 B2
Walton on the Naze 35 B6
Walton on the Wolds 41 C3
Walton-on-Trent 40 E3
Walton Park 67 D3
Walton West 16 B4
Walwick 70 C1
Walworth 63 C3
Wambrook 8 D3
Wanborough *Sry* 12 B2
Wanborough *Wilts* 22 B3
Wandsworth 24 C5
Wangford *Sflk* 35 D1
Wangford *Sflk* 44 B7
Wanlip 41 C3
Wanlockhead 74 D4
Wannock 15 A6
Wansford *Cambs* 42 D5
Wansford *Northants* 59 A2
Wanstead 24 E4
Wanstrow 21 B6
Wanswell 29 A7
Wantage 22 D3
Wapley 21 B3
Wappenbury 30 D1
Wappenham 31 B3
Warbleton 13 D5
Warblebank 69 A5
Warborough 23 A2
Warboys 43 B6
Warbstow 6 B7
Warburton 49 B3
Warcop 62 C3
Warden *Kent* 15 A1
Warden *Northld* 70 C2
Ward End 40 D6
Wardgate 50 D6
Ward Green 34 E2
Wardhouse 104 D5
Wardington 30 E3
Wardle *Ches* 49 A6
Wardle *GM* 55 D6
Wardley 42 B4
Wardlow 50 C3
Wardy Hill 43 C6
Ware *Herts* 32 E7
Ware *Kent* 15 C2
Wareham 10 A6
Warehorne 14 E5
Warenford 77 C3
Waren Mill 77 C2
Warenton 77 C2
Wareside 32 E7
Waresley 32 D3
Warfield 23 C4
Wargrave 23 B4
Warham All Saints 44 D1
Warham St Mary 44 D1
Wark *Northld* 70 B1
Wark *Northld* 76 E2
Warkleigh 7 A4
Warkton 42 B6
Warkworth *Northants* 30 E3
Warkworth *Northld* 77 D5
Warlaby 63 D5
Warland 55 D6
Warleggan 3 D2
Warley 40 C6
Warley Town 56 D5
Warlingham 13 A1
Warmfield 57 B5
Warmingham 49 B5
Warminghurst 12 D5
Warmington *Northants* 42 D5
Warmington *Warks* 30 E3
Warminster 21 C6
Warmlake 14 D3
Warmley 21 A3
Warmsworth 57 D7
Warmwell 9 D5
Warndon 29 C2
Warnford 11 C2
Warnham 12 D3
Warningcamp 12 C6
Warninglid 12 E4
Warren *Ches* 49 C4
Warren *Dyfed* 16 C6
Warrenby 64 C1
Warren Row 23 C3
Warren Street 14 E3
Warrington *Bucks* 31 D2

Warrington *Ches* 49 A3
Warroch 81 E1
Warsash 11 A4
Warse 111 D1
Warslow 50 B5
Warsop 51 B4
Warter 58 D2
Warthill 57 E2
Wartle 97 A3
Wartling 13 D6
Wartnaby 41 E2
Warton *Lancs* 61 D6
Warton *Lancs* 54 D5
Warton *Northld* 77 B5
Warton *Warks* 40 E4
Warwick *Cumb* 69 C4
Warwick *Warks* 30 C1
Warwick Bridge 69 C4
Wasbister 112 C3
Washaway 3 C2
Washbourne 5 C5
Wash Common 22 D5
Washfield 7 D5
Washfold 63 A4
Washford 7 E2
Washford Pyne 7 C5
Washingborough 52 D4
Washington *T & W* 71 B3
Washington *W Ssx* 12 D5
Wasing 22 E5
Waskerley 70 D4
Wasperton 30 C2
Wass 64 C6
Watchet 7 E2
Watchfield *Oxon* 22 B2
Watchfield *Som* 20 C6
Watchgate 61 E5
Water 55 C5
Waterbeach 33 A2
Waterbeck 69 A2
Water Eaton 31 A6
Water End *Herts* 24 C2
Water End *Herts* 32 B7
Waterfall *Staffs* 50 B5
Waterfoot *Lancs* 55 C5
Waterford *Herts* 32 E7
Waterhead *Cumb* 61 C3
Waterhead *D & G* 67 D2
Waterhill of Bruxie 105 C4
Waterhouses *Dur* 70 E4
Waterhouses *Staffs* 50 B5
Wateringbury 13 D1
Waterloo *Dors* 10 B5
Waterloo *Dyfed* 16 C5
Waterloo *Gramp* 105 D5
Waterloo *Mers* 48 C2
Waterloo *Nflk* 45 B4
Waterloo *Strath* 81 C6
Waterloo *Tays* 88 B5
Waterloo Cross 8 B2
Waterloo Port 46 D4
Waterlooville 11 C4
Watermillock 69 C7
Water Newton 42 E5
Water Orton 40 D5
Waterperry 31 B7
Waterrow 8 B1
Watersfield 12 C5
Waterside *Bucks* 23 D1
Waterside *Gramp* 96 D2
Waterside *Gramp* 105 D6
Waterside *Strath* 73 D7
Waterside *Strath* 73 D3
Waterstock 31 B7
Waterston 16 C5
Water Stratford 31 B4
Waters Upton 39 A3
Water Yeat 61 B5
Watford *Herts* 24 B3
Watford *Northants* 31 B1
Wath *N Yorks* 63 D7
Wath *N Yorks* 56 E1
Wath Brow 60 E2
Wath upon Dearne 57 C7
Watlington *Nflk* 44 A4
Watlington *Oxon* 23 A2
Watnall Chaworth 51 A6
Watten 111 C3
Wattisfield 34 E1
Wattisham 34 E3
Watton *Humb* 59 A2
Watton *Nflk* 44 D5
Watton-at-Stone 32 E7
Watton Green 44 D5
Wattstown 19 A4
Wattsville 19 C4
Waunarlwydd 18 B4

Waunclynda 27 A7
Waun Fawr 27 A2
Waunfawr 46 E5
Waun y Clyn 17 C5
Wavendon 31 E4
Waverbridge 69 A5
Waverton *Ches* 48 D5
Waverton *Cumb* 69 A5
Wawne 59 A4
Waxham 45 D3
Waxholme 59 D5
Wayford 9 A3
Way Gill 55 D1
Way Village 7 C5
Waytown 9 A4
Weald 30 D7
Wealdstone 24 B4
Weare 20 D5
Weare Giffard 6 D4
Wearne 9 A1
Weasenham All Saints 44 C3
Weasenham St Peter 44 C3
Weathercote 62 C7
Weatheroak Hill 40 C7
Weaverham 49 A4
Weaverthorpe 65 B6
Webheath 30 A1
Webton 28 D4
Wedderlairs 105 B5
Weddington 41 A5
Wedhampton 21 E5
Wedmore 20 D6
Wednesbury 40 C5
Wednesfield 40 B4
Weedon 31 D6
Weedon Bec 31 B2
Weedon Lois 31 B3
Weeford 40 D4
Week 7 B5
Weekley 42 B6
Week Orchard 6 B6
Week St Mary 6 B7
Weeley 35 A6
Weeley Heath 35 A6
Weem 87 E4
Weeping Cross 40 B2
Weethly 30 A2
Weeting 44 B7
Weeton *Humb* 59 D5
Weeton *Lancs* 54 C4
Weeton *N Yorks* 57 A3
Weir 55 C5
Weirbrook 38 C2
Welbeck Abbey 51 B3
Welborne 44 E4
Welbourn 52 C6
Welburn 64 E7
Welbury 63 D4
Welby 42 C1
Welches Dam 43 C6
Welcombe 6 B5
Weldon 42 C6
Weldon Bridge 22 D4
Welford *Berks* 22 D4
Welford *Northants* 41 D6
Welford-on-Avon 30 B2
Welham *Leics* 41 E5
Welham *Notts* 51 D2
Welham Green 24 C2
Well *Hants* 23 B7
Well *Lincs* 53 C4
Well *N Yorks* 63 C6
Welland 29 B3
Wellbank 89 A5
Well End 23 C3
Wellesbourne Hastings 30 C2
Wellesbourne Mountford 30 C2
Well Hill 24 E6
Welling 24 E5
Wellingborough 31 D1
Wellingham 44 C3
Wellingore 52 C6
Wellington *Cumb* 60 E3
Wellington *H & W* 28 D3
Wellington *Salop* 39 A3
Wellington *Som* 8 C1
Wellington Heath 29 B3
Wellington Marsh 28 D3
Wellow *Avn* 21 B5
Wellow *IOW* 10 E6
Wellow *Notts* 51 C4
Wells 20 E6
Wellsborough 41 A4

Wells-Next-The-Sea 44 D1
Wells of Ythan 104 E5
Well Town 7 D6
Wellwood 81 E3
Welney 43 D5
Welshampton 38 D1
Welsh Bicknor 28 E6
Welsh End 38 E1
Welsh Hook 16 C3
Welsh Newton 28 D6
Welshpool (*Y Trallwng*) 38 B4
Welsh St Donats 19 A6
Welton *Cumb* 69 B5
Welton *Humb* 58 E5
Welton *Lincs* 52 D4
Welton *Northants* 31 A1
Welton le Marsh 53 C5
Welton le Wold 53 A3
Welwick 59 D5
Welwyn 32 D7
Welwyn Garden City 32 D7
Wem 38 E2
Wembdon 20 B7
Wembley 24 B4
Wembury 5 A6
Wembworthy 7 A6
Wemyss Bay 80 A5
Wenallt 47 D6
Wendens Ambo 33 A5
Wendlebury 31 A6
Wendling 44 D4
Wendover 31 D7
Wendron 2 D5
Wendy 32 E4
Wenhaston 35 D1
Wenlli 47 C4
Wennington *Cambs* 32 D1
Wennington *Esx* 24 F4
Wennington *Lancs* 55 A1
Wensley *Derbs* 50 D4
Wensley *N Yorks* 63 A6
Wentbridge 57 C6
Went Hill 13 C7
Wentnor 38 C5
Wentworth *Cambs* 33 A1
Wentworth *S Yorks* 50 E1
Wenvoe 19 B6
Weobley 28 D2
Weobley Marsh 28 D2
Wepre 48 C5
Wereham 44 A5
Wergs 40 A4
Wernyrheolydd 19 D2
Werrington *Devon* 4 D2
Werrington *Northants* 42 E4
Wervil Brook 26 C5
Wervin 48 D4
Wesham 54 D4
Wessington 50 E5
West Acre 44 B4
West Allerdean 77 A1
West Alvington 5 C6
West Amesbury 22 A7
West Anstey 7 C4
West Ashby 53 A4
West Ashling 11 E4
West Ashton 21 C5
West Auckland 70 E6
West Ayton 65 B5
West Bagborough 20 A7
West Barnby 65 A2
West Barns 83 B5
West Barsham 44 D2
West Bay 9 A4
West Beckham 45 A2
West Benhar 81 C5
Westbere 38 E2
West Bergholt 34 D6
West Bexington 9 B5
West Bilney 44 B4
West Blatchington 12 E6
West Boldon 71 B2
Westborough 52 B7
Westbourne *Dors* 10 B5
Westbourne *W Ssx* 11 D4
West Bradenham 44 D5
West Bradford 55 B3
West Bradley 20 E7
West Bretton 57 A6
West Bridgford 51 B7
West Bromwich 40 C5
Westbrook 22 D4
West Buckland *Devon* 7 A5
West Buckland *Som* 8 C1

West Burrafirth 115 B2
West Burton *N Yorks* 63 A6
West Burton *W Ssx* 12 C5
Westbury *Bucks* 31 B4
Westbury *Salop* 38 C4
Westbury *Wilts* 21 C5
Westbury Leigh 21 C6
Westbury-on-Severn 29 B6
West Butterwick 57 B7
Westby 54 C4
West Caister 45 E4
West Calder 81 E5
West Carlston 81 A4
West Challow 22 C3
West Charleton 5 C6
West Chelborough 9 B3
West Chevington 77 D6
West Chiltington 12 C5
West Chinnock 9 A2
West Clandon 12 C1
West Cliffe 15 D1
Westcliff-on-Sea 25 D4
West Clyne 103 B1
West Coker 9 B2
Westcombe 21 A7
West Compton *Dors* 9 B4
West Compton *Som* 20 E6
Westcote 30 C5
Westcott *Bucks* 31 C6
Westcott *Devon* 8 B3
Westcott *Sry* 12 D2
Westcott Barton 30 E5
West Cross 18 B5
West Curry 6 B7
West Curthwaite 69 B5
Westdean 13 C7
West Dean *Wilts* 10 D2
West Dean *W Ssx* 11 E3
West Deeping 42 E4
West Derby 48 C2
West Dereham 44 A5
West Ditchburn 77 C3
West Down 6 E2
West Downham 43 D4
West Drayton *GL* 23 E4
West Drayton *Notts* 51 D3
West Dullater 80 E1
West Dunnet 111 C1
West Edington 77 C7
West Ella 59 A5
West End *Avn* 20 D4
West End *Beds* 31 E2
West End *Hants* 11 A3
West End *Herts* 24 D2
West End *Humb* 65 C7
West End *Kent* 15 B2
West End *Lancs* 54 D1
West End *Lincs* 53 B2
West End *Nflk* 45 D4
West End *N Yorks* 56 E2
West End *Oxon* 30 E7
West End *Sflk* 45 D7
West End *Sry* 24 B6
West End *Sry* 23 D5
West End Green 23 A5
Wester Badentyre 105 A3
Wester Culbeuchly Crofts 104 E2
Westerdale *Hghld* 111 B3
Westerdale *N Yorks* 64 D3
Wester Dechmont 81 E5
Westerfield *Sflk* 35 A4
Westerfield *Shet* 115 C2
Wester Fintray 97 D2
Westergate 12 B6
Wester Gruinards 102 D2
Westerham 31 B3
Wester Lealty 102 E4
Westerleigh 21 A3
Wester Lonvine 103 A4
Wester Newburn 82 E2
Wester Olrig 111 C2
Wester Ord 97 D3
Wester Parkgate 75 A7
Wester Skeld 115 B3
Wester Slumbay 93 A1
Westerton *Dur* 71 A5
Westerton *Gramp* 97 C4
Westerton *Gramp* 103 E6
Westerton *Tays* 87 E7
Westerton *Tays* 89 C3
Westerwick 115 B3
West Farleigh 13 E1
West Farndon 31 A2
West Felton 38 C2

Westfield *Cumb* 68 C7
Westfield *E Ssx* 14 D7
Westfield *Hghld* 111 A2
Westfield *Loth* 81 D4
Westfield *Nflk* 44 D5
Westfield Moor 14 D7
West Firle 13 B6
West Garforth 57 B4
Westgate *Dur* 70 C5
Westgate *Humb* 58 C7
Westgate *Nflk* 44 D1
Westgate *T & W* 70 E1
Westgate Hill 57 A5
Westgate on Sea 15 D1
West Ginge 22 D3
West Glen 79 D4
West Grafton 22 B5
West Green 23 B6
West Grimstead 10 D2
West Grinstead 12 D4
West Haddlesey 57 D5
West Haddon 41 D7
West Hagbourne 22 E3
West Hagley 40 B6
Westhall 45 D7
West Hall 69 D3
West Hallam 51 A6
West Halton 58 E5
West Ham 24 E4
Westham *Dors* 9 C6
Westham *E Ssx* 13 D6
Westham *Som* 20 D6
Westhampnett 11 E4
West Handley 50 E3
West Hanney 22 D2
West Hanningfield 25 C3
West Hardwick 57 C6
West Harptree 20 E5
West Harting 11 D2
West Hatch 8 D1
Westhay 20 D6
Westhead 48 D1
West Heath *H & W* 40 C7
West Heath *Hants* 23 C6
West Helmsdale 111 A7
West Hendred 22 D3
West Heslerton 65 B6
Westhide 28 E3
West Hill *Avon* 20 D3
West Hill *Devon* 8 B4
West Hoathly 13 A3
West Holme 9 E5
Westhope *H & W* 28 D2
Westhope *Salop* 38 D6
West Horndon 25 B4
Westhorpe *Lincs* 43 A1
Westhorpe *Sflk* 34 E2
West Horrington 20 E6
West Horsley 12 C1
West Hougham 15 C4
Westhoughton 49 A1
Westhouse 62 B7
Westhouses 51 A5
West Humble 12 D1
West Hyde 23 E2
West Hythe 15 B5
West Ilsley 22 D3
Westing 114 E2
West Itchenor 11 D4
West Jurby 60 c2
West Keal 53 B5
West Kennett 22 A5
West Kilbride *Strath* 73 B3
West Kilbride *W Is* 90 C4
West Kingsdown 25 A6
West Kington 21 C3
West Kirby 48 B3
West Knapton 65 A6
West Knighton 9 D5
West Knoyle 21 C7
Westlake 5 B5
West Lambrook 9 A2
West Langdon 15 D4
West Langwell 102 E1
West Lavington *Wilts* 21 E5
West Lavington *W Ssx* 11 E2
West Layton 63 B4
West Leake 41 C2
Westleigh *Devon* 6 D4
Westleigh *Devon* 8 B2
Westleigh *GM* 49 A1
Westleton 35 D2
West Lexham 44 C4
Westley *Salop* 38 C4
Westley *Sflk* 34 C2

Westley Waterless 33 C3
West Lilling 57 E1
West Lingo 82 E2
Westlington 31 C6
Westlinton 69 B3
West Littleton 21 B3
Westloch 82 C7
West Loch Tarbert 106 D7
West Lockinge 22 D3
West Looe 4 C5
West Lulworth 9 E5
West Lutton 65 B7
West Lydford 20 E7
West Lyng 8 E1
West Lynn 44 A3
West Malling 13 D1
West Malvern 29 B3
West Marden 11 D3
West Markham 51 D3
West Marsh 59 C6
Westmarsh 15 C2
West Marton 55 C2
West Melton 57 C7
West Meon 11 C2
West Mersea 34 E7
Westmeston 13 A5
Westmill 32 E6
West Milton 9 B4
West Minster 14 E1
West Molesey 24 B6
West Monkton 8 D1
West Moors 10 B4
West Mostard 62 C5
Westmuir 88 E3
West Muir 89 B2
West Ness 64 D6
Westness 112 C4
Westnewton Bdrs 77 A2
Westnewton Cumb 68 E5
West Newton Humb 59 B4
West Newton Nflk 44 A3
Westnewton Northld 76 E2
West Norwood 24 D5
West Ogwell 5 D3
Weston Avn 21 B4
Weston Berks 22 C4
Weston Ches 48 E3
Weston Ches 49 B6
Weston Dors 9 C6
Weston Gramp 104 C2
Weston Hants 11 D2
Weston Herts 32 D5
Weston Lincs 43 A2
Weston Northants 31 A3
Weston Notts 51 D4
Weston Salop 38 E2
Weston Salop 38 E5
Weston Staffs 40 B2
Weston W Yorks 56 E3
Weston Beggard 28 E3
Westonbirt 21 C2
Weston by Welland 41 E5
Weston Colville 33 C3
Weston Corbett 23 A7
Weston Coyney 49 D7
Weston Favell 31 C1
Weston Green Camb
 33 C3
Weston Green GL 24 B6
Weston Green Nflk 45 A4
Weston Heath 39 B3
Weston Hills 43 A2
Westoning 32 B5
Weston-in-Gordano 20 D3
Weston Jones 39 B2
Weston Longville 45 A4
Weston Lullingfields 38 D2
Weston-on-the-Green
 31 A6
Weston-on-Trent 41 B2
Weston Patrick 23 A7
Weston Point 48 E3
Weston Rhyn 38 B1
Weston Subedge 30 B3
Weston-super-Mare 20 C4
Weston Turville 31 D6
Weston-under-Lizard
 40 A3
Weston under Penyard
 29 A5
Weston under Wetherley
 30 D1
Weston Underwood Bucks
 31 D2
Weston Underwood Derbs
 50 D6

Westonzoyland 20 C7
West Overton 22 A5
Westow 64 E7
West Park Gramp 97 C4
West Park Mers 48 E2
West Parley 10 B5
West Peckham 13 D1
West Pennard 20 E7
West Pentire 2 E2
West Porlock 7 C2
Westport Som 8 E2
Westport Strath 72 A5
West Putford 6 C5
West Quantoxhead 20 A6
West Rainton 71 B4
West Rasen 52 D3
West Raynham 44 C3
Westrigg 81 D5
West Rounton 64 B3
West Row 33 C1
West Rudham 44 C3
West Runton 45 A1
Westruther 76 C1
Westry 43 B5
West Saltoun 82 E6
West Sandwick 114 D4
West Scrafton 63 A6
Westside 97 D4
West Somerton 45 D4
West Stafford 9 D5
West Stoke 11 E4
West Stonesdale 62 D4
West Stoughton 20 D6
West Stour 9 D1
West Stourmouth 15 C2
West Stow 34 C1
West Stowell 22 A5
West Street 14 E3
West Tanfield 63 C7
West Taphouse 3 D2
West Tarbert Hghld 79 C5
West Tarbert Hghld 106 E7
West Tarring 12 D6
West Thorney 11 D4
West Thurrock 25 A5
West Tilbury 25 B5
West Tisted 11 C2
West Tofts Nflk 44 C6
West Tofts Tays 88 C5
West Torrington 52 E3
West Town 20 D4
West Town 11 D5
West Tytherley 10 D1
West Tytherton 21 D3
West Walton 43 C3
West Walton Highway
 43 C3
Westward 69 A5
Westward Ho! 6 D4
Westwell Kent 14 E4
Westwell Oxon 30 C6
Westwell Leacon 14 E4
West Wellow 10 D3
West Wemyss 82 D3
West Wick 20 C4
Westwick Cambs 33 A2
Westwick Dur 63 A3
Westwick Nflk 45 B3
West Wickham Cambs
 33 C4
West Wickham GL 24 D6
West Williamston 16 D5
West Winch 44 A4
West Winterslow 10 D1
West Wittering 11 D5
West Witton 63 A6
Westwood Devon 8 B4
Westwood Wilts 21 C5
West Woodburn 76 E7
West Woodhay 22 C5
Westwood Heath 40 E7
West Woodlands 21 B6
Westwoodside 51 D1
West Worldham 11 D1
West Worlington 7 B5
West Worthing 12 D6
West Wratting 33 C3
West Wycombe 23 C2
West Yell 114 D4
Wetheral 69 C4
Wetherby 57 C3
Wether Cote 64 D5
Wetherden 34 E2
Wetheringsett 35 A2
Wethersfield 33 D5
Wethersta 115 C1
Wetherup Street 35 A2

Wetley Rocks 49 D7
Wettenhall 49 A5
Wettenhall Green 49 A5
Wetton 50 C5
Wetwang 58 E2
Wetwood 39 B1
Wexcombe 22 B6
Weybourne 45 A1
Weybread 45 B7
Weybridge 23 E5
Weydale 111 B2
Weyhill 22 C7
Weymouth 9 C6
Whaddon Bucks 31 D4
Whaddon Cambs 32 E4
Whaddon Glos 29 C6
Whaddon Wilts 10 C2
Whale 69 D7
Whaley 51 B3
Whaley Bridge 50 B2
Whaligoe 111 D4
Whalley 55 B4
Whalton 77 C7
Wham 55 B1
Whaness 113 B1
Whaplode 43 B2
Whaplode Drove 43 B3
Whaplode St Catherine
 43 B2
Wharfe 55 B1
Wharles 54 D4
Wharncliffe Side 50 D1
Wharram le Street 65 A7
Wharram Percy 65 A7
Wharton Ches 49 A5
Wharton H & W 28 E2
Whashton 63 B4
Whatcombe 9 E3
Whatcote 30 C3
Whatfield 34 E4
Whatley 21 B6
Whatlington 13 E5
Whatstandwell 50 E5
Whatton 51 D7
Whauphill 67 A6
Whaw 62 E4
Wheatacre 45 D6
Wheathampstead 32 C7
Wheathill 39 A6
Wheatley Hants 23 B7
Wheatley Notts 51 D2
Wheatley Oxon 31 A7
Wheatley Hill 71 B5
Wheatley Lane 55 C4
Wheaton Aston 40 A3
Wheatsheaf 48 C6
Wheddon Cross 7 D3
Wheedlemont 104 C6
Wheelerstreet 12 B2
Wheelock 49 B6
Wheelton 55 A5
Wheen 96 D6
Wheldrake 57 E3
Whelford 22 A2
Whelpley Hill 23 E1
Whelpo 69 B6
Whenby 57 E1
Whepstead 34 C3
Wherstead 35 A4
Wherwell 22 C7
Wheston 50 C3
Whetsted 13 D2
Whetstone 41 C5
Whicham 61 A5
Whichford 30 D4
Whickham 71 A2
Whickham Street 33 D3
Whiddon Down 7 A7
Whifflet 81 B5
Whigstreet 89 A4
Whilton 31 B1
Whim 82 C7
Whimple 8 B4
Whimpwell Green 45 C3
Whinburgh 44 E5
Whin Lane End 54 C3
Whinnyfold 105 D5
Whippingham 11 B5
Whipsnade 32 B7
Whipton 7 D7
Whisby 52 C5
Whissendine 42 B3
Whissonsett 44 D3
Whistley Green 23 B4
Whiston Mers 48 D2
Whiston Northants 31 D1
Whiston Staffs 50 B6

Whiston Staffs 40 A3
Whiston S Yorks 51 A2
Whitbeck 61 A5
Whitbourne 29 B2
Whitburn Loth 81 D5
Whitburn T & W 71 C2
Whitby Ches 48 D4
Whitby N Yorks 65 A2
Whitchurch Avn 21 A4
Whitchurch Bucks 31 D5
Whitchurch Devon 4 E3
Whitchurch Dyfed 16 B3
Whitchurch H & W 23 A4
Whitchurch Hants 22 D7
Whitchurch Oxon 23 A4
Whitchurch Salop 48 E7
Whitchurch S Glam 19 B5
Whitchurch Canonicorum
 8 E4
Whitchurch Hill 23 A4
Whitcombe 9 D5
Whitcott Keysett 38 B6
Whiteacen 104 A4
Whiteash Green 34 C5
Whitebog 105 C3
Whitebridge Hghld 111 C1
Whitebridge Hghld 94 C4
Whitebrook 28 E7
Whiteburn 76 B1
Whitecairn 66 D5
Whitecairns 97 E2
Whitecastle 75 A1
White Chapel 54 E3
White Colne 34 C5
White Coppice 55 A6
Whitecraig 82 D5
Whitecroft 29 A7
Whitecrook 66 C5
White Cross Corn 3 A2
White Cross H & W 28 D3
White End 29 C5
Whiteface 103 A3
Whitefield GM 49 C1
Whitefield Gramp 105 A6
Whitefield Hghld 94 B3
Whitefield Hghld 111 C3
Whitefield Tays 88 C5
Whiteford 105 A6
Whitegate 49 A5
Whitehall 112 F4
Whitehall Hants 11 D1
Whitehill Kent 14 E3
Whitehill Strath 80 B6
Whitehills 104 E2
Whitehouse Gramp 97 B2
Whitehouse Strath 79 C5
Whitehurst 13 D4
Whitekirk 83 A4
White Lackington Dors
 9 D4
Whitelackington Som 8 E2
White Ladies Aston 29 D2
Whitelaw 83 D7
Whiteleen 111 D4
Whitelees 73 C4
Whiteley Bank 11 B6
Whiteleys 66 B5
Whiteley Village 23 E5
Whitemans Green 13 A4
Whitemire 103 C6
Whitemoor 55 C3
White Moor 50 E6
White Notley 33 D7
Whiteparish 10 D2
White Pit 53 B4
Whiterashes 105 B6
White Roding 33 B7
Whiteshill 29 C7
Whiteside Northld 70 A2
Whitesmith 13 C5
Whitestaunton 8 D2
Whitestone Devon 7 C7
Whitestone Gramp 97 B4
Whitestone Strath 72 B4
Whitestripe 105 C3
White Waltham 23 C4
Whiteway 29 D6
Whitewell Gramp 105 C2
Whitewell Lancs 55 A3
Whiteworks 5 B3
Whitewreath 104 A3
Whitfield Avn 21 A1
Whitfield H & W 28 D4
Whitfield Kent 15 D4
Whitfield Northants 31 B4

Whitfield Northld 70 A3
Whitford Clwyd 48 A4
Whitford Devon 8 D4
Whitgift 58 D5
Whitgreave 40 A2
Whithorn 67 A6
Whiting Bay 72 E5
Whitington 44 B6
Whitkirk 57 B4
Whitlam 105 B6
Whitland 16 E4
Whitletts 73 C5
Whitley Berks 23 B4
Whitley N Yorks 57 D5
Whitley Bay 71 B1
Whitley Chapel 70 C3
Whitley Lower 57 A6
Whitley Row 13 C1
Whitlock's End 40 D7
Whitminster 29 B7
Whitmore Dors 10 B4
Whitmore Staffs 49 C7
Whitnage 8 B2
Whitnash 30 D1
Whitney 28 B3
Whitrigg Cumb 69 A4
Whitrigg Cumb 69 A6
Whitsbury 10 C3
Whitsome 83 D7
Whitson 19 D5
Whitstable 15 B2
Whitstone 6 B7
Whittingham 77 B4
Whittingslow 38 D6
Whittington Derbs 50 E3
Whittington Glos 30 A5
Whittington H & W 29 C2
Whittington Lancs 61 E6
Whittington Salop 38 C1
Whittington Staffs 40 D4
Whittington Staffs 40 A6
Whittlebury 31 B3
Whittle-le-Woods 54 E5
Whittlesey 43 A5
Whittlesford 33 A4
Whitton Clev 71 B6
Whitton Humb 58 E5
Whitton Northld 77 B5
Whitton Pwys 28 B1
Whitton Salop 38 E7
Whitton Sflk 35 A4
Whittonditch 22 B4
Whittonstall 70 D3
Whitway 22 D6
Whitwell Derbs 51 B3
Whitwell Herts 32 C6
Whitwell IOW 11 B7
Whitwell Leics 42 C4
Whitwell Nflk 45 A3
Whitwell N Yorks 63 C5
Whitwell-on-the-Hill 64 E7
Whitwick 41 B3
Whitwood 57 C5
Whitworth 55 C6
Whixall 38 E1
Whixley 57 C2
Whorlton Dur 63 B3
Whorlton N Yorks 64 B3
Whygate 70 A1
Whyle 28 E1
Whyteleafe 13 A1
Wibdon 20 E1
Wibsey 56 E4
Wibtoft 41 B6
Wichenford 29 B1
Wichling 14 E3
Wick Avn 21 A3
Wick Dors 10 C5
Wick H & W 29 D3
Wick Hghld 111 D3
Wick M Glam 18 E6
Wick Wilts 10 C2
Wick W Ssx 12 C6
Wicken Cambs 33 B1
Wicken Northants 31 C4
Wicken Bonhunt 33 B5
Wickenby 52 D3
Wickerslack 62 B3
Wickersley 51 A1
Wickford 25 C3
Wickham Berks 22 C4
Wickham Hants 11 B3
Wickham Bishops 34 C7
Wickhambreaux 15 C3
Wickhambrook 33 D3
Wickhamford 30 A3
Wickham Heath 22 D5

Wickham Market 35 C3
Wickhampton 45 D5
Wickham St Paul 34 C5
Wickham Skeith 34 E2
Wickham Street Sflk
 33 D3
Wickham Street Sflk 34 B
Wick Hill 14 D4
Wicklewood 44 E5
Wickmere 45 A2
Wick Rissington 30 B5
Wick St Lawrence 20 C4
Wickwar 21 B2
Widcombe 21 B4
Widdington 33 B5
Widdop 55 D4
Widdrington 77 D6
Widecombe in the Moor
 5 C3
Widegates 4 C5
Widemouth Bay 6 B6
Wide Open 71 A1
Widford Esx 25 B2
Widford Herts 33 A7
Widmerpool 41 D2
Widnes 48 E3
Widworthy 8 D4
Wier 25 D3
Wigan 48 E1
Wiggaton 8 C4
Wiggenhall St Germans
 43 D3
Wiggenhall St Mary
 Magdalen 43 D3
Wiggenhall St Mary the
 Virgin 43 D3
Wiggenhall St Peter 44 A
Wiggington 57 D2
Wigginton Herts 31 E6
Wigginton Oxon 30 D4
Wigginton Staffs 40 E4
Wigglesworth 55 C2
Wiggonby 69 A4
Wiggonholt 12 C5
Wighill 57 C3
Wighton 44 D2
Wigley H & W 28 D1
Wigmore Kent 14 D2
Wigsley 52 B4
Wigsthorpe 42 D6
Wigston 41 D5
Wigston Parva 41 B6
Wigthorpe 51 B2
Wigtoft 43 A1
Wigton 69 A5
Wigtown 67 A5
Wigtwizzle 50 D2
Wilbarston 42 B6
Wilberfoss 58 C2
Wilburton 33 A7
Wilby Nflk 44 E7
Wilby Northants 31 D1
Wilby Sflk 35 B1
Wilcot 22 A5
Wilcott 38 C3
Wilcrick 20 D2
Wildboarclough 49 D3
Wilden Beds 32 B3
Wilden H & W 40 A7
Wildern 22 C6
Wildsworth 52 B2
Wilford 51 B7
Wilkesley 49 A7
Wilkhaven 103 C3
Wilkieston 82 B6
Wilkins 24 B2
Willand 8 B2
Willaston Ches 48 C4
Willaston Ches 49 A6
Willen 31 D3
Willenhall W Mids 40 B5
Willenhall W Mids 41 A7
Willerby Humb 59 A4
Willerby N Yorks 65 C6
Willersey 30 B4
Willersley 28 C3
Willesborough 15 A4
Willesden 24 C4
Willett 20 A7
Willey Salop 39 A5
Willey Warks 41 B6
Williamscot 30 E3
Williamthorpe 51 A4
Willian 32 D5
Willimontswick 70 A2
Willingale 24 F2

Willingdon 15 A6
Willingham *Cambs* 33 A1
Willingham *Lincs* 52 B3
Willingon 15 A6
Willington *Beds* 32 C3
Willington *Derbs* 40 E2
Willington *Dur* 70 E5
Willington *T & W* 71 B2
Willington *Warks* 30 C4
Willington Corner 48 E5
Willisham 34 E3
Willitoft 58 C4
Williton 7 E2
Willoughby *Lincs* 53 C4
Willoughby *Warks* 31 A1
Willoughby on the Wolds
   41 D2
Willoughby Waterleys
   41 C5
Willoughton 52 C2
Willsworthy 5 A2
Wilmcote 30 B2
Wilmington *Devon* 8 D4
Wilmington *E Ssx* 13 C6
Wilmington *Kent* 24 F5
Wilmslow 49 C3
Wilnecote 40 D6
Wilpshire 55 A4
Wilsden 56 D4
Wilsford *Lincs* 52 D7
Wilsford *Wilts* 10 C1
Wilsford *Wilts* 22 A6
Wilsill 56 E1
Wilsley Green 13 E3
Wilson 41 B2
Wilsontown 81 D6
Wilstead 32 B4
Wilsthorpe 42 D3
Wilstone 31 E6
Wilton *Bdrs* 76 A4
Wilton *Clev* 64 C2
Wilton *N Yorks* 65 A5
Wilton *Som* 8 D1
Wilton *Wilts* 22 B5
Wilton *Wilts* 10 B1
Wimbish 33 B5
Wimbish Green 33 C5
Wimblebury 40 C3
Wimbledon 24 C5
Wimblington 43 C5
Wimborne Minster 10 B5
Wimborne St Giles 10 B3
Wimbotsham 44 A5
Wimpstone 30 C3
Wincanton 9 D1
Wincham 49 A4
Winchburgh 81 E4
Winchcombe 30 A5
Winchelsea 14 E7
Winchelsea Beach 14 E7
Winchester 11 A2
Winchet Hill 13 E2
Winchfield 23 B6
Winchmore Hill *Bucks*
   23 D2
Winchmore Hill *GL* 24 D3
Wincle 49 D5
Wincobank 50 E1
Windermere 61 D5
Winderton 30 D3
Windhill 102 D7
Windlesham 23 D5
Windley 50 E6
Windley Meadows 50 E6
Windmill Hill *E Ssx* 13 D5
Windmill Hill *Som* 8 E2
Windrush 30 B6
Windsor 23 D4
Windygates 82 D2
Windy Yet 80 D6
Wineham 12 E4
Winestead 59 C5
Winewall 55 D4
Winfarthing 45 A7
Winford 20 E4
Winforton 28 B3
Winfrith Newburgh 9 E5
Wing *Bucks* 31 D5
Wing *Leics* 42 B4
Wingate 71 C5
Wingates *GM* 49 A1
Wingates *Northld* 77 B6
Wingerworth 50 E4
Wingfield *Beds* 31 E5
Wingfield *Sflk* 35 B1
Wingfield *Wilts* 21 C5
Wingham 15 C3

Wingmore 15 B4
Wingrave 31 D6
Winkburn 51 D5
Winkfield 23 D4
Winkfield Row 23 D4
Winkhill 50 B5
Winkleigh 7 A6
Winksley 63 C7
Winksley Banks 63 C7
Winkton 10 C5
Winlaton 70 E2
Winlaton Mill 70 E2
Winless 111 D3
Winmarleigh 54 D3
Winnards Perch 3 B2
Winnersh 23 B4
Winscombe 20 D5
Winsford *Ches* 49 A5
Winsford *Som* 7 D3
Winsham 8 E3
Winshill 40 E2
Winskill 69 D6
Winslade 23 A7
Winsley 21 B4
Winslow 31 C5
Winson 30 A7
Winster *Cumb* 61 D5
Winster *Derbs* 50 D4
Winston *Dur* 63 B3
Winston *Sflk* 35 A2
Winstone 29 D7
Winswell 6 D5
Winterborne Abbas 9 C4
Winterborne Clenston
   9 E3
Winterborne Herringston
   9 C5
Winterborne Houghton
   9 E3
Winterborne Kingston
   9 E4
Winterborne Monkton
   9 C5
Winterborne Steepleton
   9 C5
Winterborne Stickland
   9 E3
Winterborne Tomson 9 E4
Winterborne Whitechurch
   9 E4
Winterborne Zelston 9 E4
Winterbourne *Avn* 21 A2
Winterbourne *Berks* 22 D4
Winterbourne Bassett
   22 A4
Winterbourne Came 9 D5
Winterbourne Dauntsey
   10 C1
Winterbourne Earls 10 C1
Winterbourne Gunner
   10 C1
Winterbourne Monkton
   21 E3
Winterbourne Steepleton
   9 C5
Winterbourne Stoke 21 E6
Winterburn 55 D2
Winteringham 58 E5
Winterley 49 B6
Wintersett 57 B6
Winterslow 10 D1
Winterton 58 E6
Winterton-on-Sea 45 D4
Winthorpe *Lincs* 53 D5
Winthorpe *Notts* 52 B6
Winton *Cumb* 62 C3
Winton *Dors* 10 B5
Wintringham 65 A6
Winwick *Cambs* 42 E6
Winwick *Mers* 49 A2
Winwick *Northants* 41 D7
Wirksworth 50 D5
Wirswall 48 E7
Wisbech 43 C4
Wisbech St Mary 43 C4
Wisborough Green 12 C4
Wiseton 51 D2
Wishaw *Strath* 81 B6
Wishaw *Warks* 40 D5
Wisley 12 C1
Wispington 53 A4
Wissett 35 C1
Wissington 34 D5
Wistanstow 38 D6
Wistanswick 39 A2
Wistaston 49 A6
Wiston *Dyfed* 16 D4

Wiston *Strath* 74 E2
Wiston *W Ssx* 12 D5
Wistow *Cambs* 43 A6
Wistow *N Yorks* 57 D4
Wiswell 55 B4
Witcham 43 C6
Witchampton 10 A4
Witchburn 72 B5
Witchford 33 B1
Witcombe 9 A1
Witham 34 C7
Witham Friary 21 B6
Witham on the Hill 42 D3
Withcall 44 C3
Withcote 42 B4
Witherenden Hill 13 D4
Witheridge 7 C5
Witherley 41 A5
Withern 53 C3
Withernsea 59 D5
Withernwick 59 B3
Withersdale Street 45 B7
Withersfield 33 C4
Witherslack 61 D5
Withiel 3 B2
Withiel Florey 7 D3
Withington *Ches* 49 C4
Withington *Glos* 30 A6
Withington *GM* 49 C2
Withington *H & W* 28 E3
Withington *Salop* 38 E3
Withington *Staffs* 50 B7
Withington Green 49 C4
Withleigh 7 D5
Withnell 55 A5
Withybrook 41 B6
Withycombe 7 E2
Withycombe Raleigh 8 B5
Witcham 13 B3
Withypool 7 C3
Witley 12 B3
Witnesham 35 A3
Witney 30 D7
Wittering 42 D4
Wittersham 14 D6
Witton 97 A6
Witton Bridge 45 C2
Witton Gilbert 71 A4
Witton-le-Wear 70 E5
Witton Park 70 E5
Wiveliscombe 8 B1
Wivelsfield 13 A4
Wivelsfield Green 13 A5
Wivenhoe 34 E6
Wivenhoe Cross 34 E6
Wiveton 44 E1
Wix 35 A6
Wixford 30 A2
Wix Green 35 A6
Wixoe 33 D4
Woburn 31 E4
Woburn Sands 31 E4
Wokefield Park 23 A5
Woking 12 C1
Wokingham 23 C5
Wolborough 5 D3
Woldingham 13 A1
Wold Newton *Humb* 53 A2
Wold Newton *N Yorks*
   65 C6
Wolfelee 76 B5
Wolferlow 29 A1
Wolferton 44 A3
Wolfhampcote 31 A1
Wolfhill 88 C5
Wolfpits 28 B2
Wolfsdale 16 C3
Woll 76 A3
Wollaston *Northants* 31 E1
Wollaston *Salop* 38 C3
Wollaston *W Mids* 40 A6
Wollerton 39 A2
Wolsingham 70 D5
Wolstenholme 55 C6
Wolston 41 B7
Wolvercote 30 E7
Wolverhampton 40 B5
Wolverley *H & W* 40 A7
Wolverley *Salop* 38 D1
Wolverton *Bucks* 31 D3
Wolverton *Hants* 22 E6
Wolverton *Warks* 30 C1
Wolves Newton 20 D1
Wolvey 41 B6
Wolviston 64 B1
Wombleton 64 D5
Wombourne 40 A5

Wombwell 57 B7
Womenswold 15 C3
Womersley 57 D6
Wonastow 28 D6
Wonersh 12 C2
Wonson 5 B2
Wonston 11 A1
Wooburn 23 D3
Wooburn Green 23 D3
Woodale 63 A7
Woodbastwick 45 C4
Woodbeck 51 D3
Woodbine 16 C4
Woodborough *Notts* 51 C6
Woodborough *Wilts* 22 A6
Woodbridge 35 B4
Wood Burcote 31 B3
Woodbury 8 B5
Woodbury Salterton 8 B5
Woodchester 29 C7
Woodchurch *Kent* 14 E5
Woodchurch *Mers* 48 B3
Woodcote *Oxon* 23 A3
Woodcote *Salop* 39 B3
Woodcroft 20 E1
Woodcuts 10 A3
Wood Dalling 44 E3
Woodditton 33 C3
Woodeaton 31 A6
Wood End *Beds* 32 B4
Woodend *Cumb* 61 A4
Woodend *Gramp* 97 B2
Wood End *Herts* 32 E6
Woodend *Hghld* 95 A3
Woodend *Hghld* 85 D2
Woodend *Northants* 31 B3
Woodend *Tays* 87 D4
Wood End *Warks* 40 E5
Wood End *Warks* 40 D7
Woodend *W Ssx* 11 E4
Wood Enderby 53 A5
Woodfalls 10 C2
Woodfield 24 C2
Woodford *Ches* 49 C3
Woodford *Corn* 6 B5
Woodford *Glos* 21 A1
Woodford *Northants*
   42 C7
Woodford Bridge 24 E3
Woodford Green 24 E3
Woodford Halse 31 A2
Woodgate *H & W* 40 B6
Woodgate *H & W* 29 D1
Woodgate *Nflk* 44 E4
Woodgate *W Ssx* 12 B6
Woodgreen 10 C3
Wood Green 24 D3
Woodhall 62 E5
Woodhall Spa 52 E5
Woodham *Dur* 71 A6
Woodham *Sry* 23 B6
Woodham Ferrers 25 C3
Woodham Mortimer 25 D2
Woodham Walter 25 D2
Woodhaven 89 A6
Wood Hayes 40 B4
Woodhead *Gramp* 105 A3
Woodhead *Gramp* 105 A5
Woodhill 39 B6
Woodhorn 77 D7
Woodhouse *Cumb* 61 E5
Woodhouse *Leics* 41 C3
Woodhouse *S Yorks*
   51 A2
Woodhouse Eaves 41 C3
Woodhouses 40 D3
Woodhuish 5 E5
Woodhurst 32 E1
Woodingdean 13 A6
Woodland *Devon* 5 C4
Woodland *Dur* 70 D6
Woodlands *Dors* 10 B4
Woodlands *Hants* 10 E3
Woodlands *Salop* 39 B6
Woodleigh 5 C6
Woodlesford 57 B5
Woodley 23 B4
Woodmancote *Glos* 29 D5
Woodmancote *Glos* 30 A7
Woodmancote *W Ssx*
   12 E5
Woodmancote *W Ssx*
   11 D4
Woodmancott 22 E7
Woodmansey 59 A4
Woodmansterne 24 C6
Woodmer End 32 C5

Woodminton 10 B2
Woodnesborough 15 D3
Woodnewton 42 D5
Wood Norton 44 E3
Woodplumpton 54 D4
Woodrising 44 D5
Woodseaves *Salop* 39 A1
Woodseaves *Staffs* 39 B2
Woodsend 22 B4
Woodsetts 51 B2
Woodsford 9 D4
Woodside *Berks* 23 D4
Woodside *D & G* 68 D2
Woodside *Fife* 82 C2
Woodside *Gramp* 97 E3
Woodside *Herts* 24 C2
Woodside *Salop* 38 C6
Woodside *Strath* 80 C6
Woodside *Tays* 88 D5
Woodstock 30 E6
Woodstock Slop 16 D3
Woodston 42 E5
Wood Street 12 B1
Woodthorpe *Derbs* 51 A3
Woodthorpe *Leics* 41 C3
Woodton 45 B6
Woodtown *Devon* 6 D4
Woodtown *Gramp* 97 B6
Woodville 41 A3
Wood Walton 43 A6
Woodyates 10 B3
Woofferton 28 E1
Wookey 20 E6
Wookey Hole 20 E6
Wool 9 E5
Woolacombe 6 D2
Woolaston 20 E1
Woolavington 20 C6
Woolbeding 11 E2
Wooler 77 A3
Woolfardisworthy *Devon*
   7 C6
Woolfardisworthy *Devon*
   6 C4
Woolfords Cottages 81 E6
Woolhampton 22 E5
Woolhope 29 A4
Woollage Green 15 C4
Woolland 9 D3
Woollaton 6 D5
Woolley *Avn* 21 B4
Woolley *Cambs* 32 C1
Woolley *S Yorks* 57 B6
Woolmere Green 29 D1
Woolmer Green 32 D7
Woolmersdon 20 B7
Woolpit 34 D2
Woolscott 30 E1
Woolstaston 38 D5
Woolsthorpe *Lincs* 42 B1
Woolsthorpe *Lincs* 42 C2
Woolston *Ches* 49 A3
Woolston *Hants* 11 A3
Woolston *Salop* 38 C2
Woolston *Salop* 38 D6
Woolstone *Oxon* 22 B3
Woolston Green 5 C4
Woolton 48 D3
Woolton Hill 22 D5
Woolverstone 35 A5
Woolverton 21 B5
Woolwich 24 E5
Woonton 28 C2
Wooperton 77 B3
Woore 49 B7
Wootton *Beds* 32 B4
Wootton *Hants* 10 D5
Wootton *Humb* 59 A6
Wootton *Kent* 15 C4
Wootton *Northants* 31 C2
Wootton *Oxon* 30 E6
Wootton *Oxon* 30 E7
Wootton *Salop* 38 D7
Wootton *Staffs* 40 A2
Wootton *Staffs* 50 C6
Wootton Bassett 21 E2
Wootton Bridge 11 B5
Wootton Common 11 B5
Wootton Courtenay 7 D2
Wootton Fitzpaine 8 E4
Wootton Rivers 22 A5
Wootton St Lawrence
   22 E6
Wootton Wawen 30 B1
Worcester 29 C2
Worcester Park 24 C6

Wordsley 40 A6
Wordwell 34 C1
Worfield 39 B5
Work 112 D5
Workington 68 C7
Worksop 51 B3
Worlaby 59 A6
World's End *Berks* 22 D4
Worlds End *Hants* 11 C3
Worle 20 C4
Worleston 49 A6
Worlingham 45 D7
Worlington *Devon* 7 B5
Worlington *Sflk* 33 C1
Worlingworth 35 B2
Wormbridge 28 D4
Wormegay 44 A4
Wormelow Tump 28 D4
Wormhill 50 C3
Wormiehills 89 C5
Wormingford 34 D5
Worminghall 31 B7
Wormington 30 A4
Worminster 20 E6
Wormistone 83 B2
Wormit 88 E6
Wormleighton 30 E2
Wormley 24 D2
Wormleybury 24 D2
Wormley Hill 12 B3
Wormshill 14 D3
Wormsley 28 D3
Worplesdon 12 B1
Worrall 50 E1
Worsbrough 57 B7
Worsley 49 B1
Worstead 45 C3
Worsthorne 55 C4
Worston 55 B3
Worswell 5 A6
Worth *Kent* 15 D3
Worth *W Ssx* 13 A3
Wortham 34 E1
Worthen 38 C4
Worthenbury 48 D7
Worthing *Nflk* 44 D4
Worthing *W Ssx* 12 D6
Worthington 41 B2
Worth Matravers 10 A7
Worthy 20 E2
Wortley *Glos* 21 B1
Wortley *S Yorks* 50 E1
Worton 21 D5
Wortwell 45 B7
Wotherton 38 B4
Wotton 12 D2
Wotton-under-Edge 21 B1
Wotton Underwood 31 B6
Woughton on the Green
   31 D4
Wouldham 14 C2
Wrabness 35 A5
Wrae 105 A3
Wrafton 6 D3
Wragby 52 E4
Wragholme 53 B2
Wramplingham 45 A5
Wrangham 104 E5
Wrangle 53 C6
Wrangle Bank 53 C6
Wrangle Lowgate 53 C6
Wrangway 8 C2
Wrantage 8 E1
Wrawby 59 A7
Wraxall *Avn* 20 D3
Wraxall *Som* 20 E7
Wray 55 A1
Wraysbury 23 E4
Wrea Green 54 C4
Wreay *Cumb* 69 C7
Wreay *Cumb* 69 C5
Wrecclesham 23 C7
Wrekenton 71 A3
Wrelton 64 E5
Wrenbury 48 E7
Wreningham 45 A6
Wrentham 45 D7
Wrenthorpe 57 B5
Wressle 58 C4
Wrestlingworth 32 D4
Wretton 44 A6
Wrexham 48 C7
Wribbenhall 39 B7
Wrightington Bar 54 E6
Wrightpark 81 A2
Wrinehill 49 B7
Wrington 20 D4

Writhlington 21 B5
Writtle 25 B2
Wrockwardine 39 A3
Wroot 58 C7
Wrotham 13 D1
Wrotham Heath 13 D1
Wrotham Hill 25 B6
Wrotham Park 24 C3
Wroughton 22 A3
Wroxall 11 B7
Wroxeter 38 E4
Wroxhall 40 E7
Wroxham 45 C4
Wroxton 30 E3
Wrythe, The 24 C6
Wstrws 26 C6
Wyaston 50 C6
Wyberton 53 B7
Wyboston 32 C3
Wybunbury 49 A7
Wychbold 29 D1
Wych Cross 13 B3
Wyche 29 B3
Wyck 11 D1
Wycliffe 63 B3
Wycoller 55 D4
Wycomb 41 E2
Wycombe Marsh 23 C2
Wyddial 32 E5
Wye 15 A4
Wyke *Salop* 39 A4
Wyke *W Yorks* 56 E5

Wyke, The 39 B4
Wykeham *N Yorks* 65 B5
Wykeham *N Yorks* 65 A6
Wyken 39 B5
Wyke Regis 9 C6
Wykey 38 C2
Wylam 70 E2
Wylde Green 40 D5
Wylye 10 B1
Wymering 11 C4
Wymeswold 41 D2
Wymington 31 E1
Wymondham *Leics* 42 B3
Wymondham *Nflk* 45 A5
Wyndham 18 E4
Wynford Eagle 9 B4
Wynnstay 48 C7
Wyre Piddle 29 D3
Wyresdale Tower 55 A2
Wysall 41 D2
Wyson 28 E1
Wythall 40 C7
Wytham 30 E7
Wythburn 61 C2
Wyton 32 D1
Wyverstone 34 E2
Wyverstone Street 34 E2
Wyville 42 B2

Y

Yaddlethorpe 58 D7
Yafford 11 A6
Yafforth 63 D5
Yalding 13 E1
Yanworth 30 A6
Yapham 58 C2
Yapton 12 B6
Yarburgh 53 B2
Yarcombe 8 D3
Yardley 40 D6
Yardley Gobion 31 C3
Yardley Hastings 31 D2
Yardro 28 B2
Yarkhill 29 A3
Yarlet 40 B2
Yarley 20 E6
Yarlington 9 C1
Yarm 64 B2
Yarmouth 10 E6
Yarnbrook 21 C5
Yarnfield 40 A1
Yarnscombe 6 E4
Yarnton 30 E6
Yarpole 28 D1
Yarrow 75 D3
Yarrow Feus 75 D3
Yarrowford 76 A2
Yarsop 28 D3
Yarwell 42 D5

Yate 21 B2
Yateley 23 C5
Yatesbury 21 E3
Yattendon 22 E4
Yatton *Avn* 20 D4
Yatton *H & W* 29 A4
Yatton *H & W* 28 D1
Yatton Keynell 21 C3
Yaverland 11 C6
Yaxham 44 E4
Yaxley *Cambs* 42 E5
Yaxley *Sflk* 35 A1
Yazor 28 D3
Yeading 24 B4
Yeadon 57 A3
Yealand Conyers 61 E6
Yealand Redmayne 61 E6
Yealmpton 5 A5
Yearby 64 D1
Yearsley 64 C6
Yeaton 38 D3
Yeaveley 50 C6
Yedingham 65 A6
Yelford 30 D7
Yelland 6 D3
Yelling 32 D2
Yelvertoft 41 C7
Yelverton *Devon* 5 A4
Yelverton *Nflk* 45 B5
Yenston 9 D1
Yeoford 7 B7
Yeolmbridge 4 D2

Yeomadon 6 C6
Yeo Vale 7 B6
Yeovil 9 B2
Yeovil Marsh 9 B2
Yeovilton 9 B1
Yerbeston 16 D5
Yesnaby 112 B5
Yetlington 77 B5
Yetminster 9 B2
Yettington 8 B5
Yetts o'Muckhart 81 E1
Y Fan 27 D2
Y Foel 47 B6
Yielden 32 B2
Yiewsley 23 E3
Ynysboeth 19 A4
Ynysddu 19 B4
Ynyshir 19 A4
Ynyslas 37 A6
Ynysmendwy 18 C3
Ynystawe 18 B3
Ynysybwl 19 A4
Yockenthwaite 62 E7
Yockleton 38 C3
Yokefleet 58 D5
Yoker 80 E5
Yonder Bognie 104 D4
York 57 E2
Yorkletts 15 A2
Yorkley 29 A7
Yorton 38 D2
Youldon 6 C6

Youldonmoor Cross 6 C6
Youlgreave 50 D4
Youlston 6 E3
Youlstone 6 B5
Youlthorpe 58 C2
Youlton 57 C1
Young's End 33 D7
Yoxall 40 D3
Yoxford 35 C2
Ysbyty Cynfyn 27 B3
Ysbyty Ifan 47 C6
Ysbyty Ystwyth 27 B3
Ysceifiog 48 A4
Ysgubor-y-coed 37 A6
Ystalyfera 18 C3
Ystrad 18 E4
Ystrad Aeron 26 E5
Ystradfellte 18 E2
Ystradffin 27 B6
Ystradgynlais 18 C2
Ystrad Meurig 27 B4
Ystradmynach 19 B4
Ystradowen *Pwys* 18 C2
Ystradowen *S Glam* 19 A6
Ythsie 105 B5

Z

Zeal Monachorum 7 B6
Zeals 21 B7
Zelah 3 A3
Zennor 2 B5